BUREAU OF INDIAN AFFAIRS SPECIAL AGENT HORACE B. DURANT'S 1907 DURANT ROLL FIELD NOTES

Correspondence and Field Notes Relating to the Census Roll of All Members or Descendants of Members Who Were on the Roll of the Ottawa and the Chippewa Tribes of Michigan in 1870, and Living on March 4, 1907

COMPILED AND EDITED BY

Raymond C. Lantz

HERITAGE BOOKS

2014

HERITAGE BOOKS
AN IMPRINT OF HERITAGE BOOKS, INC.

Books, CDs, and more—Worldwide

For our listing of thousands of titles see our website
at
www.HeritageBooks.com

Published 2014 by
HERITAGE BOOKS, INC.
Publishing Division
5810 Ruatan Street
Berwyn Heights, Md. 20740

Heritage Books by the author:

Bureau of Indian Affairs: Special Agent Horace B. Durant's 1907 Durant Roll Field Notes

Descendants of Johann Jacob Lantz, 1721–1789,
Immigrant Settler of Albany Township, Berks County, Pennsylvania

Lantz-Crossley: An Experience in Genealogy

Lantz-Crossley: An Experience in Genealogy, Volume I, A–E, Second Edition

Lantz-Crossley: An Experience in Genealogy, Volume II, F–J, Second Edition

Lantz-Crossley: An Experience in Genealogy, Volume III, K–O, Second Edition

Lantz-Crossley: An Experience in Genealogy, Volume IV, P–Z, Second Edition

Lantz-Crossley: An Experience in Genealogy, Supplement I to Volumes I–IV, Second Edition

Ottawa and Chippewa Indians of Michigan, 1855–1868

Ottawa and Chippewa Indians of Michigan, 1870–1909

Potawatomi Indians of Michigan, 1843–1904
Including Some Ottawa and Chippewa, 1843–1866 and Potawatomi of Indiana, 1869 and 1885

Seminole Indians of Florida: 1850–1874

Seminole Indians of Florida: 1875–1879

International Standard Book Numbers
Paperbound: 978-0-7884-5581-0
Clothbound: 978-0-7884-6031-9

Table of Contents

Foreword

All the information contained in this book has been transcribed from the records of the Department of Interior, Bureau of Indian Affairs Records which are a part of the holdings of the National Archives in Washington, D.C.

These records are hand written notes compiled by Special Indian Agent, Horace B. Durant, who was assigned the task of taking the Census of August 1, 1908 of the Ottawa and Chippewa Indian Tribes of Michigan. His assigned task consisted of determining all the living descendants of those persons found listed on the 1870 Census and Annuity Payment Record of the Grand River, Mackinac, Sault Sainte Marie and Traverse Bands of the Ottawa and Chippewa Indians of Michigan. The information that Special Agent Durant found regarding the living descendants was compiled to form the Ottawa and Chippewa Census of August 1, 1908. That census was then utilized to determine the eligibility of persons of Indian descent to receive payment of monies as the result of U.S. Congressional Legislation and Treaties signed between the Indian tribes and the government of the United States.

Special Agent Durant's records were compiled in an orderly fashion by assigning a number to each person who was listed as a head of household in the 1870 Census of the Ottawa and Chippewa of Michigan. This number was composed of the family number as it appeared in sequence on a given census page, followed by a dash and the number of the census page (i.e. 5-22, 3-63, etc.). Special Agent Durant in search for all the living descendants of those found alive in 1870 accumulated a wealth of useful genealogical information in addition to that which was used to construct the Census of August 1, 1908. His field notes contain information regarding all the known descendants that were not alive in 1908 and a considerable amount of correspondence relating to all the known descendants both living and dead which was not a part of the 1908 Census information. He also provided extensive cross-referencing throughout his notes showing relationships and references made to them by others in correspondence received by him.

Special Agent Durant compiled the name, age, place of residence, marital status, name of spouse, and names of the children of each known descendant. The hand written notes about each known descendant were organized in files numbered 1 through 65 (excluding 10, 18 & 19) matching the number of pages contained in the 1870 Census and Annuity Roll and are stored in the National Archives. Each file contains all of Special Agent Durant's notes and correspondence he received regarding the descendants of the heads of household listed on the page of the 1870 Census. These records number in excess of some 4000 pages. The utmost care has been taken to replicate completely these records as presented with only very minor and insignificant deviations to maintain a standard presentation format and readability. Where appropriate author comments have been added and identified accordingly except the following common unidentified comments which in all cases were not part of the original records:

Name or sex not given   Name not given   None Given

Any text associated with these three comments however, should be considered as part of the original record where they appear. Any transcribed correspondence contained in the original file appears in the book as italicized text.

For those who are researching their Ottawa and Chippewa ancestry this book holds a wealth of invaluable and necessary information which is a must for even the most casual researcher. Published information is quite scarce comparably for Native Americans and equally obscure and hidden in its natural state.

Raymond C. Lantz

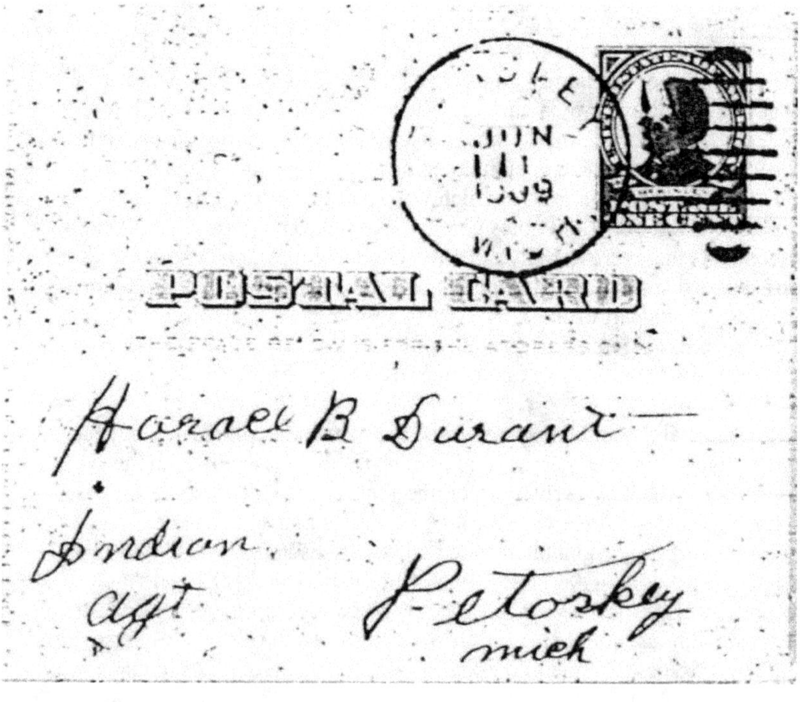

Pages 1 & 2
Sault Sainte Marie Band
Chief MAW DOSH
Marquette Dead River

Information following from: George Madosh, Marquette, May 30/09

1-1 MAW DOSH, a brother of Pi Aw Be Daw Sung # 1-9, dead.
Wife: Name not given, dead.
1-1-1 Name not given, dead.
Husband: Name not given, a Canadian.
1-1-1-1 Ellen Marshall, age 41, enrolled with her grandfather's brother Pi Aw Be Daw Sung # 1-9.
1-1-2 Kate, dead
Husband: Name not given.
1-1-2-1 Jacob Shaw, age 35, P.O. Odanah, said to belong to LaPointe Agency.
Wife: Name not given, enrolled La Pointe Agency
1-1-3 Charlotte Halfaday, age 50, L'Anse Agency
Husband 1st : Amos Craine.
Husband 2nd: Joe Halfaday, age 60, see 7-6.

Information following from: George Madosh, a brother, Margaret Madosh, widow, Marquette, May 30/09.

2-1 DAVID MADOSH, dead, all drew L'Anse in 1907.
Wife: Margaret Madosh, age 60, P.O. Marquette ar Dead River 2 miles north.
2-1-1 Name not given, dead, older the 2-1-4 and 2-1-5.
2-1-2 Name not given, dead, older the 2-1-4 and 2-1-5.
2-1-3 Name not given, dead, older the 2-1-4 and 2-1-5.
2-1-4 David Madosh, age 36, P.O. Marquette, Mich., single.
2-1-5 Annie Madosh, age 20, P.O. Marquette, single.

Information following from: Not Given

3-1 FRANCIS GURNOE, dead.
Wife: Name not given, dead.
3-1-1 Jane Nault, age 64, P.O. 311 Fisher St., Marquette, no children.
Husband: Name not given, white.
3-1-2 Carrie Plain, age 59, P.O. Toledo, Ohio, said to be dead, sister Annie does not known anything about her or her son.
Husband: Jed Plain, white.
3-1-3 Annie Gournoe, age 38, P.O. Garden River, Mich.
3-1-4 Sam Gurnoe, blind, P.O. Thornten near Chicago, never on roll with father, was sailing.

4-1 NO NOTES FOUND

Information following from: Chiefs, Bay Mills, May 10/09
5-1 JULIA NAW MAY WE NAW NE GAW BO, dead, no heirs.

Information following from: George Madosh, Marquette, May 30/09.
6-1 LOUIS NAW MAY WE NAW NE GAW BO, dead.
Wife: Name not given.
6-1-1 Name not given, dead.
Husband: Henry St. Arnold, a L'Anse Indian.
6-1-1-1 Mattie St. Arnold, age 27, P.O. Marquette, no children, drew at L'Anse.
6-1-1-2 Jane St. Arnold, age 23, single, drew at L'Anse.
6-1-2 Name not given, dead.

Information following from: George Madosh, Marquette, May 30/09.
7-1 CHARLES NAW MAY WE NAW NE GAW BO, Chiefs do not know where he is but think he is dead, lived down by Mackinaw City.

Information following from: Not Given
8-1 LOUISA PIQUETTE, dead
Husband: Name not given.
8-1-1 Louisa Brule, not heard from for years.
Husband: Name not given, white.
8-1-2 Harriett, P.O. Menomanee, not heard from for 40 years.
Husband: Dr. ___________

Information following from: Harriet MeIntyre
9-1 JULIA CONTOIS, dead, no heirs.

Information following from: Not Given
10-1 CHARLES PIQUETTE, age 67, P.O. 510 Seymore St., Sault Ste. Marie.
Wife: Angeline Piquette, age 64, see 51-4.
10-1-1 Lucy Lumsden, age 37, P.O. Carey St., "Soo."
Husband: Name not given, white.
10-1-1-1 Viola Lumsden, age 13.
10-1-1-2 Carl Lumsden, age 12.
10-1-1-3 Paul Lumsden, age 6.
10-1-1-4 Edward Lumsden, age 8.
10-1-1-5 Agnes Lumsden, age 2.
10-1-1-6 Alic Lumsden, age 10.
10-1-2 Mary Ann Boucher, age 35, P.O. Soo
Husband: Name not given, dead, see 3-3.
10-1-2-1 Roy Boucher, age 16.
10-1-2-2 John Clifton Boucher, age 14.

10-1-3 Charlotte Brooks, age 33, P.O. Soo.
Husband: Name not given, white.
10-1-3-1 Catharine Brooks, age 7.
10-1-3-2 Mary Brooks, age 6.
10-1-3-3 Maisey Brooks, age 4.
10-1-3-4 Loretta Brooks, age 2.
10-1-4 Stella Green, age 30, P.O. Soo.
Husband: Name not given, white.
10-1-4-1 John Green, age 7.
10-1-4-2 Louisa Green, age 5.
10-1-4-3 Margaret Green, age 3.
10-1-5 Agnes Piquette, age 22, P.O. Soo, single.

Information following from: George Madosh, Marquette, May 30/09.
11-1 AW KO QUAGE, dead.

Information following from: Not Given
12-1 MRS. WM. CAMERON, dead.
Husband: William Cameron.
12-1-1 Mary Jane, dead.
Husband: Samuel Denomie, P.O. Odanah, La Pointe Indian.
12-1-1-1 Samuel Denomie Jr., age 39, P.O. Odanah, enrolled La Pointe Agency.
12-1-2 Clement G. Cameron, dead, no heirs.
12-1-3 Francis James Cameron, age 54, P.O. Autrain, Mich.
Wife: Rosalie Cameron, age 48, 11-7, nee Larmond, father John Larmond at Autrain, said to belong to Mackinaw Band.
12-1-3-1 Eliza Reffrnochmini, age 24.
Husband: Joe Reffrnochmini.
12-1-3-1-1 Francis Reffrnochmini, age 4.
12-1-3-1-2 Joe Reffrnochmini. age 2.
12-1-3-2 Alice Cameron, age 19, P.O. Autraine, Mich.
12-1-3-3 Wm Cameron, age 16, P.O. Autraine, Mich.
12-1-3-4 Duncan Cameron, age 13
12-1-3-5 Henry Cameron, age 11
12-1-3-6 Julia Cameron, age 9.
12-1-4 Sophia Charlotte Cameron, dead.
12-1-5 Julia McKay, age 48, P.O. Bay Mills.
Husband: Name not given, white.
12-1-5-1 George McKay, age 29, P.O. Bay Mills, single.
12-1-5-2 Wm J. McKay, age 25, P.O. Duluth, Minn., single.
12-1-5-3 Mary Jane McKay, age 22, P.O. Bay Mills, single.
12-1-5-4 Annie J. Kerr, age 20.
Husband: Name not given, white.

12-1-5-4-1 Leslie Kerr, age 3.
12-1-5-4-2 Nellie Kerr, age 2, born March 14, 1907.
12-1-5-4-3 Wm Kerr, born March 26, 1909.
12-1-5-5 Margaret McKay, age 19, P.O. Bay Mills.
12-1-5-6 Catharine McKay, age 16, P.O. Bay Mills.

Information following from: Frank Brown, Soo, May 26/09.
13-1 ARTHUR EDWARDS, dead
Wife: Name not given, white.
13-1-1 Thomas Edward, age 32, P.O. Commercial House Soo.
13-1-2 Dave Edwards, age 27, P.O. Detroit.
13-1-3 Charles Edwards, age 25, Detroit.

Information following from: Not Given.
14-1 JANE BRULLIA, age 65, P.O. Maple St., Sault St. Marie.
Husband: Name not given, white.
14-1-1 Name not given, dead, was married.

Information following from: Joe Rouleau.
15-1 KAW CHEESE, dead.
Husband: Name not given.
15-1-1 Rosie Graff, age 41, no children, P.O. House of Corrections Detroit, March.09 for 90 days, lives at Sault St. Marie.

Information following from: Not Given.
16-1 PAW CAW CAW DOSE or JACK LAPEAKE or FRANCIS NOLAN, said to be living, old man 70 or 80, P.O. Manitoba, Canada.
Note: Joe Verette, Interpreter at L'Anse says Paw Caw Caw Dose is dead, Barage May 31/09 Durant Spl. Agt.
Note: Jake Delf, a white man a collector ar Marquette, where Jack LaPeake is. Do not enroll him till found. Delf says he goes by name of Francis Nolan & he went to Manitoba, Canada & he has not heard from him for 2 yrs. Marquette, May 31/09 Durant Spl. Agt.

Information following from: Charles & Angeline.
17-1 EDWARD O SHAW WAW NO, dead.
Wife: Ellen Shawano, age 60, see 41-3, P.O. Sault St. Marie.
17-1-1 Charles Shawano, age 49, P.O. Bay Mills, Mich.
Wife: Mary, Canadian Indian.
17-1-1-1 Maria Shawano, age 18, P.O. Bay Mills, Mich.
17-1-2 Angeline Shawano, age 39, Sugar Isle, not married, but had child by accident, Durant.
17-1-2-1 Kate Wilson, age 2 ½, born September 9, 1906, 1st roll.

Information following from: Not Given.

50-2 MARY LABUT, nee St. Cyre, dead.
Husband: Name not given.
50-2-1 Mary Labatt Carroll, age 35, P.O. Autrain, Mich., see 22-1.
Husband: Name not given.
50-2-1-1 Ed Carroll, age 19, see 22-1.
50-2-1-2 Jessie Carroll, age 17, see 22-1.
50-2-1-3 Louise Carroll, age 15, see 22-1.
50-2-1-4 Ellen Carroll, age 11, see 22-1.
50-2-1-5 Leslie Carroll, age 8, see 22-1.
50-2-1-6 Theodore Carroll, age 5 see 22-1.
50-2-1-7 Percy Carroll, age 4, see 22-1.
50-2-1-8 Howard Carroll, age 3, see 22-1.
50-2-2 Louis Labatt.

Labatt Family 50-2

28 Mary Labatt, 35 years old, whose mothers name was Mary Labatt, deceased, of Saut Ste Marie, Mich. She is married to a white man, her name is Mrs Mary Carroll, the following are their childrennow living.

29 Edmund Carroll	*19 years old*
30 Jessie Carroll	*17 " "*
31 Louise Carroll	*15 " "*
32 Ellen Carroll	*11 " "*
33 Leslie Carroll	*8 " "*
34 Theodore Carroll	*5 " "*
35 Percy Carroll	*4 " "*
36 Howard Carroll	*3 " "*

Authority Petition

We the Undersigned Chippewa Indians and descendants select and appoint Henry Cadreau to be our legal representative with full authority to represent us in any claim or claims, from any treaty or contract made by our forefathers, parents or grand parents, with the United States Government of America.

Name	Address	Age	Date *1930*
Frank Brown Jr.	*900 E. Spruce St.*	*54*	*March 25*
Mrs Frank Brown.	*900 E. Spruce St.*	*47*	"
Francis Brown.	*900 E. Spruce St.*	*25*	"

We the Undersigned Chippewa Indians and descendants select and appoint Henry Cadreau to be our legal representative with full authority to represent us in any claim or claims, from any treaty or contract made by our forefathers, parents or grand parents, with the United States Government of America.

Name	Address	Age ~~Amount~~	Date Age
Joseph Cadreau	*Sugar Isle, Mich*	*64*	*deceased*
Isabella Cadreau Brown	*Sault Ste. Marie 431 Ridge*	*68*	
Alex Cadreau	*Sault Ste. Marie*	*48*	*deceased*
Mary Cadreau	*Sault Ste. Marie 924 Ackinson*	*58*	
Louis Cadreau	*Sault Ste. Marie 557 Carrie*	*53*	*11*
Henry Cadreau	*Sault Ste. Marie 213 Brady*	*48*	*17*
Michael Cadreau	*Sugar Isle, Mich*	*35*	
Paul Cadreau	*Sault Ste. Marie, Mich*	*17*	*17*
Louis ~~Cadreau~~ Hatch	*Sugar Isle, Mich*		
Charles Hatch	*Sault Ste. Marie, Mich*	*74*	*deceased*
Lawrence ~~Catherine~~ Hatch	*Sault Ste. Marie, Mich*	*47*	
Stephen Hatch	*Sault Ste. Marie, Mich*	*45*	*deceased*
Fredric Hatch	*Sault Ste. Marie, Mich*	*41*	
George Hatch	*Sault Ste. Marie, Mich*	*39*	
Isabelle Hatch	*Sault Ste. Marie, Mich*	*37*	*deceased*
Agnes Hatch	*Sault Ste. Marie, Mich*	*35*	
Dewey Hatch	*Sault Ste. Marie, Mich*	*32*	
Beatrice Hatch (Lumsden)	*Sault Ste. Marie, Mich*	*29*	
Ply men Por Piquette	*Cedar Street*	*48*	*March 20*
Robert Thome Piquette	*SugarIsle, Mich*	*40*	*14*
Cadreau List			
Wilfred Cadreau	*SugarIsle*	*39*	*15*
Mrs. Rebecca Cadreau	*SugarIsle*	*65*	*15*
John Cadreau	*SugarIsle*	*45*	*15*
Mary Cadreau	*SugarIsle*	*34*	*15*
James Cadreau	*SugarIsle*	*31*	*15*
Archie Cadreau	*SugarIsle*	*27*	*15*
Hatch List			
Cadotte Descendants			
Louis C. Hatch Jr	*SugarIsle*	*73*	*19*
Mike Hatch	*SugarIsle*	*47*	*died 19*
Louis Hatch	*SugarIsle*	*47*	*19*
Mary Hatch	*SugarIsle*	*27*	*19*
Albert Hatch	*SugarIsle*	*25*	*19*
Margaret Hatch	*SugarIsle*	*25*	*deceased 19*
Piquette and Bonno Descendants			
Plymen Por Piquette	*Cedar Street*	*48*	*15*
Grand Children and Descendants of Chief Kegeash			

Joseph Loford	Sault Ste. Marie	54	15
Mrs. Emma Loford	Sault Ste. Marie	52	15
Tillie Loford	Sault Ste. Marie	50	15
Vernica Loford	Sault Ste. Marie	48	15
Paul Loford	Sault Ste. Marie	42	15
Cerril Loford	Sault Ste. Marie	38	15
Cadotte Descendants			
Joseph Cadreau	Sugar Isle, Mich	64	deceased
	Sault Ste. Marie		
Isabella Cadreau Brown	Sugar Isle	68	
Alex Cadreau	Sault Ste. Marie	48	deceased
Mary Cadreau	Sault Ste. Marie 924 Askmin	58	
Louis Cadreau	Sault Ste. Marie	53	11
Mike Cadreau Lamery	Sugar Isle, Mich	35	
Paul Cadreau	Sault Ste. Marie, Mich	17	17
Descendants of John Boucher			
Sarah Boucher	St. Jacques, Mich	15	
John Boucher	St. Jacques, Mich	15	
Wm Boucher	Sault Ste. Marie	deceased 1916	
Marie Boucher	Sault Ste. Marie	15	
Bonno La Coy Descendants			
Frank La Coy	Sugar Isle		19
John La Coy	Sugar Isle		19
Theodore La Coy	Sugar Isle		19
Wm La Coy	Sugar Isle		19
Leo La Coy	Sugar Isle		19
Mr. Bert McKerchie La Coy	Sugar Isle		19
Mrs. Mary Jane LaFernies La Coy	Sugar Isle		19
Cadotte Descendants			
Charles Hatch	Sault Ste. Marie	74 decesed	
Lawrence Hatch	Sault Ste. Marie	47	19
Stephen Hatch	Sault Ste. Marie	45 deceased	
Fred Hatch	Sault Ste. Marie	41	
George Hatch	Sault Ste. Marie	39 deceased	
Isabella Hatch	Sault Ste. Marie	37 deceased	
Agnes Hatch	Sault Ste. Marie	35	
Dewey Hatch	Sault Ste. Marie	32	19
Robert Thom Piquette	Sugar Isle	40	19
Descendants of Awshawassi			
Mrs. Joseph Wayishkey	Sault Ste. Marie 419 Godey	66	19
John Ojibway	Sault Ste. Marie		24
Henry Ojibway	Sault Ste. Marie		24
Joseph Ojibway	Sault Ste. Marie		24
Delia Ojibway	Sault Ste. Marie		24
Agnes Ojibway	Sault Ste. Marie		24

Georgia Ann Ojibway	*Sault Ste. Marie*		*24*
Stella Ojibway	*Sault Ste. Marie*		*24*
George Ojibway	*Sault Ste. Marie*		*24*
Leo Ojibway	*Sault Ste. Marie*		*24*
Adeline Ojibway	*Sault Ste. Marie*		*24*
Direct Descendants of Chief Shawano & John Jurnoe Headman			
Henry Thome; deceased	*616 Spruce St.*	*87*	*28*
Frank Thome	*616 Spruce St.*	*61*	*28*
Gilbert Thome	*616 Spruce St. deceased*	*46*	*28*
James Thome	*616 Spruce St.*	*52*	*28*
Harriet Thome	*616 Spruce*	*50*	*28*
Emma Thome	*616 Spruce deceased*	*48*	*28*
Lucy Thome	*616 Spruce*	*48*	*28*
~~*Harriet Thome*~~		*28*	
H. George Thome	*616 Spruce Deceased*	*26*	*28*
Al J. Thome	~~*3530*~~ *616 Spruce St.*	*40*	*28*
S. J. Thome	*616 Spruce St.*	*38*	*28*
Louis L. Thome	*616 Spruce St.*	*36*	*28*
Lorence Thome	*616 Spruce St.*	*33*	*28*
Ed thome	*616 Spruce St.*	*27*	*28*
Archie Thome	*616 Spruce*	*24*	*28*

Information following from: Not Given

18-1 WAW WE AW GE WAW NO QUAY

Note: George Madosh, at Marquette, son of Chief, & 70 yrs. old does not remember the name. Marquette, Durant, May 30/09.

Information following from: Mados, Marquette, May 30/09.

19-1 QUE WIS, dead, no heirs.

Information following from: Bay Mills head men & Marquette head men.

20-1 O HIGH ISH, dead.

Husband: Name not given.

20-1-1 Julia, dead.

Husband: Paul Pine, dead, see 26-1.

20-1-1-1 George Pine, age 32, single, P.O. Sault Ste. Marie or Bay Mills.

Information following from: Frank Brown Jr.

21-1 ELLEN EDWARDS, dead.

Husband: _________ Brown, dead

21-1-1 Frank Brown Sr., age 52, P.O. Sault Ste. Marie.

Wife: Isabelle Brown, age 50, P.O. 551 Maple St., 11-3.

21-1-1-1 Frank Brown Jr., age 29, Soo Carey St.

Wife: Blacky Brown, see 10-3.

21-1-1-1-1 Fancis Brown, age 5.
21-1-1-1-2 Name not given, born July/08, 2nd roll.
21-1-1-2 Joe Brown Jr., age 23, single, P.O. Soo Maple St.
21-1-1-3 Charlotte M. Brown, age 22, single, P.O. Soo Maple St.
21-1-2 Joe H. Brown, age 47, P.O. Minnesota, Deluth.
Wife: Name not given, white, no children.

Information following from: Not Given
22-1 MRS. JESSE ST. CYER, nee Mary Restule, dead.
Husband: Name not given.
22-1-1 ~~Eliza~~ Isabelle St. Cyre ~~Kauffman~~ Coffman, P.O. 102 Furnace Street, South Marquette.
Husband 1st: Joseph Tourner, dead.
Husband 2nd: Alfred Coffman, white
22-1-1-1 Josephine Tourner, age 33.
22-1-1-2 Eva Tourner, age 28.
22-1-1-3 Aggie Tourner, age 26.
22-1-1-4 Louis Tourner, age 24.
22-1-1-5 Eddie Tourner, age 21.
22-1-1-6 Bessie Coffman, age 17.
22-1-2 Hyacinthe St. Cyer, Milwaukee, dead.
Husband: Name not given.
22-1-2-1 Rosa
22-1-2-2 Jennnie
22-1-2-3 Louis
22-1-2-4 Freddie
22-1-3 Mary St. Cyre, dead.
Husband: John Sabut, white.
22-1-3-1 Mary Carroll, P.O. Autrain, Mich., see 50-2.
22-1-3-2 Louis Sabatt, P.O. Autrain, Mich., see 50-2.
22-1-4 Charles St. Cyre, dead.
22-1-5 Richard St. Cyre, dead.

Marquette, Mich
102 Furnace Street
July 8, 1909

Horace B. Durant
Special US. Indian Agent
Petoskey, Mich.

My Dear Sir.

I have yours of June 22 last. My mother maiden name was Mary Restule she married Servis St. Cyre at the "Soo" but I do not know the date. They raised a family of four children – there were nine children born but four died young.

Mary St Cyre oldest daughter married John Sabit. She had one daughter now Mary Carroll living now at AuTrain Alger Co Mich.
Mary St. Cyre nee Sabah died Sept 8th 1885 at AuTrain Mich.
Jessie St. Cyre my brother died several years age, but do not know place or date of his death. He left four children but I do not know their ages or where they now are. Their names are Rosa – Louis – Jennie – Freddie.
Charles St Cyre my brother is dead – was not married left no issue.
Richard St. Cyre, my brother, is also dead – not married – left no issue.
Isabell St. Cyre – myself married Joseph Tourner & raised a family of five children all living

Josephine Tourner	*33 years.*
Eva Tourner	*28 "*
Aggie Tourner	*26 "*
Louis Tourner	*24 "*
Eddie Tourner	*21 "*

My husband Joseph Tourner died Sept 4 1889 in Alger County Mich. In 1880 I married Alfred Coffman and have our daughter Bessie Coffman now age 17.

I have our grand son Louis Tourner son of my daughter Josephine Tourner said Grand son is now 14 years old.

This is all the information I can now give you regarding my family. If anything further is needed wult me will do but I can my mother Mary Restule was one of the Tribe of Chippewas.

Very Truly Yours
Isabell Coffman

Marquette, Mich Sept. 1 1909

To Horace B. Durant
Special U.S. Indian Agent
Dear Sir

Replying to yours of June 22nd which only reached ma a few days since I have to advise you that I do claim right to enrollment as afull blooded Chippewa. I was born in Marquette Mich about 55 years and have lived in Marquette County all my life.
Fathers name was Peter Cadotte – a Chippewa: died about 1859
Mothers name " Amanda Mar je ke zik " " " "
No brothers or sisters living.
Wife's name is Eliza Thebault Cadotte: she is ¼ indian: 45 years of age: P.O. Marquette, Mich: her father was French Canadian, and mother a half breed Chippewa: her fathers name was Alex Thebault and mothers Mary _______ both have been deadfor some years.
Our childrem are Charles Cadotte 22 years: Alfred Cadotte 21 years: Clifford Cadotte: 19 years : Wilfred Cadotte 13 years and Alice Cadotte, 15 years, all living in Marquette Mich.

Very Respectfully

Fred Cadotte Pr Byrne
P.O. Marquette Co Mich

Information following from: Not Given

23-1 PE NAY SE WON QUOT O QUAY, dead, cannot trace heirs Durant Spl. Agt.

Information following from: JM Johnson, wife of old Interpreter in 1870 & George Madosh, Marquette, May 30/09.

24-1 KO BAW GUM, dead.
Wife: Name not given, dead.
24-1-1 Name not given, dead.
Husband: Name not given.
24-1-1-1 Lizzie Perault, age 16, P.O. Mt. Pleasant School.
24-1-1-2 Frank Perault, age 12, P.O. Mt. Pleasant School.
24-1-2 Fred Cadotte, age 55, P.O. Marquette, Mich.
Wife: Name not given, French Canadian.
2-1-2-1 Charlie Cadotte, age 22, P.O. Marquette, Mich.
2-1-2-2 Alfred Cadotte, age 21, P.O. Marquette, Mich.
2-1-2-3 Clifford Cadotte, age 19, P.O. Marquette, Mich.
2-1-2-4 Wilfred Cadotte, age 13, P.O. Marquette, Mich.
2-1-2-5 Alice Cadotte, age 15, P.O. Marquette, Mich.

Information following from: Justina Johnson, Madosh & Andrew Waishkey, Marquette, May 30/09.

25-1 PAY ME CHE WONG, dead.
Wife 1st: Name not given.
Wife 2nd: Name not given.
25-1-1 Mary Green - Pendell, see 21-7, age 55, by 2nd wife, she had 3 children at Odanah. All drew at L'Anse.
Husband 1st : ________ Clark, dead, of Sou band.
Husband 2nd: ________ Green, dead, an Odamah Indian.
25-1-2 Henry Vanansilles
Note: ask sister where he is. Has not been heard from for some years, can't find him.

Information following from: Not Given

26-1 PAUL PINE, dead.
Wife: Name not given, daughter of 20-1
26-1-1 George Pine, age 32, single, see 20-1.

Information following from: Justina Johnson.

27-1 O DE QUAIB, dead, a sister of Chief Praiobe dawsung.
Note: had a child but both dead, & all heirs said to be dead Durant

May/09.

Information following from: Andrew & Peter Waishkey, Bay Mills, May 10/09.
28-1 Louis Pine, age 75, P.O. L'Anse, said to draw with L'Anse Band.
Wife: Name not given, L'Anse Indian, no children.

Information following from: Joseph Rouleau.
29-1 DANIEL CADOTTE, 2nd, dead, no children.

Information following from: Samuel Wawbegaykake, Bay Mills, May 10/09.
30-1 WAW BE GAY KAKE, dead.
Wife: Angeline Waw Be Gay Kake, age 80, P.O. Sault Ste. Marie.
30-1-1 Joe, dead.
Wife: Name not given, dead.
30-1-1-1 Mary Jane Wawbegakake, dead.
Husband: Gilbert Jones, Canadian Indian.
30-1-1-1-1 Edward Jones, dead.
30-1-1-2 Agnes Wawbegakake, dead.
Husband: Angus Kay.
30-1-1-2-1 Susan Waw Be Ga Kake, age 16, P.O. Sault Ste. Marie, with grandmother.
30-1-1-3 Samuel Wawbegakake, age 35, P.O. Bay Mills.
Wife: Jennie Wawbegakake, age 22, see 26-5.
30-1-1-3-1 Joe Wawbegakake, age 7.
30-1-2 Emiline Greenfield, age 64, Sault Ste. Marie, see 39-1.
Husband: Name not given, dead.
30-1-2-1 Mary Kaw We Tos, age 20.
Husband: Joe Kaw We Tos, age 23, see 17-9.
30-1-3 Name not given, dead, no heirs.
30-1-4 Name not given, dead.
Spouse: name not given, dead.
30-1-4-1 Louisa Waw Be Gay Kake, age 21, see 20-9.

Information following from: George Madosh.
31-1 NAW KEY WAY or GEORGE MADOSH or JOE, age 70, P.O. Marquette – 2 miles north near Dead River take Street Car to Power house, all on this page drew with L'Anse.
Wife: Jane Madosh, age 70, see 1-8
31-1-1 Annie Madosh, age 48, P.O. Pequaming, Mich., drew at L'Anse.
Husband 1st : Name not given, dead, L'Anse Indian.
Husband 2nd: George Johnson, age 38, see 6-6.
31-1-1-1 Sarah Marksman – GoKey (Gauthier), age 32, P.O. Marquette, all drew L'Anse.

Husband: Sam GoKey, white.
31-1-1-1-1 James GoKey, age 15.
31-1-1-1-2 Louis GoKey, age 14.
31-1-1-1-3 Wilfred GoKey, age 10.
31-1-1-1-4 George GoKey, age 4.
31-1-1-1-5 Lizzie GoKey, age 2.
31-1-1-1-6 John GoKey, born Nov 10/09.
31-1-1-2 Julia Curtis, age 21, P.O. L'Anse, Mich, draw at L'Anse.
Husband: Name not given, L'Anse Indian.
31-1-1-2-1 Name not given, draw at L'Anse.
31-1-1-2-2 Name not given, draw at L'Anse.
31-1-1-2-3 Name not given, draw at L'Anse.
31-1-1-3 Jerry Marksman, age 18, P.O. Odanah, draws at L'Anse.
31-1-1-4 Susan Johnson, P.O. Pequaming, draws at L'Anse with mother.
31-1-1-5 Hazel Johnson, P.O. Pequaming, draws at L'Anse with mother.
31-1-1-6 Rhoda Johnson, P.O. Pequaming, draws at L'Anse with mother.
31-1-1-7 Baby Johnson, P.O. Pequaming, draws at L'Anse with mother.
31-1-2 Susan Kroft, age 45, P.O. Pequaming, Mich, no children.
Husband: Name not given, white.
31-1-3 Pete Madosh, age 40, P.O. Pequaming, Mich.
Wife: Name not given, dead.
31-1-3-1 William Madosh, P.O. Pequaming, Mich.
31-1-3-2 Mary Mados, P.O. Pequaming, Mich.
31-1-4 Charles Madosh, 28, P.O. Pequaming, Mich.
Wife: Name not given, L'Anse.
31-1-4-1 Lawrence Madosh, age 5.
31-1-4-2 Clara Madosh, age 3.
31-1-5 Jannie Fountain, age 23, P.O. Pequaming, Mich.
Husband: Name not given, white.
31-1-5-1 Eliza Fountain, P.O. Pequaming, Mich.
31-1-6 Augustus Madosh, age 24, single, P.O. Duluth, Minn.
31-1-7 George Madosh, age 21, single, P.O. Marquette.
31-1-8 Maggie Belanger, dead.
Husband: Mike Belanger, white.
31-1-8-1 Evangeline or Vangie Belanger, age 12, lives with grandfather George Madosh.
31-1-8-2 Joe Belanger, age 10, lives with grandfather George Madosh.

Information following from: Madosh, Marquette, May 30/09.

32-1 SHING GWAW NAW QUOT, last heard from was down near Mackinaw, cannot find him.

Information following from: Madosh, Marquette, May 30/09.

33-1 KEY WAY DE NO QUAY's children.

33-1-1 Frank Parault or Pero, age 60, P.O. Grand Marie, Minn.

33-1-2 Henry Perault, age 59, P.O. Harvey, lives Chocolay, Mich, single, see 38-1, adopted sister's child.

33-1-1 Harvey Parault, age 4, see as 2nd child of Susan Saboo below.

33-1-3 Louisa Curtis, P.O. L'Anse, see 38-1.

33-1-4 Susan Howard Saboo, see 4-7, separated.

Husband 1st : John Brown, P.O. Munising.

Husband 2nd: James Howard Saboo, see 4-7.

33-1-4-1 Henry Brown, age 16, Reform School in Mich, child by 1st husband.

33-1-5-2 Harry Parault Jr., age 14, lives with Henry Perault Sr. an uncle, see above, child by 1st husband.

33-1-5-3 Name not given, see 4-17, child by 2nd husband.

Harvey, Mich. July 15-09
Department of the Interior
United State Indian Service
Gentlemen
My Name is Henry Pero my age 59 years, No Children, My Brothersname is Frank Pero, address, Grand Morie, Minn.
My Sisters Name Louise Cuddis herAddress Baraga, Mich, my Sisters hasfive children.

Yours Truly
Henry Pero, Harvy Mich

Information following from: Madosh, Marquette, May 30/09.

35-1 O GAW BAY AW SE GAY QUAY or MRS. JOSEPH HALFADAY, 7-6 and 1-1.

Information following from: Madosh, Marquette, May 30/09.

36-1 O ME NE SE NO QUAY, dead, heirs at Soo already enrolled on other sheets.

Information following from: Madosh, Marquette, May 30/09.

37-1 ONG O QUAY, dead.

Information following from: Charles Marshall, a half sister in law.

38-1 LOUISA PEROW (PERAULT) or LOUISA CURTIS, age 58, P.O.

L'Anse, Mich.
Husband: Name not given.
38-1-1 Louis Perow, age 22.
38-1-2 Daniel Perow, age 20.

Information following from: Not Given.
39-1 MRS. MOSES GREENBIRD, P.O. Soo, see 30-1.

Information following from: Louis Moses, P.O. St. Jacques, Dec 4 & 6/08
40-1 AW BE TAW KE ZHICK, dead,
Wife: Name not given.
40-1-1 Louis Moses, age 51, P.O. St. Jacques, Mich, spouse & children see 3-37.
40-1-2 Catharine Washo, age 38, P.O. St Jacques, spouse & children see 2-37.
40-1-3 Annie Halfaday, dead.
Husband: Name not given, dead, white.
40-1-3-1 Mary Young, age 16, P.O. St. Jacques, is non competent & half witted Durant, lives with 3-37.
40-1-3-2 Andrew Wheaton, age 26, P.O. St. Jacques, for wife & child (dead) see 20-9.

Information following from: Not Given.
43-2 KE CHE E QUAY or ELLEN MARSHALL, see 1-1 and 10-7.

Pages 3 & 4
Sault Sainte Marie Band
Chief O SHAW WAW NO
Sault Ste. Marie Vicinity

Information following from: John Andrews, The names on this aheet are vouched for by the Sugar Isle Chiefs Durant May 14/09.
A-Soo NE BE NAISH CAW MO QUAY, or MRS. PETER SMITH, no number or page assigned to this sheet, labeled as "A" "Soo", age 75, P.O. Drumonds Isle.
Husband: Peter Smith, see 8-15.
A-Soo-1 Mary Andrews Jan Ga Ge Gade, age 65, P.O. Sugar Isle, see 2-8.
Husband: Name not given, dead.
A-Soo-1-1 Veronica Nim Dos Kung, 33, see 3-8.
A-Soo-1-2 George Andrew #1, age 46, P.O. Hessell, see 3-17.
A-Soo-1-3 John Andrew, age 34, P.O. Sugar Isle.
Wife: Charlote Andrew, age 36, see 35-8, nee Naw Way Ke Zhick.
A-Soo-1-3-1 Charles Andrew, age 6.

A-Soo-1-3-2 Joe Andrew, age 4.
A-Soo-1-4-3 Sophia Andrew, born August 1907, 2nd Roll.
A-Soo-1-4 William Andrews, age 25, P.O. Sugar Isle, single.
A-Soo-1-5 Jannie Andrews, dead.
Husband: William Coleman, white.
A-Soo-1-5-1 Mary Coleman, age 8, P.O. Sugar Isle.
A-Soo-1-5-2 Lena Coleman, age 6.

Information following from: Spencer Johnston, Sugar Isle, May 25/09.

1-3 JOHN M. JOHNSON, dead.
Wife: Justina Johnson, age 85, P.O. Sailor's Encampment, Mich.
1-3-1 Spencer N. Johnston, age 66, P.O. Payment, Mich – Sugar Isle.
Wife: Name not given, white.
1-3-1-1 Pearl A. Lindberg, age 22, P.O. Astoria, Clatsop Co., Oregon.
Husband: Name not given, white.
1-3-1-1 Norvel Lindberg, born March 19,1908, 2nd Roll.
1-3-2 Maria Johnston, age 64, single, P.O. Sailor's Encampment, Mich.
1-3-3 Charlotte Johnson, single, age 62, P.O. Sailor's Encampment.
1-3-4 James Johnson, age 60, P.O. Tacoma, Wash., heard from fall of 1908, wife white, no children.
1-3-5 John Johnson, dead, no children.
1-3-6 Howard Johnston, age 54, P.O. Sailor's Encampment, wife white, no children.
1-3-7 William Johnston, age 50, P.O. Drummond's Isle.
Wife: Name not given, white.
1-3-7-1 Naida Johnston, age 22, single, P.O. Drummond's Isle
1-3-7-2 Juanita Johnston, age 20, single.
1-3-7-3 W. Evelyn, age 18, single.
1-3-8 Henry Johnston, dead.
Wife. Pricilla Johnston, white, P.O. Soo.
1-3-8-1 Lorina Johnston, single, age 24, P.O. Detroit (School).
1-3-8-2 Bernia Johnston, single, 19, P.O. Soo.
1-3-8-3 Percy Johnston, age 15.
1-3-8-4 Keith Johnstoon, age 12.
1-3-9 Archie Johnson, dead, no children.
1-3-10 Eliza Johnston Anthony, age 58, P.O. Detroit, Mich.
Husband: _________ Anthony, dead, white.
1-3-10-1 Howard Anthony, age 22, single, P.O. Detroit, Mich.
1-3-10-2 Retta Anthony, age 25, single.

Information following from: Not Given.

2-3 LOUIS O SHAW WAW NO, age 84, P.O. Soo, Sugar Isle.
Wife: Name not given, dead.
2-3-1 Charlotte Shagonaby, age 59, see 1-8, P.O. Sugar Isle.
Husband: Louis Shagonaby, 62, Sugar Isle, see 20-34.
2-3-1-1 Robert Shagonaby, age 44, single, Sugar Isle.
2-3-1-2 Eva Billington, age 40
Husband: ________ Billington, white.
2-3-1-2-1 Wilfred Billington, age 3.
2-3-1-3 Josephine Hallaway, age 30, P.O. Sugar Isle.
Husband: ________ Hallaway, white.
2-3-1-3-1 Pearl Hallaway, age 3.
2-3-1-3-2 Florence Hallaway, born September 1908, too late.
2-3-1-4 Kate Shagonaby, age 27, single, P.O. Sugar Isle.
2-3-1-5 Agnes Stearns, age 24
Husband: _________ Stearns, white.
2-3-1-5-1 John Stearns, age 2, born September 1907, 2nd Roll.
2-3-1-6 Charles Shagonabe, age 21, single, P.O. Sugar Isle.
2-3-1-7 Frank Shagonabe, age 18.
2-3-1-8 Susan Shagonabe, age 14.
2-3-2 Mary Shagonaby, dead, no heirs.
2-3-3 Jane Pereault, dead.
Husband: John Pereault, see 12-8.
2-3-3-1 Mary Pereault, age 27, single, P.O. Soo 208 Fort St.
2-3-3-2 John Pereault, dead, no heirs.
2-3-3-3 Sophia Pereault, age 19, died June 28/07.
2-3-3-4 Jennette Pereault, age 19, single.
2-3-3-5 Frank Pereault, age 14.
2-3-4 Maria Shawano, age 49, single, Sugar Isle.
2-3-5 Lizzie Shagonaby, dead, single.
2-3-6 Susan Bunno, age 51, P.O. Soo 214 Gros Cap Ave.
Husband: Joseph Bunno, age 52, see 22-5.
2-3-6-1 Joseph Bunno Jr., age 25, single, P.O. Soo.
2-3-6-2 Addie Bunno, dead.
2-3-6-3 John Bunno, age 21, single.
2-3-6-4 Sophia Bunno, 20, single.
2-3-6-5 Louis Bunno, age 18.
2-3-7 Harriet Shagonaby, dead, no child.
2-3-8 Catharine McCall, age 38, P.O. Soo Maple St.
Husband: Charles McCall, white.
2-3-8-1 Hazel McCall, age 15.
2-3-9 Frank Shawano, age 36, P.O. Sugar Isle.
Wife: Maria Shawano #3, age 28.
2-3-9-1 Edward Shawano, age 5.

2-3-10 Name not given, dead, no heirs.

Information following from: Alex Boucher, Soo, May 8/09.

3-3 JOHN B. BO SHAY or BOUCHER
Wife: Name not given.
3-3-1 Name not given.
3-3-2 Alex Boucher, age 57, see 3-8
Wife 1st : Name not given, dead.
Wife 2nd: Charlotte, age 37, see 3-8.
3-3-2-1 George Boucher, age 26, P.O. Sugar Isle, single, see 2-8, child by 1st wife.
Wife: Zoe, see 2-8.
Note: For children by 2nd wife see 3-8.
3-3-3 William Boucher, dead.
Wife: Maria Grant Boucher, see 27-8.
3-3-4 Charles Boucher, age 45, P.O. Maple St. Soo.
Wife: Name not given, white.
3-3-4-1 Evans Boucher
3-3-5 Frank Boucher #2, see 25-8.
Wife: Name not given, see 25-8.
3-3-6 Name not given, dead.
Wife: (Nettie) Mary Ann Piquette, age 35, see 10-1.

Information following from: Not Given.

4-3 EDWARD ASHMAN, dead.
Wife: Amanda (Chipman) Ashman, dead, see 30-13, P.O. Sault Ste. Marie.
4-3-1 Lucy Ripley, age 58, P.O. Sault Ste. Marie 312 Park Place.
Husband: _______ Ripley, white.
4-3-1-1 E. R. Ripley, age 38, P.O. Soo, Mich.
4-3-1-2 V. A. Ripley, age 37, P.O. Soo, Mich.
4-3-1-3 Mrs. G. A. Boyd, age 35, P.O. Soo Ontario.
4-3-1-4 Charles A. Ripley, age 33, P.O. Soo, Mich.
4-3-1-5 H. G. Ripley, age 31, P.O. R.F.D. #2 Soo, Mich.
4-3-1-6 Guy C. Ripley, age 27, P.O. Riverside, Ill.
4-3-1-7 C. W. Ripley, age 26.
4-3-1-8 B. J. Ripley, age 24.
4-3-1-9 L. Clyde Ripley, age 18.
4-3-2 Reuben Ashman, dead.
Wife: Name not given, white, living Portage Ave. Soo.
4-3-2-1 Glenn Ashman, age 22, P.O. Portage Ave. Soo, Mich.
4-3-3 Ed Ashman, dead.
Wife: Name not given, widow living at Whitier, Colo.
4-3-3-1 Elsie May Ashman, age 16, P.O. Whitier, Col.
4-3-4 Amanda Kelly, dead.

Husband: _______ Kelly, white.

4-3-4-1 Mrs. Freeman L. Gullifer, P.O. 2103 Vega Ave., Cleveland O.

4-3-4-2 Jame Kelly, P.O. 2108 W. 24th Place Chicago Ill.

4-3-5 Mrs. Ella Hecox, age 44, P.O. Bingham Ave Soo.

Husband: _______ Hecox.

4-3-5-1 Don M. Hecox, age 24.

4-3-5-2 Paul Hecox, age 21.

4-3-5-3 Florence Hecox, age 18.

4-3-5-4 Ruth Hecox, age 16.

4-3-6 Mary L. Ashman, age 42, P.O. 312 Park Place Soo.

4-3-7 Jennie Kelly, age 40, P.O. Arlington St. Soo.

Husband: _______ Kelly, white.

4-3-7-1 E. Ray Kelly, age 21.

4-3-8 Anna Ashman, age 40, Arlington St. Soo.

4-3-9 Grace Ashman, dead.

Sault Mich June 22nd/09

Horace B. Durant
Special M. I. Indian Agent
Sir.

Your communication received and in reply would say the following are the Descendants of Edward Ashman.

Reuben D. Ashman Deceased age at time of death 50 years
His Heirs.
Widow and 1 child address Portage Ave Sault Ste Marie, Mich.
Edward Ashman Deceased age at time of Death 36
His Heirs
Widow and 1 child address Whitier, Col.
Amanda Kelly Deceased age at time of death 41
Her Heirs
1 Daughter Mrs Freeman L. Gullifer 2103 Vega Ave Cleveland Ohio.
1 Son James Kelly 2108 W. 24th Place Chicago Ill.
Mrs Ella Hecox Bingham Ave, Saukt Ste. Marie Mich age 44
Miss Mary L. Ashman 312 Park Place Sault Ste. Marie Mich age 42.
Miss Jennie Kelly Arlington St. Sault Ste. Marie Mich age 40
Miss Anna Ashman Arlington St. Sault Ste. Marie Mich age 40
Miss Grace Ashman Deceased age at time of Death 20
Mrs. Lucy A. Ripley Sault Ste. Marie Mich age 58
I was on Pay Roll as head of family in 1871.
Yours Respectfully
Mrs Lucy A. Ripley
312 Park Place, Sault, Mich

Information following from: Joseph Misatago & Fam., St. Ignace.

5-3 O SAW WAW MICK, spelled (OZAMICK), dead.
Wife: Name not given, dead.
5-3-1 Name not given, dead, no heirs.
5-3-2 Name not given, dead.
Wife or Husband: Name not given.
5-3-2-1 Name not given, P.O. near Mantoulin Isle.
5-3-3 William O Saw Waw Mick, age 60, P.O. Drummond's Isle.
Wife: Angeline, age 50, nee Shawan Soo Band see 5-8.
5-3-3-1 Lizzie Boucher or Boushay, age 30, P.O.
Drummond's
Isle.
Husband: Willam Boucher or Boushay, see 23-3.
5-3-3-1-1 Ellen Boucher or Boushay, born January/08.
5-3-3-1-2 Baby (Jane) Boucher or Boushay, born January/09.
5-3-3-2 Ed O Saw Waw Mick, age 24, Drummond's Isle.
Wife: Eliza O Saw Waw Mick, nee LaRose, Canadian Indian, no children.
5-3-3-3 Mary Ann O Saw Waw Mick, age 18, Drummond's Isle.
5-3-3-4 Pete O Saw Waw Mick, age 12.
5-3-3-5 William O Saw Waw Mick, age 8.
5-3-3-6 Archangle O Saw Waw Mick, age 5.
5-3-3-7 Michael O Saw Waw Mick, age 31, single.
5-3-4 Elizabeth Misatago, see 31-15, P.O. St. Ignace.
5-3-5 Louis O Saw Waw Mick, age 48, single, P.O. St. Ignace.
5-3-6 Mary (O Saw Waw Mick) Lasage, age 44, P.O. St. Ignace.
Husband: Louis Lasage.
5-3-6-1 Duncan Lasage, age 19.
5-3-6-2 Eliza Lasage, age 15.
5-3-6-3 Benjamin Lasage, age 7.
Note: Plus grandson of 6-17 says his grandmother belonged to Beam Isle.
5-3-7 Samuel O Saw Waw Mick, age 42, P.O. St. Ignace.
Wife: Rosie (Ance) O Saw Waw Mick, age 30, see 2-15.
5-3-7-1 William O Saw Waw Mick, age 8.
5-3-7-2 Alice O Saw Waw Mick, age 4.

Information following from: Charlotte Abel, Elizabeth Johnson & Joseph Rouleau, Soo, May 7/09.

6-3 JOHN GURNOE, dead.
Wife: Name not given, dead.
6-3-1 Sarah Thorne, age 50, P.O. Goos Cap Ave., Sault Ste. Marie.
Husband: Henry Thorne, see 16-3, P.O. Goos Cap Ave., Sault Ste. Marie.

6-3-1-1 Aloisious Thorne, age 21, P.O. Goos Cap Ave., Sault Ste. Marie.
6-3-1-2 Sam Thorne, age 19, P.O. Goos Cap Ave., Sault Ste. Marie.
6-3-1-3 Louis Thorne, age 17, P.O. Goos Cap Ave., Sault Ste. Marie.
6-3-1-4 Lawrence Thorne, age 13, P.O. Goos Cap Ave., Sault Ste. Marie.
6-3-1-5 Eddie Thorne, age 8, P.O. Goos Cap Ave., Sault Ste. Marie.
6-3-1-6 Archie Thorne, age 5, P.O. Goos Cap Ave., Sault Ste. Marie.
6-3-2 Charlotte Abel, age 43, P.O. 311 Sponee, West, Sault Ste. Marie.
Husband: _______ Abel, white.
6-3-2-1 Clarence Abel, age 8.
6-3-2-2 Gertrude Abel, age 6.
6-3-3 Elizabeth Johnson, age 41, P.O. 311 Sponee, West, Sault Ste. Marie, husband white, no children.
6-3-4 Name not given, dead, no heirs.
6-3-5 Name not given, dead, no heirs.
6-3-6 Name not given, dead, no heirs.
6-3-7 Name not given, dead, no heirs.

Information following from: Frank Nolin & Clement Nolin.
7-3 JOHN B. NOLIN, dead.
Wife: Name not given, dead.
7-3-1 Mary Jandreau, age 55, P.O. Soo.
Husband: Joe Jandreau.
7-3-2 Sophia Davidson, age 52, Cedar St. Soo, husband white.
7-3-3 Jennie Prior, age 47, P.O. Soo.
Husband: James Pryor.
7-3-4 Tillie Bunno, age 46, P.O. Soo.
Husband: Leo Bunno, see son of 22-5.
7-3-5 Madeline Pryor, age 43, P.O. Soo.
Husband: Samuel Pryor.
7-3-6 Frank Nolin, age 42, Lighthouse Keeper, Sugar Isle.
Wife: Maggie Nolin, age 38, Canadian.
7-3-6-1 Ellen Nolin, age 15.
7-3-6-2 Frank Nolin, age 12.
7-3-6-3 Ada Nolin, age 10.
7-3-6-4 Cecelia Nolin, age 8.
7-3-6-5 John Nolin, age 6.
7-3-6-6 William Nolin, age 3.
7-3-7 Clement J. Nolin, age 40, P.O. Sugar Isle.

Wife: Victoria Nolin, Canadian.
7-3-7-1 Joseph A. Nolin, age 5.
7-3-7-2 Ida May Nolin, age 3.
7-3-8 Cecelia Boullia, age 37, P.O. Soo Maple St., no children.
Husband: Samuel Boullia, see 10-5.

Information following from: Thomas Fish & letter from Joe Shagonaby.
8-3 Edward SHAY GO NAY BE, dead.
Wife: Sophia Shagonaybe, age 80, P.O. Bay Mills.
8-3-1 Mary Shagonayby, dead.
Husband: Name not given, dead.
Note: Children said to be drawing in Guly Bay Canada.
8-3-2 Joseph Shagonaby, age 54, P.O. Goulais Bay, Canada.
Wife: Name not given, Canadian Indian.
8-3-2-1 Mary Shagonaby, age 21.
8-3-2-2 Joseph Shagonaby, age 15.
8-3-2-3 Margaret Shagonaby, age 10.
8-3-3 Theresa Fish, age 52, P.O. Bay Mills, see 9-7.

Goulais Bay Mission Ont.
July 3rd 1909

Mr Horace B. Durant Esq
Special U.S. Indian Agent
Petoskey Mich

Dear Sir

Your letter June 8th at hand asking me if I was member the Chippewa tribe in Michigan. Yes I was and I received the treaty in Michigan and also received the last payment was made in michigan. My name his Joseph shagonaby. My age 50 years and my wife herage 38 years and I have three children, namely, Mary her age 21 years Joseph his age 15. Margaret her age 10 years. And About my parents. My father died. And my Mother she is living yet. She is living in Michigan. place called Bay Mills. This is all I can give you Information. This time if you want to know any more particulars please write to me. And I wish to thank you for the trouble you took to write to me. Hoping this will be satisfaction.

I beg to remain Dear Sir
Very Respectfully
Joseph Shagonaby

Information following from: Letter from James Mushway or James Shawawgawbo & Chiefs, July 3/09.
9-3 SHAW WAW NO GAW BO or MUSHWAY, dead.
Wife: Name not given, dead.
9-3-1 Name not given, dead.
9-3-2 James Mushway or James Shawwawgawbo, age 56, P.O.

Goulais Bay, Canada.
Wife: Name not given, dead.
9-3-2-1 Angeline Mushway, age 29.
9-3-2-2 James Mushway, age 24.
9-3-2-3 Elizabeth Mushway, age 19.
9-3-2-4 Paul Mushway, age 18.
9-3-2-5 Mary Mushway, age 14.

9-3-3 Genevieva McKay, age 63, P.O. Goulais Bay, Canada.
Husband: Dan McKay.
9-3-3-1 Betsey McKay, age 34.
9-3-3-2 Margaret Mckay, age 30.
9-3-3-3 Elizabeth McKay, age 27.
9-3-3-4 Jennie McKay, age 23.

9-3-4 Angeline Cadron, age 60, P.O. Goulais Bay, Canada.
Husband: ________ Cadron.
9-3-4-1 Joseph Cadron, age 39.
9-3-4-2 Thomas Cadron, age 32.
9-3-4-3 Michael Cadron, age 24.
9-3-4-4 John Cadron, age 21.

9-3-5 Charlotte Reil, age 61, P.O. Goulais Bay, Canada.
Husband: Antoine Reil.
9-3-5-1 Antoine Reil, age 20.
9-3-5-2 Veronica Reil, age 19.

Goulais Bay Mission Ont.
July 3rd 1909

Mr Horace B. Durant Esq
Special U.S. Indian Agent
Petoskey Mich

Dear Sir

Your letter June 22nd at hand asking me if I was member the Chippewa tribe in Michigan. Yes I was and I received the treaty in Michigan and also received the last payment was made in Michigan. And I don't get the Canadian treaty. And I have no property In Canada. My wife died 12 years agoand I have five children kiving my age 56 years my name is James Shawanigabaw name of my children. Angeline her age 29 Lizabeth her age 19. James his age 24 oaul his age 18. Mary her age 14. And I have three sisters living and no brothers. My Sisters the received the last payment was made in Michigan. Names of my sisters Mrs Dan McKay her age 63 years. And she has four childrens Namely Bestsey her age 34 years. Margaret her age 30 years. Elizabeth her age 27 years Jennie her age 23. And my sister Mrs Joe Cadran Sr. she also received the last payment was made In Michigan. her age 60. And she has four children namely Joseph. His age 39. He also received two payments in Michigan. Thomas his age 32 years. Michael his age 24 years. John his age 21 years. And My sister Mrs.

Antroion Reil. She also received the last payment was made In Mich. Her age 58 years. she has two children. Namely Antroion his age 20. Veronica her age 19. My sister Mrs Joseph Cadran Sr. her older son his married and Joseph his wife living . And he has five children. Namely. Frank his age 6 Sarah her age 4. Joe two years old this is all I can give you Information this time. If you want to know any more particulars please write to me and hoping this will be satisfaction and I wish to thank you for the trouble you took to write to me hoping to hear from you soon.

I beg to remain Dear Sir
Your & Very Respectfully
Joseph Shawawgabaw

Our Adress Goulais River Ont Can P.O. Indian Mission

Information following from: Louis O Shawawno.

10-3 PE NAY SE WAW NAW QUOT, dead.
Wife: Name not given, dead.
10-3-1 Name not given, dead.
Wife or Husband: Name not given.
10-3-1-1 Annie Belleau, age 25, single. P.O. Sault Ste. Marie.
10-3-1-2 Blackey Brown, see 21-1.
10-3-2 Name not given, dead.
10-3-3 Name not given, dead.
10-3-4 Name not given, dead.

Information following from: Louis Hatch & Joe Cadreau, Sugar Isle.

11-3 MRS. ALEXIS CADOTTE, dead.
Husband: Alexis Codotte.
11-3-1 Charles Cadotte, dead.
Wife: Name not given, dead.
11-3-2 Louis Cadotte, dead.
11-3-3 Margaret Cadotte, dead.
11-3-4 Mary Ann Cadotte, dead.
Husband 1st : Name not given.
Husband 2nd: Louis Cadreau, dead.
11-3-4-1 Charles Hatch, age 54, P.O. Sugar Isle.
Wife: Catharine Hatch (nee Cadotte), see 5-5, dead.
11-3-4-1-1 Lawrence Hatch, age 25, single, P.O. Soo
11-3-4-1-2 Steve Hatch, age 23, single.
11-3-4-1-3 Fred Hatch, age 18.
11-3-4-1-4 Isabella Hatch, age 14.
11-3-4-1-5 Agnes Hatch, age 16.
11-3-4-1-6 Dewey Hatch, age 10.
11-3-4-1-7 Vina Hatch, age 8.
11-3-4-1-8 George Hatch, age 16.
11-3-4-2 Louis Hatch, age 50, P.O. Sugar Isle, Mich.

Wife: Mary Ann Hatch, age 45, a niece of 20-9, see 33-9, her mother was a sister of 20-9 & an allotter.

11-3-4-2-1 Mike Hatch, age 24, single.

11-3-4-2-2 Louis Hatch, age 22, single.

11-3-4-2-3 Maggie Hatch, age 16.

11-3-4-2-4 Fred Hatch, age 8.

11-3-4-2-5 Mary Hatch, age 6.

11-3-4-2-6 Albert Hatch, age 5.

11-3-4-3 Isabelle Cadreau Brown, age 50, see 21-1.

Husband: Fank Brown, see 21-1.

11-3-4-4 Joe Cadreau, age 43, P.O. Sugar Isle.

Wife: Rebecca (Cadotte) Cadreau, age 40, see 5-5.

11-3-4-4-1 John Cadreau, age 23, single, P.O. Sugar Isle.

11-3-4-4-2 Wilfred Cadreau, age 19, single.

11-3-4-4-3 Mary Cadreau, age 13.

11-3-4-4-4 James Edward Cadreau, age 11.

11-3-4-4-5 Archie L. Cadreau, age 6.

11-3-4-5 Alex Cadreau, age 38, P.O. Soo.

Wife: Name not given, white, separated.

11-3-4-5-1 Gabriel Cadreau, age 17, Haskell School.

11-3-4-6 Angeline Cadreau, P.O. St. Paul.

Husband 1st : M. F. McDonald, white, separated.

Husband 2nd: Name not given, white.

11-3-4-6-1 Mannie (girl) McDonald, age 20, P.O. Syracuse N.Y.

11-3-4-6-2 Frank McDonald, age 18, P.O. Syracuse N.Y.

11-3-4-6-3 Gerald McDonald, age 16, P.O. Syracuse N.Y.

11-3-4-6-4 Donald McDonald, age 12, P.O. Syracuse N.Y.

11-3-4-6-5 Charles McDonald, age 7, P.O. Syracuse N.Y.

11-3-4-7 Louis Cadreau, age 32, P.O. Lizzie St. Soo, wife Canadian, no children.

11-3-4-8 Mary Cadreau, dead.

11-3-4-8-1 Charles McBride, age 14, P.O. Sugar Isle, lives with Foster Family.

11-3-4-9 Louisa Downs, age 35, P.O. Carey St. Soo, husband white, no children.

11-3-4-10 Henry Cadreau, age 29, P.O. 1017 E. Portage Soo, wife Canadian, children all dead.

Information following from: Jane Cotay at her home, Soo.

12-3 JOHN COTAY, dead.

Wife: Jane Cotay (proper spelling Cota), age 73, P.O. 809 Helen St. Soo, see 60-4.

12-3-1 Henry Cotay, age 48, P.O. Port huron, Mich., wife white, no children.

12-3-2 Matilda LaFaver, age 41, P.O. 606 South St. Soo.

Husband: _______ LaFever, white.

12-3-2-1 Olive LaFaver, age 15.

12-3-2-2 Elmer LaFaver, age 14.

12-3-2-3 Clinton LaFaver, age 10.

12-3-2-4 Dorris LaFaver, age 2.

12-3-3 Annie Perry, age 38, 809 Helen St. Soo.

Husband: ________ Perry, white.

12-3-3-1 Merril Perry, age 11.

12-3-3-2 Ethel Perry, age 8.

12-3-3-3 Carl Perry, age 7.

12-3-3-4 Marian Perry, age 3.

12-3-3-5 Marie Perry, born January 21/09.

12-3-4 George Cota, age 35, P.O. Soo.

Wife: Name not given, white.

12-3-4-1 George Cota, age 7.

12-3-4-1 Laetha Cota, age 5.

12-3-5 Hattie Cotay, age 32, P.O. Soo, single.

12-3-6 Albert Cotay, age 30, P.O. Soo, single.

Information following from: Louis Oshawanaw.

13-3 HENRY THOMAS, dead, relatives of Bay Mills Indians, see 2-7, all enrolled.

Information following from: Louis Oshawanaw.

14-3 I YAW BANCE, dead.

Wife: Name not given, dead.

14-3-1 Name not given, dead.

Wife or Husband: Name not given.

14-3-1-1 Mrs. Frank Thorne, age 35, P.O. Soo.

Husband: Frank Thorne Jr., age 38, see 16-3.

14-3-1-1-1 Name not given, age 6.

June 22
Sault Ste Marie Mich

Mr Horace Durant

Dear Sir your letter Received and I and sending you my wife and child age hy wife age 35 Born March 2 1874 child age 6 Born May 21 1903 and I am sending the last of the Rest of my Brothers and sisters.

Mr Frank thorne

529 Ridge st.

Information following from: Louis Oshawanaw 2-3.

15-3 ~~LOUIS~~ OSHAW WAW NO, (Chief), dead.

Wife: Name not given, dead.

15-3-1 Name not given, dead, see 2-3 for children.

15-3-2 Name not given, dead, see 2-3 for children.

Information following from: Robert Roussain.

16-3 JOHN ROUSSAIN, dead.

Wife: Charlotte Roussain, age 84, P.O. Sugar Isle, Mich.

16-3-1 James Roussain, dead, died March 3/1909, heirs desire that share be paid to their grandmother Charlotte.

Wife: Name not given, dead.

16-3-1-1 Mary Roussain, dead.

16-3-1-2 Josephine Roussain, age 30, single, P.O. New Orleans.

16-3-1-3 Edward Roussain, age 28, single, Sugar Isle Soo.

16-3-1-4 Charlotte Shingles, age 26, husband white, P.O. Soo, Emeline St., no children.

16-3-1-5 Benjamin Roussain, age 24, P.O. Portage Ave. Soo.

Wife: Name not given, white.

16-3-1-5-1 George Roussain, age 10.

16-3-1-5-2 Kenneth Roussain, age 8

16-3-2 Harriet Roussain, dead.

Husband: Henry Thorne, as his 1st wife, 2nd wife Sarah Gurnoe & 6 children, see 6-3, P.O. Soo.

16-3-2-1 Henry Thorne Jr., age 44, see 25-3.

16-3-2-2 Frank, Thorne, age 42.

16-3-2-3 John, Thorne, age 39.

16-3-2-4 Gilbert, Thorne, age 36.

16-3-2-5 Harriet, Thorne, age 35.

16-3-2-6 James, Thorne, age 32.

16-3-2-7 Emma, Thorne, age 25.

16-3-2-8 Lucy, Thorne, age 25.

16-3-3 Robert Roussain, age 54, P.O. 625 Emeline St. Soo.

Wife: Francis Roussain, age 49, Canadian.

16-3-3-1 Joe Roussain, age 24.

Wife: Name not given, white.

16-3-3-1-1 Ryal Roussain or Buster Roussain, age 3.

16-3-3-2 Louise Roussain, age 23.

16-3-3-3 Charles Roussain, age 18.

16-3-3-4 John Roussain, age 16.

16-3-3-5 Frances Roussain, age 15.

16-3-3-6 Tom Roussain, age 12.

16-3-3-7 Harriett Roussain, age ~~2~~2.

Children of Henriette Rousson and Henry Thorne taken from the registers of St. Mary's Church.

Henry Thorne	*age 46*	*born in*	*1863*
Frank Thorne	*" 42*	*" "*	*1867*
John Thorne	*" 39*	*" "*	*1870*
Gilbert Thorne	*" 36*	*" "*	*1873*
Harriet Thorne	*" 35*	*" "*	*1874*
James Thorne	*" 32*	*" "*	*1877*
Emma Thorne	*" 25*	*" "*	*1884*
Lucy Thorne	*" 25*	*" "*	*1884*

Information following from: Louis Oshawanaw, Sugar Isle.

17-3 MRS. FRANCIS BELONGHAY, dead.
Husband: Francis Belonghay.
17-3-1 William Belongea, P.O. Hessell, Mich., see 11-15.
17-3-2 Name not given, dead.
Wife: Name not given, dead.
17-3-2-1 Frank Belongea or Baker, see 15-9.

Information following from: Joe La Coy & Chief Oshawano.

18-3 MADAM LE COY or JANE LA COY, age 65, P.O. Sugar Isle, see 22-5.
Husband: Joseph La Coy, enroll by consent of Chief Oshawano, his mother was a full blood Indian of this tribe & an allotter.
18-3-1 Alice Jandreau, age 44, P.O. Cedar St Soo.
Husband: Henry Jandreau.
18-3-1-1 Mabel Jandreau Ermatinger, Age 24, P.O. Soo.
Husband: George Ermatinger.
18-3-1-2 Eva Jandreau, age 22, single.
18-3-1-3 Addie Jandreau King, age 19.
Husband: ________ King, white.
18-3-1-3-1 Name not given.
18-3-1-3-2 Name not given.
18-3-1-4 Mary Jandreau, age 17, single.
18-3-1-5 Cecelia Jandreau, age 12.
18-3-2 ~~Charlotte~~ Augusta La Coy, dead, no children.
18-3-3 Sophia La Coy, dead, no children.
18-3-4 Augusta La Coy, dead, no children.
18-3-5 Frank La Coy, age 36, P.O. Sugar Isle.
Wife: Harriett La Coy, Canadian.
18-3-5-1 Leona La Coy, age 13.
18-3-5-2 Josepa La Coy, age 12.
18-3-5-3 Mary La Coy, age 9.

18-3-5-4 Antoine La Coy, age 7.
18-3-5-6 Teddy La Coy, age 5.
18-3-6 Joseph La Coy Jr., age 33, P.O. Bay de Wasai Sugar Isle.
Wife: Jane La Coy Jr., nee Piquette, age 34, see 25-3.
18-3-6-1 Adelaide La Coy, age 12.
18-3-6-2 Lillie La Coy, age 7.
18-3-6-3 Ada La Coy, age 4.
18-3-7 John La Coy, age 30, P.O. Sugar Isle, single.
18-3-8 Pete La Coy, age 27, P.O. Sugar Isle, single.
18-3-9 Jennie La Freniere, age 25, P.O. Sugar Isle.
Husband: Mack La Freniere, white.
18-3-9-1 Luke La Freniere, born June 1907, 2nd Roll.
18-3-10 Charlotte McCherchy, age 23, P.O. Sugar.
Husband: _______ McCherchy, white.
18-3-10-1 Alphonsine (girl) McCherchy, age 6.
18-3-10-2 Leo McCherchy, age 5.
18-3-10-3 Albert McCherchy, age 4.
18-3-10-4 Genvieve McCherchy, age 2, born July 1907, 2nd Roll..
18-3-10-5 Not named boy McCherchy, age 5, born May/1909 too late.
18-3-11 Leona La Coy, dead, no children.
18-3-12 William La Coy, age 20, single, P.O. Soo Sugar Isle.
18-3-13 Leo La Coy, age 18, single.
18-3-14 Josephine La Coy, age 13, single.

Information following from: Not Given.
19-3 O GAW BAY GE WAW NO QUAY, dead.
Husband: Name not given, dead.
19-3-1 Mary Cube, age 70, on roll with husband on 6-12.
19-3-2 Moses Nawwigigig, age 62, Indian name Ogeginung), P.O. Mackinac Isle.
Wife: Name not given, dead.
19-3-2-1 Eliza Nawwigigig, age 28, single, P.O. Mackinac Isle.
19-3-2-2 Lucy Nawwigigig, age 26, single, Mackinac Isle.
19-3-3 Mike Nawwigigig, age 58, single, P.O. Mackinac Isle.

19-3-4 Charlotte Nawwigigig, age 50, P.O. Mackinac Isle, separated, not married, lived with Robert Marshall..
19-3-4-1 Lizzie Marshall, age 21, single.

Information following from: Joseph Rouleau, May 7.
20-3 MRS. WIDOW EDWARDS, dead.
Husband: Thomas Edwards, white, 1st wife dead in 1870 but had 2

children on 1870 roll as members 13-1 & 21-1.

20-3-1 Charlotte Edwards, dead.
Husband: Allen Rains, white.
20-3-1-1 Edward Rains, P.O. Sugar Isle, see 50-4.
20-3-1-2 Ella Rains, P.O. Sugar Isle, see 50-4.
20-3-1-3 Effie Rains, P.O. Sugar Isle, see 50-4.
20-3-1-4 Ethel Rains, P.O. Sugar Isle, see 50-4.
20-3-1-5 Wilford Rains.

20-3-2 Edward Edwards, dead.
Wife 1st : Name not given, white, dead, no children.
Wife 2nd: Name not given, alive but white, no children.

20-3-3 Alice Rouleau, dead, for husband & children see 47-4.

20-3-4 Maria Edwards, age 54, P.O. Sault Ste Marie, single.

Information following from: Oshawano, Sugar Isle, May 14/09.

21-3 MRS. J. L. CHIPMAN's children.
Husband: J. L. Chipman.
21-3-1 Harry Chipman, age 54, P.O. Detroit, attorney.
21-3-2 Lizzie Buell, age 45, P.O. Detroit.
21-3-3 Edmund Chipman, age 40, P.O. Detroit, attorney at law.

Information following from: Oshawano, Chief.

22-3 CHE QUAITCH, dead.
Husband: Name not given.
22-3-1 William Meron, single, P.O. Wisconsin somewhere, died March/09, no heirs.

Information following from: Susan Riley & Frank Boucher, Soo, May 26.

23-3 CHARLES CADOTTE, dead.
Wife: Name not given, dead.
23-3-1 Isaac Cadotte 2nd , age 45, P.O. Brimley, see 11-3.
Wife Name not given, white, separated.
23-3-1-1 Charles Cadotte, age 30, P.O. 511 Ridge St. Sault Ste. Marie.
23-3-1-2 Maria Cadotte, age 28, P.O. 511 Ridge St. Sault Ste. Marie.
23-3-1-3 Anna Cadotte, age 21, P.O. 511 Ridge St. Sault Ste. Marie.
23-3-1-4 Christina Cadotte, age 19, P.O. 511 Ridge St. Sault Ste. Marie.
23-3-1-5 Wilfred Cadotte, age 18.
23-3-1-6 Mary Cadotte, age 15.
23-3-1-7 Ruby Cadotte, age 8.
23-3-2 Susan Riley, age 47, P.O. 511 Ridge St. Soo, Mich.
Husband: Name not given, Canadian, separated.

23-3-2-1 Mary Riley, age 23, single, P.O. 511 Ridge St. Soo, Mich.

23-3-2-2 Charlotte Riley, age 20, single, P.O. 511 Ridge St. Soo, Mich.

23-3-2-3 Pete Riley, age 9, single, P.O. 511 Ridge St. Soo, Mich.

23-3-3 Mary Ann Cadotte, dead.

Husband: Solomon Causley, age 50, see 15-12.

23-3-3-1 Ed Causley, age 23, P.O. Drummond's Isle.

Wife: Mary Causley, nee Whalin, see 35-8, her sister married Ed Gurnoe.

23-3-3-1-1 Name not given, born Nov/08, too late.

23-3-3-2 Fred Causley, age 24.

23-3-3-3 Perry Causley, age 18, single.

23-3-4 Maggie Cadotte, dead.

Husband: ______ Boucher or Bushay, dead.

23-3-4-1 William Boucher or Bushay, age 30, see 5-3.

Wife: Lizzie Boucher or Bushay.

23-3-4-1-1 Name not given.

23-3-4-1-2 Name not given.

Maxton June 9th/09

Horace B. Durant
U.S. Indian Agt.

Yours of the 4th inst received in reply will say I am 47 years ald, as near as I can tell., my oldest boy Fred 25, 2nd boy Ed 23 years Perry the youngest 20. My Fathers name was Steve Causley was a half Breed Frenchman and was not on the treaty. My Mothers name was Mary Mar ga onon no other name that I know off.

Respectfully yours
Solomon Causley

P.S. Mrs Mus har bo used to draw my money from the government. My Cheff name was Bay bam sa.

Department of the Interior,
United States Indian Service,

Dear Madam:

Please give me the names, ages & addresses of Isaac Cadotte's children, who are said to live at the "Soo".

I am told he is separated from his wife & I have not the names of his children.

Please use this sheet for reply, & find envelope enclosed for return.

Very respectfully
HORACE B. DURANT

Special U.S. Indian Agent

Names of Isaac Cadotte children

Anna Cadotte	*age 21*
Christena Cadotte	*" 19*
Wilfred Cadotte	*" 18*
Mary Cadotte	*" 12*
Rubie Cadotte	*" 8*
Charlie Cadotte	*" 30*
Maria Cadotte	*" 28*

	Address	
Mrs Anna Cadotte	*511 Ridge street*	*Soo Mich*
Miss Christena Cadotte	*511 Ridge street*	*Soo Mich*
Wilfred Cadotte	*511 Ridge street*	*Soo Mich*
Miss Mary Cadotte	*511 Ridge street*	*Soo Mich*
Miss Ruby Cadotte	*511 Ridge street*	*Soo Mich*
Mr Charlie Cadotte	*511 Ridge street*	*Soo Mich*
Miss May Cadotte		

Please send the letters by these addresses. For my father capable of keeping the money for he is a heavy drinker.

Information following from: Eli Gurnoe, Bay Mills.

24-3 ELI GURNOE, dead.
 Wife: Name not given.
 24-3-1 Louis Gurnoe, age 46, P.O. Bay Mills, single.
 24-3-2 Edward Gurnoe, age 44, P.O. Wash D.C., single.
 24-3-3 Lawrence Gurnoe, age 40, P.O. Bay Mills, single.
 24-3-4 Eli Gurnoe, age 38, P.O. Bay Mills, single.
 24-3-5 Joseph Gurnoe, age 49, see 2-8 & 43-3, was enrolled with 43-3 in 1870.

Information following from: Jane La Coy & Robert Thorne, Soo, May 26.

25-3 ANTOINE PIQUETTE, dead.
 Wife1st : Name not given, dead.
 Wife 2nd: Adelaide Piquette, age 67, P.O. Soo, see 22-5.
 25-3-1 Mary Ermatinger, age 44, P.O. Soo, see.
  Husband: Name not given, see 49-4
 25-3-2 Sophia Thorne, dead.
  Husband: Henry Thorne Jr., age 44, see 16-3, P.O. 1846 E. 57th St. Cleveland, Ohio.
  25-3-2-1 Robert Dan Thorne, age 24, single, P.O. Soo Maple.
  25-3-2-2 Gilbert L. Thorne, age 18.
  25-3-2-3 Hazel L. Thorne, age 17.
 25-3-3 Antoine Piquette, age 40, P.O. Sugar Isle, single.

25-3-4 John Piquette, dead, no children.
25-3-5 Addie Piquette, dead.
Husband: Jack Lathwell, white.
25-3-5-1 William Lathwell, goes by name of Jack Piquette, age 17.
25-3-6 Jane La Coy, age 34, see 18-3.
25-3-7 Philamon Parr, age 32.
Husband: _______ Parr, white.
25-3-7-1 Chester Parr, age 12.
25-3-7-2 Nellie Parr, age 10.
25-3-7-3 Frank Parr, age 8.

Information following from: Not Given.
26-3 JOSEPH KE CHE O JIB WAY, dead.
Wife: Name not given, dead.
26-3-1 Joseph O'Jibway Jr., age 50, Sault Ste. Marie R.F.D. #1.
Wife: Name not given.
26-3-1-1 John A. O'Jibway, age 28.
26-3-1-2 Henry O'Jibway, age 26.
26-3-1-3 Joseph Edward O'Jibway, age 25.
26-3-1-4 Mary Delia O'Jibway, age 23.
26-3-1-5 Agnes May O'Jibway, age 20.
26-3-1-6 George E. O'Jibway, age 17.
26-3-1-7 Georgianna O'Jibway, age 16.
26-3-1-8 Stella A. O'Jibway, age 14.
26-3-1-9 Leo A. O'Jibway, age 12.
26-3-1-10 Beatrice E. O'Jibway, age 6.

R.F.D. #1
Sault Ste. Marie, Mich.
June, 24 1909

Horace B. Durant,
Petoskey, Mich.
Dear Sir:
Herewith are the names and ages of myself and children.

John A	*28 yrs.*
Henry	*26 "*
Jos. Edward Jr.	*25 "*
Mary Delia	*23 "*
Agnes May	*20 "*
George E.	*17 "*
Georgina	*16 "*
Stella Ann	*14 "*
Leo A.	*12 "*
Beatrice Adeline	*6 "*

My age 50 "

I remain,
Joseph O'Jibway Sr.

Information following from: Not Given.

27-3 WILLIAM JOHNSON, dead.
Wife: Name not given.
27-3-1 Mary L Scott, age 50, P.O. Sault Ste. Marie 664 Court St..
Husband: _______ Scott, white, dead.
27-3-1-1 Carrie A. La Bonte, age 26, P.O. 666 Court St.
27-3-2 Margaret A. Fuller, P.O. 1008 Easterday Ave Sault Ste Marie.
Husband: _______ Fuller.
27-3-2-1 Oscar W. Fuller, age 30, P.O. 1008 Easterday Ave Sault Ste Marie.
27-3-2-2 Laura A. Fuller, age 27, P.O. 1008 Easterday Ave Sault Ste Marie.

Sault Ste. Marie, Mich.
July 26, 1909

Horace B. Durant
Special U.S. Indian Agent
Dear Sir:
I re'cd your letter some time ago. I am the daughter of H. W. Johnston, deceased.
My name is Mrs. Mary L. JohnstonScott.
(Address) 664 Court St. Soo Mich.
I have one daughter her name is Mrs Carrie A. La Bonte
(age) 26 years (address) 664 Court St. Soo Mich.
I have one sister her name is Mrs Margaret A. Johnston Fuller
(address) 1008 Easterday Ave.
My sister has two children.
Miss Laura A. Fuller
(age) 28 years (address) 1008 Easterday Ave Soo Mich.
Mr. Oscar W. Fuller
(age) 31 years (address) 1008 Easterday Ave Soo Mich.

Respectfully yours
Mrs Scott

Information following from: Oshawano, Chief.

28-3 CHING QUALK, dead.
Wife: Name not given, dead.
Note: Chief does not know anything about where this family is. Said to be all dead. Durant.

Information following from: Chief.

29-3 KOO KOOSH children.
Note: O'Shawano, Chief says he does not remember of any children enrolled in his band in a870, by this name. Durant Spl. Agt. May 14/09, Sugar Isle.

Information following from: Chief Oshawano & Frank Boucher, Sugar Isle, May 14/09.

30-3 GABRIEL KAW WE TAW KE ZHICK, or GABRIEL SHAWANO, age 70, P.O. Soo 1094 Maple St.
Wife: Charlotte Shawano, age 55, P.O. Soo 1094 Maple St.
30-3-1 Charlotte La Sage, age 33, , P.O. Soo 1094 Maple St.
Husband 1st : Alex Cadreau, age ?.
Husband 2nd: John La Sage, Canadian Indian.
30-3-1-1 Gabriel Cadreau, age 19, P.O. Soo 1094 Maple St.

Information following from: Oshawano & Apencer Johnston.

31-3 SAMUEL & JANE JOHNSON.
Note: Samuel is dead, Jane age 52 single lives Keene New Hampshire. Chiefs never heard of these people. Durant. Later this was Spencer Johnson, cousins Durant May 25/09.

Information following from: Frank Boucher.

32-3 LOUIS CADOTTE, Jr., dead, wife dead, no heirs.

Information following from: Not Given.

33-3 MRS. LE SAY, dead.
Husband: ______ Le Say, white, dead.
33-3-1 Victoria Lalone, age 72, P.O. 244 Arlinton St., Soo, see 33-8, see notes on back of 47-4.
Husband: ________ Lalone.
33-3-1-1 Peter Lalone, age 40, P.O. Soo.
33-3-1-2 Emma Lalone, age 38, P.O. Chicago.
Husband: Name not given, dead.
33-3-1-2-1 John Lalone, age 18.
33-3-1-3 Eliza Johnson, age 36, P.O. Minnesota Sandstone.
33-3-1-3-1 Peter Frank
33-3-1-4 William Lalone, age 34.

Information following from: Andrew Waishkey & Angeline Ermatringer, Soo, May 26/09.

34-3 MRS. EDWARD BOIS BAIR, dead.
Husband: Edward Bois Bair.
34-3-1 Catharine Day, dead.
Husband: _______ Day, dead.
34-3-1-1 Alex Day, age 52, P.O. Soo.
34-3-1-2 Mary Gayger, P.O. Soo.

34-3-1-3 Julia Thomas, P.O. Soo.
34-3-1-4 Henry Day, age 40, P.O. Soo.
34-3-1-5 Jennie Wilson, age 35, P.O. Soo.
Note: Chief's know nothing. Later: They did know but said nothing because they wanted to leave off the heirs of the half breeds who drew with them in 1870. The heirs have been identified and are as given on this aheet. Durant Spl. Agt. These children ~~and~~ this mother were enrolled in 1870.

34-3-2 Edward Bois Bair, dead, no children.
34-3-3 Julia Bois Bair, dead, no children.
34-3-4 Angeline Ermetinger, age 65, P.O. 431 Gros Cap Ave. Soo.
Husband: ________ Ermetinger, dead.
34-3-4-1 Catharine Stirling, age 43, 429 Gros Cap Ave. Soo.
Husband: _______ Stirling, white.
34-3-4-1-1 Charles, age 20, single.
34-3-4-1-2 Elmer, age 18.
34-3-4-1-3 Harry, age 13.
34-3-4-1-4 Eva, age 10.
34-3-4-1-5 Clyde, age 4.
Note: Do not enroll altho living they did not receive money at last payment: unless Dept. authorizes.
34-3-4-2 Edward Ermetinger, age 41, P.O. Soo, single.
Note: Do not enroll altho living they did not receive money at last payment: unless Dept. authorizes.
34-3-4-3 ______ Ermetinger, dead, no heirs.
34-3-4-4 Maris Ermetinger, dead.
Husband: Ben Liberty, white.
34-3-4-4-1 Raymond Liberty, age 7.
34-3-4-4-2 Evaline Liberty, age 5.
34-3-4-4-3 Lemore Liberty, age 3.
Note: Do not enroll altho living they did not receive money at last payment: unless Dept. authorizes.

Information following from: Frank Boucher.
35-3 FRANCIS O GAW BAY GE SHE GO and sister, enroll as Francis Boucher, age 70, P.O. Sugar Isle, ½ brother to John Boushay (Boucher).
Wife: Philimon Boucher, age 60.
35-3-1 Mary Boucher, age 10, adopted, see 5-5.
Note: Sister, on roll with 35-3, see heading, dead, no heirs.

Information following from: Not Given.
36-3 MRS. STILES, dead.
Husband: ________ Stiles, dead.
36-3-1 _______ Stiles, dead, no heirs.

Information following from: Not Given.
37-3 JUSTINE O'JIBWAY, dead, no heirs.

Information following from: Not Given.
38-3 AISH QUAY BE QUAY, dead.
Husband: Name not given.
38-3-1 Name not given, dead, said to be living at hessel, see 8-15.
Husband: John Smith.

Information following from: Joseph Rouleau.
39-3 MRS. THOMAS ERMATINGER, dead.
Husband: Thomas Ermatinger, dead.
39-3-1 Lawrence Ermatinger, age 47, P.O. Sault Ste. Marie.
Mary Ermatinger, white.
39-3-1-1 Joseph Ermatinger, age 26.
Wife: Clara Ermatinger, white.
39-3-1-1-1 Clyde Ermatinger, age 1, P.O. Sault Ste. Marie.
39-3-1-1-2 Marim Ermatinger, age 3, P.O. Sault Ste. Marie.
39-3-1-2 Thomas Ermatinger, age 24, P.O. Sault Ste. Marie.
39-3-1-3 Lawrence Ermatinger jr., age 21, P.O. Sault Ste. Marie.
39-3-1-4 Edwin Ermatinger, age 15, P.O. Sault Ste. Marie.
39-3-2 William J. Ermatinger, age 40, P.O. Sault Ste. Marie.
Wife: Dora Ermatinger, white.
39-3-2-1 Nancy Ermatinger, age 14, P.O. Sault Ste. Marie.
39-3-2-2 Irvine Ermatinger, age 11, P.O. Sault Ste. Marie.
39-3-3 Henry Ermatinger, age 37, P.O. Sault Ste. Marie.
Wife: Lillian Ermatinger, white.
39-3-3-1 Reginald Ermatinger, age 10, P.O. Sault Ste. Marie.
39-3-4 Joseph Ermatinger, age 30, P.O. Sault Ste. Marie.

Information following from: Not Given.
40-3 JOSEPHINE LALONE, age 65 or 70, P.O. Sault Ste. Marie, no children.

Information following from: Not Given.
41-3 ELLEN PE TAW WAW NAW QUOT, now goes by name of Ellen Shawano, age 60, Sault Ste. Marie, see 17-1.

Information following from: Not Given.
42-3 MICHEL NOLAN, dead, wife dead also.

Information following from: George Frishette.
43-3 MAW KOONSE, dead.
Wife: Name not given, dead.
43-3-1 George Frishette, age 48, P.O. Sugar Isle.
Wife: Charlotte Frishette, age 32, see 32-8.
43-3-1-1 Pete Frishette, age 18.
43-3-1-2 Julia Frishette, age 14.
43-3-1-3 Catharine Frishette, age 10.
43-3-1-4 Agnes Frishette, age 8.
43-3-1-5 Levi Frishette, age 5.
43-3-2 Joe Gurnoe, see 24-3 & 2-8.

Information following from: Not Given.
44-4 CAW MUSH COO, dead, no heirs.
Information following from: Not Given.
45-4 MRS. BATTIST PLANT, dead.
Husband: Battist Plant.
45-4-1 Pauline Plant Lalone, age 58, P.O. Sault Ste. Marie, 1053 E. Portage Ave.
Husband: Charles Lalone, whie.
45-4-1-1 Fred Payment, age 37, P.O. Soo.
Wife: Name not given.
45-4-1-1-1 Sadie Payment.
45-4-1-1-2 Fred Payment.
45-4-1-1-3 Cecil Payment.
45-4-2 Name not given, dead.
45-4-3 Name not given, dead.

Sault Ste. Marie Mich
June 21st 1909

Dear Sir

I receive you jus lius that you want me to send that name of my children and thay all through my Olds is.

Fred Payment, 37, and 3 children is rady. Fredy. Crieb are his children.

And my daughter Jennee Lalonde 24 and 2 cildren is Saphy, Jesy, that her children.

And my son William Plount, 27 and 4 children is Pauline, Mary, Wllie, Davit, are his children.

That is all if this is right my name is Mrs Charles LaLonde but So many by that name I go by Pauline Plaunt Lalonde.

Sault Ste. Marie Portage Ave this is all the adres East 1053.

Mrs Pauline Plount Lalonde
Sault Ste Marie Mich
Portage Ave East 1053

My brother and sister are dead 23 years ago.

Information following from: Not Given.
46-4 JOSEPH O SHAW WAW NO, dead, no heirs.

Information following from: Joseph Rouleau, Soo, May 7/09.
47-4 JOSEPH ROULEAU, age 61, P.O. 408 Sprouse St. E. Sault Ste. Marie.
Wife: Name not given, dead.
47-4-1 Laurian Rouleau, age 37, P.O. Cleveland, Ohio.
Wife: Name not given, white.
47-4-1-1 Margaret Fern Rouleau, age 8.
47-4-1-2 Vivian F. Rouleau, age 6.
47-4-1-3 Laurian J. Rouleau, age 3.
47-4-2 Bertha Rouleau, age 30, P.O. 408 Spruce St. E. Sault Ste. Marie, single.
47-4-3 Marian Rouleau, age 21, P.O. 408 Spruce St. E. Sault Ste. Marie, single.
47-4-4 Joe Rouleau, age 28, P.O. Columbus, Ohio or Soo, wife white, no children.

Information following from: Not Given.
48-4 JULIA BARRY, dead.
48-4-1 Fred Bellemar, age 37, P.O. Houghton, Mich.
Wife: Annie (Spruce) Bellemar, L'Anse, age 20, no children.

Information following from: Joseph Rouleau.
49-4 MRS. JOHN ERMATINGER, age 65, P.O. Sault Ste. Marie.
Husband: John Ermatinger, age 68, P.O. Sault Ste. Marie.
49-4-1 George Ermatinger, age 45, P.O. Sault Ste. Marie.
Wife: Mable Ermatinger, age 24, P.O. Sault Ste. Marie.
49-4-1-1 John Ermatinger, age 3, P.O. Sault Ste. Marie.
49-4-1-2 Almer Ermatinger, age 1, P.O. Sault Ste. Marie.
49-4-2 John Ermatinger, age 40, P.O. Sault Ste. Marie.
Wife: Mary Ermatinger, age 45, P.O. Sault Ste. Marie.
49-4-2-1 Julia Ermatinger, age 12, P.O. Sault Ste. Marie.
49-4-2-2 Leanard Ermatinger, age 4, P.O. Sault Ste. Marie.
49-4-3 Maria White, age 38, P.O. 156 State Street Rochester, N.Y.
Husband: Fred White, white.
49-4-3-1 William White, age 14, P.O. 156 State Street Rochester, N.Y.
49-4-3-1-1 Lena White, age 10, P.O. 156 State Street Rochester, N.Y.
49-4-4 Mary Hodgins, age 33, P.O. Gladstone, Mich.
Husband: Alfred Hodgins, white.
49-4-5 Robert R. Ermatinger, age 32, P.O. Sault Ste. Marie.

Wife: Ida Ermatinger, age 29, P.O. Sault Ste. Marie.
49-4-5-1 Frederick Ermatinger, age 10, P.O. Sault Ste. Marie.
49-4-5-2 Hazel Ermatinger, age 7, P.O. Sault Ste. Marie.
49-4-5-3 Earl Ermatinger, age 5, P.O. Sault Ste. Marie.
49-4-5-4 Ruth Ermatinger, age 3, P.O. Sault Ste. Marie.
49-4-5-5 Elmer Ermatinger, age 2, P.O. Sault Ste. Marie.
49-4-6 Charles Ermatinger, age 29, P.O. Sault Ste. Marie.
49-4-7 Lora Ermatinger, age 25, P.O. Sault Ste. Marie.
49-4-8 Lother Ermatinger, age 22, P.O. Sault Ste. Marie.
49-4-9 Matilda Ermatinger, age 20, P.O. Sault Ste. Marie.
Note: children though living at that time were not enrolled with mother, enroll with question? Durant. (Note applies all on 49-4)

Information following from: Not Given.
50-4 SHAW GAW NAW SHE QUAY, dead.
50-4-1 Maria Edwards, age 55, P.O. Sugar Isle, single, see 20-3.
50-4-2 Name not given.
50-4-2-1 Ed Rains, see 20-3.
50-4-2-2 Effie Rains.
50-4-2-3 Ethel Rains.
50-4-2-4 Wilfred Rains.

Information following from: Not Given.
51-4 MRS. JOSEPH MENECKLIER, dead.
Husband: Joseph Menecklier.
51-4-1 Angeline Piquette, age 64, see 10-1.
51-4-2 Victoria Rains, P.O. Sailor' Encampment, Neebish.
Note: Although old enough, was not enrolled with mother in 1870, should not go on now. Durant.

Information following from: Not Given.
52-4 JOHN B. BOUDRIE, dead, no children.

Information following from: Not Given.
53-4 KO STAW QUAY, dead.
Note: had a daughter who went to California.
54-4 MRS. FRANCIS DENOYER, dead.
Husband: Francis Denoyer.
54-4-1 Name not given
54-4-1-1 Joe Hudson, P.O. Sault Ste. Marie, see 57-4.
54-4-2 Name not given.
54-4-2-1 Jane Smith, P.O. Sugar Isle, see 57-4.

Information following from: Not Given.
55-4 KAW BE DAW NAW WE KE ZHICK or JOHN CAPTAIN or NAW

WE KE ZHICK, see 35-8.

Information following from: Not Given.

56-4 MRS. WILLIAM STAFFORD, dead.
Husband: William Stafford.
56-4-1 Alice Stafford, ran away with Boulie & has not been heard from.

Information following from: Jane Smith, Sugar Isle, May 14/09.

57-4 MRS. HENRY HUDSON.
Husband: Henry Hudson, white.
57-4-1 Alice Hudson, dead, P.O. Sault Ste. Marie.
Husband: Name not given.
57-4-1-1 Frank Andres, age 28, P.O. Mackinaw Isle, single.
57-4-1-2 Maggie Niffries, age 26, husband white, no children.
57-4-2 Joe Hudson, age 42, P.O. Sault Ste. Marie, see 54-4, works on the U.S. Canal.
Wife: Mary Hudson, nee Belongea.
57-4-2-1 Hester Hudson, age 16.
57-4-2-2 John Hudson, age 14.
57-4-3 Mary Hudson, dead, no children.
57-4-4 Josephine Hudson, dead.
57-4-5 Jane Smith, age 36, P.O. Sugar Isle, see 54-4.
Husband: John Smith, age 48, white.
57-4-5-1 Frank Smith, age 17.
57-4-5-2 Mary Smith, age 12.
57-4-5-3 Maggie Smith, age 8.
57-4-5-4 John Smith, age 6.
57-4-5-5 Alice Smith, age 4.
57-4-5-6 Louis Smith, born July 1908, 2nd Roll.

Information following from: Joseph Campbell, son.

58-4 MRS. J. B. CAMPBELL, deceased.
Husband: J. B. Campbell.
58-4-1 Joseph Campbell, age 64, P.O. Sault Ste. Marie, Mich.
Wife: Isabell Campbell, age 62.
58-4-1-1 Joseph Campbell Jr., age 45, P.O. Sault Ste. Marie, Mich.
58-4-1-2 Agness Campbell Laramie, age 32, P.O. Sault Ste. Marie, Mich.
Husband: John B. Laramie, age 32, P.O. Sault Ste. Marie, Mich.
58-4-1-2-1 Joseph Laramie, age 15, P.O. Sault Ste. Marie, Mich.
58-4-1-2-2 Leo Laramie, age 13, P.O. Sault Ste. Marie,

Mich.

58-4-1-2-3 Lucile Laramie, age 4, P.O. Sault Ste. Marie, Mich.

58-4-1-2-4 Thelma Laramie, age 1 y 10m, P.O. Sault Ste. Marie,Mich.

58-4-1-3 Hattie Campbell Robinson, age 27, P.O. Sault Ste. Marie, Mich.

Husband: John Robinson, 27, P.O. Sault Ste. Marie, Mich.

58-4-1-3-1 Nina Robinson, age 8, P.O. Sault Ste. Marie, Mich.

58-4-1-3-2 Earl Robinson, age 8, P.O. Sault Ste. Marie, Mich.

58-4-1-3-3 Tom Robinson, age 8, P.O. Sault Ste. Marie, Mich.

58-4-1-3-4 John Robinson, age 8, P.O. Sault Ste. Marie, Mich.

58-4-2 Theophile Campbell, deceased, P.O. Sault Ste. Marie, Mich., born April 10, 1860, died Oct 8, 1907, his heirs.

Wife: Name not given.

58-4-2-1 Sarah Campbell Madigan, age 25, P.O. Sault Ste. Marie, Mich.

Husband: _________ Madigan.

58-4-2-1-1 Bernard Madigan, age 4, P.O. Sault Ste. Marie, Mich.

58-4-2-1-2 John Madigan, age 2, P.O. Sault Ste. Marie, Mich.

58-4-2-1-3 Howard Madigan, age 10 months, P.O. Sault Ste. Marie, Mich.

58-4-2-2 Ida Campbell, age 19, P.O. Sault Ste. Marie, Mich.

58-4-2-3 Richard E. Campbell, age 21, P.O. Sault Ste. Marie, Mich.

58-4-2-4 Pearl Campbell, age 18, P.O. Sault Ste. Marie, Mich.

58-4-2-5 Walter Campbell, age 11, P.O. Sault Ste. Marie, Mich.

58-4-2-6 Melvin Campbell, age 7, P.O. Sault Ste. Marie, Mich.

58-4-3 Joe Campbell, P.O. Sault Ste. Marie, Mich., Foreman on the U.S. Canal.

58-4-4 Alice Brown, P.O. Sault Ste. Marie, Mich., born 1862.

Husband 1st : _________ Reed, white.

Husband 2nd: _________ Booker, white.

Husband 3rd : _________ Brown, white.

58-4-4-1 Blance Booker, age 22, P.O. Sault Ste. Marie, Mich.

58-4-4-2 Eva Booker, age 19, P.O. Sault Ste. Marie, Mich.

58-4-4-3 Howard Booker, age 12, P.O. Sault Ste. Marie, Mich.
58-4-4-4 Frances Booker, age 10, P.O. Sault Ste. Marie, Mich.
58-4-5 Rogers Campbell, born in 1857, died December 26, 1890.
58-4-5-1 Mary Campbell Ford, age 35, P.O. Grosse Isle, Mich.
Husband: ________ Ford.
58-4-5-1-1 Cletus Ford, age 14, P.O. Grosse Isle, Mich
58-4-5-1-2 Leonore Ford, age 12, P.O. Grosse Isle, Mich.
58-4-5-1-3 Hellen Ford, age 10, P.O. Grosse Isle, Mich
58-4-5-1-4 Maurice Ford, age 8, P.O. Grosse Isle, Mich.
58-4-5-1-5 Francis Ford, age 6, P.O. Grosse Isle, Mich.
58-4-5-1-6 Henry Ford, age 4, P.O. Grosse Isle, Mich.
58-4-5-1-7 Marguerite Ford, age 2, P.O. Grosse Isle, Mich.
58-4-5-2 Hellen Campbell Wilhelm, age 33, P.O. Sault Ste. Marie, Mich.
Husband: ________ Wilhelm.
58-4-5-2-1 Francis Wilhelm, age 4, P.O. Sault Ste. Marie, Mich.
58-4-5-2-2 Stephen Wilhelm, age 1, P.O. Sault Ste. Marie, Mich.
58-4-5-3 Rollie Campbell, age 27, P.O. Sault Ste. Marie, Mich.
58-4-5-4 Lindy Campbell, age 25, P.O. Duluth, Minn.
58-4-5-5 Russel Campbell, age 21, P.O. Sault Ste. Marie, Mich.
58-4-5-6 Leo Campbell, age 20, P.O. Sault Ste. Marie, Mich.
58-4-6 Harriet Campbell Nault, deceasd, born November 26, 1848, died June 28, 1897, her heirs.
Husband: ________ Nault.
58-4-6-1 Julia Nault Menard, age 36.
Husband: _______ Menard.
58-4-6-1-1 Joseph Menard, age 17, P.O. Sault Ste. Marie, Mich.
58-4-6-1-2 Alphonse Menard, age 15, P.O. Sault Ste. Marie, Mich.
58-4-6-1-3 Louis Menard, age 13, P.O. Sault Ste. Marie, Mich.
58-4-6-1-4 Azarie Menard, age 11, P.O. Sault Ste. Marie, Mich.
58-4-6-1-5 Eugene Menard, age 3, P.O. Sault Ste. Marie, Mich.
58-4-6-1-6 Jeanpte Menard, 10days, P.O. Sault Ste.

Marie, Mich.

58-4-6-2 William Nault, born 1871, died October 6, 1902.
Wife: Name not given.
58-4-6-2-1 Anna Nault, age 14, P.O. Sault Ste. Marie, Mich.
58-4-6-2-2 Louisa Nault, age 12.
58-4-6-2-3 Bertha Nault, age 10.
Note: Eugene Menard gaurdian of the said William Nault children.
58-4-6-3 Nelson Nault, age 34.
58-4-6-4 Henry Nault, age 30.
Wife: Name not given.
58-4-6-4-1 Geneviere Nault, age 3.

Note: Notes for 58-4 included three hand written pages by and signed at the end page three with the following:

Joseph Campbell Senear member of Mary Cambell deceased

Information following from: Not Given.

59-4 PETER MCFARLIN, dead.
Wife: Name not given, dead.
59-4-1 John McFarlin, dead, no children.
59-4-2 Alex McFarlin, dead, no children.
59-4-3 Charlotte McFarlin, dead, no children.
59-4-4 Name not given, dead.
Husband: _______ Heberly, white.
59-4-5 Annie Warner, dead.
Husband: _______ Warner.
59-4-5-1 Mary Warner Trombly, P.O. Sault Ste. Marie.

Information following from: Not Given.

60-4 MRS. CHARLES BUCK, 2nd.
Husband: Charles Buck, dead.
60-4-1 Charles Buck Jr., dead.
60-4-2 Isabelle Doan, P.O. Dick, Mich., cannot find Durant.
60-4-3 Sophia Andrews, age 43, P.O. Dick, Mich., cannot find Durant.
60-4-4 Sarah Trempe, P.O. Toledo, Ohio, cannot find Durant.
60-4-5 Josephine Van Sandt, P.O. Detroit, cannot find Durant.
60-4-6 Jane Cotay, oldest, see 12-3, on roll 1870 with husband.

Information following from: Chiefs, Bay Mills, May 11/09.

61-4 ELLEN ROUSSAIN, dead, no children.

Information following from: Chiefs, Bay Mills.
62-4 MRS. ANGELIQUE LAFOI, dead, no heirs.

Information following from: Not Given.
63-4 NARCISSA BRISBAIS, dead, no heirs.

Information following from: Not Given.
64-4 PIERRE TARDIEFFE, dead, no heirs.

Information following from: Not Given.
65-4 MRS. SHEARER, dead.
Husband: _______ Shearer.
65-4-1 Jennie Shearer, P.O. Proctro Knott, Minn., cannot locate her.

Information following from: Not Given.
66-4 PASCAL LALONE, said to be at St. Ignace, some of the Indians say he is dead, has not been at Sugar Isle for 25 yrs. or more.

Information following from: Alex La Pointe.
67-4 ISAAC CADOTTE Sr., age 72, P.O. Drummond's Isle.
Wife: Mary Cadotte, age 70.
67-4-1 Polly Ke Way Ke Zhick or Sailor, age 41, P.O. Drummond's Isle.
Husband: Joe Ke Way Ke Zhick, age 45, of the Mackinaw Band see 4-11.
67-4-1-1 Mary Ke Way Ke Zhick, age 12.
67-4-1-2 Julia Ke Way Ke Zhick, age 10.
67-4-1-3 Isaac Ke Way Ke Zhick, age 7.
67-4-1-4 Emma Ke Way Ke Zhick, born November/08.
67-4-2 Lucy La Pointe, see 9-8.
Husband: James La Pointe, see 9-8.

Information following from: Charlotte Rousain, & Chief.
68-4 JOHN ROUSAIN Jr., dead, no one ever heard of John Rousain Jr.

Information following from: Not Given.
69-4 ANGELIQUE BUSHEY, dead, no child.

Information following from: Joseph Roulran.
70-4 MARGARET PRYOR, age 71, P.O. Sault Ste. Marie.
Husband: Thomas Pryor Sr., age 81, P.O. Sault Ste. Marie.
70-4-1 Charles Pryor, age 48, P.O. Sault Ste. Marie.
Wife: Frany Pryor, white.
70-4-2 Benjamin Pryor, age 45, P.O. Sault Ste. Marie.
70-4-3 Mary Mende, age 42, P.O. Sault Ste. Marie.

Husband: William Mende, white.
70-4-3-1 Charles Mende, age 15, P.O. Sault Ste. Marie.
70-4-3-2 Hazel Mende, age 13, P.O. Sault Ste. Marie.
70-4-3-3 Eddie Mende, age 12.
70-4-3-4 Alger Mende, age 10, P.O. Sault Ste. Marie.
70-4-3-5 Doris Mende, age 4, P.O. Sault Ste. Marie.
70-4-4 Frank Pryor, age 39, P.O. Sault Ste. Marie.
70-4-5 Alice Busho, age 36, P.O. Sault Ste. Marie.
Husband: William Busho, white, P.O. Sault Ste. Marie.
70-4-5-1 Raymond Busho, age 2, P.O. Sault Ste. Marie.
70-4-6 Stephen Pryor, age 32, P.O. Sault Ste. Marie.
70-4-7 Julia Jane Cooper, age 28, P.O. Sault Ste. Marie.
Husband: George Cooper, white.
70-4-7-1 Mary J. Cooper, age 2, P.O. Sault Ste. Marie.
70-4-7-2 Francis Cooper, age 6 months, P.O. Sault Ste. Marie, off too late.
70-4-8 John Pryor, age 26, P.O. Sault Ste. Marie.
Note: children of 70-4 were not enrolled with her in 1870 although living enroll with? Durant.

Department of the Interior,
United States Indian Service,

Dear Sir:

In order to complete the Ottawa & Chippewa roll please give me the name, age & address of your mother, yourself, & your brothers & sisters.

A prompt reply will oblige.

Very respectfully
HORACE B. DURANT
Special U.S. Indian Agent

Mrs. Margrette Pryor	*age 71*
Mr. Charlie Pryor	*age 48*
Mr. Benjeman Pryor	*age 42*
Mrs. May Mende	*age 40*
Mrs. Alice Busha	*age 36*
Mr. Frank Pryor	*age 34*
Mr. Stephen Pryor	*age 32*
Mrs. Dolly Cooper	*age 28*
Mr. John Pryor	*age 26*

Mr. B. Durant,

The reason I didn't answer your letter any sooner it that your letter was delayed. I only got it the other day. So if you should write again you can address the letter to me. *Mrs. Margarette Pryor*
1049 Ceder St.

and what about my grand Children, and my Husband, are they entitled to anything or not.

Information following from: Charlotte Roussain.
71-4 JUSTINE ROUSSAIN, dead.
71-4-1 Louis Roussain. Do not know where he is unless at Badenock.

Pages 5 & 6 (Part)
Sault Sainte Marie Band
Chief JOHN WAISHKEY
Bay Mills & Waishkey Bay

Information following from: Andrew Waiskey, Sault Ste. Marie May 8/09.
1-5 JOHN WAISHKEY, dead.
Wife: Name not given, dead.
1-5-1 Peter Waishkey, on roll as 39-5.
Wife: Name not given, see 9-9.
1-5-2 Louis Waishkey, dead, single, no child, There were two sons named Louis, Draws in Canada & is Canadian Indian.
1-5-3 Eliza La Branch, age 60, P.O. Sault Ste. Marie.
Husband 1st : ______ Cameron.
Husband 2nd: Xavier La Branche, age 60, P.O. Sault Ste. Marie.
1-5-3-1 Hugh Cameron, age 44.
Wife: Mary Cameron, age 44, enroll by consent of Chiefs- Durant.
1-5-3-1-1 Joe Cameron, age 21, single.
1-5-3-2 John La Branche, age 34, single, P.O. Sault Ste. Marie
1-5-3-3 Henry La Branche, age 32, P.O. Bay Mills.
Wife: Name not given.
1-5-3-3-1 Alphonse La Branche, age 5.
1-5-3-3-2 Angeline La Branche, age 4.
1-5-3-3-3 Henry La Branche, age 3.
1-5-3-3-4 Mary La Branche, born February/08, 2nd roll.
1-5-3-4 Joe La Branche, age 27, P.O. Soo.
1-5-3-5 Jennie La Branche, age 20, single.
1-5-3-6 Annie Cavanaugh, age 35, P.O. Soo Maple St. 928.
Husband: Name not given.
1-5-3-6-1 Francis Cavanaugh, age 12.
1-5-3-6-2 Roy Cavanaugh, age 10.
1-5-3-6-3 Loretta Cavanaugh, age 7.
1-5-3-6-4 Annie Cavanaugh, age 2.
1-5-4 John Wasishkey, age 59, P.O. Bay Mills.
Wife: Christina Waishkey, age 49, P.O. Bay Mills, enroll by consent of Chief – Durant.

1-5-4-1 Jennie Lufkins, age 29, no children.
Husband: _______ Lufkins, Minnesota Indian.

1-5-5 Edward Waishkey, dead, died March 7/08.
Wife: Lizzie Waishkey, age 37, P.O. Bay Mills, see 7-6.
1-5-5-1 Cecelia Waishkey, age 18, P.O. Mt. Pleasant School.
1-5-5-2 Vina Waishkey, age 12, P.O. Mt. Pleasant School.
1-5-5-3 Lawrence Waishkey, age 8, P.O. Bay Mills School.

1-5-6 Charlotte Waishkey, dead, was on 1870 roll as adopted child of William Shaw 18-5.
Husband: Name not given, white.
1-5-6-1 Mary Shaffer, age 28, P.O. Detroit.
1-5-6-2 Jennie Jahalka, age 26, P.O. Detroit.
1-5-6-3 Frances Jahalka, twin, age 24, P.O. Detroit.
1-5-6-4 Josie Jahalka, twin, age 24, P.O. Chicago.
1-5-6-5 Victor Jahalka, age 22.
1-5-6-6 Blanche Jahalka, age 19, Alberta, B.C.

1-5-7 Andrew Waishkey, 53, P.O. Bay Mills.
Wife: Ellen Waishkey, age 48, off belongs to Beraga Band of Chippewas.
1-5-7-1 Charlotte (Waishkey) Roberts, age 24, P.O. Bay Mills, no children, husband white. On L'Anse roll 1907.
1-5-7-2 Bertha Waishkey, age 12, P.O. Bay Mills, on L'Anse roll 1907.

1-5-8 Charles Waishkey, age 50, P.O. Bay Mills, Mich.
Wife: Maria Waishkey, age 52, see 8-7, no children.
1-5-8-1 Nelson Waishkey, adopted, age 9, Chiefs say to enroll Durant.

1-5-9 Jane Cameron, age 46, P.O. Bay Mills.
Husband: Duncan Cameron, age 51, P.O. Bay Mills, see 4-6.
1-5-9-1 John Cameron, age 25, single, P.O. Bay Mills.
1-5-9-2 Lillie Holliday, age 24, P.O. Garnett, Mich, no children, husband L'Anse Indian.
1-5-9-3 Gertrude Cameron, age 14, P.O. Bay Mills.
1-5-9-4 Herman Cameron, age 9, P.O. Bay Mills.
1-5-9-5 Norman Cameron, age 7.
1-5-9-6 William Cameron, age 4.

1-5-10 Louis Waiskey, age 36, P.O. Bay Mills.
Wife: Mary Waishkey, Canadian Indian.
1-5-10-1 Manni Waishkey, age 16, P.O. Genoa School, Nebr.
1-5-10-2 Mary Jane Waishkey, age 9, Chiloceo Okla. School.
1-5-10-3 Arona Waishkey, age 7, Chiloceo Okla. School.

Information following from: Not Given.

2-5 MRS SIMON TEEPLE, dead.
Husband: Simon Teeple.

2-5-1 George Teeple, see 40-5.
2-5-2 Thomas Teeple, see 44-6.
2-5-3 Elizabeth Teeple, dead.
Husband: Silas Mason, white.
2-5-3-1 _____ Mason, dead, no heirs.
2-5-3-2 Bertha Mason, P.O. Montana, Whitefish, husband white, 6 children.
2-5-3-3 Clarence Mason, dead, no children.
2-5-3-4 May Mason, address unknown.
2-5-3-5 Alice Mason, address unknown (Mexico).
2-5-3-6 Amy Mason, dead, no children.
2-5-3-7 Cora Mason, address unknown (Mexico).
2-5-4 Catharine Parish, age 55, P.O. Bay Mills, Mich.
Husband: _______ Parish, white.
2-5-4-1 Elijah Parish, age 36, P.O. Bay Mills.
Wife: Name not given, white.
2-5-4-1-1 Clifford Parish, age 10.
2-5-4-1-2 Percy Parish, age 8.
2-5-4-1-3 Melborne Parish, age 6.
2-5-4-1-4 Harry Parish, age 2.
2-5-4-1-5 Baby Parish, born January/09, too late.
2-5-4-2 Maggie Weston, dead.
Husband: Victor Weston, white, his 2nd wife see below
2-5-4-2-1 Nora Weston, age 10, P.O. Bay Mills.
2-5-4-2-2 Wayne Weston, age 5.
2-5-4-2-3 Maggie Weston, age 4.
2-5-4-3 Daniel Parish, age 29, P.O. Bay Mills, wife white, no children.
2-5-4-4 Maud Taylor, age 27, P.O. Tacoma, Wash.
Husband: _________ Taylor, white.
2-5-4-4-1 Maxey Taylor, (male), born December 1907 2nd roll.
2-5-4-5 Wesley Parish, age 22, P.O. Bay Mills, single.
2-5-4-6 William Parish, age 18, P.O. Bay Mills, single.
2-5-4-7 Hazel Parish, age 16, P.O. Bay Mills.
2-5-5 John Teeple, age 53, P.O. Bay Mills.
Wife: Lydia Teeple, age 54, see 1-6.
2-5-5-1 George Teeple 3rd, age 14, P.O. Bay Mills.
2-5-6 Joe Teeple, dead.
Wife: Emma Teeple, age 48, P.O. Sault Ste. Marie, white.
2-5-6-1 Ina Weston, age 22, P.O. Alagonquin, Mich.
Husband: Victor Weston, see above.
2-5-6-1-1 Violet Weston, born July 1908 2nd roll.
2-5-6-2 Myrtle Teeple, age 17, P.O. Genoa School, Nebr.
2-5-6-3 Joe Teeple, age 15, P.O. Alagonquin, Mich.

2-5-6-4 Hildah Teeple, age 12.
2-5-6-5 Randall Teeple, age 6.
2-5-7 Sophia Teeple, dead, no children.
2-5-8 Lydia Richardson, age 41, P.O. Mishepocotan, Canada.
Husband: ________ Richardson, white.
2-5-8-1 Perry Richardson or Perry Teeple, age 28, P.O. Bay Mills.
Wife: Laura Richardson, age 22, see 39-5, nee Waishkey.
2-5-8-1-1 Loretta Richardson, age 4.
2-5-8-1-2 Floyd Richardson, age 3.
2-5-8-1-3 Bazil Richardson, age 2.
2-5-8-1-4 Simon Richardson Jr., born April/08 off.
2-5-8-2 Simon Richardson, age 25, single, U.S. Army.
2-5-8-3 Jennie Richardson, age 16, Mishepcotan, Canada.

Information following from: Not Given.
3-5 HENRY KAY KAY KOONSE, dead.
Wife: Name not given, dead.
3-5-1 Fannie Kay, dead, no children.
3-5-2 Charlotte Kay, dead.
Husband: Albert Menominee or Pay Ke Naw Gay, see 8-7.
3-5-3 Sarah Kay, dead, no children.
3-5-4 William Kay, age 71, P.O. Bay Mills.
Wife: Mary Kay, age 60, nee Waw Naw Kis, see 1-7, no children.
3-5-4-1 Cora Kay, adopted, see 40-5.
3-5-5 Angus Kay, age 60, P.O. Bay Mills.
Wife 1st : Susan, dead, see 17-5.
Wife 2nd: Name not given, dead.
3-5-5-1 Charlotte Pine, see 17-5, child by 1st wife.
3-5-5-2 Fannie Wasquam, see 26-5, child by 1st wife.
3-5-5-3 Joe Kay, age 24, P.O. Bay Mills, single.
3-5-5-4 Martha Kay, age 16, P.O. Bay Mills.
3-5-6 Henry Kay, age 35, died July1908.
Wife: Jane Sabastion Kay, Canadian, P.O Drummond's Island.
3-5-6-1 William Kay, age 23, P.O. Bay Mills.
Wife: Clara, see 4-5.
3-5-6-2 John Kay, age 21, P.O. Bay Mills, single.
3-5-6-3 Mary Ellen Kay, age 12, Mt. Pleasant School.
3-5-6-4 James Kay, age 10, Drummond Isle.

Information following from: Chiefs & Charlotte St. Louis.
4-5 MARY ANN MAY TWAY KE ZHICK, dead.
4-5-1 James Smith, age 50, P.O. Brimley, Mich.

Wife: Anna, dead, nee Brown, see 33-7.
4-5-1-1 Moses Smith, age 18.
4-5-1-2 Charlotte Smith, age 16.
4-5-1-3 Lucy Smith, age 14.
4-5-1-4 James Smith, age 12.
4-5-1-5 Alex Smith, age 10.
4-5-2 George Martel, age 47, P.O. Brimley.
Wife: ______, Canadian Indian, nee Pero.
4-5-2-1 Clara Martel, age 11, step child, a grandchild of 25-5, also know as Clara Shaw.
4-5-3 Charlotte St. Louis, age 45, P.O. Brimley.
Husband: _______ St. Louis, French & white.
4-5-3-1 Mary Kinney, age 27, P.O. Brimley.
Husband: ______ Kinney, white.
4-5-3-1-1 Annie Kinney, age 5.
4-5-3-1-2 Melvin Kinney, age 3.
4-5-3-1-3 James Kinney, born February 1908.
4-5-3-2 James St. Louis, age 24, P.O. Brimley.
4-5-3-3 Lucy Sylvester, age 22, P.O. Brimley, husband white, no children.
4-5-3-4 Melissa St. Louis, age 20, P.O. Brimley, Mich., single.
4-5-3-5 Clara Kay, age 18, P.O. Bay Mills, see 3-5.
4-5-3-6 Napolean St. Louis, age 7, P.O. Brimley.
4-5-3-7 Melvin St. Louis, age 5, P.O. Brimley.

Information following from: Rebecca Cadreau.
5-5 JOHN CADOTTE, dead.
Wife: Name not given, dead.
5-5-1 Philamon Boucher, P.O. Sugar Isle, no children.
Husband: Frank Boucher, see 35-3.
5-5-1-1 Mary Boucher, age 10, adopted, enroll by consent of Chief, a descendant of a member of Band Durant May 14/09.
5-5-2 Cecelia Cadotte, dead, no children.
5-5-3 Catharine Hatch, dead.
Husband: Charles Hatch, see 11-3.
5-5-4 Charlotte Cadotte, dead, no children.
5-5-5 Rebecca Cadreau, age 40, see 11-3.
5-5-6 Angeline Cadotte, dead.
Husband: James Pine, Canadian.
5-5-6-1 Edward Pine, Canadian.
5-5-7 Agnes Cadotte, age 28, P.O. Drummond's Isle.
Husband: Joe Andrew (?)
5-5-8 Pauline Gates, age 25, P.O. Sugar Isle, no children.
Husband: William Gates, white.

Information following from: Not Given.

6-5 HENRY COTAY, dead.

Wife: Name not given, dead.

6-5-1 John Cotay, on 1870 roll as 12-3.

6-5-2 Charlotte Cotay, dead.

Husband: _______ Fisher, dead.

6-5-2-1 Robert Fisher, age 42, P.O. Soo, no children.

6-5-2-2 Lucy Meloy, age 40, P.O. Soo, has children.

6-5-2-3 Joseph Fisher, age 38, P.O. Soo, no children.

6-5-3 Josephine Plante, age 67, on rollas 21-5.

6-5-4 Charles Cotay, age 65, P.O. Soo.

Wife: Name not given, of another band, L'Anse.

6-5-4-1 Myra Doran, age 25, Winnwpeg, one child.

6-5-4-2 Bertha Brown, age 20, P.O. Soo, husband white, one child.

6-5-4-3 Melissa Cotay, age 18, P.O. Soo, single.

6-5-5 Amos Cotay, age 59, P.O. Soo, single.

6-5-6 William Cotay, age 57, P.O. Soo, single.

Information following from: Not Given.

7-5 CHE MO AW WAY, dead.

Wife: Name not given.

7-5-1 Louis Cartwright (Ke Che Mo Ah Wa), Odanah, Wis., has an enrollment at L'Anse & child have Wis, made appl. for allot. at La Pointe.

Wife: Eliza, dead, see 2-7.

7-5-1-1 Antoine Cartright, age 21, Hayward School, Wis.

7-5-1-2 Sophia Cartright, age 7, Hayward School, Wis.

7-5-2 Mary, dead, see 8-7.

Husband: Albert Menomina, dead, see 8-7.

7-5-2-1 Susan Menomina, see 8-7.

7-5-2-2 Jonah Menomina, see 8-7.

7-5-3 Carolline Kish E Taw Tug, age 50, P.O. L'Anse, Mich.

Husband: Belongs to L'Anse Band, (Danl).

7-5-3-1 Mary Ann, age 18.

7-5-3-2 William, age 26.

7-5-3-3 Thomas, age 24.

7-5-3-4 Nash, age 21.

Note: Drew at L'Anse 1907 Durant, Banaga June 1/09.

Information following from: Susan, Clarissa & Charlotte Shaw & Andrew Waishkey.

8-5 THOMAS SHAW, dead.

Wife: Name not given, dead.

8-5-1 Susan Shaw, age 63, P.O. Sault Ste. Marie 530 Ridge St, single.
8-5-2 Clarissa Shaw or Clarissa Fitch, age 61, P.O. Sault Ste. Marie 530 Ridge St.
Husband: ______ Fitch, dead or separated.
8-5-2-1 Sarah Thatcher, age 34, P.O. Canon City, Colo. c/o Eldred or Soo.
Husband: _________ Thatcher, white.
8-5-2-1-1 Ralph H. Thatcher, age 9.
8-5-2-1-2 Allen W. Thatcher, age 6.
8-5-2-1-3 Lois Thatcher, age 3.
8-5-3 Charlotte Bernard, age 58, P.O. 509 9th Soo, Mich.
Husband: _________ Bernard, dead.
8-5-3-1 Frank Bernard, age 33, P.O. 509 9th Soo, Mich., single
8-5-3-2 Louis Bernard, age 30, P.O. Gros Cap, Canada.
Wife: Name not given, Canadian.
8-5-3-2-1 Delphine Bernard, age 8, born in Canada.
8-5-3-3 Susan M. Bernard, age 25, P.O. 509 9th Soo, Mich., single.
8-5-3-4 Julia C. Bernard, age 21, P.O. 509 9th Soo, Mich., single.

Information following from: Not Given.
9-5 ANTOINE ROUSSAIN.

Information following from: Charles Marshall, a nephew, Bay Mills, May 11/09.
10-5 NE GAW NAW SE NO QUAY.
10-5-1 Samuel Boullia or Bully, age 40, Drummond's Isle.
Wife: Cecelia, see 7-3, no children.
10-5-2 Edward Boullia or Bully, age 38, P.O. Sugar Isle.
Wife: Cassie or Catherine, age 40, see 2-8.
10-5-2-1 Mary Pine, age 23, husband Ed Pine, no children.
10-5-2-2 Stephen Boullia or Bully, age 21.
10-5-2-3 Vina Boullia or Bully, age 18.
10-5-2-4 Alex Boullia or Bully, age 16.
10-5-2-5 Norman Boullia or Bully, age 14.
10-5-2-6 Stella Boullia or Bully, age 12.
10-5-2-7 Louisa Boullia or Bully, age 10.
10-5-2-8 Abraham Boullia or Bully, age 8.
10-5-2-9 Marcel Boullia or Bully, age 6.
10-5-3 Jack Bully or Boullia, see 4-11.

Information following from: Chiefs, Bay Mills, May 10/09.
11-5 AIN NE ME KUCE, dead, wife & children dead, no heirs Durant.
Information following from: William Waishkey & Joe Waishkey, Bay Mills.

12-5 WILLIAM WAISHKEY, age 75, P.O. Bay Mills.
Wife: Jane Waishkey, age 63, P.O. Bay Mills.
12-5-1 Louis Waishkey, dead, single.
12-5-2 Joseph Waishkey, age 42, P.O. Bay Mills.
Wife: Sophia Waiskey, age 44, belongs to Mackinaw Band, see 14-15 but is on Canadian Rolls & draws money from Canadian Govt.
12-5-2-1 Agnes Waishkey, age 5.
12-5-2-2 James Toby, age 20, P.O. Bay Mills, child of Sophia Waishkey by James Toby, dead.
12-5-3 Annie Waishkey, dead, single.
12-5-4 _______ Waishkey, dead no heirs.

Information following from: William Marou.
13-5 WILLIAM MAROW or MIROW, age 77, P.O. Bay Mills, Mich.
Wife: Archangle Marow, age 80, P.O. Bay Mills, Mich.
13-5-1 Lawrence Marow, age 47, P.O. Bay Mills, single.
13-5-2 Agnes Le Blanc, age 43, P.O. Bay Mills.
Husband: Arthur Le blanc, white.
13-5-2-1 Addie Le Blanc, age 20, single.
13-5-2-2 Arthur Le Blanc, age 18.
13-5-2-3 Alfred Le Blanc, age 16.
13-5-2-4 William Le Blanc, age 14.
13-5-2-5 Leo Le Blanc, age 12.
13-5-2-6 Francis Le Blanc, age 9.
13-5-2-7 Bella Le Blanc, age 7.
13-5-2-8 Agnes Le Blanc, age 2, born June 6/02.
13-5-3 ________ Marow, dead no heirs.

Information following from: Not Given.
14-5 BETSEY BROWN, dead.
14-5-1 Antoine Bellaire, see 15-7.
14-5-2 Charlotte Kaw Gaw Aw Shee, see 6-7, died November 1908.
14-5-3 Mary Friday, age 55, P.O. Bay Mills, Mich.
Husband 1st : Name not given.
Husband 2nd: Joe Friday, age 57, P.O. Bay Mills, Mich., see 25-7
14-5-3-1 Angus K. Kay Jr., age 40, P.O. Bay Mills, Mich., child by 1st husband.
Wife: Nancy, off belongs to Baraga Band.
14-5-3-1-1 May Ann Kay, born May 13/08, 2nd roll.
14-5-3-2 Lydia Pine, age 35, P.O. Garden River, Canada- Draws with Canadian Gov't. make note on roll.
Husband: Frank Pine, Canadian.
14-5-3-2-1 David Pine, age 10, draws with Canadian

Gov't.

14-5-3-2-2 Frank Pine Jr., age 6, draws with Canadian Gov't.

14-5-3-3 Charlotte Hugo, age 31, P.O. Bay Mills.
Husband: Frank hugo, belongs to Baraga Band.
14-5-3-3-1 Mary Hugo, age 6.
14-5-3-3-2 Frances Hugo, age 3.
14-5-3-3-3 Carrie Hugo, born January 1908 2nd roll.

14-5-4 Name not given, a grandchild, daughter of Lydia Pine, who does not draw with Canadian Gov't.

Garden River, Ontario, Canada.
June 18 1909
Horace B. Durant
Petoskey, Mich.
Dear Sir:
Your letter at hand and contents carefully noted. I was born and raised in Bay Mills. I only left there ten years ago and am very glad that I ain't all together forgotten. Andrew Waishkey is unfriendly with our whole family that is why he didn't want me on the rool.
Parents Joseph Friday, Mary Friday, Bay Mills
Sister Mrs Frank Hugo " "
Half Brother Angus Kay, Jr " "
My Family
Husband Frank Pine, Paid in Garden River age
Son David Pine draws no pay born in Bay Mills 11 yrs
" Frank Pine, Jr., Paid in Born in Garden River 7 "
My self age 38 "
Your Very Truly
Mrs Lydia Pine

Information following from: Chiefs, Bay Mills, May 10/09.
16-5 CHARLES BUTTERFIELD, dead, nephew of William Waishkey, Sr. 12-5.
Wife: Name not given.
16-5-1 Charles Butterfield, dead.
16-5-2 Lee Butterfield, said to be in Chicago, cannot locate him.

Information following from: Samuel Waishkey, Bay Mills.
17-5 MARY WAISHKEY, dead.
17-5-1 Samuel Waishkey, age 52, P.O. Bay Mills.
Wife: Nancy, age 50, P.O. Bay Mills, see 5-6.
17-5-1-1 Henry Waishkey, age 18, P.O. Bay Mills.
17-5-1-2 Samuel Waishkey Jr., age 16.
17-5-1-3 William Waishkey, age 14.

17-5-1-4 Catharine Waishkey, age 12.
17-5-2 Susan Waishkey, dead.
Husband: Angus Kay, age 60, see 3-5.
17-5-2-1 Charlotte Pine, age 37, P.O. L'Anse, Mich.
Husband: George Pine, L'Anse Indian.
17-5-2-1-1 Fred Pine, age 17.
17-5-2-1-2 Rona Pine, age 14.
17-5-2-1-3 Georgiana Pine, age 12.
17-5-2-1-4 George E. Pine, age 10.
17-5-2-1-5 William A. Pine, age 8.
17-5-2-1-6 Eliza Pine, age 6.
17-5-2-1-7 Estie Pine, age 4.
17-5-2-1-8 ____ Pine.
Note: all children drew with L'Anse band of Chips.
17-5-2-2 Fannie Wasquaum, see 26-5.

Information following from: Chiefs, Bay Mills, May 10/09.
18-5 WILLIAM SHAW, dead.
Wife: Name not given, dead.
Note: Had no children of his own; but see note on 1-5. The child on this sheet was Charlotte Waishkey 6th child of 1-5.

Information following from: Not Given.
19-5 MRS. LOUIS GURNOE, dead, write to Jane Nault at 311 Fisher St. West Marquette, Mich. For information of this family, Durant.

Information following from: Peter Messenger.
20-5 JOHN MESSENGER, dead.
Wife: Name not given, dead.
20-5-1 Georgiana Bachand, age 37, P.O. Odanah, Wis.
Husband: Ed Bachand, member of L'Anse Band.
20-5-1-1 Esther Bachand, age 17.
20-5-1-2 Blanche Bachand, age 14, Drew at L'Anse.
20-5-1-3 Dayton Bachand, age 10.
20-5-1-4 Augustus Bachand, age 9, Drew at L'Anse.
20-5-1-5 Gilbert Bachand, age 4.
20-5-1-6 Archie Bachand, bornNov 1908, too late..
20-5-2 Peter Messenger, age 28, P.O. Bay Mills, single.

Odanah, Wis. July 20, 1909

Mr. Horace.B.Durant,
Special Agent.,
Washington, D.C.

Dear Sir:-

I am in receipt of your letter of the 17th, instant, in which you state the following:

"The name of your wife has been given me as a member of the Ottawa and Chippewa tribe of Mich.

If she claims to be a member of that band please give me the names of her parents, and her brothers and sisters, if any with ages and addresses.

Also give me her full name, her age and the names ages and addresses of all her children."

In Reply thereto as to claim, will state what I understand the facts to be, and in submitting the same can say; That my wife is a member of the tribe and of that division known as the Chippewa's of Lake Superior.

That her Father in latter years, was known as John Messenger, that he was born in the vicinity of this the La Pointe Reservation, and regarded as a member of that subdivision or what is known as the La Pointe band for which the above mentioned reservation was set apart.

That her Mother was a Mary Lightfoot, and born at Bay-Mills, Mich., that she was regarded as being a member of that part of the Chippewa tribe residing in the vicinity of Sault Ste Marie, Mich.,

That my wife has an only brother, aged__*30*__years, now residing at Bay-Mills, Mich, known as ~~John~~.J.Messenger.
Peter

That my wife's full name is Georgian Bachand, age 33, years, residing at Odanah, Wis., together with six children whose names and ages areas follows: Mary E.Bachand age 15 years; Blanch E.Bachand age 13 years; Dayton E.Bachand age II years; August J.E.Bachand age 9 years; Arthur W. Bachand age 4 years; and Gilbert M.Bachand age one year.

Believing to have fully answered your letter, I wish to request of you, that I be informed of the object of your inquiry, and as to any rights that may accrue to Georgian Bachand and children by reason thereof.

Very Respectfully,
Edward.Bachand

Information following from: Charlotte Belanger.

21-5 MRS. HENRY PLANT or JOSEPHINE (COTAY), age 67, P.O. Augusta St. Sault Ste Marie.
Husband: Henry Plant, dead.
21-5-1 Charlotte Belanger, age 42, P.O. 207 Bingham Ave Soo.
Husband: Name not given, white.
20-5-1-1 Maxson Belanger, age 19, P.O. 207 Bingham Ave Soo.
20-5-1-2 Rose Belanger, age 17.
20-5-1-3 Leo Belanger, age 15.
20-5-1-4 Ernest Belanger, age 13.
20-5-1-5 Cecelia Belanger, age 10, twin.

20-5-1-6 Lucile Belanger, age 10, twin.
20-5-1-7 Stella Belanger, age 6.
20-5-1-8 Louis Belanger, age 3.
20-5-1-9 Joseph Belanger, born September/08, off.
21-5-2 Henry Plante, age 40, P.O. Soo, single.
21-5-3 Louise Bennett, age 38, P.O. Soo.
Husband: ______ Bennett, white.
21-5-3-1 Louis Bennett, age 18.
21-5-3-2 Edna Bennett, age 16.
21-5-3-3 Francis Bennett, age 11.
21-5-3-4 Joe Bennett, age 8.
21-5-3-5 Leo Bennett, age 5.
21-5-3-6 Russell Bennett, age 3.
21-5-4 John Plante, age 35, P.O. Soo.
Wife: Mary Plante, no children.
21-5-5 Fannie Murphy, age 28, P.O. Soo Augusta St., no children.
Husband: _____ Murphy, white.
21-5-6 Joe Plante, age 23, P.O. Soo, single.

Information following from: Alice Pidgeon, Soo, May 26/09.
22-5 MRS. LEON BRUNNO, dead.
Husband: Leon Brunno.
22-5-1 Joseph Brunno or Bunno, age 52, P.O. Soo, see 15-3.
22-5-2 Adelaide Piquette, P.O. Soo.
Husband: Antoine Ermatinger, dead, on roll as 25-3.
22-5-2-1 Mary Ermatinger.
22-5-3 Jane La Coy, age 65, see 18-3.
22-5-4 Alice Pidgeon, age 48, Soo #500 Ridge.
Husband: ______ Pidgeon, white.
22-5-4-1 Peter Pidgeon, age 31, P.O. Soo 4th St.
Wife: Name not given, Canadian.
22-5-4-1-1 Julia Pidgeon, age 9.
22-5-4-1-2 Adolph Pidgeon, age 7.
22-5-4-1-3 Delphine Pidgeon, age 5.
22-5-4-1-4 William Pidgeon, age 2.
22-5-4-2 Mary Lalone, age 34, P.O. Gros Cap St. Soo.
Husband: Isaac Lalone, Canadian, white.
22-5-4-2-1 Adolph Lalone, age 11.
22-5-4-2-2 Alice Lalone, age 9.
22-5-4-2-3 Rose Lalone, age 7.
22-5-4-2-4 Lillian Lalone, age 5.
22-5-4-2-5 Bertha Lalone
22-5-4-3 Orilla Hanley, age 25, P.O. 502 South St. Soo.
Husband: ________ Hanley.
22-5-4-3-1 Lena Hanley, age 8.

22-5-4-3-2 Adolph Hanley, age 6.
22-5-4-3-3 Hilda Hanley, age 4.
22-5-4-3-4 Elizabeth Hanley, age 2.
22-5-4-4 Joseph Pidgeon, age 24, P.O. Pt. Iroquoi's Bay Mills.
22-5-4-5 Alice Kelly, age 22, 500Ridge St.
Husband: ________ Kelly.
22-5-4-5-1 Marie Kelly, age 5.
22-5-4-5-2 Adolph, age 3.
22-5-5 Josephine Parr, age 35, P.O. Soo.
Husband 1st : _________ Laramie.
Husband 2nd: _________ Parr, white.
22-5-5-1 Byrnett Laramie (boy), age 12
22-5-5-2 Leroy Parr, age 2.
22-5-6 Leo Bunno, age 32, P.O. Soo, see 7-3.

Information following from: Not Given.
23-5 GEORGE BROWN, dead.
Wife: Name not given.
23-5a Edward Brown, brother of 23-5, age 55, P.O. address unknown, In Grand Marias somewhere White Fish Point, Mich.
23-5-1 Alex Brown, age 44, single, 546 Maple St. Soo, see 33-7.
23-5-2 Mary (Brown) O'Malley, age 39, 546 Maple St. Soo.
23-5-2-1 Bessie Brown, age 21, see 33-7.
23-5-2-2 Victoria Brown, age 16, see 33-7.

Department of the Interior,
United States Indian Service,

Petoskey Mich.
June 28/09

Dear Sir:

Your name has been given me as a member of the Ottawa & Chippewa Indian Tribe of Michigan, a roll of which I am making.

If you claim to be a number of that band please give me the names and ages of your father and mother and state whether living or dead, & if living, their address.

Also give me the names & ages of yourself & family, and the names ages and addresses of your brothers and sisters if you have any.

Sheet for your reply.

Very respectfully
HORACE B. DURANT
Special U.S. Indian Agent

1 Alex Brown age 44 & single

			546 Maple St Soo Mich
George Brown		2	Mrs. Anna Smith age 42
fathers name dead			(dead)
	children		
Betsey Brown		3	Mrs. Mary O'Malley 39
Mothers name dead			546 Maple Soo Mich
		4	

Sault Ste. Marie, Mich., *July 11, 1909*

Mr. Horace B. Durant
Petoskey Mich.,
Dear Sir;

I have received the letter you sent me in regard to the payment the Indians are about to receive. I am a member of the Ottawa and Chippewa Tribe, being a great grand-son of the Old Chief Moses Gab-ba-no-dau (dead). His daughter, Ma-gequa-wis dead, was my mother's mother, so from them our Indian starts! No-doubt you will find them on the old roll.

I have two sisters, the oldest being dead, but she has seven children which are entitled to payment. They have been supported by the Government since her death. I will give you their addresses and ages on another page.

I make my house with my other sister who also has two (over) Children.

Edward Brown, my uncle is still living, but I know not his direct address. He was inFort William, Canada, two years ago.

Respectfully,
Alex Brown

Sault Ste. Marie, Mich., *July 11, 1909.*

Mrs. Anna Smith's children and their addresses.

	Age	Address
Mrs. Mary Schirmer	24	Porterville, Cal.
Mrs. Samuel Gruett	22	Mt. Pleasant, Mich
Mr. Walter Smith	18	Genoa, Nebr. (Ind. Sch.)
Miss Charlotte Smith	14	Mt. Pleasant, Mich, (Ind. Sch.)
" Lucy Smith	12	" " " " "
Mr. Jimmie Smith	8	" " " " "
" Alex Smith	5	Brimley, Mich

Some one may have enrolled these children before, but this roll is correct. Their father is not capable of handling this money, for he is not capable of even taking care of tem. So I would like this money sent directly to them, for they need it. I am also willing to take a step to see that the money will reach them. If my help is not satisfactory, I would like it put in the bank, so their

father wont use it up on them. Of course the two married daughters can look after their own. And I will look after Walter Smiths.
Mrs. Mary O'Malley's children.
Miss Bessie Brown age 21) 546 Maple St.
" Victoria Brown " 16) Soo Mich
This roll is correct and my hope is that you will give it your prompt attention. I am widely known here and should you want to find me again send my mail to 546 Maple Soo, Mich, or c/o Str. Minnie M. at Locke, Soo, Mich.
Respectfully,
Alex Brown

Information following from: Chiefs, Bay Mills.
24-5 WILLIAM WAISHKEY 2nd & brothers, all dead, no heirs.
Information following from: Celamia Shaw, a sister, Soo, May 26/09.
25-5 LOUIS SHAW, dead.
Wife: Name not given, white, Canadian.
25-5-1 William Shaw, dead.
Wife: Julia Shaw, L'Anse Indian see 1-1.
25-5-1-1 Louis Shaw, age 13, L'Anse Indian Draw's with mother, on L'Anse roll 1907.
25-5-1-2 Frances Shaw, age 6, L'Anse Indian Draw's with mother, on L'Anse roll 1907.
25-5-1-3 Sarah Shaw, age 4, L'Anse Indian Draw's with mother, on L'Anse roll 1907.
25-5-2 Frank Shaw, age 24, P.O. Oskosh, Wis., single.
25-5-3 Clara Shaw, age 11, P.O. Brimley, known as Clara Martel, see 4-5.

Information following from: Joe.
26-5 WAW SE QUA WON, dead.
Wife: Julia Wasquam, age 59, P.O. Bay Mills, see 25-7.
26-5-1 Joe Wasquam, age 33, P.O. Bay Mills.
Wife: Fanny (Kay) Wasquam, age 33, see 17-5.
26-5-1-1 Joe Wasquam, age 6.
26-5-1-2 Maggie Wasquam, age 4.
26-5-1-3 Rose Wasquam, age 2.
26-5-1-4 Manning Wasquam, born February/09 off.
26-5-2 Maggie (Wasquam) Badgers, age 26, P.O. Bay Mills.
Husband: _________ Badgers, white.
26-5-2-1 Fannie Badgers, age 10, pay share to Jane Saboo, see 18-7 with whom she has lived for several years.
26-5-2-2 Nancy Badgers, age 6.
26-5-3 Annie Teeple, age 24, see 40-5.
Husband: _______ Teeple, see 40-5.
26-5-4 Jennie Wawbegakake, age 22.

Husband: Samuel Wawbegakake, age 35, see 30-1.
26-5-5 Peter Wasquam, age 28, P.O. Bay Mills, single.

Information following from: Alice Pidgeon, Soo, May 26/09.
27-5 LOUIS CADOTTE, dead, wife dead, no heirs.

Information following from: Not Given.
28-5 MRS. FRANCIS LADEBOUCHE, dead.
Husband: Francis Ladebouche.
28-5-1 _______ Ladebouche, mother of 29-5 dead heirs see 29-5.

Information following from: Harriet McIntyre, Soo, May 26/09.
29-5 MRS. ABRAHAM MCCOY, now HARRIET MCINTYRE, age 67, P.O. 312 Ridge St. Soo.
Husband: Abraham McCoy.
29-5-1 Sophia McCoy, dead.
Husband: Charles ________, white.
29-5-1-1 Melissa Blakesley, age 27, P.O. Soo 312 Ridge St., with grandmother.
Husband: _______ Blakesley, white.
29-5-1-1-1 Ada Blakesley, age 4.
29-5-1-1-2 Madeline Blakesley, age 2.
29-5-1-2 Catharine Tilson, age 25, P.O. Ferris St. Soo Mich.
Husband: ________ Tilson, white.
29-5-1-2-1 Margarite Tilson, age 2, born June 1/07.

Information following from: Horace B. Durant, Special U.S. Indian Agent, Grand Marais, Mich, June 30 '09.
30-5 MRS. ALEXANDER MISHOE, dead.
Husband: Alexander Mishoe, white, 84, Grand Marais, Mich (living).
30-5-1 Mrs. Mary Jane Martin, age 51, Grand Marais, Mich (living).
Husband: Mr. Samuel Martin, age 63, Grand Marais.
30-5-1-1 Alexander Martin, age 18 mo., dead.
30-5-1-2 William, Anna Martin, age 26, P.O. Grd. Marais, Mich. (William dead).
30-5-1-3 Samuel Joseph Martin, age 22, P.O. Grd. Marais, Mich.
30-5-1-4 Russel Martin, age 19, P.O. Grd. Marais, Mich.
30-5-1-5 Millie Martin, age 31, Grand Marais, Mich, This girl was born before Her a and 1.
30-5-2 Charlotte Mishoe or Mr. Peter Roberson, age 45, P.O. Batchanona Bay, Ont. (l~~e~~iving).
Husband: Mr. Peter Roberson.
Note: Unable to give the ages of the children of Charlotte, but you may receive the same by writing Mrs. Peter Roberson,

Batchana Bay, Ontario, Canada.
30-5-3 William Mishoe, age 40, P.O. Manistique, Mich. (living)
30-5-4 Harrett Mishoe, age 23 years, dead.
Husband: Mr. James Beaty, age 45 yrs, dead.
30-5-4-1 Mary Beaty, age 31, P.O. grand Marais, Mich.

Information following from: Not Given.
32-5 WILLIAM WAW BAW NAW QUOT or WILLIAM CARDINAL, age 54, P.O. Baraga, said to be enrolled at L'Anse.
Wife: Name not given.
31-5-1 Veronica Cardinal, age 14, draw at L'Anse.
31-5-2 Nancy Cardinal, age 11, draw at L'Anse.
31-5-3 Mary M. Cardinal, age 21, draw at L'Anse.
31-5-4 Charles Cardinal, age 29, draw at L'Anse.
31-5-4-1 Lawrence Cardinal, age 5, draw at L'Anse.
31-5-5 William Cardinal, dead.
31-5-5-1 Mary Cardinal, age 11, draw at L'Anse.
31-5-5-2 Charles Cardinal, age 5, draw at L'Anse.

Information following from: Chiefs, Bay Mills.
33-5 MARY WAW BO GIEG, dead, sister in law of Peter Waishkey Sr., no heirs.

Information following from: Chiefs, Bay Mills, May 10/09.
34-5 ROBERT HEAD, dead, no heirs.

Information following from: Chiefs, Bay Mills, May 10/09.
35-5 MARY NO DO QUAY, dead, no heirs.

Information following from: Chiefs, Bay Mills.
36-5 ELIZA JOHNSON, dead, no heirs.

Information following from: Chiefs, Bay Mills, May 10/09.
37-5 KE WAY DE NO QUAY, dead, no heirs.

Information following from: Not Given.
38-5 JOHN LADEBAUCHE, brother of 29-5, & son of 28-5, They have not heard from him in 20 years.

Information following from: Peter Waishkey.
39-5 PETER WAISHKEY Sr., age 56, P.O. Bay Mills Mich.
Wife: Catharine Waishkey, nee Foster, age 52, see 9-9.
39-5-1 Laura Teeple, age 22.
Husband: Perry Teeple or Perry Richardson, age 28, see 2-5.

Information following from: George Teeple.

40-5 GEORGE TEEPLE, age 60, P.O. Bay Mills.
Wife 1st : Name not given, dead.
Wife 2nd: Rachel Teeple, age 44, see 1-6.
40-5-1 John Teeple, age 38, P.O. Baraga, Mich, by 1st wife, Drew with L'Anse 1907, belongs to Baraga Chippewa – L'Anse band, children are all dead.
40-5-2 Thomas Teeple, age 32, P.O. Odanah.
Wife: Lydia Teeple, age 28, see 4-6.
40-5-2-1 Cora Teeple or Cora Kay, age 8, goes by name of Cora Kay, lives with William Kay, see 3-5.
40-5-3 Joe Teeple, age 30, P.O. Bay Mills, single.
40-5-4 George Teeple Jr., age 26, P.O. Bay Mills.
Wife: Annie Teeple, age 24, see 26-5.
40-5-4-1 Jennie Teeple, age 5.
40-5-4-2 Peter Teeple, age 3.
40-5-4-3 Pearl Teeple, born August 10, 1908, 2nd roll, too late.
40-5-5 Frank Teeple, age 21, P.O. Bay Mills, single.
40-5-6 Angus Teeple, age 18, P.O. Bay Mills.
40-5-7 Henry Teeple, age 16, P.O. Bay Mills.
40-5-8 James Teeple, age 9.
40-5-9 Sophia Jane Teeple, adopted, age 3, P.O. Bay Mills, ok enroll.

Information following from: William Mirou, Bay Mills, May 8/09.

42-5 CHARLES MIROW, dead.
Wife: Name not given, dead.
42-5-1 Sophia Pope, age 35, P.O. Bay City, Mich.
Husband: ______ Pope, white.
42-5-1-1 Catharine Pope, age 7.
42-5-1-2 Charles Pope, age 4.
42-5-1-3 Marion Pope, born September 07, 2nd roll.
42-5-1-4 Charlotte Mirow, age 18, P.O. Bemidji, Minn., single, child by 1st husband.
42-5-2 Agnes Mirow, age 30, P.O. Sault Ste. Marie Glenn Ave, not married.
42-5-2-1 Jennie Mirow, age 9.

Information following from: Joseph Rouleau, Sault Ste. Marie.

43-5 MRS. CHARLES ERMATINGER, age 70, P.O. Sault Ste. Marie.
Husband: Charles Ermatinger.
43-5-1 Catherine Sterling, age 46, Sault Ste. Marie.
Husband: John Sterling, white, P.O. Sault Ste. Marie.
43-5-1-1 Charles A. Sterling, age 21, P.O. Sault Ste. Marie.
43-5-1-2 Elmer Sterling, age 18, P.O. Sault Ste. Marie.
43-5-1-3 Harry A. Sterling, age 16, P.O. Sault Ste. Marie.

43-5-1-4 Eva Sterling, age 11, P.O. Sault Ste. Marie.
43-5-1-5 Clyde Sterling, age 6, P.O. Sault Ste. Marie.
43-5-2 Edward Ermatinger, age 44, P.O. Sault Ste. Marie, single.
43-5-3 Marie Liberty, dead.
Husband: Benjamin Liberty, white.
43-5-3-1 Reymond Liberty, age 8, P.O. Sault Ste. Marie.
43-5-3-2 Aveline Liberty, age 6, P.O. Sault Ste. Marie.
43-5-3-3 Leanore Liberty, age 4, P.O. Sault Ste. Marie.

Information following from: George Teeple Sr., a brother, Bay Mills.
44-6 THOMAS TEEPLE, dead.
Wife: Name not given, dead.
44-6-1 Jennie Cadotte, age 37, P.O. L'Anse, Mich, on L'Anse roll 1907.
Husband: Ed Cadotte, age 24, on L'Anse roll 1907.
44-6-2 Lucy Teeple, age 34, P.O. Baraga, Mich. , on L'Anse roll 1907
44-6-3 Frank Teeple #2, age 30, P.O. Baraga, Mich., single, on L'Anse roll 1907.
44-6-4 John Teeple, age 26, P.O. Baraga, at Chilocao School, on L'Anse roll 1907.

Information following from: Chiefs, Bay Mills, May 11/09.
45-6 MRS. CAPT. PECK, dead, no heirs.

Information following from: Not Given.
46-6 JENEVIEVE MARTEL, dead.
Note: Do not enroll until Deptmental action Durant Spl Agt.
46-6-1 Abraham Martel, dead, has children at Cheueaux Isles.
46-6-2 Jane Paul, age 50, P.O. Detroit, who was never on 1870 roll with parent, & should not be enrolled.
Husband: _______ Paul, white.
46-6-2-1 Archie Paul.
46-6-2-2 Sam Paul.
46-6-2-3 Eugene Paul.
46-6-2-4 Raymond Paul.
46-6-2-5 Nancy De Forrest.
Husband: ________ De Forrest, dead.
46-6-3 John Martel, P.O. Detroit.

Information following from: Chiefs, Bay Mills, May 11/09.
47-6 JOSEPHINE DOLLAR, dead, no heirs.

Pages 6 (Part)
Sault Sainte Marie Band
Chief WAW-BE-GAY-KAKE

Information following from: Not Given.
1-6 O GAW BAY AW NAW QUOT
1-6-1 Lydia Teeple, see 2-5.
1-6-2 Guy, dead, no family.
1-6-3 Angus Shegud, age 48, P.O. Odanah, Wis., single.
1-6-4 Name not given, dead no heirs.
1-6-5 Rachel Teeple, see 40-5.

Information following from: joe Sabbooe & Chiefs, Mission School House, Bay Mills, May 9/09.
2-6 NORMAN AW KE NE BO WE, dead.
2-6-1 Girl, name not given, dead.
2-6-1-1 Lizzie Sabbooe, age 40, see 6-7.
Husband: William Shegud, dead, no children.
2-6-2 John Shegud, dead, no children.
Note: all others died leaving no heirs.

Information following from: Alfred Bellaire & Margaret Duffina, Mac Isle, Mack City.
3-6 ALEXIS BAZENETE, dead.
Wife: Name not given, dead.
3-6-1 Elizabeth Bazenete, dead, see 65-14.
Husband: Alfred Bellaire, P.O. Mackinaw Island, see 65-14.
3-6-1-1 Alex Bellaire, age 39.
3-6-1-2 John Bellaire, Mackinaw roll.
3-6-2 Margaret Duffina, age 44, Mackinaw City.
Husband: Peter Duffina, age 42, see 8-12.
3-6-2-1 Hattie Duffina, age 18, P.O. Mackinaw City.
3-6-2-2 Paul Duffina, age 16.
3-6-2-3 Lizzie Duffina, age 11.
3-6-2-4 Iva Andrews, age 7, adopted lives with Margaret Duffina, father is Mitchell Andrews, grand father is William Andrews Sr..
3-6-3 Eliza Bazenete.
Husband: Mitchell Andrews Sr., see 2-17.
Note: Child see above Iva Andrews, age 7.
3-6-4 Cecilia Andrews, age 42, P.O. Mackinaw Island.
Husband: Peter Andrews, see 2-17.
Note: children see 2-17.

Information following from: Dougal Cameron, Bay Mills, May 11/09.
4-6 JAMES CAMERON, dead.
Wife: Name not given, dead.

4-6-1 Charles Cameron, age 58, P.O. Odanah, Wis.
Wife: Emma Cameron, age 56, see 9-7.
4-6-1-1 Dan Cameron Jr., age 38, P.O. Odanah, Wis, no children, wife Wisconsin Indian, separated.
4-6-1-2 Fred Cameron, age 35, P.O. Odanah, Wis., no children, see 2-8.
4-6-1-3 Emily (Cameron) Houle, age 28, no children.
Husband: Alex Houle.
4-6-2 Duncan Cameron, age 51, see 1-5.
Jane Cameron, age 46, see 1-5.
4-6-3 Dan Cameron, age 54, P.O. Odanah or Bay Mills.
Wife: Name not given, now cooking for Douglas Johnson, see 6-6.
4-6-3-1 Duncan Cameron Jr., age 32, P.O. Detroit, Mich., single.
4-6-3-2 James Cameron, age 30, Odanah, Wis., single.
4-6-3-3 Lydia Teeple, age 28, see 40-5.
4-6-3-4 Angus Cameron, age 18, P.O. Odanah, Wis.
4-6-3-5 Susan Cameron, age 16.
4-6-4 Dougal Cameron, age 48, P.O. Bay Mills, single.

Information following from: Garrett Smith, Bay Mills, May 10/09.
5-6 SMITH WAWBOSE or GARRETT SMITH, age 72, P.O. Bay Mills.
Wife: Mary Smith, age 73.
5-6-1 Nancy Waishkey, age 50, see 17-5.
5-6-2 Mary Smith jr., age 45, single.
5-6-3 Name not given, dead, no heirs.
5-6-4 Name not given, dead, no heirs.

Information following from: Not Given.
6-6 JOHN GEORGE JOHNSON.
6-6-1 Susan Menominee, dead.
Husband: William Menominee, age 42, see 8-7.
6-6-2 Douglas Johnson, P.O. Sault Ste. Marie, see 1-7.
Wife: Charlotte Johnson, 1st wife of Sam Cameron, see 4-6.
Note: no children but Charlotte has children.
6-6-3 George Johnson, age 38, draw at L'Anse.
Wife: Annie Johnson, age 45, see 31-1.

Information following from: Chiefs, Bay Mills.
7-6 AW BE TAW KE ZHICK, dead, (means Halfaday).
Wife: Name not given, dead.
7-6-1 Name not given, dead.
Husband: Henry St. Arnold, P.O. Marquette, do not enroll, belongs to Beraga Band of Chiefs.

7-6-1-1 Lizzie Waishkey, age 37, P.O. Bay Mills, see 1-5.
7-6-1-2 William Halfaday, age 40, P.O. Bay Mills.
Wife: Emiline Halfaday, no children, L'Anse Indian.
7-6-2 Joe Halfaday, age 60, P.O. L'Anse Mich, said to draw at L'Anse.
Wife: Name not given, see 1-1, no children.
7-6-3 John Halfaday, dead.
Wife: Name not given, dead.
7-6-3-1 Joe Halfaday Jr., age 36, P.O. Odanah, Wis.
7-6-3-2 William Halfaday Jr., age 26, P.O. Bay Mills, single.

Information following from: Chiefs, Bay Mills, May 11/09.
8-6 WILLIAM BROWN, dead.
Note: Chiefs do not know where children are, nor if they are living, nor does anyone at Bay Mills. Durant Spl Agt.

Information following from: Chiefs, Bay Mills, May 11/09.
9-6 O MAY TOS & daughter, both dead, heirs enrolled on 1-6.

Information following from: Xavier La Brauche, Soo, May 8.
10-6 MRS. FRANCIS LA BRAUCHE, dead.
Husband: Francis La Bruche.
10-6-1 Xavier La Bruche, age 60, see 1-5.
10-6-2 Amelia Mishoe, dead, on roll as 30-5.
Husband: Alex Mishoe, Canadian Indian.
10-6-2-1 Name not given, dead, no heirs.
10-6-2-2 Mary Jane Martin, age 51, P.O. Grand Marais, Mich.,
has children(write).
10-6-2-3 Charlotte Robinson, age 30, P.O. Batchawaning, Canada.
10-6-2-4 William Mishoe, age 28, P.O. Manistique.
10-6-3 others names not given, dead, no heirs.

Information following from: Not Given.
11-6 WAW BE GAY KAKE, dead, no heirs.

Information following from: Chiefs, Bay Mills, May 11/09.
12-6 NIH SHWA WAWN NAY QUOT.
Note: Chiefs & headmen of this band do not remember anyone by that name. Durant Spl Agt.

Information following from: Chiefs, Bay Mills, May 11/09.
13-6 QUAY GAW ZHE GANCE, dead no heirs.

Information following from: Chiefs, Bay Mills, May 11/09.
14-6 O WISH TEAWE, dead, no heirs.

Information following from: James Howard Saboo, Bay Mills, May 10/09.
15-6 KE ZHICK GO QUAY, dead.
15-6-1 Johnson Brown, age 58, P.O. Port Arthur, Canada.
15-6-2 Jacob Brown, age 48, P.O. Munising, single.
15-6-3 Jack or John Brown, age 44, Munising.
Wife: Susan Saboo, separated, now wife James Howard Saboo, see 4-7.
15-6-3-1 Henry Brown, age 17, P.O. Lansing, Mich House of Correction?

Information following from: Charles Sabooe, Bay Mills.
16-6 MRS. MO CO BUAM or ELIZABETH SABOOE, age 80, P.O. Bay Mills, Mich, see 26-7.
Husband 1st : Mo Co Buam.
Husband 2nd: _________ Sabooe.

Page 7
Sault Sainte Marie Band
Chief EDWARD O-MAW-NO-MAW-NE
Bay Mills-Vicinity

Information following from: William Kay & T. C. Thomas, Bay Mills, May 9/09.
1-7 WAW NAW KIS, dead.
Wife: Name not given, dead.
1-7-1 Mary Kay, age 60, see 3-5.
Husband: William Kay, see 3-5.
1-7-2 Charlotte Johnson.
Husband: Douglas Johnson, see 6-6 & 4-6.
1-7-3 Name not given, dead.
Husband: Pete O Saw We Gush, age 60, P.O. Munising, see 20-7.
1-7-3-1 Martha O Saw We Gush, age 22, P.O. Munising, Mich., single.
1-7-4 Name not given, dead, no heirs.
1-7-5 Name not given, dead, no heirs.
1-7-6 Mrs. Clement, dead.
Husband: James Clement, white, P.O. Shingleton Mich.
1-7-6-1 Nellie Clement, age 17, Mt. Pleasant School.
1-7-6-2 Minnie Clement, age 14, Mt. Pleasant School.
1-7-6-3 Annie Clement, age 12, Mt. Pleasant School.
1-7-6-4 Fred Clement, age 8 , Mt. Pleasant School.

1-7-7 Name not given, dead, (girl).
Husband: Maxim Launderville, white.
1-7-7-1 Charles Launderville, age 30, P.O. Carlisle, single.
1-7-7-2 Annie Launderville, age 26, P.O. Houghton, Mich, married & has child.
1-7-7-3 William Launderville, age 24, P.O. Munising, single.

Information following from: William Thomas, Bay Mills.
2-7 QUAY QUAY CUB, dead.
Wife: Name not given, dead.
2-7-1 Caroline Blair, died March 6/09.
Husband: ________ Blair, dead.
2-7-1-1 Mary Jane Marshall, age 44, see 10-7 & 15-7.
2-7-1-2 Emma B, Carr, age 38, P.O. Munising.
Husband: _______ Carr, white.
2-7-1-2-1 Ray Carr, age 18.
2-7-1-2-2 Roy Carr, age 15.
2-7-1-2-3 Pearl Carr, age 14.
2-7-1-2-4 Mabel Carr, age 12.
2-7-1-2-5 Ina Carr, age 10.
2-7-1-2-6 Belle Carr, age 7.
2-7-1-3 Martha Clark, age 32, P.O.Munising.
Husband: ________ Clark, white.
2-7-1-3-1 Wesley Clark, age7.
2-7-1-3-2 Archie Clark, age 5.
2-7-1-3-3 Florence Clark, age 3.
2-7-1-4 Grace Blair, age 22, P.O. Munising.
2-7-1-4-1 Peter Jones Blair, age 2.
2-7-2 Eliza Quay Quay Cub, dead.
Husband: Louis Cartwright, P.O. Odanah, Wis., see 7-5.
2-7-3 Thomas Quay Quay Cub or T.C. Thomas, age 52, P.O. Odanah, Wis., said to draw with Wis, Inds.
Wife: Emma Pennock, L'Anse band, draw with L'Anse.
2-7-3-1 Belle Thomas, age 17.
2-7-3-2 John Thomas, age 7, draw with mother with L'Anse.
2-7-4 Edward Thomas or Nah Be Na Ashe, age 44, P.O. Munising.
Wife: Charlotte Thomas, belongs to La Pointe.
2-7-4-1 Sophia Ames, age 20, draw at La Pointe.
Husband: _____ Ames, white.
2-7-4-1-1 Virginia Ames, age 2.
2-7-5 William Thomas or William Nah Beyash,age 42, P.O. Bay Mills, wife dead and also children all 5 dead.

Information following from: Joseph Rouleau, Sault Ste. Marie.
3-7 MRS. HOSEA SMITH, dead.

Husband: Hosea Smith, white.

3-7-1 Mary S. Foster, age 53, P.O. Sault Ste. Marie.

Husband: George R. Foster, age 56, P.O. Sault Ste. Marie, white.

3-7-1-1 Hugh H. Foster, age 30, P.O. Sault Ste. Marie.

3-7-1-2 Nannie Foster Tecter, age 26, Sault Ste. Marie.

Husband: Glenn Tecter, white.

3-7-1-2-1 Bernice Tecter, age 16 months, P.O. Sault Ste. Marie.

3-7-1-3 Lulu Foster Rudell, age 24, P.O. Los Angeles Cal 736 Ruth Ave.

Husband: Herbert Rudell, white.

3-7-1-3-1 Francis Rudell, age 6. P.O. Los Angeles Cal 736 Ruth Ave.

3-7-1-4 Bernice V. Foster, age 21, P.O. Sault Ste. Marie.

3-7-1-5 George Everette Foster, age 19, P.O. Sault Ste. Marie.

3-7-2 Emma Smith Parcell, age 50, P.O. Sault Ste. Marie.

Husband: John Parcell, white.

3-7-2-1 Ruth Parcell, age 16, P.O. Sault Ste. Marie.

3-7-2-2 John E. Parcell, age 14, P.O. Sault Ste. Marie.

3-7-2-3 Libbie Parcell, age 11, P.O. Sault Ste. Marie.

3-7-3 Carles P. Smith, age 43, P.O. Sault Ste. Marie.

Wife: Agnes Smith, white.

3-7-3-1 Elmer N. Smith, age 20, P.O. Sault Ste. Marie.

3-7-3-2 Charles P. Smith Jr., age 17, P.O. Sault Ste. Marie.

West Wisconsin Conference
T. C. Thomas,
Pastor M. E. Church

Odanah, Wis., *Feb. 23rd* 1909.

Howard B. Durant U.S. Ind. Agt.
Washington, D.C.

Sir:- I see by the presses that you are soon to pay the Sault Ste Marie band Chippewas We are members of the bandand I would like to know. Whether you have our names on the Census list. We are full members of the band and received annuities up to 1871. Mother's name was Martha Smith on the pay roll. Her children and grand children's names & P.O. addresses are given on the annexed sheet here with together their places of residence.

Respy yours,

C.P. Smith

Martha Smith's children and grand children now living who are entitled to the payment to be made to the Sault Ste Marie band of Chippewa Indians. Martha Smith died Jan. 7th 1878 at Bay Mills, Michigan.

Charles P. Smith son of Martha Smith, Odanah , Wis.
Elmer H. Smith grand son of " " " "
Charles P. Smith Jr." " " " " " "

George Folster husband of Mary F. Folster, mixed, entitled, received payment, with Sugar Island band in 1871, lives at Sault Ste Marie Michigan.

Mary F. Folster daughter of Martha Smith, Sault Ste Marie, Mich.
Henry H. Folster grand child " " " Sault Ste Marie, Mich.
Nanie Folster " " " " " " " " "
now Mrs Teeter
Lula Folster 18 " " " " " " " " "
Burnice Folster " " " " " " " " "
George Folster Jr " " " " " " " " "

Emma J. Parsille daughter of Martha Smith Sault Ste Marie, Mich.
Ruth Parsille grand child of Martha Smith Sault Ste Marie, Mich.
John E. Parsille Jr. " " " " " Sault Ste Marie, Mich.
Emma Parsille " " " " " Sault Ste Marie, Mich.

Confirmed Bay Mills & "Soo" May 7/09 Enroll on sheet # 3/7 Durant Spl Agt Sault Ste Marie.

Odanah, Wis. February 23, 1909.
I hereby certify on honor, that the above is true and correct and that the parties named therein, are entitled to the benefits of the Sault Ste Marie band of Chippewa Indians, that: Charles P.Smith, Mary F. Smith, now Mrs Folster, Emma J. Smith, now Mrs Parsille, and Mr George Folster husband of Mary F. Smith, received the annuities under the treaty of 1855. And they received their annuities and was on the pay roll untl 1871. And are, themselves and their children full well entitled to the monies appropriated by the Govt about to be paid.

T. C. Thomas, Age 50 years.
Pastor M.E. Church Odanah, Wis.

Put the children on but not grand children Durant Baraga June 1/09.

Information following from: Ezekiel Saboo & James Saboo, Bay Mills, May 10/09.

4-7 NAW KE WAY, dead.
Wife: Name not given, dead.
4-7-1 James Howard Saboo, age 56, P.O. Bay Mills, see 33-1.
Wife 1st : Name not given, dead.
Wife 2nd: Susan, see 15-6, age 39, P.O. Bay Mills, enroll by consent of Chiefs.

4-7-1-1 John Saboo or John Howard, age 23, P.O. Mt. Pleasant School, child by 1st wife..

4-7-1-2 Eliza Howard, age 20, P.O. Mt. Pleasant School, child by 1st wife.

4-7-1-3 Ovinia Howard, age 5.

4-7-2 Catharine, dead.

Husband: John Foster, P.O. Sugar Island.

4-7-2-1 Eliza Foster, age 20, P.O. Sault Ste Marie.

4-7-3 Charlotte La Rose #1, age 47, P.O. Bay Mills.

Husband: John La Rose, Canadian Indian.

4-7-3-1 Emma La Rose, age 7.

4-7-4 Ezekiel Garrett Saboo, age 45, P.O. Bay Mills, single.

4-7-5 Samuel Saboo, age 39, P.O. Bay Mills.

Wife: Name not given, dead.

4-7-5-1 Name not given, dead.

Information following from: Not Given.

5-7 NAY TO NEECE, dead.

Wife: Name not given, dead.

5-7-1 Dan Sky, age 44, P.O. Bay Mills

5-7-2 No other heirs.

5-7-3 Sam, dead.

5-7-3-1 Dan Sky Jr., age 21, P.O. Odanah, see Minnesota somewhere said to draw with L'Anse Band.

Information following from: Not Given.

6-7 KAW GAW AW SHE, dead.

Wife: Charlotte Kaw Gaw Aw She, age 60, died November 9/1908, see 15-5.

6-7-1 Joe Sabbooe, age 48, P.O. Bay Mills.

Wife: Lizzie, age 40, see 2-6.

6-7-1-1 Alice Sabbooe, age 20, P.O. Bay Mills.

6-7-1-2 Rachel Sabbooe, age 7.

6-7-1-3 Alex Sabbooe, age 5.

6-7-1-4 William Sabbooe, age 3.

6-7-2 David, dead, no children.

6-7-3 Name not given, dead, no heirs.

6-7-4 Name not given, dead, no heirs.

Information following from: Not Given.

7-7 EDWARD O MAW NO MAW NE, dead, wife dead, children are all dead and no heirs.

Information following from: William Menominee, Bay Mills.

8-7 PAY KE NAW GAY or Albert Menominee, dead.

Wife 1st : Charlotte, dead, see 3-5.
Wife 2nd: Mary, dead, see 7-5.
8-7-1 Maria Waishkey, see 1-5.
8-7-2 William Menominee, age 42, P.O. Bay Mills, Mich.
Wife: Susan, dead, see 6-6.
8-7-2-1 Albert Menominee, age 8.
8-7-3 Susan Menominee, by 2nd wife, age 22, single, P.O. Odanah, Wis. or Bay Mills, see also 7-5.
8-7-4 Jonah Menominee, age 15, P.O. Mt. Pleasant School, see 7-5.

Information following from: Mary Jane McCoy.
9-7 Mrs. KE GAW GAW SAUCE, dead.
Husband: Ke Gaw Gaw Sauce.
9-7-1 Lucy Ann Jack, on roll with husband 22-7.
Husband: Francis Blackjack, known as Francis Jack, see 22-7.
9-7-2 Fred, dead.
Wife: Theresa Fish, age 52, P.O. Bay Mills.
9-7-2-1 Mary Fish, age 30, employee Mt. Pleasant School.
9-7-2-2 Solomon Fish, age 20.
9-7-2-3 Alfred Fish, age 18.
9-7-3 Mary, dead.
Husband: John Lavine, white, P.O. Sugar Island.
9-7-3-1 Mary Jane McCoy, age 34, P.O. Payment Sugar Island.
Husband: Name not given, white.
9-7-3-1-1 George L. McCoy, age 14.
9-7-3-1-2 Mary McCoy, age 12.
9-7-3-1-3 Harriet McCoy.
9-7-3-1-4 Adelaide McCoy, age 9.
9-7-3-1-5 Theodore McCoy, age 3.
9-7-3-1-6 Bernice, born November 18/1907.
9-7-4 Emma Cameron, P.O. Odanah, Wis, see 4-6.
9-7-5 Peter Kah Way Awshe or Walker, dead.
Wife: Name not given, dead.
9-7-5-1 Peter Walker Jr., age 27, single, P.O. Bay Mills, Mich.
9-7-5-2 Frank Walker, age 18, single, P.O. Bay Mills, Mich.

Information following from: Charles Marshall.
10-7 MRS. DAVID MARSHALL, dead.
Husband: David Marshall.
10-7-1 Charles Marshall, age 56, P.O. Bay Mills, Mich.
Wife: Ellen, age 41, see 1-1 & 43-2.
10-7-1-1 Martha E. Marshall. age 26, P.O. Genoa School Nebr., single.
10-7-1-2 Annie O. Marshall. age 26, P.O. Genoa School

Nebr., single.
10-7-1-3 Clinton D. Marshall. age 26, P.O. Genoa School Nebr., single.
10-7-1-4 Edgar C. Marshall. age 26, P.O. Genoa School Nebr., single.
10-7-1-5 Sarah Marshall, age 10, P.O. Bay Mills.
10-7-1-6 Ellen E. Marshall, age 9, P.O. Bay Mills.
10-7-1-7 Blanche Marshall, age 5, P.O. Bay Mills.
10-7-2 Albert Marshall, age 41, P.O. Bay Mills, single.
10-7-3 Annie Marshall Shaffer, dead.
Husband: Name not given, dead.
10-7-3-1 Ida Sebastian, age 30, P.O. Sugar Island.
Husband: David Sabastian, P.O. Payment, Mich.
10-7-3-1-1 William Sebastian, age 12.
10-7-3-1-2 Myrtle Sebastian, age 10.
10-7-3-1-3 Clara Sebastian, age 3.

Information following from: Not Given.
11-7 MRS. JOHN LARMOND, dead.
Husband: John Larmond.
11-7-1 Rosa L. Cameron, age 47, P.O. Autrain, see 12-1.
11-7-2 John Larmond, age 44, P.O. Autrain, Mich.
11-7-3 Edward Larmond, age 37, P.O. Autrain, Mich.
11-7-4 Henry P. Larmond, age 34. P.O. Autrain, Micch.
11-7-5 William J. Larmond, age 29.
11-7-6 David J. Larmond, age 26.
11-7-7 Mary Larmond, dead.
11-7-7-1 Beatrice Doucette, age 20, P.O. Autrain, Mich.

1
Louisa She-ga-gan-gega, or
Mrs John Larmond, deceased.
Children now living

1 Rosa L. (now now Mrs Frances J. Cameron) Age 47 yrs
2 John 44 "
3 Edward 37 "
4 Henry P. 34 "
5 William J. 29 "
6 David J. 26 "
Mary, deceased, who was Married to Doucette, has a daughter living.
7 Beatrice Doucette age 20 years.
Rosa L. the first name above is Married to Frances J, Cameron, The following are their children living:-
8 Mary Eliza, now Mrs Joseph Refferchini, 25 yrs

9 Alice Cecilia *21 "*
10 William Frederick *18 "*
11 Michael Duncan *14 "*
12 Henry James *10 "*
13 Julia Veronica *5 "*

Information following from: T. C. Thomas, Baraga, June 1/09.
12-7 JACK O GE MAW PE NAY SE or JACK BIRD, dead.
Wife: Charlotte Bird, age 74, P.O. Munising.
12-7-1 Daniel Bird, age 30, Munising, separated.
Wife: Maggie, L'Anse Indian.
12-7-1-1 Grace Bird, age 4, drew at L'Anse.

Information following from: Not Given.
13-7 MRS. CHARLES BUCK, dead.
Husband: Charles Buck.
13-7-1 Charitine Tardiffe, age 70, P.O. Sault Ste. Marie.
13-7-1-1 Philamine La Lone, age 50, P.O. Sault Ste. Marie.
13-7-1-2 Christine McCarrow, age 48, P.O.
13-7-1-3 Joe Tardiffe, age 46, P.O. Detroit.
13-7-1-4 Elizabeth Ford, age 44, P.O. Chassell, Mich.
13-7-1-5 George Tardiffe, age 43, P.O. Sault Ste Marie.
13-7-1-6 Cora Eckhart, age 42, Sault Ste Marie.
13-7-2 Christine Taylor, age 60, P.O. Sault Ste Marie.
Note: Not on roll with parents in 1870- altho old enough, should be enrolled Durant Spl Agt.

Information following from: Chiefs, Bay Mills, May 11/09.
14-7 SHE GAW SHE, dead, no heirs.

Information following from: Not Given.
15-7 ANTONIE BELLAIRE, dead.
15-7-1 Name not given, dead, no heirs.
15-7-2 Name not given, dead, no heirs.
15-7-3 Mary Jane Marshall, age 39, see 10-7.

Information following from: Chiefs, Bay Mills, May 11/09.
16-7 NAW BE GWON, all dead, no heirs.

Information following from: Chiefs, Bay Mills, May 11/09.
17-7 MARIA O MAW NO MAW NE, all dead, no heirs.

Information following from: Jane Saboo.
18-7 AW BE TAW KE ZHICK, dead.
Wife: Jane Saboo, age 80, P.O. Bay Mills, Mich.

18-7-1 Name not given, dead no heirs.

Information following from: Chiefs, Bay Mills, May 11/09.
19-7 A GIN DOSH, all dead, no heirs.

Information following from: Not Given.
20-7 SAMUEL O SAW WE GAW ZHENCE, dead, has no heirs, but the other name enrolled with him in 1870 was his brothe Peter, who is living.
20-7a Peter O Saw We Gunce, age 60, Munising, Mich., see 1-7.

Information following from: Not Given.
21-7 NAW NAW GUSE or JOHN CLARK, dead.
Wife: Mary Clark Green Pendell, age 55, P.O. Odanahsee 25-1, 2nd husband Edmund Green (dead), of the L'Anse band.
21-7-1 Harry Thomas Clark, age 16, at indian School.
21-7-2 Nathan Clark, age 17, P.O. Odanah or at Indian School.
21-7-3 Barlow Clark, age 18.

Information following from: Francis Jack, May 9.
22-7 FRANCIS BLACKJACK or FRANK JACK, age 64, P.O. Bay Mills, Mich.
Wife: Lucy Ann Jack, age 72, see 9-7.
22-7-1 John Jack, age 44, P.O. Bay Mills, single.
22-7-2 Hannah Menominee, age 40, P.O. Bay Mills.
Husband: ___________ Menominee, dead.
22-7-2-1 Jennie Menominee, age 20, single, P.O. Bay Mills Genoa School.
22-7-2-2 Susan Menominee, age 18, single, P.O. Bay Mills Genoa School.
22-7-2-3 Marian Menominee, age 16, single, P.O. Bay Mills Genoa School.
22-7-2-4 Emma Menominee, age 10, single, P.O. Bay Mills Genoa School.
Note: Do not pay shares to mother she is bad.
22-7-3 Gilbert Jack, age 38, P.O. Bay Mills, wife dead, no children.
22-7-4 Peter Jack, age 34, P.O. Bay Mills.
Wife: Sopia Jack, Canadian Indian, no children.

Information following from: Not Given.
23-7 WILLIAM O GE MAW PE NAY SE, age 65, P.O. L'Anse, Mich.
Wife: Name not given, dead.
23-7-1 Lucy Curtis, age 22, P.O. L'Anse, does not draw at L'Anse.
Husband: Philip Curtis, belongs to L'Anse band, no children.

Information following from: Chiefs, Bay Mills, May 11/09.
24-7 GEORGE WAW SAY QUO AM, dead, no heirs.

Information following from: Not Given.
25-7 JULIA O ME SAW DANCE or JULIA WASQUAM, see 26-5, P.O. Bay Mills.
Wife: Waw Se Qua Won, dead.

Information following from: Charles Sabooe, Bay Mills.
26-7 AW NAW QUOT or CHARLES SABOOE & sister, age 75, P.O. Bay Mills.
Wife: Elizabeth Sabooe, see 16-6, no children.

Information following from: Not Given.
27-7 TAW BE KOOSH, dead, no heirs.

Information following from: Chiefs, Bay Mills, May 11/09.
28-7 KE CHE WAW NAY DE NO QUAY, dead, no heirs.

Information following from: Chiefs, Bay Mills, May 11/09.
29-7 SAW GE MAW QUAY, dead, no heirs.

Information following from: Chiefs, Bay Mills, May 11/09.
30-7 AW MING GO, dead, no heirs.

Information following from: Chiefs, Bay Mills, May 11/09.
31-7 NAW O QUAY GAW BO, both dead, no heirs.
Information following from: Chiefs, Bay Mills, May 11/09.
32-7 JULIUS BARRY, dead.

Information following from: Not Given.
33-7 MRS. BETSEY BROWN, dead.
Husband: ________ Brown.
33-7-1 Name not given, dead.
Husband: Name not given, dead.
33-7-1-1 Annie Smith, dead, was wife of james Smith, see 4-5.
33-7-1-2 Mary (Brown) O'Malley, age 33, P.O. Sault Ste Marie.
Husband: _______ O'Malley, white.
33-7-1-2-1 Bessie O'Malley, age 20, P.O. Genoa School Nebr., see 23-5.
33-7-1-2-2 Cora O'Malley, age 17, P.O. Genoa School Nebr., see 23-5.
33-7-1-3 Alex Brown, age 43, P.O. Sault Ste Marie, see 23-5.

Information following from: Not Given.
34-7 MRS. LOUIS MINIKLIER, dead.
Husband: Louis Miniklier.
34-7-1 Jemmie Miniclier, age 48, P.O. Sault Ste Marie, single.
34-7-2 Louis Miniclier, age 46, P.O. Sault Ste Marie.
Wife: Name not given, white.
34-7-2-1 Zoe Miniclier, age 23, single, P.O. Sault Ste Marie.
34-7-2-2 Louis Miniclier, age 21, P.O. Duluth.
34-7-2-3 Joe Miniclier, age 18, P.O. Sault Ste Marie.
34-7-2-4 John Miniclier, age 16, twin.
34-7-2-5 Maggie Miniclier, age 16, twin.
34-7-2-6 Maggie Miniclier, age 14.
34-7-3 Charles Miniclier, age 44, P.O. Sault Ste Marie, single.
34-7-4 Napoleon Miniclier, age 40, P.O. Minneapolis.
Wife: Name not given, white.
34-7-4-1 John Miniclier, age 12.
34-7-4-2 Walter Miniclier, age 10.
34-7-4-3 Bert Miniclier, age 8.
34-7-4-4 Frank Miniclier, age 6.
34-7-4-5 Mary Miniclier, age 4.
34-7-5 Mary Warner, age 38, P.O. Gt. Falls Montana.
Husband: Name not given, white.
34-7-5-1 Charles Warner, age 6.
34-7-5-2 Genevieve Warner, age 4.
34-7-6 Oliver Miniclier, age 35, P.O. Sault Ste Marie, wife white, no children.

Information following from: Chiefs, Bay Mills, May 11/09.
35-7 NE BE NAY KE ZHICK, dead, no heirs.

Information following from: Chiefs, Bay Mills, May 11/09.
36-7 SAMUEL, dead, no heirs.

Information following from: William Waishkey, Sr. & others, Bay Mills, May 11/09.
37-7 MARY TALLIEN or MARY MASCOT, age 49, P.O. Sault Ste Marie, no children.

Information following from: T. C. Thomas, Baraga, June 1/09.
38-7 MARGARET BIRKHUME – COCHERE or CUTURE, age 60, P.O. Odanah, said to draw with L'Anse.
Husband: Rev. Antoine Couture, a La Pointe Indian, no children.

Sault Sainte Marie Band
Chief SHAW-WAN
Sugar Island

Information following from: Julia Bomakezhick.

1-8 SHAW WAN, Chief, dead.
Wife: Name not given, dead.
1-8-1 See 3-8.
1-8-2 See 5-8.
1-8-3 See 22-8.
1-8-4 Susan Shawano, dead.
Husband: Name not given, Traverse.
1-8-4-1 Charlotte Louis Shay Ge Na By, see 2-3.
1-8-5 Caw Baish Caw Mo Quay or Jane Madosh, P.O. Marquette, Mich, see 31-1.
1-8-6 Name not given, spouse a Canadian.
1-8-6-1 Julie Bomakezhick, age 29, single, P.O. Garden River.
1-8-6-2 James Bomakezhick, age 27, single, P.O. Garden River.
1-8-6-3 George Bomakezhick, age 25, single, P.O. Garden River.
1-8-6-4 Jennie Bomakezhick, age 23, single, P.O. Garden River.
Note: All draw from Canadian Govt.

Information following from: Edward Joseph & Moses Oller, Sugar Isle, May 14/09.

2-8 NAW TAW MAY BE or EDWARD JOSEPH, age 68, P.O. Sugar Isle
Wife: Sophia Joseph, age 67, P.O. Sugar Isle, see 6-8, see 17-8.
2-8-1 Maria Gurnoe, age 46, P.O. Sugar Isle.
Husband: Joseph Gurnoe, age 49, see 24-3.
2-8-1-1 Sam Gurnoe #2, age 30, P.O. Sugar Isle, single.
2-8-1-2 Edward Gurnoe Jr. #2, age 27, P.O. Sugar Isle.
Wife: Maggie Gurnoe, age 20, see 35-8, enroll by consent of Chiefs, Sugar Isle Durant.
2-8-1-2-1 Angus Gurnoe, age 4.
2-8-1-2-2 Sam, born January/08, 2nd roll.
2-8-1-3 Maggie (Gurnoe) Ricolais (Rickoly), age 22.
Husband: ___________ Ricolais, white.
2-8-1-3-1 Philamon Ricolais, born February 25/08.
2-8-1-4 Joe Gurnoe, age 13.
2-8-1-5 Lucy Gurnoe, age 12.
2-8-1-6 Eva Gurnoe, age 8.
2-8-1-7 Jennie Gurnoe, age 3.

2-8-2 Rosalie Oller, age 45, P.O. Sugar Isle.
Husband: Moses Oller.
2-8-2-1 Dave Oller, age 18.
2-8-2-2 Annie Oller, age 15.
2-8-2-3 Charles Oller, age 13.
2-8-2-4 Fred Oller, age 11.
2-8-2-5 Mary Oller, age 3.
2-8-2-6 Moses Oller, born December 1907. 2nd roll.
2-8-3 Cassie or Catharine Bulley, age 40.
Husband: Ed Bulley, see 10-5.
2-8-3-1 See 10-5.
2-8-4 Lizzie Cameron, 33, P.O. Sugar Isle.
Husband: Fred Cameron, see 4-6, no children, separated.
2-8-5 Zoe Boucher, age 28, P.O. Sugar Isle.
Husband: George Boucher, age 26, see 3-3, no children.
2-8-6 Peter Joseph, age 26, P.O. Sugar Isle, single.
2-8-7 Sarah Sprinkle, age 23. P.O. Sugar Isle.
Husband: Fred Sprinkle, white, no children.
Note: The two men who drew with the head of this family in 1870, were his brothers: viz.
2-8a John Joseph, age 62, P.O. Sugar Island.
Wife: Susan Joseph, dead.
2-8a-1 Alice Joseph, age 18, single.
2-8a-2 Paul Joseph, age 16, single.
2-8a-3 Thomas Joseph, age 14.
2-8a-4 William Joseph, age 12.
2-8a-5 George Joseph, age 10.
2-8a-6 Gilbert Joseph, age 8.
2-8b Andrew Joseph, dead.
Wife: Mary Andrews or Gangagegade, age 65, A-Soo page 3.

Information following from: John Mendoskung, Mike Mendoskung & Alex Boucher, Hessel, May 3/09, Sugar Isle, May 14/09.

3-8 MINDOSKUNG or SHAW WAN MIN DO SKUNG, 95, P.O. Sault Ste Marie 707 West Peck St.
3-8-1 Joe, dead.
Wife: Name not given, dead.
3-8-1-1 Name not given, dead.
3-8-1-2 Joe Min Do Skung, age 35, P.O. Pine River Jameson's Mills.
Wife: Mary, nee Moses, age 18, see 61-35.
3-8-2 Theresa Fox, P.O. Little Chanler Cobuse Isle.
Husband: _________ Fox, Canadian.
3-8-3 Mike Mindoskung, age 58, P.O. Sugar Island.
Wife: Veronica Mindoskung, age 33, see A-Soo page 3.

3-8-3-1 Jennie Mindoskung, age 17.
3-8-3-2 Robert Mindoskung, age 15.
3-8-3-3 Louisa Mindoskung, age 12.
3-8-3-4 Edward Mindoskung, age 5.
3-8-3-5 Lena Mindoskung, born August 1907.
3-8-3-6 Eliza Mindoskung, age 8.

3-8-4 Charlotte Boucher, age 37, P.O. Sault Ste Marie 707 W. Peck St.
Husband: Alex Boucher, age 57, see 3-3.
3-8-4-1 Mary Boucher Meyer, age 21, no children., P.O. Soo.
3-8-4-2 Emily Boucher, age 17, P.O. Soo.
3-8-4-3 Lizzie Boucher, age 14.

3-8-5 John Mandoskung, age 45, P.O. Hessell, Mich.
Wife 1st : Name not given, dead.
Wife 2nd: Eliza Mandoskung, age 18, see 11-15.
3-8-5-1 David Mandoskung, age 17, P.O. Hessell, Mich.
3-8-5-2 James Mandoskung, age 16, P.O. Hessell, Mich, Harbor Springs School.
3-8-5-3 Annie Mandoskung, age 12, P.O. Hessell, Mich.
3-8-5-4 Charles Mandoskung, age 9, P.O. Hessell, Mich.
3-8-5-5 Jennie Mandoskung, age 5, P.O. Hessell, Mich.
3-8-5-6 Noah Mandoskung, born March 2/08 by 2nd wife, P.O. Hessell, Mich.

Information following from: Mike St Germain.

4-8 WAY GE MAW WA BE or ST. GERMAIN, dead, a brother of Sunday St. Germain.
Wife: Angelique St Germain Mesho, age 65, P.O. Drummond's Isle.
4-8-1 John St. Germain, dead, no children.
4-8-2 Joe St. Germain, dead, no heirs.
4-8-3 Clement St. Germain, dead.
4-8-3-1 Joe St. Germain, age 23, P.O. Drummond's Isle.
Wife: Angeline, no children, Canadian.
4-8-4 Mike St. Germain, age 47, P.O. Pine River.
Wife: Josephine St. Germain, age 40, see 8-15.
4-8-4-1 Jessie St. Germain, age 19, single, P.O. Pine River.
4-8-4-2 Ellen St. Germain.
Husband: William Osawoguam, age 27, see 4-34.
4-8-4-2-1 Name not given, born March/09 too late.
4-8-4-3 Levi St. Germain, age 15, P.O. Pine River.
4-8-4-4 Joe St. Germain, age 13, P.O. Pine River.
4-8-4-5 Harry St. Germain, age 9, P.O. Pine River.
4-8-4-6 William St. German, age 6, Pine River.
4-8-5 Angeline St. Germain, dead.
Husband: Name not given, dead.

4-8-5-1 William Roule, P.O. Toledo.
4-8-5-2 John Axen, age 16, P.O. Mt. Pleasant School.
4-8-5-3 Eva Lator, age 12, P.O. Settlement, Drummond's Isle.
4-8-6 Carrie St. Germain, dead.
Husband: Mike Bellow, raised at Drunmmon'd Isle.
4-8-6-1 Name not given, in convent school, Wis.
4-8-6-2 Name not given, in convent school, Wis.
4-8-6-3 Name not given, in convent school, Wis.
4-8-6-4 Maggie Brushey or Boucher, age 6, by another man, lives with grandmother at Drummond's Isle, Angeline Mesho.
4-8-7 Mary St. Germain, dead, no heirs.

Department of the Interior,
United States Indian Service,
Mount Pleasant Indian School
Mt. Pleasant, Mich. June 25, 1909.

Mr. Horace B. Durant,
Special U. S. Agent,
Petoskey, Michigan.
Dear Mr. Durant:-

In reply to your letter asking about "John Axle and Eva Axle", I would say that we have a boy in school here named John Axen, 16 years of age, whom I think is the same as the boy you are after.

The Grandmother of John Axen was Mrs. Angeline St. Germain, of Settlement, Mich., Drummonds Island, and I think thatshe still lives there. John's mother had the same names as the Grandmother, as near as I can understand it. She married Mr. Axen, John's father, who afterwards died. Then she married Mr. Lator, and Eve Laor, their daughter, and John's hslf sister I think is the girl you mentionedas Evs Axke.

John's mother died several years ago, but Eva lives with her father on the Island; she has never attended this school, but I should think her age to be about twelve or thirteen.

Very truly yours,
R. A. Cochran
Superintendent

Information following from: Alex La Pointe, Drummonds Is;e, May 27.
5-8 AW NE WAW QUO UNG, dead.
Wife: Nezette Shawan, age 70, Drummon's Isle.
5-8-1 Cecelia Pine, P.O. Garden River, Canada, draws in Canada.
5-8-2 Sophia Sageon, age 48, see 8-15.
5-8-3 Angeline Osawwawmick, see 5-3.
5-8-4 John Shawan, age 35, single.
5-8-5 Michel, dead no heirs.

Information following from: Not Given.
6-8 A daw de win, dead.
6-8-1 Sophia Joseph, see 2-8.
6-8-2 Joseph Ojibway Sr., age 69, see 28-8.
6-8-3 Angeline O Saw O Quam, see 10-8
Husband: Joe O Saw O Quam.

Information following from: Nick Nolin, & Chief, Sugar Island.
7-8 LE GARD NOLIN or NICHOLAS NOLIN, age 70, P.O. Sugar Isle.
Wife: Name not given, de d.
7-8-1 Name not given, dead, no heirs.
7-8-2 Name not given, dead, no heirs.
7-8-3 Name not given, dead, no heirs.

Information following from: Not Given.
8-8 AW BE TAW GE SHE GO QUAY or MRS. JAMES NAW WE GE ZHICK, age 70.
Husband: James Naw We Ge Zhick, Canadian Indian, P.O. Garden River, Canada.
8-8-1 Susan Sampson, age 50, P.O. Manitoulin Island, all 8 children paid by the Canadian Govt.
Husband: Name not given, Canadian.
8-8-2 Angeline Sampson, age 45, P.O. Massey, Canada, has 5 children.
8-8-3 Wilson Sampson, age 42, P.O. Manitoulin Isle, has one child.
Note: The head of this family says she & all her children draw from Canadian Govt. Durant Spl Agt Soo May 26/09.
Information following from: Alex & whole family, Drummonds Isle, May 27/09.
9-8 MRS. LA POINTE or ARCHANGLE LA POINTE, age 74, P.O. Drummond's Isle.
Husband: __________ La Pointe.
9-8-1 Mary La Pointe, dead.
Husband: Tom Jandreau, P.O. Detour.
9-8-1-1 Lillie Abair, age 30, P.O. Detour.
Husband: ________ Abair, white.
9-8-1-1-1 Lula Abair, age 10.
9-8-1-1-2 Morris Abair, age 8.
9-8-1-1-3 Frank Abair, age 6.
9-8-1-1-4 (girl) Abair, born November/08, too late.
9-8-1-2 Alice Abair, age 28, address unknown.
Husband: ________ Abair, white.
9-8-1-2-1 Lawrence Abair, age 6, P.O. Bay City.
9-8-1-2-2 Wilford Abair, age 4, P.O. Bay City.

9-8-1-3 Maggie Jandreau, dead, husband is white, has a daughter.
9-8-1-4 Ellen Stewart, age 25, P.O. Detour.
Husband: _______ Stewart, white.
9-8-1-4-1 William Stewart, age 7.
9-8-1-5 Lena La Plant, P.O. Detour.
Husband: ______ La Plant, white.
9-8-1-5-1 Albert La Plant, age 3.
9-8-1-5-2 (boy) La Plant, age 2.
9-8-1-6 Oliver Jandreau, age 12, P.O. Harbor Springs School.
9-8-2 John La Pointe, age 49, P.O. Drummond's Isle.
Wife: Mary La Pointe, nee Key Way Ke Zhick, age 48, ok enroll see 4-11.
9-8-2-1 John La Pointe, age 16.
9-8-2-2 Joe La Pointe, age 13.
9-8-2-3 Maggie La Pointe, age 4.
9-8-3 Maggie Stevenson, age 42, Drummond's Isle.
Husband: ________ Stevenson, white.
9-8-3-1 Jennette Stevenson, age 14.
9-8-3-2 Harvey Stevenson, age 11.
9-8-3-3 Annie Stevenson, age 9.
9-8-3-4 Frank Stevenson, age 5.
9-8-4 Alex La Pointe, age 41, P.O. Drummonds Isle, single.
9-8-5 Joe La Pointe, age 34, P.O. Drummonds Isle.
Wife: Eliza La Pointe, age 26, nee Dos Ke Now Cadote, see 4-12.
9-8-5-1 Richard La Pointe, born November/07.
9-8-6 Peter La Pointe, age 31, P.O. Drummonds Isle, single.
9-8-7 James La Pointe, age 28, P.O. Drummonds Isle.
Wife: Lucy La Pointe, age 24, nee Cadotte, P.O. Drummonds Isle.
9-8-7-1 Lucy La Pointe, age 8.
9-8-7-2 Ellen La Pointe, age 3.
9-8-8 Willaim La Pointe, age 26, P.O. Drummonds Isle, single.

Department of the Interior,
United States Indian Service,

9/8

Dear Madam:

Your name has been given me as the grand child of Mrs. La Pointe, of Drummond's Isle, who was a member of the Ottawa & Chippewa Tribe of Indians, of which I am making a roll.

If this information is correct please give me the names, ages, and addresses of all of your brothers and sisters, and their children, using the back of this sheet for that purpose and return to me as soon as practicable.

Envelope enclosed for reply.

Very respectfully
HORACE B. DURANT
Special U.S. Indian Agent

If any are dead please state.
Give names in order of birth.

1| alice abear 27 mother
| of Edward abear
| Florance abear No2
| Wilford abear

2| Hillie abear mother of
| Julia abear /P.S This space
| marris abear /Should read
| Frank abear /first
| alice abear No1
| mildred aber

Mary Jandreau
Mother died
| children |
Joseph Jandreau
Father living
These are all Daughters and
Son of mary jandreau
Who is dead

3| Elen E. Stewart mother of
| Willie stewart
| Perl stewart No3

4| Lena La Plant mother of
| orvel La Plant
| Helor La Plant No4

5| oliver jandreau No5

Information following from: Joe Ka Koosh, Sugar Isle.

10-8 O SAW O QUAM, dead.
Wife: Angeline Ojibway O Saw O Quam, age 90, P.O. Sugar Isle, see 6-8.
10-8-1 Charlotte La Rose or Mishaquod, age 60, P.O. Garden River, Canada.
Husband: Joe La Rose, dead.
10-8-1-1 Mary La Rose, age 13, P.O. Garden River, Canada.
10-8-2 Charlotte Parault, age 46, P.O. Sugar Isle.
Husband: Adam Parault, Canadian Indian, no children.
10-8-3 Joe Ka Koosh or O Saw O Quam, age 44, P.O. Sugar Isle, single.

Information following from: Not Given.

11-8 SAW QUA NAW NE QUAY, dead.
11-8-1 Charlotte Tebo, dead.

Husband: ______ Tebo, dead.
11-8-1-1 Joseph Tebo, P.O. Detour.
Wife: Name not given, dead.
11-8-1-1-1 Richard Tebo.
11-8-1-2 John Tebo, dead.
Wife: Name not given, dead.
11-8-1-2-1 Thomas Tebo, P.O. Sault Ste Marie.
11-8-1-2-2 William Tebo, P.O. Sault Ste Marie.
11-8-1-2-3 Jane Tebo, dead.
11-8-1-3 Philamon Curry, age 56, P.O. Sault Ste Marie, Seymore St., husband white, has 2 children.
11-8-1-4 Christie Tebo, dead, husband white, P.O. Sault Ste Marie.
11-8-1-5 Peter Tebo, age 46, P.O. St. Ignace.
Wife: Elizabeth Tebo, age 38, see 31-15, no children.

Note: This family tho old enough, never drew with the band & should not now be enrolled. Leave off till action by Dept Durant Spl Agt.

Information following from: Not Given.

12-8 KE WAY DE NO QUAY, dead.
12-8-1 Louis Pero Curtis, P.O. Baraga, members of L'Anse band.
12-8-2 Frank Pero, went west address unknown, Grand Marias.
12-8-3 Henry Pero, P.O Harvey, Mich., cripple, wife dead, no children.
All above crossed out and annotated with "See 33-1."
Note: These (below) are said to be the right heirs of Ke Way De No Quay of this band.
12-8-4 John Perault, age 59, Sault Ste Marie, see children 2-3.
12-8-5 Frank Perault, age 53, wife Canadian, no children.
12-8-6 Catharine Gates, age 62, P.O. Homestead E. Neebish Isle.
Husband: ________ Gates.
12-8-6-1 William Gates, age 36, P.O. Homestead E. Neebish Isle.
Wife: Polly (Cadotte) Gates, no children.
12-8-6-2 Frank Gates, age 33, P.O. Payment Sugar Isle.
Wife: Name not given, see 35-8, separated.
12-8-6-3 Ed Gates, age 22, P.O. Detroit, light keeper Gros Pt., single.

Information following from: Mike Mindoskung.

13-8 A DAW WE GE ZHE GO QUAY, dead.
13-8-1 John Sayers, age 41, P.O. Payment, no children.

Information following from: Mike Mindoskung.

14-8 FRANCIS AISH QUAY GO NAY BE, dead, wife dead, no heirs.

Information following from: Mindoskung.
15-8 O SHAW WAW SKO PE NAY SE, dead, wife Canadian, children dead.

Information following from: Not Given.
16-8 PAW ZHE DAW QUO UNG, dead, wife and child dead, no heirs.

Information following from: Not Given.
17-8 WAY BE GE WAW NO QUAY or SOPHIA JOSEPH, see 17-8/2-8.

Information following from: Mike Mindoskung & Oshawano.
18-8 JOSEPH VERNORE, dead, at Garden River & draws from Canadian Govt.

Information following from: Mindoskung.
19-8 PAW WE TE GO QUAY, dead, children in Canada and paid in Canada.

Information following from: Not Given.
20-8 MARY ANN & grandson, both dead.

Information following from: Mindoskung.
21-8 O GE MAW PE NAY SE, dead, no heirs.

Information following from: Mindoskung & Elizabeth Savore.
22-8 ME GE SAW SE NO QUAY or ELIZABETH SAVORE, age 87, P.O. Payment, married to Savore after 1870, was on roll by herself, a son & daughter.
Husband: Joseph Savore, Canadian, P.O. Garden River, Canada, all draw in Canada.
22-8-1 John Savore, age 45, Garden River.
Wife: Name not given, Canadian.
22-8-1-1 John Savore Jr., age 5.
22-8-1-2 Eliza Savore, age 3.
22-8-1-3 Helen Savore, born May/08.
22-8-2 Susan Cheyney, age 43, P.O. Marquette, Mich, husband white, no children.
Note: says she never drew money from Canadian Govt.
Durant
Spl Agt May 30/09 Marquette.
Note: All parties named on this sheet draw money from Canadian Govt. This is admitted by Elizabeth Savore, the head of the family Durant Spl Agt at hotel Soo, May 26/09.

Information following from: Not Given.

23-8 PE DAW NAW QUAW DO QUAY, dead, no heirs.

Information following from: Not Given.

24-8 MRS. CATHARINE LAISK, P.O. Payment.
Husband: ________ Laisk.
24-8-1 Jane Scanlon, age 57, P.O. Payment.
24-8-1-1 Agnes Scanlon, age 32, P.O. Payment.
24-8-1-2 James Scanlon, age 29, P.O. Payment.
24-8-1-3 Alfred Scanlon, age 23, P.O. Payment.
24-8-2 Paul Laisk, age 48, has 8 children.
24-8-3 Joseph Leask, age 46, has 5 children.
Note: The other on this roll with head of family was her daughter Jane.

Sugar Island Mich June 26th 1909
Family of Late Catherine Laisk

Living Jane Laisk	*age 57 yrs & children*
Agnes Scanlan	*age 32 yrs*
James Scanlan	*age 29 "*
Alfred Scanlan	*age 23 "*
Family of Paul Laisk	*age 48 Living*
Mary Laisk Wife	*age 38 yrs*
Archie Laisk	*age 19 yrs*
Agnes Laisk	*age 14 "*
Tommy Laisk	*age 12 "*
Catherine Laisk	*" 10 "*
Joseph Laisk	*" 8 "*
Paul Laisk	*" 6 "*
Adelaide Laisk	*" 4 "*
Ambrose Laisk	*" 2 "*
Family of Joseph Leask	*age 46 yrs*
children Wife Dead	~~*age 44*~~ *yrs*
living Marion Laisk	*age 14 yrs*
Lena Laisk	*age 12 yrs*
Jane Laisk	*age 9 yrs*
Pearl Laisk	*age 6 yrs*
Rose Laisk	*age 4 yrs*

S. N. Johnston
Payment Mich.

Information following from: Not Given.

25-8 O NAW NO MAW NE, dead, Children draw in Canada & living at Garden River.

Information following from: Not Given.
26-8 CHARLOTTE GERAU, ?

Information following from: Frank Boucher, Sugar Isle.
27-8 MARIA GRANT or now MARIA G. BOUCHER, age 55, P.O. Sault Ste Marie.
Husband: William Boucher, dead, see 3-3.
27-8-1 Sarah Boucher, P.O. Marquette, husband white.
27-8-2 John Boucher, age 24, P.O. Marquette.
27-8-3 Maria Boucher, age 21, U.S. Army in Filapines, single.
27-8-4 Maria Boucher, age 18.

Information following from: Joseph O'Jibway, Sr.
28-8 PAW SHE NAW NAW QUOT or JOSEPH O'JIBWAY, Sr., age 69, P.O. Sugar Isle.
Wife: Isabelle La Rose, dead, see also 6-8, no children.

Information following from: Not Given.
29-8 NE SHAW SO GAW BO, dead.
Wife: Paw Go Naw Ge She Go Quay, on Canadian side some where, "Sobb", Canada, said to draw in Canada.

Information following from: Not Given.
30-8 SUNDAY ST. GERMAIN, dead.
Wife: Charlotte (Foster) Emery or Lemoroue, age 50, P.O. Sugar Island, see 9-9, no children.

Information following from: Not Given.
31-8 NAW GAW WAY WE DUNG, P.O. Garden River, Canada, said to be paid in Canada & has always lived there.

Information following from: George Frishette, Sugar Isle, May 15/09.
32-8 WAW BE MONG or JOE WHITE LOON, age 95, P.O. Sugar Isle.
Wife: Madeline White Loon or Ah Dah De Be Quay, age 80, P.O. Sugar Isle.
32-8-1 Julia Greensky, age 60, P.O. Sugar Island, no children.
Husband: John Greensky, age 55, P.O. Sugar Island, Saginaw Indian.
32-8-2 Charlotte Frishette, age 32, see 43-3.
32-8-3 William Whiteloon, age 45, P.O. Sugar Isle, no children, separated, wife French & now lives at Cheboygen, Indians do not know her name.
32-8-4 Nicholas Whiteloon, age 43, P.O. Sugar Isle, single.
32-8-5 E Quay Wish Ish (Martha) Riley, age 28, P.O. Neebish Isle.
Husband: Jake Riley, age 52, Canadian.

32-8-5-1 James Riley, age 12.
32-8-5-2 Henry Riley, born January 1908 2nd roll.

Information following from: Not Given.

33-8 Mrs. BAPTISTE LE LOND or LALONE or VICTORIA LALONE, P.O. Arlinton St. Soo, see 33-3.

Information following from: Mindoskung.

34-8 O TASH QUA KE ZHICK GO QUAY, dead, Chiefs do not remember who this is.

Information following from: Chief Shawan, John Naw Way Ke Zhick & Frank Boucher, Sugar Isle.

35-8 CHE CHE, dead.
35-8-1 John Naw Way Ge Zhick or John Captain, age 65, P.O. Sugar Isle, see 55-4.
Wife: Sophia Naw Way Ge Zhick, age 60.
35-8-1-1 Charlotte Andrews, age 36.
Husband: John Andrews, age 34, see A-Soo Page 3, see 3-17.
35-8-1-2 Mary Ann Boucher, age 33, P.O. Sugar Isle.
Husband: Frank Boucher #2, see 3-3.
35-8-1-2-1 Margaret Boucher, age 14.
35-8-1-2-2 Christina Boucher, age 12.
35-8-1-2-3 Frank Boucher #3, age 10.
35-8-1-3 Mary Gates, age 31, P.O. Sugar Isle.
Husband: Frank Gates, wite, separated, see 12-8.
35-8-1-3-1 William Gates, age 14.
35-8-1-4 Maria Shawano #3, age 28, see 15-3 & 2-3.
Husband: Frank Shawano.
35-8-1-4-1 Name not given.
35-8-1-5 John Naw O Way Ge Zhick, age 24, single, P.O. Sugar Isle.
35-8-1-6 Thomas Naw O Way Ge Zhick, age 22.
35-8-1-7 James Naw O Way Ge Zhick, age 17.
35-8-1-8 Isabelle Naw O Way Ge Zhick, age 15.
35-8-2 Mary Ann Sebastian, age 40, P.O. Drummond's Isle.
35-8-2-1 Maggie Gurnoe, age 20, see 2-8, P.O. Drummond's Isle.
35-8-2-2 Mary Causley, see 23-3, P.O. Drummond's Isle.
35-8-2-3 Richard Shawan, age 10, P.O. Drummond's Isle.

Page 9
Sault Sainte Marie Band
Chief PI AW BE DAW SUNG

Information following from: Dan Edwards or Dan Pi Aw Be Daw Sung, Sugar Isle, May 25.

1-9 PI AW BE DAW SUNG, dead.
Wife: Name not given, dead.
1-9-1 Name not given, dead.
Wife: Mrs. Luther Rice, dead, see 15-9.
1-9-2 Henry Pi Aw Be Daw Sung, age 30+, P.O. St Ignace or Hessel.

Information following from: Chief Pi Aw Be Daw Sung.

2-9 AW BE TAW KE ZHICK, dead.
2-9-1 Louis Aw Be Taw Ke Zhick or Halfaday, age 50, P.O. St Jacques.
Note: This is the only child of this family that the Chief at Sugar Island know to be living. Possibly I got this name at St. Jacques took up & to correct Durent. Write to Peter Kesis at St. Jacques, (Ind. Point) & ask him is Louis there & what other name he probably goes by or write to Joe Beaver, also at St. Jacques, for information about Louis Aw be taw ke zhick
This was also an A.

Information following from: Capt Aishquagon, Sugar Isle.

3-9 WAW BAW SE NO QUAY, dead.
3-9-1 Henry Saw Gaw Quot or Se Gah Quaw, age 43, P.O. Garden River, Canada, does not draw in Canada.
Wife: Ellen Saw Gaw Quot, Canadian.
3-9-1-1 John Saw Gaw Quot, age 10, draws in Canada with mother.
3-9-1-2 Lawrence Saw Gaw Quot, age 8.
3-9-1-3 Susan Saw Gaw Quot, age 5.
3-9-1-4 Richard Saw Gaw Quot, born March/08.
Note: Three youngest children do not draw in Canada so says the father and the Chief Durant Spl Agt.
3-9-2 Stephen Saw Gaw Quot, age 65, P.O. Garden River, see 32-9.
Wife: Name not given, Canadian.
3-9-2-1 Henry Saw Gaw Quot Jr., draw in Canada.
3-9-2-2 Mary Saw Gaw Quot, draw in Canada.
Note: All other children and grand children living draw with Canadian Govt.

Information following from: Dan Edwards & Capt Aishquagon, Sugar Isle.

4-9 MO KE CHE WAW NO QUAY, dead.
Husband: Name not given, a Canadian.

4-9-1 Joe Naw Qua Ke Zhick, P.O. Garden River, draws in Canada.
4-9-1-1 James Ti Bish Ko Ke Zhick, age 22, single, P.O. Garden River, Canada, see also 31-9.
4-9-1-2 Tom Wilcox, age 17, single, P.O. Garden River, Canada, see also 31-9.
Note: The Chief Pi aw be dw sung says that these two boys are the only ones of that family alive who do not draw in Canada, altho there are other heirs living. Durant Spl Agt.
4-9-2 Tom Naw Qua Ke Zhick, draw in Canada.
Note: The Chief Pi aw be dw sung says that these two

Information following from: Joseph Rouleau.
5-9 WAY ZHE BAUM or MARY BELLANGER Sr., age 83, P.O. 900 Spruce St Sault Ste Marie.
Husband: Peter Bellanger, dead.
5-9-1 Maggie Bellanger Smith, age 58, Port Authur Ont.
Husband 1st : Name not given.
Husband 2nd: Harry Smith, white.
5-9-1-1 Joseph Smith.
5-9-1-2 Maggie Smith Messiah, age 23.
5-9-1-3 Peter Smith.
5-9-1-4 Charlotte Smith.
5-9-1-5 Agnes Smith.
Note: All children Canadian born an draw money from Canadian Government.
5-9-2 Joseph Bellanger, age 56, P.O. Garden River Ont.
Wife: Charlotte Whalfen Bellanger, draws money in Canada.
5-9-2-1 James Bellanger, age 30, P.O. Garden River Ont.
5-9-2-2 Mary Bellanger, age 28, P.O. Garden River Ont.
5-9-2-3 Sophia Bellanger, age 23, P.O. Garden River Ont.
Note: All children Canadian born Charlotte Bellanger draws in Canada.
5-9-3 Andrew Bellanger, age 54, Gladstone, Mich.
5-9-4 Mary Bellanger Hudson, age 38, P.O. Sault Ste Marie.
Husband: George Hudson, age 45, P.O. Sault Ste Marie.
5-9-4-1 Hattie Hudson, age 16, P.O. Sault Ste Marie.
5-9-4-2 Francis Hudson, age 14, P.O. Sault Ste Marie.
5-9-4-3 Hester Hudson, age 15, P.O. Sault Ste Marie.
5-9-4-4 John Hudson, age 12, P.O. Sault Ste Marie.
5-9-5 Peter Bellanger, age 36, P.O. Sault Ste Marie.
Wife: Vina Bellrau Bellanger, age 32, P.O. Sault Ste Marie.
5-9-5-1 Willliam Bellanger, age 15, P.O. Sault Ste Marie.
5-9-5-2 Stephen Bellanger, age 11, P.O. Sault Ste Marie.
5-9-5-3 John Bellanger, age 9, P.O. Sault Ste Marie.
5-9-5-4 Molly Bellanger, age 7, P.O. Sault Ste Marie.

5-9-6 Joseph Bellanger Sykes, dead.
Husband: James Sykes, white.
5-9-6-1 Samuel Sykes, age 36, P.O. Sault Ste Marie.
5-9-6-2 Frederick Sykes, age 32, P.O. 5489 Jefferson Ave Chicago Ills.
Wife: Louise Sykes, white.
5-9-6-2-1 Ruth Sykes, age 6, P.O. 5489 Jefferson Ave Chicago Ills.
5-9-6-2-2 Frederick Sykes, age 34, P.O. 5489 Jefferson Ave Chicago Ills.
5-9-6-3 Frank Sykes, age 26, P.O. Sault Ste Marie 913 Ceeder St.
5-9-6-4 Mary Sykes La Drig, age 23, P.O. Sault Ste Marie 913 Ceder St.
Husband: Joseph La Drig, white.
5-9-6-4-1 Mervis La Drig, age 1, P.O. Sault Ste Marie 913 Ceder St.
5-9-6-5 Hattie Sykes Sish, age 19, P.O. Sault Ste Marie 913 Ceder St.
Husband: William Sish, white.

Information following from: Not Given.
Compilers Note: This is 2nd page numbered as 5-9, appears to be same families as above with slight different information.

5-9 WAY ZHE BAUM or MARY BELONGER, P.O. Soo 900 Spruce.
Husband: Peter Belonger, dead.
5-9-1 Maggie Bellanger Smith, age 60, Port Authur.
Husband: Name not given.
5-9-1-1 Maggie Smith Messiah, age 23.
5-9-2 Joseph Bellanger, age 56, P.O. Garden River.
5-9-2-1 James Bellanger, age 35.
5-9-2-2 Mary Bellanger, age 30.
5-9-2-3 Sophia Bellanger, age 24.
5-9-2-4 Ida May Bellanger, age 13.
5-9-2-5 Maggie Bellanger, age 11.
5-9-3 Andrew Bellanger, age 53, Gladstone.
5-9-3-1 Samuel Sykes, age 36.
5-9-3-2 Fred Sykes, age 34.
5-9-3-3 Frank Sykes, age 26.
5-9-3-4 May Sykes La Drig, age 23, P.O. 913 Cedar St Soo
5-9-3-5 Hattie Sykes Sisk, age 19.
5-9-4 Mary Hudson, age 43, P.O. 900 Spruce St Soo.
5-9-4-1 Hattie Hudson, age 14.
5-9-4-2 Francis Hudson, age 12.

5-9-5 Peter Bellanger, age 36, P.O. Corner Spruce & Greenough Sts.

5-9-5-1 Willlie Bellanger, age 15.

5-9-5-2 Stephen Bellanger, age 11.

5-9-5-3 John Bellanger, age 9.

5-9-5-4 Molly Bellanger, age 7.

Letter June 29/09 D.__
Mrs. Mary Bellanger
Indian name Way-she-bon
Spruce Street No 900
Mrs Maggie Bellanger 60 Living at Port Authur
Children Maggie Messiah age 23
Joseph Bellanger age 56 Living at Garden River

Children.	*James*	*age 35*
	Mary	*" 30*
	Sophia	*" 24*
	Ida May	*" 13*
	Maggie	*" 11*

Peter Bellanger age 41
Mrs Peter Bellanger 32

Children	*Willie*	*age 15*
	Stephen	*" 11*
	John	*" 9*
	Molly	*" 7*

Living corner of Spruce & Greenough Streets No number
Mary Bellange children and Grand children
Andrew Bellanger age53Working at Gladstone
Samuel Bellanger age 36
Frederic " 34
Frank Sykes 26
May Sykes & 1 child #913 Ceder St 23
Hattie Sykes 19
Living at 913 Ceder N.E.
Mrs Mary Bellager Hudson age 43
Children Hattie Hudson age 14
Francis Hudson 12
Spruce St 900

Information following from: Capt Aishquagwon, May 29/09.

6-9 AINE NE WAW BE, dead.

Wife: Name not given, now draws in Canada, because her father was a Canadian.

6-9-1 Name not given, dead, children dead, Chief Pe aw be daw sung say the wife is living & draws annuity from Canadian Govt. Durant.

6-9-2 Joe Shawano, age 40, Jim Island near Lake George probable enrolled on Oshawano's band though.

Information following from: Joseph Greensky & Capt Aishquagwon, Sugar Isle, May 25/09.

7-9 A DO SAY, dead.
Wife: Mary A Do Say, age 80, P.O. Garden River, Canada, does not draw in Canada.
7-9-1 Name not given, see 25-9.
7-9-2 George Greensky, age 50, P.O. Garden River, Canada, does not draw in Canada, single.
7-9-3 Philamon A Do Say, P.O. Garden River, Canada, does not draw in Canada.
Husband: Name not given, dead, draw in Canada.

Information following from: Chief Edwards & Joe Taygosbe, Sugar Isle.

8-9 TAY GOSHE, dead.
Wife: Name not given, dead.
8-9-1 Joe Tay Gosbe, age 70, P.O. Garden River Canada, single.
8-9-2 Philamon Tay Goshe, draw in Garden River Canada.
Husband: Tom Tebow, Canadian, draw in Garden River Canada.
8-9-3 Margaret Tay gosbe, age 50, P.O. Garden River Canada, does not draw in Canada, single.
8-9-4 James Tay Gosh, age 38, dead, died May 9/09.
Wife: Jennie Tay Gosh, Canadian, P.O. Garden River Canada.
8-9-4-1 Arthur Tay Gish, age 7, said to draw in Canada.
8-9-4-2 Felix Tay Gish, age 5, siad to draw in Canada.

Information following from: Not Given.

9-9 MRS. HUGH FOSTER, dead.
Husband: Hugh Foster.
9-9-1 William Foster, age 55, P.O. Sugar Island.
Wife: Lizzie (Fish) Foster.
9-9-1-1 Charles Foster, age 40, single, P.O. Sugar Isle.
9-9-1-2 "Tootsy" Wain Daw Sung or Jennie Shedowin, age 38, P.O. St Jacques.
Husband: Joe Shedowin, see 14-36.
9-9-1-3 Georgiana Foster, age 35, P.O. Sugar Isle,
9-9-1-3-1 Louisa Ann Foster.
9-9-1-3-2 ________ Foster.
9-9-2 Catharine Waishkey, see 39-5.
9-9-3 Charlotte Lamorne, see 30-8.

Information following from: Mary Edwards, Sugar Isle, May 25.

10-9 AW WAY AW SE NO QUAY, or ANGELINE KEE CHE BE NACE, age 75, P.O. Payment.

10-9-1 Louis, dead, heard he ws dead went away years ago.

10-9-2 Frank, dead, single.

10-9-3 Name not given, dead, no children.

10-9-4 Mary Edwards or Mary Pi Aw Be Daw Sung, age 43, see 15-9.

Information following from: Joe MesquawbowoKay, May 29/09.

11-9 ME SQUAW BAW NO KAY, dead.

Wife: Name not given, dead.

11-9-1 Name not given, dead.

11-9-1-1 Annie Me Squaw Baw No Kay, age 42, P.O. Garden River Canada, does not draw.

11-9-1-1-1 William Me Squaw Baw No Kay, age 7.

11-9-2 Joe Me Squaw Bo No Kay, age 53, P.O. Payment Garden River.

Wife: Name not given, dead.

11-9-2-1 Ada Me Squaw Bo No Kay, age 25, P.O. Garden River, single.

11-9-2-2 Simon Me Squaw Bo No Kay, age 19.

11-9-2-3 Elijah Me Squaw Bo No Kay, age 8.

11-9-2-4 Mary Me Squaw Bo No Kay, age 7.

Note: all others dead, but some has grand children who draw in Canada, Durant Spl Agt.

Information following from: Chief Piawbedawsung & Capt Aishquagwon.

12-9 SHAW WAW NAW QUAW DO QUAY, dead.

Husband: Name not given, Canadian.

12-9-1 Alex Waw Ba No Say, age 57, P.O. Garden River, draws in Canada.

Wife: Name not given, Canadian.

12-9-1-1 Sam Waw Ba No Say.

12-9-1-2 John Waw Ba No Say.

12-9-1-3 Eliza Waw Ba No Say.

Note: enroll Alex Waw ba no say & say in notes: "he draws in Canada & has children all of whom draw in Canada" Durant Spl Agt.

Note: all others dead.

Information following from: Chief Piawbedawsung, Sugar Isle, May 25.

13-9 JOSEPH PAYSON or DAYSON, P.O. St Jacques, see 20-9.

Information following from: Chief Piawbedawsung & Capt Aishquagwon, Sugar Isle.

14-9 QUAY KE GE ZHE GO QUAY or MARY THOMPSON, age 90,

P.O. Garden River Canada, all heirs if living draw in Canada Durant, her sister 8-8 says she draws from Canada, Durant Spl Agt, May 26/09.
Husband: Name not given, Canadian.
14-9-1 Joe La Sage, P.O. Garden River Canada.
14-9-2 Paul La Sage, P.O. Garden River Canada.
14-9-3 Moses La Sage , P.O. Garden River Canada.
14-9-4 John la Sage, P.O. Garden River Canada.
Note: Enroll, but note that they draw in Canada, as does their mother, Mary Thompson, Durant Spl Agt, May 29/09.

Information following from: Dan Edwards, Sugar Isle.
15-9 LUTHER RICE, age 75, P.O. Odanah, Wis.
Wife 1st: Name not given, dead, Luther Rice was her 2nd husband.
Wife 2nd: Name not given, mother of children 11 & 2 was 1st married to a son of 1-9.
15-9-1 Dan Pi Aw Be Daw Sung or Dan Edwards Sr., age 46, P.O. Payment, (Sugar Isle) Mich, his mother mother was 2nd wife of Luther Rice by her 1st husband, enroll as Edwards.
Wife: Mary Edwards, age 43, her mother mother was 1st wife of Luther Rice & was on roll as 10-9, enroll as Edwards.
15-9-1-1 John Pi Aw Be Daw Sung or John Edwards, age 22, P.O. Payment, single.
15-9-1-2 Joe Edwards, age 20, P.O. Payment, single.
15-9-1-3 Sophia Edwards, age 19.
15-9-1-4 Dan Edwards Jr., age 15.
15-9-1-5 Paul Edwards, age 10.
15-9-1-6 Mary. Edwards, age 8.
15-9-2 Name not given, dead.
Husband: Frank Baker, age 34, P.O. Drummond's Isle.
15-9-2-1 Sophia Baker or Belongea, age 12. See 17-3.
15-9-3 George Rice, age 35+, L'Anse, Information from Spl Agt Interpreter at L'Anse.
Wife: Theresa Rice, L'Anse Indian, no children.
15-9-4 William Rice, age 30+, P.O. Odanah.

Information following from: Justine Johnson & son Willaim Johnson, Detour, May 27.
16-9 SAW QUAW GIEN, dead, a son of Pi Aw Be Daw Sung 1-9.
Wife: Name not given, dead.
16-9-1 Henry Kay Kay Koose or Louis La Sage, see 6-17, lived at Drummond's 10 or 12 yrs ago, probably at Hessel or Pine River.
Wife: Mary la Sage, daughter of O Saw Waw Mick 5-3.
16-9-2 ~~Joe Kaw We Tos~~.

16-9-2-1 Joe Kaw We Tos, P.O. Sugar Isle, see 17-9.
16-9-2-2 Sarah Kaw We Tos, age 28.

Information following from: old Capt Aishquagwon, St Jacques, December 5/08, Sugar Isle, May 29/09.

17-9 KAW WE TOS, dead.
Wife: Name not given, dead.
17-9-1 Name not given, dead, Traverse.
Wife: Name not given, dead, Traverse.
17-9-1-1 Mary Ann Lambert, see 4-34 & 52-35.
17-9-1-2 ~~Joe Kaw We Tos, see 30-1~~.
17-9-2 ~~Sarah Kaw We Tos, age 28, P.O. Payment, single~~.
17-9-2-1 Joe Kaw We Tos, see 30-1 & 16-9.
17-9-2-2 Sarah Kaw We Tos, age 28, P.O. Payment, Mich. Sugar Isle, single.

Information following from: Chief Piawbedawsung, Mrs Haller & Mrs. Supe, May 29/09, Sugar Isle, May 25.

18-9 MRS. CHARLES LINK, dead.
Husband: Charles Link.
18-9-1 Joe Linke, age 48, P.O. Soo, Seymore St., wife white, no children.
18-9-2 Mary Ann Haller, age 43, P.O. Soo 345 Maple St.
Husband: Name not given, white, a policeman.
18-9-2-1 Theresa Haller, age 12.
18-9-2-2 Joseph Haller, age 10.
18-9-3 Matilda L. Supe, age 40, P.O. 823 Lizzie St. Soo, husband white, no children.
18-9-4 Charles A. Link, age 35, P.O. 823 Lizzie St. Soo, wife white, no children.

Information following from: Chiefs & Capt Aishquagwon, Sugar Isle, May 25 & 29.

19-9 EDWARD PI AW BE DAW SUNG, dead, wife dead, no heirs.

Information following from: John Aishquagwon, May 29/09, Information as to Identity, St. Jacques, December 4 & December 6/08.

20-9 CAPT. or JOHN AISH QUA GWON, age 69, P.O. Payment, Mich.
Wife: Margaret Aish Qua Gwon, age 69, P.O. Sugar Island.
20-9-1 No child.
20-9-2 Louisa Waw Be Gay Kake, adopted, age 21, P.O. Payment, Mich (Sugar Isle), single, father & mother dead, a niece of Angeline Waw Be Gay Kake, see 30-1.
20-9-3 John Jarvis, age 11, P.O. Payment, Mich (Sugar Isle), single
20-9-4 Joe Dason, age 45, P.O. Namah, on roll as Joe Payson 13-9,

father , a Canadian & mother Ottawa & Chippewa Indian, former living at Sugar Island; mother dead, this man was brought up at Sugar Island & has lived at Namah 21 yrs. Believe he is entitled to enrollment ask John Shedowan at Rapid River about this man.
Wife: Mary Dason, age 36, see 67-35.
20-9-4-1 Mary Wheaton, age 20, P.O. Namah, see 18-7.
Husband: Andrew Wheaton, see 40-1.
20-9-4-1-1 Name not given, born June/08 died August/08.
20-9-4-2 Peter Dason, age 18.
20-9-4-3 Nancy Dason, age 16.
20-9-4-4 Bessie Dason, age 8.
20-9-4-5 Barney Dason, age 6.
20-9-4-6 Joseph Dason, age 2.

Information following from: Not Given.
21-9 O GAW BAY AW SE GAY QUAY or MRS. JOE HALFADAY, age 50, lives near L'Anse, see 7-6.
Husband 1st : Amos Crane, dead.
Husband 2nd: Joe Halfaday.

Information following from: Not Given.
22-9 MRS. GEORGE BRITT, P.O. Odanah, Wis.

Information following from: Not Given.
24-9 MRS. CHARLES CRUSHIER, dead.
Husband: Charles Crushier.
24-9-1 Jane Lasley, P.O. Little Current, Manitoba Isle, Canada.
24-9-2 Joe Crushier, P.O. Soo.

Information following from: Joseph Greensky.
25-9 O SHAW WAW SQUAW QUOT or JOSEPH GREENSKY, age 65, P.O. Payment (Sugar Isle), draws with Canadian Government.
Wife: Susan or Susette Greensky, age 50.
25-9-1 James Greensky, age 20, single, P.O. Payment, Mich.
25-9-2 Jemmie Greensky, age 18, single, P.O. Payment, Mich.
25-9-3 Edith Greensky, age 16, single, P.O. Payment, Mich.

Information following from: Capt Aishquagwon & Chiefs, Sugar Isle, May 25 & 29.
26-9 JOSETTE NAW WAW DE GO, dead.
Husband: John Pine, Canadian, Garden River (Chief).
26-9-1 William Erskine or William Pine, P.O. Garden River, Canada.
26-9-2 Jennie Tay Go She.

Note: Both draw in Canada so says Chief, Durant.

Information following from: Capt Aishquagwon.
27-9 O ME NAW CAW WE GO QUA, dead, mother of Pi Aw Be Daw Sung.
27-9-1 Name not given.
26-9-1-1 Dan Edwards, see 15-9.
27-9-2 Chief Madosh, dead, see 1-1.

Information following from: Dan Edwards – Pi Aw Be Daw Sung (Chief) & Capt Aishquagwon.
28-9 ISABELLE KEE CHE PE NACE, dead.
28-9-1 Frank Mindo, age 28, P.O. Sugar Isle, single.
28-9-2 Mary Oliver, draws in Canad with husband, a Canadian, so says Chief.

Information following from: Chief Pi Aw Be Daw Sung & Capt Aishquagwon, Sugar Isle, May 25/09, May 29/09.
29-9 MIN DE MO YEA, dead.
Husband: Name not given, Canadian.
29-9-1 William Kabaoosa, has two children both draw in Canada through this father, so says Chief, Durant.
29-9-2 George Kabaoosa, draws in Canada.

Information following from: Not Given.
30-9 MARY ME YAW BE NANCE.
Heirs all draw in Canada, has only 2 grandchildren living who draw there, so says Chief et al, Durant Spl Agt.
30-9-1 Name not given, see 31-9
30-9-2 Name not given.
30-9-2-1 John James, age 11, lives with John Aish Qua Gwon & does not draw in Canada, see 30-9.

Information following from: Capt Aishquagwon, Sugar Isle.
31-9 ONG GE O QUAY, dead, daughter of 30-9.
31-9-1 Tom Wilcox, age 17, see 4-9.
31-9-2 James Tibish Ke Ke Zhick, age 22, see 4-9.

Information following from: Stephen Saw Gaw Quot.
32-9 STEPHEN SAW GAW QUOT, age 65, P.O. Garden River, Canada, does not draw.
Wife: Mary Saw Gaw Quot, age 60
32-9-1 Henry Saw Gaw Quot, age 30, P.O. Garden River, single.
32-9-2 Mary Saw Gaw Quot.
32-9-2-1 George Saw Gaw Quot, age 12.

32-9-2-2 Philip Saw Gaw Quot, age 10.

Note: This mans wife and children draw in Canada he admits so, except 2 grand children daughter of Mary 2nd child who lives with grandfather & do not draw in Canada.

Information following from: Mary Ann Hatch & Chiefs, Sugar Isld, May 15/09.

33-9 KAW GAY QUAY, dead, mother of 17-9 & 20-9.

33-9-1 See 17-9.

33-9-2 See 20-9.

33-9-3 O Ge She Aw Be No Quay, dead.

Husband: ________ Parault, dead.

33-9-3-1 Mary Ann Hatch, see 11-3 for children.

33-9-3-2 Dan Parault, age 35, P.O. Sugar Isle, single, no children.

Information following from: Not Given.

34-9 SWAW SWAW NAW QUOT, dead, no heirs.

Author Note: There are no entries for Page 10 on the original roll.

Page 11

Mackinaw Band

Pine River Sub-Band

Chief NE SWAW SO BE

Information following from: Pete Waw Say Ke Zhick see 16-12, Pine River, May 19/09.

1-11 NE SWAW SO BE, Jr., Chief, dead.

Wife: Name not given, dead.

1-11-1 Christine Muscoe, P.O. Pt. Aux Chesne, see 14-15.

Note: all other heirs dead.

Information following from: Not Given.

2-11 NE SWAW SO BE, Sr.

2-11-1 See 1-11.

Note: all other children dead and no heirs. Ask wife of Frank Muscoe (St. Ignace) as she is a grandchild, see 14-15.

Information following from: Not Given.

3-11 PAW ACE, dead, a son of 4-12, see 4-12 for children.

Information following from: Alex La Pointe, Drummonds, May 2.

4-11 KE WAY KE ZHICK or "BIG ALICK" or ALEX SAILOR, age 75, P.O. Drummonds.

Wife: Name not given, dead.
4-11-1 Mary La Pointe, see 9-8.
4-11-2 Joe Ke Way Ke Zhick or Joe Alick, age 41, P.O. Drummonds Isle.
Wife: Polly Cadotte, see 67-4.
4-11-3 Julia Bully, age 35, P.O. Drummond's Isle.
Husband: Jack Bully or Boullie, age 42, enroll by consent of Chief, Soo Band, see 10-5.
4-11-3-1 Louise Bully, age 8.
4-11-3-2 Pete Bully, age 6.
4-11-4 Alex John Ke Way Ke Zhick, age 30, P.O. Drummond's Isle, single.

Information following from: John Naw Gaw Ne Gwon, St. Ignace, April 20/09.

5-11 NAW GAW NE GWON or JOHN NAW GAW NE GWON, age 76, P.O. Oscoda.
Wife: Name not given, dead.
5-11-1 Dan Naw Gaw Ne Gwon, age 44, P.O. Oscoda.
Wife: Martha Naw Gaw Ne Gwon, Saginaw Indian, off.
5-11-1-1 Lydia Naw Gaw Ne Gwon, age 6.
5-11-1-2 John Naw Gaw Ne Gwon, age 4.
5-11-1-3 Naw Gaw Ne Gwon Go Quay, age 2, female.
5-11-2 Amos Naw Gaw Ne Gwon, age 42, P.O. Oscoda, single.
5-11-3 Name not given, dead, female, no heirs.

Information following from: Not Given.

6-11 NAW WAW CHE KE ZHICK WAY BE.
Note: Mackinac head men do not recall the name & this family cannot be identified. Durant.

Information following from: Angeline, Pine River.

7-11 O KE CHE GUM & Sisters, dead, sister of Chief, sisters all dead and no heirs.
7-11-1 Angeline Wandal Alterman, age 43, P.O. Pine River.
Note: lives with Louis Osawmick 5-3, see if she is enrolled as his wife. No she is not enrolled with him. Durant
Husband: Isaac Alterman, dead, Canadian.
7-11-1-1 George Alterman, age 8.
7-11-2 Name not given, dead.

Information following from: Not Given.

8-11 KE CHE GAW NAW QUO UM or JAKE SHEDOWIN, age 72, P.O. Pt. Aux Chesne.
Wife: Name not given, dead.
8-11-1 Shedowin, dead.

Wife: Mary Ann Shedowin, age 47, see 14-15.

Information following from: Not Given.
9-11 WAW BE GUM, this family cannot be identified.

Information following from: head of family, Pine River.
10-11 KEY WAY AW SE NO QUAY, age 75, P.O. Charles Pine River.
Husband 1st : Name not given, dead.
Husband 2nd: Name not given, dead.
10-11-1 Joe, dead, by 1st husband.
Wife: Name not given, dead.
10-11-1-1 Name not given, dead.
10-11-2 James Jake, age 36, see 11-15 for wife and child.
10-11-3 Saw Waw Qua Do Quay, mother says she the daughter draws in Canada, by 1st husband.
Husband: Jake, Canadian.
10-11-4 Susan Moses, 48, Pine River, see 61-35.
Husband: ______ Moses, see 61-35, by 2nd husband.
10-11-5 Name not given, dead, no heirs, by 2nd husband.
10-11-6 Margaret Moses, age 30, by 2nd husband.
Husband 1st : Joe Moses, dead, see also 61-35.
Husband 2nd: Louis Moses, age 30, see 61-35, see 76-21, this his 2nd wife the other is at Rapid City.
10-11-6-1 Antoine Moses, age 2.
10-11-6-2 Dan Moses, born February/09 too late.
10-11-6-3 William Moses, age 14.
10-11-6-4 Dan Moses, age 7.
10-11-7 Young Jake Paw Qudge Nin, age 28, P.O. Pine River, single.

Information following from: Not Given.
11-11 WAW SAY GE WAW NO QUAY, dead, mother of 10-11 heirs on 10-11.

Information following from: Eliza Ance.
12-11 Aw No Ke Ke Zhick, dead.
Wife 1st : Eliza Ance, see 1-15.
Wife 2nd: Name not given, dead.
12-11-1 Name not given, dead, no heirs.

Information following from: Thomas Sagatoe, Pt. Aux Chesne.
13-11 O TISH QUAY KE ZHE GE QUAY or Theresa Sagatoe, age 75, P.O. Pt. Aux Chesne, see also 2-36.
13-11-1 Angeline Chippeway, age 47, P.O. Cross Village, see 2-36 & 15-36 for children, husband dead.
13-11-2 Mary Keshawas, P.O. Cross Village, see 31-30.

Husband: William Keshawas, see 31-30.
13-11-3 Jane Odemin, age 44, P.O. Pt. Aux Chesne.
13-11-4 Eliza Annemequam or Eliza Sam, see 39-20.

Information following from: Not Given.
14-11 PAW ME GE WAW NO QUAY or MARY ANN ALICK, age 70, see
3-17.

Information following from: Not Given.
15-11 O MAW NO MAW NE QUAY, children dead, no heirs.

Information following from: Not Given.
16-11 PAY TAW QUAW SE NO QUAY, dead, children dead, no heirs.

Information following from: Not Given.
17-11 KE CHE GE WAW NO QUAY, Chiefs do not remember this family.

Information following from: Not Given.
18-11 O SAW WAW BE CO QUAY, Chiefs do not remember her.

Information following from: Not Given.
19-11 MAW CHE GO NOW AW SHE, dead, no heirs.

Information following from: Joe Labelle, Mac Isle, April 12/09.
20-11 GEORGE LABELLE, dead.
Wife 1st : Name not given, dead.
Wife 2nd: Name not given, dead.
20-11-1 Nezette Labelle, age 44, P.O. Cheboygan.

Information following from: Not Given.
21-11 SHE BYE AW WAY QUAY or MRS. CECELIA GERUE, age 64, P.O. Mullett Lake.
21-11-1 Cornelia Cotey, age 41, P.O. Cheboygan.
Husband: _______ Cotey, white.
21-11-1-1 Joseph Cotey, age 16.
21-11-1-2 Eugene Cotey, age 15.
21-11-1-3 Olive Cotey, age 14.
21-11-1-4 Phillis Cotey, age 11.
21-11-1-5 Mabel Cotey, age 4.
21-11-2 Name not given.
Wife: Florence Roberts Lafond, white
21-11-2-1 Bernie Gerue, age 17, P.O. Torver, Mich.
21-11-2-2 Fred Gerue, age 14, P.O. Torver, Mich.
21-11-2-3 Ruth Gerue, age 9, P.O.Torver, Mich.

21-11-2-4 Loretta Gerue, age 8, P.O. Torver, Mich.
21-11-2-5 Beatrice Gerue, age 6, P.O. Torver, Mich.
21-11-3 Louis Gerue, age 38, P.O. Mullett Lake, see 95-22.
21-11-4 Charles S. Gerue, age 36, Cheboygan, wife white, no children.

Information following from: Not Given.
22-11 WAW BE GE NIECE, dead.
Wife: Mary Andrews #1 or O Dish Quay, age 80, P.O. Sugar Isle, see 13-36.
22-11-1 George Wah Be Ge Niece, age 55, P.O. Garden Island, see 1-34.
Wife: Name not given, dead, daughter of Antoine Pean 1-34.
22-11-1-1 Mitchell Wah Be Ge Niece, age 5.
22-11-2 Pete Wah Be Ge Niece, age 42, P.O. Namah, Mich or Baker's Camp Rapid River, Mich, single, no children.
22-11-3 Joe Wah Be Ge Niece, age 35, P.O. Hessell, Mich., see 4-34.
22-11-4 James Wah Be Ge Niece, age 52, P.O. Pine River, see 13-36.
Wife: Name not given, see 5-17.
22-11-4-1 Elizabeth Wah Be Ge Niece, age 14.
22-11-4-2 Patrick Wah Be Ge Niece, age 12.
22-11-4-3 Enos Wah Be Ge Niece, age 5.

Information following from: Alex La Pointe, Drummonds.
23-11 PE TAW SE GAY QUAY, age 70, P.O. Drummonds Isle, a sister of 4-11.
23-11-1 Joe Andrew, age 34, P.O. Drummond's Isle.
Wife: Agnes Andrew, nee Cadotte, age 20, no children.

Information following from: Leon Beloungea, Mc Isle, April/09.
24-11 LEON or PAUL BELOUNGEA or BELONZHAY, age 75, P.O. Mackinac Isle.
Wife: Name not given, dead, see 26-13.
24-11-1 John Beloungea, age 50, P.O. Sarnia, Mich.
Wife: Name not given, white.
24-11-1-1 Eva Beloungea, dead, no heirs.
24-11-1-2 Edith Beloungea Walker, age 20, P.O. Escanaba.
24-11-2 William Beloungea, age 46, P.O. Namah, Mich., single.
24-11-3 Henry Beloungea, age 48, P.O. Namah.
Wife: Mary (Martin) Beloungea, age 52, P.O. Namah, see 37-15.
24-11-3-1 Lizzie Beloungea, age 22.
24-11-3-2 Charlie Beloungea, age 20, see 26-13.

Information following from: Lucy King, et al, Mac Isle, April 2/09.

25-11 PAUL ASLIN, dead.
Wife: Jane Aslin, age 60, P.O. Gould City, Mich., see 74-21.
25-11-1 George Aslin, dead, no heirs.
25-11-2 Lucy King, age 34, Mack Isle.
Husband: Frank king, Canadian Indian.
25-11-2-1 Stella King, age 13.
25-11-2-2 Jennette King, age 7.
25-11-2-3 Rachel King, age 4.
25-11-2-4 Bessie King, born January 17/1908, 2nd roll.

Information following from: Not Given.

26-11 MO DOR DOPHENA, dead.
Wife: Name not given, dead.
26-11-1 Theodore Duffina, age 32, P.O. Macinaw City.
Wife: Name not given, white.
26-11-1-1 Frank J. Duffina, age 10.
26-11-1-2 Helen Duffina, age 4.
26-11-1-3 Christie Duffina, born May 24, 1908.

Information following from: Not Given.

27-11 ALEX DOPHENA or DUFFINA, age 75, P.O. Mackinaw Island.
Wife: Name not given, white, see 23-13.
27-11-1 Julia Davenport, age 46, P.O. Naubinway, Mich.
Husband: John Davenport, see 31-13.
27-11-2 Theodore Duffina, age 34, P.O. Mac Isle.
27-11-2-1 Susie Duffina, age 13.
27-11-2-2 Philip Duffina, age 11.
27-11-2-3 Florence Duffina, age 9.
27-11-2-4 Emerson Duffina, age 7.
27-11-2-5 Ellen Duffina, age 5.
27-11-2-6 James Duffina, born May 1908.
27-11-3 Annie Kniffin, see 19-13.
27-11-4 George Duffina, age 32, P.O. Mac Isle, single.
27-11-5 Rosie Duffina, age 36, P.O. Mac Isle, single.
27-11-6 Lena Duffina, age 30, P.O. Mac Isle, single.
27-11-7 Frank Duffina, age 26, P.O. Mac Isle, single.

Information following from: Nicholas Andrews, Mac Isle, April 12/09.

28-11 THOMAS WARD, dead.
Wife: Virginia (McGulphine) Belote, white, her 2nd husband _______ Belote is white.
28-11-1 Mary Ward, dead, no children.
28-11-2 Name not given, dead, no children.
28-11-3 Ebert Ward, age 37, P.O. Cheboygan, no family.

Information following from: Not Given.
29-11 #1 LOUIS BELONZHAY Sr. or BELONGEA, age 55, P.O Cross Village

Wife: Maria Belongea, nee McGalphin, said to belong to Mackinaw, P.O. Cross Village.

Note: Connect this Louis Belongea with his mother's sheet of the Mackinaw Band.

Note: This family is half French & half Indian. The mother of Louis Belonzhay was an Indian woman of Mackinaw band, who died 16 years ago. It seems that her child Louis was put on 1870 roll by himself altho, then only 17 years old. Durant Spl Agt.

29-11-1 Jennie Marshall, age 25, P.O. Cross Village.

Husband: _______ Marshall, white.

29-11-1-1 Melvina Marshall, age 8.

29-11-1-2 Elmer Marshall, age 6.

29-11-1-3 Mamie Marshall, age 2.

29-11-2 Blanche Lewar, age 23, P.O. Cross Village.

Husband: ______ Lewar, white.

29-11-2-1 Earl Lewar, age 2.

29-11-3 Louis Belongea Jr., age 21, P.O. Cross Village, single.

29-11-4 James Belongea, age 18, P.O. Cross Village.

29-11-5 Wilbert Belongea, age 16.

29-11-6 Evangeline Belongea, age 14.

29-11-7 Charles Belongea, age 12.

Information following from: Louis Belongea, St. Ignace, January 5/09.
29-11 #2 LOUIS BELONGEA, age 64, P.O. St. Ignace.

Wife: Name not given, white.

Note: This man claims to be the rightful one enrolled in 1870 as # 29-11 which is also claimed by the Louis Belongea at X Village.

Note: This sheet is correct. However, the other Louis Belongea (No. 1) is as much entitled by having him enrolled with his mother. Durant, Spl. Agt. April/09.

29-11-1 Oliver Belongea, age 38, P.O. St. Ignace.

Wife: Name not given, white.

29-11-1-1 Joe Belongea, age 5.

29-11-1-2 Abraham Belongea, age 4.

29-11-1-3 James Belongea, age 2

29-11-1-4 ______ Belongea, born December/07, 2nd roll.

29-11-2 Mary Trombly, age 34, P.O. St. Ignace.

Husband: Louis Trombly.

29-11-3 Joe Belongea, age 32, P.O. St. Ignace.

Wife: Minnie (Levake) Belongea, see 66-16.

29-11-4 Lizzie Johnson, age 30, P.O. St. Ignace.

Husband: _______ Johnson, white.

29-11-5 Rosie Larsow, age 28, P.O. St. Ignace.

Husband: _______ Larsow, white.

Information following from: Joe Mesawtego Et als., St. Ignace.

30-11 MRS. MARY WALKERTON children.

Husband: John Walker, dead, white.

Note: Chiefs do not know where children are, whether living or dead. Durant.

Information following from: Not Given.

31-11 NA TUM BE TWA WE DUNG.

Note: Chiefs remember the name but do not know where he went or where he is. Durant.

Information following from: Not Given.

32-11 NE GAW NE KE ZHICK GO QUAY.

Note: Chiefs say she is dead with no heirs and was wife of 5-17.

Information following from: Not Given.

33-11 KE CHE NAY GO, dead.

Wife: Name not given, dead.

Note: No heirs, Chiefs. Durant.

Page 12

Mackinaw Les Cheneaux Band

Chief PAY BAW ME SAY

Information following from: Rosie Shomin & mother, Hessel, June 18/09.

0-12 a brother of Pay Baw Me Say, dead.

Wife: Mary Ann Aw Ne Me Quong, age 82, P.O. Hessel, Mich.

0-12-1 Joe Cube, dead.

Wife: Mary Cube, see 6-12.

0-12-2 Mary Dixon, age 55, P.O. Hessel.

Husband: Name not given, a Saginaw Indian.

0-12-2-1 Rosie Dixon, dead, see 8-15.

0-12-2-1-1 Mollie Smith, age 18, P.O. Detroit, single.

0-12-2-2 Susan Dixon, dead.

Husband: _______ Stevenson, now married to Charlotte Cube, see 6-12.

0-12-2-2-1 Nellie Stevenson, age 10, see 6-12.

0-12-2-2-2 Russell Stevenson, age 9, see 6-12.

0-12-2-2-3 Mary Jane Stevenson, age 10, see 6-12.

0-12-2-3 George Dixxon, age 23, single.

0-12-3 Rosie Shomin, age 50, P.O. Hessel, no children.

Husband: Pete Shomin, dead, see 9-20, a son on 9-20.
0-12-4 Louis Aw Ne Me Quong or Louis Cube, age 40, P.O. Hessel.
Wife: Name not given, dead.
0-12-4-1 Margaret Aw Ne Me Quong, age 20, P.O. Petoskey, single, lives with Blackbirds or Wah Be Min Ke, maybe this girl is enrolled at Petoskey look up, see on 24-26.

Information following from: Not Given.
1-12 PAY BAW ME SAY, dead.
Wife: Pay She Nay Ne Quay or Mrs. Shabway, age 110, P.O. Hessell.
1-12-1 Name not given, dead.
1-12-1-1 Joe Besoyea, age 28, P.O. Albany Island, 16 miles east of Hessell.
Wife: Mary Besoyea, a Canadian.
1-12-1-1-1 Eliza Besoyea, age 10.
1-12-1-1-2 Fred Besoyea, age 6.
1-12-1-1-3 Tillie Besoyea, age 5.
1-12-1-1-4 Ellen Besoyea, age 3.
1-12-1-1-5 Alex Besoyea, age 2, born July 6, 1908.
1-12-2 Name not given, dead.
1-12-3 Name not given, dead.

Gatesvill Mich June 6th

Dear Sir
In reply of your letter dated May 26th Just reached this morning my oldest girl Lizzie Besayeashe is going on 9 years 29th of September and Fredie Besayea is 7 years 4th May last month and Matilda Besayea is 6 years 13th of December and Ellen Besayea will be 4 years old 11th of September and I have another baby boy he will be a year old his name is Alex Lawrence will be 1 year old 6th of July. *Yours truly*
Joe Besoyea
Address to *Joe Besoyea Gatesvill*
C/o W. J. Johnston Camp Mich

Information following from: Pete Waw Say Ke Zhick 16-12, Pine.
2-12 WAW BE KE ZHICK, dead, children at Cackburn Island east of Drummond's Isle Canada.

Information following from: Not Given.
3-12 JOHN B CADOTTE, dead, wife and all children dead.
Wife: Name not given, dead.
3-12-1 Name not given, dead.
3-12-2 Charles Cadotte, dead.

Information following from: Joe La Pointe, Les Cheveaux, Drummond's Isle May 27.

4-12 O DO SKE NOW, dead.
Wife: Name not given, dead.
4-12-1 Name not given, dead.
4-12-1-1 Louisa Tuskenow, age 35, P.O. Drummond's Isle, single.
4-12-1-2 Eliza Tuskenow, age 26, wife of Joe La Pointe 9-8.
4-12-1-3 James Tuskenow, age 24, single.
4-12-2 Name not given, dead, a girl.
Husband: Name not given, dead.
4-12-2-1 Theresa Mitchell, age 29, P.O. Pine River, no children.
Husband: Joe Mitchell or Mitchell Key Wan De Way, see 9-36, Traverse.

Information following from: Not Given.

5-12 AUGUSTUS CADOTTE, dead, children all dead.
Wife: Name not given, dead.
5-12-1 Name not given, dead.
5-12-2 Madeline Cadotte, dead.
5-12-2-1 Dufina, dead.

Information following from: Mary Cube, Mack Isle, April 12/09..

6-12 AW ME NE KE WAW BE or Joe Cube, dead.
Wife: Mary Cube or Mary Aw Me Ne Ke Waw Be, age 70, P.O. Hessel, Mich, see 19-3.
6-12-1 Joe Cube, age 40, P.O. St. Ignace, see 45-42, no children.
6-12-2 Dave Cube, age 38, P.O. Pine River St. Ignace, see 62-16.
6-12-3 Pete Cube, age 36, has one arm, single.
6-12-4 Mike Cube, age 20, P.O. Hessel, Mich, single.
6-12-5 Charlotte Steveson, age 30, P.O. Cedarville.
Husband: ________ Stevenson, white.
6-12-5-1 Nellie Stevenson, age 10, twin, by Stevenson's 1st wife, see 0-12.
6-12-5-2 Russell Stevenson, age 9, by Stevenson's 1st wife, see 0-12.
6-12-5-3 Mary Jane Stevenson, age 10, twin, by Stevenson's 1st wife, see 0-12.
6-12-6 Ellen Obey, age 44, P.O. Pine River.
Husband: ________ Obey, white.
6-12-6-1 Mary Obey, age 15.
6-12-6-2 Harry Obey, age 12.
6-12-6-3 William Obey, age 7.
6-12-6-4 Virginia Obey, age 4.

6-12-6-5 Ellen Obey, born April 23/09 too late.
6-12-7 William Cube, age 46, P.O. Pine River, single.
6-12-8 Charles Louis, age 45, see 11-15, child by 1st husband who was a Canadian.
6-12-9 James Cube, age 19, P.O. Pine River.

Information following from: Not Given.
7-12 O MAY YAW BAW NO QUAY, dead, mother of 10-12.
7-12-1 White Loon, oldest son, see 32-8, on roll by himself, P.O. Sugar Island.
Note: Chiefs know of no other heirs.

Information following from: Not Given.
8-12 MRS. HYACINTHE DOPHENA Jr. or MRS. JOSEPHONE DOPHINA or DUFFINA, age 69, P.O. Mackinaw City.
Husband: Name not given, dead.
8-12-1 Frank Duffina, Sr., age 52, P.O. Mackinaw City.
Wife: Lucy Duffina, age 50, nee Bennett.
8-12-1-1 Josie (Duffina) Oleson, age 24, P.O. Mackinaw City.
Husband: ________ Oleson, white, no children.
8-12-1-2 William Duffina, age 20, P.O. Mackinaw City.
8-12-1-3 Frank Duffina Jr., age 18, P.O. Mackinaw City.
8-12-1-4 Aggie Duffina, age 16.
8-12-1-5 Mary Duffina, age 14.
8-12-2 William Duffina, age 50, P.O. Mackinaw City.
Wife: Name not given, dead.
8-12-2-1 Pearl Duffina, age 9.
8-12-2-2 Emma Duffinw, age 4.
8-12-2-3 Mary Duffina, born May 1908.
8-12-3 Peter Duffina, age 42, P.O. Mackinaw City.
Wife: Margaret Duffina, age 44, see 3-6 for children.
8-12-4 Louis Duffina, age 30, P.O. Mackinaw City.
Wife: Louisa Duffina, age 20, nee Andrews, see 2-17.
8-12-4-1 Mary Duffina, age 4.
8-12-4-2 Emily Duffina, born March 18, 1907.

Information following from: Not Given.
10-12 WAY ZHE BUN A WAY, dead.
Wife: Name not given, dead.
10-12-1 Name not given, dead.
10-12-2 Stephen Bunaway, age 47, P.O. Pine River.
Wife: Madaline Bunaway, age 32, OK enroll, see 11-51 & 8-31, separated from Pete Shaw Waw Naw Se Gay 11-52.
10-12-2-1 Mary Ann Bunaway, age 2, same child as enrolled on 8-31 as Mary Shaw Waw Naw Se Gay Durant.

Information following from: Pete Waw Say Ke Zhick, Pine River.
11-12 PE TAW WAW NAW QUAW DO QUAY, dead, don't know where children are.

Information following from: Not Given.
12-12 MRS. FRANCIS DOPHENA, age 62, P.O. Cheboygan.
Husband: Francis Dophena.
12-12-1 Augustus Duffina, age 45, P.O. Cheboygan, single.
12-12-2 Samuel Duffina, age 42, died April 15, 1908.
Wife: Anna Duffina, white, P.O. Mackinaw City.
12-12-2-1 Joseph Duffina, age 7, P.O. Mackinaw City.
12-12-3 John Duffina, age 39, P.O. Cheboygan, single.
12-12-4 Josie Gouler, age 26, P.O. Cheboygan.
Husband: ______ Gouler, white.
12-12-4-1 Eddie Gouler, age 9.
12-12-4-2 Dora Gouler, age 8.
12-12-4-3 Henry Gouler, age 10.
12-12-5 Elizabeth Johnson, age 42, P.O. Brimley, Mich.
Husband: ________ Johnson, white.
12-12-6 Annie Kush, age 24, P.O. Cheboygan, twin 12-12-7.
Husband: ________ Kush, white.
12-12-6-1 Vina Kush, age 7.
12-12-6-2 Rosie Kush, age 2.
12-12-6-3 Nellie Kush, age 6 months.
12-12-7 Mary Duffina, age 24, P.O. Cheboygan, single, twin 12-12-6.
12-12-8 George Duffina, age 22, P.O. Cheboygan.
12-12-9 Ida Bourassa, age 20, P.O. Cheboygan.
Husband: Paddy Bourassa, age 28, see 7-31, Traverse.
12-12-9-1 Laura Bourassa, age 4.
12-12-9-2 Frank Bourassa, age 2.
12-12-9-3 George Bourassa, age 6 months.

June, Tuesday 8 1909
Cheboygan Mich

Dear sir I just received your Kind letter, and about my sister Elizabeth johnson when you came around to take the names. I give you her address as bay mills it yous to be bay mills but it is changed now. But I will give you the right address her address is Mrs. Elizabeth Lees Johnson, Brimley Mich.
From yours truly John Duffina

Information following from: Not Given.
13-12 MAY YAW WAW GE WON, dead, wife dead, Chiefs at Les Cheveaux do not know.

Information following from: Joe Mesawtego, Louis La Sage Inter. & Sosette Bodwaince, St. Ignace.
14-12 MARY A PERROW, dead, P.O. Mac Isle.

Information following from: Not Given.
15-12 MAW CHE O NAW, dead.
15-12-1 Solomon Cosley or Causley, age 50, P.O. Drummond Isle, see 23-3.

Information following from: Pete Waw Say Ke Zhick & Mike St. German, Pine River, May 19/09.
16-12 WAW SAY KE ZHICK or PETE WAW SAY KE ZHICK, age 64, P.O. Charles Pine River.
Wife: Name not given, dead.
16-12-1 Margaret Waw Say Ke Zhick, age 35, P.O. Pine River, single.
16-12-2 John Waw Say Ke Zhick, age 24, P.O. Pine River.
Wife: Mary Waw Say Ke Zhick, age 17, see 11-15.
16-12-2-1 George Waw Say Ke Zhick, age 2.
16-12-2-2 William Waw Say Ke Zhick, born January/09 too late.
16-12-3 Pete Waw Say Ke Zhick Jr., age 22, P.O. Pine River, single.
16-12-4 James Waw Say Ke Zhick, age 18.
16-12-5 Moses Waw Say Ke Zhick, age 16.

Information following from: Joe Mesawtego, Pine River.
17-12 NOTE NO KUNG, dead.
Wife: Martha Cloud, see 1-17, children all dead.

Information following from: Peter Smith, Drummonds, May 27.
18-12 PE TAW BE NO QUAY, dead, a sister of Mrs. Peter Smith 8-15, no heirs.

Information following from: Not Given.
19-12 NE BE NAW SHE NO QUAY, acannot trace this family.

Information following from: Joe Mesawtego, Joe Smith & letter from Joe Pond 8/9/09, St. Ignace, June 20/09.
20-12 JOSET POND, or (nee) JOSIE PERRAULT, dead.
20-12-1 Neal Pond, dead.
20-12-2 Josephine Pond, dead.
20-12-3 Jane (Pond) Bouchard, age 50, P.O. St. Ignace.
Husband: Oliver Bouchard, dead.
20-12-4 Sophia (Pond), age 27, P.O. St. Ignace.
Husband: Name not given, dead.

20-12-5 Joe Pond, age 42, P.O. St. Ignace, see 65-16.
20-12-6 Edward Pond, age 52, P.O. St. Ignace, no children.

Information following from: Harriet Belonga, a granddaughter, Pine River.
21-12 PAY ME SAW DUNG, dead, grandfather of Harriet Belonga 11-15.
Wife: Name not given, dead.
21-12-1 Name not given, wife of 11-15, see 11-15 for children.

Information following from: Not Given.
22-12 WAW SAY KE ZHICK GO QUAY
Husband: Name not given, dead.
22-12-1 Salmond, P.O. Stonington, Mich.

Information following from: Not Given.
23-12 KE NUC & Brother

Information following from: Not Given.
24-12 KE WAY TE NO QUAY.

Information following from: Not Given.
25-12 MRS. PHILLIMAN FARTAN, age 69, P.O. Cross Village.
Husband: John Fartan, white.
25-12-1 Kate Redmond, age 49, P.O. Cross Village.
25-12-1-1 Henry Redmond, adopted.
25-12-2 Cecilia Owen, age 47, P.O. Cross Village, has 9 children.
25-12-3 John Fartan, dead, one child Henry who lives with 25-12-1 above.
25-12-4 Philip Fartan, age 38, P.O. Cross Village, no children.
25-12-5 Josephine Meyers, age 37, P.O. Arian, Washington State, no children.
25-12-6 Eliza Baddean, age 35, P.O. Detroit, Mich place called 3 flats, has 2 children.
25-12-7 Myra Campbell, age 28, P.O. Cross Village, has one child a boy.
25-12-8 Lottie Perkins, age 26, P.O. Lake Odessa, has 5 children.
25-12-9 Lenora Drake, age 25, P.O. Cross Village, no children.
25-12-10 Victoria Kellar, age 23, no children.
Note: See report on sheet 6-37. This family is of very little Indian blood. I am of opinion that they were erroneously enroled as Indians in 1870. Mrs. Philliman Fartan's father was French & her mother part Indian according to her own statement. Horace B. Durant Spl. Agt. Report: In as much as her name is on the 1870 roll. I am of opinion that she might with propriety be enrolled now, but believe that, injustice to the full blood Indians, her children should not be enrolled. Horace B. Durant Spl Agt Oct 19/08 Cross Village, Mich.

November 11, 1908, Cheboygan, Mich, The above report applies with equal force to numerous families & persons of the Macinac Band, whose sheets have been marked "F." Horace B. Durant Spl Agt. Sent (copy) to Mrs. Catharine Kellar, Cross Village, Mich, January 20/09 Durant.

(Information Returned on reverse of form received from Mrs. Catharine Keller.)

The Children of Cecelia Owens are.

Harvey Owens	*29 age*
Amanda Holmes	*27 "*
John Owens	*24*
James Owens	*23*
Eugene Owens	*22*
Catharine Keller	*20*
Cecelia Wilsey	*18*
Minnie Owen	*15*
Charley Owen	*5*

The Children of Catharine Keller are Agnes 3 years, James 1 year, Henry 6 moths, are dead.

Children of Amanda Holmes are.

Dewey Holmes	*10 years old*
Mildred "	*7 " "*
Hazel "	*5 " "*
George "	*3 " "*
Henry "	*3 months old*

Adress all to Cross Village Mich.

Cross Village Mich
June 1-1909

Horace B Durant,

Dear sir: Here are the names.

Henry Readmond age 24
Katherine Parker age 14
Mary Fertia age 8
John Campbell age 9

Yours Respectfully
Mrs. Kate Readmond

Lake Odessa Mich
June 22 1909

Mr. H. Durant
Petoskey, Mich

Dear Sir

Has you advertised that Letter I wrote to you and that the paper stated I was to draw $12.250 dollars I would like to Have the money now has every Body around L. O. knows now I am the only one from C. V. I dident know I had eny Indian Blood has mother always talked agin the Indians so she must be foolish. If we were Indians why didn't she raise us that way.
I wont If to come By express an oblige the children name is
Philip B. Perkins
Cecil J. Perkins
Vera A. "
Harold R. "
I am sorry this come out like this to disgrace us and children.
Yours truly
Lottie Perkins

Pages 13 & 14
Pine River Band
Chief MRS. AGATHA BIDDLE

Information following from: Not Given.
1-13 MRS. AGATHA BIDDLE, dead.
1-13-1 Sarah (Biddle) Durfee, age 80, P.O. St. Ignace.
1-13-1-1 Ed Biddle Durfee, age 43, P.O. Detroit.
1-13-1-2 Sophia Biddle Bath, age 49, P.O. St. Ignace, married to a bookkeeper in St. Ignace.
1-13-1-2-1 Creighton Bath, age 20.
1-13-1-2-2 Agatha Bath, age 18.
1-13-1-2-3 Clara Bath, age 15.
1-13-1-2-4 William Bath, age 13.
1-13-2 John Biddle, dead.
1-13-2-1 Sophia A. Biddle.
1-13-2-2 Agatha McNaughton, see 30-13.
1-13-2-3 Grace Rankin.

1-13-3 Others, dead.

St. Ignace June 30th 1909

Horace B. Durant
Sir,
Why I did not go to see you when here last write this is the third time that a roll has been taken. So I did not have any faith in the work I will say, as sone no remarke thet the are waiting for then to all diefor so many have gone. Enclose you will find a brother who is dead but three of his children are living.
Yours respectfully
Sarah Biddle Durfee

Information following from: Not Given.

2-13 MRS. LOUIS MAISH TANN, dead.

2-13-1 Christian St. Peter, age 70, P.O. Harbor Springs, see 43-28.

2-13-2 Mary Laquea, age 52, Mackinaw City,

Husband: Amab Laquea, white.

2-13-2-1 George Laquea, age 34, U.S.Army in Calif., single.

2-13-2-2 Ida Parker, age 32, P.O Grand Rapids c/o GR & I Ry.

Husband: Lynn Parker, white.

2-13-2-2-1 Reba Parker, age 7.

2-13-2-2-2 Rena Parker, age 5.

2-13-2-2-3 Earl Parker, age 3.

2-13-2-2-4 Infant Parker, born June 1908.

2-13-2-3 Fred Laquea, age 30, P.O. Ionia, Mich., single.

2-13-2-4 Amab Laquea, age 28, P.O. Mackinaw City, single.

2-13-2-5 Barney Laquea, age 26, P.O. Mackinaw City.

Wife: Ruth Laquea, age 26, see 2-20.

2-13-2-5-1 Ruth Laquea, born May 1908.

2-13-2-6 Joseph Laquea, age 24, P.O. Mackinaw City, single.

2-13-2-7 Ruben Laquea, age 22, P.O. Mackinaw City.

2-13-2-8 William Laquea, age 20, P.O. Mackinaw City.

2-13-2-9 Chester Laquea, age 17, P.O. Mackinaw City.

2-13-3 John Mastaw, age 52, P.O. Mackinaw City.

Wife: name not given, dead.

2-13-3-1 Christine Peterson, age 36, P.O. Detroit, Mich.

Husband: Name not given, white.

2-13-3-1-1 Louis Peterson, age 4.

2-13-3-1-2 ______ Peterson, age 3.

2-13-3-2 Louis Mastaw, age 22, P.O. Harbor Springs, single.

2-13-4 Joseph Mastaw, age 50, P.O. Mackinaw City, see 30-28.

2-13-5 Tillie Kintcel Sr., age 48, P.O. Mackinaw City.

Husband: Alford Kintcel, white.

2-13-5-1 Fred Kintcel, age 24, P.O. Mackinaw City.

2-13-5-2 Henry Kintcel, age 22, P.O. Mackinaw City.

2-13-5-3 Tillie Kintcel Jr., age 20, P.O. Mackinaw City.

2-13-6 Margaret Terrient.

Husband: Charles Terrient, see 54-14 and 15-13.

Information following from: Not Given.

3-13 MRS. ANDREW MORAW or MOREAU, dead.

Husband: Andrew Moraw, not enrolled.

3-13-1 Oliver Moreau, age 44, P.O. Cheboygan.

Wife: Name not given, white.

3-13-1-1 Mary Gilland, age 18, no children.

3-13-1-2 Rosie Moreau, age 16.

3-13-1-3 George Moreau, age 12.
3-13-1-4 William Moreau, age 10.
3-13-1-5 Henry Moreau, age 8.
3-13-1-6 Minnie Moreau, age 2.

3-13-2 Maggie Davis, age 40, P.O. 394 Grand Ave. E. Lincoln St. Portland, Ore.
Husband: Name not given, white.
3-13-2-1 Minnie Schelien, age 21, P.O. Cheboygan, has 2 children names not given.
3-13-2-2 George Davis, age 19, P.O. Cheboygan.
3-13-2-3 Emma Davis, age 14, P.O. Portland.
3-13-2-4 Ethel Davis, age 9, P.O. Portland.

3-13-3 Angeline Demorrow, P.O. Grace Harbor.

3-13-4 Name not given, dead.
Wife: Name not given, dead.
3-13-4-1 William Moreau, age 34, P.O. Cheboygan, single.

Cheboygan Mich.
May 30, 1909

Mr. Horace B. Durant
Petoskey Mich.
Dear Sir in regards to your request of the adress of my sister and her children. Mrs Maggie Davis born feb 26, 1868 394 Grand ave E lincoln St. Portland Oregon.
Her oldest Daughter Mrs. Minnie E. Schelien Cheboygan Mich Born april 29 1887.
Son Mr. Geo. E. Thompson Cheboygan Mich Born March 23 1889.
Tow youngest children with their mother
Emma Blando Born Dec 7, 1894.
Ethel Blando Born July 21, 1899 and Oblige your truly.
Mr. Olive Morrow Cheboygan Mich

Information following from: Not Given.

4-13 MRS. EDWARD LASLEY, dead.
4-13-1 Julia Plant, age 60, P.O. Mackinaw City or Cross Village.
Husband: Name not given, white.
4-13-1-1 James Plant, age 35, P.O. Mackinaw City.
4-13-1-2 Ed Plant, age 34, died May 6/08.
4-13-1-3 Kate Plant, age 25, P.O. Cross Village.
4-13-1-4 Grace Belonghay, age 36, P.O. Mackinaw Island.
Husband: Clement Belonghay, age 48, P.O. Mackinaw Island, see 26-13.
4-13-1-4-1 Joe Belonghay, age 10.
4-13-1-4-2 Clement Belonghay, age 8.
4-13-1-4-3 Barbara Belonghay, age 7.

4-13-1-4-4 Arthur Belonghay, age 4.
4-13-1-5 Mary Brooks, age 28, P.O. Sturgeon Bay.
Husband: Name not given, white.
4-13-1-5-1 Sadie Brooks, age 6.
4-13-1-5-2 Minnie Brooks, age 2.
4-13-1-5-3 Susie Brooks, age 1.
4-13-1-6 John Plant, age 30, P.O. Mackinaw City.
Wife: Grace Margaret Plant, age 25, Traverse, see 3-32 and 39-13.
4-13-1-6-1 George Plant, age 6.
4-13-1-6-2 Josephine Plant, age 2.
4-13-1-7 Louis Plant, age 23, P.O. Cross Village.
4-13-1-8 Rosie Plant, age 21, P.O. Cross Village.
4-13-1-9 Julia Plant, age 19, P.O. Cross Village.
4-13-2 Louis Lasley, age 58, P.O. Cross Village.
Wife: Louisa Lasley, age 54, P.O. Cross Village, daughter of Louis Robinson of Mackinaw Band, Traverse.
4-13-2-1 Frank Lasley, age 36, P.O. Cross Village.
Wife: Cynthia (Shomin) Lasley, see 37-20.
4-13-2-2 Henry Lesley, age 29, P.O. Cross Village.
Wife: Name not given, white.
4-13-2-2-1 Leo Lesley, age 7.
4-13-2-2-2 Lyda Lesley, age 5.
4-13-2-2-3 Vina Lesley, age 3.
4-13-2-2-4 Margaret Lesley, born March 1908, 2nd roll.
4-13-2-3 Sam Lesley Jr., age 23, P.O. Cross Village, single, known as Ed Lasley, Haskel Institute Lawrence, Ks.
4-13-2-4 Albert Lesley, age 21, P.O. Cross Village.
4-13-2-5 William Lesley, age 19. P.O. Cross Village.
4-13-2-6 Isadore Lesley, age 12.
4-13-2-7 John Lesley, age 16, P.O. Carlisle School, Pa.
4-13-2-8 Ida Lesley, age 9.
4-13-3 Samuel Lesley Sr., age 43, P.O. Elk Rapids.
Wife: Name not given, white, separated, no children.
4-13-4 John Lesley, age 35, P.O. Cross Village, single.

Sturgeon Bay Mich 1909 May 31

Dear Sar
Mrs Mary Brooks age 28
Sadie age 6 year old
Minnie age 2 year old
Susie 2 year old
Mrs Mary Brook

Information following from: Not Given.

5-13 MRS. JOSEPH KARROW, Indians call it (Crow) that's the corruption in English Karrow, said to be dead but do not know.

Information following from: Not Given.

6-13 MRS. CHARLES BENNETT, age 73, P.O. Mackinaw City.
Husband: Charles Bennett, white.
6-13-1 Lucy Duffina, age 50, see 8-12.
6-13-2 Jane Onenagos, age 45, P.O. Cross Village, see 6-20.
6-13-3 Therese Cadron, age 40, P.O. Mackinaw Island.
Husband: Alford Cadron, age 43, see 25-13.
6-13-3-1 Sophia Cadron, age 18.
6-13-3-2 Charles Cadron, age 8.
6-13-3-3 Margaret Cadron, age 6.
6-13-4 Eliza Bennett, age 27, single, died March 17, 1907.

Information following from: Not Given.

7-13 MRS. WILLIAM KARROW or CAROW, age 80, P.O. Cheboygan.
7-13-1 Isabel Carow.
Husband: Name not given, white.
7-13-1-1 Mary Derry, age 35, P.O. Cheboygan.
Husband: _______ Derry, white.
7-13-1-1-1 Herbert Derry, age 18.
7-13-1-1-2 Cora Derry, age 14.
7-13-1-1-3 George Derry, age 13.
7-13-1-1-4 Tom Derry, age 10.
7-13-1-1-5 Russell Derry, age 8.
7-13-1-1-6 Iabelle Derry, age 4.
7-13-1-1-7 Colonel Derry, age 6.
7-13-1-1-8 John Derry, born September/07.
7-13-1-2 Julia Carow, age 39, P.O. Cheboygan
7-13-1-2-1 William Carow, age 26.
7-13-1-2-2 Gertie Carow, age 20.
7-13-2 Andrew Karrow or Carow, age 56, P.O. Cheboygan, keeps barber shop.
Wife: Name not given, white.
7-13-2-1 Mary Lishman, age 22.
Husband: _______ Lishmsn, white.
7-13-2-1-1 William Lishman, age 4.
7-13-2-1-2 Mary Lishman, age 2.
7-13-2-1-3 John Lishman, born July 11/08.
7-13-2-2 William Carow, age 18.
7-13-2-3 Anthony Carow, age 15.
7-13-3 Madelien Carow.
Husband: Charles Chevalier, Canadian Indian.
7-13-3-1 Charles Cavalier Jr., age 32, P.O. Cheboygan.

7-13-4 Jane Jarvis, age 39, P.O. Cheboygan.
Husband: ________ Jarvis, white.
7-13-4-1 Mary Jarvis Young, age 22.
7-13-4-2 Lizzie Jarvis, age 18.
7-13-4-3 Eva Jarvis, age 13.
7-13-4-4 Bernie Jarvis, age 10.
7-13-4-5 William Jarvis, age 4.
7-13-4-6 Joseph Jarvis, born April 1, 1908, off.

May 27/09

Mr. Horace B. Durant
Special U,S, Indian Agt.
Dear Sir
You will find All the names of my family inclosed.
Herbert Derry Born June 22/1890 age 19
Cora Derry Born Oct 28 1894 Age 15
George Derry Born May 14/1895 Age 14
William Tom Derry Born Dec 12/1897 Age 11
Russell Derry Born Jan 15/1900 Age 9
Curnal Derry Born Feb 15/1902 Age 7
Isabell Derry Born Feb 9 1904 Age 5
John Derry Born Sept 3 1907 Age 2
Mrs Mary Derry mother Age 35
We Remain Yours Very Respt
Mrs Mary Derry
Cheboygan, Mich

Information following from: Not Given.
8-13 MRS. LOUIS CADOTTE, dead.
Husband 1st : ________ Lavake, dead.
Husband 2nd: Louis Cadotte, dead.
8-13-1 Xavier Lavake, age 80, P.O. Manistee, cannot find this man Durant.
8-13-2 Rosalie Lozou or Lalotte, dead.
Husband: Name not given, dead.
8-13-2-1 Lizzie La Pine, age 40, P.O. Mac Isle, has three children names not given.
Husband: John La Pine.
8-13-2-2 Minnie Lalotte, dead.
8-13-3 Mary Lalone Deloria, age 67, P.O. Mac Isle.
Husband: ________ Lalone, dead.
8-13-3-1 Charles A. Lalone, age 47, P.O. Mac. Isle (Boise Blanc), single.
8-13-3-2 Mary Lalone, age 38, P.O. Chicago, cannot locate her

Durant.

8-13-4 Louis Cadotte, dead.

Wife: Name not given, dead.

8-13-4-1 Sophia Andres, dead.

Husband: Alex Andres, P.O. Mac. Isle Bois Blanc Isle see 2-17.

8-13-4-1-1 Lucy Andres, age 8.

8-13-4-1-2 Josephine, age 11.

8-13-5 Edward Cadotte, age 58, Mac. Isle (Bloise Blanc).

Wife: Sophia Cadotte, nee Levake, see 16-15.

8-13-5-1 Louise Cadotte, age 12.

8-13-5-2 James Cadotte, age 7.

8-13-5-3 Frank Cadotte, age 5.

8-13-5-4 Fred Cadotte, age 3.

8-13-5-5 Mary Cadotte, Born July 25, 1907.

8-13-6 Frank Cadotte, dead, no children.

Information following from: Jackson Chapman.

9-13 MRS. ALICE CUSHWAY, dead.

Husband: John B. Cushway, dead.

9-13-1 Ganet Cushway, said to be in Chicago, has 2 children in Chicago, but do not know address Durant Spl Agt.

9-13-2 (Daughter) Cushway, said to be in Chicago, but do not know her name or address.

May 28th 1909

Well I have receive your letter and I must tell you that my little girls there is one July Andrews She is Eight 8 years of age and Josie Andrews She is Eleven 11 years of age and the oldest one died at Eleven years of age it now one year and a half Since She died.

From Alex Andrews

Mackinac Island Mich

To Mr. Horace B. Durant

Special U.S. Indian agent Per B.

Information following from: Not Given.

10-13 MRS. HENRY KARROW or CAROW

Husband 1st: Henry Karrow, dead.

Husband 2nd: Henry Hudson, white.

10-13-1 (Daughter) Carow, dead.

Husband: _______ Fisher.

10-13-1-1 Maria Fisher Lablanc, P.O. Cheboygan 537 First St.

10-13-1-1-1 Celia Lablanc Keeton, age 20.

10-13-1-1-2 Marie Lablanc, age 19.

10-13-1-1-3 Eugene Lablanc, age 17.
10-13-1-1-4 Benjamin Lablanc, age 15.
10-13-1-1-5 Maggie Lablanc, age 13.
10-13-1-1-6 Samuel Lablanc, age 11.
10-13-1-1-7 Evaline Lablanc, age 9.
10-13-1-1-8 Stanley Lablanc, age 8.
10-13-1-1-9 Iven Lablanc, age 6.
10-13-1-1-10 Garnet Lablanc, age 4.
10-13-1-1-11 Donald Lablanc, age 2.
10-13-1-2 Ellen Fisher, age 36, P.O. Deer River, Minn Box 141.
10-13-1-3 George Fisher, age 38, P.O. Chebygan.
10-13-1-4 John Fisher, age 34, P.O. Cheboygan.
10-13-1-5 Joe Fisher, age 32, P.O. Cheboygan.
10-13-1-6 Jum Fisher, age 25, P.O. Cheboygan.
10-13-1-7 Lina Fisher Hudson, age 30, P.O. Cheboygan.
10-13-2 Angeline McCarty, age 43, P.O. Cleveland, Ohio 1418 W. 32nd St..
Husband: _______ McCarty, white.
10-13-2-1 Alex McCarty, age 27.
10-13-2-2 Alice E. McCarty, age 24.
10-13-3 Napole or Hudson, age 54, P.O. Cheboygan.
Wife: Name not given, white.
10-13-3-1 Lizzie Golden, age 29, P.O. Cheboygan.
Husband: ________ Golden, white.
10-13-3-1-1 Maggie Golden, age 3.
10-13-3-1-2 Harry Golden, born August 1908. Off.
10-13-3-2 Mary Bellow, age 27, P.O. Cheboygan.
Husband: ________ Bellow, white.
10-13-3-2-1 Pearl Bellow, age 3.
10-13-3-2-2 Luke Bellow, age 2.
10-13-3-3 Bertie Hudson, age 25, P.O. Cheboygan.
10-13-3-4 Fred Hudson, age 24, P.O.Cheboygan.
10-13-3-5 Emma Hudson, age 22, P.O. Cheboygan.
10-13-3-6 Lilly Kanousky, age 19.
Husband: _______ Kanousky, white.
10-13-3-6-1 Name not given, born October/08 off.
10-13-3-7 Clyde Hudson, age 15, P.O. Cheboygan.
10-13-3-8 Susie Hudson, age 13, P.O. Cheboygan.
10-13-3-9 Jessie Hudson, age 9.
10-13-3-10 Tom Hudson, age 5.

Cheboygan Mich June 30 1909
Mr. Horace B. Durant
Dear Sir please find enclose the names of my Brothers & Sisters as follow

Mr George Fisher age38 his address Cheboygan Mich.
Miss Ella Fisher " 36 Dear River Minnisota Box 141
Mr Johnie Fisher age 34
Mr Josie Fisher " 32
Mrs Linie Hudson age 30
Mrs Jimmie Fisher age 25
The four last one on this paper I don't know there addresses this is all I can inform you about them your.

Respeckfully Mrs Marie Fisher LaBlanc 537 first St Cheboygan, Mich

Department of the Interior,
United States Indian Service,

June 28/09

Dear Madam:

Please give me the names of your brothers and sisters, if any, their ages and addresses.

Very respectfully
HORACE B. DURANT
Special U.S. Indian Agent

Donald LaBlanc age 3 years and as for Angeline McCarthy I can~~t~~ give ~~I~~ her address But I cant tell you the ages of ~~your~~ her children her address is 1418 W. 32 St Cleveland Ohio. I have a Daughter Celia Ahe is married her name now is Mrs. Celia Keaton her address is 5109 Rooselvet St Duluth Minn.
I remaine ~~as~~
Mrs Maria Fisher Lablanc Cheboygan Mich First St 537.

Cheboygan Mich May 31 1909
Horace B. Durant
Special U.S. Indian Agent
Dear Sir I read your letter please find enclose the following names of my family.

Miss Marie LaBlanc		*age 20 years old*	
Mr Eugene	"	*age 18*	" "
" *Benjamin LaBlanc*	"	*16*	
Maggie	"	*14*	
Samuel	"	*12*	
Eveline	"	*10*	
Stanley	*LaBlanc*	*9*	
Iven	"	*7*	
Garnet	"	*5*	
Donald	*LaBlanc*	*3*	

Cleveland June 7/09

Mr Horace B. Durant

Dear Sir your Letter at hand in Regards about our a yes my age is 44 years and my son Alexander was 27 years the Seventh of last November and my Daughter Alice Emily was 25 years the first of last March.
Hoping to Hear from you Soon

I Remain Yours Truly
Angeline McCarthy
C/o 1418 W. 32 St Cleveland, O.

Information following from: Not Given.
11-13 MRS IGNATIUS PELOTTE, dead.
11-13-1 Eliz Pellotte, dead.
Husband: Charles Fountain, dead.
11-13-1-1 Ellen Fountain, dead.
Husband: ______ Smith, P.O Baltimore, Md.
11-13-2 Agatha Fountain, dead.
Husband: James McGulphin, P.O. Sault Ste. Marie.
11-13-2-1 Perry McGulphin, P.O. Mack Isle, lives with Mrs. Eliz. McGulphin grandmother.
11-13-2-2 Catharine McGulphin, age 18, P.O. Mack Isle, lives with Mrs. Eliz. McGulphin grandmother.
11-13-2-3 Charles McGulphin, P.O. Mack Isle, lives with Mrs. Eliz. McGulphin grandmother.
11-13-3 Rose Fountain, dead.
Husband: _____ Simmons, dead.
11-13-3-1 George Simmons, age 24, P.O. St. Ignace.
11-13-3-2 Charles Simmons, age 22.
11-13-2 Rose Pellotte, dead.
Husband: Jack Gallagher, white.
11-13-2-1 Ivy Andres, age 25, P.O. Les Cheveaux.
Husband: John Andres, age 34, see 9-17.
11-13-4 Mary Pellotte, dead, no heirs.
11-13-5 Christine Pellotte, dead.
Husband: Sam Decatur, white.
11-13-5-1 Lottie Decatur, age 32, P.O. Mack Isle, single.
11-13-5-2 Grace Cadron, age 29, P.O. Mack Isle.
Husband: John Cadron, age 52, P.O. Mack Isle.
11-13-5-2-1 Edward Cadron, age 9.
11-13-5-2-2 Rose Cadron, age 8.
11-13-5-2-3 Christina Cadron, age 6.
11-13-5-2-4 Mary Cadron, age 4.
11-13-5-2-5 Wilfred Cadron, age 2, born January 1, 1907 1st roll.
11-13-5-3 Edward Boyles, age 22, P.O. Cuba.

11-13-5-4 Reben Boyles, age 19, P.O. Cheboygan, single.
11-13-6 Harriet Chapman, dead.
Husband: Levi Chapman, see 30-13
11-13-7 Angeline La Pin, dead.
Husband: Isaac La Pin, dead.
11-13-7-1 (Daughter) La Pin, dead.
Husband: _______ Moore, white.
11-13-7-1-1 Mamie Moore, age 10, P.O. Cheboygan.

Information following from: Paul Lancour, Mack Isle, April 10/09.
12-13 MRS. SARAH LALOTTE or LOZON, now Sarah Lancour, age 46, see 51-14.
12-13-1 Louisa Lalotte Parper, age 45, P.O. Cheboygan, a sister of the head of the family.
12-13-1-1 Alex Parper, age 22.
12-13-1-2 Olive Parper, age 20.
12-13-1-3 Josie Parper, age 16.
12-13-1-4 Charles Parper, age 14.
12-13-1-5 Lizzie Parper, age 12.
12-13-2 Charles Lalotte or Charles Lozon, age 58, P.O. St. Ignace, see 6-15, a brother of the head of the family.

Dear Sir
I rec'd the letter and I write to let you know my age and family age.
Mrs. Louisa Parper age 46 years
Alex Parper age 23 years
Olive Parper age 21 years
Josie Parper age 17 years
Charles Parper age 15 years
Lizzie Parper age 13 years
Your truly
Mrs. Louisa parper

Information following from: Isabelle Anderson, Mackanaw City 3 miles East & South, April 6/09.
13-13 MRS. FRANCIS RESTOOL, dead.
Husband: Frank Restool, white, living Mackinaw City.
13-13-1 Isabelle Anderson, age 48, P.O. Mackinaw City, no children.
Husband: Niles Anderson, white.
13-13-2 Tom Restool, died when young, no heirs.
13-13-3 Charles Restool, died when young, no heirs.
13-13-4 Maggie Dunwald, age 38, P.O. Petoskey, Mich, husband white, no children.
13-13-5 Jane Morris, age 35, P.O. Petoskey.
Husband: Milton Morris, white.

13-13-5-1 Gertie Morris.
13-13-5-2 Maggie Morris.
13-13-6 Lizzie Restool, age 32, P.O. Petoskey, single.
13-13-7 Frank Restool, age 30, P.O. Sault Ste.Marie, U.S. Army Fort Brady, single.

Information following from: Joseph Fountain, Mack Isle, June 19/09.
14-13 MRS. JOSEPH FOUNTAIN, dead.
14-13-1 Name not given, see 20-17.
14-13-2 Agatha Martin, dead.
Husband: Frank martin, dead, see 38-15.
14-13-2-1 Joe Martin, P.O. Mac Isle, see 21-13.
14-13-2-2 Frank Martin, P.O. Mac Isle, see 21-13.
14-13-2-3 Agatha Martin Parrow, P.O. Mac Isle, see 21-13.
14-13-2-4 Mary Martin Bezinaw, P.O. Bois Blanc Isle, see 21-13
14-13-3 Jane Fountain, dead, no children.
14-13-4 Joseph Fountain, age 67, P.O. St. Helena Isld. Gros Cap Mich.
Wife: Christine Fountain, nee Lazon, age 68.
14-13-4-1 Eugene Fountain, age 36, P.O. St. Helena Island.
Wife: _______ Gendreau, white.
14-13-4-1-1 William Fountain, age 10.
14-13-4-1-2 Joe Fountain, age 8.
14-13-4-1-3 John Fountain, age 6.
14-13-4-1-4 Mary Rosie, age 2.
14-13-4-1-5 Phoebe, born February/09.
14-13-4-2 Mary Jane Fountain, age 31, single.

Information following from: Not Given.
15-13 MRS FRANCIS JOHNSTON, age 80, P.O. Mackinaw City.
Husband: Francis Johnston, white.
15-13-1 Mary Johnston.
Husband: Charles Terrient, age 62, see 54-14, Mary was his 1st wife and for his 2nd see 2-13.
15-13-1-1 Eliza Terrient Donner, age 38, P.O. Mackinaw City.
Husband: _______ Donner, white.
15-13-1-1-1 Mary Donner, age 20, P.O. Mackinaw City.
15-13-1-1-2 Alex Donner, age 18.
15-13-1-1-3 Harriet Donner, age 12.
15-13-1-1-4 Fred Donner, age 8.
15-13-2 Julia Johnston, dead.
Husband: Name not given, dead.
15-13-2-1 Frank Cadotte, age 39, P.O. Minnesota, single,

cannot locate him Durant.

Information following from: D. L. Hudson, Cheboygan, Jan 5/09, supported by affidavits as to identity.

16-13 MRS. CATHARINE HUDSON, dead, her children, a sister of William Andrews, Sr. 2 –17 and a sister-in-law of Mrs. John Andrews 16-17.

16-13-1 Andrew Hudson, age 58, P.O. Cheboygan.
Wife: Name not given, white.
16-13-1-1 David Hudson, age 26, P.O. Cheboygan, single.
16-13-1-2 Catharine McCauley, age 33, P.O. Cheboygan, husband white, no children.
16-13-1-3 Fred E. Hudson, age 24, P.O. Cheboygan.

16-13-2 George Hudson, dead.
16-13-2-1 Charles T. Hudson #2, age 27, P.O. Cheboygan.
Wife: Name not given, white.
16-13-2-1-1 Bertha Hudson, age 6.
16-13-2-2 Fred G. Hudson, age 25, P.O. Tower.
Wife: Name not given, white.
16-13-2-2-1 Minie Hudson, age 5.

16-13-3 Charles Theodore Hudson #1, age 52, P.O. Cheboygan.
Wife: Name not given, white.
16-13-3-1 Joseph Hudson, age 20.
16-13-3-2 Edith Hudson, age 18.
16-13-3-3 Mary Hudson, age 16.
16-13-3-4 Rachel Hudson, age 14.
16-13-3-5 Russel Hudson, age 12.
16-13-3-6 Maggie Hudson, age 8.
16-13-3-7 Madeline Hudson, age 6.
16-13-3-8 Isabelle Hudson, age 4.
16-13-3-9 Julius Hudson, age 2.

16-13-4 D. L. Hudson, age 50, P.O. Aloha.
Wife: Name not given, white.
16-13-4-1 Grace M. Hudson, age 24, single, P.O. Aloha.
16-13-4-2 George Hudson, age 22.
16-13-4-3 Jerome F. Hudson, age 17.
16-13-4-4 Frank B. Hudson, age 14.
16-13-4-5 Josephine C. Hudson, age 12.
16-13-4-6 Agnes S. Hudson, age 10.
16-13-4-7 Lillian G. Hudson, age 9.
16-13-4-8 William D. Hudson, age 6.
16-13-4-9 Andrew J. Hudson, born April/08.

16-13-5 Emily E. Jewett, dead.
Husband: Name not given, white.
16-13-5-1 Blanche Whitney, age 23, husband white, P.O.

Cheboygan.
16-13-5-2 Mamie Byers, age 21, husband white, P.O. Cheboygan.
16-13-5-3 Violet Jewett, age 19.
16-13-5-4 Ernest Jewett, age 17.
16-13-5-5 Addie Jewett, age 15.
16-13-5-6 Bert Jewett, age 14.
16-13-5-7 Emma Jewett, age 12.
16-13-5-8 Ella Jewett, age 10.
16-13-5-9 William Jewett, age 8.

16-13-6 Jennie Lincoln, dead.
Husband: Name not given, white.
16-13-6-1 William J. Lincoln, age 24, P.O. Cheboygan.
16-13-6-2 Gertrude Beeman, age 22, P.O. Frederick, Mich.
16-13-6-3 Ella Lincoln, age 19, P.O. Cheboygan.
16-13-6-4 Leonard Lincoln, age 16, P.O. Cheboygan.

16-13-7 Julius Hudson, age 43, P.O. Cheboygan.
Wife: Name not given, white.
16-13-7-1 Charlotte C. Hudson, age 16.
16-13-7-2 Susan A. Hudson, age 13.
16-13-7-3 Albert J. Hudson, age 11.
16-13-7-4 Rosie C. Hudson, age 9.
16-13-7-5 Myrtle J. Hudson, age 5.

Report: The head of this family was living in Cheboygan in 1870, but for some reason was <u>not</u> enrolled as <u>was</u> her sister & brother. They show no Indian blood. HBDurant Spl. Ind. Agt., St. Ignace January 5/09. Her half bro. Thos Ward #28/p11, is also on the roll.

Further Report: D. L. Hudson and brother brought Francis Graham in for purpose of him making affidavit to facts to prove his claim, but upon being questioned by me Graham refused to swear that Hudson's mother was of Indian blood or that she was a sister of William Andrews as stated at the beginning of this sheet. Horace B. Durant, St. Ignace January 6/09.

State of Michigan,

–SS–

County of Cheboygan.

_______*Alfred Roberge*_______, being duly sworn, deposes and says that he is a resident of the ___*City*___ of ____*Cheboygan*____, County ~~and~~ *of* Cheboygan and State of Michigan; and that he has so resided for *forty-five* years last past; that during her lifetime *he was* ~~they were~~ personally acquainted with Catherine Hudson, now deceased; and that ~~they were~~ *he was* personally acquaited with Margaret Andrews, John Andrews and William Andrews all now deceased, who during the time deponent knew them lived in Cheboygan, Michigan; that *he was* ~~they were~~ personally acquainted with allthe members of the Andrews family and that the said Margaret Andrews was the mother of John Andrews, William Andrews, and Cathherine Hudson, now deceased; that ~~they~~ *he* knows these facts from having lived in the same town with them and from ~~their~~ *his* knowledge of the parties; that ~~they are~~ *he is* personally acquainted with David L. Hudson, having known him for *forty* years last past and that said David L. Hudson is the son of the said Catherine Hudson is the son of the said Catherine Hudson.

his
Alfred X Robarge
mark

Subscribed and sworn to before me this 14th day of January, A.D.1909.

James T. Shepherd
Notary Public in and for said County.
My commission expires Sept. 15, 1909

State of Michigan,
–SS–
County of Cheboygan.

Maxim Jarvis, being duly sworn, deposes and says that he is a resident of the *City* of *Cheboygan*, County ~~and~~ *of* Cheboygan and State of Michigan; and that he has so resided for *forty* years last past; that during her lifetime *he was* ~~they were~~ personally acquainted with Catherine Hudson, now deceased; and that ~~they were~~ *he was* personally acquaited with Margaret Andrews, John Andrews and William Andrews all now deceased, who during the time deponent knew them lived in Cheboygan, Michigan; that *he was* ~~they were~~ personally acquainted with allthe members of the Andrews family and that the said Margaret Andrews was the mother of John Andrews, William Andrews, and Cathherine Hudson, now deceased; that ~~they knew~~ *he knows* these facts from having lived in the same town with them and from ~~their~~ *his* knowledge of the parties; that ~~they are~~ *he is* personally acquainted with David L. Hudson, having known him for *forty* years last past and that said David L. Hudson is the son of the said Catherine Hudson is the son of the said Catherine Hudson.

his
Maxim X Jarvis
mark

Subscribed and sworn to before me this 14th day of January, A.D.1909.

James T. Shepherd
Notary Public in and for said County.
My commission expires Sept. 15, 1909

State of Michigan,
–SS–

County of Cheboygan.

_______*John Breggo*_________, being duly sworn, deposes and says that he is a resident of the ___*City*___ of ___*Cheboygan*___, County ~~and~~ *of* Cheboygan and State of Michigan; and that he has so resided for *forty-two* years last past; that during her lifetime *he was* ~~they were~~ personally acquainted with Catherine Hudson, now deceased; and that ~~they were~~ *he was* personally acquaited with Margaret Andrews, John Andrews and William Andrews all now deceased, who during the time deponent knew them lived in Cheboygan, Michigan; that *he was* ~~they were~~ personally acquainted with allthe members of the Andrews family and that the said Margaret Andrews was the mother of John Andrews, William Andrews, and Cathherine Hudson, now deceased; that ~~they knew~~ *he knows* these facts from having lived in the same town with them and from ~~their~~ *his* knowledge of the parties; that ~~they are~~ *he is* personally acquainted with David L. Hudson, having known him for *forty* years last past and that said David L. Hudson is the son of the said Catherine Hudson is the son of the said Catherine Hudson. *his*

John X Breggo

mark

Subscribed and sworn to before me this 14th day of January, A.D.1909.

James T. Shepherd

Notary Public in and for said County.

My commission expires Sept. 15, 1909

OFFICE OF

E. A. BOUCHARD

REAL ESTATE

NOTARY PUBLIC

JUSTICE OF THE PEACE

PENSION CLAIMS

FIRE AND MERCHANTILE INSURANCE

CASUALTY, ACCIDENT AND SICK INSURANCE

INDEMNITY BONDS

*Cheboygan, Mich.,*____________________*190*__

State of Michigan,

SS

County of Cheboygan.

That we the undersigned duly sworn that Cathrine Andress was a sister of William Andress, we know that being acquainted with boath of them for fifty years, and upwards *his*

sworn before me a notary Public *(William X Carrow*

on the ist day of March 1909 *(mark*

Edward A. Bouchard *(his*

Notary Public *(Charles X Shevelier*

My commision Expires march 14th 1909 *(mark*

Information following from: Charles Terrient and William A. Fountain, Gould City, April 27/09.

17-13 MRS. BETSEY CHAMPAIGN, dead, children dead and no heirs.

Information following from: Not Given.

18-13 MRS. DAVID MOORE or DANIEL MOORE, dead, head of the La Pine family, dead.

Husband 1st : _________ La Pine.

Husband 2nd: David or Daniel Moore.

18-13-1 Joe La Pine, dead.

Wife: Elizabeth La Pine, age 73, P.O. Gould City, Mich.

18-13-1-1 Mrs. Mary Pemble.

18-13-1-2 Mrs. Jane McGulphin, see 49-14.

18-13-1-3 Clara Freeman.

18-13-1-4 William La Pine.

18-13-1-5 Theodore La Pine.

18-13-1-6 Frank La Pine.

18-13-1-7 Wilson La Pine.

18-13-2 Louis La Pine

18-13-3 Victor La Pine, P.O. Mackinaw Island.

18-13-4 Isaac La Pine, on roll as 19-17.

Dear Sir
My childres name are as affollow home are living
Mrs Mary Pemble

" Jane McGulpine
" Clara Freeman
William Lapine
Theodore "
Frank "
Wilson "

Yours Respectfully
Elizabeth Lapine

Dear Sir
My Brothers and Sisters all dead. I have one sister living in Cheboygan Mich her name is Mrs. John Corraw don't know I would advise you to write to her and She could tell you better then I could in Regard of her family names and ages.

My father name was Joe Aslin
" mother " " Mary Aslin

1. Elizabeth age age 73 (Father Joe Aslin English & Indian
(Mother Mary "
Died about 24 years ago Joe age

2. Louis dead age
His children's names & ages don't know

3. Victor is living at Mackinaw Island his age can not tell don't know

4. Isaac died years ago

Information following from: Not Given.
19-13 MRS. DAVID KNIFFIN, age 88, P.O. Mackinaw City, husband white.
- 19-13-1 Ellen Plaunt, age 54, P.O. Mackinaw City, no children.
  Husband: Augustus Plaunt, white.
- 19-13-2 Marie Kniffin, age 46, P.O. Mackinaw City, no children.
  Husband: Frank Kniffin, white, a cousin.
- 19-13-3 Samuel Kniffin, age 44, P.O. Mackinaw City.
  Wife: Annie Kniffin, nee Dophina, see 27-11.
  - 19-13-3-1 Sampson Kniffin, age 22, single, P.O. Mackinaw City
  - 19-13-3-2 Rosa Kniffin, age 19, single, P.O. Mackinaw City.
  - 19-13-3-3 Edith Kniffin, age 9.
  - 19-13-3-4 (name not given), age 7.
- 19-13-4 Charles Kniffin, age 42, P.O. Mackinaw City. no children.
  Wife: Maggie Kniffin, nee Andrews, see 2-17.
- 19-13-5 James Kniffin, age 36, P.O. Mackinaw City, single.

Information following from: Mrs Angeline Bourassaw Terrient, Mac Isle, Apr 14/09.
20-13 MRS. VITAE BOURASSAW, dead.
- 20-13-1 Frank Bourassaw, age 55, P.O. Mac Isle, see 2-20.
  Wife: Babe Hattie Bourassaw, nee Lasley, age 56.
- 20-13-2 Gabriel, dead.
  Wife: Name not given, dead.
  - 20-13-2-1 Josephine Hall, see 24-13.
- 20-13-3 Garratt, dead, single.
- 20-13-4 Vital, dead, single.

Information following from: Agatha Pero, Mac Isle, Apr 1, 2/09.
21-13 MRS. FRANCIS MARTIN, dead.
- 21-13-1 Name not given, dead, no heirs.
- 21-13-2 Name not given, dead, no heirs.

21-13-3 Joseph Martin, age 44, P.O. Mack Isle, see 14-13.
Wife: Ellem Martin, white.
21-13-4 Agatha Martin, nee Pero or Perrerult, age 42,Mack Isle, see 14-13.
Husband: Name not given, white.
21-13-4-1 Hattie Martin, age 22, single.
21-13-4-2 Volia Martin, age 19, single.
21-13-4-3 Delia Martin, age 18.
21-13-4-4 Charles Martin, age 15.
21-13-4-5 Jank Martin, age 13.
21-13-4-6 Mary Martin, age 10.
21-13-4-7 Celia Martin, age 8.
21-13-4-8 Robert Martin, age 6.
21-13-4-9 Lawrence Martin, age 4.
21-13-4-10 Duward Martin, age 2.
21-13-4-11 P__l, born Aug 16/1907.
21-13-5 Frank Martin, age 36, P.O. Mack Isle, see 14-13.
Wife: Mary (Lozon or Lalotte) Martin, age 38.
21-14-5-1 Frank Martin, age 6.
21-14-5-1 Julia Martin, age 4.
21-13-6 Mary (Bazenet) Bazenet Andres, age 40, P.O. Mack Isle, see 14-11.
Husband 1: Tom Bazenett, dead, see 4-17.
Husband 2: Julius Andres, see 2-17.
21-13-6-1 Tom Andres, age 14.
21-13-6-2 Agatha Andres, age 16.
21-13-6-3 Susie Andres, age 10.
21-13-6-4 Robert Andres, age 5.
21-13-6-5 Annie Andres, age 2.

May 30, 1909
Mackinac Island, Mich

Dear Sir:
I have recive your letter. I'll gave you thes children names
Susie is 9 year old.
Tommy is 14 year old.
Robert is 5 year old.
Annie is 2 year old.
Agatha is 16 year old.
John Gasper is 4 months old.
Mrs. Mary Andress c/o Julis Andress
Boblo Island, Mich.

Information following from: Not Given.
22-13 MRS. PETER JACOBEAR, dead.
    22-13-1 Name not given, dead, no heirs.

Information following from: Not Given.
23-13 MRS. HYACINTH DOPHENA, SR.
    23-13-1 Francis Dolphena, see 12-12.
    23-13-2 Name not given, dead.
        Wife: Mrs. Hyacinth (or Josephine) Dophena Jr., see 8-12.
    23-13-3 Alex Dophena, see 27-11.
    23-13-4 Madar Dophena, dead, see 26-11.
    23-13-5 Peter Doneville, age 64, P.O. Mackinaw City, no children.
        Wife 1st : Name not given, dead.
        Wife 2nd: Name not given, white.

Information following from: Peter Terrient, Mack Isle, Apr/09.
24a-13 MISS HESTER TORRIEW, 24a-13 & SISTER (JANE), 24b-13 & PETER 24c-13.
    24a-13-1 William Hildrethe, age 35, P.O. ~~Alpena~~, no children.
    24a-13-2 Esther Hildreth, age 27, P.O. Alpena, no children.
    24a-13-3 Ellen Hildreth, age 26, P.O. Alpena, single, Bookeeper J. Cohen's Store.
    24a-13-4 Clarence Hildreth, P.O. Cleveland Ohio, has 3 male children names not given.

Alpena Mich July 1, 09

Mr Horace B. Durant.
Petoskey, Mich.
Dear Sir:

Your letter of June 29th received. The information given you by my Uncle Mr. Peter Terrent is correct.

My mother Mrs. Wm. D. Hildreth (nee Hester Terrient) has four children.

Mr. Clarence G. Hildreth age 33
5437 Lake Shore Blvd.
Collinwood, Ohio
Mrs. Mae Timms (nee Agnes Mary Hildreth) age 30 years.
Pittsburg, Pa. Gen. Del.
Mr. Wm. J. Hildreth age 27
50 Manhatten St.
N. Tonawanda, New York
and myself Ellen A. Hildreth age 24 years
112 State St.
Alpena, Mich.

Any further information you may desire will be gladly given.

Thanking you for the enquirey, I remain.
Respectfully yours,
Ellen A. Hildreth

Information following from: Peter Terrient, Mack Isle, Apr/09.
24b-13 JANE CHEESEMAN, age 49, P.O. St. Ignace, no children.
Husband: Down Cheeseman, white

Information following from: Peter Terrient, Mack Isle, Apr/09.
24c-13 PETER TORRIENT, age 53, P.O. Mack. Isle.
Wife: Angeline Belongea Torrient, age 53, see 26-13.
24c-13-1 Scott Torrient, age 19.
24c-13-2 Rome Torrient, age 17, a girl.
24c-13-3 Florence Torrient, age 14.
24c-13-4 Herbert Torrient, age 12.
Children of Angeline Belongea Terrient by 1st Husband Dan. Donovan, dead.
24c-13-5 Walter Donovan, age 38, P.O. Chicago, Light House Service, Evanston.
Wife: Name not given, white.
24c-13-5-1 Florence Donovan.
Children of Angeline Belongea Terrient by 2nd Husband Wm. Hall, dead.
24c-13-6 Wallace Hall, age 24, Light House Service at Squaw Island near Beaver.
Wife: Josephine Hall, age 26, nee Bourassaw, see 20-13.
24c-13-6-1 Walter Hall, age 3.

Information following from: Sophia Cadotte, Mack Isle, Apr 1/09.
25-13 MRS. MICHAEL KUTHRON or KEDRON or CADRON now Sophia Cadott, age 75, P.O. Mack Isle.
Husband 1st : Michael Cadron, dead.
Husband 2nd: Frank Cadott, dead.
25-13-1 Michael, dead, no children.
25-13-2 Mary, dead.
Husband: Theodore Hammond, P.O. Mac Isle, white.
25-13-2-1 Jennie Keller, age 36, 7 children names not given, P.O. Cross Village.
Husband: Name not give, white, a brother of the husband of Victoria Kellar, see 25-12.
25-13-2-2 Theodore Hammond Jr., single, age 31.
25-13-2-3 Clara Foltz, age 32, P.O. Petosky, not heard from for 2 yrs., has 3 children in school at Harbor Springs Catholic School.
25-13-2-3-1 Annie Foltz, age 16.

25-13-2-3-2 Lillie Foltz, age 13.
25-13-2-3-3 Lamenee Foltz, age 11.
25-13-2-4 Lillie Sheffield, age 29, P.O. X Village, 4 children.
25-13-2-4-1 Francis Sheffield, age 8.
25-13-2-4-2 Sylvia Sheffield, age 6.
25-13-2-4-3 Ernie Sheffield, age 3.
25-13-2-4-4 Ethel Sheffield, too late.
25-13-2-5 Minnie Walters, age 26, P.O. West Virginia, heard from her March/09, has 1 child.
25-13-2-5-1 Name not given, age 3.
25-13-2-6 John Hammond, age 23, P.O. Mac Isle, single.
25-13-2-7 Joe Hammond, age 21, P.O. Mac Isle, single.
25-13-3 Joe Cadron, age 47, P.O. Mackinaw Isle.
Wife: Maggie, off Canadian., P.O. Mackinaw Isle.
25-13-3-1 Sophia Cadron Jr., age 12, P.O. Mt. Pleasant School.
25-13-3-2 Bessie Cadron, age 10.
25-13-3-3 Veronica Cadron, age 7.
25-13-4 Alford Cadron, age 43, P.O. Mack Isle.
Wife: Therese (Bennett), age 40, P.O. Mack Isle, see 6-13.
25-13-4-1 Name not given, see 6-13.

May 31/09

Horace B. Durant
Dear Sir:
I am sending you the following names and ages of my children and my sisters children and my own age and sisters ages.
Jennie Kellers children names and ages.
My ages is 36 years
May Keller 18
Willie Keller 16
Harry " 14
Louis Keller 13 years
Georgia " 11 "
Lawrence " 8 "
Laura " 5 "
Melvina " 4 months
Clara Foltz names and ages of children.
Clara Foltz age 32 years
Annie " " 17 "
Lillie " " 14 "
Lawrence " " 12 "
Minnie Walters names and age of child.
Minnie Walters age 26 years
1 child name unknown age 3 years

Lillie Sheffields ages and names of childrens.
Lillie Sheffields age 29 years
Trancïe " " 9 "
Sylvia " " 7 "
Ermie " " 4 "
Ethel " " 6 months
Yours Truly,
Mrs Jennie Keller
Cross Village, Mich.

Information following from: Not Given.
26-13 MRS. PAUL BELONZHAY, dead.
26-13-1 Leon Belonzhay, see 24-11.
26-13-1-1 Henry Belonzhay, P.O. Namah, see 37-15 and 24-11.
Wife: Mary Ann Belonzhay, age 52, P.O. Namah see 37-15.
26-13-2 Charles Belonzhay, dead.
26-13-3 Name not given, dead.
26-13-4 Name not given, dead.
26-13-5 Sophia Chapman, see 30-13.
26-13-6 Louis Belonzhay or Belongea, P.O. X Village.
26-13-7 Angeline Beongea or Belonzhay Terrient, age 53, see 24-13.
26-13-8 Clement Belongea, age 46, P.O. Mack Isle, see 20-17.
Wife 1st : Name not given.
Wife 2nd: Grace (Plaunt) Belongea, see 4-13.
Children by 1st wife:
26-13-8-1 Fountain Boulongea, age 18, P.O. Gould City.
26-13-8-2 Sadie Boulongea, age 16, P.O. Gould City.
Child by 2nd wife see 4-13.

Information following from: Antoine Bebineau, St. Ignace.
27-13 MRS. CHARLES ROUSSAIN
27-13-1 Antoine Bebineau, age 55, P.O. St. Ignace
Wife: Name not given, dead.
27-13-1-1 Charles Bebineau, age 15, adopted, P.O. Bayfield, Wis., this boy's mother lives at Mackinaw Island, her name is Marcellene Champaign, sister of Simon Champaign, at Gullier near Manistequa.

Information following from: James Vallier, Jan 7/09.
28-13 MRS. THOSMAS VILLAIRE, dead.
28-13-1 James Vallier, age 66, P.O. St. Ignace.
Wife: Name not given, white, dead.
28-13-1 Frank Vallier, age 30, P.O. St. Ignace.

28-13-2 John Vallier, age 28.
28-13-3 Joe Vallier, age 20.
28-13-4 Oliver Vallier, age 18.
28-13-2 Thomas Vallier, age 62, P.O. St. Ignace.
Wife: Name not given, white, separated.
28-13-2-1 Thomas Vallier Jr., age 35, P.O. Engadine.
28-13-2-2 Martha Vallier, age 33, P.O. Namah.

Information following from: Not Given.
29-13 MARY A. KARROW or CARROW, age 111, P.O. County Poor House Cheboygan.
29-13-1 Louis Carow, no heirs.
29-13-2 Joseph Carow, no heirs.
29-13-3 John B. Carow, on roll as 17-17.
29-13-4 Mary Carow.
Husband: Name not given, dead.
29-13-4-1 Ed, dead.
29-13-4-2 Julia, dead.
29-13-4-3 Jane Cox, age 40, P.O. Cheboygan.
Husband: ________ Cox, white.
29-13-4-3-1 Josephine Parkey.
Husband: Tome Parkey, see 3-31.
29-13-4-3-1-1 Rosie Parkey, age 4.
29-13-4-3-1-2 Evaline Parkey, age 2.
29-13-4-4 Joe Dumas, age 42, P.O. Pellston, no children.
29-13-4-5 Frank Dumas, age 32, P.O. Pellston, Mich., wife white, single.
29-13-4-6 Louis Dumas, age 41, P.O. Drummond's Isle.
29-13-4-6-1 Eliza Dumas, age 11.
29-13-4-6-2 William Dumas, age 9.
29-13-4-6-3 Lizzie Dumas, age 7.

June 7 1909
Drummond

Mr. HB Durant
Dear Sir
When you went to Marton I did not see you I was to lateyou had gone well My name is Lewie Duman.
My mother name was Eliza Duman My father was John Duman and my grandmother name wa Mary Morran and my great granmother Maryann Corrow.

My girl name is Eliza Duman are 12 Willie Duman age 10 years Lizzie Duman age 7 years and my age is 41 years and we use to get payed at Mackinaw Island.
My father and mother and grand mother are all dead except my great grandmother is still living in Cheboygan.
Dear Sir, had one sister her name Lizzie but she is dead and no brothers.
Yours truly Lewie Duman

My Chief name was Bamamsa.
Dear Sir;
Please send me the names of your brothers & sisters if you have any & their addresses.
Return this letter.
Very respy,
HORACE B. DURANT
Special U.S. Indian Agent

Pellston, Mich
June 1 – 1909

Mr. Horace B. Durant
Dear Sir
I am writing in answer to your letter. I am 32 years old, and my brother Joe is 42 years old, his address is Joseph Dumas Pellston Mich.
Resptfly yours
Frank Dumas
Pellston Mich

Information following from: John B. Shomin, Jackson Chapman & Levi Chapman, Mackinaw Isle, April/09.
30-13 MRS. BELA CHAPMAN, dead.
30-13-1 Amanda Ashman, dead, see 4-3.
30-13-2 Reuben Chapman, dead.
Wife: Name not given, dead.
30-13-2-1 Junie Chapman, dead.
Husband: Claud Cable, white, P.O. Lake View Hotel, Mac Isle.
30-13-2-1-1 Bessie Cable, age 28, P.O. Mac Isle, single.
30-13-2-1-2 Harry Cable, age 23, P.O. Mac Isle, single.
30-13-2-1-3 Gale Cable, age 20, P.O. Mac Isle, single.
30-13-3 Eliza Chapman, dead.
30-13-3-1 John Chart, age 35, P.O. Sault Ste Marie, single, both legs cut off.
30-13-4 Mary Chapman Shomin, age 65, see 81-21, Traverse.

30-13-5 Lucy Chapman, dead.
Husband: _______ Biddle, see 1-13
30-13-5-1 Elizabeth Sophia Biddle, age 56, P.O. Sault Ste Marie, single.
30-13-5-2 Agatha McNaughton, age 52, P.O. Sault Ste Marie, husband white, has 2 children.
30-13-5-3 Grace Rankin, age 41, P.O. St. Ignace, husband white (Co. Cleark at St Ignace), no children.
30-13-6 John Chapman, dead.
Wife: Mrs. Annie Bourassaw, P.O. Mackinaw Isld, 2nd husband dead.
30-13-6-1 Mary A. Legget, age 50, P.O. Mack Isld., husband white, no children.
30-13-6-2 James R. Chapman #1, age 47, P.O. Sand Pt., Idaho.
Wife: Name not given, white.
30-13-6-2-1 Annie Chapman, age 10.
30-13-6-3 William Chapman #1, age 45, P.O. Mack Isld, wife dead no children.
30-13-6-4 Edna Grace La Pine, age 32, P.O. Mack Isld.
Husband: Eugene La Pine, age 38.
30-13-6-4-1 Lawrence G. La Pine, age 11.
30-13-6-4-2 William J. La Pine, age 4.
30-13-7 Levi Chapman, age 70, P.O. Mackinaw Island.
Wife: Name not given, dead.
30-13-7-1 Reuben Chapman, age 48, P.O. Mack Isld., 5 children.
30-13-7-2 Minnie Coughlin, age 46, P.O. St. Joe Mich., 5 children.
30-13-7-3 Lottie Johnson, age 44, P.O. Idaville, Indianna., 10 children.
30-13-7-4 Amanda La Pine, age 42, P.O. Mack Isld., 3 children.
30-13-7-5 Lena McGulpin, age 40, P.O. Mack Isld., no children.
30-13-7-6 Hattie Gallagher, age 38, P.O. Alpena, Mich.
30-13-7-7 Bela M. Chapman, age 36, P.O. Mac Isle., 4 children.
30-13-7-8 Jennie Chapman, dead.
30-13-7-8-1 Sarah Gallagher Latour, age 28, P.O. Cedarville.
30-13-7-8-2 Lillian Gallagher, age 24, P.O. Mac Isle.
30-13-7-8-3 William Gallagher, age 26, P.O. Mac Isle.
30-13-7-8-4 Grace Gallagher, age 22, P.O. Mac Isle, see 42-14.

30-13-8 Jackson Chapman, age 62, P.O. Mackinac Island.
Wife: Sophia (Belongea) Chapman, age 57, see 26-13.
30-13-8-1 William A. Chapman, age 28, P.O. 700 N Water St Chicago.
30-13-8-2 Lucy Chapman, age 26, P.O. Mackinaw Isle.
30-13-8-2 Henry Chapman, age 24, P.O. Mackinaw Isle.
30-13-8-2 James Chapman, age 21, P.O. Mackinaw Isle.
30-13-8-2 John Chapman, age 19, P.O. Mackinaw Isle.

Sault Ste Marie June 22nd 1909

Mr. Horace B. Durant,
Dear Sir.
Your letter came several days ago. But-I was away from home at the time. But trust I am not too late in answering it.
My Fathers name is John Biddle and Mothers, Lucy Biddle. A am fifty two years of age.
My childrens names are Leroy McNaughton, twenty none years of age and Otto McNaughton twenty five years. Sophia Biddle's age is fifty six years, and Grace Rankin is forty one. I have two Grand Son's, Urswell, and Robert, respectively six and four years of age. I do not know whether they would be enrolled or not.
Respectfully yours,
Mrs Agatha McNaughton

Information following from: Henry L. Davenport, Mack Isle, April 10/09.
31-13 MRS. AMBROSE DAVENPORT, dead.
Husband: Ambrose Davenport.
31-13-1 John Davenport, age 65, P.O. Naubinway, Mich.
Wife: Julia Davenport, age 46, see 27-11.
31-13-1-1 John Davenport Jr., age 26, P.O. Naubinway, Mich.
31-13-1-2 Emily Davenport, age 17.
31-13-1-3 Millie La Blanc, age 24.
Husband: Joseph La Blanc, P.O. Cheboygan.
31-13-1-3-1 Christina La Blanc, age11.
31-13-1-3-2 Theodore La Blanc, age 9.
31-13-1-3-3 Mamie La Blanc, age 5.
31-13-1-3-4 Marion La Blanc, age 2.
31-13-1-4 R. V. Davenport, age 20.
31-13-1-5 Mary Viola Davenport, age 10.
31-13-2 William Davenport, dead.
Wife: Mrs. Harriet Hearst, nee Flynn, age 70, P.O. Mullet Lake, see 26-31.
31-13-2-1 Eliza Ball, age 52, husband white, no children, P.O. Mullet Lake.
31-13-3 Henry L. Davenport, age 81, P.O. Mac Isle.
Wife: Name not given, dead.

31-13-3-1 Melissa J. Dewey, age 58, P.O. Detroit corner Bellevue & Strong.
Husband: James S. Dewey, white.
31-13-3-1-1 Elmer Dewey, age 40, P.O. Detroit corner of Bellevue & Strong.
31-13-3-1-2 James Dewey, age 38, P.O. Detroit.
31-13-3-1-3 Clarence Dewey, age 36.
31-13-3-1-4 Henry Dewey, age 34.
31-13-3-1-5 Melissa Dewey Jr., age 32.
31-13-3-2 Henry Davenport, dead.
Wife: Name not given, dead.
31-13-3-2-1 Myrtle Davenport, age 21, P.O. Detroit corner Antoine & (?), single.
31-13-3-3 Lewis A. Davenport, age 53, P.O. Detroit, wife white, no children.
31-13-3-4 Lucretia G. Davenport, age 42, P.O. Detroit Glove Dept. Hutchinson's Store.
31-13-3-5 Blanche S. Davenport, dead, no heirs.
31-13-3-6 Blanche V. Perault or Pero, age 37, P.O. Mac Isle.
Husband: Louis Perault, white.
31-13-3-6-1 Lawrence Perault, age 17.
31-13-3-6-2 Clarence Perault, age 15.
31-13-3-6-3 Wolford Perault, age 13.
31-13-3-6-4 Herbert Perault, age 11.
31-13-3-6-5 Davenport Perault, age 4.
31-13-3-7 William G. Davenport, age 35, P.O. Augusta, Ga. R.F.D. #2.
Wife: Name not given, white.
31-13-3-7-1 Clarence Davenport, age 6.
31-13-3-7-2 Harold Davenport, age 4.
31-13-3-7-3 Billy Davenport, age 2.
31-13-3-8 Frank Davenport, dead, no children.
31-13-3-9 Clarence Davenport, dead, no children.
31-13-4 Mary Davenport, dead, no children.
31-13-5 Elizabeth Belongea, dead.
Husband: Leon or Paul Belongea, P.O. Mac Isle, see 24-11.
31-13-6 Jospeh Davenport, dead, no children.
31-13-7 Jane Davenport, dead, no children.
31-13-8 Julia Duklin, age 63, P.O. Eagle Bluff Wisconsin, In Light House Service.
Husband: ________ Duklin, white.
31-13-9 Susan Davenport, dead, single.
31-13-10 James Davenport, age 58, P.O. home at Mackinaw City, Light House Service at Old Mission.
Wife: Madeline Davenport, nee Lasley, dead daughter of Mrs.

James Lasley, see 2-20.

31-13-10-1 Harry Davenport, age 38, P.O. Mack City, single.
31-13-10-2 Lizzie Bourroughs, age 36, P.O. Mack City.
31-13-10-3 Edith Davenport, age 34, P.O. Mack City.
31-13-10-4 Joseph Davenport, age 32.
31-13-10-5 Louise Davenport, age 30.
31-13-10-6 Rachel Desy, age 28, has 1 child.
31-13-10-7 James Davenport, age 22, P.O. Mack City.
31-13-10-8 Overtan Davenport, age 19, P.O. Mack City.

31-13-11 Margaret Morris or Mosier, age 55, P.O. Village.
Husband: ________ Morris, white.

31-13-11-1 Jennie Morris, age 33, single.
31-13-11-2 Wilbert Morris, age 28.
31-13-11-3 Rosa Augusta Morris or Mrs. James Ried, P.O. 606 Grove at Petoskey.

31-13-12 Jackson Davenport, age 50, P.O. Light Service, So. Chicago, wife white.

Naubinway, Mich.
April 30, 1909

Horace B. durant
Special U.S. Indian agent.
Dear Sir:-

I have been informed by John Davenport in regards of Ottawa and Chippaway race which I do not know whether you have my name and my wife which was Emma Davenport before marriage and which is now Emma King and also I will enclude you all of my families names.

John King	*age 42 – off – white*
Emma King	*age 41*
Martha King	*age 17*
Bertha King	*age 15*
Olive King	*age 13*
Gregory King	*age 10*
Ella King	*age 7*
Ernest King	*age 5*

Now Mr. Durant if there is any information that you desire please write me and I will be glad to furnish you with and information that I am able to.

Yours Respt,
John King

Mackinac Co. Naubinway Mich

Naubinway, Mich.
April 30/09

Horace B Durant

Special U.S. Indian agent.
Dear Sir

Your Letter of the 29 Received in Regard to the ages of my children as follows 9 including my wife & myself.
Mr. John Davenport Sr
Mrs Julia Davenport wife

Yours Respt.
John Davenport Naubinway Mich

Miss Molley Davenport age 42 now Mrs. Molley Lorenson Sawyer, Wis.
Miss Emma Davenport, age 40 now Mrs. Emma King Naubinway Mich
Miss Minnie Davenport, age 29 now Mrs. Minnie White 208 # 6th Street Cheboygan Mich
John A Davenport age 27 Naubinway Mich
R. V. Davenport age 20 Naubinway Mich

Department of the Interior,
United States Indian Service,

Petoskey, Mich.
May 28/09

Mrs. Margaret Morris,
Cross Village, Mich.
Dear Madam:

Will you please send me the names and ages of your childrento complete the Ottawa and Chippewa payroll & oblige.

Yours truly,
HORACE B. DURANT
Special U.S. Indian Agent

Jennie	*Morris born*	*July 24, 1878*
Wilbert	*" "*	*Aug 2, 1879*
Rosa Agusta	*" "*	*Feby 11, 1882*

The latter is now Mrs. James A. Ried, 606 Grove St., Petoskey, Mich.

Information following from: Charles Teriant & William A. Fountain, Gould City, Apr 27/09.

32-13 MRS. JOSEPH LALOTTE or LAZONE, dead.
Husband: Joseph Lalotte or Lazone.
32-13-1 Alford Lalotte, dead.
Wife: Josephine Lalotte or Lazone, P.O. Mac.Isle, member "Soo" band.

Information following from: Mrs. Lucy King, Mac Isle, April 13/09.

33-13 DAVID ROBINSON, age 59, P.O. Gould City Scott's Point, single.

Information following from: Not Given.

34-13 MRS. SARAH CHAMPAIGN, dead.
Husband: ________ Champaign.
34-13-1 Sarah Champaign, dead.
Husband: Name not given, dead.
34-13-1-1 Patrick Halland, age 22, P.O. Mack. City, cannot locate him Durant.
34-13-2 John Champaign, age 48, P.O. Naubinway, single.
34-13-3 Charles Champaign, age 46, P.O. Beaver Island, wife white, see 16-15.
34-13-4 Mary Cadran, age 44, P.O. Mac. Island.
Husband: _______ Cadran, dead.
34-13-4-1 Louis Cadran, age 24, P.O. Mac. Isle.
34-13-4-2 Alford Cadran, age 22, P.O. Mac. Isle.
34-13-4-3 Mary Cadran, age 12, P.O. Mac. Isle.
34-13-5 William Champaign, age 40, P.O. Gawas Bay, Canada, cannot locate them Durant.
Wife: Name not given, white.
34-13-5-1 Sarah Champaign, age 4.
34-13-5-2 Mary Champaign, age 2.

Information following from: Joe Mesawtego et al, St Ignace, June 20/09.
35-13 MRS. ALIXSE LELONE, dead, do not know of any children Durant.

Information following from: Not Given.
36-13 MRS. ISAAC BLANCHARD, dead.
36-13-1 Phobe Recolley, see 58-16.
36-13-2 Elvira Corp, age 57, see 13-15.
Note: Relates to head of family, She has 2 other children living at St Ignace, but they did not draw in 1870 & they are not now enrolled with their mother for that reason Durant Spl Agt Dec 18/08. Later: One of these 2 children were found at St Ignace & enrolled with husband, who is Indian "Corp" Durant St Ignace Jany 6/09.

Information following from: Everybody, Mac Isle, April 13/09.
37-13 MRS. MARTHA TANNER, dead, no heirs.

Information following from: Charles Terrient, Gould City, April 27/09.
38-13 MRS. LOUIS BEAUBIEN, dead, grandmother of Maggie Terrient nee Mastaw wife of Charles Terrient, see 54-14 and 2-13.

Information following from: Not Given.
39-13 MRS. JOSEPH CHEVEROW or SHIVREY or ASHLIN, dead.
39-13-1 Alex Aslin, age 59, P.O. Newberry, Mich., single.
39-13-2 Elizabeth Johnson, age 53, P.O. St. Ignace, husband white, no children.

39-13-3 Peter Aslin, age 52, P.O. St. Ignace.
Wife: Agatha (Peck) Aslin, age 50, Traverse, sister to Joe & Peter Peck, see 5-32.
39-13-3-1 Cynthia Mary Grundain, age 25, P.O. St. Ignace, no children.
Husband: Joe Grundain
39-13-3-2 Grace Plaunt, age 24, P.O. Mac. City, see 5-32 and 4-13.
39-13-3-3 Peter Aslin Jr., age 19.
39-13-3-4 William Aslin, age 17.
39-13-3-5 Eva Aslin, age 15.
39-13-3-6 Albert or Bertie Aslin, age 13.
39-13-3-7 Charles Aslin, age 11.
39-13-3-8 Bessie Aslin, age 7.
39-13-4 Esther Aslin, dead.
Husband: John Dailey, white, off.
39-13-4-1 Laura Fisher, age 27, P.O. Dryed, Washington.
Husband: _______ Fisher, white.
39-13-4-1-1 Verne Fisher, age 7.
39-13-4-1-2 Clifford Fisher, age 5.
39-13-4-1-3 Virgil Fisher, age 2.
39-13-4-2 Thomas Dailey, age 21, P.O. Cheboygan, single.
39-13-4-3 John Dailey, age 19, P.O. Cheboygan, single.
39-13-5 Mary Jane Landry, age 48, Mac. Isle, no children.
Husband: Ed Landry, white.
39-13-6 Harriet Martin, age 42, see 37-15, Mac Isle, for children see 37-15.
39-13-7 William Aslin, age 35, P.O. Newberry, Mich.
Wife: Myrtle Aslin, white, off.
39-13-7-1 Esther May Aslin, age 13.
39-13-7-2 Theodora Aslin, age 11.
39-13-7-3 Harley Aslin, age 7.
39-13-7-4 William Aslin, age 5.
39-13-8 Edmund Aslin, age 32, P.O. St Ignace, single.
39-13-9 Paul Aslin, age 27, P.O. Germfask, Mich.
Wife: Name not given, white.
39-13-9-1 Gladys Aslin, age 6, P.O. Germfask, Mich.

Information following from: Charles Terrient, Gould City, April 27/09.
40-13 MRS. JOSEPH LASLIN should be ASLIN, dead.
40-13-1 Alex Aslin, age 52, P.O. Newberry, single.
40-13-2 Elizabeth Johnson, P.O. Pt St Ignace.
Husband: Charles Johnson, white.
40-13-3 Pete Aslin, age 46, P.O. St. Ignace, see 5-32.
40-13-4 Jane Aslin Landry, P.O. Mack Isle.

40-13-5 William Aslin, P.O. Newberry.
40-13-6 Edmund Aslin, P.O. Cheboygan, single.
40-13-7 Paul Aslin, P.O. Germfast, Mich, no children.

Information following from: Not Given.
41-13 MISS NANCY MCGALPHIN, dead, no heirs.

Information following from: Not Given.
42-14 MRS. WILLIAM DAVENPORT, dead.
42-14-1 Robert Davenport, dead.
Wife: Name not given, dead.
42-14-1-1 Albert Davenport, age 38, P.O. Munising, wife white.
42-14-1-2 Robert Davenport, age 30, P.O. Mac Isle.
Wife: Grace (Gallagher), white.
42-14-1-2-1 Nellie Davenport, age 4.
42-14-1-3 Walter Davenport, age 28, P.O. Scotts Point Gould City.
Wife: Laura, see 37-15.
42-14-1-3-1 Franklin Davenport, age 2.
42-14-1-3-2 Cecelia Davenport, born Nov/08 too late.
42-14-1-4 Paul Davenport, age 25, P.O. Mac Isle, single.
42-14-1-5 Joseph Davenport, age 23, P.O. Gould City, MI, single.

Information following from: Not Given.
43-14 MRS. LOUIS BELONZHAY, dead.
43-14-1 Louis Blongea, P.O. Carp River, Mich., see 29-11 number 2.

Information following from: Not Given.
44-14 MRS. JOSEPH ME NAW SAW, P.O. Cheboygan.
44-14-1 Joe Me Naw Saw, said to live in Wisconsin either at Armipie or Kewena, Wis. Cannot trace this family Cheboygan, June 8/09 Durant Spl Agt.

Information following from: Joseph Cowett, white, knows all the old French families, Gould City, April 27.
45-14 MRS. SAMUEL LE BLANC, dead.

Information following from: Amabele Ance and Mary Garrison, St. Ignace.
46-14 MRS. LOUIS ST. ONGE, dead.
45-14-1 John St. Onge, age 60, see 24-15.
45-14-2 Angeline McGulphin, age 78, P.O. Mac Isle.
Husband: Name not given, dead.
45-14-2-1 Mary Garrison, see 52-14.

45-14-2-2 Ellen Culp, age 39, P.O. Mac Isle, husband white, no children.

45-14-3 Ed St. Onge, has not been heard from for years.

Wife: Name not given, now wife of AntoineAnce.

45-14-4 Mary Cotey, age 55, P.O. St. Ignace.

Information following from: Charles Terrient.

47-14 MRS. ROSALIE LOUISIGNON, dead.

47-14-1 Name not given, dead, no heirs.

Information following from: Not Given.

48-14 MRS. BENJAMIN RICE, dead.

48-14-1 Hattie Dabb, P.O. Chicago, husband white.

48-14-2 Ellen Sharp, dead.

Information following from: Annie Lasley, Mac Isle, April 13/09.

49-14 MRS. BENJAMIN MCGULPHIN or ELIZABETH MCGULPHIN

49-14-1 Benjamin McGukphin, age 54, P.O. Village.

Wife: Jane (LaPine) McGulphin, age 42, see 18-13.

49-14-1-1 Annie Lasley, age 25, see 28-15

Husband: George Lasley.

49-14-1-2 Lydia DeLong, age 23, P.O. River Rouge, Mich.

Husband: Robert DeLong, white.

49-14-1-2-1 Marian DeLong, age 6.

49-14-1-2-2 Harry Delong, age 4.

49-14-1-2-3 Robert DeLong, age 2.

Information following from: Vincent Valencourt, Mac Isle, April 12/09.

50-14 MRS. HENRY VALENCOUR, dead.

50-14-1 Daughter, dead no children.

50-14-2 Henry Valencour, dead, no children.

50-14-3 Andrew Valencour, dead, single.

50-14-4 Vincient Valencourt, age 67, P.O. Mack Isle.

Wife: Mary Bodeosin(? or Bodeonin), dead, ist husband Augustus Rebouskaw or Pond, dead.

50-14-4-1 Name not given, dead.

Children of wife Mary by her 1st husband:

50-14-4-2 Archie Pond, age 40, P.O. Mack Isle.

Wife: Agnes (nee Wilmette) Pond, see 46-16.

50-14-4-2-1 William Pond, age 25.

Wife: ________ nee Perault.

50-14-4-2-1-1 Marian Pond, age 3.

50-14-4-2-2 Lucy Pease, age 23, husband white.

50-14-4-2-2-1 Guy Pease, born May/08.

50-14-4-2-3 Annie Michalke, age 21, husband white.
50-14-4-2-3-1 Francis Michalke, age 3.
50-14-4-2-4 Ruth Pond, age 18.
50-14-4-2-5 Esther Pond, age 12.
50-14-4-2-6 Mary Pond, age 10.
50-14-4-2-7 Margaret Pond, age 8.
50-14-4-3 Dan Pond, dead.
Wife: Jane, white, P.O. Bay City.
50-14-4-3-1 Artie Pond, age 22, P.O. Bay City.

Northport Mich., July 3rd 1908
To Mr. Horace B. Durant
Petoskey Mich.

Dear Sir.
In reply to your last letter to me, will say that my Father was George Bourissaw of Mackinac and he also lived at St. Ignace. My mother was Agatha Lancord of St. Ignace her mothers, name was Miss Jane Pond of St. Ignace. I have one Brother name William G. Bourissaw and think his post office adress is Naubinway MackinawCo. Mich.
Very Respectfully
Lewis Bourissaw
Keeper of South Fox Island Lighthouse

Northport Mich May 6, 1909
Dear Sir,
Your notice of the 29th April 1909. Has just came to hand. I am sorrie it was not sent unto the Light House. I can not say any thing of my parents. They died before 1870. At least my father did. My mother died in 1870. My father George Bourissaw received 3 payments or so that I can remember before the pay Master was last on saginaw bay. When the Steamer City of Detroit was lost. Any thing before that I could not say anything of after as my father was burnt on the steamer Grace Dormer shortly after that. And about my wife people I never inquired or thought of it. Some of my children are married. They are Mrs. Fred Berlin Traverse City that is Josephine J. Bourissaw. Mrs. Agatha Stafford St. James. Mrs. Phillomena Mason St. James. This is all I can say of my people hoping this will be satisfactory to you. I am
Very Respectfully
L. G. Bourissaw
Keeper of South Fox Island Lighthouse

Information following from: Not Given.

51-14 MRS. JANE LANCOUR, dead.

51-14-1 Jane Lancour, dead.

Husband: Duffield Fountain, dead.

51-14-1-1 Pete Fountain, age 38, P.O. Traverse City, cannot locate.

51-14-1-2 Alex Fountain, age 26, P.O. Traverse City, cannot locate.

51-14-2 Flora Lancour, dead, husband dead, no heirs.

51-14-3 Agnes Lancour, dead, husband dead.

51-14-3-1 William Bourassaw, P.O. Seul Choix.

51-14-4-2 Louis Bourassaw, P.O. Charlevoix.

Wife: Lillie Bourassaw, nee Nontay, see 27-57.

51-14-4 Justina Lancour, dead.

Husband 1st: ________ Bouchard, dead.

Husband 2nd: Joseph Terrien, P.O. St. Ignace, white.

51-14-4-1 Henry Bouchard, age 40, P.O. Trout lake, working on R.R.

51-14-4-2 Eugene Terrien, Iron Mountain, Mich., cannot locate.

51-14-4-3 Alford Terrien, Iron Mountain, Mich., cannot locate.

51-14-5 Mary Ann Lancour, dead, husband dead, no children.

51-14-6 Adeline Lancour, dead, no children.

Husband: _______ Primo, white.

51-14-7 Paul Lancour, age 58, P.O. Mackinaw Isle.

Wife: Sarah Lalotte, see 12-13.

51-14-7-1 Harry Lancour, age 38, P.O. Cheboygan.

51-14-7-2 Addie McGuire, age 36, P.O. Cheboygan, husband brother of sister Gertrude's husband.

51-14-7-3 Gertrude McGuire, age 34, P.O. Cheboygan, husband brother of sister Addie's husband.

51-14-7-4 Charles Lancour, age 24, P.O. Cheboygan.

51-14-7-5 Albert Lancour, age 22, P.O. Mackinac Isle.

51-14-7-6 Alfred Lancour, age 20, P.O Mackinac Isle.

51-14-7-7 Eva Lancour, age 18, P.O. Mackinac Isle, single.

51-14-7-8 Lizzie Lancour, age 31, P.O. Mackinac Isle, single.

Letters to those people April 29/09, 27-57 & 51-14
Louie E. Bourissaw age 29.
Lillie M. Noantay Bourissaw age 30 and son.
Louis William Bourissaw age 4 of Charlevoix, Mich.
Also

Josephine and Lewie G. Bourissaw.
Parents of Lewie E. also William Josephine Philomene Gettie James and Frank address L. G. Bourissaw c/o S. Fox Island L. H. North Port Mich.
Also a cousin Josephine Bourissaw the all Squaw Island Mich
Mrs L. E. Bourissaw Charlevoix, Mich.

Information following from: Mary McGalphin or Mrs Garrison, Mac Isle, April 13/09.

52-14 MISS MARY MCGALPHIN now MARY GARRISON, age 52, P.O. Mac. Isle, see 46-14.
Husband: John Garrison, white.
52-14-1 Mary Newton, age 30, P.O. Grand Rapids 86 Goodrich St., no children.
Husband: William Newton.
52-14-2 John Garrison, age 28, P.O. Grand Rapids or Mac. Isle, separated from wife.
Wife: Rose, white, P.O. Mac. Isle.
52-14-3 Winnifred Garrison, age 6, liveswith mother.
52-14-3 Catharine Sayles, age 25, Grand Rapids, no children.
Husband: Delos Sayles, white.
52-14-4 Fred Garrison, age 23, P.O. Grand Rapids Wealthy Ave.
Wife: Name not given, white.
52-14-4-1 Fred Garrison Jr., age 3.
52-14-4-2 Delos V. Garrison, born June 1908.

Information following from: Not Given.

53-14 MRS. MOSES MAILLET, dead, said to be the wife of Mases Naw Wi Gigig, see 19-3.

Information following from: Annie Lasley, Lucy King and Charles Terrient, Mac. Isle, April 13/09, April 27/09.

54-14 MRS. ANGELINE LOUISIGNON, dead.
54-14-1 Charles Terrient, age 62, P.O. Gould City, Mich., see 15-13.
Wife: Maggie (Mastors) Terrient, age 47, see 2-13.
54-14-1-1 Charles Terrient, age 29, P.O. Manistique, no children.
54-14-1-2 Fred Terrient, age 26, P.O. Scott's Point Gould City, single.
54-14-1-3 Annie Bellant, age 24, P.O. Epoufette, has seven children.
Husband: Name not given.
54-14-1-3-1 Jos Bellant.
54-14-1-3-2 Name not given.
54-14-1-3-3 Name not given.
54-14-1-3-4 Name not given.

54-14-1-3-5 Name not given.
54-14-1-3-6 Name not given.
54-14-1-3-7 Name not given.
54-14-1-4 Blanche Terrient, age19, P.O. Gould City.
54-14-1-5 Nellie Terrient, age 16.
54-14-1-6 James Terrient, age 13.
54-14-1-7 Mary Terrient, age 11.
54-14-1-8 Herbert Terrient, age 8.
54-14-1-9 Francis Terrient, age 6.
54-14-2 Lucy Bailey, age 34, P.O. Detroit
Husband: Fred Bailey, white.
54-14-2-1 Fred Bailey, age 14.
54-14-2-2 Blanche Bailey, age 13.
54-14-23 George Bailey, age 10.

Information following from: Mrs. ElizaTruckey, St. Ignace.
55-14 MISS LIZZETTE MARTIN or MRS. ELIZABETH TRUCKEY, age 70, P.O. St. Ignace.
55-14-1 Joe Truckey, age 28, P.O. St. Ignace, single.
55-14-2 Name not given, dead, no heirs.
55-14-3 Mary McGormet, age 26, P.O. St. Ignace, husband white.

Information following from: Not Given.
56-14 MISS MARY BAZINETT (child).
56-14-1 Augustus Bazinaw, age 46, P.O. Mack. Isle, see 4-17 & 17-15.
Wife: Emma Bazinaw, age 40.

Information following from: Mrs. Mallett, June 8/09, Cheboygan.
57-14 EDWARD KARROW or CAROW, age 48, P.O. Grace Harbor Mich, lame.
Wife: Name not given, dead.
57-14-1 Rachael Carow, age 17, P.O. Cheboygan.
57-14-2 Eddie Carow Jr., age 20, P.O. Cheboygan.
57-14-3 Herbert Carow, age 21, P.O. Cheboygan.
57-14-4 Joseph Carow Jr., age 13, P.O Cheboygan Corner Sutherland & James St., Note well! Lives with & adopted legally by Alex Mallette.

Information following from: Not Given.
58-14 MARY ANN LA DUKE or LUDUC, P.O. Cheboygan, cannot get track of her, ask or write Durant. Later see letter from her.

St. Ignace, Mich. July 6/09

Horace B. Durant

Petoskey Mich.

Dear Sir,

In answer to your inquiry of else – no d ale ~~see~~ will say first. I gelong to band of Ottawa & Chippewa Indians. Louis Grondin my father, Mary Ann Martin my mother.

My Daughter family name Lucy Luduc, married name Bodwin, 34 years of age.

My Daughter family name Josephine Luduc, married name Gasper Massway, age 31 years.

My daughter Mary Luduc, married name St. Onge, aged 29years of age.

My Daughter May Luduc, married name Joe Bodwin aged 26 years.

My Son Noah Luduc, 16 uears of age.

My Grand Son, Edward Ludu, 11 years of age.

The Post address of all these partiesl is St. Ignace, Mich.

My name is Mary Ann Luduc age 58 of age address St, Ignace Mich.

I remain yours Truly,

Mary Ann Luduc

St. Ignace, Mich.

Information following from: Joe Cowett, French, Gould City, April 27/09.
59-14 ANGEL ROBINSON, dead.

Information following from: Not Given.
60-14 ALEXSIE DOPHENA, dead no heirs.

Information following from: Not Given.
61-14 MARGUARETTA THOMPSON, a sister of Mrs. Philamon Fartan of Village, cannot trace her Durant.

Information following from: Joe Cowett, white, knows all French families, Gould City.
62-14 JOSEPHINE LA PIERRE, dead.
62-14-1 Sarah Lafond, age 40, P.O. Manistique, Mich., cannot locate her Durant.
Husband: John Lafond.

Information following from: Not Given.
63-14 MAMA WALCH, dead, never heard of her Chiefs.

Information following from: Mrs. Peter Closs.
64-14 MRS. PETER CLOSS, age 61, P.O. St. Ignace.
Husband: Peter Closs, dead.
64-14-1 Julia Bouchard, age 48, P.O. St. Ignace.
Husband: Name not given, dead.

64-14-1-1 Philip Bouchard, age 15.
64-14-1-2 Otis Bouchard, age 12.
64-14-1-3 John Bouchard, age 5.
64-14-2 Oliver Closs, age 30, P.O. St. Ignace, single.
64-14-3 Peter Closs Jr., age 29, Sault Ste. Marie, husband white, no children.

Information following from: Alford Bellaire, Mack Isle, April/09.
65-14 VICTORIA PELTIER, dead.
65-14-1 Alford Bellair, age 55, P.O. Boise Blanc Isle.
Wife: Lizzie Bazinet, dead, daughter of 3-6.
65-14-1-1 John Bellair, age 22, P.O. Sault Ste. Marie.
65-14-2 Theodore Bellair, age 54, P.O. Mack Isle., single.

Information following from: Not Given.
66-14 WILLIAM VALIER, dead.
Wife: Rosalie Valier, P.O. St. Ignace.
66-14-1 Antoine Vallier, age 60, P.O. St. Ignace.
66-14-2 Joe Vallier, age 58, P.O. St. Ignace.
66-14-3 John Vallier, age 56, P.O. St. Ignace.
66-14-4 Rose Martins, age 50, P.O. St. Ignace.
66-14-5 Josephine Johnson, age 48, St. Ignace.
Note: These children should not be enrolled, for, altho living in 1870, they were not enrolled as members of the tribe, Durant Spl Agt.

Pages 15 & 16
St. Ignace Band
Chief AMABLE ANCE

Information following from: Amable Ance, St. Ignace.
1-15 AMABLE ANCE, Chief, age 64, P.O. St. Ignace.
Wife 1st: Name not given, dead.
Wife 2nd: Eliza Ance, age 60, P.O. St. Ignace, on roll 1870 as 22-17.
1-15-1 Name not given, dead, no children.
1-15-2 Margaret Clausen, age 45, P.O. St. Ignace.
Husband 1st: Name not given.
Husband 2nd: Name not given, white.
Child by 1st husband:
1-15-2-1 Peter Ance McIntosh, age 24, P.O. St. Ignace, single.
Children by 2nd husband:
1-15-2-2 Kate Clausen, age 18, P.O. St. Ignace.
1-15-2-3 Marie Clausen, age 16.
1-15-2-4 Ruby Clausen, age 12.
1-15-2-5 Maggie Clausen, age 9.
1-15-3 Leo Ance, age 41, P.O. St. Ignace.

Wife 1st: Name not given, dead.
Wife 2nd: Agnes (Petoskey) Ance, age 25, P.O. St. Ignace, see 19-28.
Child by 1st wife:
1-15-3-1 Joseph Ance, age 17, P.O. St. Ignace.
1-15-4 Esther Ance, dead.

Information following from: George Ance #2, St. Ignace.
2-15 AISH CAW BAY WIS or ANTHONY ANCE #2, age 97, P.O. St. Ignace.
Wife: Name not given, dead.
2-15-1 Anthony Ance, dead.
Wife: Therese ______, white, age 65.
2-15-1-1 Anthony Ance #3, age 47, P.O. St. Ignace.
Wife: Sophia _______, white, no children.
2-15-1-2 George Ance #3, age 38, P.O. St. Ignace.
2-15-1-3 Jane Ance, age 32, P.O. St. Ignace.
Husband: Archie Paquin, white.
2-15-1-3-1 John Paquin, age 17.
2-15-1-3-2 Ed Paquin, age 12.
2-15-1-3-3 Phil Paquin, age 10.
2-15-1-3-4 Melvina Paquin, age 8.
2-15-1-3-5 Alice Paquin, age 5.
2-15-1-3-6 Leon Paquin, age 2.
2-15-1-4 Rosie O Saw Waw Mick, age 30, P.O. St. Ignace.
2-15-1-5 Edward Ance, age 28, P.O. St. Ignace.
Wife: Name not given, white.
2-15-1-5-1 Clara Belle Ance, age 2.
2-15-1-6 Joseph Ance, age 26, P.O. St. Ignace, single.
2-15-1-7 Therese Lamyont, age 34, P.O. St. Ignace.
Husband: Name not given, white.
2-15-1-7-1 Kate Lamyont, age 14.
2-15-1-7-2 Annie Lamyont, age 12.
2-15-1-7-3 John Lamyont, age 10.
2-15-1-7-4 Louise Lamyont, age 8.
2-15-1-7-5 Jessie Lamyont, age 6.
2-15-1-7-6 Alice Lamyont, age 4.
2-15-1-7-7 Christian Lamyont, age 2.
2-15-1-8 Mary Massey, age 34, P.O. Brevoort Lake, near Allenville, husband white, no children.
2-15-2 George Ance #2, age 63, P.O. St. Ignace.
Wife: Susan Ance #1, nee Keogiwa, age 48, see 23-20.
2-15-2-1 Susan Ance, age 20, single P.O. St. Ignace.
2-15-2-2 Mary Jane Ance, age 18.
2-15-2-3 George Ance #4, age 15.

2-15-2-4 Louisa Ance, age 7.
2-15-3 Kate Ance, dead.
Husband: Name not given, dead.
2-15-3-1 Ed Boucha, age 30, P.O. St. Ignace.
Wife: Susan (Davenport) Boucha, age 32, see 104-22.
2-15-3-1-1 Fred Boucha, age 14.
2-15-3-1-2 Wilber Boucha, age 7.
2-15-3-2 Isaac Boucha, age 28, see 9-36.
Wife: Rhetta, see 9-36.
2-15-3-2-1 Joseph Boucha
2-15-3-3 Lucy Johnson
Husband: Name not given.
2-15-3-3-1 Clarence Johnson, age 4.
2-15-3-4 Susie Boucha, age 19.
2-15-3-5 Annie Boucha, age 11.

2/15

Department of the Interior,
United States Indian Service,

Dear Sir:

Your name has been given me as a member of the Ottawa & Chippewa Tribe of Indians of Michigan, as a grand child of Anthony Ance.

If this information is correct please give me the names, ages, & post office of yourself, and all of your brothers & sisters, if you have any.

Give names in the order of age, & use the back of this sheet for reply, Envelope enclosed for reply,

Very respectfully
HORACE B. DURANT
Special U.S. Indian Agent

Names	*Age*	*Post Office*
Mr. Ed. Boucha	*31*	*St. Ignace, Mich.*
Mrs. Susan Boucha	*32*	*St. Ignace, Mich.*
Freddie Boucha	*14*	*St. Ignace, Mich.*
Wilbur Boucha	*7*	*St. Ignace, Mich.*
	Age	*Post Office*
Isaac Boucha	*29*	*St. Ignace, Mich.*
Mrs IsaacBoucha	*25*	
Joseph Boucha	*4*	
	Age	*Post Office*
Mrs. Lucy Johnston	*21*	*Charles, Mich.*
Clarence Johnston	*4*	*Charles, Mich.*
		Post Office
Miss Susie Boucha	*Age 19*	*Allenville, Mich.*

Annie Boucha *Age 11* *Naubinway, Mich.*

2/15

Kate Lamyotte	*14 year old*
Annie Lamyotte	*12 year old*
John C. Lamyotte	*10 " "*
Louise Lamyotte	*8 " "*
Jessie Lamyotte	*6 " "*
Alice Lamyotte	*4 " "*
Christa M. Lamyotte	*2 " "*

Therisa Lamyotte

Clara Belle Ance 2 year and half
Edward Ance

From Mr. Ed Ance
St. Ignace, Mich

2/15

Dear Sir:
Here are the names of them you ask for.

John Paquin	*17 age old*
Eddie Paquin	*12 = =*
Philippe Paquin	*10 = =*
Malvina Paquin	*8 = =*
Alice Paquin	*5 = =*
Lean Paquin	*2 = =*

Jane Paquin

Information following from: Not Given.

3-15 NAW WE KE ZHE GO QUAY, age 95, dead, mother of 62-16 Francis Me Sway O Wince.
- 3-15-1 Charles, dead, no heirs.
- 3-15-2 Enos, dead, no heirs.
- 3-15-3 Alixse, dead, no heirs.
- 3-15-4 Ellen, dead, no heirs.
- 3-15-5 Oldest, see 62-16.

Information following from: Joe Mesawtego, St. Ignace, June 20/09.

4-15 AISH QUAY KE ZHICK, dead, children gone to Canada, Chiefs do not know where but think Little Currents, Ontario, Spanish River Georgian Bay –Durant Spl. Agt.

Information following from: Not Given, Jan 06/09.

5-15 MRS. SAMUEL VELLAIRE or MARGARET, dead.
Husband 1st: Key Wan De Way, dead.
Husband 2nd: Samuel Vallier, dead.
5-15-1 Joe Ke Wand De Way, age 57, on roll as 9-36 Traverse Band.
5-15-2 James Vallier, Jr., age 50, P.O. St. Ignace.
Wife: Name not given, dead.
5-15-2-1 Maggie (Vallier) Gamble, age 21, P.O. Saginaw.
5-15-3 John Vallier, age 47, P.O. St. Ignace.
Wife: Name not given, white.
5-15-3-1 Alexander Vallier, age 20. P.O. St. Ignace.
5-15-3-2 Addie Vallier, age 18, P.O. St. Ignace.
5-15-3-3 Albert Vallier, age 12.
5-15-3-4 Bertha Vallier, age 6.
5-15-4 Isaac Vallier, age 41, P.O. St. Ignace.
Wife: Name not given, white.
5-15-4-1 Willard Vallier, age 16.
5-15-4-2 Victor Vallier, age 14.

Information following from: Not Given.

6-15 PA BISH KO KE ZHICK or JOSEPH ME SAW TE GO, age 97, P.O. St. Ignace.
Wife: Name not given, dead.
6-15-1 Angeline Belongea, dead, on roll as Mrs. Joseph Belonzhay 12-15
6-15-2 Josit Bodwaince, on roll as 18-15.
6-15-3 Joseph Me Saw Te Go, Jr., on roll as 31-15.
6-15-4 Antoine Me Saw Te Go or Santago, age 60, P.O. The Snows Hessel.
Wife: Margaret Me Saw Te Go, age 46, enroll although can't trace family.
6-15-4-1 Frank Antoine Santago, age 22, P.O. Hessel.
Wife: Name not given, white.
6-15-4-2 Pete William Santago, age 20, single, P.O. Hessel.
6-15-4-3 Catharine Santago
Husband: John Alick, see 3-17.
6-15-5 Mary Lazon or Lalotte, age 55, P.O. St. Ignace, sometimes this family is called Lazon & Lallotte, see 12-13.
Husband: Charles Lozon or Lalotte, age 67.
6-15-5-1 Alixse Lozon
6-15-6 Name not given, dead, single.
6-15-7 Name not given, dead, single.

Information following from: Augustus Hamlin, St. Ignace.

7-15 ROSALIE HAMLIN, dead.

7-15-1 Ellen Hamlin, dead no children.
7-15-2 Name not given, dead, no children.
7-15-3 James Hamlin, age 50, P.O. St. Ignace, single.
7-15-4 Augustus Hamlin, age 48, P.O. St. Ignace, see 18-15.
7-15-5 Moses Hamlin, dead.
Wife: Eliza Hamlin, age 35, P.O. Ashland, Wis., daughter of 12-15.
7-15-5-1 Stella Hamlin, age 14.

Information following from: Joseph Smith, St. Ignace, Dec 31/08, Jany 2/08.
8-15 PAY SHE GO GAW BO WE, dead.
Wife 1st : Name not given, dead.
Wife 2nd: Name not given, dead.
8-15-1 John Smith, age 73, P.O. Hessel, Mich, see 11-15.
Wife: Name not given, see 38-3.
8-15-2 Therese Smith, dead.
Husband: Name not given, dead Sault Ste. Marie Band.
8-15-2-1 Josephine (Shedowan) St. Germain, age 40, P.O. Charles, Mich, near Jenison's Mills.
Husband: Mike St. Germain, see 4-8.
8-15-2-1-1 Ellen Shedowin La Pointe, age 37, P.O. Chicago, husband white, no children.
8-15-3 Pete Smith, age 66, P.O. Drummond Island.
Wife: Mary Smith, age 75, see A-3.
8-15-3-1 Philamon Francis, age 40, P.O. Georgian Bay, Canadian.
Husband: Alex Francis, P.O. Georgian Bay, Canadian.
8-15-3-1-1 Louise Francis, age 12, Canadian.
8-15-3-1-2 Agnes Francis, age 8, Canadian.
8-15-3-1-3 Daughter not named, age 2, Canadian,
Note: Mary Smith has 1 child by 1st husband, dead.
Peter Sageon, age 50, P.O. Drummond Isle.
Wife: Sophia Sageon, age 48, nee Showan.
1. Mary Sabastian, age 28.
Husband: James Sabastian, age 35.
1. Ida Sabastian, age 5.
2. Joe Sageon, age 24, single.
3. Julia Cadotte, age 18.
Husband: Charles Cadotte, age 24, son of Isaac Cadotte 67-4.
4. John Sageon, age 10, deaf & dumb.
5. Archangel Sageon, age 6.
8-15-4 Joseph Smith, age 65, St. Ignace.
Wife: Veletine Smith, age 54, P.O. St. Ignace, see 19-15.
8-15-4-1 Louis Smith, dead.

Wife: Annie (Smith) Petoskey, P.O. Petoskey, see 3-26 and 15-20.
8-15-4-1-1 Rosie Smith, dead.
8-15-4-2 Paul Smith, age 34, P.O. St. Ignace, single.
8-15-4-3 Frank Smith.
Wife: Name not given, white.
8-15-4-3-1 Clarence Smith, age 5, P.O. Vanderbilt, Mich., lives with grandfather Shriowisky(?) 24 miles below Cheboygan.
8-15-4-4 Mary Sweetland, age 30, P.O. Diboll, Texas.
Husband: Name not given, white.
8-15-4-4-1 Guy Sweetland, age 11.
8-15-4-4-2 Lester Sweetland, age 8.
8-15-4-5 Kate Dupont, age 28, P.O. Fosterville, Wis.
Husband: Name not given, white.
8-15-4-5-1 Violet Dupont, age 8.
8-15-4-5-2 Tessie Dupont, age 6.
8-15-4-5-3 Harry Dupont, age 4.
8-15-4-5-4 Clayton Dupont, age 2.
8-15-4-6 Edward Smith, age 23, P.O. St. Ignace, single.
8-15-4-7 John Smith #2, age 19, P.O. Marquette or St. Ignace.
8-15-4-8 William Smith, age 18.
8-15-4-9 Eveline Smith, age 13.
8-15-4-10 Ida Smith, age 10.

Information following from: Not Given.
9-15 FRANCIS GRAHAM, age 71, P.O. Pt. St. Ignace.
Wife: Angeline Graham, age 64.
9-15-1 Henry Graham, age 48, P.O. Goodheart, see 16-28.
Wife: Name not given, see 16-28.
9-15-2 Angeline Graham, dead.
9-15-3 Ellen E. La Grill, age 43, P.O. St. Ignace.
Husband: Name not given, white.
9-15-3-1 Albert E. La Grill, age 10.
9-15-3-2 Adelia E. La Grill, age 9.
9-15-3-3 Amabelle E. La Grill, age 5.
9-15-3-4 Joseph F. La Grill, age 3.
9-15-3-5 Mary E. La Grill, born Dec. 22/07, died May 22/08.
9-15-4 Mary Graham, age 40, P.O. St. Ignace, single.
9-15-5 Jennie Graham, age 34, P.O. St. Ignace, single.
9-15-6 Oral Graham, age 32, P.O. St. Ignace, single.
9-15-7 William Graham, age 30, P.O. St. Ignace, single.
9-15-8 Frank Graham, age 24, P.O. St. Ignace.
9-15-9 Bridget Jenkins, age 28, P.O. Viola, Corinne, Mich.
Husband: Charles H Jenkins, white.

9-15-9-1 Francis Jenkins, age 4.
9-15-9-2 Name not given, female, born 22/07.
9-15-10 Susan Jones, age 38, P.O. Sault Ste. Marie, no children.
Husband: J. C. Jones, white.
9-15-11 Kate Russell, age 36, P.O. St. Ignace.
Husband: Name not given, white.
9-15-11-1 Harry Russell, age 12.
9-15-11-2 Dolores Russell, age 10.
9-15-11-3 Beatrice Russell, age 8.

Information following from: Not Given.
10-15 MRS. AUGUSTINE MARTIN, Mary Ann Martin, a sister of Amable Ance 1-15, age 64. P.O. St. Ignace.
Husband: Name not given, dead.
10-15-1 Jane Guyer, age 46, P.O. Bessemer, Mich.
Husband: name not given, white.
10-15-1-1 Fannie Guyer, age 23.
10-15-1-2 Ida Guyer, age 21.
10-15-1-3 Emma Guyer, age 19.
10-15-1-4 William Guyer, age 17.
10-15-1-5 Elizabeth Guyer, age 15.
10-15-2 Antoine Martin, age 45, P.O. Bessemer, Mich.
Wife: Name not given, dead, P.O. St. Ignace.
10-15-2-1 John Martin #2, age 21, in U.S. Army at Sault St. Marie.
10-15-2-2 William Martin, age 18.
10-15-3 Emma Harris, age 20, died July 6/08.
Husband: William Harris, white, P.O. St. Ignace.
10-15-3-1 Victoria Harris, age 2.
10-15-3-2 Amy Harris, born too late.
10-15-4 John Martin #1, age 38, P.O. Ashland, Wis. or Odenah, Wis., single.
10-15-5 Ambrose Martin, age 33, P.O. St. Ignace, single.

Taconite Minn
June 15, 1909

Dear Sir.

I have received your letter and I will give you the names that you wish to know. My Father name is Mr. Augus Martin and my Mother is name is Mary Ann Martin, and before marriage, Mary Ann Ance, Adress Stignace Mich and my brothers names are Antoine, John, and Ambro Martin, Antoine Martin is my brother and he has two suns, one is named John age 21. William, age 18 and the names of my family is Fannis age 23 Ida age 21 Emma age 19 William age 17Elizabeth age 15.

Antoine and Ambro are in Stignace and John is ~~in~~ Martin is in Udenah, Wis.

Your's Truly
Mrs Jane Guyer
Taconite
Minn

Information following from: Not Given.

11-15 WAY WE GAW NAY BE or JOHN SMITH, age 73, see 8-15.
Wife: Name not given, dead.
11-15-1 Harriet Baker Belongea, age 51, P.O. Pine River.
Husband: William Belongea, age 56, P.O. Pine River, see 17-3.
11-15-1-1 Frank Belongea, age 22, P.O. Pine River, single.
11-15-1-2 John Belongea, age 19.
11-15-1-3 Mike Belongea, age 17.
11-15-1-4 Agnes Belongea, age 11.
11-15-2 Louisa Louis, age 48, P.O. Pine River.
Husband: Charles Louis, age 45, see 6-12.
11-15-2-1 Jennie Nongaishcawnaw, age 25.
Husband: John Nongaishcawnaw, see 3-31.
11-15-2-2 Eliza Mindoskung, age 18, P.O. Pine River.
Husband: John Mendoskung, age 45, see 3-8.
11-15-2-2-1 Noah Mendoskung, born Mach 25/08 2d Roll.
11-15-2-3 Mary Louis Wawsaykezhick, age 17, see 16-12.
Husband: John Wawsaykezhick, see 16-12.
11-15-2-4 Joe Louis, age 15.
11-15-2-5 Louise Louis, age 12.
11-15-2-6 Harriet Louis, age 10.
11-15-2-7 Frank Louis, age 6.
11-15-3 Margaret Smith, age 45.
Husband 1st: George Bolton, separated, Canadian.
Husband 2nd: Pete Taylor, , P.O. Cap Cooker, lived there about 5 yrs.
11-15-3-1 Dan Bolton, age 21, single.
11-15-4 Rosie Jake, age 30.
Husband: James Jake, see 10-11.
11-15-4-1 Peter Jake, age 15.
11-15-4-2 Jonas Jake, age 10.
11-15-4-3 Mary Jane Jake, age 8.
11-15-4-4 Sam Jake, age 7.
11-15-4-5 Elizabeth Jake, age 6.

Information following from: Not Given.

12-15 MRS. JOSEPH BELONGHAY, or ANGELINE BELONGAY, dead.
Husband: Joseph Belonghay, dead.

12-15-1 Angeline Pond, age 50.
Husband: William Pond, son of 20-12.
12-15-2 Eliza Hamlin, see 7-15.
12-15-3 Esther Askin, age 44, P.O. St. Ignace.
Husband: Ed Askin.
12-15-3-1 Margaret Askin, age 15.

Information following from: Not Given.
13-15 GE-MAW-KE-NIN-NE or AMBROSE CORP, age 67, P.O. Gros Cap, 8 miles form St. Ignace.
Wife: Elvira Corp, age 57, daughter of 36-13.
13-15-1 Catharine Lavake, age 48, P.O. Gulliver, Mich.
Husband: Paul Lavake, age 49, see 16-15.
13-15-1-1 Harry Lavake, age 24.
13-15-1-2 Nancy Lavake, age 22.
13-15-1-3 Edith Lavake, age 18.
13-15-1-4 Grace Lavake, age 16.
13-15-1-5 Agnes Lavake, age 14.
13-15-1-6 Napoleon Lavake, age 12.
13-15-1-7 Esther Lavake, age 5.
13-15-2 David Corp, age 45, P.O. Gulliver or Gros Cap, Mich., single.
13-15-3 Lizzie Kelly, age 42, P.O. Gros Cap, Mich.
Husband: Name not given, dead.
13-15-1 Perry Kelly, age 21.
13-15-4 Susan Erskine, age 39, P.O. Allenville, Mich.
Husband: Name not given, white.
13-15-4-1 Jennie Erskine, age 19.
13-15-4-2 Ruby Erskine, age 17.
13-15-4-3 James Erskine, age 16.
13-15-4-4 Nellie Erskine, age 14.
13-15-4-5 John Erskine, age 12.
13-15-4-6 Elsie Erskine, age 10.
13-15-4-7 Esther Erskine, age 8.
13-15-5 Isaac Corp, age 37, P.O. St. Ignace, Mich.
Wife: name not given, white.
13-15-5-1 Philip Corp, age 13.
13-15-5-2 Winifred Corp, age 12.
13-15-5-3 Herbert Corp, age 8.
13-15-5-4 Elmer Corp, age 2.
13-15-6 Fred Corp, age 35, P.O. Gros Cap, Mich.
Wife: Name not given, white.
13-15-6-1 Edmund Corp, age 5.
13-15-6-2 Alice Corp, age 4.
13-15-6-3 Grace Corp, age 2.

13-15-7 Agnes Simpson, age 32, P.O. Cranbrook, BC.
Husband: Name not given, white.
13-15-7-1 Frank Simpson, age 13.
13-15-7-2 Violet Simpson, age 6.
13-15-7-3 Agnes Simpson, age 4.
13-15-8 Rosa Bryce, age 29, P.O. Gros Cap, Mich.
Husband: Name not given, white.
13-15-8-1 Elaine Bryce, age 8.
13-15-8-2 Loris Bryce, age 6.
13-15-8-3 Marion Bryce, age 4 (male).
13-15-8-4 Helena Bryce, age 3.
13-15-8-5 Wilford, age 1 yr born Dec. 1907.
13-15-9 Elmer Corp, age 27, P.O. Gros Cap, Mich.
Wife: Agnes Corp, age 19, nee Parkey.
13-15-10 Belva Goudreau, age 24, P.O. Gros Cap.
Husband: Louis Gourdreau, age 26.
13-15-10-1 James Gourdreau, 8 months old Jany 6/09, born Apr 1908.
13-15-11 Amable Cheeseman, age 21, P.O. Gros Cap, Mich.
Husband: Name not given, white.
13-15-11-1 Elvira Cheeseman, 2 mos old Jany 6/09, born Nov/08.

Information following from: Anthony and Frank Muscoe, St. Ignace, Dec/08 and Pt. Aux Chenes, Apr/09.
14-15 O-MUSH-KO-GOS.
Wife: Name not given, dead.
14-15-1 Frank Mush Ko Gos or Muscoe or Ance, age 65, P.O. Pt. Aux Chenes, on roll as 43-16.
Wife: Christine Muscoe, age 52, see 1-11.
14-15-1 Joe Muscoe, age 38, P.O. Snow Island.
Wife: Name not given, dead.
14-15-1-1 Fred Muscoe, age 5.
14-15-2 Isaac Muscoe, age 36, P.O. Gros Cap.
Wife: Jennoe Muscoe, age 21, nee Petosegay.
14-15-2-1 Isaac Muscoe, age 9.
14-15-2-2 George Muscoe, born July 28, 1908.
14-15-3 John Muscoe, age 20, P.O. Gros Cap, single.
14-15-4 Mitchel Muscoe, age 16, single.
14-15-5 Mary Muscoe, age 27, P.O. Gros Cap.
14-15-6 William Muscoe, age 15, P.O. Gros Cap, Mich.
14-15-7 Moses Muscoe, age 10, P.O. Gros Cap, Mich.
14-15-8 Christina M. Muscoe, age 6, P.O. Gros Cap, Mich.
14-15-9 Christine Andreson, age 34, P.O. Cedarville, Mich.
Husband: Name not given, white.

14-15-9-1 Annie Anderson, age 10.
14-15-9-2 Mary Anderson, age 8.
14-15-9-3 Helen Anderson, age 5 (twin).
14-15-9-4 Angeline Anderson, age 5 (twin).
14-15-9-5 George Anderson, age 3 (twin).
14-15-9-6 Maggie Anderson, age 3 (twin).

14-15-2 Anthony Mush Ko Gos or Ance, age 54, P.O. St. Ignace or Charles.
Wife: Philamon Ance, age 33, P.O. St. Ignace, see 45-21.
14-15-2-1 Rosie Ance, age 16.

14-15-3 Mary Ann Shedowin, age 47, P.O. Pt. Aux Chenes.
Husband: Name not given, dead.
14-15-3-1 Joe Shedowin, age 30, single.
14-15-3-2 Moses Shedowin, age 28, single.

14-15-4 Isaac Muscoe, dead no children.

14-15-5 Elizabeth Corbiere, dead.
Husband: Name not given, dead.
14-15-5-1 Sophia Waishkey, age 44, off draws on Canadian rolls, see 12-5.
Husband: name not given, see 12-5.

Information following from: Joe Mesawtego and Amable Ance.

15-15 O-GAW-BAY-GE-ZHE-GO-QUAY, dead, children dead.
Husband: Name not given.

Information following from: Not Given.

16-15 FREDERICK LEVAKE JR., dead.
Wife: Name not given, dead.

16-15-1 Napoleon Levake or Paul Levake, age 54, P.O. Gulliver, Mich.
Wife: Catharine Levake, age 50, nee Corp, see 13-15 of Gros Cap.
16-15-1-1 Harry Levake, age 25, P.O. Manistique.
16-15-1-2 Nancy Levake, age 24, P.O. Manistique.
16-15-1-3 Edith Bellant, age 22, P.O. Gulliver.
16-15-1-4 Grace Levake, age 18, P.O. Gulliver.
16-15-1-5 Ida Levake, age 14.
16-15-1-6 Nepoleon Levake, age 12, P.O. Gulliver.
16-15-1-7 Esther Levake, age 5.

16-15-2 Mary Levake.
Husband: Tullis View, P.O. Cheboygan, white.
16-15-2-1 Denny View, age 19, P.O. Cheboygan.
16-15-2-2 Mary View, age 17, P.O. Cheboygan.
16-15-2-3 Adolphus View, age 15, P.O. Cheboygan.
16-15-2-4 Erminie View, age 13, P.O. Cheboygan.

16-15-2-5 Fred View, age 11, P.O. Cheboygan.
16-15-2-6 Joe View, age 9, P.O. Cheboygan.
16-15-2-7 Rosa View, age 7, P.O. Cheboygan.
16-15-2-8 John View, age 5, P.O. Cheboygan.
16-15-3 Libby Archambo, age 40, P.O. Cheboygan.
Husband: Name not given, white.
16-15-3-1 John Archambo, age 17.
16-15-3-2 Nicholas Archambo, age 13.
16-15-3-3 Agnes Archambo, age 10.
16-15-3-4 Elsie Archambo, age 8.
16-15-3-5 Melvina Archambo, age 5.
16-15-3-6 Napoleon Archambo, age 3.
16-15-4 Jennie Poirier, age 35, P.O. Cheboygan, no children.
Husband: Name not given, white.
16-15-5 Rosie Champine, age 31, P.O. Beaver Island.
Husband: Charles Champine, son of 34-13.
16-15-6 Sophia Cadotte, age 38, P.O. Boise Blanc, Mac. Isle, children see 8-13.
Husband: Edward Cadotte, see 8-13.

Information following from: Not Given.
17-15 MRS. PETER MAY-SE-SWAY-WE-NIN-NE, dead.
17-15-1 Ellen Andrews, age 43, see 9-17.
17-15-2 Hyacinth May-Se-Sway-We-Nin-Ne, dead, no heirs.
17-15-3 Gaspar May-Se-Sway-We-Nin-Ne, age 38, P.O. St. Ignace.
Wife: Josephine May-Se-Sway-We-Nin-Ne, age 30, see 65-16.
17-15-3-1 Philamon May-Se-Sway-We-Nin-Ne, age 13.
17-15-3-2 Frank May-Se-Sway-We-Nin-Ne, age 11.
17-15-3-3 Paul May-Se-Sway-We-Nin-Ne, age 8.
17-15-3-4 Charles May-Se-Sway-We-Nin-Ne, age 6.
17-15-3-5 Hyacinth May-Se-Sway-We-Nin-Ne, age 4.
17-15-3-6 Irene May-Se-Sway-We-Nin-Ne, born Jany 28/07, 2nd roll.
17-15-4 Emma Bazinaw, age 40, P.O. Mackinaw Island.
Husband: Augustus Bazinaw, age 46, son of 56-14 and 4-17.
17-15-4-1 Ellen Bazinaw, age 20.
17-15-4-2 Alex Bazinaw, age 16.
17-15-4-3 Delia Bazinaw, age 7.
17-15-4-4 Anita Bazinaw, age 4.
17-15-4-5 Michael Bazinaw, born Nov 2/07.

Information following from: Mrs. Josette Bodwaince, St. Ignace.
18-15 MRS. JOSETTE BODWAINCE, age 66, P.O. St. Ignace.
Husband: Name not given.

18-15-1 Name and sex not given, dead.
18-15-2 Hyacinthe Bodwin, age 44, P.O. St. Ignace.
Wife: Lucy Bodwin, white.
18-15-2-1 Pete Bodwin, age 10.
18-15-2-2 Antoine Bodwin, age 6.
18-15-2-3 Lucy Annie Bodwin, born Apr 5/07.
18-15-3 Mary Hamlin, age 36, P.O. St. Ignace.
Husband: Augustus Hamlin, age 48, see 7-15.
18-15-3-1 Rose Hamlin, age 19.
18-15-3-2 Albert Hamlin, age 14.
18-15-3-3 George Hamlin, age 11.
18-15-3-4 Hyacinth Hamlin, age 8.
18-15-3-5 William Hamlin, age 4.
18-15-3-6 Paul Hamlin, born Feby. 3/08.
18-15-4 Joseph Bodwin, age 33, P.O. St. Ignace.
Wife: Mary (Misatago) Bodwin, white, formerly wife of Joe Misatago, see 31-15.
18-15-4-1 George Bodwin, age 7.
18-15-4-2 Sophia Bodwin, age 6.
18-15-5 Angeline Frazer, age 30, P.O. St. Ignace.
Husband: Name not given, white.
18-15-5-1 Abram Frazer, age 8.
18-15-5-2 Nellie Frazer, age 6.
18-15-5-3 Daniel Frazer, age 3.
18-15-5-4 John Frazer, born Nov 23/08 too late.
18-15-6 Name and sex not given, dead.
18-15-7 Name and sex not given, dead.
18-15-8 Name and sex not given, dead.
18-15-9 Name and sex not given, dead.

Information following from: Veletine Smith, St. Ignace.
19-15 LOUIS POND, dead.
Wife 1st : Name not given, white, dead.
Wife 2nd: Mary Ann Pond, age 84, P.O. St. Ignace, on roll as 63-16, mother of Amable Ance.
19-15-1 Mary Prue, age 58, P.O. St. Ignace, by 1st wife of Louis Pond.
Husband 1st: _______ Boucha
Husband 2nd: _______ Prue.
19-15-1-1 Ed Boucha, age 41, P.O. St. Ignace.
19-15-1-2 Ezra Boucha, age 34, P.O. Munising.
19-15-1-3 Mrs. William Paquin, age 37, P.O. Munising.
19-15-1-4 Mrs. Charles Dumas, age 26, P.O. Shoreham, Vermont.
19-15-1-5 Mrs. Jennie Grundin, age 23, P.O. St. Ignace.

19-15-1-6 Mrs. Lavina Valley, age 21.
19-15-1-7 Miss Anna Prue, age 19, P.O. St. Ignace.
19-15-1-8 Flora Prue, age 12, P.O. Ignace.
19-15-2 Veletine Smith, age 54, see 8-15.

9/15

Department of the Interior,
United States Indian Service,

Dear Madam:

Please give me the names, ages and addresses of all your children, for the Ottawa & Chippewa Enrollment which I am making.

Also, give the names of your father & mother.

Envelope enclosed for reply, please use the back of this sheet in reply.

Very respectfully
HORACE B. DURANT
Special U.S. Indian Agent

Dear Sir,

The names and addresses of my children are as follows

1st family.	*Mr. Ed Boucha*	*Age*	*41*	*St. Ignace Mich*
	Mr. Ezra "	*"*	*34*	*Munising Mich*
	Mrs. Wm Paquin	*"*	*37*	*Munising Mich*
	Mrs. Charles Dumas		*26*	*Shoreham Vermont*
2nd family.	*Mrs. Jennie Grondin*		*23*	*St. Ignace Mich*
	Mrs. Lavina Vallie		*21*	*" " "*
	Miss Anna Prue		*19*	*" " "*
	Miss Flora Prue		*12*	*" " "*
	Father Mr. Louis Pond			
	Mother Mrs. Cathrine Pond (nee Massey)			*" "*

From Mrs Mary Prue,
St. Ignace, Mich

Information following from: Joe Mesawtego.
20-15 MICHEL MACANUCT-GO, dead, has children living at Little Channel on other side of Detroit 18 miles in Canada, Durant.

Information following from: Not Given.
21-15 MRS. CHARLES BELONZHAY, cannot trace this family, Durant.

Information following from: Not Given.
22-15 CYRIL REBASKAW or CYRIL POND, dead.
Wife: Name not given, dead.

22-15-1 Pete Pond, age 50, P.O. St. Ignace.
Wife: Name not given.
22-15-1-1 Boy, name and age not given.
22-15-1-2 Boy, name and age not given.
22-15-1-3 Girl, name and age not given.
22-15-2 Napoleon Pond, age 48, P.O. St. Ignace.
Wife: Name not given.
22-15-2-1 Boy, name and age not given.
22-15-2-2 Girl, name and age not given.
22-15-3 Charles Pond, P.O. St. Ignace.
22-15-4 Fred Pond, P.O. St. Ignace.
22-15-5 Philamon Martino, P.O. St. Ignace.
22-15-6 Velaline Martino, P.O. St. Ignace.

Information following from: Joe Mesawtego and Amab Ance.
23-15 MRS. FRED'K LEVAKE Sr., dead, no children living.

Information following from: Note: The persons enrolled in 1870 were Pean Ance, his Sister (Lizzie Mullen) & Lizzie Mullen's two children & Mrs. Alice Gudreau, & Louis Mellon.
24-15 PEAN ANCE, dead, died single & SISTER or LIZZIE MULLEN, living.
24-15-1 Sister Lizzie Mullen or Lizzie Mellon, age 56, P.O. Epoufette, Mich.
Husband: Name not given, white.
24-15-1-1 Louis Mellon, age 40, P.O. Epoufette, Mich.
Wife: Name not given, white.
24-15-1-1-1 Name or sex not given.
24-15-1-2 Alice Goudreau, age 39, P.O. Epoufette, Mich.
Husband: Peter Goudreau, white.
24-15-1-2-1 Francis Goudreau, age 14.
24-15-1-2-2 Mary Goudreau, age 12.
24-15-1-2-3 Alvin Goudreau, age 9.
24-15-1-2-4 Nelson Goudreau, age 7.
24-15-1-2-5 Robert Goudreau, age 6.
24-15-1-2-6 Elizabeth Goudreau, age 5.
24-15-1-2-7 Wilbur Goudreau, age 4.
24-15-1-2-8 Fidel Goudreau, age 2, girl.
24-15-1-3 Frank Mellen, age 37, P.O. Epoufette, Mich., single.
24-15-1-4 Robert Mellen, age 25, P.O. Epoufette, Mich., single.
24-15-1-5 Daniel Mellen, age 27, P.O. Epoufette, Mich., single.

24-15-1-6 Charles Mellen, age 17, P.O. Epoufette, Mich., single.

24-15-1-7 Grace Mellen, age 19, P.O. Epoufette, Mich., single.

24-15-1-8 Mollie Mullen, age 15, single.

24-15-1-9 Nora Beheydt, dead.

Husband: Clement Beheydt, P.O. Epoufette, Mich, white.

24-15-1-9-1 Francis Beheydt, age 12.

24-15-1-9-2 Ralph Beheydt, age 6.

24-15-1-9-3 Raymond, age 3.

24-15-2 Sister Mary St. Onge.

Husband: John St. Onge, age 60, P.O. St. Onge, see 46-14.

24-15-2-1 Louis St. Onge, age 30, P.O. St. Ignace, single.

24-15-2-2 John St. Onge, age 26, P.O. St. Ignace, single.

24-15-2-3 Mary Larsen, age 28, P.O. St. Ignace.

Husband: Name not given, white.

24-15-2-3-1 William Larsen, age 6.

24-15-2-3-2 Floyd Larsen, age 4.

24-15-2-3-3 Unnamed Infant, born Jany 1908.

24-15-3 Nora McDermott, age 38, P.O. Chicago, Ill.

Husband: Name not given, white.

24-15-3-1 James McDermott, age 24, P.O. Chicago, Ill. 9114 Cottage Grove Ave.

Wife: Name not given, white.

24-15-3-1-1 Sarah McDermott, age 7.

24-15-3-1-2 Florence McDermott, age 6.

24-15-3-1-3 James L. McDermott, age 2 ½ .

24-15-3-2 William McDermott, age 22, P.O. St. Ignace.

Wife: Name not given, white.

24-15-3-2-1 John Isaac McDermott, age 3.

24-15-3-2-2 William H. McDermott, born Apr 1907, 2nd roll.

24-15-3-3 Eugene McDermott, age 20, P.O. 9119 Cottage Grove Ave., Chicago.

24-15-3-4 Alice McDermott, age 18, P.O. 9119 Cottage Grove Ave., Chicago.

Information following from: Amab Ance and John Bourassaw, Jany 6/09.

25-15 MRS. LOUIS BOURASSAW, dead.

25-15-1 Se-Ge-Nock, as 56-16.

25-15-2 George Bourassa, as 61-16.

25-15-3 Battise Bourassaw, dead no heirs.

Information following from: Charles Terrient, Gould City, Apr 27/09.

26-15 MRS. LOUIS BENNETT, dead, an aunt of Charles Terrient.
26-15-1 Name not given, girl, probably dead, but don't know.

Information following from: Joe Mesawtego, Joe Smith, Peter Tebo Inter. and Louis LaSage, St. Ignace, June 20/09.

27-15 FRANCIS HUBERT, Chiefs cannot remember this name & I cannot trace him, Durant Spl. Agt.

Information following from:Jane Lasley visiting her son at Mack Isle, Apr/09.

28-15 GEORGE LASLEY, dead.
Wife: Jane Lasley, age 67, P.O. Scott's Point, Gould City.
28-15-1 Mary Jane Gillespie, age 42, P.O. Gould City.
Husband: Robert Gillespie, white.
28-15-1-1 Eva Berry, age 19, P.O. Gould City.
Husband: Name not given, white.
28-15-1-1-1 John Berry, age 2.
28-15-1-2 Lucy Gillespie, age 15, P.O. Gould City.
28-15-1-3 Robert A. Gillespie, age 12.
28-15-1-4 George Gillespie, age 10.
28-15-2 George Lasley, age 34, P.O. Mack Isle.
Wife: Annie (McGulphin) Lasley, age 25, see 49-13.
28-15-2-1 May Lasley, age 6.
28-15-2-2 Catharine Lasley, age 4.
28-15-2-3 Ellen Lasley, age 3.
28-15-3 Barney Lasley, age 33, P.O. Gould City.
Wife: Mary Jane Lasley.
28-15-3-1 Irene Lasley, age 5.
28-15-3-2 Hattie Lasley, age 2.

Information following from: Amab Ance.

29-15 LOUIS MARTIN, dead no heirs.

Information following from: Charles Levake, Brevoort, Apr 21/09.

30-15 CHARLES LEVAKE, age 65.
Wife: Name not given, dead, white.
30-15-1 Mary Prout, age 42, P.O. Epoufette, Mich, St. Ignace.
Husband: Name not given, white.
30-15-1-1 Mary Prout, age 17.
30-15-1-2 Phoebe Prout, age 15.
30-15-1-3 Ellen Prout, age 12.
30-15-1-4 William Prout, age 9.
30-15-1-5 John Prout, age 8.
30-15-1-6 Charles Prout, age 6.
30-15-1-7 Annie Prout, age 3.

30-15-2 Sophia Kirridge, age 38, P.O. Levering, 5 miles north.
Husband: Charles Kirridge, white.
30-15-2-1 Charles Kirridge, age 19.
30-15-2-2 Lena Kirridge, age 18.
30-15-2-3 Nora Kirridge, age 15.
30-15-2-4 Fred Kirridge, age 10.
30-15-2-5 Chester Kirridge, age 8.
30-15-2-6 William Kirridge, age 6.
30-15-3 Lucy Champaign, age 36, P.O. Epoufette.
Husband: Fred Champaign, Canadian, off.
30-115-3-1 Rosie Champaign, age 13.
30-115-3-2 Henry Champaign, age 10.
30-115-3-3 Fred Champaign, age 9.
30-115-3-4 Catharine Champaign, age 5.
30-115-3-5 Ida Champaign, age 2.
30-15-4 Amab Levake, age 32, P.O. Epoufette, Mich., single.

Information following from: Joe Misawtego Sr., St. Ignace.
31-15 ME-SAW-TE-GO or JOSEPH MISATAGO, age 64, P.O. St. Ignace.
Wife: Elizabeth Misatago, age 54, P.O. St. Ignace, see 5-3.
31-15-1 Joseph Misatago Jr., age 27, died Sept 9/07 1st roll.
Wife: May Misatago, now wife of Joe Bodwin, see 18-15.
31-15-1-1 Joseph Thomas Misatago, age 3, P.O. St. Ignace.
31-15-2 Frank Misatago, age 41, P.O. St. Ignace.
Wife: Almay Misatago, age 36, belongs to "Soo" Band.
31-15-2-1 Della Mariam Misatago, born Nov 1907.
31-15-2-2 Eva Misatago, age 2, died Sept 8, 1907.
31-15-3 Elizabeth Tebo, age 38, P.O. St. Ignace, no children.
Husband: Peter Tebo, age 46, belongs to "Soo" Band, see 11-8.

Information following from: Not Given.
32-15 CATHARINE PIEROUGAY or PE-NOU-GAY, dead, mother of Francis Graham.
Husband: Name not given.
32-15-1 Kate Grant, age 65, P.O. Bellingham City, Washington, no children.
Husband: Jno. Grant, white.

Information following from: Amab Ance, Jany 6/09.
33-15 ANGELINE & PAUL HAMLIN, both dead & none had any children.

Information following from: Amab Ance.
34-15 ANTOINE JAUNDREAU, dead, no heirs.

Information following from: Joe Mesawtego, Joe Hinish.
35-15 ALEXSE PERANCE or PEROW, dead, no heirs.

Information following from: Mrs. Joe Kaw-Kye-Yea.
36-15 MRS. JOSEPH KAW-KYE-YEA or MARY ST. ONGE, age 70, P.O. St. Ignace.
Husband: Joseph St. Onge, white, separated.
36-15-1 Louise Saintoush or St. Onge., age 44, P.O. Trout lake, single

Information following from: Not Given.
37-15 ANTOINE MARTIN, dead.
Wife: Name not given, dead.
37-15-1 Mary Louise Goudreau, age 58, P.O. St. Ignace.
Husband: Name not given, dead.
37-15-1-1 Henry Goudreau, age 30, P.O. St. Ignace (Cody, Wyoming).
37-15-1-2 Antoine Goudreau, age 28, P.O. St. Ignace.
37-15-1-3 Alex Goudreau, age 26, P.O. St. Ignace.
37-15-1-4 Leander Goudreau, age 24, P.O. St. Ignace.
37-15-1-5 Fred Goudreau, age 22, P.O. St. Ignace.
37-15-1-6 Agnes Goudreau, age 19, P.O. St. Ignace.
37-15-1-7 Ellen McDonald, age 20, P.O. St. Ignace.
37-15-1-8 Josephine Raby Goudreau, age 32, P.O. St. Ignace.
37-15-1-9 Amab Goudreau, dead.
Wife: Name not given, white, now wife of John Bourassaw, see 56-16.
37-15-1-9-1 Clifford Goudreau, age 11.
37-15-1-9-2 Lawrence Goudreau, age 8.
37-15-1-9-3 Eugene Goudreau, age 6.
37-15-2 Antoine Martin, age 56, P.O. Scott's Point, Mich.
Wife: Harriet Martin, age 42, see 39-13.
37-15-2-1 Laura Davenport, age 26, Scott's Point, Mich.
Husband: Name not given, see 42-14.
37-15-2-2 Franklin Martin, age 25, P.O. Gould City, single.
37-15-2-3 Joseph Martin, age 22, P.O.Gould City, single.
37-15-2-3 Abraham Martin, age 20, P.O.Gould City, single.
37-15-2-3 Mary Ella Martin, age 18, P.O.Gould City, single.
37-15-2-3 Fred Martin, age 16, P.O.Gould City, single.
37-15-2-3 Lena Jane Martin, age 14, P.O.Gould City, single.
37-15-3 Catharine Goudreau, age 54, P.O. St. Ignace.
Husband: Name not given, white.
37-15-4 Mary Ann Belonghay, age 52, P.O. Namah.
Husband: Henry Belonghay, see 24-11.
37-15-5 Junius Martin, age 50, P.O. St. Ignace.
Wife: Name not given, dead.

37-15-6 John (Baptiste) Martin, age 48, P.O. St. Ignace, has 10 children names not given.
Wife: Name not given, white.
37-15-7 Jane Miles, age 42, P.O. St. Ignace, has 5 children names not given.
Husband: Name not given, white.

Information following from: Joe Mesawtego, Joe Smith.
38-15 FRANCIS MARTIN, dead.
Note: These children though living in 1870 were not enrolled with parent in 1870, who was a half breed & the Inds did not enroll children of half breeds, as members of tribe, Durant Spl Agt.
38-15-1 Hyacynthe Martin, age 48, P.O. St. Ignace.
38-15-2 William Martin.

Information following from: Amab Ance.
39-15 NAW-O-QUAISH-CAW-MO-QUAY, dead, no heirs.

Information following from: Not Given.
40-15 MOSES HAMLIN, age 78, P.O. Brutus.
Wife: Name not given, on roll 1870 with husband.
Note: A son of wife of Moses Hamlin, whose mother was regularly enrolled in 1870, & he, therefore is entitled to enrollment. HBDurant Spl Agt, Oct 24/08 Burt Lake.
40-15-1 Eugene Hamlin, age 33, P.O. Pellston.
Wife: Hattie Hamlin, age 33, nee Shaw-Waw-Naw-Quab, see 29-31.
40-15-1-1 Maggie Hamlin, age 8.
40-15-1-2 Dick Hamlin, age 6.
40-15-1-3 James Hamlin, age 10, died Apr 1908.
40-15-2 Moses Hamlin Jr., age 31, P.O. Pellston.
Wife: Justina Hamlin, age 29, Traverse, see 34-32.
40-15-3 William Hamlin, age 40, P.O. Brutus, see 3-31 and 16-31.

Information following from: Not Given.
41-15 ANTHONY ANCE #1, age 70, P.O. Suttons Bay, no children by 2nd wife.
Wife 1st: Name not given, a Pottawatomie.
Wife 2nd: Mary Ann Ance, age 58, see 24-41.
41-15-1 Peter Ance, age 45, P.O. Elk Rapids.
Wife 1st: Name not given, dead.
Wife 2nd: Eliza (King) Ance, age 41, see 3-40.
41-15-1-1 Isaac Ance, age 10, P.O. Northport, see 10-40, Traverse.
41-15-1-2 Daniel Ance, age 6, P.O. Northport, see 10-40,

Traverse.

Information following from: Amab Ance.
42-16 MRS. HIGGINS, dead.
Husband: __________ Higgins
42-15-1 Mike or Mitchell Higgins, P.O. St. Ignace.

Information following from: Not Given.
43-16 FRANCIS O-MUSH-KO-GOS or FRANK MUSHGOSE ANCE or MUSCOE, age 63, P.O. Gros Cap, Mich, see 14-15.
Wife: Christine Mush-Ko-Gos.
43-15-1 Joe Muscoe, see 14-15.
43-15-2 Isaac Muscoe, see 14-15.
43-15-3 John Muscoe, see 14-15.
43-15-4 Mitchell Muscoe, see 14-15.
43-15-5 Mary Muscoe, see 14-15.

Information following from: Francis Graham, brother, St. Ignace, Jany 2/09.
44-16 JOHN GRAHAM, age 70, P.O. Tower, Min. (or Michigan) Tower Lumber Co., separated from wife.
Wife: Name not given, white.
44-16-1 Mary McDonald, P.O. Garnett or Welch between Trout Lake & Manistique, cannot locate her, Durant.

Report: This man was enrolled in 1870 by himself, altho. He had children at that time: from which it appears that the tribe did not recognize the children as members, and the question now is: shall they be now recognized & enrolled.

Information following from: Amab Ance, Mrs Louis Lushway.
45-16 MRS. LOUIS LUSHWAY, formerly MARGARET ROBINSON, age 75, P.O. St. Ignace.
Husband: Louis Lushway.
46-16-1 Joe Lushway.

Information following from: Jackson Chapman, Vincent Valencourt, Mac. Isle, Apr 12/09.
46-16 MRS. ALICE LABUTT, dead.
Husband: Name not given.
46-16-1 Daughter, name not given, dead.
Husband: Name not given, dead.
46-16-1-1 Agnes Pond, see 50-14
46-16-1-2 Rose Crosby, age 40, P.O. Mack. Isle.
Husband: Name not given, white.
46-16-1-2-1 Ineze Crosby, age 23, P.O. Mack. Isle.

46-16-1-3 Joe Wilmette, age 45, P.O. Light House at Frankfort.

Wife: Name not given.

46-16-1-3-1 Robert Wilmette, age 23, single, address unknown.

46-16-1-3-2 Albert Wilmette, age 21.

46-16-1-3-3 Harold Wilmette, age 19, married no children, P.O. Detroit.

46-16-1-3-4 Florence Wilmette, age 18, P.O. Frankfort.

46-16-1-3-5 Leo Wilmette, age 16. P.O. Frankfort.

46-16-1-3-6 Marie Wilmette, age 12, P.O. Frankfort.

46-16-2 Name not given, dead, no heirs.

(Author Note: The relationship of these people is not at all clear as written in Durants notes. They are listed above as best as could be determined based on his notes.)

Information following from: Amab Ance.

47-16 PAW-GE-NAY, dead, children dead with no heirs.

Information following from: Not Given.

48-16 LOUIS GRAHAM, P.O. St. Ignace, cannot locate him, Durant.

Information following from: Amab Ance.

49-16 MADAM BODWAINE, dead.

Husband: Name not given.

49-16-1 Isabelle Cheney Grondin, P.O. St. Ignace.

49-16-1-1 Annie Grondin, age 18.

49-16-1-2 Clara Grondin, age 15.

49-16-1-3 Blanche Grondin, age 13.

49-16-1-4 Eva Grondin, age 8.

City of St. Ignace
Clerk's Office

To HoraceB. Durant *St. Ignace, Mich., May 31 1909*
Special U.S. Indian Agt

Dear Sir: In answer to your favorof 28 Mch relatin/to~~My~~ age and the names and age of my children. Were, Say, my family name is Isabella Cheney. My children name and ages are as follows:

1 Annie Grondin 18 years of age
2 Clara Grondin 15 " " "
3 Blanch Grondin 13 " " "
4 Eva Grondin 8 " " " hoping the

Above were prove satisfactory to you.
I remain yours Respectfully
Isabelle Cheney family name
By Isabelle Grondin

Information following from: Amable Ance, Chief, St. Ignace, Jany 2/08
50-16 MADAM CHAMPAIGN
Husband: Name not given.
50-16-1 Simon Champaign, age 63, P.O. Gulliver, Mich (near Manistique).
See attached sheet for statement, & for his family.
Simon Champaign is sufficiently identified with this sheet by testimony of Amable Ance, Chief of the band, now living near St. Ignace. Durant, Spl Agt, St. Ignace Jany 2/08

The mother of Simon Champaign was an Indianof theOttawa & Chippewa tribe of the Mackinaw Band; Simonsays she died before 1870, that he used to draw with his mother; that his father was a Frenchman:_ Simon's mother was a cousin of wife of Chief Kesic, of the Nahuna sub-band; his mother also had an allotment of land near Mackinaw Island.

His statements are corroborated by Chief Kesic or Kesie, and I have no doubt as to his identity. However he appears to be ~~weaky~~ of littleIndian blood, and, inas much as neither his mother's name, nor his own, appears on the 1870 roll as a member of this band, I do not believe it proper to permit his family to share in this payment but would ~~limit~~ permit the enrollment & participation of Simon Champaign.

Simon Champaign, 63 ____ Gulliver P.O. Mich
Wife: white
Children 1. Wm Champaign 37_ Whitedale, Mich
Wife: whiteMadeline or Mary – nee Lalotte, was a Lalotte, of the Mackinaw Band.
Childn: 1.
2.
3.
4.
2. Simon Champaign Jr, 34 __ Canary, Mich
single
3. John Champaign, 32__ Garden Bay, Mich
single
4. Ellen Clare, 31 Manistique, "
Husb: white
Childn: 1.
2.
3.

4.
5.
6

5. Louisa Flora *29 __ Manistique,*
Husb: white
Childn: 1.
2.

6. Emily Holling *27 Manistique*
Husb: white
Childn: 1.
2.

7. Ida Champaign *25 Gladstone*
single

8. Oliver Champaign *22 Whitedale*
single

9. Henry Champaign *19* *"*
10. Lillie " 16 *"*
11. Charley " 14 *"*

Information following from: Amab Ance.
51-16 CATHARINE LAZUINE or LALOTTE, dead, an aunt of Amab Ance
Never had any children.

Information following from: Amab Ance.
52-16 MRS. TRUMBLY, dead, no heirs.

Information following from: Amab Ance et al and Joe Misawtego, St. Ignace.
53-16 SHAW-WE-GAW, died single.

Information following from: Gould City, Apr 27/09
54-16 ANGELIQUE MARTIN, dead.
54-16-1 Dead girl, no heirs.

Information following from: Joe Mesawtego, Joe Smith, Peter Tebo Interpreter, Louis LaSage Interpreter, St. Ignace, June 20/09.
55-16 JOHN B. REBAURE, dead, left no children.

Information following from: St. Ignace, Jany 6/09.
56-16 SE-GE-NOCK or JOHN BOURASSAW
Wife: Name not given.
56-16-1 John Bourisaw, age 38, P.O. St. Ignace
Wife: white, formerly wife of Amab Goudreauy, dec'd, see 37-15, no children.
56-16-2 Theresa Bourassaw, age 21, P.O. Gros Cap, single.

Information following from: Amab Ance.

57-16 ANGELINE TRUCKEY, dead.
Husband: Name not given.
57-16-1 Antoine Truckey, P.O. St. Ignace
57-16-2 Angelique Pamble, age 57, St. Ignace, separated, no children.

St. Ignace June 6 1909
Horace B. Durant
Dear Sir
Yours of the 20th of May received and you want to know of my age and also my family my age is 58 years and my father when he died was 80 years old and he has bin dead 23 years and my mother was 65 years old when she died and she has bin dead 19 years my father's name was Peter Truckey and my mother's name was Angeline Chenia before she was married when she died was Angeline Truckey now about their age I think I am forety neer right and about myself I am alone I have one brother and I don't see him very often I could not write before
Yours Truly
Mrs Angeline Pemble St IgnaceMich

Information following from: Louis Recolley, Dec 18/08.
58-16 LOUIS ROCKLOE or RECOLLEY, age 68, P.O. Mullett Lake.
Wife: Phoebe Recolley, age 65, daughter of 36-13.
58-16-1 Phoebe Slocum, age 42, P.O. 77 Palinas St., Grand Rapids, Mich.
Husband: Name not given, white.
58-16-1-1 Leslie Slocum, age 17.
58-16-1-2 Deway Slocum, age 12.
58-16-1-3 Louis Slocum, age 10.
58-16-1-4 William Slocum, age 8.
58-16-1-5 Lawrence Slocum, age 6, duplicate twin.
58-16-1-6 Clarence Slocum, age 6, duplicate twin.
58-16-1-7 Walter Slocum, age 2.
58-16-2 Meredith Recolley, age 40, P.O. Mullet Lake, single.
58-16-3 Lillian Recolley, age 36, P.O. Mullet Lake, single.
58-16-4 Elenor Stone, age 32, Mullet Lake.
Husband: Name not given, white.
58-16-5 Lester Recolley, age 29, P.O. Mullet Lake.
Wife: Name not given, white.
58-16-5-1 Jake Recolley, born Dec 1907.
58-16-6 Susan Recolley, age 20, Mullet Lake.

Information following from: Amab Ance.
59-16 HYACINTHE HAMLIN, dead, no children.

Information following from: Lizzie Shomin, et al, Jos. Labelle, Mack Isle, Apr 10/09, Apr 12/09.

60-16 JOSEPH LABELLE, age 66, P.O. Mackinaw Island.
  Wife: Name not given, dead.
  60-16-1 Lizzie Shomin, age 38, P.O. Mackinaw Isld.
    Husband: See 81-21.
  60-16-2 Joe Labelle Jr., age 40, P.O. Vietage or Lakewood.
    Wife: Name not given, white, no children.
  60-16-3 Lena Chamberlain, age 36, Ishpeming, Mich.
    Husband: John Chamberlain, white.
    60-16-3-1 William Chamberlain, age 14.
    60-16-3-2 Earl Chamberlain, age 12.
    60-16-3-3 Robert Chamberlain, age 4.

Ishpeming Mich June 10 1909

Pulaskey Mich
Mr Durant

Dear sir your letter to hand. I am sure you are wrongly informaed as to my being Indian or part Indian.
My mother was white her mother was german & French & her maiden name was Veletine St. Andrew & her Father was French too, & my Father is French I never knew much aboiut my father but I know he is white, I lay no claim to the Indian Nationality who ever said in my name as my being Indian were mistakenyou could find out all you want to by writing to my father Joe LaBelle Mackinac Island Mich.
I am sure you Trust be mistaken.
Mrs Lina Chamberlain

Dear ~~Madam:~~
~~Your father, Jos. LaBelle was enrolled in 1870 as a member of the Ottawa & Ch~~

Information following from: Not Given.

61-16 GEORGE BOURASSA, dead.
  Wife: Christian (Standre) Bourassa, white.
  61-16-1 Tiorge Bourassaw, age 21, P.O. Gros Cap, single.
  61-16-2 Mary Pacquin, age 22, P.O. St. Ignace.
    Husband: Louis Pacquin, pronounced Parkey.
    61-16-2-1 George L. Pacquin, age 2.
    61-16-2-2 Antoine Pacquin, born March/08.
  61-16-3 Lucy St. Louis, age 18, St. Ignace.
    Husband: Jasper St. Louis, white.
    61-16-3-1 Julian St. Louis, born Jany 5/09 too late.
  61-16-4 Garrett Bourassaw, age 17, P.O. St. Ignace.
  61-16-5 Vetal Bourassaw, age 14, (m).

61-16-6 Edmund Bourassaw, age 13.
61-16-7 Isaac Bourassaw, age 12.
61-16-8 Levi Bourassaw, age 10, see 11-63 Grand River.
61-16-9 Philip Bourassaw, age 3.

Information following from: Joe Noah, St. Ignace.

62-16 RANCIS ME-SWAY-O-NIN-NE, age 66, P.O. Allenville, Mich.
Wife: Mary Me-Sway-O-Ninne, age 54, P.O. Allenville, Mich.
62-16-1 Angelin Noah, age 41, P.O. Allenville, Mich.
Husband: Joe Noah, age 43, P.O. Allenville, Mich, see 2-23.
62-16-2 Mary Ann Cube, age 35, P.O. St. Ignace (Pine River).
Husband 1st: _______ Hoban.
62-16-2-1 Kate (Hoban) Andres, age 20, P.O. Mac Isle
Husband: ________ Andres See 9-17.
Husband 2nd: Dave Cube, see 6-12.
62-16-2-1 Mary Cube, age 7.
62-16-2-2 Elizabeth Cube, age 5.
62-16-2-3 Maggie Cube, age 4.
62-16-2-4 Lucy Cube, born Aug/08 off.
62-16-3 Agatha Brown, dead.
Husband: Charles Brown, white, P.O. Duluth, Minn.
62-16-3-1 Mary Brown Meswayoninne, age 14.
62-16-3-2 Maggie Brown Meswayoninne, age 12.
Children live with Francis the grandfather pay shares to him.
62-16-4 Mitchell Meswayoninne, age 31, P.O. Allenville.
Wife: Anna Meswayoninne, age 19, Traverse, no children.
62-16-5 Ellen Thompson, age 28, P.O. Allenville.
Husband: Name not given, white.
62-16-5-1 Blanch Thompson, age 5.
62-16-5-2 Emma Thompson, age 2.
62-16-5-3 Joseph R. Thompson, age 5 months, born Apr/07, died Sept 25/07.
62-16-6 Charles Meswayoninne, age 26, P.O. Allenville.
Wife: Jane Meswayoninne, age 50, nee St. Onge, children none, has children by 1st husb Any Robinson, dead sec 21-25.
62-16-7 Alixse Meswayoninne, age 24, P.O. Allenville, Mich, single.
62-16-8 Agnes Meswayoninne, age 19, P.O. Allenville, Mich.
62-16-9 Elizabeth Meswayoninne, age 17.
62-16-10 Mary Meswayoninne, age15.
62-16-11 Peter Meswayoninne, age 13.

Information following from: Not Given.

63-16 MRS REBOUSKAW or MARY ANN POND, age 84, P.O. St. Ignace, see 19-15, mother of Amab Ance 1-15.

Information following from: Amab Ance.

64-16 NANCY NEWTON, dead, a sister of Francis Graham.
Husband: Name not given.
Note: Jany 6/09 Later; She (Nancy Newton) had children in 1870 but they were not enrolled with her & did not draw money because, at that time, the children (who were half breeds & well-to-do) did not want to be known as Indians & did not want to be enrolled. HBDurant Spl Agt Gould City, Mich (Scott's Point, Apr 27/09).
64-16-1 Jane Garrion, age 52, has two children somewhere but they are pure white, Durant.
Husband: Name not given, white.
64-16-2 Wilson Newton, age 48, P.O. Gould City, Mich.
Wife: Name not given, white.
64-16-2-1 Mark Newton, age 6.
64-16-2-2 Mary Newton, age 4.
64-16-3 Orrillia (Newton) Feurt, age 46, P.O. Franklin Furnace, Ohio.
Husband: Name not given, white.
64-16-3-1 Edith Feurt, age 22. no children.
64-16-4 Obediah Newton, age 44, P.O. Gould City, single.
64-16-5 Mary Newton, age 40., P.O. Norfolk, VA, Supt. Of hospital, "Grace Hospital."

Information following from: Louis Groudin, Petroskey (nephew) and Wm. H. Groudin, St. Ignace (son), Petroskey, Nov 8/08.

65-16 ROSE GRUNDAIN, age 75, P.O. St. Ignace.
Husband: Name not given.
65-16-1 Charles V. Grondin, age 45, P.O. St. Ignace.
Wife: Name not given, white, no children.
65-16-2 Frank A. Grondin, age 43, P.O. St. Ignace.
Wife: Name not given, white.
65-16-2-1 George Grondin, age 11.
65-16-2-2 Louisa Grondin, age 9.
65-16-2-3 Phil Grondin, age 8 (f).
65-16-3 Rose Archambo, age 38, P.O. St. Ignace, see 70-16.
Husband: Name not given, white.
65-16-3-1 Maggie Archambo, age 16.
65-16-3-2 Harry Archambo, age 14.
65-16-3-3 William Archambo, age 12.
65-16-4 Lucy Pond, age 36, P.O. St. Ignace, see 20-12.
Husband: Joe Pond, age 42.
65-16-4-1 Philina Pond, age 13.
65-16-4-2 Levi Pond, age 8.
65-16-4-3 John Pond, age 3.
65-16-5 William H. Grondin, age 34, P.O. St. Ignace.
Wife: Name not given, white.

65-16-5-1 Pearl M. Grondin, age 6.
65-16-5-2 Violet A. Grondin, age 5.
65-16-5-3 William S. Grondin, age 2.
65-16-5-4 Cecelia Grondin, born Aug 1907.

Information following from: John Levake et al, St. Ignace, Jany 5/09.

66-16 BATIS LEVAKE or JOHN B. LEVAKE, age 68, P.O. St. Ignace.
Wife 1st : Name not given, dead.
Wife 2nd: Name not given, white.
66-16-1 John Levake Jr., age 49, P.O. St. Ignace (by 1st wife)
Wife: Mary (Lejoie) Levake, white, age 44.
66-16-1-1 Jack Levake, age 28.
Wife: Name not given, white.
66-16-1-1-1 Amelia Levake, age 3.
66-16-1-1-2 Alice Levake, age 2.
66-16-1-1-3 Name not given, born Dec/07.
66-16-1-2 Augustus Levake, age 26.
66-16-1-3 Alex Levake, age 16.
66-16-1-4 Garrett Levake, age 14.
66-16-1-5 Josephine Levake, age 12.
66-16-1-6 Hannah Levake, age 10.
66-16-1-7 Nelson Levake, age 7.
66-16-1-8 Caroline Levake, age 5.
66-16-2 Louis Levake, age 47, P.O. Manistique. (by 1st wife)
Wife: Name not given, white, separated, no children.
66-16-3 Jane Ross, age 34, P.O. St. Ignace. (by 2nd wife)
Husband: Name not given, white.
66-16-3-1 Elsie Ross, age 17.
66-16-3-2 George Henry Ross, age 13.
66-16-4-3 Frances Ross, age 10.
66-16-4 Helen Pond, age 32, P.O. St. Ignace. (by 2nd wife)
Husband: Name not given, white.
66-16-4-1 Janice Pond, age 13.
66-16-4-2 Lillie Pond, age 9.
66-16-4-3 Katherine Pond, age 7.
66-16-4-4 Joseph Pond, age 5.
66-16-4-5 Annie Pond, age 2.
66-16-5 Marie Champaign, age 28, P.O. Cheboygan. (by 2nd wife)
Husband: Joe Champaign.
66-16-5-1 No name given?
66-16-6 Minnie Belongea, age 22, P.O. Carp River. (by 2nd wife)
Husband: Joseph Belongea #1, see 29-11.
66-16-6-1 No name given?
66-16-6-2 No name given?
66-16-6-3 No name given?

66-16-6-4 No name given?

66-16-7 Tiny Levake, age 17, P.O. Detroit, (by 2nd wife), married name not known.

66-16-8 Joe Levake, age 24, P.O. St. Ignace. (by 2nd wife)
Wife: Name not given.
66-16-8-1 George Levake, age 8.
66-16-8-2 Katherine Levake, age 6.
66-16-8-3 John Levake, age 4.
66-16-8-4 Frank Levake, age 2.
66-16-8-5 Ellen Levake, age 1.

66-16-9 Gaspar or Jaspar Lavake, age 19, P.O. St. Ignace, (by 2nd wife), single.

St. Ignace June 2 1909
Mr. Horas B. Durant
Please find Enclosed the names of my Children
Elsie Ross 18 years old married
George Henry Ross age 14 years
Frances Ross age 11 years

Mrs. Ellen Pond Children

Jamse Pond	*age 14 years*
LilliePond	*age 10 years*
Kathrine Pond	*age 8 years*
Joseph Pond	*age 6 years*
AnniePond	*age 2 years*

Joe Lavake Children

George Lavake	*age 8 years*
Kathrine Lavake	*age 6 years*
John Lavake	*age 4 years*
Frank Lavake	*age 2 years*
Ellen Lavake	*age 1 year*

Information following from: Amab Ance.
67-16 JOHN JAUNDRIAN, dead, no heirs.

Information following from: Not Given.
68-16 MARGARET AW-DAY-NE-ME
Note: Amab Ance and others do not remember any such person, as a child on the roll of 1870. But they recollect a Margaret Awdayname who was living with Frank Williams #19-36 (Aw-day-ne-me) but since separated & she went to Ashland, Wis. Where she died. Durant Spl Agt, St. Ignace, Mich, Jany 6/09.

Information following from: Amab Ance.

69-16 SHAW-BWAY-WAY or NEWELL POND, dead.
 Wife: Name not given.
 69-16-1 Name not given, dead.
 69-16-2 Name not given, dead.

Information following from: Amab Ance and Louis Martin Jr..

70-16 LOUIS MARTIN Sr., dead.
 Wife: Name not given.
 70-16-1 Isabelle Truchey, dead.
 Husband: Name not given.
 70-16-2 LaRose Martin or Rose Grundain as 65-16.
 Husband: Name not given, see 65-16.
 70-16-3 Charles Martin, dead.
 Wife: Name not given, dead.
 70-16-4 Louis Martin, age 50.

Page 17
Naw-o-quaish-cum Band
Chief NAW-O-QUAISH-CUM

Information following from: Dave Cloud, Hubbard Lake, June 9/09.

1-17 (HENRY) NAW-O-QUAISH-CUM, dead.
 Wife 1st: Name not given.
 Wife 2nd: Martha Cloud. Age 69, P.O. Hubbard Lake, Mich 20 miles from Alpena, Mich, South West, Mich, see 13-17.
 1-17-1 Waw-say-ah Emma Joseph, age 40, P.O. Hubbard Lake, Mich.
 Husband: John Joseph, Saginaw Indian.
 1-17-1-1 Lyman Joseph, age 19.
 1-17-1-2 Nay-so-be-quay Annie Joseph, age 17.
 1-17-1-3 Waw-say-ab-be-no-quay Amy Joseph, age 15.
 1-17-1-4 Pe-taw-ay-ke-zhick-go-quay Jane Joseph, age 9.
 1-17-1-5 Ah-be-so-be-quay Martha Joseph, age 8.
 1-17-1-6 Me-sah-be Timothy Joseph, age 6.
 1-17-1-7 Ah-be-te-go Pius Joseph, age 4.
 1-17-1-8 Josephine Joseph, age 2½.
 1-17-1-9 Mary Joseph, age 1½.
 1-17-2 Eliza Henry, age 25, P.O. Hubbard Lake, single, went to Mackinaw Island.
 1-17-3 Simon Henry, age 17, Carlisle School, Pa.

Information following from: Nicholas Andres, Mac Isle, Apr/09 and Dave Andrews, Mac Isle, Apr 13/09.

2-17 WILLIAM ANDREWS Sr.
 Wife 1st: Name not given, dead.

Wife 2nd: Susan Andrews, age 80, P.O. Mac Isle (Boise Blanc).
2-17-1 Josephine Duffina, see 8-12.
2-17-2 William Andrews Jr., see 9-17.
2-17-3 David Andrews, age 62, P.O. Boise Blanc, Mich.
Wife 1st: Margaret (Aslin) Andrews.
Wife 2nd: Mary (St. Onge) Andrews, age 47, daughter of Mrs. Joseph Aslin.
2-17-3-1 Mary Bazinaw, age 24, see 4-17.
2-17-3-2 Ed Andrews, dead.
Wife: Christie(Gardner) Andres (Soo Band).
2-17-3-1 Edmund Andres, age 9.
2-17-3-2 Nora Andrews, age 6.
2-17-3-3 Wilford Andres, age 2.
2-17-3-3 Julius Andres, age 35, P.O. Boise Blanc Isle.
Wife: Mary Martin, see 21-13.
2-17-3-4 Peter Andrews, age 23, P.O. Boise Blanc Isle, single.
2-17-3-5 Charles Andrews, age 11.
2-17-3-6 Nancy Andrews, age 9.
2-17-4 John Andrews #1, age 58, P.O. Mackinaw Island (Bois Blanc).
Wife: Name not given, dead.
2-17-2-1 Maggie Kniffin, see 19-13.
2-17-2-2 Frank Andres, age 29, P.O. Mack Isle, single.
2-17-5 Mitchell Andrews Sr., age 54, P.O. Boise Blanc, Mich.
Wife: Eliza Andrews nee Bazenette, see 3-6.
2-17-3-1 Thomas Andrews, age 18.
2-17-3-2 Henry Andrews, age 13.
2-17-3-3 Felix Andrews, age 9.
2-17-3-4 Virginia Andrews, age 10, lives with Emily Plant see over (below).
2-17-3-5 Eber Andrews, died Nov 1907.
2-17-3-6 Iva Andrews, see 3-6.
2-17-6 Peter Andrews, age 50, P.O. Mackinaw City.
Wife 1st: Cecelia Andrews, age 45, P.O. Mackinaw City, see 3-6.
Wife 2nd: Louisa Duffina , see 8-12.
2-17-6-1 William Andrews, age 27, P.O. Mackinaw Island.
Wife: Ida Andrews, no children.
2-17-6-2 Mitchell Andrews Jr., age 25, P.O. Mackinaw City.
Wife: Philamon Andrews, white, no children.
2-17-6-3 Fred Andrews, age 22, P.O. Mackinaw City.
2-17-6-4 (This number was unintentionally skipped by Durant)
2-17-6-5 Augustus Andrews, age 17, P.O. Mackinaw City.
2-17-6-6 Kate Andrews, age 10, P.O. Mackinaw City.
2-17-6-7 Joe Andrews, age 8.

2-17-7-8 Melissa Andrews, age 5.
2-17-7 Alex Andrews, age 47, P.O. Boise Blanc.
Wife: Name not given, dead.
2-17-7-1 Rosie Andrews, age 12, died Dec 1907.
2-17-7-2 Josephine Andrews, age 10.
2-17-7-3 Lucy Andrews, age 7.
2-17-8 Emily Plaunt, age 45, P.O. Mackinaw City.
Husband: Chris Plaunt or Plant (white), no children.
2-17-9 Nicholas Andrews, age 44, P.O. Boise Blanc, single.

Information following from: Catharine Blackbird and Peter Alick et al, Hessel.

3-17 AINE-NE-ME-KE-WAW-BE, dead.
Wife: Mary Ann Alick or Peme-che-no-quay or Mary Ann Cube, age 70, on roll as 14-11.
3-17-1 John Alick, age 52, P.O. Pine River.
Wife: Catharine Alick, age 32, nee Santigo, see 6-15.
3-17-1-1 Abram Alick, age 18.
3-17-1-2 Sophia Alick, age 16.
Husband: Pete Moses, 61-35, Traverse/
3-17-1-3 Joe Alick, age 14.
3-17-1-4 Mary Alick, age 8.
3-17-2 Ben Ellick or Aleck, age 50, see 1-37 & 5-20.
Wife: Mary Ellick or Aleck, no children.
3-17-3 Margaret Andrew, age 40, P.O. Hessel.
Husband: George Andrew, age 46, P.O. Hessel, see "A Soo."
3-17-3-1 Joe Andrew, age 22.
3-17-3-2 Mary Andrew, age 12.
3-17-3-3 Mitchell Andrew, age 10.
3-17-3-4 John Andrew, age 8.
3-17-3-5 Josephine Andrew, age 6.
3-17-3-6 Enos Andrew, age 4.
3-17-4 George Alick, age 38, P.O. Hessel, single.
3-17-5 Christine or jane Blackbird, age 35, P.O. Hessel, Mich.
Husband: Truman Blackbird, age 44, see 24-26, Traverse.
3-17-5-1 William Blackbird, age 15.
3-17-5-2 Mary Blackbird, age 10, died Apr 12/09.
3-17-5-3 Lydia Blackbird, age 8.
3-17-5-4 Louisa Blackbird, age 6.
3-17-5-5 Catharine Blackbird, age 4.
3-17-5-6 Jeremiah Blackbird, age 2.
3-17-5-7 Cecelia Blackbird, born Mar 26/09 off.
3-17-6 Sophia Mandosking, dead.
Husband: John Mandosking, see 3-8.
3-17-6-1 David Mandosking.

3-17-6-2 James Mandosking.
3-17-6-3 Annie Mandosking.
3-17-6-4 Charles Mandosking.
3-17-6-5 Jennie Mandosking.
3-17-7 Peter Alick, age 33, P.O. Hessel.
Wife: Elizabeth Alick, age 35, see 24-26, no children.

Information following from: Mack Isle, Apr 10/09.
4-17 JOHN B. BAZINET, dead.
Wife: Mary Bazinaw #1, age 73, P.O. Mackinaw Island.
4-17-1 John Bazinaw, dead, no heirs.
4-17-2 Augustus Bazinaw, age 46, P.O. Mack Isle, on roll 1870 as child 56-14.
Wife: Emma Bazinaw, age 40, see 17-15.
4-17-3 William Bazinaw, age 42, P.O. Mack Isle.
Wife: Mary (Andres) Bazinaw #2, age 24, P.O. Mack Isle, see 2-17.
4-17-3-1 Jack Bazinaw, age 6.
4-17-4 Thomas Bazinaw, dead.
Wife: Mary (Martin) Bazinaw, P.O. Boise Blanc, Mich, see
21-
13, 2nd husband Julius Andres 2-17.
4-17-4-1 Jennie Bezinaw, age 18, P.O. Cedarville, Mich, see 21-13.
Husband: Jack Bezinaw
4-17-4-1-1 Frank Bezinaw, born Nov 1908, too late.
4-17-4-2 Agatha Bazinaw, age 16, P.O. Boise Blanc.
4-17-4-3 Thomas Bazinaw, age 13, P.O. Boise Blanc.
4-17-5 Jennie Bazinaw, dead, single.
4-17-6 Julius Bazinaw, 38, P.O. Mack Isle, single.
4-17-7 Elizabeth Campeau, age 34.
Husband: Frank Compeau (white), P.O. Mack Isle.
4-17-7-1 Eddie Compeau, age 13.
4-17-7-2 Dorothy Compeau, age 11.
Information following from: Not Given.
5-17 WAY-GE-MAW-WAW-BE, dead.
Wife: Name not given, dead.
5-17-1 See 3-17.
5-17-2 Naw-o-quo-mo-qual (girl), P.O. Canada Spanish River, brother
says she draws money from Canadian Govt.
Husband: Name not given, Canadian Indian, dead.
5-17-3 Name not given, dead, no heirs.
5-17-4 Name not given, dead, no heirs.
5-17-5 Joseph Osawgwon, age 58, P.O. Hessel, Mich.

Wife: Therese Osawgwon, age 45, P.O. Hessel, Mich., see 4-34.

5-17-6 Awgonay-gezhick-go-quay Margaret, age 50, P.O. Pine River, see 22-11.
Husband: Jim Wabegennse.

Information following from: Louis Lasage and Joe Mesawtego.

6-17 MRS. SIMON MARTIN, dead.
Has two children living on Mac Isle. Durant Spl Agt.

Information following from: Enroll this man with consent of Chiefs of Mackinaw Band Amab Ance, Joe Mesawtego & Joe Smith st al, St. Ignace, June 20/09, Durant Spl Agt., attach to 6-17.

7-17 LOUIS LASAGE, age 50, P.O. St. Ignace.
His grandmother belonged to Beaver Island Band, his mother to Mac. Island Band, he was born at St. Ignace & is ½ Indian. Mrs. Simon Martin was his uncle's wife.
Wife: Name not given, see 5-3.

Information following from: Neswawsobe, Hubbard Lake.

8-17 WAW-SAW-NAW-QUO-DE-QUAY, dead, no children.

Information following from: Not Given.

9-17 WILLIAM ANDREWS Jr.
Wife: Name not given, dead.
9-17-1 George Andrews, age 38, P.O. St. Ignace.
Wife: Ellen Andrews, age 43, see 17-15.
9-17-1-1 George Andrews Jr., age 15, P.O. St. Ignace.
9-17-1-2 Albert Andrews, age 7, P.O. St. Ignace.
9-17-1-3 Esther V. Andrews, age 6, P.O. St. Ignace.
9-17-2 John Andrews, age 34, P.O. Cedarville, Snow Island, Mich.
Wife: Ivy Andres, see 11-13, no children.
9-17-3 Samuel Andrews, age 33, P.O. Mackinaw Island.
Wife: Kate (Hoban) Andrews, age 20, grand daugh. of 62-16.
9-17-3-1 Albert Andrews, age 2?.
9-17-3-2 Name not given, born summer 1908, too late.
9-17-4 James Andrews, age 21, P.O. Onaway, Mich, near Cheboygan.

Information following from: William A. Fountain #1, a cousin, see 20-17, Gould City, Apr 27/09.

12-17 MRS CHARLES FOUNTAIN, dead.
Husband: Charles Fountain, dead?.
12-17-1 Name not given, dead, no heirs.
12-17-2 William Fountain #2, age 4, P.O. Ontonagon, Mich, cannot locate him Durant.

Information following from: Dave Cloud, Hubbard Lake, June 9/09.
13-17 AW-BE-WAY-NAY, dead.
Husband: Name not given.
13-17-1 Ne-Swaw-So-Be, age 90, P.O. Hubbard Lake, Mich.
Wife: Name not given, dead?
13-17-1-1 Martha Cloud, see 1-17.
13-17-1-2 Thomas Ne-Swaw-So-Be or Tom Onaquot, age 55, P.O. Alvin, Mich.
Wife: Name not given, Saginaw Indian.
13-17-1-2-1 boy, single.
13-17-1-2-2 boy, single.
13-17-1-2-3 boy, single.
13-17-1-2-4 girl, single.

Information following from: Not Given.
16-17 MRS. JOHN ANDREWS or ANDRES.

Information following from: Not Given.
17-17 JOHN B. KARROW, spelled now Carow, age 60, P.O. Cheboygan.
Wife: Mary Karrow (or Carow), age 57, with husband 1870.
17-17-1 Reuben Carow, age 41, P.O. Cheboygan.
Wife: Name not given, white.
17-17-1-1 William Carow, age 15.
17-17-1-2 Charles Carow, age 13.
17-17-1-3 Walter Carow, age 10.
17-17-1-4 Agnes Carow, age 9.
17-17-1-5 Roy Carow, age 7.
17-17-1-6 Eva Carow, age 5.
17-17-1-7 Richard Carow, age 3.
17-17-1-8 Ruth Carow, age 1, born Oct/07.
17-17-2 Mary Hipkins, age 38, P.O. Cheboygan.
Husband: Name not given, white.
17-17-2-1 Ed Hipkins, age 18.
17-17-2-2 Nettie Hipkins, age 16.
17-17-2-3 Fred Hipkins, age 15.
17-17-2-4 Reuben Hipkins, age 13.
17-17-2-5 Mary Hipkins, age 11.
17-17-2-6 David Hipkins, age 9.
17-17-3 Frank Carow, age 35, P.O. Cheboygan, single.
17-17-4 George Carow, age 33, P.O. Cheboygan.
Wife: Name not given, no children.
17-17-5 Paul Carow, age 32, P.O. Cheboygan.
Wife: Name not given, white.
17-17-5-1 Pansy Carow (f), age 6, P.O. Cheboygan.

17-17-6 Julia Richmond, dead.
Husband: William Richmond, white, address unknown, children live with grandmother Mary Carow.
17-17-1 Charles Richmond, age 14.
17-17-2 Joe Richmond, age 10.
17-17-3 Freda Richmond, age 8.
17-17-4 William Richmond, age 7.
17-17-5 Blanch Richmond, age 6.
17-17-7 Rosie Laduke, age 28, P.O. Cheboygan.
Husband: Name not given, white.
17-17-7-1 Dorris, age 9.
17-17-7-1 Rena, age 7.
17-17-7-1 Elmer, age 4.
17-17-7-1 Clyde, age 2.
17-17-8 Lucy Boda, age 23, Cheboygan.
Husband: Name not given, white.
17-17-8-1 Herbert Boda, age 9.
17-17-8-2 Mabel Boda, age 5.
17-17-8-3 Ida Boda, age 1½, born Mch 21/07.

Information following from: Not Given.
18-17 PA-ZHICK-WA-BE, dead.
Wife: Name not given, dead.
18-17-1 Dan Pay-Zhick-Wa-Be or Pay-Zhick-Go-Be or Dan Williams,
age 45, P.O. Mackinaw same place Newberry, Mich, single.
18-17-2 Name not given, dead.
Husband: John Naw-Gaw-Ne-Gwon, age 68, P.O. Alvin, Mich, used to live at Mackinaw, see 5-11. This man is enrolled on another card, find it, I saw him at St. Ignace, ask Joe Smith.
18-17-2-1 Amos Naw-Gon-E-Quon, age 22, P.O. Au Sable, Alvin, used to live at Mackinaw.
18-17-2-2 Dan Naw-Gon-E-Quon, age 25, P.O. Au Sable, Alvin, used to live at Mackinaw.
18-17-3 (This number was unintentionally skipped by Durant)
18-17-4 Eliza Ance, see 1-15, wife of 1-15.

Information following from: Andrew Fountain and William A. Fountain.
20-17 ANDREW FOUNTAIN, age 75, P.O. Gould City, Mich.
Wife: Mary Ann Fountain, age 70, P.O. Gould City, Mich, with husband 1870.
20-17-1 Mary Ann LaBlanc, age 39, P.O. Cheboygan.
Husband: Alex, LaBlanc, white.
20-17-1-1 Sam LaBlanc, age 24.

20-17-1-1 Ellen LaBlanc Stevenson, age 22.
20-17-1-1 Josephine LaBlanc Laforest, age 20.
20-17-1-1 Louis LaBlanc, age 18.
20-17-1-1 Mary LaBlanc, age 16.
20-17-1-1 Myrtle LaBlanc, age 14.
20-17-1-1 John LaBlanc, age 12.
20-17-1-1 William LaBlanc, age 10.
20-17-1-1 Herman LaBlanc, age 8.
20-17-1-1 Marie LaBlanc, age 6.

20-17-2 William A. Fountain, age 37, P.O. Gold (Gould) City, Mich, single.

20-17-3 Libby Belongea, dead.
Husband: Clemen Belongea, P.O. Mac Isle, see 26-13, his 2nd wife Grace Plant Belongea, see 4-13.
20-17-3-1 Sadie Belonga, age 16, P.O. Gould City.
20-17-3-2 Alvin Belonga, age 18.

20-17-4 Joseph Fountain, age 34, P.O. Gold City, single.

20-17-5 Edward Fountain, age 26, P.O. Gold City.
Wife: Name not given, white.
20-17-5-1 Alex Fountain, age 2.
20-17-5-2 Name not given, born Apr/09. too late.

Information following from: Eliza Ance, St. Ignace.

22-17 WAW-WAW-SE-MO-QUAY, now ELIZA ANCE, wife of 1-15, age 60, P.O. St. Ignace.
Husband 1st: Name not given, dead, see 12-11.
22-17-1 Matilda Aw-No-Ke-Kezhick, age 42, P.O. St. Ignace, single.

Information following from: Enroll by consent of Chiefs at meeting held at St. Ignace June 19/09, HBDurant Spl Agt.

UNK SUSAN PAQUIN, age 70, P.O. St. Ignace, Mich.
Note: She is enrolled by special consent of Chiefs & headmen, being a sister of Batis Levake 66-16. She has children & grandchildren but they do not desire to be enrolled under the circumstances & do not insist. Durant Spl Agt. (This person was later identified with 56-16 on the final Durant Roll.)

Author Note: There are no entries for Pages 18 & 19 on the original roll.

Page 20
Cross Village Band
Chief NAW-WE-MAISH-CO-TAY

1-20 NAW-WE-MAISH-CO-TAY, dead.
Wife: Name not given, dead.

1-20-1 Name not given, dead, no heirs.

Information following from: Margaret Lasley, Mac Isle, Apr 13/09.

2-20 MRS. JAMES LASLEY of BETSEY LASLEY, dead, Land Patent #623, Recorded Vol. 2 p. 123.
Husband: James Lasley, dead?
2-20-1 Oliver Lasley, age 67, P.O. St. Mary's Mission, Kansas.
Wife: Mary Lasley, Kansas Indian, Pottawatomie, off.
2-20-1-1 James Lasley, P.O. St. Mary's Mission, Kansas.
2-20-2 John Lasley, age 63, P.O. Mac Island, single.
2-20-3 Matilda Tourtillotte, age 61, P.O. Mack City.
Husband: Charles Tourtillotte, dead.
2-20-3-1 Ruth Tourtillotte
Husband: Name not given, see 2-13.
2-20-3-2 Harry Tourtillotte, age 23, P.O. Mack City, twin.
2-20-3-3 Leah Tourtillotte, age 23, P.O. Mack City, twin (f).
2-20-4 Hattie Bourassaw, age 56, P.O. Mac Isle.
Husband: Frank Bourassaw, see 20-13.
2-20-4-1 James Bourassaw #2, age 24, single.
2-20-4-2 Ruth Bourassaw, age 21, single.
2-20-4-3 Morton Bourassaw, age 20, single.
2-20-4-4 Harry Bourassaw, age 15, single.
2-20-5 James Lasley #1, age 48, P.O. Mac Isle, single.
2-20-6 Frank Lasley, age 45, P.O. Mac Isle, single.
2-20-7 Margaret Lasley, age 42, P.O. Mac Isle, single.
2-20-8 Madeline Davenport, dead.
Husband: James Davenport, P.O. Mac City, see 31-13.

Emmett June 14/1909
Sir

I received your letter and will answer it I and my family enroll with the Pottawatmies Pand here iff you will write to (John Lasley) MackinacMich he will tell you there ages.

Oliver Lasley

Information following from: Not Given.

3-20 SHAW-WAW-NE-PE-NAY-SE, dead.
Wife: Name not given, dead.
3-20-1 Madeline Edowegonaby, age 62, P.O. Cross Village, see 61-21.
Husband: Name not given, dead.
3-20-1-1 Mary Ann Francis, age 25, P.O. Cross Village.
Husband: William Francis, age 30, see 8-42 & 18-28, no children.
3-20-2 Mary Paul, age 51, P.O. Pecestore, Mich.

Husband: Francis Paul, age 51, see 4-30 & 27-30, no (other) children.
3-20-2-1 Christina Paul, age 16, died Nov 1907.

Information following from: Oct 16/08, X Village.
4-20 TWA-GNAW-GAW-NAY, dead.
Wife: Name not given, dead.
4-20-1 Alex (Poneshing) spelled now Bwanishing, age 59, P.O. Cross Village.
Wife: Rosie Bwanishing, age 41, P.O. Cross Village, nee Shaw-Waw-Non-Quot, see 43-32.
4-20-1-1 John Bwanishing, age 18, P.O. Cross Village.
4-20-1-2 Henry Bwanishing, age 12, P.O. Cross Village.
4-20-1-3 Louisa Bwanishing, age 10, P.O. Cross Village.
4-20-1-4 Joseph Bwanishing, age 8, P.O. Cross Village.
4-20-1-5 David Bwanishing, age 6, P.O. Cross Village.
4-20-1-6 Margaret Bwanishing, age 2, P.O. Cross Village.
4-20-2 Louis Bwanishing, age 56, Cross Village, single.
4-20-3 Theresa Shomin, age 54, P.O. Cross Village.
Husband: Bazil Shomin, dead.
4-20-3-1 Agnes Wahkazoo, age 17, adopted child, see 13-32.
4-20-4 Madeline Leo, age 52, P.O. Cross Village.
Husband: Joe Leo, age 55, see 7-20.
4-20-5 Lucy Shomin, P.O. Cross Village.
Husband: Angus Shomin, see 14-20.
4-20-6 Anna Leece, age 43, P.O. Cross Village.
Husband: William Leece, white, off.
4-20-6-1 John Leece, age 14.
4-20-6-2 Ida Leece, age 11.
4-20-6-3 James Leece, age 9.
4-20-7 Name not given, dead, no heirs.

Information following from: Not Given.
5-20 FRANCIS GILBERT, age 100, P.O. Cross Village.
Wife: Elizabeth Gilbert, age 70, P.O. Cross Village.
5-20-1 Francis Gilbert Jr., age 57, P.O. Cross Village.
Wife: Mary Gilbert Ellick, separated, age 42, P.O. Kennish, Mich North Shore, see 1-37.
5-20-1-1 Mary Gilbert Hardwick, age 21, P.O. Ogaiitz North Shore.
Husband: George Hardwick, age 26, see 12-37.
5-20-1-1-1 Frank Hardwick, age 2.
5-20-2 Rosie Gilbert, age 49, P.O. Traverse City, single.
5-20-3 Agnes Engstron, age 44, P.O. Cross Village.
Husband: Name not given, separated, white.

5-20-3-1 Stella Waldo, age 20, Cross Village.
5-20-3-2 Fred Engstron, age 12, P.O. Cross Village.
5-20-3-3 Lillie Engstron, age 9, P.O. Cross Village.
5-20-4 Joe Gilbert, age 42, P.O. Cross Village, single.
5-20-5 Theodore Gilbert, age 38, P.O. Cross Village, single.
5-20-6 Andrew Gilbert, dead, no heirs.

Information following from: Harbor Springs, Oct 9/08.
6-20 PETER O-MAY-NAW-GOONSE, dead.
Wife: Josette Onenagos or Onenanegos, age 75, P.O. Cross Village, Mich.
6-20-1 William Onenagos, age 59, P.O. Cross Village, Mich.
Wife: Jane Onenagos nee Bennett, age 45, see 6-13.
6-20-2 Francis Onenagose, age 57, P.O. Cross Village, Mich.
Wife: Margaret Onenagose, age 57, see 106-22 & 33-20.
6-20-3 Alex Onenagos, age 55, P.O. Cross Village, Mich, dead.
Wife: Name not given, dead, children dead, no heirs.
6-20-4 Margaret Kagigebitang, age 53, P.O. Cross Village, see 98-22.
Husband: Name not given, dead.
6-20-5 Sophia (Omay-Na-Goonse), age 40, P.O. Petroskey, Mich, now lives with white man by name of Birch.
Husband: Stanalus Ni-Gan-Kwa-Am, age 44, P.O. Cross Village, separated, see 10-20.
6-20-5-1 Benjamine Ni-Gan-Kwa-Am, age 17.
6-20-5-2 Aaron Birch, age 6.
6-20-5-3 Eddie Birch, age 2.
6-20-6 Isaac Onenagos, dead.
Wife: Sarah Nanagose, age 33, P.O. Cross Village, see 25-20.

Information following from: Not Given.
7-20 AGATHA NAW-WE-MAISH-CO-TAY, dead.
Husband: Name not given, dead?
7-20-1 Name not given, dead, no heirs.
7-20-2 Veronica Medwagin or Maydwagon, age 53, see 62-21.
7-20-3 Joseph Leo, age 55, P.O. Cross Village.
Wife: Madeline Leo nee Po-Ne-Shing, age 52, see 4-20.
7-20-3-1 Frank Leo, age 28, P.O. Cross Village, single.
7-20-3-2 John Leo, age 22, P.O. Cross Village.
7-20-3-3 George Leo, age 19, P.O. Cross Village.
7-20-3-4 Edward Leo, age 16, P.O. Cross Village.
7-20-3-5 Esther Leo, age 14, P.O. Cross Village.
7-20-4 Jonas Leo, dead.
Wife: Rosie Shaw-Waw-Naw-Se-Gay, P.O. Pellston, 2nd husband James Shaw-Waw-Naw-Se-Gay 8-31.
7-20-4-1 Sampson Leo, age 15, P.O. Mt. Pleasant School.

7-20-4-2 Joseph Leo, age 17, P.O. Cross Village.

Information following from: Not Given.

8-20 NAW-DO-WAY-QUA-SAW, dead.
Wife: Mary Ann Agosa, age 60, P.O. Cross Village.
8-20-1 Sarah Francis, age 35, P.O. Goodheart, see 3-41.
Husband: Joseph Francis or joe Oke-No-Te-Go, age 46, see 18-28.
8-20-1-1 Ed Francis, age 15.
8-20-1-2 Albert Francis, age 13.
8-20-1-3 Louis Francis, age 9.
8-20-1-4 Mary Francis, age 7.
8-20-1-5 Solomon Francis, age 4.
8-20-1-6 Eliza Francis, age 2.
8-20-1-7 Agnes Francis, born Aug 11, 1908, too late.
8-20-2 Angeline Aniwaskey, age 29, P.O. Austin's Bay.
Husband: William Aniwaskey, see 13-40.
8-20-3 Peter Agosa, age 28, P.O. Beaver Island.
Wife: Susan Agosa nee Wah-Be-Minkse, see 10-38, no children.
8-20-4 George Agosa, age 26, P.O. Cross Village, single.
8-20-5 Philamon (Agosa) Meangwa or May-On-Go-We, age 24, P.O. Cross Village.
Husband: Joseph Meangwa, age 28, P.O. Cross Village, see 49-29.
8-20-5-1 Cecilia Warren, age 5.
8-20-5-2 Benjamin Warren, age 1, born May 1907.

Information following from: In 2 Sheets.

9-20a MITCHELL O-SAW-KEENY-CAMP, dead. (SHEET #1)
Wife: Name not given, dead.
9-20a-1 John B. Shawmin, see 81-21.
9-20a-2 Louis Shomin, see 43-21.
9-20a-3 Enos Shomin, see 9-20 Sheet #2.
9-20a-4 Mike Shomin, age 57, P.O. Cross Village, see 4-51.
Wife: Sophia Shomin, age 50, see 19-20.
9-20a-4-1 Angeline Shomin, age 28, P.O. Cross Village.
Husband: Name not given, separated, see 66-21, no children.
9-20a-4-2 Joseph Shomin, age 21, P.O. Cross Village, single.
9-20a-5 Pete Shomin, dead.
Wife: Rosie Shomin, see 0-12.

9-20b ENOS SHOMIN, dead, child #3. (SHEET #2)
Wife: Elizabeth Shomin, age 61, P.O. Cross Village.

9-20b-1 MaryShomin or Gaiashk, age 32, separated, have not heard from her for 4 years, last heard from was in Chicago.
Husband: Adam Kiosk, dead, an Indian from Walpole Island, Canada.
9-20-1-1 William Davis, age 12, P.O. Tomah Indian School, Wis., (illegitimate), lives with grandmother when home.
9-20b-2 Christina Thompson, age 30, P.O. Cross Village, separated.
Husband: Edmund Thompson, white, see 32-32.
9-20-2-1 Edna Thompson, age 10, P.O. Tomah School. Wis.
9-20-2-2 Alvina Thompson, age 5, P.O. Cross Village.
9-20b-3 Bennett Shomin, age 23, P.O. Cross Village, not married.
9-20b-4 Edmund Shomin, age 20, P.O. Cross Village, single.
9-20b-5 Peter Shomin, age 17, P.O. Cross Village.

Information following from: Oct 16/08, X Village.
10-20 MICK-SAW-QUAY, dead.
Husband: name not given, dead?
10-20-1 Peter Nigankwaam, age 59, P.O. Cross Village, see 100-22.
Wife: Angeline Nigankwaam, age 48, P.O. Cross Village.
10-20-1-1 Frank Nigankwaam, age 17, P.O. Cross Village.
10-20-2 Name and sex not given, dead.
Spouse: Name not given, dead?
10-20-3 Alphonse (Lee) O-Taw-Naw-Zhe, age 35, P.O. Harbor Springs or Boyne City Camp #11.
Wife: Anna O-Taw-Naw-Zhe, age 33, see 30-32 and 50-29.
10-20-3 Mary Nigankwaam, age 53, P.O. Cross Village, single.
10-20-4 Stanalus V, age 44, P.O. Cross Village.
Wife: Sophia Birch, age 40, P.O. Petroskey, separated, see 6-20, living with _______ Birch.
10-20-4-1 Benjamin Nigankwaam, age 17.

Information following from: Not Given.
11-20 AS-SE-BUN, dead.
Wife: Name not given, dead, all children dead, no heirs.

Information following from: Not Given.
12-20 FRANCIS WAW-SAY-KE-ZHICK, dead.
Wife: Name not given, dead.
12-20-1 Francis Waw-Say-Ke-Zhick, dead.
Wife: Madeline Manitou, P.O. Beaver Island, see 21-34 and 19-34, 2nd husband Pete Manitou.
12-20-1-1 George Waw-Say-Ke-Zhick, age 24, P.O. Beaver Island.

Wife: Sarah Waw-Say-Ke-Zhick, see 10-34.
12-20-1-1-1 Esther Waw-Say-Ke-Zhick.
12-20-1-2 Enos Waw-Say-Ke-Zhick #2, age 20, P.O. Beaver Island, single.
12-20-1-3 William Waw-Say-Ke-Zhick, age 16, P.O. Beaver Island.
12-20-1-4 James Waw-Say-Ke-Zhick, age 12.
12-20-2 Catharine Starr, age 50, P.O. Cross Village.
Husband: Howard Starr, white, dead, off.
12-20-2-1 Mary Starr, age 19, P.O. Cross Village.
12-20-3 Mitchell Waw-Say-Ke-Zhick, age 40, P.O. Petroskey, single.
12-20-4 Enos Waw-Say-Ke-Zhick #1, age 38, P.O. Petroskey.
Wife: Jane Waw-Say-Ke-Zhick, age 33, see 72-21 & 24-20.
12-20-4-1 Howard Waw-Say-Ke-Zhick, age 5, P.O. Petroskey.
12-20-4-2 Christine Waw-Say-Ke-Zhick, age 2, P.O. Petroskey.
12-20-4-3 Dan Wassigijig, age 13, see 42-21.
12-20-5 Elizabeth Mick-Saw-By, see 21-20.
12-20-6 Philamon Moses, age 38, Cutler, Ontario, Canada.
Husband: Moses or Alex Moses, Canadian Indian.
12-20-6-1 Alex Moses Jr., age 17.
12-20-6-2 Rose Moses, age 15.
12-20-6-3 George Moses, age 12.
12-20-6-4 Mary Jane Moses, age 10.
12-20-6-5 Frank Moses, age 8.
12-20-6-6 Cecelia Moses, age 6.
12-20-6-7 Edmund Moses, age 4.

Information following from: Not Given.
13-20 AW-NE-ME-QUO-UM or PAYSON, dead.
Wife: Name not given, dead?
13-20-1 Agatha Ma-Ong-Quay or May-On-Go-We, age 56, P.O. Cross Village, see 49-29.
Husband Name not given, dead.
13-20-1-1 Theresa Otayemin, age 30, P.O. Cross Village.
Husband: Benedict Otayemin, see 40-20.
13-20-1-2 Joseph May-On-Go-We spelled now Me-On-gwa, age 28.
Wife: Philamon May-On-Go-We, age 24, see 8-20.
13-20-1-3 Samuel Meongwa, age 21, P.O. Cross Village.
13-20-1-4 Cecelia Meongwa, age 17, P.O. Cross Village.
13-20-2 Christina Macdagin, age 52, P.O. Cross Village, see 37-28.
13-20-3 Mary Ann Pay-Son-Etaw-Naw-Caw-We-Go, age 50, P.O. Cross Village.
Husband: Daniel Pay-Son-Etaw-Naw-Caw-We-Go, age 52,

P.O. Cross Village, see 17-20.

Information following from: Caspar, Oct 15.
14-20 KEY-ME-WAW-NAW-UM, dead.
Wife: Name not given, dead.
14-20-1 Caspar Shomin, age 59, see 101-22.
14-20-2 Angus Shomin, age 49, P.O. Cross Village.
Wife: Lucy Shomin, age 48, see 4-20.
14-20-2-1 John Shomin, age 14.
14-20-2-2 Martha Sshomin, age 6.
14-20-3 Name not given, dead, no children.
14-20-4 Name not given, dead, no children.

Information following from: Not Given.
15-20 PETER SHAWMIN, dead.
Wife: Name not given, dead.
15-20-1 Jasper Shomin, age 48, P.O. Cross Village.
Wife: Annie Shomin, see 17-20.
15-20-1-1 Mary Shomin, age 19, died May 1907.
15-20-2 Theresa Paul nee Shomin, age 46, P.O. Cross Village.
Husband: Peter Paul, Canadian Indian, off.
15-20-2-1 George Paul, age 8.
15-20-2-2 Rosie Monroe, age 22, P.O. Harbor Springs, single.
15-20-3 Annie (Shomin) Petroskey, P.O. Petroskey, see 8-15.
Husband: Paul Petroskey.
15-20-4 Sabatian Shomin, age 36, P.O. Cross Village, see 3-26.
Wife: Catharine Shomin (nee Chippeway), see 27-20.
15-20-4-1 Peter Shomin, age 4.
15-20-4-2 Guy Shomin, age 3.
15-20-4-3 Wesson Shomin, born May 1907, died Aug 1908, 2nd roll.
15-20-5 Stella (She-Qua-Gaw)Anderson, a niece, wife of Jacob Anderson see 14-58.

Information following from: Not Given.
16-20 ANDREW KE-CHE-PE-NAY-SE, dead.
Wife: Name not given, dead.
16-20-1 Martin Ke-Ja-Bin, age 47, P.O. Cross Village.
Wife: Mary Ann Pay-Son-Etaw-Naw-Caw-Me-Go, age 50, separated, see 13-20.
16-20-1-1 Rosie Martin, age 15, see 17-20.
16-20-2 Name not given, dead, no heirs.

Information following from: Not Given.
17-20 WILLIAM ETAW-NAW-CAW-ME-GO, dead.

Wife: Name not given, dead.
17-20-1 Baldine Warren, age 54, P.O. Cross Village, see 18-24.
Husband: Charles Warren, dead, white.
17-20-1-1 Charle Warren, age 24, P.O. Cross Village, single.
17-20-1-2 Grace King, age 19, P.O. Cross Village.
Husband: John King, age 29, see 11-31.
17-20-1-2-1 Mary King, born July 20, 1908, 2nd roll.
17-20-1-3 Sam Warren, age 18, P.O. Cross Village.
17-20-1-4 George Warren, age 13, P.O. Cross Village.
17-20-1-5 Alex Warren, age 11, P.O. Cross Village.
17-20-2 Daniel Etaw-Naw-Caw-Me-Go, age 52, P.O. Goodheart.
Wife: Mary Ann Payson Etaw-Naw-Caw-Me-Go, daughter of 13-20, separated.
17-20-2-1 Paul Etaw-Naw-Caw-Me-Go or Paul Williams #2, age 28, P.O. Cross Village.
Wife: Annie Sargonqotto, age 27, see 47-21.
17-20-2-1-1 Julius Etaw-Naw-Caw-Me-Go, age 9, P.O. Cross Village.
17-20-2-1-2 Infant Etaw-Naw-Caw-Me-Go, born Sept 1908, do not enroll.
17-20-2-1-3 Lucy Etaw-Naw-Caw-Me-Go, age 2, born Dec 1906, died Mch 1908.
17-20-2-2 Rosie Martin, age 15, child by wife's 1st husband.
17-20-3 Sophia Taylor, age 50, P.O. Cross Village.
Husband: Joseph Taylor, white, off.
17-20-3-1 Mary Taylor, age 27, P.O. Cross Village.
Husband: Name not given, white.
17-20-3-1-1 Francis Taylor, age 3, P.O. Cross Village.
17-20-3-2 Helena Taylor Munson, age 22, P.O. Cross Village.
Husband: Steve Munson, see 16-45, no children.
17-20-4 Elizabeth Ransom, age 46, P.O. Cross Village.
Husband: Charles Ransom, white, do not enroll.
17-20-4-1 Susan Ransom, age 21, P.O. Cross Village.
17-20-4-2 Ida Ransom, age 19, P.O. Cross Village.
17-20-4-3 Fred Ransom, age 17, P.O. Cross Village.
17-20-4-4 Nancy Ransom, age 11, P.O. Cross Village.

Information following from: Not Given.
18-20 JOSEPH SAW-WAW-QUOT, dead.
Wife Name not given, dead.
18-20-1 Name or sex not given, dead, see 10-28.
Spouse: Name not given.
18-20-1-1 Agnes Mosnaw, P.O. Goodheart, see 10-28.
18-20-2 Name or sex not given, dead.
18-20-3 Name or sex not given, dead.

Information following from: Not Given.
19-20 OGE-MAW-MAW-PE-NAY-SE ANTOINE, age 85, P.O. Petoskey, Mich.
Wife: Name not given, dead.
19-20-1 Sophia Shomin, age 50, P.O. Cross Village, Mich.
Husband: Mike Shomin, age 50, P.O. Cross Village, see 9-20.
19-20-1-1 Angeline Shomin, age 30, P.O. Cross Village.
19-20-1-2 Joseph Shomin, age 21, P.O. Cross Village.
19-20-2 Jane Oge-Maw-Maw-Pe-Nay-Se Petoskey, age 45, P.O. Petoskey, see 3-26.

Information following from: Not Given.
20-20 JOHN B. CHAW-ME, dead.
Wife: Name not given, dead.
20-20-1 Moses Chawme, dead.
Wife: Margaret Chawme, age 55, P.O. Cross Village, see 10-32.
20-20-1-1 Joseph Chawme, age 26, P.O. Cross Village.
Wife: Rosie Chawme, age 23, P.O. Cross Village.
20-20-1-1-1 Cramer Chawme, age 6, P.O. Cross Village.
20-20-1-1-2 Moses Chawme, age 2, P.O. Cross Village
20-20-2 Name not given, dead, no heirs.

Information following from: Not Given.
21-20 FRANCIS MICKSAWBAY, dead.
Wife: Name not given, dead.
21-20-1 Moses Micksawbay, age 48, P.O. Cross Village.
Wife: Elizabeth Micksawbay, age 38, P.O. Cross Village, see 12-20.
21-20-1-1 Mary Micksawbay, dead.
21-20-1-2 Rosie Micksawbay, age 14, P.O. Cross Village.
21-20-1-3 Mabel Micksawbay, born Sept 1907, died Jany 14, 1907, off. (Durant recorded wrong year of death?)
21-20-2 Susan Shawan, age 46, P.O. Cross Village, see 39-20.
21-20-3 Joseph Ne-Saw Waw-Quot or Joseph Micksawbay, age 56, see 25-20 and 31-20.
21-20-4 Mary Ann Micksawbay, dead.
21-20-5 Philamon Mixmong, P.O. Cross Village, see 42-21.

Information following from: Oct 15/08.
22-20 JOSEPH SHAW-MIN, dead.
Wife: Name not given, dead.
22-20-1 Catharine Shomin, age 66, P.O. Cross Village. Single.

22-20-2 Lucy Shaw-Min, dead, lived with.
Husband: William Deveney.
22-20-2-1 Rosie Anderson, age 30, P.O. Cross Village.
Husband 1st : Alex McGalphin, age 33, see 59-33
Husband 2nd: ________ Anderson, white.
22-20-2-1-1 Harvey (McGalphin) Shomin, age 7, see 59-33.
22-20-3 Other Children Dead.

Information following from: X Village.
23-20 CHARLES KEY-O-GE-MAW, age 75, P.O. Cross Village.
Wife: Name not given, dead.
23-20-1 Name not given, dead, no heirs, see 46-21.
23-20-2 ~~Lucy~~ Susan Ance, age 48, P.O. St. Ignace.
Husband: George Ance #2, age 63, P.O. St. Ignace, see 2-15.
23-20-2-1 Rosie Susan Ance, age 21, single.
23-20-2-2 Mary Jane Ance, age 19.
23-20-2-3 George Ance, age 14.
23-20-2-4 Louisa Ance, age 10.
23-20-3 Annie (Supnee) Norton, age 42, P.O. Cross Village, see 36-32, separated from husband.
Husband: William Norton, no children.
23-20-4 John Kiogima, age 35, P.O. Cross Village.
Wife: Hattie Kiogima, nee Deveoney, age 32, P.O. Cross Village.
23-20-4-1 Annie J. Kiogima, 13, twin.
23-20-4-2 Mary J. Kiogima, 13, twin.
23-20-4-3 Michael Kiogima, 11.
23-20-4-4 Clementia Kiogima, 11.
23-20-4-5 Nancy Kiogima, 11.
23-20-4-6 Sophia Kiogima, 11.
23-20-4-7 Clara Kiogima, 11, born Dec 26/06, died Feby 17/07.
23-20-4-8 Anastatia Kiogima, born March 9/08, 2nd roll.

Information following from: Not Given.
24-20 NAW-O-SIS-NAY-BE, dead.
Wife: Name not given, dead.
24-20-1 Name or sex not given, dead.
Spouse: Nmae not given, dead?
24-20-1-1 Jane Waw-Say-Ke-Zhick, age 38, P.O. Petoskey.
Husband: Enos Waw-Say-Ke-Zhick, see 12-20.
24-20-2 Name or sex not given, dead.
24-20-3 Name or sex not given, dead.

Information following from: Not Given.

25-20 JOHN B. KEY-O-GEMAN or KIOGIMA, age 76, P.O. Cross Village.

Wife: Name not given, dead.

25-20-1 Christina Micksawbay ~~Ne-Saw-Waw-Quot~~, age 50, P.O. Cross Village.

Husband: Joseph Micksawbay or Joseph Ne-Saw-Waw-Quot, age 56, P.O. Cross Village.

25-20-1-1 Bazil Micksawbay, age 24, single.

25-20-1-2 Rosie Micksawbay, age 22, single.

25-20-1-3 Joe Donatus or Joe Micksawbay, age 35, P.O. Goodheart.

Wife: Rosie Sinaway Donatus, see 8-28, no children.

25-20-2 Victoria Macdagin ~~Maw-Caw-Day-Gon~~, age 43, P.O. Cross Village.

Husband: Jasper Macdagin, age 46, P.O. Cross Village see 37-28.

25-20-2-1 Peter Macdagin, age 19.

25-20-2-2 Edmund Macdagin, age 17.

25-20-3 Pian Kiogima, age 41, P.O. Harbor Springs, see 8-32.

Wife: Mary Ann Kiogima, age 38, P.O. Harbor Springs, see 48-33.

25-20-3-1 Augustus Kiogima, age 5.

25-20-3-2 Susan Ida Kiogima, age 3.

25-20-4 Sarah ~~Naw-~~O-Naw-Naw-Goose, spelled now Naugos, age 33, P.O. Cross Village.

Husband: Isaac Naugose, died Jany 1907, off.

25-20-4-1 Stephen Naugos, age 11.

25-20-4-2 Angus Naugos, age 8.

25-20-4-3 Cecelia Naugos, age 3.

Information following from: Not Given.

26-20 JOSEPH SHE-GWAW-JAW, dead.

Wife: Name not given, dead.

26-20-1 James She-Gwa-Jaw, age 47, P.O. Elk Rapids.

Wife: Jane (Petosky) She-Gwa-Jaw, age 62, P.O. Elk Rapids, on roll 1870 with 3-25, jane has child see 3-25.

26-20-2 ~~Catharine~~ Mary Ann, dead.

Husband: Name not given, his children who live with Rosie Shomin, see 27-20.

26-202-1 Thomas Shomin or Thomas Pond, age 8, P.O. Cross Village.

26-20-3 Catharine Dalmas, age 40, P.O. Cross Village.

Husband: Name not given, a Frenchman, white.

26-20-3-1 Mary Delmas, age 12, P.O Cross Village.
26-20-3-2 Benedict Delmas, age 9.
26-20-3-3 Louis Delmas, age 7.
26-20-3-4 Peter Delmas, age 5.
26-20-3-5 Aurelia Delmas, age 3.
26-20-4 Philaman Odemin, (female), P.O. Cross Village, see 40-20.

Information following from: Not Given.
27-20 E-DO-WE-KE-ZHICK-WAY-BE, dead.
Wife: Name not given, dead.
27-20-1 Name not given, see 107-22.
27-20-2 Peter E-Do-We-Ke-Zhick-Way-Be, age 59, P.O. Cross Village. Known as Peter Chippeway.
Wife: Name not given, dead.
27-20-2-1 John E-Do-We-Ke-Zhick-Way-Be, age 29, P.O. Cross Village, single, known as John Chippeway.
27-20-2-2 Annie Dominick, age 24.
Husband: Edmund Dominick, see 35-20.
27-20-2-3 Sophia E-Do-We-Ke-Zhick-Way-Be or Chippeway, age 17, P.O. ~~Cross Village~~ Genoa School Nebr.
27-20-3 Enos E-Do-We-Ke-Zhick-Way-Be, dead.
Wife: Angeline Chippeway #2, age 47, P.O. Cross Village.
27-20-3-1 Mary Kaw-Way-Go-Mo-Aw, age 25.
Husband: Jonas Kawagomoah, age 44, see 34-28, Goodheart see 11-28.
27-20-3-1-1 John Kawagomoah, age 5.
27-20-3-1-2 Alice Kawagomoah, age 3.
27-20-3-1-3 Joseph Kawagomoah, born July 16, 1908 2nd Roll.
27-20-3-2 Catharine Shomin, age 23.
Husband: Sebastian Shomin, see 15-20.
27-20-3-3 Louisa Chippeway, age 16, P.O. Cross Village – at Tomah Sch. Wis.
27-20-4 Mary Sainwick, age 49, P.O. Cross Village, see 31-28.
27-20-5 Daniel Chippeway #2, age 43, P.O. Cross Village, single.
27-20-6 Rosie Shomin, age 42, P.O. Cross Village.
Husband: Mitchell Shomin, dead.
27-20-6-1 Thomas Pond, age 8, adopted, see 26-20.
27-20-7 Name not given, dead no heirs.

Information following from: Not Given.
28-20 NE-ZHO-TO-GE, dead.
Wife: Name not given, dead.
28-20-1 Catharine, age 58.
Husband: Joseph May-Dway-Gown, age 60, see 66-21.

28-20-2 Charles Shomin, age 57, P.O. Cross Village.

Wife: Mary Shomin (nee Dailey), age 58, P.O. Cross Village, see 17-28, children none.

28-20-2-1 Benedict Shawanabin, adopted, age 25, P.O. Cross Village, see 17-28.

28-20-3 Sarah Saganakwado, age 44, P.O. Cross Village.

Husband: Joseph Saganakwado, age 46, P.O. Cross Village, see 47-21.

28-20-4 Name not given, dead, no heirs.

Information following from: Not Given.

29-20 FRANCIS TAW-BAW-SOSH, age 81, P.O. Cross Village.

Wife: Name not given, dead.

29-20-1 Madeline, dead, no children.

29-20-2 John Tabasash, age 50, P.O. Cross Village.

Wife: Anna Tabasash (nee Jackson), Age ~~42~~, dead.

29-20-2-1 Angeline Tabasash, age 22, P.O. Cross Village, single, no children.

Information following from: Not Given.

30-20 ISAAC NAW-DO-WAY-QUAY-SAW, dead.

Wife: Josette Naw-Do-Way-Quay-Saw, age 66, P.O. Cross Village.

30-20-1 Mary Animequam, age 28, P.O. Cross Village, see 39-20.

30-20-2 Bennett Shingawkose, age 47, P.O. Cross Village.

Wife: Josie (Michigan), age 38, see 45-42.

Note: Bennett has children by 1st wife, see 56-21.

Information following from: Not Given.

31-20 AUGUSTUS NAW-WE-MAISH-CO-TAY, dead.

Wife: Name not given, dead.

31-20-1 Name not given, dead.

Husband: Joe Micksawbay, see 21-20.

31-20-1-1 Donatus Ne-Saw-Waw-Quot or Joe Donatus, age 35, P.O. Goodheart.

Wife: Rosie Sinaway Donatus (Aw-Se-No-Ung), age 30, see 15-28.

31-20-2 Name not given, dead.

Information following from: Not Given, Harbor Springs, Oct 6/07.

32-20 KIN-NE-QUAY, dead.

Husband: Name not given.

Step Children:

32-20-1 Mary Petoskey, age 50, P.O. Harbor Springs, see 50-21.

32-20-2 Peter Poyat, age 53, P.O. near Sault St. Marie, cannot find him, Durant.

Information following from: Not Given, Oct 19/08 Cross Village.
33-20 NESETTE A-GAW-WAW-NE-GAY, noe known as Elizabeth Ketch Baptist, age 88, P.O. Cross Village.
Husband: Name not given.
33-20-1 Margaret Onanagose, age 57, P.O. Cross Village.
Husband: Francis Onanagose, age 57, 6-20 and 106-32.
33-20-2 Rosie Shaw-Waw-Naw-Se-Gay, P.O. Burt Lake, see 8-37.
Husband 1st : Name not given, dead, see 7-20.
Husband 2nd: James Shaw-Waw-Naw-Se-Gay, see 3-31.
33-20-3 Name not given, dead, no heirs.
33-20-4 Name not given, dead, no heirs.
33-20-5 Name not given, dead, no heirs.

Information following from: Not Given, Oct 19/08 Cross Village.
34-20 MAY-DWAY-GO-NAY-AW-SHE, dead.
Wife: Name not given, dead.
34-20-1 Name not given, dead, no heirs.
34-20-2 Name not given, dead.

Information following from: Not Given.
35-20 LOUIS O-GE-DAW-NAW-QUOT, dead.
Wife: Name not given, dead.
35-20-1 Dominick O-Ge-Daw-Naw-Quot, age 53, P.O. Cross Village.
Wife: Eliza O-Ge-Daw-Naw-Quot, age 48, P.O. Cross Village,
see 3-28.
35-20-1-1 Edmund Dominick, age 27, P.O. Cross Village.
Wife: Annie Dominick, age 25, P.O. Cross Village, see 27-20, no children.
35-20-2 Name not given, dead.
Wife: Lucy Blackman, age 29, P.O. Suttons Bay, see 17-41.
35-20-3 Agnes, dead.
Husband: Name not given.
35-20-3-1 Agnes Paul, age 25, see 4-30 and 28-28.

Information following from: Not Given, Oct 16 Cross Village.
36-20 KE-SIS-WAW-BAY, dead.
Wife: Theresa Ke-Sis-Waw-Bay, age 77, P.O. Cross Village, children all dead and no heirs.

Information following from: Not Given.
37-20 THOMAS SHAWMIN, age 73, P.O. Cross Village.
Wife: Name not given, dead.
Note: Two oldest children dead, no heirs.

37-20-1 Cynthia Lesley, age 33, P.O. ~~Lansing~~ Cross Village.
Husband 1st : Ed Mellett (white), separated.
37-20-1-1 Elizabeth Mellett, age 13, died July 1908.
Husband 2nd: Frank Lesley, Age 36, P.O. ~~Beaver Island~~ Cross Village, see 4-13.
37-20-1-2 Mary Lesley, age 9.

Information following from: Not Given.
38-20 JOSEPH NAY-ONG-GAY-BE, age 68, P.O. Cross Village.
Wife: Sarah Nay-Ong-Gay-Be, age 63, died July 8, 1907.
38-20-1 Julia Ko-Se-Quot, age 48, P.O. Cross Village.
Husband: Peter Ko-Se-Quot, age 48, P.O. Cross Village, see 2-28.
38-20-1-1 Titus Ko-Se-Quot, age 25, P.O. Cross Village, single.
38-20-1-2 Rosie Ko-Se-Quot Chawme, age 23, P.O. Cross Village, see 20-20.
Husband: Joe Chawme, children see 20-20.
38-20-1-3 Agnes Ko-Se-Quot, age 21, P.O. Cross Village.
38-20-1-4 Sam Ko-Se-Quot, age 17, P.O. Cross Village.
38-20-2 Mary Anemiquom, age 31, P.O. Cross Village.
Husband: Simon Anemiquom, age 41, P.O. Cross Village, see 39-20.
38-20-2-1 Amelia Anemiquom, age 7.
38-20-3 Name not given, dead, no heirs.

Information following from: Not Given.
39-20 SAMUEL AW-NE-ME-QUO-UM, age 75, P.O. Cross Village.
Wife: Name not given, dead.
39-20-1 Moses Shawan, age 62, P.O. Cross Village, a half brother of Samuel enrolled with 39-20 in 1870.
Wife: Susan Shawan, age 46, P.O. Cross Village, daughter of Francis Micksawbay 21-20.
39-20-1-1 Francis Shawan, age 26, P.O. Cross Village, not married.
39-20-1-2 Therese Shawan, age 19, P.O. Cross Village
Husband: Name not given.
39-20-1-2-1 Mary Shawan, born March 1908, died Aug 1908, P.O. Cross Village, 2nd Roll.
39-20-1-3 Jennie Shawan, age 14, P.O. Cross Village.
39-20-2 Mitchell Awnemequom or Mitchell Sam, age 46, P.O. Pt. St. Ignace.
Wife 1st : Name not given, dead.
39-20-2-1 Joseph Sam Animequoum, age 15, P.O. Carlisle

School, enroll with Sophia Nishigebinese, see 13-28.
39-20-2-2 Charles Sam Animequoum, age 15, P.O. Cross Village, enroll with Sophia Nishigebinese, see 13-28.
Wife 2nd: Eliza Sam, nee Say-Ge-Tos, see 15-36.
39-20-2-3 Patrick Awnemequoum, age 3.
39-20-2-4 Emma Awnemequoum, born Dec/08, 2nd Roll.
39-20-3 Simon Awnemequom or Simon Sam, age 41, P.O. Cross Village.
Wife: Mary Awnemequom, nee Nay-Ong-Gay-Be, see 38-20.
39-20-4 Felix Awnemequom or Animequam, age 35, P.O. Cross Village.
Wife: Mary Awnemequom, age 28, see 30-20.
39-20-4-1 James Awnemequom, age 11.
39-20-4-2 Pius Awnemequom, age 9.
39-20-4-3 Therese Awnemequom, age 7.
39-20-4-4 Rosie Awnemequom, age 2, died June 30/08.

Information following from: Not Given.
40-20 MICHAEL O-TAY-E-MIN, dead.
Wife: Name not given, dead.
40-20-1 Jonas ~~Otayemin~~ Odeimin, age 45, P.O. Cross Village, see 52-21.
40-20-2 Ambrose ~~Otayemin~~ Odeimin, age 43, P.O. Cross Village.
Wife: Philamon Odeimin, age 39, P.O. Cross Village.
40-20-2-1 Mary Odeimin, age 11.
40-20-2-2 Rosie Odeimin, age 7.
40-20-2-3 Anna Odeimin, age 5.
40-20-2-4 Stella Odeimin, age 3.
40-20-3 Paul ~~Otayemin~~ Odeimin, age 37, P.O. Cross Village, single.
40-20-4 Regina Shaw, age 35, P.O. Cross Village.
Husband: William Shaw, white.
40-20-4-1 Ida Shaw, age 15, P.O. Cross Village.
40-20-4-2 Edward Shaw, age 12, P.O. Cross Village.
40-20-5 Barbara Chingway, age 33, P.O. Cross Village, sparated from husband.
Husband: William Chingway, P.O. Middle Village.
40-20-5-1 Mary Chingway, age 15, P.O. Tomas Indian School Wis.
40-20-5-2 Anna Chingway, age 8, P.O. Harbor Springs School
40-20-6 Louis Odeimin, age 21, P.O. Cross Village, single.
40-20-7 Joe Odeimin or Odemon, age 39, P.O. Pt. Aux Chene, has son on 2nd Roll.
Wife: Jane Odeimin, nee Sagato, age 41, P.O. Pt. Aux Chene, see 2-36.
40-20-7-1 Edward Odeimin, age 9.

Page 21
Cross Village Band
Chief NAW-WE-MAISH-CO-TAY

Information following from: Not Given, Oct 16.

42-21 JOSEPH ME-GE-SE-MONG, spelled Mixmong, age 66, P.O. Cross Village.
Wife: Philomena MixMong, age 59, P.O. Cross Village, on 1870 Roll with husband.
42-21-1 Jasper Mixmong, age 40, P.O. Cross Village.
Wife: Mary Ann Mixmong, nee Agosa, age 32, see 36-43.
42-21-1-1 William Mixmong, age 12.
42-21-2 John Mixmong, age 38, P.O. Cross Village, single.
42-21-3 Clara Cutler, age 36, P.O. Cross Village.
Husband: Jacob Cutler, white.
42-21-3-1 John Cutler, age 13.
42-21-3-2 Nellie Cutler, age 12.
42-21-3-3 Mary Ann Cutler, age 10.
42-21-3-4 Christina Cutler, age 8.
42-21-3-5 Barney Cutler, age 3.
42-21-3-6 Jerone Cutler, born Oct 15/08. Off.
42-21-4 Sophia Wilmet, age 34, P.O. Cross Village.
Husband: Moses Wilmet, white.
42-21-4-1 Dan Wassigijig (Wah-Sa-Ke-Zhick), age 13, see 12-20.
42-21-4-2 Mary Wilmet, age 10.
42-21-5 Christina, dead.
Husband: Name not given, dead.
42-21-5-1 Jennie Mixmong, age 20, P.O. Cross Village.
42-21-5-2 Peter Mixmong, age 16, P.O. Cross Village.
42-21-6 Marlina Jenkins, age, 47, a cousin, parents dead, P.O. 356 ½ E. Ohio St. Chicago.
Husband: Charles Alfred Jenkins, age 54, white.
42-21-6-1 George Kewekahkam McLeod, age 26, P.O. Chicago, Ill.

356 ½ East Ohio St.
Chicago
July 18/09

Horace B. Durant Esq.
Washington D.C.

Dr Sir.

Yours of the 12th instant received and contents carefully noted will say in reply that My wife's Mothers brother MosesShowan is still living at Cross Village Mich as to whether thay were ever enrolled . I personally am unable to say. But my wife is pretty sure they where. Her Grandfather was a man who fought with the Indians against the British troops. and his name was Mikisemay. and his brother has a son named Joseph Mikisemay. Still living ar Cross Village. But these tribes have intermarried in different parts of the country that it is very difficult. Neather to trace them so late in the day but there is one sure thing about it. My wife is clearly entitled to enrollment. They seem to me to take any or eachothers name whenever they felt like it. For instancemy wife's fathers name was Tehkumah but his Fathers name was (as before stated). Miksemay. Will you please let me hear from you further in this matter. if I can render you any more information I shall be glad ot the oppurnity. I do not want anything that is not quik on the lerd. but I am concerned she is entitled to enrollment.

Yours faithfully,
Chas. A. Jenkins

Cross Village November 5

Simo nogo sa kitojibiamon kawi ni gi kachkitosi na gaie mi awi wabamina agi bi ijaieg Mano dach na gaie ni kibagose- nimin tchi bositoiaba Ni dano Sowin kichpin iji kachkitoian Mi jaikwa 25 bibon eko tani Siia Mandapi kitchi Mokoman aking *Mi Sa Minig Pojo*
60 years old

Nin Elizabeth Tekama

Kawika Nigotchi Nida

Tosin Nidanosowin Mi go eta Mijiiganig agi waba Minaba agi atoiaba gaieni ni danosowin

Information following from: Not Given.
43-21 LOUIS SHAWMIN
Wife 1st : Name not given, dead.
Wife 2nd: ~~Mrs. Isaac Blackman~~ Rosie Blackman wife of Isaac Blackman, white, see 42-41.
43-21-1 Name not given, dead.
43-21-2 Lucy Blackman, see 17-41.

Information following from: Not Given.
44-21 PAUL O-MAW-WE-NIN-NE, dead.
Wife: Name not given, dead.
44-21-1 Jeremiah Waukazoo, age 45, P.O. Cross Village, single.
44-21-2 Annie Stafford, age 43, P.O. Petoskey, no children.
Husband: Name not given, white.
44-21-2-1 Agatha Stafford, age 13, mother is Catharine

Crandall oe Kate Kezhegowe, see 9-31 and 27-54.

44-21-3 Name not given, dead.

Information following from: Not Given, Oct 24/08 Burt Lake.

45-21 MRS. MARY PAW-CAW or Parkey, dead.

Husband: Name not given.

45-21-1 Joseph Parkey, age 48, P.O. Brutus, see 3-31.

45-21-2 Philamen Ance, age 33, P.O. Charles Mich. near St. Ignace.

Husband: Anthony Mush-Ko-Gos Ance, age ~~43~~ 54, see 14-15, P.O. Charles Mich. near St. Ignace.

45-21-2-1 Rosie Ance, age 16, P.O. Charles Mich. near St. Ignace.

Information following from: Not Given, Oct 19/06 X Village.

46-21 DANIEL KEY-O-GE-MAW, dead.

Wife: Name not given, dead.

46-21-1 Name not given, dead, no heirs.

Information following from: Not Given.

47-21 PAUL SAW-GAW-NAW-GWAW-DO or SARGONQUATTO, dead

Wife: Name not given, dead.

47-21-1 Francis Saganakwado, dead, no heirs.

47-21-2 Joseph ~~Sargonquatto~~ Saganakwado, age 46, P.O. Cross Village, see 28-20.

Wife 1st : ~~Angel~~, dead Saganakwado.

Wife 2nd: ~~Josette~~ Sarah ~~Saganakwado~~, age 44.

47-21-2-1 Annie Etaw-Naw-Caw-Me-Go, Age 27, P.O. Cross Village, see 17-20.

47-21-2-2 David Saganakwado, age 16, P.O. Cross Village.

Information following from: Not Given.

48-21 AW-SE-NAW-BAY, dead, no heirs.

Wife: Name not given, dead.

Information following from: Not Given.

49-21 BENJAMIN O-TAY-E-MIN, dead.

Wife: Name not given, dead.

49-21-1 Joe O-Tay-E-Min or Odamon, age 39, P.O. Port Auxchene.

Wife: Jane O-Tay-E-Min (nee Sageto), age 41, see 2-36.

49-21-1-1 Edward O-Tay-E-Min, age 9.

49-21-1-2 George O-Tay-E-Min, born July 1907 2d Roll.

Information following from: Not Given.

50-21 SHAW-GAW-WAW-BUN-NO, dead.

Wife: Name not given, dead.

50-21-1 Joseph Petoskey, age 60, P.O. Harbor Springs.
Wife: Mary Petoskey, nee: Kin-Ne-Quay, age 50, see 32-20.
50-21-1-1 John Petoskey, age 32, P.O. Harbor Springs.
Wife: Victoria Petoskey, age not given, P.O. Charlevoix or Harbor Springs, nee daughter of James Cooper & Margaret Key-Way-O-Say, Indian of Ottawa Tribe.
50-21-1-1-1 John Petoskey Jr., age 7, see 48-33.
50-21-1-1-2 Margaret Petoskey, age 3, see 48-33.
50-21-1-2 Stephen Petoskey, age 22, Harbor Springs.
50-21-1-3 Ellen Petoskey, age 12, P.O. Harbor Springs.
50-21-1-4 Leander Petoskey, age 7, P.O. Harbor Springs.

Information following from: Not Given.
51-21 SAW-GAW-CHE-WAY-O-SAY, dead.
Wife: Name not given, dead.
51-21-1 Name Not Given, dead, no heirs.

Information following from: Not Given.
52-21 LOUIS KEY-O-GE-MAW
Wife: Name not given, dead.
Note: Two oldest children dead no heirs.
52-21-1 Flora Odeimin, age 35, P.O. Sturgeon Bay, Mich. or Cross Village.
Husband: Jonas Odeimin, age 45, P.O. Cross Village, see 40-20.
52-21-1-1 Sam Odeimin, age 18, P.O. Genoa School, Nebr.
52-21-1-2 Angeline Odeimin, age 8.
52-21-1-3 George Odeimin, age 2.
53-21-2 Thomas Kiogina, age 28, P.O. Cross Village.
Wife: Mary Jane Kiogina, age 27, see 104-22.
53-21-2-1 Margaret Kiogina, age 5.
53-21-2-2 Levi Kiogina, age 3.
53-21-2-3 Olive Kiogina, born Jany 1908 2nd Roll, died Oct 4/1908.
53-21-3 Jennie Kiogina, age 26, P.O. Cross Village, single.

Information following from: Not Given.
53-21 JOHN NE-SAW-WAW-QUOT, dead.
Wife: Name not given, dead.
53-21-1 Name not given, dead.
Spouse: Name not given.
53-21-1-1 Margaret Blackbird or Isaac, age 51, see 3-39.
Husband: Isaac Blackbird or Isaac Sig-A-Nock or Bert Issac, see 9-37.

53-21-2 Name not given, dead.
53-21-3 Jeremiah Saw-Wah-Quot or Joe Edowegonaybe or Joe Nishaw, age 29, P.O. Cross Village, see 76-21.
Wife: Catharine Saw-Wah-Quot, age 31, see 61-35.
53-21-4 Susan Nishaw Moses, age 26, P.O. Rapid City ~~Jameson's Mills, Mich.~~, separated.
Husband: Louis Moses, see 61-35 & 10-11.

Information following from: Not Given.
54-21 PE-NAY-SE-QUAY, dead.
Spouse: Name not given.
54-21-1 Margaret Wahbegog, age 52, P.O. Cross Village, not married, no children.
54-21-2 Name not given, dead, no heirs.

Information following from: Not Given.
55-21 WILLIAM NAW-DO-WAY-GWAY-SAW, age 62, P.O. Cross Village.
Wife: Margaret Naw-Do-Way-Gway-Saw, age 50, on 1870 Roll with him.
55-21-1 Name not given, dead, no heirs.

Information following from: Not Given.
56-21 SHE-GWAW-MEIG, dead.
Wife: Name not given, dead.
56-21-1 Elizabeth (Shingwakos) Williams, age 40, P.O. Goodheart, see 31-28.
Husband 1st: Bennett Shinggwakose, age 47, P.O. Cross Village, see 30-20, separated, 2nd wife Josie (Michigan) Shinggwakose.
56-21-1-1 Mary Shingwakos, age 20, P.O. Cross Village, single.
56-21-1-1-1 James Shingwakose, age 2 months, died Aug 3/1908 2nd Roll.
56-21-1-2 Charles Shingwakose, age 17, P.O. Tomah School,
Husband 2nd: Jacob Williams, age 42, P.O. Goodheart.
Wis. Said to be a Canadian Indian, his father is alive & lives at Wekwamikong, Mantobin Island, & if entitled to enrollment at all, might be found with the Mackinawband, but I cannot trace him with the Cross Village of Middle Village Bands, Horace B. Durant Spl. Agt Oct20/08 Middle Village, Mich.
56-21-2 Name not given, dead, no heirs.

Information following from: Not Given, Oct 19/08.

57-21 THOMAS PE-NOY-GON, dead.
Wife: Name not given, dead.
57-21-1 Name not given, dead, no heirs.

Information following from: Not Given.
58-21 WILLIAM KE-ZHICK-WAW, dead.
Wife: Name not given, dead.
58-21-1 Name not given, dead, no heirs.

Information following from: Not Given, Sept. 25/08.
59-21 MARGARET AISH-KE-BAW-GOSH.
Husband: Name not given.
59-21-1 Jeremiah Skibogosh, age 62, P.O. Elk Rapids, RFD #1, see 26-42..
59-21-2 Name not given, dead, no heirs.

Information following from: Not Given.
60-21 NE-SHE-KE-PE-NAY-SE, dead.
Wife: Sophia Ne-She-Ke-Pe-Nay-Se or Sophia Nishigebinese or Sophia Bird, see 13-28.
60-21-1 Name not given, dead, no heirs.

Information following from: Not Given.
61-21 PETER NE-SAW-WAW-QUOT, dead.
Wife: Madeline Edowegonaybe, age 62, P.O. Cross Village.
61-21-1 Name not given, dead, no heirs.
61-21-2 Mary Francis, age 25, P.O. Cross Village.
Husband: William Francis, age 32, see 8-42.

Information following from: Not Given, Oct 16/08 X Village.
62-21 MOSES MAY-DWAW-GON, spelled Midwagin, age 63, P.O. Cross Village.
Wife: Veronica May-Dwaw-Gon, spelled by them: Midwagin, age 53.
62-21-1 Moses May-Dwaw-gon Jr., age 43, P.O. Manistique.
Wife: Angeline May-Dwaw-Gon, nee Siganock, off Canadian Indian.
62-21-1-1 Benjamin May-Dwaw-Gon, age 12, P.O. Manistique.
62-21-1-2 George May-Dwaw-Gon, age 5.
~~62-21-1-3 Infant~~ taken off because father says he has only 2 children.
62-21-2 Therese Swartout, age 38, P.O. Cross Village.
Husband: Arthur Swartout, white, dead.
62-21-2-1 Esther Swartout, age 17.
62-21-2-2 Nellie Swartout, age 15.

62-21-2-3 Eddie Swartout, age 9.
62-21-2-4 Willie Swartout, age 6.
62-21-3 Jonas May-Dwaw-Gon, age 28, P.O. Cross Village, single.
62-21-4 Anna May-Dwaw-Gon, age 18, died June 1907.

Information following from: Not Given.
63-21 MARY KEY-NO-ZHAY, dead.
Husband: Name not given.
63-21-1 Peter Pike, age 60, P.O. Cross Village, see 61-35.

Information following from: Not Given, Oct 19/08.
64-21 MRS. A-PAW-POW-KEY, dead.
Husband: Name not given.
64-21-1 Name not given, dead, no heirs.

Information following from: Not Given.
65-21 JOHN GILBERT, age 61, P.O. Cross Village.
Wife: Margaret Gilbert, age 61, P.O. Cross Village.
Note: First two children died young with no heirs.
65-21-1 Paul Gilbert, age 32, P.O. Cross Village, single.
65-21-2 Gabriel Gilbert, age 28, P.O. Cross Village, single.
65-21-3 William Gilbert, age 22, P.O. Cross Village, single.
65-21-4 Lena Gilbert, age 20, P.O. Genoa School Nebr.
65-21-5 Mary Gilbert, age 15, P.O. Cross Village.
By 1st husband of Margaret Gilbert:
65-21-6 Anna Tabasash, see 29-20, dead, for children see 29-20.

Information following from: Not Given.
66-21 JOSEPH MAY-DWAW-GWON, age 60, P.O. Cross Village.
Wife: Catharine May-Dwaw-Gwon, age 58, P.O. Cross Village.
66-21-1 Angeline Shomin, age 28, P.O. Cross Village, adopted, no children.
Husband: Peter Bourassaw, age not given, P.O. North Shore, separated, see 79-21.

Information following from: Not Given.
67-21 O-GE-DAW-NAW-QUOT, dead.
Wife: Name not given.
67-21-1 Name not given, dead, no heirs.

Information following from: Not Given.
68-21 MRS. William Lasley.
No further information given.

Information following from: Not Given, Oct 19/08.

69-21 WAW-BE-GAY, dead, no heirs.
Wife: Name not given.
No further information given.

Information following from: Not Given.
70-21 O-GAW-O-QUAY, dead.
Spouse: Name not given.
70-21-1 Name not given, dead, no heirs.

Information following from: Not Given, Oct 19/08 X Village.
71-21 AISH-KE-BAW-GAW-WAW, dead.
Wife: Name not given.
71-21-1 Name not given, dead, no heirs.

Information following from: Not Given.
72-21 AW-POW-TOO, dead.
Spouse: Name not given.
72-21-1 Name not given, dead.
Husband: Name not given, whereabouts unknown.
72-21-1-1 Jane Waw-Say-Ke-Zhick, age 33, P.O. Petoskey, see 12-20.

Information following from: Not Given, X Village.
73-21 O-TE-NE-GON or LOUIS OTENEGON, age 72, P.O. Cross Village, no children..
Wife: Name not given.

Information following from: Lucy King & George Lasley, Mac Isle Apr 13/09.
74-21 MAW-CO-DAY-WE-KOONSE-QUAY or MARY LASLEY, dead.
Husband: Name not given.
74-21-1 George Lasley, on roll as 28-15.
74-21-2 Jane Aslin, age 60, P.O. Gould City Mich, see 25-11.
74-21-3 Henry Lasley, age 58, P.O. Gould City, sometimes called Senah Lasley.
Wife: Clara Lasley, white.
74-21-3-1 Ellen Perkins, age 31, P.O. Gould City.
Husband: Name not given, white.
74-21-3-1-1 Crawford Perkins, age 6.
74-21-3-2 Josephine Lafond, age 26, P.O. Manistique, no children.
Husband: Eugene Lafond.
74-21-3-3 Arthur Lasley, age 24, P.O. Manistique.
Wife: Name not given, white.
74-21-3-3-1 Henry Lasley, age 1.

74-21-3-4 Albert Lasley, age 22, P.O. Gould City, single.
74-21-3-5 Ed Lasley, age 20, P.O. Gould City, single.
74-21-3-6 Mike Lasley, age 17, P.O. Gould City.
74-21-3-7 Belle or Cora Lasley, age 11, P.O. Gould City.
74-21-3-8 Mary Lasley, age 9.
74-21-3-9 Alice Lasley, age 7.

Information following from: Not Given.
75-21 NAW-GAW-NAW-SHE, dead.
Wife: Name not given, dead.
75-21-1 Name not given, dead, no heirs.

Information following from: Not Given, X Village Oct 10/08.
76-21 PAUL NE-SAW-WAW-QUOT, dead.
Wife: Name not given, dead.
76-21-1 Name not given, see 53-21.
Spouse: Name not given.
76-21-1-1 Jere Nishaw, age 30, P.O. Cross Village, see 61-35.
76-21-1-2 Susie Moses, age 25, P.O. ~~Jameson's Mills Mich.~~ Rapid City, see 53-21 & 10-11.
Husband: Louis Moses, see 61-35 & 10-11.

Information following from: Not Given.
77-21 JOHN MICK-SE-MONG, dead.
Wife: Name not given, dead.
77-21-1 Joseph Mick-Se-Mong, see 42-21.

Information following from: Not Given.
78-21 LOUIS SAW-GAW-NAW-GWAN-DO, dead.
Wife: Sophia Shomin, now wife of Mike Shomin, see 19-20 & 4 -51.
No further information given.

Information following from: Not Given.
79-21 SAW-KE, dead, no heirs.
Wife: Name not given, dead.

Information following from: Not Given.
80-21 MAW-CO-QUAY, dead, no heirs.

Information following from: Not Given, John B. Shomin, Mackinac Island Apr/09.
81-21 JOHN B. SHOMIN, age 63, P.O. Mackinac Island Mich.
Wife: Mary (Chapman) Shomin, age 65, P.O. Mackinac Island Mich, see 30-13.
81-21-1 Nicholas Shomin, age 40, P.O. Mackinac Island.

Wife: Elzzie Shomin, age 32, see 60-16.
81-21-1-1 Veta Shomin, age 18.
81-21-1-2 Agatha Shomin, age 17.
81-21-1-3 John Shomin, age 16.
81-21-1-4 Wilfred Shomin, age 15.
81-21-1-5 Edna Shomin, age 13.
81-21-1-6 Nicholas Shomin, age 10.
81-21-1-7 Margarette Shomin, age 8.
81-21-1-8 Hastings Shomin, age 6.
81-21-1-9 Rowena Shomin, age 3.
81-21-2 George Shomin, age 38, P.O. Mackinac Island, single.

Information following from: Not Given.
82-21 NAW-PAW-WAW-CHE-QUAY, dead, no heirs, no further information given.

Page 22
Cross Village Band
Chief NAW-WE-MAISH-CO-TAY

Information following from: Not Given.
83-22 JAMES WAW-SHAW-WAW-NAW-SHE or Joe Aishconock, age 62, P.O Cross Village.
Wife: Elizabeth Aishconock, age 60., P.O. Cross Village.
83-22-1 William Aishconock, age 34, P.O. Cross Village, single.
83-22-2 Bruno Aishconock, age 32, P.O. Cross Village, single.
83-22-3 Therese Aishconock, age 30., P.O. Cross Village, single.

Information following from: Not Given.
84-22 AISH-PE-GAW-BO-WAY, dead, no heirs, no further information.

Information following from: Not Given.
85-22 NIN-DO-BAW-NE-QUAY, dead.
Spouse: Name not given.
Note: Children al enrolled by themselves in 1870.
85-22-1 Tom Shomin
85-22-2 Jo Shomin, see 22-20.
85-22-3 Louis Shomin, see 43-21.

Information following from: Not Given.
86-22 MICHAEL KIN-NEECE, dead, no heirs, no further info given.

Information following from: Not Given.
87-22 KIN-NE-O-QUAY, dead, no heirs, no further info given.

Information following from: Not Given.
88-22 MARY SHOMIN, dead, no heirs, no further info given.

Information following from: Not Given.
89-22 AW-SHAW-WAW-CHE, dead, no heirs, no further info given.

Information following from: Not Given.
90-22 ME-TAW-SAW, dead, no heirs, no further info given.

Information following from: Not Given.
91-22 MAW-CHIT-O-GO-QUAY, dead.
SPOUSE: Name not given
91-22-1 George Dailey, dead, no heirs.
91-22-2 Margaret Flint, dead.
Husband: Name not given, white.
91-22-2-1 Hattie Gerne, see 95-22.

Information following from: Not Given.
92-22 CATHARINE NAW-WE-MAISH-CO-TAY, gone to Canada, Mantolin Island, have not heard from her for many years – 10 years. Cannot trace her Durant.

Information following from: Not Given.
93-22 MARTHA N. CHANCE, dead, no heirs, no further info given.

Information following from: Not Given.
94-22 DANIEL DAILEY, age 62, P.O. Cross Village.
Wife: Angeline Dailey, age 57, on 1870 roll with husband, no children.

Information following from: Mrs. Hattie Gerne, Mullet Lake, Dec 18/08.
95-22 MARGARET FLINT, should be FLYNN, dead.
Husband: Name not given.
95-22-1 Hattie Flynn Gerne, age 34, P.O. Mullet Lake Mich.
Husband: Louis Gerne, age 38, see 21-11.
95-22-1-1 Lawrence Gerne, age 12.
95-22-1-2 Helen Gerne, age 10.
95-22-1-3 Ethel Gerne, age 8.
95-22-1-4 Bertha Gerne, age 5.

Information following from: Not Given.
96-22 THERESA LABELLE, dead.
Husband: Name not given.
96-22-1 Mary Shomin, see 17-28.
96-22-2 Eliza Shawanabon, see 17-28.

Information following from: Not Given, X Village.
97-22 FRANCIS LACROIX, dead, no heirs.
Wife: Name not given, dead.

Information following from: Not Given.
98-22 PETER KAW-GE-GAY-BE-TUNG, dead.
Wife: Margaret Kagigebetang, age 53, P.O. Cross Village, see 6-20.
98-22-1 Moses Kagigebitang, age 33, P.O. Cross Village.
Wife: Mary Kagigebitang #1, nee Bwanishing, age 28, see 43-32.
98-22-1-1 Samuel Kagigebitang, age 11.
98-22-1-2 Clara Kagigebitang, age 9.
98-22-1-3 Peter Kagigebitang, age 4.
98-22-1-4 Julius Kagigebitang, age 2.
98-22-1-5 Theresa Kagigebitang, born July 10, 1908 2nd Roll.
98-22-2 Mary Kagigebitang #2, age 28, P.O. Cross Village, single.
Husband: Not Married.
98-22-2-1 William Kagigebitang, age 6.
98-22-2-2 George Kagigebitang, age 3.
98-22-3 Susan Kagigebitang, age 26, P.O. Cross Village, single.
Husband: Not Married.
98-22-3-1 John Kagigebitang, born & died July 22, 1908.
98-22-4 Thomas Kagigebitang, age 19, P.O. Elm Grove Wis.
98-22-5 Alex Kagigebitang, age 10, Harbor Springs School.

Elm Grove Wis.,
June 24, 1909

Mr. Horace B. Durant,
Dear Sir:

Yours of inst, should have been noticed sooner. Deferred doing so, excepting to go to Petoskey before this. Am delayed a few days longer so will comply by sending names of Brothers & Sisters now.

Their ages and addresses will send in about four days. Their names are__

(over)

Father	–	*Peter*	*Kagigebitang*
Mother	–	*Margaret*	" "
Sisters	–	*Mary*	" "
" "	–	*Susie*	" "
Brothers	–	*Moses*	" "
" "	–	*Alex*	" "

Respectfully

Information following from: Not Given.
99-22 LOUIS LA CROIX.
Wife: Josett La Croix, age 78, died Jany 21/08.
99-22-1 Name not given, dead.
Husband: William Shield, white, age not given, P.O. Brutus.
99-22-1-1 Eugene Shield, age 7, P.O. Brutus.
99-22-1-2 William Shield, age 6, P.O. Brutus.
99-22-2 Isadore La Croix, age 41, P.O. Cross Village, no children.

Information following from: Not Given.
100-22 JOSEPH KAW-O-GO-MAW, dead.
Wife: Name not given, dead.
100-22-1 Mary Kee-Me-Che-Chaw-Gan, age 69, P.O. Petoskey.
Husband: Name not given.
100-22-1-1 Hyacinth Kee-Me-Che-Chaw-Gan, see 40-26.
100-22-1-2 Mitchell Kaogoma, age 53, P.O. Cross Village, wife dead, no heirs.
100-22-1-3 Angeline She-Go-Meig Nigankwaam, age 48, P.O. Cross Village.
Husband 1st: Peter She-Go-Meig, dead
Husband 2nd: Peter Nigankwaam, age 59, see 10-20.
100-22-1-3-1 Frank Nigankwaam, age 17.
100-22-1-4 Name not given, dead, no heirs.
100-22-1-5 Name not given, dead no heirs.
100-22-1-6 Alex Kaogoma, age 38, P.O. Petoskey.
Wife: Theresa Kaogoma, age 38, nee Nanagoonse.
100-22-1-6-1 Annie Kaogoma, age 13, P.O. Mt. Pleasant School.

Information following from: Casper, Oct 15.
101-22 CASPER SHAWMIN or SHOMON, age 59, lives with Mrs. Peter Lasley, enroll separately.
Wife: Mary Ann Shomin, age 62, P.O. Cross Village, no children.

Information following from: Not Given, Burt Lake, Oct 24/08.
102-22 MARGARET MOSIER or MASIER, pronounced Massey, age 75, P.O. Manistique, French except head of family.
Note: (N.B.) This is one of the nearly French families, see my report on 25-12 HBDurant Spl. Agt.
Husband: Joe Mosier, French.
102-22-1 Mary (Petoskey) McArthur, age 50, ~~Deluth~~ Ballclub Minn.
Husband: Name not given, white.
102-22-1-1 Dennis McArthur, age 14, P.O. Ballclub Minn.

102-22-2 Louisa Lapointe, age 48, P.O. Asylum at Newberry Mich, see 9-8, brother has not heard from her for 5 or 6 years. Said to be in Asylum, but does not know where.
Husband: Frank Lapinte, white.
102-22-2-1 Bertha Hancock, age 24, P.O. Charlevoix
Husband: Name not given, white.
102-22-2-1-1 William Hancock, P.O. Charlevoix.
102-22-2-1-2 Girl ~~Hancock~~, P.O. Charlevoix.
102-22-2-2 Wilson Hancock, age 25, P.O. Deluth Minn., single.
102-22-2-3 Vina Hancock, age 18, P.O. Manistique.
102-22-3 Charles Massey, age 49, P.O. Brutus, see 2-31.
102-22-4 Adalaide Duparow, age 45, P.O. Manistique.
Husband: Allen Duparow, off.
102-22-4-1 William Duparow, age 24, P.O. Manistique.
Wife: Name not given, white.
102-22-4-1-1 Marie Duparow, age 2.
102-22-4-1-2 Marian Duparow, born Sept 1908.
102-22-4-2 Rose Duparow Gibson, age 20, P.O. Detour Mich, has not been heard from for 8 to 10 years.
Husband: Name not given, white.
102-22-4-2-1 Catharine Gibson, age 3.
102-22-5 Joe Massey, age 43, P.O. Detour.
Note: Has a brother Charles Massey 55 living between Mack. City & Petoskey. Has 3 sisters in Manistique 1. Mary, 2. Louise LaPointe 3. Adelaide Duparrow.
Wife: Philamon Paquin (Parkey), age 40, P.O. Detour, Mackinaw Band, brother Frank Paquin St Ignace.
102-22-5-1 Charles Massey, age 19.
102-22-5-2 Jerry Massey, age 17.
102-22-5-3 Mary Massey, age 13.
102-22-5-4 William Massey, age 11.
102-22-5-5 Albert Massey, age 9.
102-22-5-6 Victoria Massey, age 7.
102-22-5-7 Delia Massey, age 5.
102-22-5-8 Pearl Massey, age 3.
102-22-5-9 Frank Massey, born July 1907.
102-22-6 Victoria Demarah, age 34, P.O. Manistique, no children.
Husband: Name not given, white.

The Upper Peninsula
Hospital for the Insane
Newberry, Mich.

1353

June 10, 1909

Department of the Interior,
Petoskey, Mich.
Dear Sir:-

Yours of the 8th inst. Relative to Mrs.Louisa Lapoint received. In reply beg to say that Mrs. Lapoint was admitted to this institution from Manistique, Schoolcraft County, Michigan, on January 23, 1900, and has resided here continuously since that date.

Trusting the above will be satisfactory, I am

Very truly yours,
E. H. Campbell
Medical Supt.

Ball Club, Minn. June 19, 1909.

Horace B. Durant,
Special U. S. Indian Agent,
Petoskey, Mich.
Dear Sir:

Your esteemed favor of the 9th inst. At hand. In reply beg to advise that I belong to the Ottawaand Chippewa Indians of Michigan. My father's name Joseph Massey, of Manistique, Mich. My mother's name is Marguerite (cote) Massey.

I have brothers and sisters in Michigan. Also a son, Dan McArthur, aged sixteen.

Yours very resp'y,
Mrs Mary McArthur

Information following from: Not Given.

103-22 MARGARET WAGLEY, dead, father white, mother Indian named Vallier.
Husband, Name not given, white.
103-22-1 John Wagley, age 60, P.O. Cross Village.
Wife: Name not given, white.
103-22-1-1 Willie Wagley, age 34, P.O. Cross Village.
103-22-1-2 Mary Louise Taylor, age 28, P.O. Cross Village.
103-22-1-3 Maud Emmous, age 26.
103-22-1-4 Glen Wagley, age 19.
103-22-2 Catharine Burnett, age 57, P.O. Charlevoix.
Husband: Name not given, white.
103-22-2-1 Edward Burnett, age 34.
103-22-2-2 Nellie Chency, age 28.
103-22-2-3 Bertie Burnett, age 26.
103-22-3 Edward Wagley, age 54, P.O. Traverse City.
Wife: Name not given, white.
103-22-3-1 Lynn Wagley, age 25.

103-22-3-2 Leslie Wagley, age 19.
103-22-3-3 Rosana Wagley, age 10.
103-22-4 Willie Wagley, age 50.
Wife: Name not given, white.
103-22-4-1 Leo Wagley, age 19.
103-22-4-2 Lester Wagley, age 10.
103-22-5 Cynthia Hough, age 47.
Husband: Name not given, white.
103-22-5-1 Ethel Hough, age 26.
103-22-5-2 Christina Hough, age 24.
103-22-5-3 Elmer Hough, age 22.
103-22-5-4 Jimmie Hough, age 19.
103-22-5-5 Morgan Hough, age 10.
103-22-6 Louise Cole, age 44.
Husband: Name not given, white.
103-22-6-1 Oliver Cole, age 23.
103-22-6-2 Guy Cole, age 21.
103-22-6-3 Stanley Cole, age 14.
103-22-6-4 Alma Cole, age 3.
103-22-7 Mary Davis, age 39.
Husband: Name not given, white.
103-22-7-1 James Howden, age 17.
103-22-8 Amos Wagley, age 36.

Report:

This family is pure white and do not claim to be Indians and only one, Amos Wagley, lives among the Indians, or claims any Indian blood.

However, the mother, & head of this family appears on the 1870 roll and her descendants are given herewith for such action as seems to the Dept. to be right & proper.

Horace B Durant, Spl. Agt.

Cross Village, Mich, Oct 16, 1908
Note: The identity of the names on this sheet has been fully established by testimony of many Indians at Cross Village.

Horace B Durant, Spl. Agt.

Information following from: Not Given.
104-22 TERESA DAVENPORT, age 67, P.O. Cross Village.
Husband: Name not given.
104-22-1 William Davenport, age 38, P.O. Cross Village, separated.
Wife: Josephine Aniwaskey, age 30, P.O. Sutton's Bay, now living with & as wife of James Blacksmith, see 20-52 & 13-40, Grand River Band.
104-22-2 Susan ~~Bushey~~ Boucha, age 32, P.O. Port St. Ignace.
Husband: Ed Boucha, see 2-15.

104-22-3 Nancy Kewandeway, age not given, P.O. Port St. Ignace.
Husband: Harry Key-Wan-Da-Way age 31, see 9-36.
104-22-4 Mary Jane Kiogima, age 26.
Husband: Thomas Kiogima, see 52-21.
104-22-5 Lucy Davenport, age 25, P.O. Cross Village, single.
104-22-6 Robert Davenport, age 21, P.O. Carlisle Pa.

Information following from: Joe Mish-Qua-Do, finished at St. Ignace, Dec 4/08.

105-22 O-MO-QUAW-DO, dead.
Wife: Margaret Mashaqueto, age 75, died Aug 15, 1908.
105-22-1 Joe ~~Mish-Qua-Do~~ or Mashaqueto, age 55, P.O. Nawah.
Wife 1st: Name not given, dead.
105-22-1-1 Catharine Mashaqueto, age 21, died June 1908.
Wife 2nd: Mary Mishequeto, age 50, see ~~100-5~~ 4-34
105-22-1-2 Mary Mashaqueto, age 15, P.O. Mt. Pleasant Sch.
105-22-2 Mary Peter, age 40, P.O. Rapid River in Baker's Camp.
Husband: John Peter, age 50, see 32-30.
105-22-2-1 Mary Peter Jr., age 11.
105-22-2-2 Sam Peter, age 8.
105-22-2-3 Edward Peter, age 6.
105-22-2-4 John Peter, age 2.
105-22-3 Name not given, dead, no heirs.
105-22-4 Name not given, dead, no heirs.

Apr 18 1909
Rapid River, Mich

Dear Sir

I now write these few lines . in order to ask you if My Name appears on your Book. I am the Nephew of Wabenigum and received My Payment in Escanaba formerly. and___ I as Member of Ottawa Tribe. and also I send you Names of My____ Childrens and there age if you have Not received them from any one in St Jacqnes.

Yours Truly

Address
Rapid River R. D.
Delta Co. Mich
John Peter

Names

Mr. John Peter	*49 years of age*
Mrs. Mary Peter	*32*
Miss Mary Peter	*12*
Mr. Sam Peter	*9*
Mr. Edward Peter	*6*

Mr Johnny Peter 2 yrs.

Information following from: Not Given.

106-22 FRANCIS O-NAW-WAW-GOOSE, now spelled Nanegos, age 59, P.O. Cross Village.

Wife: Margaret (O-Naw-Waw-Goose) Nanegos, age 57, P.O. Cross Village, see 33-20.

106-22-1 Mary Petoskey Lawrence, age 35, P.O. Cross Village, separated.

Husband 1st :Eson Petoskey, age 38, P.O. Goodheart, see 21-28

106-22-1-1 Levi Petoskey, age 9, lives with grandfather.

Husband 2nd: Mobis Lawrence, see 21-57.

106-22-2 Mitchell Nanegos, age 26, P.O. Cross Village, single.

106-22-3 William Nanegos, age 23, P.O. Cross Village, single.

Information following from: Not Given.

107-22 FRANCIS ETO-WAY-KE-ZHICK-WAY-BE, age 61, P.O. Cross Village, no children.

Wife 1st : Name not given, left him at Goodheart.

Wife 2nd: Name not given, dead.

Information following from: Not Given.

108-22 MAY-DWAY-GE-WEN-NO-QUAY, dead, no heirs, no further information given.

Page 23
Charlevoix Band
Chief SHAW-WAN-DAY-SE

Information following from: Not Given.

1-23 SHAW-WAN-DAY-SE #2

Wife: Name not given, dead.

1-23-1 Lewis Shaw-Waw-Day-Se, see 14-23.

1-23-2 Moses Shaw-Waw-Day-Se, P.O. Pashabatown, see 36-23.

1-23-3 Mway-Ke-We-Naw or Peter Shaw-Waw-Day-Se, P.O. Northport.

1-23-4 Mary Coon (Asebun), age 76, P.O. Pashabatown.

Husband: John Wain-Bway-Go-Nay-By of John Coon, P.O. Pashabatown, see 5-23.

Information following from: Not Given.

2-23 WAIN-DAW-SAW-MO-SAY or NOAH WAIN-DAW-SAW-MO-SAY, age 95, died April 1908.

Wife: Bedah Wain-Daw-Saw-Mo-Say, age 90, died April 1908 two days before husband.

2-23-1 Joe Noah, age 43, P.O. ~~St. Ignace~~ Bay Shore or Allenville.
Wife: Angeline Noah, age 40.
2-23-1-1 Frank Noah, age 12.
2-23-1-2 Mitchell Noah, age 10.
2-23-1-3 Antoine Noah, age 5.
2-23-1-4 Sam Noah, age 2.

2-23-2 Name not given, dead.
Wife: Name not goiven, dead.
2-23-2-1 Sarah Noah, age 26, P.O. Bay Shore, single.
2-23-2-1-1 Alice Noah, age 5.
2-23-2-2 Martha Redbird, see 17-25.

June 21 1909

Dear Sir
I got your letter all wright

My folks aunt, living my father died and so is my mother am only me self here. My age is 43 years my wife is age 41 years old my Boy is age 13 years is name frank. Michael is age 8 years old and Antoine is age 5 years old Same is age 3 years old.

yours Truly
Joe Noah
Allenville Mich P.O.
Mackenac County Mich

Information following from: Not Given.

3-23 SHE-GWAW-GAW, dead.
Wife: Name not given, dead.

3-23-1 Rubin Willis, dead see 39-23.
Wife 1st: Name not given, dead.
Wife 2nd: Esther Willis Greensky Aniwasky, age 67, P.O. Bay Shore, 2nd husband Thomas Aniwasky age 53, see 5-38 and 24-23.
3-23-1-1 Isabella Francis, age 30, P.O. Bay Shore.
Husband: Louis Francis, age 50, P.O. Bay Shore, see 4-23 for children.
3-23-1-2 Levi Willis, age 22, P.O. Chilocco Indian School.

3-23-2 Susan Walker, age 56, P.O. Charlevoix, see 38-26.
Husband: Abraham Walker, dead.
3-23-2-1 Martha Walker, age 36, P.O. Charlevoix, single.
3-23-2-1-1 Edna Walker, age 2.
3-23-2-2 Edwin Walker, age 28, P.O. Charlevoix, single.

3-23-3 Benjamin Willis, age 50, P.O. Charlevoix.
Wife: Angeline Willis (nee Micksawbay), age 48, P.O.

Charlevoix, see 13-25 and 13-26.
3-23-3-1 Annie (Willis) Green, age 24, P.O. Horton Bay.
Husband: James Green, age 35, P.O. Horton Bay.
3-23-3-1-1 Alberta Green, age 6, see 17-25.
3-23-3-1-2 Blanche Green, age 4.
3-23-3-1-3 Lucy Green, age 3.
3-23-3-1-4 Leander Green, born March 1908.
3-23-4 Mary Ann Nah-Quam, age 48, P.O. Charlevoix R.F.D. #3.
Husband: Philip Nah-Quam, age 65, see 16-23.
3-23-5 Lazarus Willis, age 45, P.O. Bay Shore.
Wife: Lucy Willis, nee Scott, said to be a Grand River Indian.
3-23-5-1 Isaac Willis, age 12, P.O. Tomah School, Wis.

Information following from: Not Given.
4-23 O-KINGE-WAW-NO
Wife: Name not given, dead.
4-23-1 Louis Francis, age 58, P.O. Bay Shore.
Wife: Isabelle Francis, nee Willis, age 33, P.O. Bay Shore, see 3-23.
4-23-1-1 Jennie Francis, age 12.
4-23-1-2 Lena Francis, age 10, died July 13/08.
4-23-1-3 Clarence Francis, age 8.
4-23-1-4 Cecelia Francis, age 6.
4-23-1-5 Irene Francis, age 2, died July 8/07.
4-23-1-6 Lee Francis (Twin), born Dec 2, 1907.
4-23-1-7 Leva Francis (Twin), born Dec 2, 1907.
4-23-2 Thresa Taylor, see 29-32.
4-23-3 Lucy Penawse, age 56, P.O. Kewadin, see 34-46.

Information following from: Not Given, Sept 25/08.
5-23 WAIM-BWAY-GO-NAY-BE or JOHN COON, age 81, P.O. Sutton's Bay.
Wife: Mary Coon, age 76, P.O. Sutton's Bay, see 1-23.
5-23-1 Mitchell Coon, age 57, P.O. Sutton's Bay.
Wife 1st: Name not given, dead.
Wife 2nd: Jane Coon, nee Johnson, age 40, off Saginaw Indian.
5-23-1-1 Joe Coon, age 24, P.O. Sutton's Bay, not married.
5-23-2 George Coon, age 40, P.O. Sutton's Bay.
Wife: Mary Coon, nee Pequongay, see 2-39 and 11-38.
5-23-2-1 Samuel Coon, age 18, P.O. Sutton's Bay.
5-23-2-2 Margaret Coon, age 16.
5-23-2-3 William Coon, age 14.
5-23-2-4 Cecelia Coon, age 10.
5-23-2-5 Elizabeth Coon, age 7.
5-23-2-6 Edwin Coon, born Nov 17/07, 2nd Roll.

Information following from: Not Given.

6-23 TAW-BAW-SOSH or JOSEPH TAW-BAW-SOSH, age 81, P.O. Charlevoix.

Wife: Name not given, dead.

6-23-1 William Tabasash, age 47, P.O. Charlevoix, single no children.

6-23-2 Mary Ann Kew-A-Gish-Kon or Mary Ann Tabasosh, age 45, P.O. Charlevoix.

Husband: Name not given, dead.

6-23-2-1 William Key-Was-Cush-Ean or William Mitchell, age 22, P.O.Charlevoix, not married.

6-23-2-2 Thomas Mitchell, age 10, P.O. Charlevoix.

6-23-3 Jane Oliver, age 43, P.O. Charlevoix, no children.

Husband: Joe Oliver Jr., age 38, see 30-42 and 16-34.

6-23-4 Solomon Tabasosh, age 36, P.O. Charlevoix, see 11-38, separated.

Wife: Jane Tabasosh, nee Quonga or Pequonga, age 34, P.O. Bay Shore daughter of Peter Shedonquot, see 35-38 and 11-38,

children none(?).

6-23-4-1 Pete Wahbaose, age 16, P.O. Mt. Pleasant School.

6-23-5 Annie Boulton, age 33, P.O. Charlevoix.

Husband: Richard Boulton, age 42, mother said to be an Ottawa, father a white man, Indians say he is a Canadian Indian, do not enroll without further evidence, Durant.

6-23-5-1 Edward Boulton, age 12, P.O. Mt. Pleasant School.

6-23-5-2 Ida Boulton, age 9, P.O. Mt. Pleasant School, died Jany 16/08.

6-23-5-3 Prudence Boulton, age 8, P.O. Mt. Pleasant School.

6-23-5-4 Richard Boulton, age 4, P.O. Charlevoix.

6-23-5-5 Laura Boulton, age 2, P.O. Charlevoix.

Information following from: Not Given.

7-23 NAY-WAW-DAY-KE-ZHICK or GEORGE NADY, dead, for family see 2-38.

Information following from: Not Given.

8-23 MWAY-KE-WE-NAW or PETER SHAW-WAW-DAY-SE, age 78, P.O. Northport.

Wife: Name not given, dead.

8-23-1 Louis Shaw-Wan-Day-Se, age 51.

Wife: Sarah Wan-Say-Quoun, age 55, see children 1-38.

8-23-2 James Shaw-Wan-Day-Se, age 48, P.O. Northport, no children.

Wife: Name not given, dead.

8-23-3 Martha Nay-Ge-O-Ma, age 44, P.O. Northport.
Husband 1st : Daniel Wa-Say-Quom or Wayashe, dead.
8-23-3-1 Alex Waw-Say-Quom, age 16, P.O. Northport.
8-23-3-2 Rhoda Waw-Say-Quom, age 14, P.O. Northport.
8-23-3-3 Charles Waw-Say-Quom, age 8, P.O. Northport.
Husband 2nd: Name not given, dead.
8-23-4 Louise Nay-O-To-Shing, see 13-38 and 6-38.
8-23-5 Mary Ann Fisher, age 35, P.O. Northport, no children.
Husband: George Fisher, age 40, P.O. Northport, son of 17-38.
8-23-6 Jackson Brown, age 27, P.O. Northport, adopted child, said to be a relative of 67-33.
Wife: Agnes Shaw-Waw-Non-Quot, age 17, P.O. Traverse City, left him and lives at Traverse City, see 29-31. Child by 1st husband: Lizzie Shaw-Waw-Non-Quot, age 6 months, born Mch 19/08, 2nd Roll, enrolled with mother.

Information following from: Not Given, Sept 25/08.
9-23 NAW-O-QUAW-UM.
Wife: Mary Naw-Quo-Um, age 90, P.O. Charlevoix.
9-23-1 Mary (Naw-Quo-Um) Waw-Say-Quo-Um, age 58, P.O. Charlevoix.
Husband: Peter Waw-Say-Quo-Um, P.O. Charlevoix, see 26-23.
9-23-2 Joe Naw-Quo-Um, age 56, see 22-41 and 9-43.
9-23-3 Name not given, dead.
9-23-4 Name not given, dead.

Information following from: Not Given.
10-23 BENJAMIN NAW-KAY-O-SAY, dead.
Wife: Maria Walker, age 65, P.O. Charlevoix.
10-23-1 Peter Walker, age 42, P.O. Charlevoix.
Wife: Angeline Walker, nee Odamin or Otayemin, age 27, see 40-20, an Ottawa Indian of Cross Village Band.
10-23-1-1 Mary Ann Walker, age 3.
10-23-1-2 Lucy Walker, born June 23, 1908, 2nd Roll.
10-23-2 Jackson Walker, age 38, P.O. Charlevoix.
Wife: Thresa Walker, nee Wahsaquon, age 36, see 26-23.
10-23-2-1 Frank Walker, age 10.
10-23-2-2 Veronica Walker, age 8.
10-23-2-3 William Walker, age 3.
10-23-2-4 Irene Walker, born Mch 18, 1908.
10-23-3 Agnes Walker, age 36, P.O. Charlevoix, not married.
10-23-3-1 Ella Walker, born June 1907, 2nd Roll.
10-23-4 Charlotte Walker, age 30, P.O. Charlevoix, single.

Information following from: Not Given.

11-23 WAW-SAY-KE-ZHICK or JAMES WAW-SAY-KE-ZHICK, age 70, P.O. Omena.

Wife 1st : Name not given, dead.

11-23-1 Thomas Anawasky, age 53, see 5-38 and 27-23 (This Eliza was his 1st wife).

Wife: Mary Andrews or Anawasky, age 25, P.O. Charlevoix.

11-23-2 Daughter, name not given.

Husband: Levi Genereaux, age 40, P.O. Petosky, Grand River Indian, Ok enroll see 12-59.

11-23-2-1 Rena Genereaux now Smith, age 18, P.O. Petosky, see 8-55 and 11-55 and 12-59.

Wife 2nd: Louisa Waw-Say-Ke-Zhick, age 37, P.O. Charlevoix, separated, see 9-40.

Information following from: Not Given, Nov 24/08, Charlevoix.

12-23 NE-GAW-NE-KE-ZHICK, dead.

Wife: Name not given, dead.

12-23-1 Joe Ne-Gone-Ge-Zhick, age 44, died Sept 1907, see 5-41 and 14-41.

12-23-2 Eliza Sands, see 7-41.

Information following from: Not Given, Nov 24/08, Charlevoix.

13-23 TAW-BAW-KE-YAW, dead.

Wife: Name not given, dead.

13-23-1 John Chingwa, dead, no heirs.

13-23-2 Enos Taw-Baw-Ke-Yaw, dead.

Wife: Margaret Tap-Keah, see 23-28 for children.

13-23-3 Pean, dead.

Wife: Eliza Tap-Keah Na-Quo-Um, see 9-40 and 22-41.

13-23-4 Therese, dead, no heirs.

13-23-5 Eliza, dead, no heirs.

13-23-6 Sophia, dead, no heirs.

13-23-7 Margaret, dead, no heirs.

Information following from: Not Given.

14-23 LEVI SHAW-WAW-DAY-SE.

Wife: Jane Clemens, age 65, P.O. Charlevoix, her 2nd husband is James Clemens, a Saginaw Indian not entitled to enrollment.

14-23-1 Name nor sex not given, dead.

Spouse: Name not given.

14-23-1-1 Isabella Francis, age 30, see 4-23.

Husband: Louis Francis, see 4-23.

14-23-1-1-1 Jennie Francis, age 12, see 4-23.

14-23-1-1-2 Lena Francis, dead, see 4-23.

14-23-1-1-3 Clarence Francis, age 8, see 4-23.
14-23-1-1-4 Cecelia Francis, age 7, see 4-23.
14-23-1-1-5 Irene Francis, see 4-23.
14-23-1-1-6 Lena Francis, age 1½ , born Dec 2/07.
14-23-1-1-7 Lee Frances, male, age 1½, born Dec 2/07.

Information following from: Not Given, Nov 24/08, Charlevoix.
15-23 O-GE-SHE-WAY, dead, children all dead, no heirs.

Information following from: Not Given, Sept 25/08.
16-23 PHILIP NAW-O-QUOUNG, spelled now NAHQUAM, age 71, P.O. Charlevoix RFD #2.
Wife 1st : Name not given.
16-23-7 David Naquoum, age 35, P.O. Bay Shore, see 39-41.
Wife 2nd: Mary Ann Naquam, nee Willis, age 52, see 3-23.
16-23-1 Sarah Naquam, age 28, P.O. Charlevoix, not married.
16-23-2 Agnes Naquam, age 23, P.O. Charlevoix Mt. Pleasant School, not married.
16-23-3 William Nahquam, age 19, P.O. Mt. Pleasant School.
16-23-4 Samuel Nahquam, age 14, P.O. Charlevoix.
16-23-5 Thomas Nahquam, age 9, P.O. Charlevoix.
16-23-6 Philip Nahquam Jr., age 7, P.O. Charlevoix.

Information following from: Not Given.
17-23 THOMPSON NAW-O-QUOUM, dead.
Wife: Name not given, dead.
17-23-1 Name or sex not given, dead, no heirs.
17-23-2 James Naw-Quoum, age 16, see 26-23.

Information following from: Not Given.
18-23 NAW-BE-SKAW-WAW-QUOUM, dead.
Wife: Name not given, dead.
18-23-1 William, dead, see 34-23.
Wife: Name not given.
18-23-1-1 Paul Smith, age 31, see 25-26 and 34-23.
18-23-1-2 John Smith, age 20, see 2-30 and 34-23.
18-23-2 Name or sex not given, dead, no heirs.

Information following from: Not Given.
19-23 ISAAC GREENSKY, dead.
Wife: Name not given, dead.
19-23-1 Martha Groundy, age 58, died Apr 20/08, no children, enrolled on Grand river as 19-59.
Husband: Louis Groundy, white, P.O. Petosky

Information following from: Not Given.
20-23 O-GE-MAW-KE-GE-DO, dead.
Wife: Name not given, dead.
20-23-1 Jasper Shay-Go-Naby, dead, see 2-40, died Mch 1908.
Wife: Nancy Shay-Go-Naby, age 42, P.O. Omena, see 2-40.
20-23-1-1 Mitchell Shay-Go-Naby, age 23, P.O. Rex Mich.

Information following from: Not Given.
21-23 ME-SKO-PE-NAY-SE or REDBIRD.
Wife: Name not given, dead.
21-23-1 Steve Redbird, on roll as 3-45.
Wife: Name not given.
21-23-1-1 Simon Redbird.
21-23-2 Name or sex not given, dead.
21-23-3 ~~Joseph Redbird~~ Kaw-Zhe-Quaw-Ne-Gay, see 1-45.
21-23-4 Joseph Aish-Quay-Ke-Zhick, age 76, P.O. Northport, 13-38 and 15-38.

Information following from: Not Given.
22-23 O-GE-SHE-AW-BAW-NO-QUAY, dead.
22-23-1 Name or sex not given, dead.
Spouse: Name not given.
22-23-1-1 Thomas Shawandase or Tom Isaac, age 26, P.O. Charlevoix, Ill. 2.36.23, single.
22-23-2 Name of Sex not given, dead, no heirs.

Information following from: Not Given.
23-23 AISH-KE-BAW-GOSH, dead.
Wife: Name not given,dead.
23-23-1 ~~Mar Lucy~~ Rose Trombly, age 30, P.O. ~~Charvoix or Bay Shore~~
Pellston.
Husband: Benjamin Thrombly, see 36-57.
23-23-1-1 Therese Thrombly or Esther Gilbert, age 7, adopted child of Indian parents both dead.
23-23-1-2 Grace Thrombly, age 6, see 19-28

Information following from: Not Given.
24-23 JACOB GREENSKY, dead.
Wife: Esther Greensky Aniwasky, age 67, P.O. Bay Shore, see 3-23, now wife of Thomas Aniwasky, age 53, see 5-38, 3-23 and 27-23.
24-23-1 Name or sex not given, dead, no heirs.
24-23-2 George Greensky, age 23, see 26-46.
24-23-3 John Willis, age 20, P.O. Bay Shore, not married.

24-23-4 Enos Willis, age 18, P.O. Bay Shore, not married.

Information following from: Not Given.
25-23 SAMUEL WAY-WIN-GE-GWAN.
Wife: Name not given, dead.
25-23-1 Mary Robinson, age 43, P.O. Charvoix, see 12-32.
Husband: John E. Robinson, white, P.O. Charlevoix.
25-23-1-1 William D. Robinson, age 19, P.O. Charlevoix.
25-23-1-2 Ed Robinson, age 17, P.O. Charlevoix.
25-23-2 Susan Agosa, age 40, see 12-40 and 12-32.
25-23-3 David Owner, age 25, P.O. Traverse City, single.

Information following from: Not Given.
26-23 WAW-SAY-QUO-UM or PETER WASAYQUOM #2, age 70, P.O. Charlevoix.
Wife: Mary Wasaquom, age 60, P.O. Charlevoix.
26-23-1 Thomas Wahsaqum, see 14-44.
26-23-2 Threse Walker, see 10-23.
26-23-3 Isaiah Wahsaquom, age 34, P.O. Charlevoix.
Wife: Thresa Wahsaquom, nee Antoine, age 32, see 22-38 and 5-60.
26-23-3-1 Emma Wahsaquom, age 3.
26-23-3-2 Sarah Wahsaquom, age 2.
26-23-3-3 Jerome Wahsaquom, born Sept 1908, not enrolled.
26-23-4 Andrew Wahsaquom, age 22, P.O. Charlevoix, no children.
Wife: Margaret Wahsaquom, nee Peters, age 16, P.O. Carlisle School, separated.
26-23-5 James Nahquom, age 16, adopted, son of Thomas Naquom, see 17-23.

Information following from: Not Given, Nov 24/08, Charlevoix.
27-23 WAY-WAW-TE-SO, dead.
27-23-1 Thomas Aniwasky, age 53, see 5-38, 24-23 and 3-23.

Information following from: Not Given, Nov 24/08, Charlevoix.
28-23 ME-NAW-QUOT, dead.
Wife: Name not given, dead.
28-23-1 Name nor sex given, dead, no heirs.

Information following from: Not Given.
29-23 GEORGE SHIPPARD, dead.
Wife: Name not given, dead.
29-23-1 Name or sex not given, dead.

Information following from: Not Given.

30-23 PE-NAY-SE-WAW-NAW-QUOT, dead.
Wife: Name not given, dead.
30-23-1 Simon Shaw-Koo, age 52, P.O. Northport.
Wife: Lucy Jacobs Mendowash, now wife Wing Mendowash, see 7-45.
30-23-1-1 Thomas Shaw-Koo, age 23, P.O. Bellair Mich.
30-23-1-2 Sophia King.
Husband: Louis King, see 8-62.
30-23-1-3 George Shaw-Koo, age 16, P.O. Northport.
30-23-1-4 Peter Shaw-Koo, age 9, P.O. Northport.
30-23-2 Susan Shaw-Koo NawQuom, age 57, see 22-41.

Information following from: Not Given, Nov 24/08, Charlevoix.
31-23 MAW-WEE, dead, no heirs.

Information following from: Not Given.
32-23 AS-SE-BUN, dead, no others with him in 1870.

Information following from: Not Given.
33-23 SUSAN WALKER #1 or SUSAN GREENSKY, age 70, P.O. Charlevoix, no children.

Information following from: Not Given.
34-23 WAW-BE-SKAW-NAW-QUOM, dead.
Wife: Name not given, dead.
34-23-1 Paul Smith, age 31, see 25-26 and 18-23.
34-23-2 John Smith, age 20, see 2-30 and 18-23.

Information following from: Not Given.
35-23 O-PAY-SHAW, dead.
Wife: Name not given, dead.
35-23-1 James Waw-Say-Ge-Zhick, age 70, on roll as 11-23.

Information following from: Not Given.
36-23 MOSES SHAW-WAW-DAY-SE, better known as MOSES ISAAC, age 56, P.O. ~~Pashabatown~~ Sutton's Bay Mich.
Wife: Name not given, dead.
36-23-1 Thomas Shawandase or Thomas Isaac, age 26, P.O. ~~Washington State~~ was at Charlevoix in Summer of 1908, single.

Information following from: Not Given.
37-23 DANIEL WALKER, dead, no heirs.

Information following from: Not Given.

38-23 KAW-KEE, dead.
Wife: Name not given, dead.
38-23-1 Mary Ann Key-Way-Cush-Cum Tabasosh, see 6-23.

Information following from: Not Given.
39-23 SIG-A-NOCK or RUBIN WILLIS, dead see 3-23.
Wife: Catharine Blackbird, dead, see 21-26.

Page 24
Bay Shore Band
Chief SHAW-WAW-NE-GWAW-NAY-BE

Information following from: Not Given.
1-24 SHAW-WAW-NE-GWAW-NAY-BE, dead.
Wife: Esther Shaw-Waw-Ne-Gwaw-Nay-Be, said to be living near Georgian Bay, Mantoulin Island.
1-24-1 Name not given, dead.
Wife: Name not given, dead.
1-24-1-1 Simon Shaw-Waw-Ne-Gwaw-Nay-Be, age 35, P.O. Mantoulin Island, Massey, Ontario.
Wife: Mary Shaw-Waw-Ne-Gwaw-Nay-Be.
1-24-1-1-1 David Shaw-Waw-Ne-Gwaw-Nay-Be.
1-24-1-1-2 John Shaw-Waw-Ne-Gwaw-Nay-Be.
1-24-1-1-3 Angel Shaw-Waw-Ne-Gwaw-Nay-Be.
1-24-1-1-4 Francis Shaw-Waw-Ne-Gwaw-Nay-Be.
1-24-1-2 Eliza Evans, age 30, P.O. Mantoulin Island, Massey, Ontario.
Husband: Name not given, dead.
1-24-1-2-1 Louisa Evans, age 6.
1-24-1-2-2 Angeline Evans, age 8.
1-24-1-3 Sam Shagonabe, age 26, P.O. Harbor Springs.
1-24-1-4 Peter Shagonabe, age 17, P.O. Mantoulin Island.

Information following from: Mitchell Odagamiki, Ke-Che-Ga-Me-Quay & headmen Sagoning: Jany 27/09, Dec 16/08 near Bay Shore.
2-24 NE-SAW-WAW-QUOT, dead.
Wife: Name not given, dead.
2-24-1 Josett Key-Way-Cush-Cum or Susan Miscogeon, age 80, P.O. Bay Shore, see 5-24.
2-24-2 Ke-Che-Ga- Me-Quay, age 68, P.O. Pinconning Mich.
Spouse: Name not given.
2-24-2-1 Josephine James,age 38, P.O. Sagoning Mich.
Wife: Name not given, a Saginaw Indian.
2-24-2-1-1 Tena James, age 9.
2-24-2-1-2 Sarah James, age 3.

2-24-2-2 Agnes Williams, age 16, Sagoning.
2-24-3 Name not given, see 22-24.

Information following from: Mitchell Odagamiki, Dec 16/08, Bay Shore.
3-24 ELIAS TAY-BAW-SE-GAY, dead, has children in Georgian Bay Manatolin Island Canada. Cannot Trace Durant.
Wife: Name not given, dead.

Information following from: Mitchell Odagamiki, Dec 16/08, Bay Shore.
4-24 WAW-BE-CHING-GWAY, dead. It is not known whether children are living or dead. None of the Indians know. They are not in this section of country Durant.
Wife: Name not given, dead.

Information following from: Not Given.
5-24 LOUIS AW-KE-BE-MO-SAY, dead.
Wife: Susan Miscogeon or Josett Key-Way-Cush-Cum, age 80, P.O. Bay Shore, see 2-24.
5-24-1 Moses Key-Way-Cush-Cum, dead.
Wife: Name not given.
5-24-1-1 Thomas Key-Way-Cush-Cum, age 11, P.O. Charlevoix.
5-24-2 John Key-Way-Cush-Cum, age 43, died Apr 24, 1907. His name also spelled Kewagoskum this spelling givin by the Indians.
5-24-3 Frank Kewagoskum, age 41, P.O. Bay Shore, not married.
5-24-4 James Kewagoskum, age 36, P.O. Bay Shore.
Wife: Alice Kewagoskum, nee Aniwasky, age 31, P.O. Bay Shore, see 5-38.
5-24-4-1 John Kewagoskum, age 14, P.O. Bay Shore.
5-24-5 Name not given, dead.
Husband: Name not given.
5-24-5-1 Margaret Kewagoskum, age 23, P.O. Bay Shore.
5-24-5-2 Minnie Kewagoskum, age 19, P.O. Bay Shore.
5-24-6 Joe Kewagoskum, age 55, P.O. Bay Shore. This is oldest child should have been #1.
Wife: Rosie Kewagoskum, nee see 7-24, age 50.
5-24-6-1 Mitchell Kewagoskum, age 35, P.O. Bay Shore, no wife or child.
5-24-6-2 Robert Kewagoskum, age 20, P.O. Bay Shore.
5-24-6-3 Sophia Kewagoskum, age 17, P.O. Bay Shore.

Information following from: Not Given, Oct ?/08, Harbor Springs, Tuttle.

6-24 MICHL WAY-KE-ZHE-GO-WE or MITCHELL OTAWGAWMEKE or ODAGAMIKI as it is spelled now, age 71, P.O. Bay Shore.

Wife: Name not given, dead.

6-24-1 Angeline Otawgawmeke, age 34, P.O. Bay Shore Mich, not married and no children.

6-24-2 Annie Otawgawmeke, age 32, P.O. Bay Shore Mich, single and no children.

6-24-3 Agnes Gibson, age 30, P.O. Bay Shore, no children, see 8-24.

Husband: Joe Gibson, see 12-26.

Information following from: Not Given.

7-24 CHARLES MAW-TWANCE, dead.

Wife: Name not given, dead.

7-24-1 Mary Ann, dead.

Husband: Name not given.

7-24-1-1 Eliza Shaw-Waw-Non-Quot, age 30, P.O. ~~Brutus~~ Aloha Mich.

Husband: Albert Shaw-Waw-Non-Quot, age 36, P.O. Aloha Mich, see 29-31.

7-24-1-1-1 Mary Ann Shaw-Waw-Non-Quot, age 7.

7-24-1-2 Moses Shaw-Waw-Non-Quot, age 20, P.O. Brutus Mich.

7-24-2 Catharine, dead, no heirs.

7-24-3 ~~Mary Sayningwawbay~~ Rosie Kewaycushcum, age ~~80~~ 50, ~~see 5~~ for husband & children see 5-24.

Information following from: Not Given.

8-24 LOUIS O-TAW-GAW-ME-KE, dead.

Wife: Name not given, dead.

8-24-1 Mitchell O-Taw-Gaw-Me-Ke or Odagamiki, Blind, age 80, P.O. 3 miles S.E. Bay Shore, on roll as 6-24.

Wife: Name not given, dead.

8-24-1-1 Angeline O-Taw-Gaw-Me-Ke, age 36, P.O. Bay Shore.

8-24-1-2 Anna O-Taw-Gaw-Me-Ke, age 33, P.O. Bay Shore.

8-24-1-3 Agnes Gibson, see 12-26.

8-24-2 Simon O-Taw-Gaw-Me-Ke, dead.

Wife: Name not given.

8-24-2-1 Eliza Shaw-Waw-Non-Quot, age 30, P.O. Aloha, see 29-51 and 7-24.

8-24-3 ~~Simon dead~~

8-24-3-1 ~~Eliza~~

8-24-4 Joseph King or Joseph Odagamiki, age 61, see 52-29.

Information following from: Not Given.
9-24 MAW-CAW-DAY-PE-NAY-SE, dead.
Wife: Mary Pabo, age 60, P.O. Horton's Bay.
9-24-1 Joe Thomas, age 44, P.O. Barker Creek.
Wife: Lucy Thomas, nee Keshawtaw, age 35, see 35-46.
9-24-1-1 Rennie Thomas, age 4.
9-24-2 Margaret Joe, age 35, P.O. Horton's Bay.
Husband: William Joe, age 46, P.O. Horton's Bay, see 3-25.
9-24-2-1 Hazel Joe, age 9.
9-24-2-2 Josie Joe, age 2.
9-24-3 Moses Peters, age 18, P.O. Horton's Bay, sister's child.
9-24-4 John W. Robinson, age 25, P.O. Northport, sister's child?

Information following from: Mitchell Odagamiki, Bay Shore.
10-24 AW-WAW-NISH-CUM, dead.
Wife 1st: Name not given, dead.
Wife 2nd: Ke-Che-Ga-Ne-Quay, see 2-24, at Pinconning where they moved years ago.
Information following from: Mitchell Odagamiki, Dec 16/08.
11-24 O-ME-SQUAW-BAW-NO-QUAY, dead, no heirs.

Information following from: Mitchell Odagamiki, Dec 16/08, Bay Shore.
12-24 SHAW-WAW-NAW-NAW-QUAW-DO-QUAY, dead, no heirs.

Information following from: Mitchell Odagamiki, Dec 16/08.
13-24 GABRIEL & MICHAEL MAW-DWANICE, both dead, no heirs.

Information following from: Mitchell Odagamiki, Dec 16/08.
14-24 MOOK-KO-ME-TAY-QUAY, dead, no heirs.

Information following from: Not Given, Dec 16/08.
15-24 AW-WAW-ZHE-ME-GAY-QUAY, dead.
15-24-1 Name not given, dead.
15-24-2 Esther Greensky Aniwasky, see 3-23 & 24-23.
15-24-3 Name not given, dead.
Wife: Susan Black, see 4-30

Information following from: Not Given, Dec 16/08.
16-24 WAW-SAY-AW-NO-QUAY, dead, no heirs.

Information following from: Not Given.
17-24 MARY SHAW-BWAW-SWIG, dead.
17-24-1 Name nor sex given, dead.
17-24-1-1 Joe Norton #2, age 8, see 8-25.

Information following from: Mitchell Odagamiki, Dec 16/08, Bay Shore.

18-24 PAY-WAW-NAW-QUOT, cannot trace Durant. Son of Chief Shaw-Waw-Ne-Gwaw-Nay-Be said to be living at Mantulin Island, Canada, left Bay Shore years (ago).
Wife: Baldine Warren, whom he left years ago, see 17-20.

Information following from: Not Given, Dec 16/08.

19-24 PAY-MAW-SAY-WAY-QUAY, dead, no heirs.

Information following from: Not Given, Dec 16/08.

20-24 JULIA WAW-KAY-ZOO, dead, no heirs.

Information following from: Mitchell Odagamiki, Dec 16/08.

21-24 AW-WAW-NE-GE-ZHE-GO-QUAY, dead, no heirs.

Information following from: Not Given, Dec 16/08, Bay Shore, Jany 27/09 Sagoning.

22-24 O-TSH-QUAY-KE-ZHICK-GO-QUAY, lives near Pinconning is a daughter of 2-24, now the wife of 14-63, no heirs.

Information following from: Mitchell Odagamiki, Dec 16/08.

23-24 OBE-YAW, dead, no heirs.

Page 25
Charlevoix Band
Chief LOUIS MICK-SAW-BAY

Information following from: Not Given.

1-25 LOUIS MICK-SAW-BAY, dead, no heirs.

Information following from: Not Given, Oct 20/08.

2-25 LOUIS WAYMEGWANCE, dead.
Wife: Name not given, dead.
2-25-1 Louis Waymegwance Jr., age 58, P.O. Goodheart, see 27-25.
Wife: Name not given, dead.
2-25-1-1 Mitchell Waymegwance, age 27, P.O. Goodheart, single.
2-25-1-2 Agnes Waymegwance, age 18, P.O. Goodheart.
2-25-1-3 Caroline Waymegwance, age 15, P.O. Goodheart.
2-25-1-4 Theresa Waymegwance, age 13.
2-25-2 Name nor sex given, dead, no heirs.

Information following from: Not Given.

3-25 JOSEPH O-SHAW-WAW-NO, dead.

Wife: Jane She-Qwa-Jaw, age 62, now wife of James She-Gway-Aw, see 26-20.

3-25-1 William Tagwansong or Dagwason or William Joe, enroll as William Joe, age 46, P.O. Charlevoix.

Wife: Margaret Joe, age 38.

3-25-1-1 Hazel Joe, age 9.

3-25-1-2 Josie Joe, age 2.

3-25-2 Name nor sex given, dead, no heirs.

3-25-3 Name nor sex given, dead, no heirs.

Information following from: Not Given.

4-25 JOSEPH MICK-SAW-BAY, dead, no heirs.

Information following from: Not Given.

5-25 STEPHEN WAW-WE-KE-ZHICK, dead.

Wife: Name not given, dead.

5-25-1 Name nor sex given, dead, no heirs.

5-25-2 Name nor sex given, dead, no heirs.

5-25-3 Sophia Williams, age 48, P.O. Harbor Springs, see 39-32.

Information following from: Not Given, Nov 24/08, Charlevoix.

6-25 WAW-SAY-GE-ZHE-GO-QUAY, dead.

6-25-1 Margaret Abinaw, age 50, see 6-32.

Information following from: Not Given.

7-25 ALBERT PAY-SHAW-BAY, dead.

Wife: Therese Peshabay, age 72, died Jun 11/08, 1st husband Dailey dead, see 51-43.

7-25-1 Mary Pay-Shaw-Bay, age 30, P.O. In correction house at Detroit, single.

7-25-2 Eliza (Dailey) Key-Way-Ken-Do, age 40, P.O. Cross Village, see 11-26 & 51-43, child of wife.

Information following from: Not Given.

8-25 THERESE MIK-SAW-BAY, age 71, P.O. Harbor Springs, not married, no children.

Information following from: Joseph Wakazoo, Ebro Minn., by mail, Dec/08.

9-25 (Rev) JOSEPH WAW-KAY-ZOO #1, age 74, P.O. Ebro Minn.

Wife: Nessettie Wakazoo Indian, age 50, P.O. Ebro Minn, belongs to Minnesota Tribe.

9-25-1 Sophia Wakazoo, age 14, died in 1900.

9-25-2 Bruno Wakazoo, age 12, died 1901.

9-25-3 Frank Wakazoo, age 30, P.O. Ebro Minn.

Wife: ~~Mrs. Edithiot Wakazoo, age 23 P.O. Ebro Minn~~ belongs

to Minnesota band.
9-25-3-1 Amos Wakazoo, age 2½, P.O. Ebro Minn.
9-25-3-2 Pete Wakazoo, age 1, P.O. Ebro Minn, 2nd Roll
9-25-4 Edman Wakazoo, age 21, P.O. Ebro Minn.
9-25-5 Lizzie Wakazoo, age 18, died 1900.
9-25-6 John Wakazoo, age 7, died 1890.
9-25-7 Sarah Wakazoo, age 8, died 1905.

Information following from: Not Given.
10-25 PO-GO-NAY-KE-ZHICK, dead, no heirs.

Information following from: Not Given.
11-25 WILLIAM MICK-SAY-BAY, age 62, P.O. Sutton's Bay.
Wife: Annie Mick-Saw-Bay, age 56, on 1870 roll with husband.
11-25-1 Frank Mick-Saw-Bay, age 35, P.O. Sutton's Bay, no children.
Wife: Rosie (or Lucy) nee Keshatah, age 35, separated, see 52-27, now lives with Joe Thomas.
11-25-2 Abbie or Eva Mick-Saw-Bay, age 17, P.O. Sutton's Bay.
11-25-3 Enos Mick-Saw-Bay, age 6, P.O. Sutton's Bay.
Note for 11-25-2 & 11-25-3: Adopted children of Indian parents & undoubtedly entitled to Enrollment, HB Durant Spl. Agt, Sept 24/08 Pashabatown, Mich.

Information following from: Not Given, Oct 20/08, Middle Village Goodheart.
12-25 MARY A. GREENSKY, known as MARY A. TUSH-QUAY-AW-BAW-NO, age 70, P.O. Goodheart, no heirs.

Information following from: Not Given.
13-25 ALEXANDER MICK-SAW-BAY, dead.
Wife: Angeline Willis, age 48, P.O. Charlevoix, now wife of Benjamin Willis, see 3-23.
13-25-1 Edward Mick-Saw-Bay, now spelled McSaby, age 29, P.O. Charlevoix, not married.
13-25-2 Daniel Mick-Saw-Bay, spell McSaby, age 17, P.O. Charlevoix.
13-25-3 Rosie McSaby, age 4, P.O. Charlevoix.

Information following from: Not Given, Nov 28/08.
14-24 MARY MICK-SAW-BAY, dead.
Husband: Name not given, dead.
14-24-1 John Mick-Saw-Bay, age 38, P.O. ~~Charlevoix~~ Bay Shore Mich, no children.
14-25-2 Jonas Mick-Saw-Bay, age 32, P.O. Bay Shore.

Wife: Hestie (Gibson) Mick-Saw-Bay, age 20., P.O. Bay Shore, see 45-42.

Information following from: Not Given.
15-25 SAMUEL AW-SAY-GON, dead.
Wife: Lucy Naw-Quay-Ge-Zhick, see 2-28.

Information following from: Not Given.
16-25 LOUIS WAW-SAY-QUOUM, dead, no heirs.

Information following from: Not Given.
17-25 O-KE-CHE-GAW-ME or SIMON GREEN, age 69, P.O. Horton Bay.
Wife 1st: Name not given, dead.
Wife 2nd: Agnes Green, age 66, P.O. Horton Bay, see 8-38.
17-25-1 Charles Green, twin , age 35, P.O. Horton's Bay.
Wife: Ellen Green, nee Wahbegokake, age 23, see 9-28.
17-25-1-1 Mary Jane Green, age 5 months, born Apr 1908.
17-25-2 James Green, twin, age 35, P.O. Horton's Bay.
Wife: Anna (Willis) Green, age 22, see 35-26.
17-25-2-1 Alberta Grenn, age 5.
17-25-2-2 Blanche Green, age 4.
17-25-2-3 Lucy Green, age 2.
17-25-2-4 Leander Green, born March 1908.
17-25-3 Jonah Redbird, age 35, P.O. Charlevoix, son of Agnes Green by 1st husband.
Wife: Martha Redbird, nee Noah, age 23, see 2-23.
17-25-3-1 Emory Redbird, age 8.
17-25-3-2 Hazel Redbird, age 3.
17-25-3-3 Moses Redbird, age 2 months, born Aug 3, 1908.

Information following from: Not Given.
18-25 SHE-BOSH-CAW-MO-QUAY, dead, no heirs.

Information following from: Not Given.
19-25 MADDELAINE ROBINSON, age 65, P.O. Pt. St. Ignace, all alone no children.
19-25-1 Joe Belongea, not her own son, do not enroll, investigate his right to Enrollment at Pt. St. Ignace.

Information following from: Margaret Robinson & James Lajoy, St. Ignace.
20-25 MARGARET ROBINSON, age 71, P.O. Pt. St. Ignace.
20-25-1 Joe Lajoy, age 38, P.O. St. Ignace.
Wife: Name not given, white.
20-25-1-1 Joe Lajoy Jr., age 16, P.O. St. Ignace.
20-25-1-2 Henry Lajoy, age 14, P.O. St. Ignace.

20-25-1-3 Alvin Lajoy, age 10.
20-25-2 James Lajoy, age 35, P.O. St. Ignace.
Wife: Name not given, white.
20-25-2-1 James Lajoy Jr., age 11.
20-25-2-2 Edward Lajoy, age 9.
20-25-2-3 Frank Lajoy, age 7.
20-25-2-4 Genevieve Lajoy, age 4.
20-25-2-5 Eliza Lajoy, age 2.
20-25-2-6 ~~Josephine Lajoy~~
20-25-3 Josephine Marts, age 28, P.O. St. Ignace
Husband: Name not given, white.
20-25-3-1 Isaac Marts, age 6.
20-25-3-2 Josephine Marts, age 4.

Information following from: Louis Robinson July 5/09 at St. Ignace & Louisa Lesley in Nov/08 at Cross Village.

21-25 LOUIS ROBINSON, age 87, P.O. St. Ignace 9 miles.
Wife: Name not given, dead.
21-25-1 Louis Robinson, age 54, P.O. St. Ignace, single.
21-25-2 Ony, son, dead, age 50, P.O. St. Ignace.
Wife: Jane St. Onge Meswayoninne, see 62-16, now husband of Charles Meswayoninne.
21-25-2-1 Anna Meswayoninne, age 19, see 62-16.
21-25-3 Louisa Lesley, age 56, see 4-13.
21-25-4 Joe Robinson, age 43, P.O. St. Ignace, single.
21-25-5 Isadore Robinson, age 41, P.O. St. Ignace, single.
21-25-6 Jane McFarland, age 44, P.O. Carp River St. Ignace.
Husband: Name not given, white.
21-25-6-1 Lillie McFarland, age 27.
21-25-6-2 Anna McFarland, age 24
21-25-6-3 Agnes McFarland, age 22
21-25-6-4 Amelia McFarland, age 20
21-25-6-5 Vina McFarland, age 18
21-25-6-6 Mae McFarland, age 15
21-25-6-7 Louisa McFarland, age 13
21-25-6-8 Ernest McFarland, age 11
21-25-6-9 Edward McFarland, age 7
21-25-6-10 Earl McFarland, age 5
21-25-6-11 Roy McFarland, age 2
21-25-7 Mary Robinson, age 38, P.O. St. Ignace, single.

St. Ignace Mich
June 7, 1909

Mr Horace B Durant
Petoskey Mich

Dear Sir
Your letter was recived the fifth the Names of my Children are Lillie age 27 years Anna 24 Agnes 22 Amelia 20 Vina 18 Mae 15 Louisa 13 Ernest 11 Edward 7 Earl 5 Roy 2

Yours sincerely
Mrs Jane MeFarland
St. Ignace Mich

Information following from: Not Given.
22-24 SOPHIA VALIER, dead.
22-24-1 ~~Maria~~ Jane Chessseman, age 49, P.O. St. Ignace, see 24-13.
Husband: Name not given, white.
Note: The Indians of this band do not remember any person by this name Durant Spl Agt Nov 24/08 Charlevoix; Later: The Indians of Mackinaw band say she has a daughter Maria Cheeseman, ___ & have fully identified Sophia Valier, dec'd Durant St. Ignace Jany 5/09.

Information following from: Not Given.
23-24 PETER RAW-BE-CAW, Indians say it should be WAW-BE-SCAW, dead, no heirs.

Information following from: Not Given.
24-25 FLEVE SHAW-BAW-NO, dead, no heirs.

Information following from: Not Given.
25-25 ISAAC MICK-SAW-BAY, dead, single, unmarried, no heirs.

Information following from: Not Given.
26-25 PETER MWAW-KO-WE-NOW, dead, no heirs.

Information following from: Not Given.
27-25 LOUIS WAY-ME-GWANCE Jr., see 2-25.

Pages 26 & 27
Petoskey Band
Chief AW-ME-GWAW-BAY

Information following from: Not Given.
1-25 AW-ME-GWAW-BAY, dead.
Wife: Name not given.
1-25-1 Angeline Blackbird, age 69, P.O. Petosky, see 21-26.
Husband: John B. Blackbird.

Information following from: Not Given.

2-26 CHARLES WAW-BE-WE-ME-KE or CHARLES BLACKBIRD.
Wife: Name not given, dead.
2-26-1 James Blackbird or James Waw-Be-We-Me-Ke, age 52, P.O. Northport, no children.
Wife: Mary (Nayotoshing) Blackbird, age 62, Apr 21/08.
2-26-2 Jeremiah Waw-Be-We-Me-Ke or Blackbird, dead, same as 24-26.
Wife: Catharine Blackbird, age 60, P.O. Petoskey.
2-26-3 Mary Waw-Be-We-Me-Ke or Blackbird, dead, no heirs.
2-26-4 Agnes Naongaby, see 41-29.
2-26-5 ~~Madeline~~ Nettie Waw-Be-We-Me-Ke or Blackbird, dead, not identified.
Husband: Louis Kezhick, P.O. Hessel Mich St. Ignace.
2-26-5-1 Maggie Kezhick, age 22, P.O. Petoskey, single.
2-26-6 Madaline Waw-Be-We-Me-Ke or Blackbird, age 49, P.O. Petoskey, separated from husband.
Husband: Name not given, white.
2-26-6-1 George McClellan, age 16, P.O. Petoskey, adopted child, his mother is Rosie Key-Way-Ke-Zhick, see 13-58 & 4-26.

Information following from: Not Given.
3-26 FRANCIS PETAWSEGAY, age 90, P.O. Petoskey.
Wife: Name not given, dead.
3-26-1 Thomas Petoskey, age 50, P.O. Petoskey.
Wife: Emma Jerico, white.
3-26-2 William Petoskey, age 51, P.O. Petoskey.
Wife: Jane O-Ge-Maw-Pe-Nay-Se Petoskey, age 45, see 19-20, no children.
3-26-3 Paul Petoskey, age 42, P.O. ~~Bay Shore~~ Petoskey.
Wife: Annie Petoskey, nee Shomin, age 43, P.O. Petoskey.
3-26-3-1 ~~Emma~~ James Smith, age 11, P.O. Tomah School.
3-26-3-2 Emma Smith, age 6, P.O. Petoskey.
3-26-3-3 Delia Smith, age 8 months, died Apr 1907.
3-26-4 Mary Ann Petoskey, age 38, P.O. Montana, has not been heard from for 4 or 5 years by family.
3-26-5 Jennie Petoskey, age 35, P.O. West Virginia, has not been heard from by family for 6 or 7 years.

Information following from: Peter Walker & John Ke-Way-Ke-Zhick, Dec 14/08.
4-26 JOHN B. O-TAW-NAW-A-ZHE, dead.
Wife: Name not given, dead.
4-26-1 John Ke-Way-Ke-Zhick, age 51, P.O. Petoskey.
Wife: Mary Ke-Way-Ke-Zhick, age 32, seee 16-26,

nee Shabwansong.
4-26-1-1 John R. Ke-Way-Ke-Zhick, age 9.
4-26-1-2 Charles R. Ke-Way-Ke-Zhick, age 6.
4-26-1-3 Grace R. Ke-Way-Ke-Zhick, age 4.
4-26-1-4 Ruby Lizzie Ke-Way-Ke-Zhick, age 2.
4-26-1-5 Jane Eunice Ke-Way-Ke-Zhick, born Aug 25, 1908, Too late.

4-26-2 Enos Ke-Way-Ke-Zhick, age 45, P.O. Petoskey.
Wife: Rosie Ke-Way-Ke-Zhick, age 40, see 13-58 also 2-26 for child by 1st husband.
4-26-2-1 Mary Ke-Way-Ke-Zhick, age 12.
4-26-2-2 Ida Ke-Way-Ke-Zhick, age 10.
4-26-2-3 Thomas Ke-Way-Ke-Zhick, age 8.
4-26-2-4 William Ke-Way-Ke-Zhick, age 6.
4-26-2-5 Dennison Ke-Way-Ke-Zhick, age 4.
4-26-2-6 Chester Ke-Way-Ke-Zhick, age 3.
4-26-2-7 Lester Ke-Way-Ke-Zhick, age 2.

4-26-3 Jane Bradley, age 43, P.O. Rosebush 7 miles North of Mt. Pleasant.
Husband: Joe Bradley, belongs to Swan Creek Band, off Saginaw Indian, has two more children who will be carried as Saginaw Indians.
4-26-3-1 Elizabeth Bradley, age 5.
4-26-3-2 Jonas Bradley, age 4.

Information following from: Not Given.

5-26 ANDREW KEY-WAY-KEN-DO, dead.
Wife: Angeline Key-Way-Ken-Do, age 75, P.O. South Hampton, Ontario, has children but all moved to Canada about 30 years ago. So says Abram Key-Way-Ken-Do 11-26 a brother of Andrew Key-Way-Ken-Do HB Durant Spl Agt Petoskey Mich Nov 19, 1908.

Information following from: Not Given.

6-26 MICHAEL KEY-WAY-KEN-DO, dead, no heirs, Information from Abram Key-Way-Ken-Do 11-26 a brother HB Durant Spl Agt Petoskey Mich Nov 19/08..

Information following from: Not Given.

7-26 MAW-CO-ME-WON, dead.
Wife: Angeline Maw-Co-Me-Won, age 65, P.O. Petoskey.
7-26-1 Mary Peck, age 47, P.O. ~~Petoskey~~ in Insane Asylum at Traverse City, no children.
Husband Joe Peck, see 5-32.
7-26-2 Elizabeth Maw-Co-Me-Won, dead, no heirs.
7-26-3 Susan Maw-Co-Me-Won, dead.

Husband 1st : Fred Harrington, white.
7-26-3-1 Jay Harrington, age 24, P.O. Petoskey, single.
7-26-3-2 Mary Smith, nee Harrington, age 19, P.O. Petoskey, no children, see 2-30.
Husband: John Smith, see 2-30.
Husband 2nd: Jake Adams, white, P.O. Petoskey.
7-26-3-3 Thomas Adams, age 11, P.O. Petoskey.
7-26-4 Lucy Stewart, age 37, P.O. Petoskey.
Husband: Name not given, white.
7-26-4-1 Bessie Stewart., age 18.
7-26-4-2 Bertha Stewart., age 16.
7-26-4-3 Jennie Stewart., age 14.
7-26-4-4 Kerim Stewart., age 12.
7-26-4-5 Levi Stewart., age 10.
7-26-5 Peter ~~Makean~~ Makomenaw, age 30, P.O. Petoskey.
Wife: May Makomenaw, nee Jackson, age 30, see 10-59, & 3-56.
7-26-5-1 Agnes Makomenaw, age 5.
7-26-5-2 Louise Makomenaw, age 3.
7-26-5-3 Arvella Makomenaw, born Sept/08 Too late.
7-26-5-4 Paul Makomenaw, oldest child, lives with David Fox, see 10-59.

Information following from: Peter Walker & John Ke-Way-Ke-Zhick, Dec 14/08.
8-26 O-TAW-WAW-A-ZHE, dead.
Wife: Name not given.
8-26-1 See 4-26.
8-26-2 See 38-26.
8-26-3 See ~~5-29~~
8-26-4 Peter Walker, age 62, P.O. Petoskey or Fountain Mich.
Wife: Name not given, dead, 1st husband Micko dead, child James Micko or James Elliot, see 3-50 & 7-55.
8-26-4-1 Maggie Walker, age 45, P.O. Millerton, no children.
Husband: Robert Genereaux, also know as Robert Wind or Robert Nodin or Newton, see 25-57.
8-26-4-2 Louis Walker, age 37, P.O. Freesoil or Fountain, see 2-54, no children.
Wife: Susan Walker, nee Shay-Go-Nay-Be, age 22, see 2-54.

Information following from: Not Given.
9-26 LOUIS CHING-GWAW, age 76, P.O. Harbor Springs.
Wife: Name not given, dead.
9-26-1 ~~Agnes~~ Frank Chingwaw, age ~~54~~ 52, P.O. Petoskey.

Wife: Eliza Chingwaw, nee Aw-Ne-Way-Ne-Mo, age 48, see 10-34.
9-26-1-1 Louis Chingwaw Jr., age 24, P.O. Mt. Pleasant Sch.
9-26-1-2 Joe Chingwaw, age 22, P.O. Petoskey.
9-26-1-3 Jonas Chingwaw, age 20, P.O. Petoskey.
9-26-1-4 John Chingwaw, age 17, P.O. Tomah Indian School.
9-26-1-5 Elizabeth Chingwaw, age 14, P.O. Tomah Ind Sch.
9-26-1-6 Daniel Chingwaw, age 12, P.O. Tomah Ind School.
9-26-1-7 Sarah Chingwaw, age 10, P.O. Tomah Ind School.
9-26-2 John Chingwaw, dead, no heirs.
9-26-3 Agnes Esttawegezhick, age 44, see 19-32.
9-26-4 Rosie Naskaw, age 35, see 26-46.
9-26-5 Sarah Chingwaw, dead, no heirs.
9-26-6 Annie Chingwaw, dead, no heirs.

Information following from: Not Given.
10-26 MICHAEL PETOSKEY, dead.
Wife: Name not given, dead.
10-26-1 John Petoskey, dead, no heirs.
10-26-2 Mary Ann Russell, dead.
Husband: Name not given, dead.
10-26-2-1 James Russell, age 31, single, went to Oregon about a year ago. Was in Manistique before he left.
10-26-3 Agnes Taylor, age 43, P.O. Petoskey, no children, see 26-40.
Husband: Name not given, white.
10-26-4 Mary Hinds, age 37, P.O. Petoskey, no children, see 26-40.
Husband: Name not given, white.
10-26-5 Sarah Petoskey, dead, no heirs.

Information following from: Not Given.
11-26 AMABEL KE-WAY-KEN-DO, also known as ABRAM KEY-WAY-KEN-DO, age 74, P.O. Petoskey.
Wife: Mary Key-Way-Ken-Do, age 73, P.O. Petoskey.
11-26-1 Kate Abram, age 42, P.O. Petoskey, no children, living with Enos Petoskey, age 59, see 14-26.
11-26-2 Sampson Abram, age 40, P.O. Petoskey.
Wife: Lucy Abram, age 36, see 21-28 & 50-29.
11-26-3 Hazen Ke-Way-Ken-Do, age 38, P.O. Petoskey, separated.
Wife: Eliza Ke-Way-Ken-Do, age 40, P.O. Petoskey, see 51-43 & 7-25, 1st husband Naw-Ga- Naw-She see 20-28.
11-26-3-1 David Ke-Way-Ken-Do, age 15, P.O. Mt. Pleasant School, see 7-25.
11-26-3-2 Lizzie Ke-Way-Ken-Do, age 3, P.O. Petoskey.
11-26-3-3 Daniel Ke-Way-Ken-Do, age 7, P.O. Harbor Springs School.

11-26-4 Name nor sex given, dead, no heirs.

Information following from: Not Given.

12-26 PAUL NE-GAW-NE-QUOUM, dead.

Wife: Sophia Isaac, age 73, P.O. Bay Shore, 2nd husband William Isaac, age 67 died Mch 15/07, do not enroll not a member of this tribe.

12-26-1 Name nor sex given, dead.

12-26-1-1 Joe Gibson, age ~~28~~ 35, P.O. ~~Cross~~ Bay Shore, see 6-24.

Wife: Agnes Gibson, nee see 8-24, age 21, grand daughter of 8-24.

Information following from: William Petoskey, Dec 30/08, Petoskey.

13-26 MARY SHAW-BWAW-SUNG, dead.

Husband 1st: Antoine Ance, dead.

Husband 2nd: Liberty Ingalls, dead.

13-26-1 Angeline Willis, age 50, P.O. Charlevoix, see 3-23 & 13-25.

13-26-2 Louis Antoine, age 46, P.O. Bay Shore Mich, see 16-26.

Wife: Julia Antoine, nee Wasson, age 42, P.O. Bay Shore Mich, see 15-32.

13-26-3 Edmund Antoine or Ed Ingalls, age 44, P.O. Charlevoix or Chicago, has not been heard from for many years, William Petoskey says 25 or more.

13-26-4 Agnes Antoine or Ingalls, age 42, P.O. Kalamazo or Battle Creek, a nurse, sister has not heard from her since 1904.

Information following from: Not Given.

14-26 IGNATUS PE-TAW-SE-GAY, dead.

Wife: Name not given, dead.

14-26-1 Francis Petoskey, see 3-26.

14-26-2 Michael Petoskey, dead, see 10-26.

14-26-3 Louis Petoskey, dead, see 17-26.

14-26-4 Mary Petoskey, dead.

14-26-5 Joseph Petoskey, 1-62, has 2 children.

14-26-6 Simon Petoskey, dead, see 18-26.

14-26-7 James Petoskey, dead.

Wife: Ella Petoskey, white, P.O. Mt. Pleasant Mich.

14-26-7-1 Kingsley Petoskey, age 21, P.O. Petoskey Mich, single.

14-26-7-2 Howard Petoskey, age 17, P.O. Mt. Pleasant Sch.

14-26-7-3 Elliott Petoskey, age 15, P.O. Mt. Pleasant Sch.

14-26-7-4 Brazil Petoskey, age 13, P.O. Mt. Pleasant Sch.

14-26-7-5 William Garland Petoskey, age 8, P.O. Mt. Pleasant Sch.

14-26-8 Elizabeth Petoskey, dead, no heirs.
14-26-9 Enos Petoskey, age 59, P.O. Petoskey.
Wife: Name not given, separated.
14-26-9-1 Huron Petoskey, age 24, P.O. Petoskey.
Wife: Sarah Petoskey, nee Meme, age 30, P.O. Petoskey, see 1-62.
14-26-9-10 Bazile Petoskey, age 55, died May 1908, no wife or child, Legal Administrator William Petoskey, age 51, Petoskey Mich, see 3-26..

Information following from: Not Given.
15-26 SHAY-GWAW-CO-SHING, dead.
Wife: Name not given, dead.
15-26-1 Name nor sex given, dead.
15-26-1-1 Daniel Shay-Gwaw-Co-Shing, age 23, P.O. Carlisle School.
15-26-2 Name nor sex given, dead, no heirs.

Information following from: Not Given.
16-26 FRANCIS SHAW-BWAW-SUNG, dead.
16-26-1 Name nor sex given.
16-26-1-1 Mary Ke-Way-Ke-Zhick, age 32, see 4-26.
16-26-2 Mary Shaw-Bwaw-Sung, dead, see 13-26.
16-26-2-1 Louis Antonie, age 46, P.O. Bay Shore, see 13-26 & 15-32

Information following from: Not Given.
17-26 LOUIS PETOSKEY, dead.
Wife: Belle Petoskey, age 67, Milwaukee Wis, on 1870 roll with husband.
17-26-1 Hattie McNeil, age 44, P.O. Charlevoix.
Husband: Name not given, white.
17-26-1-1 Isabelle McNeil, age 27, P.O. Charlevoix, single.
17-26-1-2 Ed McNeil, age25, P.O. Charlevoix.
17-26-2 Charles William Petoskey, age 33, P.O. Milwaukee Wis.
Wife: Name not given, white.
17-26-2-1 Louisa Isabelle Petoskey, age 5.
17-26-3 Name nor sex given, dead, no heirs.
17-26-4 Name nor sex given, dead, no heirs.

Information following from: Not Given.
18-26 SIMON PE-TAW-SE-GAY, dead, no heirs, So say all the Petoskey's of Petoskey. HB Durant Spl Agt, Petoskey Mich Nov 19/08.

Information following from: Not Given.

19-26 AUGUSTUS OTTOWAW, dead.
Wife: Philamon Ottawa, age 70, P.O. Cross Village.
19-26-1 Amos Augustus, age 30, P.O. Petoskey, single.
19-26-2 Sophia Lawrence, age 13, P.O. Cross Village.
19-26-3 Name nor sex given, oldest child, dead, no heirs.

Information following from: Mitchell LaCroix & Mary E. LaCroix, Dec 15, 1908, 2 ½ miles from Boyne.

20-26 MICHAEL LACROIX, age 76, P.O. Boyne City.
Wife: Mrs. Mary E. LaCroix, age 68, P.O. Boyne City.
20-26-1 Benjamin F. LaCroix, age 41, P.O. Boyne City Mich.
Wife: Name not given, white.
20-26-1-1 Vivian E. LaCroix, age 14.
20-26-1-2 Tracy M. LaCroix, age 13.
20-26-1-3 Lillian A. LaCroix, age 11.
20-26-1-4 Garnet M. LaCroix, age 8.
20-26-1-5 Harley W. LaCroix, age 5.
20-26-2 William W. LaCroix, age 39, P.O. Boyne City.
20-26-3 Victor A. LaCroix, age 34, P.O. East Jordan Mich.
Wife: Name not given, white.
20-26-3-1 Leo Guy LaCroix, age 11.
20-26-3-2 Greta LaCroix, age 8.
20-26-3-3 Agnes LaCroix, age 5.
20-26-3-4 Theodore LaCroix, age 3.
20-26-3-5 Velma LaCroix, age 1.
20-26-4 Esther (LaCroix) Hoy, age 31, P.O. Boyne City.
Husband: Name not given, white, dead.
20-26-4-1 Alvin Hoy, age 9.
20-26-4-2 Wynight Hoy, age 7.

Information following from: Not Given.

21-26 JOHN B. MAW-CAW-DAY-PE-NAY-NE or
JOHN B. BLACKBIRD, age 71, P.O. Petoskey.
Wife 1st : Name not given, dead.
Wife 2nd: Angeline Blackbird, age 69, P.O. Petoskey, see 1-26 & 49-27.
21-26-1 Gabriel Blackbird, age 41, P.O. Petoskey, single, no children.
21-26-2 Susan George, age 44, P.O. Petoskey.
Husband 1st : Name not given, dead, see 1-46 & 2-46.
21-26-2-1 Agnes Wabose, age 21, P.O. Petoskey, single, no children.
Husband 2nd: Paul George or Paul Tabawse-Kezhick, age 32, P.O. Petoskey, see 1-46.
21-26-2-2 Minnie George, age 11.
21-26-2-3 Joseph George, age 4.

21-26-3 Catharine, dead.
Husband: Name not given, see 39-23.
21-26-3-1 Levi Willis, age 22, P.O. Chilorco Ind Sch, see 3-23

Information following from: Not Given.
22-26 JACOB ANTOINE, age 55, P.O. Petoskey.
Wife: Nancy Ottawa, separated, see 54-27.
22-26-1 Name nor sex given.
22-26-1-1 Emory Nada, see 2-38.

Information following from: Not Given.
23-26 DAVID ME-NAW-NAW-QUOT, dead.
Wife: Name not given, dead.
23-26-1 Daughter, name not given, dead.
23-26-1-1 Mitchell Pesney, age 62, see 28-26 & 25-26.
23-26-2 Name nor sex given, dead.
23-26-3 Name nor sex given, dead.

Information following from: Not Given.
24-26 JAMES WAW-BE-WE-ME-KE or BLACKBIRD, dead.
Wife: Catharine Blackbird, age 60, P.O. Petoskey.
24-26-1 Truman Blackbird or Clement Blackbird, age 44, P.O. Pt. St. Ignace Mich.
Wife: Jane (Alick) Blackbird, also called Christine Blackbird, age 40, P.O. Hessel Mich, see 3-17.
24-26-1-1 William Blackbird, age 16.
24-26-1-2 Mary Blackbird, age 10, died Apr 12/09.
24-26-1-3 Lida Blackbird, age 6.
24-26-1-4 Louise Blackbird, age 4.
24-26-1-5 Catherina Blackbird, age 3.
24-26-1-6 Jeremiah Blackbird, age 1, born Jany 1908.
24-26-2 Jennie ~~Philander~~ Fridlander, age 39, P.O. Petoskey.
Husband: William ~~Philander~~ Fridlander, age 45, see 41-32.
24-26-3 Elizabeth ~~Antoine~~ Kejigobinase or Elizabeth Alick, age 34, P.O. ~~Pt. St. Ignace~~ Hessel Mich.
Husband: Antoine Kejigobinase or Kejigobinase Alick or Pete Alick, see 3-17.
24-26-4 Julia Perry, age 23, P.O. ~~Boyne City Mich~~ Elk City Okla, no children.
Husband: Name not given, white.
24-26-5 Lydia Blackbird, age 17, P.O. Petoskey, not married.
24-26-6 ~~Loui~~ Mary, dead.
Husband: John Edwageshig, P.O. Harbor Springs, see 19-32 & 27-20.
24-26-7 Edward Blackbird, age 32, P.O. Petoskey.

Wife: Name not given, white.
24-26-7-1 Minnie Blackbird, born May 1/08.
24-26-8 Amelia Paul, nee Blackbird, age 29, P.O. Petoskey.
Husband: Peter Paul, see 4-30.

Information following from: Not Given.
25-26 PETER TAY-GWAW-GAW-NAY, dead.
Wife: Name not given, dead.
25-26-1 Mitchell Peter or Mitchell Pesney, P.O. Petoskey, see 28-26.\
25-26-2 Simon Peters, age 47, P.O. Bay Shore, see 36-55.
Wife: Angeline Peters, nee Monebahdum, age 48, P.O. Bay Shore, see 35-26 & 41-26.
25-26-2-1 Julia Smith, age 20, P.O. Bay Shore.
Husband: Paul Smith, age 31, see 18-23.
25-26-2-1-1 William Smith, age 5.
25-26-2-1-2 Jinnie Smith, age 3.
25-26-2-1-3 Adeline Smith, age 6 mos, born May/08
25-26-2-2 Margaret Peters, age 16, P.O. Bay Shore.
25-26-2-3 Name not given: parents dead, P.O. Bay Shore.
25-26-2-3-1 George Thompson, age 6, grand child of ~~Simon Key-Wa-We-Ge-Zhick~~ John Pay-Quay-Nay, see 11-30 & 31-30.
25-26-2-3-2 Amos Thompson, age 8, grand child of ~~Simon Key-Wa-We-Ge-Zhick~~ John Pay-Quay-Nay, see 11-30 & 31-30.
25-26-3 Name nor sex given, dead.

Information following from: William Petoskey etal & John Kwayghezhick, 12/14/08, Petoskey.
26-26 KE-ME-WE-SHAW-GUM, dead, no heirs

Information following from: William Petoskey etal, 12/14/08, Petoskey.
27-26 WAW-WAS-SE-MAW-QUAY, dead, no heirs.

Information following from: Not Given.
28-26 MICHAEL TAY-GWAW-GAW-NAY or MICHAEL PESNEY, age 62, P.O. Petoskey, see 25-26 & 23-26.
Wife: Mary Pesney, age 60.
28-26-1 Name nor sex given, dead, noheirs.
28-26-2 Name nor sex given, dead, noheirs.
28-26-3 Alice Key-Way-Quoum, age 36, see 27-54.
Husband 1st: Louis Lindell, white.
28-26-3-1 Grace Pesney, age 16, P.O. Petoskey.
Husband 2nd: Name not given, see 27-54.

Information following from: William Petoskey etal, 12/14/08, Petoskey.
29-26 MRS. DANIEL RODD, dead, no heirs.

Information following from: William Petoskey, 12/14/08, Petoskey.
30-26 PETER SHAW-MIN, dead.
Wife: Name not given, dead.
30-26-1 Daughter, name not given, dead.
30-26-1-1 Annie Stevens(?), age 45, P.O. Grand Rapids, married, cannot locate her.

Information following from: William Petoskey etal, 12/14, Petoskey.
31-26 MARGARET STEVENS, dead.
Husband: Name not given, dead, white.
31-26-1 Jo Annie Stevens, age 45, see 30-26.
31-26-2 John Stevens, dead, no heirs.

Information following from: William Petoskey etal, 12/14/08, Petoskey.
32-26 ROSINE TRO-TO-CHO, now wife of John Duverney.
Husband: John Duverney, age 62, P.O. Petoskey, see 36-55.

Information following from: William Petoskey etal, 12/14, Petoskey.
33-26 AW-SAW-NAW-QUAY, dead.
33-26-1 Peter Aw-Saw-Naw-Quay, last heard from at Georgian Bay Manitoulin Island, Canada, has not been heard from for 25 years, cannot trace Durant.

Information following from: William Petoskey etal, 12/14/08, Petoskey.
34-26 JANE AW-ZHE-DAY-QUOT, dead., no heirs.

Information following from: William Petoskey etal, 12/14/08, Petoskey.
35-26 O-CUM-DAY, dead.
Wife: Name not given, dead.
35-26-1 Name nor sex given, dead.
35-26-1-1 Angeline Peters, age 48, see 25-26 & 41-26.
35-26-1-1 Name nor sex given.
35-26-1-1-1 Anna Green, see 17-25.

Information following from: William Petoskey etal, 12/14/08, Petoskey.
36-26 JOHN AW-SE-NE-WAY, dead, no heirs.

Information following from: William Petoskey etal, 12/14/08, Petoskey.
37-26 JOHN MWAW-KE-WE-NAW and
GEORGE MWAW-KE-WE-NAW, both dead, no heirs

Information following from: Peter Walker & John Kewaykezhick, Dec 14/08.

38-26 ABRAM O-TAW-NAW-A-ZHE or ABRAM WALKER, dead.
Wife: Susan Walker, age 56, see 3-23.

Information following from: William Petoskey etal, 12/14/08, Petoskey.
39-26 MOSES SHAW-WON, dead, no heirs.

Information following from: Not Given.
40-26 HYACINTHE KEE-ME-CHE-CHAW-GUN, or SCOCO, age 75, P.O. Petoskey.
Wife: Mary Kee-Me-Che-Chaw-Gun, age 69, see 100-22.
40-26-1 Joseph Scoco, age 37, P.O. Petoskey, single.
40-26-2 ~~Victoria Petoskey #3~~ Victoria Scoco, age 17, P.O. Petoskey, see 4-28, adopted child.

Information following from: William Petoskey etal, 12/14/08, Petoskey.
41-26 SAW-GAW-CHE-WAY-QUAY, dead.
41-26-1 Angeline Peters, age 48, see 35-26 & 25-26, she is neice enrolled in 1870 with 41-26.

Information following from: Not Given.
42-26 ABRAHAM KEY-WAY-KEN-DO & his son, both dead, no heirs.

Information following from: William Petoskey etal, 12/14/08, Petoskey.
43-26 MARY A. ME-SQUAW-WALK, dead, no heirs.

Information following from: William Petoskey etal, 12/14/08, Petoskey.
44-27 SAHW-WAW-NAW-AW-NO-QUAY, dead, no heirs.

Information following from: William Petoskey etal, 12/14/08, Petoskey.
45-27 AW-WAW-TE-NAISH-QUO-UM, dead, no heirs.

Information following from: William Petoskey etal, 12/14/08, Petoskey.
46-27 PE-NAY-SE-WAW-TE-NO-QUAY, dead, no heirs.

Information following from: William Petoskey etal, 12/14/08, Petoskey.
47-27 MOSES WAW-KAY-ZOO #1, age 65, P.O. Petoskey, no heirs.

Information following from: William Petoskey etal, 12/14/08, Petoskey.
48-27 STEPHEN WAW-KAY-ZOO, no heirs.

Information following from: William Petoskey etal, 12/14/08, Petoskey.
49-27 ELIZA AW-ME-GWAW-BAY, age 69, P.O. Petoskey, same person as ANGELINE BLACKBIRD, see 1-26 & 21-26.

Information following from: William Petoskey etal, 12/14/08, Petoskey.

50-27 LOUIS NE-BE-NAY-AW-SUNG, dead, no heirs

Information following from: Not Given.

51-27 TRO-TO-CHOW or JOHN THRUSHO, age 70, P.O. Pellston Mich, see 38-41.

51-27-1 Caspar ~~Thr~~ Trosho, age 36, see 38-41.

51-27-1-1 Julius Trosho, age 17.

51-27-2 Name not given, dead.

Wife: Angeline Aniwasky, age 29, see 3-41.

51-27-2-1 Edmund Trosho Aniwasky, age 12, P.O. Harbor Springs.

51-27-2-2 Mary Trosho Aniwasky, age 2, P.O. Suttons Bay.

Information following from: Not Given.

52-27 LEWIS TRO-TO-CHAW or KE-SHA-TAY, P.O. ~~Elk Rapids~~ Rapid City, see 51-43 & 35-46. This Indian appears to have been enrolled twice on the 1870 roll, as the testimony of all Indians whom I have consulted fully identify Louis Troto chaw, (No 52 page 27) and, Louis Ke-Shaw-Taw (No. 35 p. 46) as one and the same person. Durant Spl Agt Petoskey Dec 16/08.

Information following from: Not Given.

53-27 VINCENT SHAY-GWA-GOO-SHING, dead.

Wife: Name not given, dead.

53-27-1 Thomas, dead, no heirs.

53-27-2 James, dead, no heirs.

53-27-3 Daniel Vincent, age 25, Tomah Wis, no children.

Information following from: William Petoskey etal, 12/14/08, Petoskey.

54-27 NANCY OTTAWA or NANCY ANTOINE or NANCY HENRY, age 55, P.O. ~~Petoskey~~ Ocqueoe.

54-27-1 Daughter, name not given, dead.

Husband: Sam Nada, age 41, see 2-38.

54-27-1-1 Emory Nada, age 9, P.O. Alden Mich, see 2-38.

Note: Other children living with father, see 2-38.

Information following from: William Petoskey etal, 12/14/08, Petoskey.

55-27 ISAAC NE-SA-GOT, dead, no heirs.

Information following from: William Petoskey etal, 12/14/08, Petoskey.

56-27 ME-SQUAW-NAW-QUOT-O-QWOY, dead, no heirs.

Pages 28 & 29

Goodheart or Middle Village Band

Chief NAW-O-GE-MAW

Information following from: Not Given.

1-28 NAW-O-GE-MAW, dead.
Wife: Name not given, dead.
1-28-1 Name nor sex given, dead.
1-28-1-1 James Naw-O-Ge-Maw, age 22, see 16-28.

Information following from: Not Given.

2-28 JOSEPH SHAW-NAW-NE-GAW-BA-WE or JOE KOSEQUOT, dead.
Wife: Name not given, dead.
2-28-1 Lucy Naw-Quay-Ge-Zhick, age 50, P.O. Harbor Springs, see 15-25.
Husband 1st: Name not given, dead.
Husband 2nd: ~~Harry Naw~~ Canadian Indian.
2-28-1-1 Louis Awsaygon, age 17, died March 1908.
2-28-2 Peter Kosequot, age 48, P.O. Cross Village, see 38-20.
2-28-3 William Kosequot, age 46, P.O. Goodheart.
Wife: Sarah Kosequot, age 39, see 18-31.
2-28-3-1 Julius Kosequot, age 11.
2-28-3-2 Edward Kosequot, born Sept 23/06 1st roll, died July 29/07.
2-28-4 Harriet Keway, age 43, see 27-32
~~2-28-4 Peter Kosequot~~ see 38-20
2-28-5 Mary Gibson, nee Kosequot, age 41, see 45-42, enroll children (see 45-42) with Mary Gibson, as her husband has left her & lives with other woman.
2-28-6 Seraphine Kenoshemeig, age 42, see 35-28.
Husband: Mattias Kenoshemeig, age 45, P.O. Goodheart.

Information following from: Not Given.

3-28 MARY SHAW-WAW-NAY-SE #1, age 96, P.O. Cross Village.
3-28-1 Mary Shaw-Waw-Nay-Se #2, age 50, P.O. Cross Village.
Husband: Peter Shaw-Waw-Nay-Se, age 58, separated now living with Mary Ann Wasson, see 34-32 & 3-32.
3-28-2 Louisa McGalphin, age 38, P.O. Harbor Springs.
Husband: William McGalphin, age 40, P.O. Harbor Springs, son 59-33.
3-28-2-1 Harold McGalphin, age 18.
3-28-3 Eliza O-Ge-Daw-Naw-Quot, age 48, P.O. Cross Village, see 35-20.
3-28-4 Stephen Hamlin, dead?
Wife: Eliza ~~Ermilar~~ Hamlin, age 46, P.O. Burt Lake, see 3-31.
3-28-4-1 Agnes Hamlin.
3-28-4-2 Annie Hamlin.

3-28-4-3 William Hamlin.
3-28-4-4 Mary Hamlin.
3-28-5 Name nor sex given, dead, no heirs.
3-28-6 Name nor sex given, dead, no heirs.

Information following from: Not Given.
4-28 WAY-DAY-SHE-NAY-MAW, dead.
Wife: Name not given, dead.
4-28-1 Mary Mitchell, age 54, P.O. Goodheart, see 9-28.
4-28-2 Name nor sex given, dead.
4-28-2-1 Margaret Naw-Gaw-Naw-She, age 40, P.O. Harbor Springs, see 22-28.
Husband: Andrew Naw-Gaw-Naw-She, see 10-32.
4-28-3 Name nor sex given, dead.
4-28-4 William, dead.
Wife: Therese Bunaway, a Canadian Indian, do not enroll.
4-28-4-1 Robert Way-Day-She-Nay-Waw, age 24, P.O. Cross Village, single.
4-28-4-2 Jonas May-Se-Nin-Ne, age 12, P.O.Cross Village,
his
father is son of 21-30, see 12-30.
4-28-4-3 Victoria Scoco, age 17, P.O. Petoskey, see 40-26.

Information following from: Not Given.
5-28 MO-KE-CHE-WON, dead.
Wife: Name not given, dead.
5-28-1 Threse, dead.
Husband: Name not given, dead.
5-28-1-1 John Wenscoby, age 52, P.O. Bay Shore, no
children,
his wife had child by another see 1-30.
5-28-1-2 Name nor sex given, dead.
5-28-1-2-1 William Gilbert, age 18, P.O. Alpena Mich.
5-28-2 Name nor sex given, dead, no heirs.
5-28-3 Name nor sex given, dead, no heirs.
5-28-4 Name nor sex given, dead, no heirs.

Information following from: Not Given.
6-28 MAY-ON-GO-WAY, dead.
Wife: Name not given, dead
6-28-1 Joe, see 49-29.
6-28-2 Alexander, dead.
Wife: Name not given, dead.
6-28-2-1 Cecelia Abinaw, age 27, P.O. Harbor Springs, no children.

Husband: Paul Abinaw, age 35, P.O. Harbor Springs, see 6-32.

6-28-3 Mary, dead.

Husband: Name not given, dead.

Andrew Pete, age 18, P.O. Beaver Island, went to Beaver Island when a child, try to connect this boy with Beaver Island Band may be enrolled twice Durant.

Information following from: Not Given.

7-28 WILLIAM PO-NE-SHING, age 85, died Mch 27, 1908, 1st roll.

Wife: Name not given, dead.

7-28-1 Elizabeth Chingwa, age 55, P.O. Goodheart.

Husband: John Chingwa, age 70, P.O. Goodheart, see 53-29

7-28-2 ~~John~~ Louis Bwanishing, age 52, P.O. Goodheart, see 8-28.

Wife: Name not given, dead.

7-28-2-1 Sam Bwanishing, age 20, P.O. Goodheart.

7-28-2-2 Annie Bwanishing, age 16, P.O. Goodheart.

7-28-3 Name nor sex given, dead, no heirs.

7-28-4 Name nor sex given, dead, no heirs.

Information following from: Not Given.

8-28 SIMON AW-SE-NE-WAY, dead.

Wife: Sophia Assinaway, age 78, P.O. Goodheart.

8-28-1 Mitchell Assinaway, age 54, P.O. Goodheart.

Wife: Anatasia Assinaway, age 48, see 13-32.

8-28-1-1 Rosie Donatus, age 30, P.O. Goodheart, no children.

Husband: Joe Donatus, age 35, see 25-20.

8-28-1-2 Jasper Assinaway, age 27, P.O. Goodheart.

Wife: Therese Assinaway, age 23, P.O. Goodheart, see 45-42.

8-28-1-3 Thomas Assinaway, age 16, P.O. Goodheart.

8-28-1-4 Stephen Assinaway, age 14, P.O. Goodheart.

8-28-1-5 Joe Assinaway, age 10, P.O. Goodheart.

8-28-1-6 Louisa Assinaway, age 5.

8-28-1-7 Peter Assinaway, age 3.

8-28-2 Annie, dead.

Husnband: Name not given, dead.

8-28-2-1 Ellen (Way-Be-Ga-Kake) Green, age 23, see 9-28.

Husband: Charles Green, see 9-28.

8-28-2-2 John Way-Be-Ga-Kake, see 9-28.

8-28-3 Lucy, dead.

Husband: Louis Bwanishing, age 52, see 7-28.

Information following from: Not Given.

9-28 WAW-BE-GAY-KAKE, or MITCHELL WAW-BE-GAY-KAKE, age 80, P.O. Middle Village.

Wife 1st: Name not given, dead.

Wife 2nd: Mary Waw-Be-Gay-Kake, nee Weise, age 58, see 13-28.

9-28-1 Louis Mitchell or Waw-Be-Gay-Kake, age 46, P.O. Bay Shore.

Wife: Name not given, dead.

9-28-1-1 Emma Mitchell or Waw-Be-Gay-Kake, age 20, P.O. Bay Shore, see 7-41.

9-28-1-2 William Mitchell or Waw-Be-Gay-Kake, age 18, P.O. Bay Shore, see 7-41.

9-28-1-3 Agnes Mitchell or Waw-Be-Gay-Kake, age 12, died Sept 1908.

9-28-1-4 Amos Mitchell or Waw-Be-Gay-Kake, age 10, died Sept 1907.

9-28-1-5 Joe Mitchell or Waw-Be-Gay-Kake, age 2, died April 1908.

9-28-2 Daniel Mitchell, age 37, P.O. Middle Village.

Wife 1st: Francis Chippeway.

Wife 2nd: Mary (Waydash) Mitchell, age 54, P.O. Goodheart, see 4-28.

9-28-2-1 Rose Ann Mitchell, age 18, P.O. Goodheart.

9-28-3 Mary Ettawagezhick, age 33, P.O. Harbor Springs.

Husband: Benedict Edowakezhick, age 39, P.O. Harbor Springs, spelled by them Ettawegejig, see 19-32.

9-28-3-1 Lacy Ettawagezhick, age 10, P.O. Mt. Pleasant Sch.

9-28-4 Isaac, dead.

Wife: Name not given, dead.

9-28-4-1 Ellen Green, age 23, P.O. Bay Shore, see 8-28.

Husband: Charles Green, age 35, see 17-25.

9-28-4-1-1 Mary Jane Green, age 4 mos, born June/08.

9-28-4-2 John Waw-Be-Gay-Kake, age 18, P.O. Harbor Springs, see 8-28.

9-28-5 James Waw-Be-Gay-Kake, age 29, died Apr 24/07.

Wife: Annie Waw-Be-Gay-Kake, nee Mixcenine, age 22, P.O. Brutus Cheboygan, see 12-31, no children.

Information following from: Not Given.

10-28 NE-TWAW-QUO-UM, dead.

Wife: Name not given, dead.

10-28-1 Name nor sex given, dead, no heirs.

10-28-2 Anna, dead.

Husband 1st: Name not given, dead.

10-28-2-1 Jonas Nibaquam, age 25, P.O. Goodheart, single.

10-28-2-2 Martha Nibaquam, age 22, P.O. Goodheart.
10-28-2-3 Stephen Nibaquam, age 14, P.O. Goodheart, enroll with Agatha Mosenaw.
Husband 2nd: Mitchell Okedonaquot, see 3-46.
10-28-2-4 Joe Okedonaquot, age 2, enroll with Agatha Mosenaw.
10-28-2-5 Thomas Okedonaquot, age 2, enroll with Agatha Mosenaw.
10-28-3 Agatha Mosenaw, age 52, P.O. Goodheart, see 18-20.
Husband: Name not given, dead.
10-28-3-1 Agnes Mosenaw, age 21, P.O. Goodheart, single, see 18-20.

Information following from: Not Given.
11-28 JNO KAW-WAY-GO-MO-AW, age 77, died July 24, 1907.
Wife: Name not given, dead.
11-28-1 William ~~Kawegoah~~ Kawegomoah, age 54, P.O. Goodheart.
Wife: Harriet Kawegomoah, now Hattie Gould, age 41, P.O. Elk Rapids, separated, for her children & husband see 18-42.
11-28-2 Jonas Kawegomoah, age 44, P.O. Goodheart.
Wife: Mary Kawegomoah, age 25, ok Durant, see 27-20.
11-28-2-1 John Kawegomoah, age 5.
11-28-2-2 Alice Kawegomoah, age 3.
11-28-2-3 Joseph Kawegomoah, born July 16, 1908.
11-28-3 Name nor sex given, dead, no heirs.
11-28-4 Name nor sex given, dead, no heirs.
11-28-5 Name nor sex given, dead, no heirs.

Information following from: Not Given.
12-28 MAW-GE-SON-GAY, dead.
Wife 1st: Name not given, dead.
Wife 2nd: Mary (Maw-Ge-Son-Gay) Say-Nin-Gwaw-Day, age 76, P.O. Bay Shore Mich, see 5-31.
Note: 4 children on 1870 roll are now all dead and left no heirs.
Note: Maw-Ge-Son-Gay first wife on 1870 roll died and he then married Mary, who, after his death married Say-Nin-Gwaw-Day; Tuttle, Harbor Springs, 19/9/08.

Information following from: Not Given.
13-28 KE-NO-ZHE-NUG, dead.
Wife: Name not given, dead.
13-28-1 Mary (Weiss) Waw-Be-Gay-Kake, age ~~70~~ 58, P.O. ~~Middle~~ Goodheart Village, now wife of 9-28.
Husband: Name not given.
13-28-1-1 Mary Chingwa.

Husband: William Chingwa, see 52-29.
Note: For other children of Mary Waw-Be-Gay-Kake see 9-
28.
13-28-2 Sophia Nishigebinesi or Sophia Bird, age 57, P.O. Cross Village, see 60-21.
Husband: Name not given, dead.
13-28-2-1 Louis Nishigebinesi or Louis Bird, age 30, died Apr 1908.
Wife: Mary Nishigebinesi or Bird, age 30, P.O. Beaver Island, see 5-34.
13-28-2-1-1 Amelia Bird, age 3.
13-28-2-2 Name not given, dead.
Husband: Mitchell Animiquoum, P.O. Cloquett Mich, see 39-20.
13-28-2-2-1 Joseph Animiquoum, age 15, P.O. ~~Cross Village~~ Carlile School.
13-28-2-2-2 Charles Animiquoum, age 14, P.O. Cross Village, see 39-20.
13-28-3 Victoria Petoskey #1, age 51, P.O. Middle Village
Goodheart,
for children see 19-28.
Husband: Name not given, dead.
13-28-4 Name nor sex given, dead, no heirs.
13-28-5 Name nor sex given, dead, no heirs.
13-28-6 Name nor sex given, dead, no heirs.

Information following from: Not Given, Dec 26/08.
14-28 ZEP-HERE-KAW-GAY-GE-WON, dead.
Wife: Christine St. Peter, age 70, P.O. Harbor Springs, daughter of 2-13.
14-28-1 John Kaw-Gay-Ge-Wan or Kahgajiwan, age 44, P.O. Goodheart Mich, see 32-32.
14-28-2 Edmund Kahgajiwan, age 42, P.O> Harbor Springs.
Wife: Annie, now living with William Norton see 23-20.
14-28-3 Alex St. Peter, age 12, P.O. Harbor Springs, single.
14-28-4 George St. Peter, age 10, P.O. Harbor Springs, single.

Information following from: Not Given.
15-28 CATHARINE AW-SE-NO-WAY, dead, no heirs.

Information following from: Not Given, Oct 20, Goodheart Middle Village.
16-28 ANDREW AW-SE-NO-WAY, dead.
Wife: Name not given, dead.
16-28-1 Elizabeth Graham, age 45, P.O. Goodheart, no children.
Husband: Henry Graham, age 48, son of 9-15.

16-28-2 Matthew Assinaway, age 42, P.O. Goodheart.
Wife: Annie Assinaway, nee Pay-Mo-Say-Way, age 34, see 17-32.
16-28-3 Catharine Assinaway, dead, was wife of 1-28.
Husband: Name not given, dead.
16-28-3-1 Jonas Neogamaw, age 22, P.O. Goodheart, see 1-28.
16-28-4 Peter Assinaway, age 39, P.O. Goodheart.
Wife: Mary Assinaway, nee Oge-Maw-Ke-Ge-Do, age 35, see ~~16-28~~ 6-46.
16-28-4-1 George Assinaway, age 13.
16-28-4-2 Louisa Assinaway, age 7.
16-28-4-3 Agnes Assinaway, age 5.
16-28-4-4 Ellen Assinaway, born Dec 1907 2nd roll.

Information following from: Not Given.
17-28 ROBERT DAILEY, dead.
Wife: Name not given, dead.
17-28-1 Mary Shomin, age 58, P.O. Cross Village, see 96-22.
Husband: Charles Shomin, see 28-20.
17-28-2 Eliza Shawanabin, age 57, P.O. Cross Village, see 96-22.
Husband: Name not given, dead.
17-28-2-1 John Shawanabin, age 30, P.O. Cross Village.
Wife: Threse Shawanabin, age 26, see 50-29 & 45-33.
17-28-2-1-1 Clara Meshekey, age 8.
17-28-2-1-2 Joe Meshekey, age 5.
17-28-2-1-3 Ellen Shawanabin, born July 1908 2nd roll.
17-28-2-2 Benedict Shawanabin, age 24, not married.
17-28-2-3 Charles Shawanabin, age22, P.O. Cross Village.
17-28-2-4 Francis Shawanabin, age 18, P.O. Cross Village.
Note: others died when young.

Information following from: Not Given.
~~29-41~~ 18-28 CATHARINE, known as CATHARINE OKE-NO-TEGO, age 90, P.O. Middle Village Goodheart.
18-28-1 Name nor sex given, dead.
18-28-2 Leo Francis, age 60, P.O. Sutton's Bay.
Wife 1st : Madeline, dead.
18-28-2-1 William O-genotego or William Francis, age 27, P.O. Cross Village, see 3-20.
Wife 2nd: Philaman (P.Ance) Francis, age 44, P.O. Sutton's Bay, see 8-42.
18-28-3 Joe Francis, age 50, P.O. Giidheart Middle Village, see 8-20.
Note: This sheet should be numbered 18-28 and 18-28 should be numbered 29-41 as there has been a mistake in identityof Chiefs

where "Catharine" was enrolled. However it will not change the status of the persons enrolled HB Durant Spl Agt Oct 21, 1908 Middle Village Mich.

Information following from: Not Given.

19-28 MAW-TE-NO, dead.

19-28-1 Pete Petoskey, dead.

Wife: Victoria Petoskey #1, age 51, see 13-28.

19-28-1-1 Sophia Petoskey Kejigobinessi, age 33, P.O. Goodheart.

Husband: Joe Kejigobenessi, age, 36, P.O. Goodheart, see 45-33.

19-28-1-1-1 Julia Ann Kejigobenessi, age 15, P.O. Goodheart.

19-28-1-1-2 Agnes Kejigobenessi, age 10, P.O. Goodheart

19-28-1-1-3 Ida Kejigobenessi, age 8.

19-28-1-1-4 Amelia Kejigobenessi, age 5.

19-28-1-2 Madeline Shagonaby, age 30, P.O. Pine Lake North Shore.

Husband: Name not given, dead.

19-28-1-2-1 Louisa Shagonaby, age 6.

19-28-1-2-2 Susan Shagonaby, age 3.

19-28-1-2-3 Antoine Shagonaby, age 8.

19-28-1-3 Susan Gilbert, dead.

Husband: Name not given, dead.

19-28-1-3-1 Mary Gilbert, age 11, child lives with Victoria Petoskey grandmother.

19-28-1-3-2 Christina Gilbert, age 9, child lives with Victoria Petoskey grandmother.

19-28-1-3-3 Esther Gilbert also known as Esther Twombly, age 6, lives with Rose (Aish-Ke-Baw-osh) Twombly at Pellston Mich see 36-57 & 23-23.

19-28-1-4 Agnes Ance, age 25, P.O. Pt. St. Ignace, no children.

Husband: Leo Ance, age 41, P.O. Pt. St. Ignace, see 1-15

19-28-1-5 William Petoskey, age 22, P.O. Goodheart.

Wife: Mary Petoskey, nee Keway, age 18, P.O. Goodheart, see 27-32.

19-28-1-6 Rosie Petoskey, age 20, P.O. Goodheart.

19-28-2 William Miksawbi (Micksawbay), age 47, P.O. Goodheart.

Wife: Philomon Miksawbi, age 46, P.O. Goodheart, see 37-28 & 27-32.

19-28-2-1 Mary Miksawbi, age 23, P.O. Goodheart, single.
19-28-2-2 James Miksawbi, age 17, P.O. Goodheart, single.
19-28-2-3 Catharine Miksawbi, age 11, P.O. Goodheart, single.
19-28-2-4 Ambrose Miksawbi, age 8, P.O. Goodheart, single.
19-28-2-5 Cecelia Miksawbi, age 6, P.O. Goodheart, single.
19-28-2-6 Moses Miksawbi, age 4, P.O. Goodheart, single.

19-28-3 Louis, dead, ½ brother.
Wife: Name not given, dead.
19-28-3-1 Alphonse O-Taw-Naw-Zhe, see 50-29.

Information following from: Not Given.

20-28 ELIAS AW-BE-TAW-CAW-MICK, dead.
Wife: Name not given, dead.
20-28-1 Name nor sex given, dead.
20-28-1-1 Eliza Abram Ke-Way-Ken-Do nee Dailey, age 40, P.O. Petoskey, see 11-26.
20-28-2 Name nor sex given, dead.

Information following from: Not Given.

21-28 THERESA AW-WAW-NAW-QUOT known as THERESA PETOSE, age 75, P.O. Goodheart.
Husband: None.
21-28-1 Eson Petoskey, age 38, P.O. Goodheart.
Wife: Name not given, separated, see 106-32.
21-28-1-1 Levi Petoskey, age 9, see 106-32.
21-28-2 Lucy ~~Abraham~~ Abram, age 36, P.O. Goodheart, separated, no children.
Husband: Sam Abram or Sam Key-Way-Ken-Do, age 40, P.O. Petoskey.
21-28-3 Benjamin Petose, age 46, P.O. ~~Harbor~~ Goodheart, see 50-29.
Wife: Name not given, dead.
21-28-3-1 Louisa Shomin, age 21, see 39-32.

Information following from: Not Given, Oct 21/08, Middle Village.

22-28 BENJAMIN ME-SHAW-BE-MAY, dead.
Wife: Name not given, dead.
22-28-1 Name nor sex given, dead, no heirs.
22-28-2 Name nor sex given, dead, no heirs.
22-28-3 Name nor sex given, dead, no heirs.
22-28-4 Margaret Naw-Gaw-Naw-She, age 40, P.O. Harbor Springs, see 4-28.

Information following from: Not Given.

23-28 MARY ANN MAW-DWAY-AW-SHE, dead.

23-28-1 Margaret Tapkeah, age 51, P.O. Horton Bay,
see 29-28 & 19-23.
Husband: Name not given, dead.
23-28-1-1 Sam Tapkeah, age 33, P.O. Horton's Bay.
Wife: Angeline Tapkeah, age 30, see 25-32.
23-28-1-1-1 Jennie Tapkeah, age 2.
23-28-1-1-2 John Tapkeah, born March 8/08.

Information following from: Not Given.
24-28 BENEDICT AISH-KE-BAW-GOSH, age 70, P.O. Goodheart.
Wife: Mary Aish-Ke-Baw-Gosh, age 68, P.O. Goodheart.
24-28-1 Nancy Aish-Ke-Baw-Gosh, dead.
Husband: Frank Michigan, see 45-42.
24-28-2 Mary Ann Aish-Ke-Baw-Gosh, dead.
Husband: Joseph Waukozoo, dead.
24-28-2-1 George Waukazoo, age 10, P.O. Mt. Pleasant Sch.
24-28-3 Joseph Aish-Ke-Baw-Gosh, ag e34, P.O. Goodheart.
Wife: Barbara Aish-Ke-Baw-Gosh, dead, see 38-32.
24-28-3-1 Lizzie Aish-Ke-Baw-Gosh, age 10.
24-28-3-2 Rose Aish-Ke-Baw-Gosh, age 7.
24-28-4 Joseph Aish-Ke-Baw-Gosh, age 33, P.O. Goodheart, single.
24-28-5 Barbara Mixcenene, age 12, adopted, see 18-31, enroll with
Benedict Aish-Ke-Baw-Gosh her grandfather.

Information following from: Not Given.
25-28 NAY-AW-BAW-NO-CAW-WON, dead.
Wife: Name not given, dead, no heirs, say so all Chiefs & Headmen of Middle Village Band Horace B. Durant Spl Agt Oct 21/08.

Information following from: Not Given, Oct 21/08, Middle Village.
26-28 O-NAY-AW-SE-NO, dead, no heirs.

Information following from: Not Given, Oct 21/08, Middle Village.
27-28 WAW-WE-NE-KONG, dead.
27-28-1 Name nor sex given, dead, no heirs.
27-28-2 Name nor sex given, dead, no heirs.
27-28-3 John Louis, age 38, see 1-38.

Information following from: Not Given.
28-28 PETER MAW-CO-SAW, dead.
Wife: Mary Maw-Tance, age 80, P.O. Bay Shore, see next.

Information following from: Not Given, Supplement to 28-28, No Number.
??-28 JOHN MAW-TWANCE, dead, died Apr 2/08 1st roll, son of
Charles 7-24. I cannot find his name on 1870 roll but he and wife are

undoubtedly entitled to enrollment Durant Bay Shpre Mich Oct 5/08.
Wife: Mary Maw-Tance, age 80, P.O. Bay Shore, see 28-28.
??-28-1 Joe Keshawas, dead, nephew of Mary Maw-Tance.
Wife: Agnes Keshawas, dead, see 35-20.
??-28-1-1 Agnes Paul, age 25, P.O. Bay Shore.
Husband: Mob Paul, age 32, P.O. Bay Shore, see 4-30.
??-28-1-1-1 James Paul, age 6.
??-28-1-1-2 Clara Paul, age 2, died Dec 6/07
??-28-1-1-3 Walles Paul, born April 1907, 2nd roll.
??-28-1-2 Levi Keshawas, age 11, P.O. Bay Shore, live with grandmother.
??-28-1-3 Lena Keshawas, age 9.
??-28-1-4 Louis Keshawas, age 6.
??-28-1-5 Harry Keshawas, age 4.

Information following from: Not Given.
29-28 MAY-SHE-NIN-NE, dead.
Wife: Margaret Tapkeah, see 23-28.
29-28-1 Name nor sex given, dead, no heirs.

Information following from: Not Given.
30-28 BENEDICT KO-SE-QUOT, age 57, P.O. Goodheart.
Wife: Name not given, dead.
30-28-1 Name not given, dead, the child enrolled with him (Benedict Ko-Se-Quot) in 1870 was his younger sister.
Husband: Joe Mastaw, age 50, P.O. Mackinaw City, see 2-13.
30-28-1-1 Mitchell Mastaw, age 27, see 52-29.

Information following from: Not Given.
31-28 SAIN-WICK, dead.
Wife: Name not given, dead.
31-28-1 Madeline Sainwick, age 56, P.O. Middle Village, separated.
Husband: Jacob or Benjamin Frenchman, age 70, see 28-41.
31-28-2 Jonas Sainwick, age 48, P.O. Cross Village, no children.
Wife: Mary Sainwick, age 49, P.O. Cross Village.
31-28-3 Benedine Sainwick, dead.
31-28-3-1 Elizabeth (Shingwakos) Williams, age 40, P.O. Pellston, see 56-21.

Information following from: Not Given, Oct 21/08, Middle Village.
32-28 NAY-GO-TOOKE, dead.
Wife: Mary Aw-Se-No-Way, known as MARY NAGODOC, age 70, P.O. Goodheart.
32-28-1 Name nor sex given, dead, no heirs.

Information following from: Not Given.
33-28 MAW-CHE-WE-TAW, dead.
Wife: Name not given, dead.
33-28-1 Simon Maw-Che-We-Taw, age 47, P.O. Goodheart, died July 22, 1908.
Note: Must living all at wife of 14-56 Angeline Aw-Se-Ge-Nock his aunt who is his father's sister.

Information following from: Not Given.
34-28 PAUL KAW-WAY-GO-MO-AW, dead.
Wife: Name not given.
34-28-1 Name nor sex given.
34-28-2 Jonas.
Wife: Name not given.
34-28-2-1 Jonas Kawegomoah, see 27-20 & 11-28.

Information following from: Not Given.
35-28 FRANCIS KE-NO-ZHE-MEIG, dead.
Wife: Name not given, dead.
35-28-1 Mathias Kenoshemeig, age 45, P.O. Goodheart
Wife: Seraphine Kenoshemeig, nee see 2-28, age 42, P.O. Goodheart.
35-28-1-1 John Kenoshemeig, age 16, P.O. Goodheart.
35-28-1-2 Edward Kenoshemeig, age 14
35-28-1-3 Julius Kenoshemeig, age 3
35-28-1-4 Aline Kenoshemeig, age 1, born Apr 13/08 2nd roll.
35-28-2 Mary Abinaw, age 40, P.O. Harbor Springs, no children.
Husband: Robert Abinaw, age 44, see 6-32.
35-28-3 Eliza king, age 29, P.O. Goodheart, see 52-29.
35-28-4 Rosie Chinggwa, age 24, P.O. Goodheart, no children.
Husband: Willis Chinggwaw, dead.
35-28-5 William Kenozhemeig, age 20, P.O. Goodheart, single.

Information following from: Not Given.
36-28 THAD. AISH-KE-BAW-GOSH, dead, no heirs

Information following from: Not Given.
37-28 MAW-CAW-DAY-GEN, dead.
Wife: Name not given.
37-28-1 David Maw-Caw-Day-Gon or Macdagen, age 60, P.O. Cross Village, no children.
Wife: Christina Maw-Caw-Day-Gon or Macdagen, nee Anemequom, age 52, P.O. Cross Village, see13-20.
37-28-2 Name nor sex given, dead.
37-28-3 Paul Macdagin, age 48, P.O. Namah Mich, single, no

children.

37-28-4 Philamon Micksawbay, age 46, P.O. Middle Village, see 19-28.
Husband: William Micksawbay.

37-28-5 Jasper Macdagin, age 46, see 25-20.

37-28-6 Susan Macdagin, known as Susan Mixceney, age 38, P.O. Manistique Ossawinamaker Hotel, single.
37-28-6-1 Catharine Naongaby, age 17, P.O. Petoskey, illegitimate child, see 41-20.

37-28-7 Joe Macdagin or Mixceney, ag e36, P.O. Namah Mich.
Wife: Mary Macdagin or Mixceney, nee Jesse, age 38, see 2-36.

Information following from: Not Given.
38-28 IGNATUS NAY-O-GE-MAW, age 71, P.O. Goodheart, no children.
Wife: Mary Nay-O-Ge-Maw, age, 62, died Jany 20/08.

Information following from: Not Given.
39-28 MAW-DWAY-ZE-GE-NAW, dead, no heirs, mother to Benedict Aishkibogosh.

Information following from: Not Given.
40-28 PATRICK NAW-GAW-NAW-SHE, age 61, P.O. Goodheart.
Wife: Sarah Naw-Gaw-Naw-She, age 55, P.O. Goodheart.
40-28-1 Louis Naw-Gaw-Naw-She, age 35, P.O. Goodheart, single.
40-28-2 Angeline Naw-Gaw-Naw-She, age 21, P.O. Goodheart, single
40-28-3 Eliza King, dead.
Hisband: Charles King, P.O. Goodheart, see 52-29.

Information following from: Not Given, Oct 20/08, Middle Village.
41-28 KYE-YOSH-KOONSE, dead, no heirs.

Information following from: Not Given.
42-28 CATHARINE AISH-KE-BAW-GOSH, P.O. Mancelona Mich.

Information following from: Not Given, Dec 26/08.
43-28 KAW-GAY-GE-WON, dead.
Wife: Name not given.
43-28-1 Name nor sex given, see 14-28.

Information following from: Not Given, Oct 1/08, Middle Village.
44-29 MARY SHAW-WAW-NAW-NAY-BEECE, dead, no heirs.

Information following from: Not Given.

45-29 KAW-BE-ME-NE-GAW-NE, dead.
Wife: Name not given, dead.
45-29-1 Name not given, dead.
Husband: Simon Green, see 17-25.
45-29-1-1 Charles Green, age 35, P.O. Bay Shore or Horton's Bay.
45-29-1-2 James Green, age 35, see 17-25.

Information following from: Not Given.
46-29 KAY-GWAY-DAW-SUNG, dead, no heirs.

Information following from: Not Given.
47-29 AUGUSTUS MEEK-SE-NAY-SAW, dead, no heirs.

Information following from: Not Given.
48-29 LOUIS PAUN-DE-GAY-COW-WAW, P.O. Mantolin Island, cannot trace.

Information following from: Not Given.
49-29 JOSEPH MAY-ON-GO-WAY, dead.
Wife: Agatha May-On-Go-Way, age 56, P.O. Cross Village, see 13-20.
49-29-1 Joe May-On-Go-Way, age 28, P.O. Cross Village, see 8-20.

Information following from: Not Given, Oct 7/08.
50-29 LOUIS O-TAW-NAW-ZHE, dead.
Wife: Name not given, dead.
50-29-1 Alphonse O-Taw-Naw-Zhe, age 35, P.O. Boyne City Camp #11, see 19-28.
Wife: Anna O-Taw-Naw-Zhe, nee Naw-Gaw-Naw-She, age 33, see 30-32.
50-29-1-1 Augustus O-Taw-Naw-Zhe, age 12.
50-29-1-2 Angeline O-Taw-Naw-Zhe, born Sept 1907.
50-29-2 Benjamin ~~Wonawquot~~ Petose, age 48, P.O. Goodheart Mich.
Wife: Name not given, dead.
50-29-2-1 Louisa Shomin, age 21, P.O. Harbor Springs, no children.
Husband: Joe Shomin, age 28, see 39-32.
50-29-3 Lucy Key-Way-Ken-Do known as Lucy Abram, age 36, see 11-26 & 21-28, separated.
Husband: Sam Key-Way-Ken-Do or Sam Abram, age 40, see 11-26.
50-29-4 Name nor sex given, dead.
50-29-4-1 Therese Shawanabin, age 26, P.O. Cross Village, see 17-28 & 45-33.

Information following from: Not Given.
51-29 ANDREW MAY-DWAY-ZAW-SHE, dead, no heirs.

Information following from: Not Given.
52-29 JOSEPH O-TAW-GAW-MAW-KE known as JOSEPH KING, age 61, P.O. Goodheart.
Wife: Name not given, dead.
52-29-1 Thomas King, age 35, P.O. Goodheart.
Wife: Eliza King, nee Ke-No-She-Meig, age 29, see 35-28.
52-29-1-1 Agnes King, age 13.
52-29-1-2 Louisa King, age 9.
52-29-1-3 Isabelle King, age 5.
52-29-1-4 Lucy King, age 1½, born Aug 6, 1907.
52-29-2 Charles King, age 32, P.O. Goodheart, see 40-28.
Wife: Name not given, dead.
52-29-2-1 Leander King, age 8, P.O. Goodheart.
52-29-2-2 Martin King, age 6, P.O. Goodheart.
52-29-3 Mary Mastaw, age 25, P.O. Goodheart.
Husband: Mitchell Mastaw, age 27, P.O. Goodheart, see 30-28
52-29-3-1 Amelia Mastaw, age 5, P.O. Goodheart.
52-29-3-2 Edmund Mastaw, age 2, P.O. Goodheart.
52-29-4 Benkamin King, age 21, P.O. Goodheart, single.

Information following from: Not Given.
53-29 JOHN CHING-GWAW, spelled now CHINGWA, age 70, P.O. Goodheart.
Wife: Elizabeth Chingwa, age 55, P.O. Goodheart, see 7-28.
53-29-1 William Chingwa, age 38, P.O. Goodheart, separated.
Wife 1st : Barbara Odemin, age 33, P.O. Goodheart, see 40-20.
Wife 2nd: Mary Chingwa, age 37, P.O. Goodheart.
53-29-1-1 Lucius Chingwa, age 10.
53-29-1-2 Joe Chingwa, age 7.
53-29-1-3 Alice Chingwa, age 5.
53-29-1-4 Agnes Chingwa, age 3, died Sept 24, 1908.
53-29-1-5 Lena Chingwa, age 1, born Oct 1907 2nd roll.
53-29-2 Jane Chingwa, age 35, P.O. Goodheart, single.
53-29-3 Esther Chingwa, age 21, P.O. Goodheart, not married.
53-29-3-1 May Chingwa, age 3 months, born June 1908, died Sept 6, 1908 2nd roll.
53-29-3-2 John Chingwa, born May 2, 1907, died May 11, 1907 2nd roll.

Page 30
Harbor Springs Band

Chief SIMON KEY-NAWEK-E-ZHICK

Information following from: Not Given, Sunday Oct 25/08, Burt Lake.

1-30 SIMON known as SIMON KEYNAWEKEZHICK, age 80, P.O. Pellston or Bay Shore.
Wife 1st : Name not given, dead.
Wife 2nd: Mary Ann Keynawekezhick, age 50, P.O. Pelston or Bay Shore, daughter of 3-30.
1-30-1 Moses Keynawekezhick or Moses Simon, age 50, P.O. St. Jacques Mich.
Wife 1st : Rosie Keynawekezhick, age 40, died Mch 1908.
Wife 2nd: Josette Simon, see 28-30.
1-30-1-1 Elizabeth Keynawekezhick or Elizabeth Simon, age 17, P.O. St. Jacques, see 66-35.
1-30-2 Eliza Keynawekezhick, dead.
Husband: Name not given, dead.
1-30-2-1 George O-Ge-Ma-Ke-Do, age 23, P.O. Bay Shore, see 5-38.
1-30-3 Mary Ann Keynawekezhick, dead.
Husband: John Wenscoby, age 52, P.O. Bay Shore, see 5-28 Tuttle.
1-30-3-1 Sophia Jocko, age 17, P.O. Genoa Sch. Nebr.

Children of 2nd wife by her deceased husband:
1. Enos Mitchell, dead several years, see 9-30.
Wife 1st : Name not given, see 9-30.
Wife 2nd: Emma Mitchell, age 38, children see 5-41.

Information following from: Not Given.

2-30 PAW-KE-CAW-NAW-NAW-QUOT, dead.
Wife: Name not given, dead.
2-30-1 Jane Shegwajaw, age 47, P.O. Elk Rapids, see 26-20.
2-30-2 Joseph Jackson , age 54, P.O. Charlevoix.
Wife: Mary Ann Jackson, nee Smith, age 46, P.O. Charlevoix, sec 18-38.
2-30-2-1 Name not given, dead.
Husband: Amos John.
2-30-2-1-1 Mabel John, age 7, P.O. Charlevoix, lives with grandfather.
Children of Mary Ann Jackson by 1st husband:
2-30-2-1-2 Paul Smith, age 31, P.O. Bay Shore.
Wife: Julian Smith, neePeters, age 21.
2-30-2-1-2-1 William Smith, age 6.
2-30-2-1-2-2 James Smith, age 3.
2-30-2-1-2-3 Adeline Smith, born May/08.

2-30-2-1-3 John Smith, age 20, P.O. Charlevoix, see 18-23.
Wife: Mary Smith, nee Harrington, age 18, daughter of 7-26., no children.
2-30-3 Name nor sex given, dead, no heirs.
2-30-4 Name nor sex given, dead, no heirs.

Information following from: Not Given, Sunday Oct 25/08, Burt Lake.
3-30 PAY-ME-SAW-AW, dead.
Wife: Name not given, dead.
3-30-1 Moses Pay-Me-Saw-Aw, see 8-30.
3-30-2 Mitchell Pay-Me-Saw-Aw, see 29-30.
3-30-3 Mary Ann Kenawekezhick, age 50, P.O. Bay Shore, see 1-30.
3-30-4 Peter Pay-Me-Saw-Aw, said to be dead left no children. So says Simon Kezhegopenayse of Harbor Springs Dec 28/08 Durant. His sister #3 says he went to Canada years ago & has not been heard from for 8 or 10 years HB Durant Spl Agt Oct 25/08, cannot trace.

Information following from: Not Given.
4-30 MAW-CAW-DAY-O-QUOT, dead.
Wife: Name not given, dead.
4-30-1 Name not given, dead, 1st wife of Francis Paul.
Husband: Francis Paul, age 51, P.O. Pellston, see 3-20 & 7-30.
4-30-1-1 Mob Paul, age 32, P.O. Bay Shore, see 28-28.
Wife: Agnes Paul, see 35-20 & 27-30.
4-30-1-2 Peter Paul, age 25, P.O. Petoskey, N.B. killed by train in Petoskey Feb 13 1909.
Wife: Amelia Paul, nee Blackbird, age 26, P.O. Petoskey, see 24-26 & 2-26.
4-30-1-2-1 Mabel Paul, age 4.
4-30-1-2-2 Lawrence Paul. Age 5 months, born May/08.
4-30-2 Peter Gibson, age 53, P.O. ~~Dowagcac~~ Hartford Mich.
Wife: Elizabeth Gibson, a Pottaeatomi, off.
4-30-2-1 Marsha Wesaw, age 21, P.O. Hartford Mich, no children.
Husband: Frank Wesaw, a Pottawatomie, off.
4-30-2-2 James Gibson, age 18.
4-30-2-3 Isaac Gibson, age 16.
4-30-2-4 Paul Gibson, age 14.
4-30-3 Susan Black, age 48, P.O. Bay Shore.
Husband: Antoine Black, dead.
4-30-3-1 John Black, age 20, P.O. Tomah Ind. Sch.
4-30-3-2 Alice Black, age 17, P.O. Bay Shore.

Husband: George Pewash, see 9-40.
4-30-3-3 Peter Black, age 14, P.O. Genoa School.

Information following from: Not Given.
5-30 SHAW-BWAW-SUNG, dead, no heirs.

Information following from: Not Given.
6-30 PAY-QUAY-NAY, dead.
Wife: Name not given, dead.
6-30-1 Name not given, dead, wife of Alex. Nanagoonse dead, see 12-32.
6-30-2 Son name not given, dead.
Wife: Name not given.
6-30-2-1 Daughter, name not given, dead.
Husband: Pius Norton, see 36-32.
6-30-2-1-1 Joe Norton, age 8, see 8-25.

Information following from: Not Given.
7-30 FRANCIS SHAY-GO-NAY-BE, dead.
Wife: Therese Shagonaby, age 67, P.O. Bay Shore, see 27-30.
7-30-1 Jacob Francis #2 or Jacob Shagonaby, age 45, P.O. Bay Shore, separated.
Wife: Nancy Francis or Shagonaby, nee Bird or Nancy Ponillott, age 50, P.O. Bay Shore, sister of 22-40, step daughter of 12-45 lives at St James Beaver Island, see 12-45, no children.
7-30-2 Name not given, dead.
Husband: Name not given, dead.
7-30-2-1 Angeline Shagonaybe, age 15, P.O. Bay Shore.

Information following from: Not Given.
8-30 MOSES PAY-ME-SAW-AW, age 64, P.O. Petoskey Mich, see 3-30.
Wife: Mary Sophia Pay-Me-Saw-Aw, age 50, died Sept 1907.
8-30-1 Name not given, dead.
Husband: Name not given, dead.
8-30-1-1 Thresa Anderson.
Husband: Ed. Anderson, see 14-58.
8-30-2 Name nor sex given, dead.
8-30-3 Eliza Paymesaw, age 20, P.O. Petoskey.

Information following from: Not Given, Oct 25/08, Burt Lake.
9-30 MICHAEL WE-AW-BE-MIND, dead.
Wife: Name not given.
9-30-1 Enos Mitchell, dead.
Wife: Name not given, dead, see 1-30.

9-30-1-1 Elizabeth Mitchell, age 19, P.O. ~~Genoa Sch Nebr~~ Pellston.
9-30-1-2 Julia Mitchell, age 14, P.O. Genoa Sch Nebr, enroll with 1-30 her grandmother.
9-30-2 Name nor sex given, dead, no heirs.

Information following from: Not Given.
10-30 JOHN B. SHAY-GO-NAY-BE, dead.
Wife: Name not given, dead.
10-30-1 Mary Wahkazoo, age 60, P.O. Bay Shore, see 17-30.
Husband: ~~John~~ George Wahkazoo, dead.
10-30-1-1 Antoine Shaygonabay, age 5, adopted, ~~parents dead~~, see 15-30, mother Madeline Petoskey P.O. Mackinaw.
10-30-2 John B. Shagonaby, age 51, P.O. Bay Shore.
Wife: Elizabeth Shagonaby, nee Pontiac, age 47, P.O. Bay Shore.
10-30-2-1 Matthew Shagonaby, age 26, P.O. Tomah Ind Sch.
10-30-2-2 Francis Shagonaby, age 24, P.O. Bay Shore.
10-30-2-3 Mary Shagonaby, age ~~18~~ 21, P.O. Bay Shore.
10-30-2-3-1 Rosanna Shagonaby, born Oct 7/1907.
10-30-2-4 Joe Shagonaby, age 18, P.O. Bay Shore.
10-30-2-5 Jonas Shagonaby, age 14.
10-30-3 Antoine Shagonaby, dead, see 15-30.
10-30-3-1 James Shagonaby, age 22, P.O. Bay Shore.

Information following from: Not Given.
11-30 JOHN PAY-QUAY-NAY or JOHN SMOKE, dead.
Wife: Name not given, dead.
11-30-1 Name nor sex given, dead.
Spouse: Name not given.
11-30-1-1 George Thompson, age 6, see 25-26.
11-30-1-2 Amos Thompson, age 8, see 25-26.
11-30-2 Julia Smoke, dead, see 4-54.
Husband: Isaac Lewis, dead.
11-30-2-1 Angeline Lewis or Louis, age 17, P.O. Elk Rapids or Bay Shore.
11-30-2-2 Joseph Lewis or Louis, age 11.
11-30-3 Jonas Mitchell, age 30, blacksmith, P.O. Kalamazoo, son of John Smoke so says John Deverney.
Wife: Name not given, white.

Information following from: Not Given, Dec 16.
12-30 JOSEPH WE-AW-BE-MIND, dead.
Wife: Name not given, dead.
12-30-1 Daughter, name not given, dead.

12-30-1-1 Jonas May-Se-Nin-Ne, age 12, see 21-30 & 4-28.

Information following from: Not Given, Dec 16/08.
13-30 MARY WE-AW-BE-Mind, dead, no heirs.

Information following from: Not Given, Dec 16/08.
14-30 JAMES AISH-KE-BWAW, dead, no heirs.

Information following from: Not Given., Dec 16.
15-30 ANTOINE SHAY-GO_NAY-BE, dead.
Wife: Name not given, dead.
15-30-1 Thomas Shay-Go-Nay-Be, dead.
Wife: Madeline Petoskey, P.O. Mackinaw.
15-30-1-1 Louisa Shay-Go-Nay-Be, age 7.
15-30-1-2 Antoine Shay-Go-Nay-Be, age 5, see 10-30.
15-30-2 James Shay-Go-Nay-Be, age 22, see 10-30.

Information following from: Not Given, Dec 16/08.
16-30 MARY AW-BE-TAW-KE-ZHICK, dead, nothing more known.

Information following from: Not Given, Dec 16/08.
17-30 PEANE PAW-GAW-ME-SAY, dead.
Wife: Mary Wahkazoo, age 60, see 10-30.
17-30-1 Name nor sex given, dead, no heirs.

Information following from: Not Given.
18-30 O-GE-ZHE-AW-BAW-NO-QUAY, dead, no heirs.

Information following from: Not Given.
19-30 MARY ANN, dead, no heirs.

Information following from: Not Given, Dec 16/08.
20-30 KE-SHE-GO-QUAY, dead, no heirs.

Information following from: Not Given.
21-30 JOSEPH MAY-SE-NIN-NE, dead.
Wife: Name not given, dead.
21-30-1 Son, name not goven, dead.
Wife: Name not given.
21-30-1-1 Jonas May-Se-Nin-Ne, age 12, P.O. Cross Village, see 12-30 & 4-28

Information following from: Not Given, Dec 16/08.
22-30 BAW-NAW-BAY-QUAY, dead, no heirs.

Information following from: Not Given.
23-30 SCOTT O-TAW-NAW-AZHE, dead, no heirs.

Information following from: Not Given.
24-30 AW-NAW-NAISH-CUM, dead, no heirs.

Information following from: Not Given.
25-30 MEN-DAW-GO-QUAY, dead, no heirs.

Information following from: Not Given.
26-30 ME-SAW-NE-QUAY, dead, no heirs.

Information following from: Not Given.
27-30 PAW-ZHE-DAW-AW-MO-QUAY, dead.
27-30-1 Name nor sex given, see 61-35.
27-30-2 Name not given, wife of 28-30.
27-30-3 Threse Shaygonayby, see 7-30.
27-30-4 Francis Paul #1, age 51, P.O. Pellston.
Wife 1st : Name not given, dead, daughter of 4-30.
27-30-4-1 Mob Paul, see 4-30 & 28-28.
27-30-4-2 Peter Paul, see 4-30.
27-30-4-3 Eliza Thrusko, dead.
Husband: Casper Thrusko, see 38-41.
27-30-4-3-1 Julius Thrusko, see 38-41.
Wife 2nd: Mary Paul, ~~nee Shaw~~, age 51, see 3-20.
27-30-4-4 Christina Paul, age 16, died Nov 1907 1st roll.

Information following from: Not Given, Oct 25/08, Burt Lake.
28-30 KE-ZHICK, dead.
Wife: Name not given, dead.
28-30-1 Rosie, dead, no heirs.
28-30-2 Joseph Kezhick, age 36, P.O. St. Jacques, see 4-34.
Wife: Name not given, dead, see 4-34.
28-30-2-1 Joseph Kezhick, age 11, P.O. Mt. Pleasant Sch.

Information following from: Not Given, Oct 25/08, Burt Lake.
29-30 MITCHELL PAY-ME-SAW-AW, dead.
Wife: Victoria Petoskey #2, see 19-28, no children.

Information following from: Not Given, Dec 16/08.
30-30 ALIXE MAW-CAW-DAY-ME-GE-SE, dead, son of Nanegos, see 12-32. Oldest Indians at Bay Shore do not remember anyone by this name. Durant.
Wife: Name not given.
30-30-1 Name nor sex given.

30-30-2 Theresa Kaogomo, age 38, see 12-32.
Husband: Alex Kaogomo, age 38, see 100-22.
30-30-3 Bonapart Alexander, see 12-32.
30-30-4 Moses Alexander, see 12-32.

Information following from: Not Given.
31-30 MARY ANN SHAW-BWAW-SUNG, dead.
31-30-1 William KE-SHA-WASH, known as Buffalo Bill, P.O. Cross Village.
Wife: Mary Ke-Sha-Wash, nee Sagatoe, see 15-36 & 2-36.
31-30-2 Joe, dead.
Wife: Catharine Smoke, dead, see 11-30.
31-30-2-1 George Thompson, age 6, with Simon Peter at Bay Shore, see 25-26.
31-30-2-2 Amos Thompson, age 8, with Simon Peter at Bay Shore, see 25-26.
31-30-3 Name nor sex given.

Information following from: Not Given.
32-30 WAW-BE-NE-GWON, dead.
Wife: Name not given, dead.
32-30-1 James Williams, age 72, see 12-37.
32-30-2 John Williams, age 50, P.O. Stonington.
Wife: Name not given, dead.
32-30-2-1 Duncan Williams, age 15, P.O. Stonington Tomah Wis.
32-30-3 Name nor sex given.
Spouse: Name not given.
32-30-3-1 John Peter, age 50, for wife and children see 105-22.

Pages 31
Burt Lake Band
Chief JOSEPH WAY-BWAY-DUM

Information following from: Jane, Oct 24/08, Burt Lake.
1-31 JOSEPH WAY-BWAY-DUM, dead.
Wife: Name not given, dead.
1-31-1 Jane Grant, age 46, P.O. Brutus.
Husband: John Grant, dead.
1-31-1-1 Joseph Grant, age 22, P.O. Brutus, single.
1-31-1-2 Lizzie Grant, age 9, P.O. Brutus
1-31-1-3 Thomas Grant, age 5, P.O. Brutus
1-31-1-4 Julia Grant, age 16, died June 22, 1908.
1-31-2 Mary Brady, age 45, P.O. Topinabee Mich or Brutus, see 2-31.

1-31-3 Lucy Key-Way-Quo-Um, dead.
Husband: John Key-Way-Quo-Um, age 49, P.O. Brutus, see 6-54.
1-31-4 Martha, dead.
Husband 1st: Joe Gabriel or Joe Okedonaquot, dead.
1-31-4-1 Agnes Gabriel or Agnes Oketanaquot, age 13, P.O. Brutus, lives with Mary Brady see above.
Husband 2nd: Manie Hoig, white, off.
1-31-4-2 Harry Hoig, age 9, P.O. Topinabee Mich or Brutus.
1-31-4-3 Louisa Hoig, age 7, P.O. Topinabee Mich or Brutus.
1-31-4-4 Fred Hoig, age 5.

Topinabee Mich

June 14 1909

Extra Name

Mr Horace B. Durant

Also there is a little girl Stay with my wife mother Mary Brady Since She was a baby her father and mother is both dead She is 14 years old now her name is Agnes Gabriel Oketanaqwat and her father name was Joseph Gabriel Okitanaqwat and mother name Martha Gabriel Okitanaqwat both Ottawa. This girl mother was a sister to my wife mother. Yours truly

Louis Massey

Information following from: Not Given.
2-31 NON-QUAISH-CAW-WAW, dead.
Wife: Name not given, dead.
2-31-1 Christina Non-Quaish-Caw-Waw, age 67, P.O. Harbor Springs, no children.
2-31-2 ~~Joseph A~~ Moses Non-Quaish-Caw-Waw, age 60, P.O. Brutus Mich, see 3-31.
2-31-3 Mary Cabanaw, age 56, P.O. Brutus.
Husband: Enos Cabanaw, age 58, P.O. Brutus, see 33-31.
2-31-4 Sarah Massey, age 52, P.O. Brutus.
Husband: Charles Massey, age 49, P.O. Brutus, see 102-22.
2-31-4-1 Henry Massey, age 21, for wife & child see 61-35.
2-31-4-2 Francis Massey, age 19.
2-31-5 Paul Non-Quaish-Caw-Waw, dead.
Wife: Mary Brady, age 45, see 1-31, husband is now _____ Brady, white.
2-31-5-1 Mary Brady Massey, age 26, P.O. Brutus.
Husband: Louis Massey, age 27, see 15-31 & 13-42.
2-31-5-1-1 Lena Massey, born July 1907 2nd roll.
2-31-6 Eliza Norton Moses, age 42, P.O. ~~Cheboygan~~ Pellston.
Husband 1st: Name not given, separated, see 36-32.
Husband 2nd: Pete Moses, dead, see 61-35.

2-31-6-1 Mary Moses, age 15, P.O. Pellston.
~~2-31-7 Harry Massey see 61-35~~

Information following from: Not Given, Ocy 7/08 & Oct 23/08, Indian Point.
3-31 ANTOINE SHAW-WAW-NAW-NAW-QUOT, age 87, P.O. Brutus.
Wife: Sophia Shaw-Waw-Naw-Naw-Quot, age 88, P.O. Brutus.
3-31-1 Mary, dead.
Husband: Name not given, dead, see 8-31.
3-31-1-1 James Shaw-Waw-Naw-Naw-Quot, age 48, P.O. ~~Brutus~~ Pellston.
Wife 1st : Philamon Shaw-Waw-Naw-Naw-Quot, dead.
Wife 2nd: Rosie Shaw-Waw-Naw-Naw-Quot.
3-31-1-1-1 Stephen Shaw-Waw-Naw-Naw-Quot, age 14, see 22-31 & 8-31
3-31-2 Francis Shaw-Waw-Naw-Naw-Quot, age 60, see 43-32.
3-31-3 Isaac Shaw-Waw-Naw-Naw-Quot, age 58, see 29-31.
3-31-4 Susan Parkey, age 48, P.O. Brutus.
Husband: Joseph Parkey, age 44, see 45-21.
3-31-4-1 Thomas Parkey, age 25, P.O. Cheboygan.
Wife: Josephine Parkey, age 22, for children see 29-13.
3-31-4-2 Annie Boda, age 23, P.O. Brutus.
Husband: John Boda, age 23, white, off.
3-31-4-2-1 Barnard Boda, born Mch 5, died March 6/08 2nd roll.
3-31-4-3 Edmund Parkey, age 18, P.O. Brutus.
3-31-4-4 Charles Parkey, age 16, P.O. Brutus.
3-31-4-5 John Parkey, age 8, P.O. Brutus.
3-31-5 Eliza Hamlin, age 46, P.O. Brutus.
Husband 1st : Stephen Shaw, dead, see 3-28.
3-31-5-1 Amos Shaw-Waw, age 24, P.O. Brutus.
Husband 2nd: William Hamlin, age 40, P.O. Brutus, see 40-15 & 16-31.
3-31-5-2 Annie Hamlin, age 14, P.O. Brutus.
3-31-5-3 William Hamlin, age 12, P.O. Brutus.
3-31-5-4 Mary Hamlin, age 10, P.O. Brutus.
3-31-5-5 Agnes Hamlin, age 18, P.O. Genoa Sch Nebr, child by his 1st wife.
3-31-6 Elizabeth Non-Quaish-Caw-Waw, age 44, P.O. Brutus.
Husband: Moses Non-Quaish-Caw-Waw, age 60, see 2-31.
3-31-6-1 John Non-Quaish-Caw-Waw, age 28, P.O. Brutus.
Wife: Jennie Non-Quaish-Caw-Waw, age 25, see 11-15, OK from Snow Islands.
3-31-6-1-1 Emma Non-Quaish-Caw-Waw, age 5.
3-31-6-1-2 Daniel Non-Quaish-Caw-Waw, age 3.
3-31-6-1-3 Harry Non-Quaish-Caw-Waw, age 2.

3-31-6-1-4 William Non-Quaish-Caw-Waw, born May 1907 2nd roll.

3-31-6-2 William Non-Quaish-Caw-Waw, age 21, dead years ago

3-31-7 Sophia Josephine Non-Quaish-Caw-Waw, age 6, P.O. Brutus, adopted, father dead, mother Sarah Shawwanawsegay or Sarah Moses see 8-31.

Information following from: Not Given, Oct 24/08, Burt Lake.

4-31 SAW-GE-TON-DE-WAY, dead.

Wife: Name not given, dead.

4-31-1 Joseph Antoine, age 70, ~~Manistee~~ Boyne Falls single, no children.

4-31-2 Angeline (Captain) Bennett, P.O. Mackinaw City, Mackinaw head of family in 1870 see 6-13.

Husband: Charles Bennett, white.

4-31-3 David Antoine, dead, no heirs.

~~4-31-4 Joseph Antoine~~

4-31-4 Ambrose Antoine, dead, P.O. Manistique, said to be dead, had family, see Grand River 3-19 & 2-50, later: Is dead, died Aug/08 Durant.

Information following from: Not Given.

5-31 SAY-NIN-GWAW-DAY, dead.

Wife 1st: Name not given, dead.

Wife 2nd: Mary Say-Nin-Gwaw-Day, age 76, P.O. Bay Shore Mich.

Note: No living descendants, Say-Nin-Gwaw-Day is dead and four children on 1870 roll are all dead having no living descendants. Tuttle, Harbor Springs, Oct 9/08

Information following from: Not Given, Oct 23/08, Burt Lake.

6-31 PE-WAW-BE-KOONSE, dead.

Wife: Name not given, dead.

6-31-1 Louis Pewabiscaunce, age 54, P.O. Indian River Mich, single.

6-31-2 Mary Ann Nawakaw, age 52, P.O. Elk Rapids, see 26-46 & 20-32.

Husband: Edward Nawakaw, age 89, P.O. Elk Rapids, see 26-46.

6-31-3 Kate King, age 46, P.O. Alanson RFD#1.

Husband: Name not given, white.

6-31-3-1 Guy King, age 25, P.O. Alanson RFD #1, single.

6-31-3-2 Charles King, age 13, P.O. Alanson RFD #1.

Information following from: Not Given.

7-31 MAW-CO-PAW or Francis ~~Louis~~ L. Bourassaw, age 66,

P.O. Elk Rapids.
Wife: Cloe (Bourassaw) Piercy, P.O. Cheboygan, now wife of George Piercy, Frenchman, white.
7-31-1 Francis Bourassaw, age 41, P.O. Sturgeon River Northern Peninsula.
Wife: Name not given, white, has six children.
7-31-1-1 Daisey Bourassaw, age 14.
7-31-1-2 Frank Bourassaw, age 12.
7-31-2 John Bourassaw, age 39, P.O. Cheboygan Mich, no children.
7-31-3 Peter Bourassaw, age 36, lives in Canada somewhere heard from last summer (1908) Durant, no children.
7-31-4 Mary Russell, age 33, Elk Rapids.
Husband: George Russell, white, off, P.O. Elk Rapids.
7-31-4-1 George Russell, age 16.
7-31-4-2 Lawrence Russell, age 14.
7-31-4-3 Cloe Russell, age 12.
7-31-4-4 Clara Russell, age 10.
7-31-4-5 Myrtle Russell, age 6
7-31-4-6 Alice Russell, age 5
7-31-4-7 Stella Russell, born March 6, 1907 2nd roll.
7-31-5 Joseph Bourassaw, age 30, P.O. Cheboygan, not married.
7-31-6 Patrick Bourassaw, age 28, P.O. Cheboygan.
Wife: Ida Bourassaw, children see 12-12.
7-31-7 Laura O'Brian, age 25, P.O. Cheboygan.
Husband: Charles O'Brian, white, no children.

Information following from: Not Given.
8-31 AW-BE-TAW-GE-ZHE-GO, dead.
Wife: Name not given, dead.
8-31-1 James Shaw-Waw-Naw-Se-Gay, age 47, P.O. ~~Brutus~~ Pellston.
Wife 1st : Name not given, dead.
Wife 2nd: Rosa Shaw-Waw-Naw-Se-Gay, nee Aniwaskey, see 33-20, 7-20, 3-31, 10-31 & 22-31.
8-31-1-1 Name not given, of wife by 1st husband, see 7-20.
8-31-1-2 Name not given, of wife by 1st husband, see 7-20.
8-31-1-3 Mary Shaw-Waw-Naw-Se-Gay, age 9.
8-31-1-4 Benjamin Shaw-Waw-Naw-Se-Gay, age 7.
8-31-1-5 Frank Shaw-Waw-Naw-Se-Gay, age 2.
8-31-1-6 Steve Shaw-Waw-Naw-Se-Gay, age 14, by 1st wife, lives with grandmother, see 10-31.
8-31-2 Peter Shaw-Waw-Naw-Se-Gay, age 30, P.O. Pt. St. Ignace.
Wife 1st : Madeline Shaw-Waw-Naw-Se-Gay, age 20, separated.
Wife 2nd: Christina Shaw-Waw-Naw-Se-Gay, nee Key-Way-Qua-Um, age 28, see 11-52 Grand River

8-31-2-1 Cecelia Shaw-Waw-Naw-Se-Gay, age, age 5, P.O. Brutus, enroll with Angeline Negake, see 11-52.

8-31-2-2 Mary Shaw-Waw-Naw-Se-Gay, age 2.

8-31-3 Sarah Moses, age 30, P.O. Pt. St. Ignace.

Husband: Moses Shaw-Waw-Na-Ge-Zhick, known as Francis Moses or Frank Key-To-Naw-Be-Me, age 43, P.O. Allenville, see 9-34.

8-31-3-1 Josephine Shaw-Waw-Naw-Se-Gay, age 6, P.O. Brutus, see 3-31.

8-31-3-2 Francis Moses, born Aug 28/08.

8-31-4 Agatha.

Information following from: Not Given.

9-31 IGNATUS KE-ZHE-GO-WE, dead.

Wife: Susan Ke-Zhe-Go-We, age 70, P.O. Brutus.

9-31-1 Alex Ke-Zhe-Go-We, dead.

Wife: Victoria Cooper, now wife of James Cooper, children see 48-33.

9-31-2 Samuel Ke-Zhe-Go-We, age 39, P.O. Brutus.

Wife: Katie Ke-Zhe-Go-We, age 32, P.O. Brutus, see 27-54.

9-31-2-1 Katie Ke-Zhe-Go-We, age 17, P.O. Brutus.

9-31-2-2 Agnes Ke-Zhe-Go-We, age 14, P.O. Brutus.

9-31-2-3 Caroline Ke-Zhe-Go-We, age 12, P.O. Brutus.

9-31-2-4 Enos Ke-Zhe-Go-We, age 10, P.O. Brutus.

9-31-2-5 Mary Ke-Zhe-Go-We, age 3.

Information following from: Not Given, Oct 24/08, Burt Lake.

10-31 JOSEPH SHAW-WAW-NE-QUOUM, dead.

Wife: ~~Sophia~~ Susan Norton, age 67, P.O. Brutus, now wife of 54-33.

10-31-1 Philamon, dead.

Husband: James Shaw-Waw-Naw-Se-Gay, age 47, see 8-31.

10-31-1-1 Stephen Shaw-Waw-Naw-Se-Gay, age 14, P.O. Brutus, enroll with Susan Norton.

Information following from: Not Given.

11-31 MO-KE-CHE-WAW-NO-QUAY or CATHARINE BOURASSAW, age 80, P.O. Alanson Mich RFD #1 c/o Mrs Neff.

11-31-1 Louis Bourassaw, age 58, P.O. Sutton's Bay, see 7-31.

11-31-2 Mary Ann Ance, see 18-42.

11-31-3 Margaret Mark, see 30-41.

Husband: Joe Mark, dead, see 10-46.

11-31-4 Mitchell Barrow, age 58, P.O. Sutton's Bay.

Wife: Marian Barrow, nee Ance, see 8-42.

11-31-5 Elizabeth Parrow, age 48, P.O. Alanson Mich c/o Mrs Neff RFD #1.

Husband 1st: Joe King, white.
11-31-5-1 John King.
Wife: Name not given, see 17-20 Cross Village.
11-31-5-2 Eliza Frances Feather, age 22, P.O. Sturgeon River
Namah, see 22-34.
Husband: Joe Feather.
11-31-6 Name nor sex given, dead, no heirs.

Information following from: Not Given, Oct 23/08, Burt Lake.
12-31 ME-SE-SOW-GWAY, dead.
Wife: Name not given, dead.
12-31-1 Frank Mixcenena, age 52, P.O. Brutus.
Wife: Mary Mixcenena, age 48, P.O. Brutus, see 16.45.
12-31-1 Annie Wawbegakake, age 23, P.O. Brutus, see 9-28,
no children.
Husband: Name not given, dead.
12-31-2 Frank Mixcenena, age 11, P.O. Brutus.
12-31-3 Stella Mixcenena, age 6.
12-31-2 Mary Megwance, age 50, P.O. Mantolin Island, cannot trace.
Husband: John Megwance, Canadian Indian.

Information following from: Not Given.
13-31 O-GE-SHE-AW-NAW-QUOT, dead.
Wife: Name not given, dead.
13-31-1 Sophia Mag-Ge-Se-Tay, age 50, P.O. Harbor Springs,
see 15-32.
13-31-2 Name nor sex given, dead, no heirs.
13-31-3 Name nor sex given, dead, no heirs.

Information following from: Not Given, Oct 24/08, Burt Lake.
14-31 MICHAEL KAY-GWAITCH, dead, no heirs.

Information following from: Not Given.
15-31 LOUIS SHAW-BWAW-SUNG, dead.
Wife: Name not given, dead.
15-31-1 Joseph Shaw-Bwaw-Sung, age 70, P.O. Brutus, see 31-31.
15-31-2 Name nor sex given.
Spouse: Name not given.
15-31-2-1 Name not given, dead, see 13-42.
Husband: Name not given, white, dead.
15-31-2-1-1 Louis Massey, age 27, P.O. Brutus.
15-31-3 Name nor sex given, dead.
Spouse: Name not given.
15-31-3-1 Angeline Norton, age 39, see 20-32.
15-31-3-2 John Wangezhick, age 31, P.O. Brutus, see 7-46.

Information following from: Not Given.
16-31 THERESA WAY-WIN-DUND, dead.
16-31-1 William Hamlin, age 40, P.O. Brutus, see 40-15 & 3-31.

Information following from: Not Given.
17-31 JAMES KAY-DAW, dead, no heirs.

Information following from: Not Given, Oct 24/08, Burt Lake.
18-31 WILLIAM MICK-SE-NIN-NE, dead.
Wife: Name not given, dead.
18-31-1 Son, name not given, dead.
Wife: Name not given, daughter of 35-32.
18-31-1-1 Sarah Ko-Se-Quot, age 39, P.O. Goodheart, see 35-32.
Husband: William Ko-Se-Quot, age 46, see ~~30-50~~ 2-28
18-31-1-1-1 Julius Ko-Se-Quot, age 11.
18-31-1-2 Harry Mixcenene, age 36, P.O. Harbor Springs, ~~single~~.
Wife: Name not given, dead.
18-31-1-2-1 ~~George~~ dead
18-31-1-3 John Mixcenene, age 34, P.O. Chicago address unknown, see Benjamin Keway at Beaver Island.
18-31-1-4 Mary Portman, age 30, P.O. Petoskey.
Husband: Name not given, white, separated.
18-31-1-4-1 Clarence Portman, age 10, P.O. Harbor Springs.
18-31-1-4-2 Benjamin Portman, age 8, P.O. Traverse City.
18-31-1-5 Christina Shaw-Waw-Naw-Se-Gay, age 28, P.O. Ellenville, north of St. Ignace.
Husband: Peter Shaw-Waw-Naw-Se-Gay, see 8-31.
18-31-1-5-1 Mary Shaw-Waw-Naw-Se-Gay, age 2.
18-31-1-6 Hattie Nanega, age 22, P.O. High Island St. James.
Husband: George Nanegon, age 22, P.O. High Island St. James, see 3-34, no children.
18-31-1-7 Barbara Mixcenene, age 12, P.O. Harbor Springs Sch, enrollment see 24-28.
18-31-2 Enos ~~Kenebaw~~ Kabenaw or Cabenaw, see 2-31 Burt Lake & 33-31.

Information following from: Not Given, Oct 24/08, Burt Lake.
19-31 KAW-NO-TE-NISH-KUNG, dead, no heirs.

Information following from: Mrs. Harriett Davenport, Dec 18/08, Mullett Lake.

20-31 MRS WILLIAM O'FLYNN, dead.

20-31-1 Sam, dead.

Wife: Name not given.

20-31-1-1 Viola Trudo, age 32, P.O. 127 North St. Cheboygan

Husband: Name not given, white.

20-31-1-1-1 Florence Trudo, born Sept/08 Too late.

20-31-1-2 Maria Enault, age 20, P.O. Mullett Lake Box 91, husband white, no children.

20-31-2 John Flint, see 51-33.

20-31-3 William Flint, dead.

Wife: Name not given.

20-31-3-1 Hattie Gerne, see 95-22.

20-31-3-2 Ollivan Gower, age 30, P.O. Harbor Springs.

Husband 1st: Name not given.

Husband 2nd: Name not given, white.

20-31-3-2-1 William Flynn or William McGalphin, see 59-33.

Information following from: Not Given, Oct 24/08, Burt Lake.

21-31 O-TAW-NE-ME-KE-ZHE-GO-QUAY, dead, no heirs.

Information following from: Not Given.

22-31 PAW-SE-QUE, dead.

22-31-1 Susan Norton, age 67, P.O. Brutus, see 54-33.

22-31-1-1 Philamon Shaw-Waw-Naw-Se-Gay, dead, see 3-31.

22-31-1-1-1 Stephen Shaw-Waw-Naw-Se-Gay, see 3-31 & 10-31.

Information following from: Not Given.

23-31 SOPHIA SHAW-WAW-NE-QUOUM, dead.

22-31-1 Simon Boyd, age 42, P.O. Harbor Springs, single no children.

22-31-2 John Boyd, age 32, P.O. Harbor Springs, single.

Information following from: Not Given, Oct 14/08, Burt Lake.

24-31 NE-GANSE, dead, heirs on roll by themselves.

Information following from: Not Given, Oct 24/08, Burt Lake.

25-31 JOSEPH O-GAW-BAY-AW-NAW-QUOT, age 60, P.O. Brutus Mich, heirs all dead.

Information following from: Not Given.

26-31 MRS. HARRIET DAVENPORT, now MRS. HARRIET HURST, age 70, P.O. Mullett Lake.

26-31-1 Eliza Ball, age 52, P.O. Mullet Lake.
Husband: Name not given, white.

Information following from: Not Given, Oct 24/08, Burt Lake.
27-31 AW-SE-NAW-QUAY, dead, no heirs.

Information following from: Not Given, Oct 24/08, Burt Lake.
28-31 Elizabeth Harris.
Note: The Chiefs of the Burt Lake Band of Traverse Inds, say that Elizabeth Harris was a Canadian Indian who was enrolled with them in 1870, but afterwards returned to Canada, & she has not been heard from for 30 years or more. They no nothing of her or her heirs or her whereabouts. Horace B Durant Spl Agt Oct 24/08.

Information following from: Not Given, Oct 23/08, Burt Lake.
29-31 ISAAC SHAW-WAW-NAW-NON-QUOT, age58, P.O. Traverse City Mich.
Wife 1st: Name not given, dead.
29-31-1 Jonas Shaw-Waw-Non-Quot, age 38, P.O. Brutus.
Wife: Susan Shaw-Waw-Non-Quot, nee Negake, age 38, P.O. Brutus, see 11-52.
29-31-1-1 Susan (Jr) Shaw-Waw-Non-Quot, age 14, P.O. Brutus.
29-31-1-2 Samuel Shaw-Waw-Non-Quot, age 12, P.O. Brutus.
29-31-1-3 Mary Shaw-Waw-Non-Quot, age 9, P.O. Brutus.
29-31-1-4 Rose Ann Shaw-Waw-Non-Quot, age 7, P.O. Brutus.
29-31-1-5 Robert Shaw-Waw-Non-Quot, age 3.
29-31-2 Albert Shaw-Waw-Non-Quot, age 36, P.O. Aloha Mich.
Wife: Eliza Shaw-Waw-Non-Quot, age 30, see 8-24 & 7-24.
29-31-2-1 Cora Shaw-Waw-Non-Quot, age 8.
29-31-3 Hattie Hamlin, see 40-15.
Wife 2nd: Lizzie Shaw-Waw-Non-Quot, nee Keway, age 47, see 21-32
29-31-4 Clara Davis, age 28, P.O. Omena.
Husband: Tompkin Davis, a Mt. Pleasant Saginaw Indian.
29-31-5 Dennis Shaw-Waw-Non-Quot, age 23, P.O. Fox Island.
29-31-6 Levi Shaw-Waw-Non-Quot, age 21, P.O. Mt. Pleasant Sch.
29-31-7 Agnes Shaw-Waw-Non-Quot, age 17, separated.
Husband: Jackson Brown, age 27, see 8-23, do not enroll said to be a relative of 67-33.
29-31-7-1 Lizzie Shaw-Waw-Non-Quot #2, born Mch 1908, illegitimate, see 8-23.
29-31-8 George Shaw-Waw-Non-Quot, age 8, P.O. Traverse City.

Information following from: Not Given.
30-31 JOHN MAY-SE-NIN-NE, dead, no heirs.

Information following from: Not Given, Oct 24/08, Burt Lake.
31-31 JOSEPH SHAW-BWAW-SUNG, all dead, no heirs.

Information following from: Not Given.
32-31 JOHN BRIGGS, age 69, P.O. Cheboygan 1257 Mackinaw Ave.
Wife: Name not given, white.
32-31-1 Charles E. Briggs, age 29, P.O. Cheboygan.
32-31-2 Flora Briggs, age 38, P.O. Cheboygan.
Note: Cheboygan Chiefs say John Briggs had no right on roll in 1870; is a half breed. HBDurant Spl Agt Oct 24/08. (~~should be left off~~) Durant Dec 26/08.

Information following from: Not Given, Oct 23, Burt Lake Brutus.
33-31 IGNATUS KAW-BE-NAW, known as ENOS CABANAW, age 50, P.O. Brutus, see 18-31.
Wife: Mary Cabanaw, age 56, see 2-31.
33-31-1 Alice Deshner, age 36, P.O. Brutus.
Husband 1st: Name not given.
~~33-31-1-1 Louisa Deshner~~
33-31-1-1 Louisa Boda, age 17, P.O. Brutus.
33-31-1-2 Maud Boda, age 11, P.O. Brutus.
Husband 2nd: John Deshner, age 36, white, off.
33-31-1-3 John Deshner, age 5, P.O. Brutus.
33-31-2 Lucius Cobenaw, age 30, P.O. Brutus.
Wife: Margaret Cobenaw, age 28, white, off.
33-31-2-1 Nellie Cobenaw, age 9.
33-31-2-2 Leo Cobenaw, age 7.
33-31-2-3 Henry Cobenaw, age 5.
33-31-2-4 Paul Cobenaw, age 3.
33-31-2-5 Clementa, age 9 months, born Feb 1, 1908 2nd roll.
33-31-3 Emma Cobenaw, age 24, P.O. Brutus.
33-31-3-1 Ida Cobenaw, age 3, P.O. Brutus.
33-31-4 Rosie Burrell, age 21.
Husband: Thomas Burrell, white, off.
33-31-4-1 Jennie Burrell, born Oct 27, 1907.

Pages 32 & 33
Harbor Springs Band
Chief DANIEL NE-SAW-WAW-QUOT

Information following from: Not Given, Oct 27/08, Harbor Springs.
1-32 DANIEL NE-SAW-WAW-QUOT, dead.

Wife: Philomen Ne-Saw-Waw-Quot, age 60, died Sept 1907.
Note: All dead, leaving no heirs. Her nearest relations are brothers & sisters, as follows:
Bro. 1. Louis Sigance, Benton Harbor, see 14-56.
Sist. 2. Margaret, Grand Haven, probably Margaret Seanlan, see 6-56.

Information following from: Not Given, Oct 27/08, Harbor Springs.
2-32 PETER KEY-NO-ZHAY, dead.
Wife: Name not given, dead.
2-32-1 Name nor sex given, dead, no heirs.
2-32-2 Name nor sex given, dead, no heirs.
2-32-3 Name nor sex given, dead, no heirs.
2-32-4 Name not given, dead.
Husband: ~~Julius~~ James Wasso, age 62, see 34-32.
2-32-4-1 Mary Ann Wasson, age 32, see 34-32.
2-32-4-2 Justina Hamlin, age 30, see 34-32.

Information following from: Not Given.
3-32 JOSET SHAW-WAW-NAY-SE, age 70, P.O. Harbor Springs.
3-32-1 Peter Shawnese, age 55, P.O. Harbor Springs, separated, see 3-28 & 63-33 & 34-32.
Wife 1st : Mary Shawnese, nee Shawwon, age 55, P.O. Cross Village.
Wife 2nd: Mary Ann (Waw-So) Shawnese, age 35, see 34-32.
3-32-1-1 Cornelius Shawnese, age 8, P.O. Tomah Wis.
3-32-1-2 Martha Shawnese, age 6, Harbor Springs.
3-32-1-3 Junis Shawnese, age 4.
3-32-1-4 Benedict Shawnese, age 2, born Apr 1907.
3-32-2 Tedmus Shawnese (male), age 45, P.O. Harbor Springs, no children.
3-32-3 Annie Pyant, age 36, P.O. Harbor Springs.
Husband: John Bryant, age 45, P.O. Harbor Springs, see 18-32.

Information following from: Not Given, Oct 27/08, Harbor Springs.
4-32 TERESA CHING-GO-BE-QUAY, dead, all children dead.
Note: She has grandchildren:
(1) Agnes Hamlin, age 18, seee 3-31, child of William Hamlin by ist wife who was grand child of 4-32.
(2) Mary Key-Way-Ke-Zhick wife of John Key-Way-Ke-Zhick is a grandchild.

Information following from: Not Given, Susan, Oct 27/08, Harbor Springs.
5-32 Pay-Me-Ke-Zhick-Way-Skung, dead.
5-32-1 Josephine (or Susan) Condon, age 56, P.O. Cloquet Minn.

Husband: Name not given, dead, no children.
5-32-2 Joseph Peck or Kokosh, age 55, P.O. Petoskey.
Wife 1st : Mary Peck, in Insane Asylem, see 7-26.
5-32-2-1 Elizabeth Wawso, see 48-33.
Wife 2nd: Name not given.
5-32-3 ~~Agatha~~ Harriet Aslin, age 51, P.O. Pt. St. Ignace Mich.
Husband: Pete Aslin, age 51, see 39-13.
5-32-3-1 Mary Julia Grondin, age 27, P.O. St. Ignace, no children.
5-32-3-2 Grace Margaret Plant, age 25, P.O. Mackinaw City, see 4-13.
5-32-3-3 Joe Aslin, age 17, P.O. St. Ignace.
5-32-3-4 Eva Aslin, age 15, P.O. St. Ignace.
5-32-3-5 William Aslin, age 14.
5-32-3-6 Bert Aslin, age 12.
5-32-3-7 Charles Aslin, age 10.
5-32-3-8 Sophia Aslin, age 6.
5-32-4 Peter Peck or Kokosh (Blind), age 49, P.O. Pt. St. Ignace Brutus Poor House, no family.
5-32-5 Jane Kniffin, in hospitalat Ann Arbor, no children.

Cloquet Minn
June 14th 1907

Mr Horace Durant
Petoskey, Mich.
Dear Sir:

Your letter of recent date to hand and same noted.

My parents names are Margaret Pay-Me-Ke-Zhick-Way-Skung and Harry Pay-Me-Ke-Zhick-Way-Skung.

There are five children in the Pay-Me-Ke-Zhick-Way-Skung family living namely. Joe, Pete, Harriett, Jane and Jusell or Josephine which is myself. I am 56 years of age and have no family of my own only an adopted daughter.

My father fought in the Civil War under the same name, that of Pay-Me-Ke-Zhick-Way-Skung.

The Chief Simon Kyigopenasay of Harbor Springs is my mother's first cousin and he with the residents of Harbor Springs can testify as to my indentity.

If I have not given you all the desired information, kindly inform me and I will be greatly obleyed.

Very sincerely
Josephine Condon

Information following from: Not Given.
6-32 AW-BE-NAW-BE, dead.

Wife: Name not given, dead.
6-32-1 Robert Abinaw, age 44, P.O. Harbor Springs.
Wife: Mary Abinaw, nee Kenozhemeig, age 40, see 35-28, no children.
6-32-2 Name not given, dead.
Wife: Margaret Abinaw, age 50, P.O. Harbor Springs, see 6-25
6-32-2-1 Paul Abinaw, see 6-28.
6-32-3 Name nor sex given, dead, no heirs.
6-32-4 Name nor sex given, dead, no heirs.
Child of wife of Abenaw 6-32:
6-32-5 Goosma Chingwa, age 60, P.O. Pellston, see 55-33

Information following from: Not Given, Oct 27/08, Harbor Springs.
7-32 PAUL EDO-WE-KE-ZHICK, dead.
Wife: Name not given, dead.
7-32-1 Name nor sex given, see 19-32.
7-32-2 Pete Edo-We-Ke-Zhick, dead.
Wife: Mary Edo-We-Ke-Zhick, age 34, P.O. Harbor Springs, see 9-~~25~~ 28.
7-32-3 Louis Edo-We-Ke-Zhick, dead, no children.
7-32-4 Madaline Edo-We-Ke-Zhick, P.O. Canada Manatolin Island, cannot trace.
7-32-4-1 Cecelia ~~Pelthia~~ Pielther.
7-32-5 Agatha Williams, age 43, P.O. Manistique.
Husband: John Williams or John O-Saw-Waw-Neme-Ke, age 45, P.O. Manistique, see 8-34.
7-32-5-1 Cecelia Williams, age 15.
7-32-5-2 Julius Williams, age 13.
7-32-5-3 Josephine Williams, age 11.

Information following from: Not Given.
8-32 SIMON KE-ZHE-GO-PE-NAY-SE, spelled now KIJIGUBENESE, age 71, P.O. Harbor Springs.
Wife: Name not given, dead.
8-32-1 Sarah Kijigubenese, age 44, P.O. Harbor Springs, no children.
8-32-2 Dan Ke-Zhe-Go-Pe-Nay-Se, age 41, P.O. Walpole Island.
Wife: Name not given, now lives with Gosmes Chingwaw, see 55-33.
8-32-2-1 Agnes Chingwa or Agnes Ke-Zhe-Go-Pe-Nay-Se, age 12, P.O. Harbor Springs.
8-32-3 Jane Bowen, age 30, P.O. Pellston.
Husband: George Bowen, white, dead.
8-32-3-1 John Bowen, age 8.
8-32-3-2 Julia Bowen, age 5.

8-32-4 Martin Ke-Zhe-Go-Pe-Nay-Se, dead.
Wife: Mary Ann Kiogima, age 38, P.O. Harbor Springs, 2nd husband Pian Kiogima age 41, see 25-20.
8-32-4-1 William Ke-Zhe-Go-Pe-Nay-Se, age 13, P.O. Harbor Springs.
8-32-4-2 Charles Ke-Zhe-Go-Pe-Nay-Se, age 9.
8-32-4-3 Mary Ann Ke-Zhe-Go-Pe-Nay-Se, age 10, died Feby 1908.
8-32-5 Name nor sex given, dead, no heirs.

Information following from: Not Given.
9-32 PETER MAG-GE-SE-TAY or PETER BIGFOOT, age 70, P.O. Harbor Springs.
Wife: Theresa Mag-Ge-Se-Tay, age 70.
9-32-1 Margaret, dead.
Husband: John Okedonquot, see 3-46.
9-32-2 Joe Mag-Ge-Se-Tay, died Dec 20/07, see 15-32.
9-32-3 Name nor sex given, dead, no heirs.
9-32-4 Name nor sex given, dead, no heirs.
9-32-5 Name nor sex given, dead, no heirs.

Information following from: Not Given, Oct 7/08.
10-32 NAW-GAW-NAW-SHE, dead.
Wife: Name not given, dead.
10-32-1 Joseph Naw-Gaw-Naw-She, see 30-32.
10-32-2 Margaret Chaw-Me, age 55, P.O. Cross Village.
Husband: Name not given, dead, see 20-20.
10-32-3 Andrew Naw-Gaw-Naw-She, age 57, P.O. Harbor Springs.
Wife 1st : Name not given, dead.
Wife 2nd: Margaret Naw-Gaw-Naw-She, nee Way-Day-She-Nay-Maw, age 40, P.O. Harbor Springs, see 4-28.
10-32-3-1 Samuel Naw-Gaw-Naw-She, age 33, P.O. Harbor Springs, not married.
10-32-4 Patrick Naw-Gaw-Naw-She, P.O. Goodheart, see 40-28.
Wife: Name not given.
10-32-4-1 Name nor sex given.
10-32-4-2 Name nor sex given.

Information following from: Not Given.
11-32 WILLIAM SAW-GE-MAW, dead.
Wife: Name not given, dead.
11-32-1 Name nor sex given, ~~dead~~, see 61-33
11-32-2 Name nor sex given, dead, no heirs.
11-32-3 Name nor sex given, dead, no heirs.

11-32-4 Name nor sex given, dead, no heirs.

Information following from: Not Given.

12-32 O-NAY-NAW-GOONSE or ALEXANDER, dead.

Wife: Name not given, dead.

12-32-1 Alex Nanagoonse, dead, on roll as 30-30.

Wife: Name not given, dead.

12-32-1-1 Theresa Cogmo or Kaogoma, age 38, P.O. Petoskey, see 9-40.

Husband: Alex Cogmo, see Kaogomo 100-22.

12-32-1-1-1 George Pewash, age 20, see 9-40.

12-32-1-1-2 Joe Pewash, age 18, see 9-40.

12-32-1-1-3 William Pewash, age 16, see 9-40.

12-32-1-1-4 Annie Cogmo, age 13, P.O. Mt. Pleas. Sch

12-32-1-2 Bonapart Alexander, age 48, P.O. Custer RFD #2.

12-32-1-3 Moses Alexander, age 34, P.O. ~~address unknown~~, see 29-59.

12-32-2 Name nor sex given, dead.

Spouse: Name not given, dead.

12-32-2-1 Mary Robinson, see 25-23.

12-32-2-2 Susan (Owner) Agosa, see 25-23.

12-32-2-3 David Owner, see 25-23.

12-32-3 Name nor sex given, dead.

Spouse: Name not given, dead.

12-32-2-1 Victoria Cooper, see 48-33.

12-32-2-2 Mary Ann Cooper, see 48-33.

12-32-2-3 Robert Wasson, see 48-33.

12-32-2-4 Catharine Blackbird, see 48-33.

12-32-2-5 Mary Wasson, see 48-33.

12-32-2-6 Veronica Wasson, see 48-33.

12-32-2-7 Wasson Wasson, see 48-33.

12-32-4 Christina, dead.

Husband: Name not given, dead.

12-32-4-1 Paul Taybyant, age 40, see 25-32.

12-32-5 John Mobis Nannagoonse, age 66, P.O .Harbor Springs.

Wife: Therese Nannagoonse, dead.

12-32-5-1 John Nannagoonse, age 25, P.O. Boyne City Mich, separated.

Wife: Caroline Nannagoonse, age 24, P.O. Beaver Island.

12-32-5-1-1 Agnes Nannagoonse, age 5.

12-32-5-1-2 Ellen Nannagoonse, age 3.

~~12-32-5-2 Ellen~~

12-32-6 Pete Alexander, age ~~40~~ 35, ~~Harb~~ Bradley Mich, see 2-50 & 2-57.

Information following from: Not Given.
13-32 MARY KEY-O-GE-MAW, dead.
13-32-1 David Francis, age 49, P.O. Horton's Bay, no married, no children.
13-32-2 Name nor sex given, dead.
Spouse: Name not given.
13-32-2-1 Peter Waw-Ka-Zoo, age 25, Carlise School.
13-32-2-2 William Waw-Ka-Zoo, age 20, P.O. Bay Shore.
13-32-2-3 Agnes Waw-Ka-Zoo, age 17, Cross Village, see 4-20.
13-32-3 Name nor sex given, dead.
Spouse: Name not given.
~~13-32-3-1 Agnes~~
13-32-4 Anatasia Assinaway, age 48, P.O. Goodheart, see 8-28.

Information following from: Not Given, Oct 27/08, Harbor Springs.
14-32 PAUL WASSO, dead.
Wife: Name not given, dead.
14-32-1 Name nor sex given, dead.
Spouse: Name not given.
14-32-1-1 Annie Assinaway, see 17-32.
14-32-1-2 William Pay-Mo-Say-Way or Bourassa, see 17-32.
14-32-2 Name nor sex given, dead.

Information following from: Not Given, Oct 6, Harbor Springs.
15-32 FRANCIS WAW-SO, dead.
Wife: Name not given, dead.
15-32-1 Name not given, dead.
Wife: Sophia Mag-Ge-Se-Tay, age 50, P.O. Harbor Springs.
Husband 1st: Name not given.
Husband 2nd: Joseph Mag-Ge-Se-Tay, died Dec 20, 1907, see 9-32 & 13-31.
15-32-1-1 Mary Annie Wasso #2, age 20, P.O. Harbor Springs
15-32-1-1-1 Mary Wasso, age 5.
15-32-2 Name nor sex given, dead, no children.
15-32-3 Julia Antoine, age 46, P.O. Bay Shore, ~~see 31-3~~, no children.
Husband: Louis Antoine, age 46, see 13-26 & 16-26.

Information following from: Not Given.
16-32 SIMON WASSO, all dead, no heirs.

Information following from: Not Given, Oct 20, Middle Village.
17-32 AUGST PAY-MO-SAY-WAY or BOURASSA, dead.
Wife: Name not given, dead.

17-32-1 William Pay-Mo-Say-Way or Bourassa, age 40, P.O. near Soo City or Bay Mills.
Wife: Elizabeth Graham, separated, see 16-28.
17-32-2 Annie Assinaway, age ~~42~~ 34, see 16-28.
Husband: Mathew Assinaway, age 42.
17-32-2-1 Paul Assinaway, age 9.
17-32-2-2 Henry Assinaway, born Jany 1908, 2nd roll.

Information following from: Not Given.
18-32 JOSEPH PAYANT, dead.
Wife: Name not given, dead.
18-32-1 John Payant, age 46, P.O. Harbor Springs, see 3-32.
Wife: Annie Payant, age 36, P.O. Harbor Springs.
18-32-1-1 Elizabeth Pyant, age 12, P.O. Harbor Springs.
18-32-2 Name nor sex given, dead, no heirs.

Information following from: Not Given.
19-32 AMABEL E-DO-WE-KE-ZHICK, dead.
Wife: Nancy Hoover, age 60, P.O. Harbor Springs.
19-32-1 Joe Ettawegeshik, age 44, P.O. Harbor Springs.
Wife: Agnes Ettawegeshik, nee Chingway, age 44, P.O. Harbor Springs, see 9-26.
19-32-1-1 Jennie Ettawegeshik, age 20, P.O. Harbor Springs.
19-32-1-2 William Ettawegeshik, age 17, P.O. Harbor Springs.
19-32-1-3 Fred Ettawegeshik, age 12, P.O. Harbor Springs.
19-32-1-4 Julia Ettawegeshik, age 9, P.O. Harbor Springs.
19-32-1-5 Emanuel Ettawegeshik, age 6.
19-32-2 John Ettawegeshik, age 42, P.O. Harbor Springs.
Wife: Julia Ettawegeshik, nee Naongabay, see 41-20.
19-32-2-1 Luisa Ettawegeshik, age 17, P.O. Chilocco Ind Sch.
19-32-3 Benedict Ettawegejig, age 39, see 9-28.
Wife: Mary (Wawbegakake) Ettawegejig, age 33.
19-32-3-1 Lacy Ettawegejig, age 10.
19-32-4 ~~Nancy Ellen~~

Information following from: Not Given.
20-32 PIUS O-WAW-TE-NIASH-CUM, dead.
Wife: Name not given, dead.
20-32-1 Mary Naskaw, age 52, see 26-46 & 6-31.
20-32-2 Joseph Norton #1, age 45, P.O. ~~Cheboygan~~ Brutus.
Wife: Angeline Norton, age 39, see 15-31.
20-32-2-1 Lizzie Norton, age 7.
20-32-2-2 Edward Norton, age 3.

Information following from: Not Given.

21-32 LOUIS SHAW-WAW-NE-QUOUM, now LOUIS KEYWAY, this man has been identified as Louis Keyway see next.

Information following from: Not Given, Oct 7, Harbor springs, No Number. Note: Louis Keyway is an Ottawa Indian by the testimony of the oldest & most reliable Indians of Harbor Springs, although his name does not appear on 1870 roll. The old Chief Simon, exhibited an old list of numbersof this band on which is the name of Louis Kiway or Keway. HB Durant Spl Agt, Oct 7, 1908

??-32 LOUIS KEYWAY, age 73, P.O. Harbor Springs (21-32).
Wife: Eliza Keyway, age 62, P.O. Harbor Springs.
21-32-1 Lizzie Shaw-Waw-Non-Quot, age 47, P.O. Traverse City.
Husband: Isaac Shaw-Waw-Non-Quot, age 60, see 29-31.
21-32-2 Edmund ~~Keyway~~ Keway, age 43, P.O. Harbor Springs, not married, lived with:
Sophia Nawahquagezhick, age 50, P.O. Alden Mich, see 16-46
21-32-2-1 Rosie Keway, age 17, P.O. Alden Mich.
21-32-3 Emma Gilbault, age 35, P.O. Harbor Springs 288 29th St now in Chicago ~~526 Wabash Ave~~ in ~~rear~~, separated.
Husband: Gaerrett Gilbault, age 44, P.O. Harbor Springs, see 31-32.
21-32-3-1 Frank Gilbault, age 23, P.O. Harbor Springs.
21-32-3-2 Edward Gilbault, age 21, P.O. Haskell Inst. Lawrence.
21-32-3-3 Clarence Gilbault, age 20, P.O. Mt. Pleasant Sch.
21-32-3-4 Henry Gilbault, age 19, died Feby 1908.
21-32-3-5 Jessie Gilbault, age16, P.O. Harbor Springs, with Grandmother.
~~21-32-3-6 Bessie Gilbault, age.~~
21-32-4 Rosie Cola, age 32, P.O. Harbor Springs.
Husband: Howard Cole, white.
21-32-4-1 Cecelia Cole, age 12, P.O. Harbor Springs.
21-32-5 Agnes Callis, age 30, P.O. Chicago 526 Wabash in rear, no children.
Husband: John D. Callis, white.

June 23rd 1909

Mr. H. Durant; In regards to the Ottawa Mich. Indians, I am a decendent of the Tribe- and as you are seeking information will assist you as much as lays in my power. My Father's name Lewis Kewi – Harbor Springs Mich. his age would be 73 yrs. He died Feb, 21 1909. Mother's name Liza Benequoi from
^maiden

now of Harbor Springs Omena Mich. I have 3 sisters. Making 4 girls. 1 Brother living. Our names are Lizzie Shawnanaquot. Nee Kewi . Emma
*Omena Mich^*
Gilbow nee Kewi. Rose Cole nee Kewi harbor Springs Mich. Agnes Callis
^2951 Armour Av Chi Ill
526 Wabash Av(rear) Chi. Ill. Brother's name Edmund Kewi Harbor Springs Mich. Hoping this will assist you some & hoping to hear from you again; I remain.
Respe= Mrs. Agnes Callis nee Kewi 536 Rear Wabash Av. Chi. Ill.

Information following from: Not Given, Oct 28/08.
22-32 SUSAN MICK-SE-WAY-WAY, dead, mother of 8-32.
22-32-1 Name nor sex given, dead, no heirs.

Information following from: Not Given, Oct 28/08, Harbor Springs.
23-32 ME-SHE-KAY, dead.
Wife: Name not given, dead.
23-32-1 Name nor sex given, see 45-33.
23-32-2 Bazil Me-She-Kay, age 56, P.O. Harbor Springs, for wife and children see 39-32.

Information following from: Not Given.
24-32 LOUIS KEY-WAY-E-SAY, dead.
Wife: Name not given, dead.
24-32-1 Margaret, dead.
24-32-1-1 Louis Cooper, see 48-33.
24-32-1-2 Victoria Petoskey, see 48-33.
24-32-2 Name nor sex given, dead, no heirs.

Information following from: Not Given, Oct 7/08.
25-32 ANTOINE FAY-BYE-YAW, dead.
Wife: Mary Ann Taybyant, age 90, P.O. Harbor Springs.
25-32-1 Name nor sex given, dead.
25-32-1-1 Paul Taybyant, age 40, P.O. Cross Soo in Canada, cannot find him Durant.
25-32-2 Name nor sex given, dead.
25-32-2-1 Angeline Tapkeah, age 30, see 23-28.
Husband: Sam Tapkeah, age 33.
25-32-2-1-1 Jennie.
25-32-2-1-2 John, born Mch 8/08.

Information following from: Not Given, Oct 28/08, Harbor Springs.
26-32 JOSEPH WY-YEA-SHAY, all dead, no heirs.

Information following from: Not Given, Oct 7, Harbor Springs.

27-32 JOHN B. KEY-WAY-QUOUM, dead.
Wife: Mary Key-Way-Quoum, age 82, P.O. Harbor Springs.
27-32-1 Samuel Keway, see 69-33.
Wife: Name not given, dead.
27-32-1-1 ~~William Andrew Keway, age 38~~.
27-32-1-2 ~~Andrew Keway~~ dead.
27-32-2 Threse Keway, dead.
Husband: Francis Shaw-Waw-Non-Quot, age 60, see 43-32.
27-32-3 Enos Keway, dead.
Wife: Name not given, dead.
27-32-3-1 Agatha Keway, age 35, P.O. Harbor Springs, husband dead, no children.
27-32-4 Gabriel Keway, dead.
Wife: Philaman Mick-Saw-Bay, P.O. Middle Village, 2nd husband William, see 19-28.
27-32-5 Simon Keway, age 50, P.O. Middle Village Goodheart.
Wife: Harriet Keway, nee Kosequot, age 43, P.O. Goodheart.
27-32-5-1 Clara Keway, age 24, P.O. Goodheart.
27-32-5-2 Mary Ann Keway, age 22.
Husband: Moses Shaw-Waw-Non-Quot, see 43-32.
27-32-5-3 Agnes Keway, age 20.
27-32-5-4 Mary Keway Petoskey, age 18.
Husband: William Petoskey, see 19-28.
27-32-5-5 Hattie Keway, age 16.
27-32-5-6 Lizzie Keway, age 14.
27-32-5-7 Charles Keway, age 10.
27-32-5-8 Edward Keway, age 8.
27-32-5-9 Rosie Keway, age 4.
27-32-5-10 Samuel Keway, age 2.
27-32-5-11 William Keway, born 4, 1908 2nd roll.
27-32-5-12 Joseph Keway, age 6, died June 8, 1907 1st roll.
27-32-6 Benjamin Keway #2, age 40, P.O. Boyne City Camp #11.
Wife: Angeline Keway, age 36, see 30-42.
27-32-6-1 Julius Keway, age 17.
27-32-7 Name nor sex given, dead, no heirs.
27-32-8 Name nor sex given, dead, no heirs.

Information following from: Not Given, Oct 28/08, Harbor Springs.
28-32 JOHN STEVENS, dead.
28-32-1 Rosie Stephens, age 38, P.O. Harbor Springs, see 41-32.

Information following from: Not Given.
29-32 KIN-NE-QUAY, dead.
29-32-1 Name nor sex given, dead.
Spouse: Name not given.

29-32-1 Peter Taylor, age 55, P.O. Bay Shore.
Wife: Thresa Taylor, nee John, age 55, see 4-23.
29-32-1-1 Josie Taylor, age 20, P.O. Bay Shore.
29-32-1-2 Lizzie Taylor, age 13, P.O. Bay Shore.
29-32-1-3 Louisa Taylor, age 11, P.O. Bay Shore.
29-32-2 Alexander Cooper, age 51, P.O. Bay Shore.
Wife: Josie Cooper, age 38, died May 27, 1907, see 3-40.
29-32-2-1 Mitchell Cooper, age 13, P.O. Bay Shore.
29-32-2-2 Francis Cooper, age 11, P.O. Bay Shore.
29-32-2-3 Alex. A. Cooper, age 9, P.O. Bay Shore.
29-32-3 Edmund Taylor, age 40, P.O. Bay Shore.
Wife: Name not given, dead.
29-32-3-1 Nellie Taylor Webster, age 14, P.O. Mt Pleasant Sch, see 7-41.

Information following from: Not Given, Oct 7/08.
30-32 JOSEPH NAW-GAW-NAW-SHE or NAGANASHE, age 70, P.O. Harbor Springs RFD #.
Wife: Name not given, dead.
30-32-1 Thresa Gasco, age 42, P.O. Harbor Springs.
Husband: Amos Gasco, age 49, white.
30-32-1-1 Ida Gasco, age 22, P.O. Harbor Springs.
30-32-1-2 Louis Gasco, age 16, P.O. Harbor Springs.
30-32-1-3 Joseph Gasco, age 14, P.O. Harbor Springs.
30-32-1-4 Sarah Gasco, age 12, P.O. Harbor Springs.
30-32-1-5 Albert Gasco, age 10, P.O. Harbor Springs.
30-32-1-6 Fred Gasco, age 7, P.O. Harbor Springs.
30-32-1-7 Alex Gasco, age 3, P.O. Harbor Springs.
30-32-2 Anna O-Taw-Naw-Zhe, age 33, P.O. Boyne City Camp 11.
Husband: Alphonse O-Taw-Naw-Zhe, age 35, see 50-29.
30-32-3 Bozelle Naganashe, age 30, P.O. Harbor Springs.
Wife: Aggie Naganashe, nee Shaw-Naw-Se-Gay, age 20, grand daughter of 3-31.
30-32-3-1 George Naganashe, age 7 months, born Mch 1908.
30-32-4 Mary Naogama or King, age 23, P.O. Middle Village Goodheart.
Husband: Francis King, 26, see 33-34.
30-32-4-1 Clarence King, born Apr 16, 1908, died Apr 19/08 2nd roll.
30-32-5 John Naganashe, age 20, Harbor Springs, not married.

Information following from: Not Given.
31-32 MRS. MARY GILBAULT, age 72, P.O. Harbor Springs.
Husband: Name not given, dead.

31-32-1 Alice, dead.

Husband: Name not given.

31-32-1-1 John Hubbin, age 26, P.O. Petoskey, wife is white, no children.

31-32-1-2 Bert Hubbins, age 23, P.O. Traverse City, single.

31-32-2 Alex Gilbault, age 50, P.O. Harbor Springs, saloon keeper.

Wife: Name not given, white, no children.

31-32-3 Jane, dead.

Husband: Name not given, dead.

31-32-3-1 Frank Wells Jr., age 20, P.O. Milwaukee, wife white, no children.

31-32-4 James, dead, single no children.

31-32-5 John Gilbault, age 48, P.O. Chicago Ill 10016 Ewing Ave.

Wife: Name not given, white.

31-32-5-1 Earl Gilbault age 17.

31-32-6 Jarrett Gilbault, age 46, P.O. Harbor Springs, separated.

Wife: Emma Keway Gilbault, P.O. 288 29th St Chicago.

31-32-6-1 Frank Gilbault, age 23, P.O. Harbor Springs.

31-32-6-2 Eddie Gilbault, age 21, P.O. Haskell Institute.

31-32-6-3 Clarence Gilbault, age 19, P.O. Mt. Pleasant Ind. Sch.

31-32-6-4 Henry Gilbault, age 17, died Mar 17, 1908

31-32-6-5 Jessie Gilbault, age 15, P.O. Harbor Springs.

31-32-7 Oliver Gilbault, age 40, P.O. Harbor Springs, wife white, no children.

31-32-8 Norman Gilbault, age 35, P.O. Milwaukee Wis 526 Greenbush St.

Wife: Name not given, white.

31-32-8-1 Margaret Gilbault, age 3.

31-32-9 Pearl Gilbault Hutchinson, age 27, P.O. Petoskey, husband white, no children.

Note: Very little Indian blood in this family. Harbor Springs Oct 28/08 Tuttle. Jarrett Gilbault says his wife deserted him and the children and that he is and has cared for them and wants their shares to be paid to him. Oct 28/08 Tuttle.

So. Chicago , Ill
June 11th 1909

Horace B. Durant

Dear Sir:

In reply to yours of the 9th inst. Will state that parents names are Alex. and Mary Guilbault, sister Pearl and brothers Alex., Garrett, Oliver and Norman. Sone Earl O. Gulbault of 545 Hanover St. Milwaukee, Wis. Is 17 years and may be able to give you the information about Frank Wells Jr. as he was in that City awhile ago. My age is 43 or 44.

Yours Respt.
John E. Guibault
10016 Ewing Ave.

Milwaukee Wis.
Jun 11-09

Mr H. B. Durant.
Petoskey Mich.
Dear Sir:

I rec'd your letter inqurying for the names and ages of my brothers and sisters. I am sorry to say that I cant give their ages. You see I have been away from home so long that I dout remember there ages any more.

I will give you the names of those how is living.
There are six ~~due~~ dead, and dout suppose you want their names.
Alexander Guilbault. father.
Mrs Mary Guilbault. mother.

Brothers and sisters

Mrs. J. R. Hutchsion Petoskey age 28.
Garrett Guilbault. Harbor Spgs.
Oliver Guibault " "
Alex Guilbault " "
John Guilbault So. Chicago, Ill.
And my self Norman Guilbault age 37 and a little daughter Margaret age 33 months
This is all I can do in regards to their names and ages.

Yours truly
Norman Guilbault.
625 Greenbush st.
Milwaukee Wis.

Information following from: Not Given.
32-32 JOSEPH CHURCH or JOE CHING-GWA, dead.
Wife: Josette Ching-Gwa., also known as Josette Church, age 60, P.O. Harbor Springs, now married to John St. Onge.
32-32-1 Lucy Kahgajiwan, called Rosie, age 42, P.O. Pellston
Husband: John Kahgajiwan, grandson of 43-28.
32-32-1-1 William Kahgajiwan, age 21 P.O. Pellston.
32-32-1-2 Moses Kahgajiwan, age 14.
32-32-1-3 Levi Kahgajiwan, age 12.
32-32-1-4 Charles Kahgajiwan, age 10.
32-32-1-5 Alvina Kahgajiwan, age 8.
32-32-1-6 Agatha Kahgajiwan, age 6.
32-32-1-7 Nancy Kahgajiwan, age 4 months, died Aug 1908.
N.B. a nephew – Ed. Thompson (off), age 36, P.O. Harbor Springs, son of Margarite Pouillot: wife: Christine Shomin, see 79-21,

separated.
Josette; She says that her mother was an Indian and her father a Frenchman: her mother's name was Josette Pouillot, nee Larioirre who was a daughter of Jos. Larivirre & Margaret Tetabanokwe, an Indian. Her grandmother was an Ind.grd tribe cannot be identified. HB Durant Spl Agt

Information following from: Not Given.
33-32 CHRISTIAN, dead, no heirs, no such person can be remembered by any old members of this band now at Harbor Springs, HB Durant Spl Agt Oct 28/08 Harbor Springs Mich.

Information following from: Not Given.
34-32 JUNIUS WASSO or JONAS WASSON, age 62, P.O. Harbor Springs RFD. The 4 enrolled with this number were: (1) himself (Junius); his (3) mother (Julia) now dead; (3) his sister (now dead) & another sister (dead) leaving no heirs.
Wife: Name not given, dead.
34-32-1 Mary Ann Wasson ~~dead~~, age 32, P.O. Harbor Springs, living with but not married:
Pete Shaw-Waw-Nay-Se, age 58, P.O. Harbor Springs, see 63-33, he has another wife living: Mary Shaw-Waw, age 50, P.O. Cross Village, see 3-28.
34-32-1-1 Cornelius Shaw-Waw-Nay-Se, age 9.
34-32-1-2 Martha Nancy Shaw-Waw-Nay-Se, age 5.
34-32-1-3 Jonas Shaw-Waw-Nay-Se, age 3.
34-32-1-4 Benedict Shaw-Waw-Nay-Se, age 2.
34-32-2 Justina Hamlin, age 30, P.O. Brutus Mich.
Husband: Moses Hamlin, age 31, P.O. Brutus, see 40-15.
34-32-2-1 Charles Hamlin.
34-32-2-2 Howard Hamlin.

Information following from: Not Given.
35-32 MICHAEL SAW-WAW-NE-QUOUM, dead.
Wife: Name not given, dead.
35-32-1 Benjamin Keway #1, age 60, P.O. Beaver Island St. James.
Wife: Louisa Keway, see 12-59, separated, no children by this marriage.
35-32-2 Daughter, name not given, dead.
Husband: Name not given, dead, son of 18-31.
35-32-2-1 Sarah Kosequot, age 39, see 18-31 for children.
35-32-2-2 Henry Mixcenene, age 36, see 18-31.
35-32-2-3 John Mixcenene, see 18-31.
35-32-2-4 Mary Porkman, see 18-31.
35-32-2-5 Christina Shaw-Waw-Naw-Se-Gay, see 18-31.

35-32-2-6 Hattie Nanegon, see 18-31.
35-32-2-7 Barbara Mixcenene, see 18-31.
35-32-3 Louis Keway, see 21-32

Information following from: Not Given.
36-32 JOSEPH O-MWAW-TE-NAISH-CUM, dead.
Wife: Name not given, dead.
36-32-1 Pius Norton, age 46, P.O. Boyne City.
Wife: Name not given, dead.
36-32-1-1 Joe Norton #2, age 8, see 8-25.
36-32-2 William Norton, age 38, Sturgeon Bay Mich.
Wife 1st: Eliza Norton, now Mosco, age 42, P.O. ~~Cheboygan~~ Pellston Mich, see 2-31, separated.
Wife 2nd: Annie Kiogoma Norton, see 23-20.
36-32-2-1 William Norton Jr., age 13, P.O. Beaver Island, enroll with family at the Island, as he has not lived with father since infancy. Ind. Name of this boy is "Ke-Zhick" see 10-34 & 26-34.

Information following from: Not Given, Oct 24/08, Burt Lake.
37-32 PETER WASSO, dead.
Wife: Name not given, dead.
37-32-1 Paul Wasso, age 48, P.O. Aloaha Mich, see 54-33.
Wife: Jane Wasso, age 38.
37-32-1 Louisa Wasso, age 20.

Information following from: Not Given.
38-32 KE-SIS-WAW-BAY, dead.
Wife: Name not given, dead.
38-32-1 Name nor sex given, dead.
Spouse: Name not given.
38-32-1-1 Daughter, name not given, dead.
Husband: Francis Aish-Ke-Baw-Gosh, see 24-28.
38-32-1-1-1 Lizzie Aish-Ke-Baw-Gosh, age 10, see 24-28.
38-32-1-1-2 Rose Aish-Ke-Baw-Gosh, age 7, see 24-28.

Information following from: Not Given.
39-32 THERESA MWAW-KE-WE-NAW, age 74, P.O. Harbor Springs.
39-32-1 Mike Williams, age 53, P.O. Harbor Springs.
Wife: Sophia Williams, age 48, P.O. Harbor Springs, see 5-25.
39-32-1-1 John Williams, age 29, P.O. Harbor Springs.
39-32-1-2 Thomas Williams, age 25, in N. O Army in Philippines.

39-32-1-3 Paul Williams, age 23, P.O. Harbor Springs.
39-32-1-4 Wallace Williams, age 18, P.O. Harbor Springs.
39-32-1-5 Mary Williams, age 15, P.O. Harbor Springs.

39-32-2 Cynthia Meshekey, age 45, P.O. Harbor Springs.
Husband 1st : Shomin, dead.
39-32-2-1 Joseph Shomin, age 28, P.O. Harbor Springs.
Wife: Louisa O-Saw-Waw-Naw-Quot, age 21, no Children, see 50-29.
39-32-2-2 William Shomin, age 21, P.O. Harbor Springs.
39-32-2-3 Paul Shomin, age 16, P.O. Harbor Springs.
39-32-2-4 Lena Shomin, age 15, P.O. Harbor Springs.
~~39-32-2-5 Clarence Shomin~~
Husband 2nd: Bazil Meshekay, age 56, P.O. Harbor Springs, see 23-32.
23-32-2-1 Mary Mishekey, age 30, P.O. 11310 So. Park Ave. Pullman Ill. (Chicago), known as Sister Assumpta, by Bazil's 1st wife.
23-32-2-2 William Mishekey, age 25, P.O. Harbor Springs, not married, by Bazil's 1st wife.
23-32-2-3 James, age 22, P.O. Harbor Springs, by Bazil's 1st wife.
23-32-2-4 Louis, age 18, P.O. Harbor Springs, by Bazil's 1st wife.
23-32-2-5 Hattie, age 16, P.O. Harbor Springs, by Bazil's 1st wife.
23-32-2-6 or 39-32-2-5 Clarence, age 9, P.O. Harbor Springs, by Bazil's 2nd wife Cynthia.

Information following from: Not Given.
40-32 A-TAW-ZHE-WAY-GE-ZHE-GO-QUAY, all dead, no heirs.

Information following from: Not Given, Oct 7/08.
41-32 MARY ANN KEY-WAY-QUOUM #2, age 70, P.O. Harbor Springs.
Husband: Peter ~~Philander~~ Fridlander, age 72, white.
41-32-1 James Cooper, age 52, see 48-33.
41-32-2 William Fridlander, age 45, P.O. Petoskey.
Wife: Jennie Fridlander, nee Blackbird, age 39, see 24 -26, no children.
41-32-3 Name nor sex given, dead, no children.
41-32-4 Rosie Stephen, age 38, P.O. Harbor Springs, see 28-32.
Husband: ~~lived with~~ Name not given.
41-32-4-1 David O'conner, age 18, P.O. Mt Pleasant Sch.
41-32-4-2 Clarence O'conner, age 16, P.O. Mt Pleasant Sch.
41-32-4-3 Charles O'conner, age 11, P.O. Harbor Springs Sch.

Information following from: Not Given.
42-32 LEON TUSH-QUAY-AW-BAW-NO, dead, no heirs

Information following from: Not Given.
43-32 FRANCIS SHAW-WAW-NON-QUOT, age 60, P.O. Burt Lake Mich.
Wife: Name not given, dead.
43-32-1 Rosie Bwanishing, age 41, P.O. Cross Village, see 4-20.
43-32-2 Mary Kagigebitang, age 33, see 98-22.
43-32-3 Moses Shaw-Waw-Non-Quot, age 21, Aloha Mich.
Wife: Mary Ann Shaw-Waw-Non-Quot, age 22, see 27-32, no children.

Information following from: Not Given.
44-33 CASPER QUAY-CHE-OH, spelled QUACHIO, dead.
Wife: Mary Quay-Che-Oh, age 56, P.O. Harbor Springs.
44-33-1 Name nor sex given, dead, no heirs.
44-33 -2 Mary Pfister, age 34, P.O. Harbor Springs.
Husband: Ed. Pfister, white.
44-33-2-1 Ida Pfister, age 10.
44-33-2-2 Clements Pfister, age 8.
44-33-2-3 Hattie Pfister, age 5.
44-33-3 Jane Quachio, age 24, P.O. Harbor Springs, not married.
44-33-3-1 Albert H. Haighe, age 7, P.O. Harbor Springs.
44-33-3-2 Mary A. Miksawby, age 2.

Information following from: Not Given.
45-33 DOMINICK ME-SHE-KAY, age 65, P.O. Harbor Springs.
Wife 1st: Name not given, dead.
Wife 2nd: Christina Kijigoenasey, dead.
45-33-1 Name nor sex given, dead, no heirs.
45-33-2 Joseph Kijigoenasey, age 36, P.O. Goodheart, see 19-28.
45-33-3 Paul Kijigoenasey, age 19, P.O. Tomah Ind Sch Wis, not married.
45-33-4 William Me-She-Kay, dead.
Wife: Threse Me-She-Kay, age 26, P.O. Cross Village, 2nd husband ~~Joe Shaw~~ John Shawanabin, age 30, see 17-28 & 50-29.
45-33-4-1 Clara Me-She-Kay, age 7.
45-33-4-2 Joe Me-She-Kay, age 4.

Information following from: Rosie Wright.
46-33 MRS. HENRY GRAVEREAT, dead.
Husband: Dead.
46-33-1 Rosine Wright, age 73, P.O. Harbor Springs.

Husband 1st: Name not given, white, dead.
Husband 2nd: Name not given, white, dead.
46-33-1-1 Robert Wright, age 40, P.O. Green Bay Wis, Editor of Review.
Wife: Name not given, white.
46-33-1-1-1 Robert Wright Jr., age 15, P.O. Green Bay Wis.
46-33-1-1-2 Lloyd Wright, age 13.
46-33-1-1-3 Beulah Wright, age 11.
46-33-1-1-4 George Wright, age 9.
46-33-1-2 John Wright, age 30, P.O. Harbor Springs, not married.

Information following from: Not Given.
47-33 ANDREW J. BLACKBIRD, age 90, died Sept 7/08.
Wife: Lizzie Blackbird, white, P.O. Harbor Springs.
47-33-1 William E. Blackbird, age 40, P.O. Harbor Springs, single.
47-33-2 Fred Blackbird, age 38, P.O. ~~Peto~~ Harbor Springs, see 48-33.
47-33-3 Bert Blackbird, age 35, P.O. Harbor Springs, single.
47-33-4 Nettie (Blackbird) Schofield, age 31, P.O. San Francisco Calif., husband white, no children.

Information following from: Not Given.
48-33 MICHAEL WAWSO, dead.
Wife: Name not given, dead.
48-33-1 Victoria Cooper, age 40, P.O. Harbor Springs.
Husband 1st: Name not given, dead.
48-33-1-1 William Keshegowe, age 20, P.O. Harbor Springs.
48-33-1-2 Joseph Keshegowe, age 15, P.O. Harbor Springs.
48-33-1-3 Madeline Keshegowe, age 9, P.O. Harbor Springs.
48-33-1-4 Mike Keshegowe, age 7.
Husband 2nd: James Cooper, age 52, P.O. Harbor Springs, see 41-32, children by his 1st wife Margaret Keways who is now dead.
41-32-1-1 or 48-33-1-5 Victoria (Cooper) Petoskey #2, age 29,
P.O. Harbor Springs.
Husband: John Petoskey, separated.
41-31-1-1-1 John Petoskey Jr., age 7 see 50-21.
41-31-1-1-2 Margaret Petoskey, age 3, see 50-21.
41-32-1-2 or 48-33-1-6 Louis Cooper, age 27, P.O. Harbor Springs, not married.
48-33-2 Mary Ann Kiogima, age 38, see 25-20.
48-33-3 Robert Wawso, age 34, P.O. Alba Mich.
Wife: Elizabeth Wawso, age 30, daughter of Joseph Peck,

see 5-32, no children.
48-33-4 Catharine (Wasson) Blackbird, age 30, Petoskey, separated.
Husband: Fred Blackbird, see 47-33.
48-33-4-1 Clara Blackbird, age 9, P.O. Tomah Ind Sch Wis.
48-33-4-2 Alice Blackbird, age 7, P.O. Tomah Ind Sch Wis.
48-33-4-3 Infant Blackbird, born Apr/08.
48-33-5 Mary Wasso #1, age 28, P.O. Harbor Springs, single.
48-33-6 Veronica Wasso, age 25, Harbor Springs, not married.
48-33-7 Annie Wasso, age 22, Harbor Springs.

Information following from: Not Given.
49-33 KE-ZHE-GO-QUAY, dead.
49-33-1 Name nor sex given, dead.
Spouse: Name not given.
49-33-1-1 Mary Pfister, see 44-33.
49-33-1-2 Jane Quachio, age 24, see 44-33.
49-33-1 Name nor sex given, dead, no heirs.
49-33-1 Name nor sex given, dead, no heirs.

Information following from: Not Given.
50-33 JOHN B. PAY-BAW-MAW-SHE, dead.
Wife: Name not given.
50-33-1 Name nor sex given, dead.
Note: Chiefs & headmen of this band never heard of this name HB Durant Spl Agt Oct 28/08 Harbor Springs.

Information following from: Not Given.
51-33 JOHN FLINT, age 60, P.O. Harbor Springs.
Wife: Mary Ann Flint, age 52, Canadian Indian.
51-33-1 Name nor sex given, dead, no heirs.
51-33-2 Louisa Flint, age 15, P.O. Harbor Springs Sch.

Information following from: Not Given.
52-33 O-SAW-WAW-NE-ME-KE, dead.
Wife: Name not given, dead.
52-33-1 Son, name not given, dead.
Wife: Name not given, dead.
52-33-1-1 John O-Saw-Waw-Ne-Me-Ke, age 24, P.O. Goodheart, single.

Information following from: Not Given, Oct 28/08.
53-33 ANGELIQUE AW-SAY-GON, dead, grandmother of 14-32 et als.
53-33-1 Name nor sex given, dead, no heirs.
53-33-2 Name nor sex given, dead, no heirs.

Information following from: Not Given, Oct 24/08, Burt Lake.

54-33 THOMAS O-NAW-TE-NAISH-CUM or THOMAS NORTON, age 67, P.O. Brutus.

Wife 1st : Name not given, dead.

Wife 2nd: Susan Norton, age 67, see 22-31.

54-33-1 Jane Wasso, age 38, P.O. Aloaha Mich.

Husband: Paul Wasson, age 48, see 37-32.

54-33-1-1 Louisa Wasson, age 10, Aloaha Mich, single.

Information following from: Not Given.

55-33 MRS. ALIXSE PELLOTTE, dead.

55-33-1 Elizabeth Chingwa, nee Pellotte, age 60, P.O. Harbor Springs, separated.

Husband: Goosma Chingwa, age 60, P.O. Pellston, see 8-32, ½ brother of Robert Abinaw, see 6-32.

55-33-1-1 George Clayton, white, adopted, age 30, P.O. Harbor Springs.

Wife: Julia Clayton, white, no children.

Information following from: Not Given, Oct 28.

56-33 WILLIAM CHING-GWAW, dead.

Wife: Name not given.

56-33-1 Name nor sex given, see 53-29.

Information following from: Not Given.

57-33 NAW-WE-KE-ZHE-QUOUM, dead.

57-33-1 Name nor sex given, dead, no heirs.

Information following from: Not Given.

58-33 MARY PE-TWAY-WE-TUNE, dead, wife of 1-31..

Information following from: Not Given.

59-33 MRS. ALIXSE MCGALPHIN, age 65, P.O. Harbor Springs.

59-33-1 Rose Furguson, age 44, P.O. Petoskey 5112 Michigan St.

Husband: Name not given, white.

59-33-1-1 Rex Furgusdon, age 24, P.O. Kalamazoo 120 S. Edward St.

Wife: Name not given, white, no children.

59-33-1-2 Myrtle Owens, ag e22, P.O. ~~Seattle Wash~~ Petoskey 512 Michigan St.

Husband: Name not given, white.

59-33-1-2-1 George Owens, age 5.

59-33-1-2-2 Carl Owens, age 4.

59-33-1-2-3 Earl Owens, age 15 months.

59-33-1-3 George Furguson, age 19, P.O. Petoskey

59-33-2 William McGalphin #1, age 40, P.O. Harbor Springs, see 3-28.
59-33-3 Alex McGalphin, age 38, P.O. Pellston Mich.
Wife: Name not given, separated, see 22-20.
59-33-3-1 Harvey Shomin, age 7, see 22-20, his right name should be McGalphin.
59-33-4 Mary Metniv, age 36, P.O. Pellston.
Husband: Name not given, white.
59-33-4-1 Frank Metniv, age 18.
59-33-4-2 Edward Metniv, age 11.
59-33-4-3 Margaret Metniv, age 5.
59-33-5 George McGalphin, age 34, P.O. Cross Village.
Wife: Name not given, white.
59-33-5-1 William McGalphin #2, age 14, P.O. Harbor Springs, goes by name of William Flynn.

Petoskey Jun 3 1909

Dear Sir
My Daughter came home 2 months ago and will make her home with me here in Petoskey she is alone to care for 3 little boys of hers the first is George 5 years old the next is 4 years and his name Carl and the third one 15 months old his name Earl.
I have 2 sons George Ferguson 19 make his home with me and Rexford Ferguson 25 years lives in Kalamazoo Mich 120 Edward St.
Dear Sir
I thank you very much for letting me no about Mr. Myrtle Owen our street No is 512 Michigan St

Yours truly
Mrs Rose Ferguson
Petoskey Mich

Information following from: Not Given.
60-33 ANGELIQUE BUSHAY, dead, no heirs.

Information following from: Not Given, Oct 7/08.
61-33 DOMINICK SAW-GE-MAW, age 70, P.O. Harbor Springs.
Wife: Catharine Saw-Ge-Maw, ~~dead~~, separated, age 65, P.O. Starr City, daughter of 1-62.

Information following from: Not Given.
62-33 PAW-QUAD-GE-NIN-NE, dead, no heirs.

Information following from: Not Given.
63-33 KE-ZHE-GO-YAW-SE-NO-QUAY, dead.
63-33-1 Name not given.

Wife: Joset Shaw-Waw-Nay-Se, age 70, see 3-32.
63-33-1-1 Pete Shawnese, see 3-32 & 34-32 & 3-28.

Information following from: Not Given.
64-33 CHARLES KE-ZHE-GO-PE-NAY-SE, age 68, Harbor Springs, dead, no heirs.

Information following from: Not Given.
65-33 MARY PE-MO-SAY-WAY-QUAY, dead, no heirs.

Information following from: Not Given.
66-33 WAW-BE-NO-Way, dead, no heirs.

Information following from: Not Given.
67-33 JOSEPH MAW-DWAINCE, dead, heirs by themselves on othe cards.

Information following from: Not Given.
68-33 AGNES KE-CHE-GO-PE-NAY-SE, all dead, no heirs.

Information following from: Not Given.
69-33 SAMUEL KEY-WAY, dead.
Wife: Mary Paul Key-Way, age 59, P.O. Harbor Springs, sister of 21-42.
69-33-1 William Keyway, age 38, P.O. Harbor Springs.
Wife: Katie Keyway, nee ~~Bashanena~~ Pay-She-Nin-Ne, age 34, P.O. Harbor Springs, see 5-34.
69-33-1-1 William Keyway Jr., age 4.
69-33-1-2 Andrew Keyway, age 3.
69-33-1-3 Eva Keyway, age 1, born Aug 6, 1907.

Information following from: Not Given.
70-33 MARGARET SAW-GE-MAW, dead, no heirs.

Information following from: Not Given.
71-33 JOSEPH SHAW-WAW_NAY-SE, dead, no heirs.

Pages 34 & 35
Beaver Island Band
Chief PAY-ZHICK-WAY-WE-DUNG

Information following from: Not Given.
1-34 PAY-ZHICK-WAY-WE-DUNG, dead.
Wife: Mary Ann Pay-Zhick-Way-We-Dong, age 90, P.O. Beaver Island.
1-34-1 Antoine Pean, age 65, P.O. ~~Beaver~~ Garden Island St. James

Mich.
Wife: Mrs Antoine Pean, see 11-41.
1-34-1-1 Agatha Comstalk, age 45, P.O. High Island St. James, see 13-34.
1-34-1-2 Lucy Comstalk, age 43, see 13-34.
1-34-1-3 Daughter, name not given.
Husband: George Wah-Be-Geneece, age 55, see 22-11.
1-34-1-3-1 Mitchell Wah-Begeneece, age 5, see 22-11.
1-34-1-4 John Pean, age 30, P.O. Garden Island, single.
1-34-1-5 James Pean, age 40, P.O. Garden Island.
Wife: Name not given, dead.
1-34-1-5-1 Jacob Pean, age 23, P.O. Garden Island.
1-34-1-5-2 Eliza Pean, age 7, P.O. Garden Island.
1-34-2 Peter Pean, same as 21-34, wife dead.
1-34-3 Mary Francis, age 48, P.O. Sutton's Bay, see 5-40.

Information following from: Not Given.
2-34 WAY-GE-WE-WE-GWON, dead.
Wife: Name not given, dead.
2-34-1 Mitchell Way-Ge-We-We-Gwon or Wagner, age 52, P.O. ~~Namah~~ St. Jacques Mich.
Wife: Margaret Way-Ge-We-We-Gwon or Wagner, nee Bourasaw, age 52, see 66-35.
2-34-1-1 Mary Beaver.
Husband: Name not given, see 4-34.
2-34-2 Paul Way-Ge-We-We-Gwon, dead.
Wife: Name not given, dead.
2-34-2-1 Paul Way-Ge-We-We-Gwon or Wagner, age 16, P.O. Mt. Pleasant Sch., see 8-37.
2-34-2-2 Therese Way-Ge-We-We-Gwon or Wagner, age 14, P.O. Mt. Pleasant Sch., see 8-37.
2-34-3 Charles Way-Ge-We-We-Gwon, dead.
Wife: Name not given, dead.
2-34-3-1 Mary Ann Feathers, age 27, for husband and children see 22-34.
2-34-4 David Way-Ge-We-We-Gwon or Wagner, age 18, P.O. Namah.
2-34-5 John Way-Ge-We-We-Gwon, age 16, P.O. St. Jacques.

Information following from: Not Given.
3-34 NAY-WE-GE-GWAW-NAY-AW-SHE, dead.
Wife: Mary Nanega, age 82, P.O. High Island.
3-34-1 Mary Baptiste, age 56, P.O. High Island.
Husband: John Baptiste, age 60, P.O. High Island, see 38-34.
3-34-1-1 Male, would not give his name. Late: William

Baptiste, age 39, P.O. High Island, no wife or child.
3-34-2 Mary Ann Thomas, age 42, see 36-34.
3-34-3 Catharine Ne-Be-Ne-Gwaw-Nay-Be, age 50, P.O. High Island.
Husband: Caspar Ne-Be-Ne-Gwaw-Nay-Be, known as Caspar Napow or Nanpaw, P.O. High Island, see 6-34.
3-34-3-1 Peter Ne-Be-Ne-Gwaw-Nay-Be or Napow or Nanpaw, age 17.
3-34-4 Peter Nanega, age 48, P.O. High Island.
Wife: Name not given, dead.
3-34-4-1 George Nanega, age 22, P.O. High Island.
Wife: Hattie Nanega, age 22, see 18-31, no children.
3-34-4-2 Madeline Nanega, age 13.
3-34-4-3 Peter Nanega Jr., age 9.

Information following from: Joe & Mary Mashequeto, Peter John, Joe Beaver et als., Dec 4, Dec 5, Dec 6, St Jacques.
4-34 PAW-ZHE-DAW-NAW-QUOT, dead.
Wife: Catharine Penaysequay, age 80, P.O. Namah Mich.
4-34-1 Peter John or Peter Paw-Zhe-Daw-Naw-Quot, age 56, P.O. Namah.
Wife: Harriet John, age 40, see 39-34.
4-34-1-1 Angeline Williams, age 31.
Husband: Norman Williams, age 40, see 12-37.
4-34-1-1-1 Mary Williams, age 14.
4-34-1-1-2 Sophia Williams, age 12.
4-34-1-1-3 Norman Williams, age 10.
4-34-1-1-4 Jennie Williams, age 6.
4-34-2 Mary Mashequeto, age 50, P.O. Namah Mich.
Husband 1st: Name not given, dead.
4-34-2-1 Peter Tenesis or Tennyson, age 35, P.O. Namah Mich, single, has one eye, also known as Pete Moses #2.
4-34-2-2 Margaret, dead.
Husband: Name not given, white.
4-34-2-2-1 ~~Addy Froman~~ Adolph Romer, age 20, P.O. Mt. Pleasant School.
4-34-2-3 Mary, dead.
Husband: Joe Kezhick Sr., age 38, see 28-30.
4-34-2-3-1 Joe Kezhick, age 12, P.O. Mt. Pleasant School.
Husband 2nd: Augustus Moses, dead.
4-34-2-4 William Moses, age 29, P.O. Namah Mich.
Wife: Madeline Moses, nee Saganeck, age 19, P.O. Namah Mich, no children, see 23-34.
4-34-2-5 Lizzie Lucia, Age 23, P.O. Namah Mich.

Husband: Name not given, white.
4-34-2-5-1 Leo Lucia, age 1, born Nov. 1907.
4-34-2-6 Ellen Oga, age 21, P.O. Namah Mich.
Husband: Edward Oga, age 32, see 3-36.
4-34-2-6-1 David Oga, age 7.
4-34-2-6-2 Albert Oga, age 5, died Oct. 1908.
4-34-2-6-3 Amos Oga, age 3.
4-34-2-6-4 Stella Oga, age 2.
4-34-2-6-5 George Oga, born Aug 20, 1908.
4-34-2-7 Josephine Moses Elsley, age 19, died Sept 1908, no children.
Husband: Cyrus Elsley, white, left his wife before her death, pay share to mother.
4-34-2-8 Benjamin Moses, age 19.
Husband 3rd: Joe Mashequeto, age 55, see 105-22.
4-34-2-9 Mary Mashequeto Jr., age 15, P.O. Mt. Pleasant Sch.
4-34-2-10 Catherine Mashequeto, age 21, died June 1908, see 105-22, daughter by Jos Mashequeto former wife.
4-34-3 Therese Osawogwan, age 45, P.O. Hessell Mackinaw Co. Mich.
Husband: Joe Osawogwan, age 45, P.O. Hessell Mackinaw Co. Mich, see 5-17.
4-34-3-1 Joe Osawogwan Jr., age 31, P.O. Hessell Mackinaw Co. Mich, single.
4-34-3-2 John Osawogwan, age 29, P.O. Hessell Mackinaw Co. Mich, single.
4-34-3-3 William Osawogwan, age 27.
Wife: Ellen Osawogwan, see 4-8.
4-34-3-3-1 Mary Osawogwan, dead.
4-34-3-4 Margaret Osawogwan, age 25, Hessell Mich.
Husband: Joe Wawbekineece, see 22-11.
4-34-3-4-1 Daisy Wawbekineece, age 13.
4-34-3-4-2 Agnes Wawbekineece, age 10.
4-34-3-4-3 William Wawbekineece, age 8.
4-34-3-4-4 Eddie Wawbekineece, age 7.
4-34-3-5 Frank Osawogwan, age 23, single.
4-34-3-6 Kate Osawogwan, age 21.
4-34-3-7 Mike Osawogwan, age 19.
4-34-3-8 Mary Osawogwan, age 17.
4-34-4 Daughter, name not given, dead.
Husband: Name not given, dead, ist wife was 3rd child of 8-36.
4-34-4-1 Joseph Nadeaw, age 36, P.O. Garden Bay Mich.
Wife: Name not given, white.
4-34-4-1-1 Peter Nadeaw, age 6.
4-34-5 Margaret Saw-Gaw-Taw-Gun, age 44, P.O. Namah Mich.

Husband 1st: ______ Lambert, see 52-35.
4-34-5-1 George Lambert, see 52-35.
Wife: Mary Ann Lambert, see 17-9.
Husband 2nd: John Saw-Gaw-Taw-Gun, age 44, see 4-37, no children.

4-34-6 Joe Beaver, age 48, P.O. Namah Mich.
Wife 1st: Name not given, dead.
Wife 2nd: Mary Beaver, nee Way-Ge-Ne-We-Gwon, age 18, see 2-34.
4-34-6-1 Joseph Beaver Jr., age 17, P.O. Namah.

4-34-7 Mary Ann Moses, age 35, P.O. Namah Mich.
Husband: Pete Moses, age 39, see 9-34.
4-34-7-1 Dan Moses, age 19.
4-34-7-2 Jacob Moses, age 17.
4-34-7-3 Sophia Moses, age 15.
4-34-7-4 Mary Moses, age 13.
4-34-7-5 Isaac Moses, age 11.
4-34-7-6 Moses Moses, age 9.
4-34-7-7 Angeline Moses, age 7.
4-34-7-8 Marian Moses, age 5.
4-34-7-9 Elizabeth Moses, age 2.
4-34-7-10 Frank Moses, age 1, born Sept. 1907.

4-34-8 Moses Beaver, age 44, P.O. Namah Mich.
Wife: Lizzie Beaver, age 33, P.O. Namah Mich.
4-34-8-1 Joe M Beaver, age 11.
4-34-8-2 Peter Beaver, age 8.
4-34-8-3 Susan Beaver, age 5.
4-34-8-4 Nancy Beaver, age 3.
4-34-8-5 Eva Beaver, born Nov/07.

4-34-9 Elizabeth Mishigand, age 36, P.O. Namah Mich.
Husband: Doty Mishigand, age 42, said to belong to Mackinaw Band: his father & 2 brothers live at Barker River Mich.
4-34-9-1 Isaac Mishigand, age 20, single.
4-34-9-2 Maggie Mishigand, age 17.
4-34-9-3 Julian Mishigand, age 14.
4-34-9-4 Mary Ann Mishigand, age 11.
4-34-9-5 Bessie Mishigand, age 8.
4-34-9-6 Louis Mishigand, age 6.
4-34-9-7 Pete Mishigand, born Apr 7/07.

Apr. 18
Rapid River Mich

Dear Sir

I now take the Pleasure of sending you the Names of my five children and also the names of my wife and her sisters and brothers they are all half breed Indians the children of Susan Wabenigwn. There mother got her Payment from the Government in Escanaba and there Grandfather Wahenigwn and also they are Member of the Ottawa Tribe.

Yours Truly
Moses B. Beaver

2

here is the Names of my childrens and these age
Mr Joseph M. Beaver 12 yrs
Mr Peter Beaver 9
Miss Susan Beaver 6
Miss Nancy Beaver 4
Miss Eva Beaver 11 months old
Mrs. Lizzie Beaver age 28
Nephews of Wabenigwn
Mr. Geo. Shaskey age 22
Miss Josie Shaskey 19
Mr. Joseph Shaskey 16
Our Post office Address is
Rapid River P.O. Delta Co. Mich

Cant trace wife's family nor brothers & sisters
Letter to him
May 1/09 D

May 4/09
Rapid River Mich

Dear Sir.

I take a Pleaseure in calling your attention That I made mistake in mentioning the names of there Relations that Received there Payment in 1870.

Mabenigwn Father Mr. Jim Williams his there Grand Father who received his Pay at Escanabe and also his daughter Susan Williams. Who is now Mrs Shorkey. Is mother of my wife.

2

and there Parents are Dead there Father was a English and also uncle Norman Williams Received his Payment: sister and brothers of my as Following.
Mr. Geo. Shaskey age 22
Joseph Shaskey 16
Lusie Shaskey 18
I trust that you will accept the names

yours Truly
Moses Beaver

Information following from: Head of Family, Nov 21/08, Beaver Island.
5-34 ~~JOHN~~ STEPHEN PAY-SHE-NIN-NE, age 75, P.O. Beaver Island.
Wife: Threse Pashenine, age 68, P.O. Beaver Island, see 20-34.
5-34-1 Mary (Bomaway) Nishigepinese or Bird, age 36, P.O. Beaver Island.
Husband: Louis Bird or Nishigepenese, age 40, died April 1908, see 13-28.
5-34-1-1 Angeline Bird or Bomaway or Andrews, age 18, P.O. ~~Mt. Pleasant Sch~~ or Beaver Island.
5-34-1-2 Agnes Andrews, age 14.
5-34-1-3 Clara (Bird) Andrews, age 11, Mt. Pleas. Sch.
5-34-1-4 Amelia (Bird) Andrews, age 3.
5-34-2 Katie Keway, see 69-33.
5-34-3 Elizabeth Paysheninne, age 20, P.O.Beaver Island Garden Island St. James, not married.
5-34-4 Name nor sex given, dead, no heirs.
5-34-5 Name nor sex given, dead, no heirs.
5-34-6 Name nor sex given, dead, no heirs.

Information following from: Not Given, Beaver Island & St. Jacques.
6-34 NE-BE-NE-GWAW-NAY-BE, dead.
Wife: Name not given, dead.
6-34-1 Casper Ne-Be-Ne-Gwaw-Nay-Be, known as Casper Napon, age 45, see 3-34.
6-34-2 Pete Ne-Be-Ne-Gwaw-Nay-Be or Pete Nanpaw, age 37, P.O. Namah Mich, see 22-34.
6-34-3 Simon Ne-Be-Ne-Gwaw-Nay-Be, died Nov 1907.
Wife: Name not given, dead.
6-34-3-1 Sophia Ne-Be-Ne-Gwaw-Nay-Be, age 14, died Mch 1908.

Information following from: Not Given.
7-34 MAY-YAW-WE-KE-ZHICK, all dead, no heirs.

Information following from: Not Given.
8-34 O-SAW-WAW-NEME-KE, dead.
Wife: Name not given.
8-34-1 ~~Enos~~ Ignace O-Saw-Waw-Neme-Ke, age 71, P.O.~~Manistique~~ Ogantz Mich, see 63-35.
Wife: Name not given.
8-34-1-1 Pete Neiass, age 42, see 63-35 & 52-35.
8-34-1-2 George Neiass, age 40, see 63-35 & 15-37.
8-34-2 John Williams, age 45, P.O. In Jail at Manistique Mich,

see 7-32.

Information following from: Not Given, Oct 6, Harbor Springs, Dec 5/08, St Jacques.

9-34 KAY-TE-NAW-BE-ME, dead.
Wife: Name not given, dead.
9-34-1 Isabella Chingwashe, age 45, P.O. Harbor Springs, see 1-62
9-34-2 Frank Shaw-Way-Ne-Ge-Zhick, know as Frank Moses, age 43,
P.O. Allenville Mich.
Wife: Sarah Shaw-Way-Ne-Ge-Zhick, nee Shaw-Naw-Se-Gay, age 30, see 8-31.
9-34-3 Peter Kay-To-Naw-Be-Me, or Peter Moses, age 39, P.O. St. ~~Jacq~~ Nahma Mich.
Wife: Mary Ann Moses, age 35, P.O. Nahma Mich, see 4-34.
9-34-4 William Moses or William Kay-To-Naw-Be-Me.
9-34-5 Ben Moses or Ben Kay-To-Naw-Be-Me.

Information following from: Not Given, Nov 18, Petoskey, Nov 21, Beaver Island.

10-34 AW-NE-WAY-NE-MO, or Peter ~~Ike~~ High, dead.
Wife: Josie High, age 80, died Mch 1907.
10-34-1 Joe High or Joe Pete, dead.
Wife 1st: Name not given, dead, see 26-34 for children.
Wife 2nd: Name not given, dead.
10-34-1-1 Mary Blackbird or Mary Thomas, age 30, P.O. High
Island.
Husband: Pete Thomas or Pete Blackbird, age 25, P.O. High Island, see 36-34.
10-34-1-1-1 Mary Thomas, age 8.
10-34-1-1-2 Thomas Thomas.
10-34-1-2 Sarah Wah-Say-Ke-Zhick, see 21-34.
10-34-1-3 Joe Pete, see 26-34.
10-34-2 Margaret Anthony, age 50, P.O. High Island St. James, separated, pay minor shares to mother.
Husband: William Anthony or William Kinnewawby, age 65, P.O. ~~Namah Mich~~ St. Ignace, see 13-36.
10-34-1-1 John or Jake Anthony, age 23, P.O. High Island.
Wife: Sarah Anthony, nee Cornstalk or Kay-Bay-O-Say, see 13-34.
10-34-1-1-1 Jacob Anthony, age 7.
10-34-1-1-2 Daniel Anthony, age 3.
10-34-1-1-3 Moses Anthony, age 1, 2nd roll born Nov/07.

10-34-1-2 William Anthony, age 19, P.O. High Island.
10-34-1-3 Rosie (Anthony) McKinney, age 16, P.O. High Island.
Husband: Pete McKinney, white.
10-34-1-3-1 Susan McKinney, born June 1908 2nd roll.
10-34-1-4 Catharine Anthony, age 7, P.O. High Island.
10-34-3 Eliza Chingwaw, age 48, P.O. Petoskey, see 9-26.
10-34-4 Mary Palmer, age 46, P.O. High Island.
Husband: Name not given, white.
10-34-4-1 Name not given, dead.
10-34-5 ~~John~~ Georg ~~Ike~~ High, age 35, ~~Beaver Island~~ Manistique Mich.
Wife: Eliza (Olliver) High, age 35, see 16-34.
10-34-5-1 Peter ~~Ike~~ High, age 12, P.O. Manistique.
10-34-5-2 Joseph ~~Ike~~ High, age 8.
10-34-5-3 John ~~Ike~~ High, age 6.
10-34-5-4 George ~~Ike~~ High, age 2.

Information following from: Not Given.
11-34 WAY-WIN-DAW-BAW-NO-QUAY, dead.
Husband: Charles Bourassa, age 88, died Jany 14/08.
11-34-1 Madeline Neff, age 44, P.O. Alanson RFD #1.
Husband: Name not given, white.
11-34-1-1 Angeline Howell, age 26, P.O. Alanson Mich.
Husband: Name not given, white.
11-34-1-1-1 Mary Howell, age 7.
11-34-1-1-2 Ethel Howell, age 2.
11-34-1-1-3 Gordon Howell, age 3, died June 1908.
11-34-1-2 Ella West, age 23, P.O. ~~All~~ Arlinton Washington.
Husband: Name not given, white.
11-34-1-2-1 Lorraine West, age5, Arlington Washington.
11-34-1-3 Frank Neff, age 21, P.O. Alanson RFD #1.
11-34-1-4 Charles Neff, age 18, P.O. Alanson RFD #1.
11-34-1-5 Myron Neff, age 14, P.O. Alanson RFD #1.
11-34-1-6 John Neff, age 8, P.O. Alanson RFD #1.
11-34-2 Name nor sex given, dead, no heirs.
11-34-3 Name nor sex given, dead, no heirs.
~~Note: Louis La Sage of St. Ignace, 44 claims that his grandmother lived at Beaver Island & her name was Way-Win-Daw-Baw-No-Quay.~~

Information following from: Not Given.
12-34 MOSES, dead.
Wife: Name not given, dead.

12-34-1 Name not given, dead.
Husband: Name not given, dead.
12-34-1-1 Eliza Awdayneme, age 40, P.O. Bark River near Esanaba, see 14-34.
12-34-1-2 Josett Sagonock, age 29.
Husband: Gabriel Sagonock, age 40, see 23-34.

Information following from: Not Given.

13-34 KAY-BAY-O-SAY or CORNSTALK, dead.
Wife: Name not given, dead.
13-34-1 Name nor sex given, dead.
13-34-2 Daniel Cornstalk or Daniel Kay-Bay-O-Say, age 55, P.O. High Island St. James.
Wife: Agatha Cornstalk, age 45, see 1-34.
13-34-2-1 Sarah Anthony, age 22, see 10-34.
13-34-2-2 Nancy Wabininkee, age 19, see 2-41.
13-34-2-3 Alex Cornstalk, age 8, P.O. High Island.
13-34-2-4 Catharine Cornstalk, age 2.
13-34-3 Frank Cornstalk, age 50, P.O. Garden Island.
Note: Frank Cornstalk is not an own child but an Indian of this tribe & was on roll & takes the name of the head of this sheet. HB Durant Spl Agt.
Wife: Lucy Cornstalk, age 43, see 1-34.
13-34-3-1 Agatha ~~Vansan~~ Vincent, age 25, P.O. St. James.
Husband: ~~Francis~~ white.
13-34-3-1-1 Louis Vincent, age 6.
13-34-3-1-2 Albert Vincent, age 4.
13-34-3-1-3 Frank Vincent, age 2.
13-34-3-2 Francis Cornstlak, age 15.

Sr. James Garden Island Mich.

May 3rd__09

Horace B. Durant
Special U.S. Indian Agent
Petoskey Mich

Dear Sir.

Your letter of the 26th duly received asking the ages of my three children.

The ages are as follows
Louis Vincent 6 years old.
Albert Vincent 4 years old.
Francis Vincent 2 years old.

Hope they will be ~~pbut~~ properly enrolled on the Ottawa & Chippewa pay roll.

over

Yours Truly
Kate Vincent or Gatha Vincent in Indian.

Information following from: Not Given.
14-34 JOHN AW-DAY-NE-ME #1, dead, died July 1908.
Wife: Name not given, dead.
14-34-1 John Aw-Day-Ne-Me, age 45, P.O. Beaver Island St. James.
Wife: Eliza Aw-Day-Ne-Me, age 40, see 12-34.
14-34-1-1 John Aw-Day-Ne-Me, age Jr., age 16.
14-34-1-2 Catharine Wah-Be-Nin-Ke, age 22, P.O. Beaver Island, see ~~2-43~~.
Husband: Peter Wah-Be-Nin-Ke, age 23, see 2-41.
14-34-1-2-1 Annie Wah-Be-Nin-Ke, age 5.
14-34-1-2-2 Mary Wah-Be-Nin-Ke, age 2.
14-34-1-2-3 Amos Wah-Be-Nin-Ke, born Sept 1908, Too Late.
14-34-2 Pete Aw-Day-Ne-Me, died May 16, 1908, no wife or children.

Information following from: Not Given.
15-34 AW-NAW-QUOT-O-QUAY, all dead, no heirs.

Information following from: Not Given.
16-34 WAW-SAISH-CUM, dead.
Wife: Name not given, dead.
16-34-1 Joe She-No-Din or Bundy White, age 45, P.O. Beaver Island.
Wife: Mary She-No-Din, , age 53, see 12-46, no children.
16-34-2 Louis She-No-Din, age 54, P.O. Beaver Island, no wife or children.
16-34-3 Mary Ann Alliver, age 63, P.O. High Island, separeated.
Husband: Joe Olliver, now has another wife, see 30-42.
16-34-3-1 William Oliver, age 42, P.O. High Island.
Wife: Name not given, dead.
16-34-3-1-1 Sophia Oliver, age 22, P.O. High Island, single.
16-34-3-1-2 Mary Oliver, age 19, P.O. High Island.
16-34-3-2 Joe Oliver Jr., age 38, P.O. Charlevoix, see 6-23 & 30-42.
16-34-3-3 Eliza Oliver High, age 35, P.O. Manistique.
Husband: George High, see 10-34.

Information following from: Not Given.
17-34 KEY-NO-GWAW-GAW-WAY-QUAY, dead.
17-34-1 Mary Ann Aw-Day-Ne-Me, age 57, P.O. Petoskey, not married.

17-34-1-1 Agatha O-Saw-Waw-Ne-Me-Ke, age 32, P.O. Petoskey, single.

17-34-1-2 Enos Graham, age 30, P.O. Detroit Mich, mother knows nothing about his family, said to be married & has children & lives in Wapole Island. Found him at Wapole Island Canada he & children do not draw from Canadian Govt. wife does. Durant.

Wife: Name not given, Canadian Indian.

17-34-1-2-1 Joseph Graham, age 8.

17-34-1-2-2 Simpson Graham, age 6.

17-34-2 Frank Williams, age 74, P.O. Harbor Springs, see 19-36.

17-34-3 Joseph Aw-Day-Ne-Me, dead, see 24-34.

17-34-4 Jesse Aw-Day-Ne-Me, as Waw-Be-Kake in 1870, age 60, P.O. Namah Mich (North shore), see 67-35.

Information following from: Not Given, Nov 21/08, Beaver Island.

18-34 KIN-NE-WE-GE-ZHE-GO-QUAY, dead.

18-34-1 Joe, dead.

Wife: Name not given, dead.

18-34-1-1 Mary Nineece, age 25, P.O. High Island, separated.

Husband: Mike Nineece, St. James Beaver Island, Canadian Indian, now husband of Nancy Pontiac, see 5-58.

18-34-1-1-1 Name not given, age 2.

18-34-2 Mitchell, dead, no heirs.

Information following from: Not Given, Nov 21/08, Beaver Island.

19-34 WE-TAW-MAY-SAW, dead.

Wife: Name not given, dead.

19-34-1 Name not given, dead.

Husband: Name not given, dead.

19-34-1-1 Peter Manitou, age 37 45, P.O. Garden Island St. James Beaver Island.

Wife 1st: Name not given, dead, children dead also.

Wife 2nd: Madline Manitou, see 21-34.

19-34-1-1-1 Pete Manitou, age 15, died Aug 1908.

19-34-2 Name nor sex given, dead, no heirs.

Information following from: Not Given.

20-34 SHAY-GO-NAY-BE, dead.

Wife: Name not given, dead.

20-34-1 Therese Pay-She-Nin-E, age 68, P.O. Beaver Island, see 5-34.

20-34-2 Louis Shay-Go-Nay-Be, age 62, went to Canada about 20 years ago across the Sault Ste. Marie, see ~~18~~2-3.

20-34-3 Name not given, this child went to Canada about 20 years ago.

Information following from: Not Given.

21-34 PETER SHAW-WAW-NON-GAY-O-SAY or PETER PEAN, dead, see 1-34.

Wife: Name not given, dead.

21-34-1 Name nor sex given, dead, no heirs.

21-34-2 Name nor sex given, dead, no heirs.

21-34-3 Madaline Manitou, age ~~38~~ 45, P.O. Garden Island.

Husband 1st : Wah-Say-Ke-Zhick, dead.

21-34-1-1 George Wah-Say-Ke-Zhick, age 20, P.O. Garden Island.

Wife: Sarah Wah-Say-Ke-Zhick, age 26, see 10-34 & 26-34.

21-34-1-1-1 Esther Wah-Say-Ke-Zhick, age 2.

21-34-1-2 Eno Wah-Say-Ke-Zhick, age18, P.O. Garden Island, single.

21-34-1-3 William Wah-Say-Ke-Zhick, age 15, P.O. Garden Island.

21-34-1-4 James Wah-Say-Ke-Zhick, age 12, P.O. Garden Island.

Husband 2nd: Pete Manitou, age ~~37~~ 45, see 19-34.

21-34-4 Christine Shaw-Waw-Non-Gay-O-Say, age 30, P.O. Garden Island, single.

Information following from: Sarah Feathers, Dec 5/08, St. Jacques Mich.

22-34 WAY-SHE-GWAW-NAY, dead.

Wife: ~~E-E-Tig~~ Sarah Way-She-Gwaw-Nay or Sarah Feathers, age 70, P.O. Namah.

22-34-1 Daughter, name not given, dead, no heirs.

22-34-2 Daughter, name not given, dead, no heirs.

22-34-3 Joe Feathers, age 32, P.O. St. Jacques Mich, see 11-31.

Wife: Eliza Feathers, age 22, P.O. St. Jacques Mich, see 11-31.

22-34-3-1 Francis Feathers, age 5.

22-34-3-2 Julius Feathers, age 3.

22-34-3-3 Walter Feathers, born Jany 21/08

22-34-4 Gabriel Feathers, age 26, P.O. St. Jocques.

Wife: Mary Ann Feathers, age 27, P.O. St. Jocques.

22-34-4-1 Ella Feathers, age 3.

22-34-4-2 Alice Feathers, born Dec 1907, 2nd roll.

22-34-5 Amos Feathers, age15.

22-34-6 Agnes (Feathers) Naupaw, age30.

Husband: Pete Naupaw, age 37, see 6-34.
22-34-6-1 Mary Naupaw, age 11.

Information following from: Not Given.
23-34 SAY-SAY-GO-NAW-NAW-QUOT, dead.
Wife: Name not given, dead.
23-34-1 Name not given, dead.
Wife: Name not given, dead.
23-34-1-1 Thomas Sagonock, age 25, dead, no heirs.
23-34-1-2 Madeline Saganock or Madeline Moses, age 19, P.O. Namah, see 4-34 & 37-34.
23-34-2 Gabriel Saganock, age 40, P.O. Beaver Island St. James.
Wife: Josette Saganock, age 29, see 12-34.
23-34-2-1 James Saganock, age 19, P.O. Beaver Island
23-34-2-2 Joseph Saganock, age, 17, P.O. Beaver Island.
23-34-2-3 William Saganock, age 16.
23-34-2-4 Enos Saganock, age 13.
23-34-2-5 Stephen Saganock, age 11.
23-34-2-6 Eliza Saganock, age 9.
23-34-2-7 Elizabeth Saganock, age 7.
23-34-2-8 Annie Saganock, age 5.
23-34-3 Name nor sex given, dead, no heirs.

Information following from: Not Given.
24-34 JOSEPH AW-DAY-NE-ME, married a widow and 3 children, all dead, no heirs.

Information following from: Not Given.
25-34 SAY-SAY-GAW-NAW-QUO-UM, dead.
Wife: Name not given, lives in Cross Village & so do children &, as all in that place are recorded their names must be enrolled, but the Beaver Island people do not remember the names they now go by, Durant.

Information following from: Not Given.
26-34 PAY-BAW-MWAY-WAY, dead.
Wife: Name not given, dead.
26-34-1 Therese, dead.
Husband: John Smith, white.
26-34-1-1 Name not given, dead.
Husband: Joe Pete, dead, see 10-34.
26-34-1-1-1 Sarah Wah-Sa-Ke-Zhick, age 26, P.O. Garden Island St. James.
Husband: George Wah-Sa-Ke-Zhick, age 26, P.O. Garden Island, see 21-34.

26-34-1-1-1-1 Esther Wah-Sa-Ke-Zhick.
26-34-1-1-2 Joe Pete or Joe Pe-Nay-Se-Way-Ke-
Zhick,
age 13, P.O. Beaver Island, see 36-32 & 10-34.
26-34-1-2 John Smith Jr. or John Wah-Be-Ne-Ke, age 25,
address unknown, see 12-45.
Wife: Caroline, for children see 12-45 & pay share to mother.
26-34-2 Name nor sex given, dead, no heirs.
26-34-3 Name nor sex given, dead, no heirs.

Information following from: Not Given.
27-34 No Notes.

Information following from: Not Given.
28-34 No Notes.

Information following from: Not Given.
29-34 No Notes.

Information following from: Not Given.
30-34 No Notes.

Information following from: Not Given.
31-34 No Notes.

Information following from: Not Given.
32-34 KAW-ZEE, dead.
Wife: Name not given, dead.
32-34-1 Name not given, dead.
Wife: Name not given, dead.
32-34-1-1 John Quay-Ke-Gwance, age 29, P.O. Petoskey, single.

Information following from: Simon Ke-Zhe-Go-Pe-Nay-Se, Dec 28/08, Harbor Springs.
33-34 O-GE-DAW-CAW-MIG, dead.
Wife: Name not given, dead.
33-34-1 Daughter, name not given, dead.
33-34-1-1 Francis King, ag e26, P.O. Goodheart.
Wife: Mary King, nee Naganashe, see 30-32.

Information following from: Not Given.
34-34 No Notes.

Information following from: Not Given.
35-34 No Notes.

Information following from: Not Given.
36-34 NAW-GAW-NE-GWAN, or THOMAS BLACKBIRD,
age 66, P.O. High Island St. James Beaver Island.
Wife: Name not given, dead.
36-34-1 William Thomas, age 39, P.O. High Island Mich.
Wife: Mary Ann Thomas, nee Nanega, age 42.
36-34-1-1 Name nor sex given, dead.
36-34-2 Peter Thomas, age 25, P.O. High Island.
Wife: Mary Thomas #1, nee Pete, age 30, see 10-34.
36-34-2-1 Mary Thomas #2, age 8.
36-34-2-2 Thomas Thomas, age 3.
36-34-3 Mary Thomas ~~Antoine~~ Blackbird, age 29, P.O. High Island, no children.

Information following from: Not Given.
37-34 JOHN ME-SHE-BE-SHE-WAY, dead.
Wife: Julia Me-She-Be-She-Way, age 50, P.O. Cross Village.
37-34-1 Name nor sex given, dead.
37-34-1-1 ~~Lucy~~ Madeline Saganock, age ~~14~~ 19, P.O. ~~Beaver Island~~ Namah Mich.
Husband: William Moses, age 29, P.O. Namah, see 23-34 & 4-34.
37-34-2 Peter Me-She-Be-She-Way known as & spelled as Kin-Aw-Be-Ke-Say, age 35, P.O. Cross Village, not married

Information following from: Not Given.
38-34 JOHN BAPTISTE, age 60, P.O. High Island.
Wife: Mary Baptiste, age 56, see 3-34.
38-34-1 William Baptiste, age 39, P.O. High Island, wife & child dead.

Information following from: Not Given.
39-34 AW-GAW-DO, dead.
39-34-1 Harriet Johns, age 40, see 4-34.
39-34-2 Mary Ann Pay-She-Nine, age 47, see 42-34.

Information following from: Not Given.
40-34 No Notes.

Information following from: Not Given.
41-34 No Notes.

Information following from: John Pay-She-Nine & Catharine Jacob, Dec 4/08, St Jacques, Nov 21/08, Beaver Island.

42-34 TAW-CAW-MAW-NAW-QUOT or JOHN PAY-SHE-NINNE, age 61, P.O.Namah.

Wife: Mary Ann Pay-She-Nine, age 47, see 39-34.

42-34-1 Christina Pay-She-Nine, age 28, P.O.Namah, single.

Sister:

??-34 Catharine (Pay-She-Nine) Jacobs, age 48, P.O. Namah, sister of 5-34.

Husband: John Jacobs, age 47, P.O. Namah, a Wisconsin Indian, off.

??-34-1 Mary Ann Moses, see 51-35, by 1st husband.

??-34-2 John Way-Saw, age 30, P.O. Garden Island St. James Beaver Island, ~~see sheet no number attach~~.

Wife: Name not given, dead.

??-34-2-1 Joseph Way-Saw, age 7, P.O. Garden Island St. James Beaver Island.

??-34-2-2 George Way-Saw, age 3, P.O. Garden Island St. James Beaver Island.

Information following from: Not Given.

43-34 No Notes.

Information following from: Not Given.

44-35 No Notes.

Information following from: Not Given.

45-35 SHAW-WAW-NAW-SE-GAY-QUAY, all dead, no heirs.

Information following from: Not Given.

46-35 No Notes.

Information following from: Not Given.

47-35 PAY-SHE-GO-PE-NAY-SE-QUAY, dead, no heirs.

Information following from: Not Given.

48-35 O-CHEW-WON, dead, no heirs

Information following from: Not Given.

49-35 NE-SAW-WAY-WAY, dead, no heirs.

Information following from: Not Given.

50-35 WAY-SHE-NOW, all dead, no heirs.

Information following from: Not Given. Nov 21/08, Beaver Island.

51-35 SIMON O-SAW-WAW-NE-ME-KE, dead.

Wife: Mary Lambert O-Saw-Waw-Ne-M-Ke, age 65, died Feby 1908, has children by 1st husband who is dead.

51-35-1 Madeline Kin-Waw-Be-Ke-Say, age 35, see 68-35.
Husband: Paul Kin-Waw-Be-Ke-Say, see 68-35.

51-35-2 Ellen O-Saw-Waw-Ne-Me-Ke Hartwick, age 19, P.O. ~~Namah Namah Mich~~ Martin Bay Mich, ~~do not know her married name~~.
Husband: David Hartwick, age 22, see 12-37, no children.

51-35-3 Lucy O-Saw-Waw-Ne-Me-Ke, age 17, P.O. High Island

Children of Mary Lambert, deceased, by her 1st husband:

51-35-4 Pe-To-Wa-Ke-Zhick, age 45, P.O. Namah Mich, right name ~~unknown~~ John Moses.
Wife: Eliza Moses, age 33.
51-35-4-1 Frank Moses, age 12.

51-35-5 Swasha Moses,age 28, P.O. Namah.
Wife: Mary Ann Moses, age 22, P.O. Namah, see 42-34 & 51-35, no children.

Information following from: Not Given, Dec 5/08, St. Jacques.

52-35 GEORGE LAMBERT, dead.
Wife 1st: Name not given, dead.

52-35-1 Margaret Neiss, age 38, P.O. Martin's Bay Mich.
Husband: Pete Neiass, age 42, see 8-34.
52-35-1-1 Amab Neiss, age 10.

52-35-2 Jennie Hardwick, age 32, P.O. Martin's Bay.
Husband: Moses Hardwick, age 32, see 12-37, brother of David Hardwick, see 51-35.
52-35-2-1 Eddie Hardwick, age 6.
52-35-2-2 Lucy Hardwick, age 3.

Wife 2nd: Margaret Saw-Gaw-Taw-Gun, age 44, see 4-34 & 11-37.

52-35-3 Adam Lambert, age 22, P.O. St. Jacques.
Wife: Mary Ann Lambert, age 19, see 17-9, said to belong to Soo Band, no children.

52-35-4 Roman Lambert or Raymond Lambert, age 19, P.O. St. Jacques, single.

52-35-5 Albert Lambert, age 17, P.O. St. Jacques.

52-35-6 Joseph Lambert, age 10, P.O. St. Jacques.

52-35-7 Caroline Lambert, age 8.

Information following from: Not Given.

53-35 MARY OTTAWA, dead, no heirs.

Information following from: Not Given.

54-35 ME-ZHOW-BAY, dead, no heirs.

Information following from: Not Given.
55-35 ME-ZHAW-GAW or MICHIGAN, all dead, no heirs, see note 45-42.

Information following from: Not Given.
56-35 No Notes.

Information following from: Not Given.
57-35 No Notes.

Information following from: Not Given.
58-35 No Notes.

Information following from: Not Given.
59-35 KE-NO-ZHAY or PETE PIKE, age 55, P.O. Cross Village, see 61-35.

Information following from: Not Given.
60-35 No Notes.

Information following from: Not Given, Oct 14, Cross Village.
61-35 SAW-GAW-NAW-QUOT, dead.
Wife: Sophia Moses, age 79, P.O. Cross Village.
61-35-1 ~~Susan~~ Josie Pike, age 60, P.O. Cross Village.
Husband: Pete Pike, age 55, P.O. Cross Village, on roll as 59-35, no children.
61-35-2 Margaret, dead.
Husband: Name not given, dead.
61-35-2-1 Catharine Nishaw, age 31, P.O. Cross Village, see 53-21.
Husband: Jere Nishaw, age 30, P.O. Cross Village, grandson of 76-21.
61-35-2-1-1 Eva Leo Nishaw, age 8, P.O. Cross Village.
61-35-2-2 Jeremiah Martell, age 27, P.O. Cross Village.
Wife: Christina Martell, died Aug 1907, off.
61-35-2-2-1 Name nor sex given, dead.
61-35-2-3 Esther Massey, age 25, Burt Lake Pellston.
Husband: Henry Massey, age 21, P.O. see 2-31.
61-35-2-3-1 Margaret Massey, age 1.
61-35-2-4 Moses Martell, age 22, P.O. Cross Village.
Wife: Rosie Martell, nee Mushcose, no children.
61-35-2-5 Elizabeth Griswald, age 18, P.O. Cross Village.
Husband: Harvey Griswald, white, off, no children.
61-35-2-6 Jane Martell, age 16, P.O. Cross Village.
61-35-2-7 Abe Martell, age 14, P.O. Cross Village.
61-35-2-8 Charles Martell, age 12, P.O. Cross Village.

61-35-3 Simon Moses, age ~~44~~ 50, P.O. Pine River at Jamesson's Mill Mich, see 61-35.
Wife: Susan Moses, age 48, see 10-11.
61-35-3-1 Sam Moses or Sam Simon, age 25, P.O. Pine River, single.
61-35-3-2 Pete Moses, age 23.
Wife: Sophia (Ellick) Moses, see 3-17, no children.
61-35-3-3 Mary Mandosking, age 18, P.O. Pine River.
Husband: Joe Mandoskung, see 3-8, no children.
61-35-3-4 Moses Moses or Moses Simon, age 10.
61-35-3-5 Agnes Moses or Agnes Simon, age 5.
61-35-4 Peter Moses, dead.
Wife: Eliza (Non-Gaish-Caw-Waw) Moses, P.O. ~~Cheboygan~~ Pellston.
61-35-4-1 Mary Moses, age 15, see 2-31.
61-35-5 Joe Moses, dead.
Wife: Margaret Moises, age 30, P.O. Jameson's Mills, after Joe's death she married his brother Louis see below.
61-35-5-1 by Joe see 10-11 as child 3.
61-35-5-2 by Joe see 10-11 as child 4.
61-35-6 Christina, dead.
Husband: Charles Coby, see 14-60, Grand River.
61-35-7 Louis Moses, age 30, P.O. Jameson's Mills Mich, left this wife & has wife at Pine River, see 10-11.
Wife: Susie Moses, age 25, P.O. Jameson's Mills Mich, see 76-21 & 53-21.
61-35-8 Angeline Kenewabay, age 28, P.O. Cross Village.
Husband: Pete Kenewabay, age 36, P.O. Cross Village, Canadian Indian, off.
61-35-8-1 Anna Kenewabay, age 5.
61-35-8-2 Rosie Kenewabay, born July 1907 2nd roll.

Information following from: Not Given.
62-35 No Notes.

Information following from: Not Given.
63-35 IGNACE O-SAW-WAW-NE-ME-KE, age 71, P.O. Stonnington Mich.
Wife 1st: Name not given, dead.
Wife 2nd: Angeline O-Saw-Waw-Ne-Me-Ke, age 68.
63-35-1 Christine Sigwate or Sigataw, age 46, P.O. Ogantz Mich.
Husband: George Sigwate, age 54, see 12-57.
63-35-1-1 Alex Segwate, age 26, P.O. Ogantz.
Wife: Josephine Sigwate, age 18.
63-35-1-1-1 Pauline Sigwate, born July 1908.

63-35-1-2 Lawrence Sigwate, age 21, P.O. Ogantz.
Wife: Agnes Sigwate, nee Kezhick, ~~Canadian Indian~~.
63-35-1-2-1 Levi Sigwate, too late, born Nov 1908.
63-35-1-3 Emma Sigwate, age 19, P.O. Ogantz, single.
63-35-1-4 Benedict Sigwate, age 17.
63-35-1-5 Martin Sigwate, age 15.
63-35-1-6 Joseph Sigwate, age 13.
63-35-1-7 Anna Sigwate, age 11.
63-35-1-8 Martha Sigwate, age 9.
63-35-1-9 Lucy Sigwate, age 7.
63-35-2 George O-Saw-Waw-Ne-Me-Ke or George Neiass, age 41, P.O. Stonnington.
Wife: Mary Ann O-Saw-Waw-Ne-Me-Ke, age 22, see 15-37 & 8-34.
63-35-2-1 Eddy O-Saw-Waw-Ne-Me-Ke, born Sept/07, died Sept/08.
63-35-3 Pete, dead.
Wife: Margaret Neiass, age 37, P.O. Stonington, see 52-35.
63-35-4 Name nor sex given, dead, no heirs.

Information following from: Not Given.
64-35 No Notes.

Information following from: Not Given.
65-35 No Notes.

Information following from: Margaret Bourasaw, Dec 5/08, Indian Point St. Jacques.
66-35 PETER MAY-TWAY-WAY or PETER BOURASAW, dead.
Wife: Margaret Bourasaw, age 52, P.O. St. Jacques, now wife of Mitchell Way-Ge-We-We-Gwon, see 2-34.
66-35-1 Josette Simon, age 37, P.O. St. Jacques.
Husband 1st: Joe Mitchell, age 40, P.O. St. Jacques, separated.
66-35-1-1 Charles Mitchell, age 15.
66-35-1-2 Elizabeth Mitchell Simon, age 16, see 1-30 or Elizabeth Kenawekezhick.
Husband 2nd: Moses Simon or Kewanekezhick, age 50, P.O. St. Jacques.
66-35-1-3 Agnes Simon, born Dec 1907.
66-35-2 Margaret Jackson, age 29, P.O. St. Jacques.
Husband: Joe Jackson, age 45, P.O. St. Jacques, no children.
Note: Chief says: Joe Jackson's parents were dead in 1870 but he was enrolled with his aunt 23-37 Durant Spl Agt.
66-35-3 Thomas Bourasaw, age 24, P.O. St. Jacques, single.
66-35-4 Frank Bourasaw, age 22, P.O. St. Jacques.

Information following from: Not Given.

67-35 WAW-BE-KAKE or JESSE AW-DAY-NE-ME or JESSE WILLIAMS, age 60, P.O. Namah Mich North Shore near Escanaba.
Wife: Elizabeth Williams, age 60.
67-35-1 Mary Dasan, see 20-9.
67-35-2 Frank Williams, age 17, P.O. Namah.

Information following from: Not Given, Nov 21/08, Beaver Island.

68-35 PAW-BE-ZHE-WAY, dead.
Wife: Name not given, dead.
68-35-1 Paul Kin-Waw-Be-Ke-Say, age 35, P.O. High Island St. James Beaver Island.
Wife: Madaline Kin-Waw-Be-Ke-Say, age 35, P.O. High Island St. James Beaver Island, no children.

Information following from: Not Given.

69-35 No Notes.

Information following from: Not Given.

70-35 No Notes.

Pages 36
Manistique Band
Chief NAW-O-QUAY-GAW-BOWE

Information following from: Not Given.

1-36 NAW-O-QUAY-GAW-BOWE, dead.
Wife: Name not given.
Note: Only child left is at Cross Village.

Information following from: Not Given, Dec 6/08.

2-36 PE-TWAY-WE-KE-ZHICK or JESSE, dead.
Wife: Name not given, dead.
2-36-1 William Jesse, age 60, P.O. Namah, ~~dead~~.
Wife: Marian Jesse, age 50, see 8-36.
2-36-1-1 Mary or Marian Sagatoe or ~~Sag~~ Sacattor, age 24, P.O. Namah.
Husband: Frank Sagatoe, age 35, no children, see 15-36.
2-36-1-2 Louis Jesse, age 21, P.O. Namah, single.
2-36-1-3 Julius Jesse, age 4, P.O. Namah.
2-36-2 Mary Macdagon, age 41, P.O. Namah.
Husband: Joe Macdagin or Joe Mixceney, see 37-28, no children.

2-36-3 Name nor sex given, dead, no heirs.
2-36-4 Name nor sex given, dead, no heirs.
2-36-5 Name nor sex given, dead, no heirs.

Information following from: Therese Sagatoe, Apr 21/09, Pt. Aux Chense. Note: This woman claims to belong to this card (family) as does William Jesse & according to her statements both her husband & William Jesse's father were named Pe-Tway-We-Ke-Zhick; although I am unable to find but one by that nameon the 1870 roll. All parties are undoubtebly entitled to enrollment. Durant Spl Agent. Supplement:

2-36 PE-TWAY-WE-KE-ZHICK or John Sagatoe, dead.
Wife: Terese ~~Aw-So-Quay-Ke-She-Go-Quay~~ O-Tish-Quay-Ke-Zhick-Go-Quay or Tenese Sagatoe, age 75, P.O. Pt. Aux Chense, on roll
as 13-11.
2-36-1 Angeline Chippewa, age 47, P.O. Cross Village, see 27-20 & 15-36 & 13-11.
2-36-2 No information given.
2-36-3 Mary Keshawas, P.O. Cross Village, see 31-30.
Husband: William Ke-Sha-Was, see 31-30
Note: An uncle to Levi Keshawas & brothers see 28-28 get William's family card. The family at Pt. Aux Chenes say William Keshawas does not want to be enrolled. Durant Spl Agt.
2-36-4 Jane Odeimin, age 44, P.O. Pt. Aux Chene.
Husband: Joseph Otaymin, age 44, a son of 49-21.
2-36-4-1 Ed Otaymin, age 8.
2-36-4-2 George Otaymin, age 2.
2-36-5 No information given or missing?.

Information following from: Not Given, Dec 4/08.

3-36 O-GE-MAW-BE-NAY-SE, dead.
Wife: Theresa Oga, age 80, P.O. ~~Gold~~ Gould City Mich.
3-36-1 Name nor sex given, dead, no heirs.
3-36-2 Name nor sex given, dead, no heirs.
3-36-3 Name nor sex given, dead, no heirs.
3-36-4 Edward Oga, see 4-34.
3-36-5 Alex Peters, age 60, P.O. ~~Gold~~ Gould City Mich.

Information following from: Not Given.

4-36 MRS. FRANCIS BOURASSA, dead.
4-36-1 Sampson Bourasaw, age 53, P.O. Ogantz Mich Martin's Bay.
Wife: Annie Bourasaw, age 24, ~~parents belong to Harbor Springs band~~, see 12-37.
4-36-1-1 Rosie Bourasaw, born Aug 26, 1907.

4-36-2 Name nor sex given, dead, no heirs.
4-36-3 Name nor sex given, dead, no heirs.
4-36-4 Name nor sex given, dead, no heirs.

Information following from: Not Given.
5-36 NE-BE-NAY-GWON or GEORGE SHEDOWIN, dead.
Wife: Name not given, dead.
5-36-1 Josephine Shedawin, P.O. St. Germain Pine River ~~near Pincoming~~, see 8-15 & 4-8.

April 12 1909
Nahma Mich

Horace Durant
Dear Sir:
This man Ne-be-nay-gwon was living in St. Ignace, Mich. and his all childrens. So I do not know. I think you can find it out from Jack Shedowen from St. Ignace, Mich.
This man Ne-be-nay-gwon he is Chippewa and also all his childrens.
Yours Truly
John Shedowen

Information following from: Not Given.
6-36 ME-SAW-TE-GO, dead, no heirs.

Information following from: Therese Muscoe, Apr 21/09, Pt. Aux Chene.
7-36 O-TUSH-E-TAW-WON or SHEDOWIN, dead.
Wife: Therese Mush Muscoe, age 75, P.O. Pt. Aux Chene.
7-36-1 Wain-Daw-Sung or John Shedowin, see 14-36.

Information following from: William Jesse & Mildred Nadeau, Dec 6/08, St. Jacques.
8-36 ME-SKO-PWAW-GON, dead.
Wife: Mrs. Joe Mitchell or Mary Mitchell, age 80, P.O. Namah.
8-36-1 Marian Jesse, age 50, P.O. Namah Camp 8.
Husband: William Jesse, age 60, Namah, see 2-36 & for children 2-32.
8-36-2 Name not given, dead.
Husband: Name not given, dead.
8-36-2-1 Anna Wagner, age 8, P.O. Namah, lives with grandmother.
8-36-3 Mary Ann, dead.
Husband: F. Nadeau, white, this was his 2nd wife: his first wife was child 4 of 4-34.
8-36-3-1 Mitchell Nadeau, age 21, P.O. Namah Mich.
Wife: Susan (Paul) Nadeau, age 17, see 2-37.

8-36-3-1-1 Bertha Nadeau, born 4/08 too late.

Information following from: Simon Champaign, Dec 10/08, Manistique & Joseph Ke-Wan-De-Way, St. Ignace.

9-36 KE-WAND-DE-WAY, age 57, P.O. St. Ignace ~~living on North Shore somewhere~~, see 5-15.

Wife 1st : Name not given, dead.

Wife 2nd: Name not given, dead.

Wife 3rd: Josette (Gondreau) Ke-Wan-De-Way

9-36-1 Mary Bellant, age 32, P.O. St. Ignace.

Husband: Name not given, white.

9-36-1-1 Aloisious Bellant, age 12.

9-36-1-2 Daniel Bellant, age 10.

9-36-1-3 Alexander Bellant, age 8.

9-36-1-4 Antoinette Bellant, age 6.

9-36-1-5 Norman Bellant, age 2.

9-36-2 Harry Ke-Wan-De-Way, age 31, P.O. Seulshoix Mich.

Wife: Nancy Ke-Wan-De-Way, ~~white~~, age 30, P.O. Seulshoix Mich., no children.

9-36-3 Peter Ke-Wan-De-Way, age 29, P.O. Gulliver Mich Chicago Ills. In Light House since, single.

9-36-4 Louis Ke-Wan-De-Way, age 28, P.O. St. Ignace, single.

9-36-5 Retta Boucha, age 25, P.O. St. Ignace.

Husband: Isaac Boucha, age 28, P.O. St. Ignace, see 2-15.

9-36-5-1 Joseph Boucha, age 3.

9-36-6 Berndettie Repin, age 23, P.O. St. Ignace, husband white, no children.

9-36-7 Margaret Smith, age 21, P.O. St. Ignace.

Husband: Name not given, white.

9-36-7-1 Harry Smith, age 3.

9-36-8 Caroline Ke-Wan-De-Way, age 18, P.O. St. Ignace.

9-36-9 Lenore Ke-Wan-De-Way, age 16, P.O. St. Ignace.

9-36-10 Amy Ke-Wan-De-Way, age 12, P.O. St. Ignace.

9-36-11 Joseph Ke-Wan-De-Way, age 34, P.O. In U.S. Army in Philipines, single, child ny ~~1st~~ 2nd wife.

9-36-12 Mitchell Ke-Wan-De-Way, age 36, P.O. St. Ignace, child by 1st wife.

Wife: Annie Ke-Wan-De-Way, nee Sagetoe, age 26, P.O. St. Ignace, dead, see 15-36, off.

9-36-12-1 Mitchell Ke-Wan-De-Way Jr., age 7, P.O. St. Ignace, died July 1908, off.

Gulliver Mich
June 14th 2909

Mr Horace B Durant

Petoskey Mich

Dear Sir

As you would like to know my brother Peter's address it is Peter Kewandeway Gulliver P.O. Mich

I remain your Struly
Louis Kewandeway,
Gulliver P.O. Mich

Information following from: Not Given.
10-36 No Notes.

Information following from: Not Given.
11-36 No Notes.

Information following from: Not Given.
12-36 No Notes.

Information following from: Not Given, May/09, Pine River.
Note: There are others at Pine River who claim this sheet as head of family & I am inclined to believe they are the proper parties, see duplicate 13-36 Durant.

13-36 PAY-SHE-NE-NE-BEA, dead.
Wife: Name not given, dead.
13-36-1 Name nor sex given, dead, no heirs.
13-36-2 Name nor sex given, dead, no heirs.
13-36-3 Mary P. Giuld, age 85, P.O. Manistique, cannot locate her.
Husband: Augustus Gould, P.O. Manistique.
13-36-4 William Kinnewanby or William Anthony, age 64, P.O. St. Ignace, see 10-34.

Information following from: Not Given, see note on other sheet numbered 13-36, May 4/09, Pine River Hessell.

13-36 PAY-SHE-NE-NE-BEA, dead. DUPLICATE
Wife: Mary or O-Dish-Quay or Mary Andrews #1, age 80, P.O. Sugar Island, 2nd husband Andrews, dead, Soo Band, see 22-11.
13-36-1 James Wah-Be-Kineece, age ~~60~~ 52, P.O. ~~Sugar Island~~ Pine River, see 22-11 & 5-17.
13-36-2 George Andrews, age 46, P.O. Hessell, see A-3.
Wife: Margaret Andrews #2, age 40, see 3-17.
Children of Mary Andrews #1 by 2nd husband:
13-36-3 John Andrews, P.O. Sugar Island, see A-3 Soo.
13-36-4 Mike Andrews, P.O. Sugar Island.

Information following from: James Shedowan, Dec 5/08, St. Jacques.
14-36 WAIN-DAW-SUNG or JOHN SHEDOWAN, age 67, P.O. St.

Jacques, ~~son of 7-36~~.
Wife: Name not given, dead.
14-36-1 George Shedowan, age 41, Rapid River Mich Bakers Camp or Namah Mich.
Wife: Mary Ann Shedowan #2, age 38, no children, see child of wife by1st husband on 15-36.
14-36-2 James Shedowan, age 36, grandson of 7-36, see 2-37.
14-36-3 Joe Shedowan, age 33, P.O. Rapid River Mich Bakers Camp, see 9-9.
Wife: Jennie Shedowan or Tostey, age 38, no children.

Information following from: Not Given.
15-36 SAY-GE-TOE, dead.
Wife: Name not given, dead.
15-36-1 Simon Sagato, age 73, P.O. Namah Mich, on roll as 11-36.
Wife: Name not given, dead.
15-36-1-1 Frank Sagato, age 35, see 2-36.
15-36-1-2 Simon Sagato, age 30.
Wife: Mary Ann Sagato, age 18.
15-36-1-2-1 Frank Sagato, age 1, born Sept 1907 2nd roll.
15-36-1-2-2 Lizzie Sagato, age 5.
15-36-1-3 Mary Ann Shedowan, age 38, see 14-36.
Husband: Name not given, dead.
15-36-1-3-1 Frank Bird, age 7, P.O. Baker's CampRapid river Namah with mother.
15-36-1-4 John Sagato, age 24, single.
15-36-1-5 Mary Chingquay, age 32, see 11-41.
15-36-2 Eliza Sam, see 39-20.

Information following from: Not Given, Oct 19/08, Cross Village.
Note: This woman says that her father's name was Sag-a-toe who has a brother by name of Simon Sag-a-toe, living on North Shore, at a place called Louis. When the proper family sheet is found put this family on that sheet, as they are all undoubtedly entitled to enrollment, her father Sagatoe, was living in 1870. Durant.
15-36B SAY-GE-TOE, dead.
Wife: Name not given, dead.
15-36-1 Mary Ann Stone, age 57, P.O. Cross Village.
Husband: Name not given, dead.
15-36-1-1 Christina Jackson, age 26, P.O. Cross Village.
Husband: Mike Jackson, see 3-44.
15-36-1-1-1 Name not given, see 3-44.
15-36-1-2 Louis Stone, age 21, P.O. Cross Village, single.
15-36-2 Angeline (Sagatoe) Chippeway, age 47, see 2-36 & 27-20

& 13-11.
15-36-3 Mary (Sagatoe) Ke-Sha-Was, P.O. Cross Village.
Husband: William Ke-Sha-Was.
15-36-4 Annie (Sagatoe) ~~Key-Way-Ken-Do~~ Key-Wan-De-Way, age 26, P.O. St. Ignace, dead.
Husband: Mitchell Ke-Wan-De-Way or Joe Mitchell, age 36, see 9-36 & 4-12.

Information following from: Not Given.
16-36 No Notes.

Information following from: Not Given.
17-36 No Notes.

Information following from: Not Given.
18-36 No Notes.

Information following from: Not Given, Oct 9/08, Harbor Springs.
19-36 FRANCIS AW-DAY-NE-ME or FRANK WILLIAMS, ag 74, P.O. Petoskey Mich., on roll by himself in 1870, not married and no children.

Information following from: Not Given.
20-36 No Notes.

Information following from: Not Given.
21-36 No Notes.

Information following from: Not Given.
22-36 No Notes.

Information following from: Not Given.
23-36 No Notes.

Information following from: Not Given.
24-36 No Notes.

Information following from: Not Given.
25-36 No Notes.

Information following from: Not Given.
26-36 No Notes.

Pages 37
North Shore Band

Chief KAW-GE-GAY-PE-NAY-SE

Information following from: Not Given.
Note: The head of this family is said to have had an allotment of land & therefore the heirs claim rights. Investigate for her.
??-37 O-MIS-SQUAW-NAW-QUOT or O-SAW-WAW-GUSH
or JOHN ANCE, dead, see if this name appears on allotment roll.
??-37-1 John Ance #1, age 59, P.O. St. Ignace.
Wife 1st: Name not given, white, dead.
Wife 2nd: Name not given, white.
??-37-1-1 Louise (Ance) Tabosegay, age 30, P.O. Canada Mantoulin Island.
??-37-1-2 Angeline Ance, age 27, P.O. Canada Mantoulin Island.
??-37-1-3 Alixse Ance, age 25, P.O. Canada Mantoulin Island.
??-37-1-4 John Ance #2, age 20, P.O. Canada Mantoulin Island.
??-37-1-5 Isaac Ance, age 18, P.O. Canada Mantoulin Island.
Note: This man, John Ance, 59, now lives at St. Ignace having came from Canada about 2 years ago. Says he belongs to this band but was absent in Canada in 1870 which accounts for his name not being on the roll of 1870. I am inclined to the opinion that his children should not be enrolled, as they are closely identified by marriage with Canadian Indians, & reside in Canada where they were born & raised. This man, John Ance, is only temporarily residing in St. Ignace, working in lumber camps; his wife & family are still in Canada & he calls Canada his home, all of which leads me to believe the he, too, should not be enrolled. He is a cousin of Amable Ance, a Chief of one of the Macinac bands. St Ignace Jany 2/08 Durant Spl Agt.

Information following from: Peter Kesis Chief, Dec 5/08.
1-37 KAW-GE-GAY-PE-NAY-SE, dead.
Wife: Elizabeth Kaw-Ge-Gay-Pe-Nay-Se, dead.
1-37-1 Mary Morris, age ~~80~~ 76, P.O. Indian Town near Martin's Bay Stonington Mich.
Husband: Nicholas Morris, ~~white~~, age 80, see 5-37 & 14-37.
1-37-1-1 Caroline Langley, age 46, P.O. Stonington Mich.
Husband: Peter Langley, P.O. Stonington Mich.
1-37-1-2 Mary Ellick, age 42.
Husband: Ben Ellick, P.O. 7 miles below Trout Lake Kenneth Mich, see 3-17 & 5-20.

Stonington Mich
June 15. 1909.

Dept of Interior

W.S. Indian Service
Mr Horace B Durant
Dear Sir:

In Ansewer to your letter of June 8/09. My name is Mrs Mary Morris and I am a member of the Chippewa band of Michigan I am 76 years of age.

My parents names were Mr Peter Silverband and Mrs Elizabeth Silverband. I have only one half sister who's name is Mrs Elizebeth Gilbert and I do not know her right age the only address that I know her to be at is Cross Village Mich

I have only two Daughters their names are Mrs Caroline Langley her age is 46 and she lives at Stonington Mich and Mrs Mary Elick her age is 43 and she Lives at Kenith Mackinaw Co. Mich.

Hoping I have ansewered all correctly.

Im Yours truly
Mrs Mary Morris

Information following from: Not Given.
2-37 WAW-SHOW, dead.
Wife: Name not given, dead.
2-37-1 Name nor sex given, dead, no heirs.
2-37-2 Name nor sex given, dead, no heirs.
2-37-3 Name nor sex given, dead, no heirs.
2-37-4 Name nor sex given, dead, no heirs.
2-37-5 Andrew Washo, age 46, P.O. St. Jacques.
Wife: Catharine Washo, age 38, see ~~18~~ 40-1.
2-37-1-1 Clara Washo, age 9.
2-37-6 Name nor sex given, dead, no heirs.
~~2-37-7 Mary, dead.~~
~~Husband: Ed Paul, P.O. St. Ignace.~~
~~2-37-7-1 Ed Paul Jr., age 15, P.O. Mt. Pleasant Sch.~~
~~2-37-7-2 Ellen Paul, age 21, P.O. Sturgeon Rivier Namah.~~
~~2-37-7-3 Susan Paul, age 17, P.O. Sturgeon Rivier Namah.~~
2-37-7 Mary, dead.
Husband: Ed Paul, P.O. St. Ignace.
2-37-7-1 Ellen (Paul) Shedowin, age 21.
Husband: James Shedowan, age 36, P.O. Namah, see 14-36.
2-37-7-1-1 Henry Shedowan, age 3.
2-37-7-1-2 Gabriel Shedowan, born April 1908.
2-37-7-2 Ed Paul Jr., age 19, P.O. Mt. Pleasant Sch.
2-37-7-3 Susan Paul ~~Nateau~~ Nedeau, age 17, P.O. Namah.
Husband: Mitchell Nateau, age 21, see 8-36.
2-37-7-3-1 Bertha ~~Nateau~~ Nedeau, born Aug 4/08.

Information following from: Peter Kesis present Chief, Dec 4/08, Indian Point 5 miles from St. Jacques.

3-37 KESIC or PETER KESIS, age 75, P.O. St. Jacques.

Wife: Name not given, dead.

3-37-1 Frank Kesis, age 46, P.O. Manistique.

Wife: Mary Kesis, ok belongs to Beaver Island, no children.

3-37-2 Catharine Moses, age 41, P.O. St. Jacques.

Husband: Louis Moses, age ~~45~~ 51, see ~~18-7~~ 40-1.

3-37-2-1 Ambrose Moses, age 28, P.O. Mt. Pleasant Sch, see 9-37

3-37-2-2 Jacob Moses, age 19, Mt. Pleasant Sch.

3-37-2-3 Mathias Moses, age 18, P.O. St. Jacques.

3-37-2-4 George Moses, age 11, Mt. Pleasant.

3-37-2-5 Rosie Moses, age 15, Mt. Pleasant.

3-37-2-6 Lizzie Moses, age 7, P.O. St. Jacques.

3-37-2-7 Barney Moses, age 5, P.O. St. Jacques.

3-37-2-8 Philamon Moses, age 3, P.O. St. Jacques.

3-37-3 Name nor sex given, dead, no heirs.

Information following from: John, Dec 4/08 & 5/08, St. Jacques.

4-37 SAW-GAW-TAW-GUN, dead.

4-37-1 John Saw-Gaw-Taw-Gun, age 48, P.O. Namah Mich, see 4-34.

Information following from: Not Given.

5-37 MRS. NICHOLAS MORRIS, JR.or MARY MORRIS, age 76, see 1-37.

Husband: Nicholas Morris, age 73, see 1-37 & 14-37.

Information following from: Not Given, Oct 18/08.

6-37 MRS. JOHN FORTAIN, age 69, P.O. Cross Village.

Husband: John Fortain, white.

Note: This family was not paid on 1870 roll and therefore no enrollment is made by me. Horace B. Durant Spl. Ind. Agent Cross Village Oct 18, 1908.

Note: This family is pure French descent. Mrs. John Fortain appeared before me in person. HBDurant Spl. Agt.

Later: Oct. 19/08. Cross Village: This woman has been fully identifiedand her name found enrolled as Mrs. Phillimen Fartan, No. 25 p. 12 on 1870 roll with Mackinaw Band, which agrees with her statements and those of other Indians present who know her. However she is a French woman & of very little Indian blood; Horace B Durant Spl. Agt.

Information following from: Peter Kesis Chief, Dec 5/08, St. Jacques.

7-37 WAY-WAY-SO-MAW, dead, no heirs.

Wife: Name not given, dead.

Information following from: Peter Kesis Chief, Dec 5/08, St. Jacques.
8-37 JOHN B. BERTRAND, dead.
Wife: Name not given, dead.
8-37-1 Name not given, dead.
Husband: Paul, dead.
8-37-1-1 Paul Wagner, see 2-34.
8-37-1-2 Therese Wagner, see 2-34.

Information following from: Annie Isaac, Dec 3/08, Manistique.
9-37 PAY-BAW-MAW-SHE, dead.
Wife: Name not given, dead.
9-37-1 Annie Isaac, age 49, P.O. Manistique.
Husband 1st: Louis Moses.
9-37-1-1 Ambrose Moses, age 28, P.O. Mt. Pleasant Sch., single, see 3-37 & 40-1.
Husband 2nd: Louis Isaac or Louis Siganock, afe 57, P.O. Manistique, see report sheet #C.
9-37-1-2 Mary Isaac, age 12.
9-37-1-3 Della Isaac, age 9, died July 1908.
9-37-2 Augustus Gould, nephew, age 36, see 18-42.

Sheet #C

Report on 9-37 3-39 62-21
Report:
Louis Isaac or Louis Siganoe, husb of Annie Isaac, see #9 page 37, and Bert Isaac, husband of Margaret Isaac, nee (Pay-she-ge-zhick) see #3 p 39, and Angeline May dwa gon – 43 – wife of Moses May dwa gon see #62 p. 21 are undoubtedly Ottawa & Chippewa Indians of Michigan; but their father was not enrolled in 1870. They lived in Cross Village (now live in Manistique) in 1870 and their mother had an allotment of land there.

#80 p. 21 – Maw-co-quay, was their father's sister, and Francis Tabasosh #29 p. 20 is their cousin, and they have numerous relatives among this band.

They are nearly full blood Indian, and would seem to be entitled both from their own testimony and the statements of others of their band.

As a reason why their father & themselves were not enrolled with the Cross Village band in 1870, they state that because of the adherence of their grandfather to the Brittish Cause in war of 1812 the Inds would not permit his enrollment with them. It is my opinion that they should be enrolled & given rights in this tribe.

Horace B Durant
Special Agent

Manistique, Mich. Dec. 3, 1908

Information following from: Peter Kesis.
10-37 AW-BE-DAW-NAW-QUOT, dead.
Wife: Susan Laplant, age 63, P.O. Stonnington, no children.

Information following from: Not Given.
11-37 MRS. GEORGE LAMBERT, now
MRS. MARGARET SAW-GAW-TAW-GUN, see 4-34 & 52-35

Information following from: Not Given, Dec 5/08.
12-37 O-KE-WASH or SOPHIA WILLIAMS, age 78, P.O. Stonington.
Husband: James Williams, age 72, P.O. Stonington Mich.
12-37-1 George Sigwate or Sigataw, age 54, see 63-35.
12-37-2 Sophia Hardwick, age 52, P.O. Stonington.
Husband: George Hardwick, age 55, white off.
12-37-2-1 Moses Hardwick, age 32, see 52-35.
12-37-2-2 Kate Ross, age 29, P.O. Stonington.
Husband: Name not given, white.
12-37-2-2-1 Henry Ross, age 7.
12-37-2-3 George Hardwick Jr., age 26, P.O. Stonington.
Wife: Mary Gilbert Hardwick, age 21, see 5-20.
12-37-2-4 David Hardwick, age 24, see 51-35.
12-37-2-5 Ellen Hardwick #2, age 19.
12-37-2-5-1 Hazel Bourassaw, age 2, died summer of 1908.
12-37-2-6 John Hardwick, age 17.
12-37-2-7 Elizabeth Hardwick, age 15.
12-37-2-8 Joseph Hardwick, age 8.
12-37-3 Mary Macabee, age 44, P.O. Ogontz Mich.
Husband: Moses Macabee, white.
12-37-3-1 Jennie Thorsen, age 24, P.O. Stonington, husband white, no children.
12-37-3-2 Annie Bourasaw, age 22, P.O. Ogontz.
Husband: Sampson Bourasaw, see 4-36.
12-37-3-2-1 Rosie Bourasaw, born Sept 26/07.
12-37-3-3 Frank Macabee, age 21, P.O. Ogontz, single.
12-37-3-4 May Macabee, age 17, P.O. Ogontz
12-37-3-5 Rosie Macabee, age 15, P.O. Ogontz
12-37-3-6 Eva Macabee, age 12, P.O. Ogontz
12-37-4 Name nor sex given, dead, no heirs.
12-37-5 Norman William, age ~~36~~ 40, P.O. Namah.
Wife: Angeline William, age 31, P.O. Namah, for children see 4-34.

Information following from: Not Given, Dec 5/08.

13-37 NE-SWAN-SO-GAW-NAY, dead, no heirs.

Information following from: Not Given.
14-37 NICHOLAS MORRIS SR., dead.
Wife: Name not given, dead.
14-37-1 Nicholas Morris, ~~dead~~, see 1-37 & 5-37.

Information following from: Battise Shomin, Dec 5/08, St. Jacques.
15-37 PE-NAY-SE-QUAY, dead.
Wife: Name not given.
15-37-1 Battise Shomin, age 45, P.O. Stonington Mich.
Husband: Name not given, dead.
15-37-1-1 Angeline Shomin, age 24, P.O. Stonington.
15-37-1-2 Mary Ann (Shomin) Neiass, age 22.
Husband: George Neiass, age 40, see 8-34 & 63-35.
15-37-1-2-1 Eddy Neiass, born Sept/07, died Sept 1908.

Information following from: Not Given.
16-37 SHAW-BE-NE-GUN, dead, no heirs.
Note: Chiefs say they remember the head of family but do not remember any of children. Durant.

Information following from: Not Given.
17-37 WAW-KAW-GO-NAW, dead, no heirs.

Information following from: Peter Kesis Chief, Dec 5/08, St. Jacques.
18-37 WAW-GE-NAW, dead, these were 4 children, all dead.
Report: The Chief and other Indians of this band say that the father of these children was a white man; that their mother was a Wisconsin Indian who lived here and upon her death her 4 children were enrolled with this band; that they do not know what has become of these 4 children or their parents. Horace B. Durant Spl. Agt. Indian Point St. Jacques P.O. Dec 5/08.

Information following from: Not Given.
19-37 FRANCIS WAW-WAW-GE-BO, dead, no heirs.

Information following from: Not Given.
20-37 NO-TE-NO-PE-NAY-SE, dead.
Wife: Name not given.
20-37-1 Name nor sex given.
20-37-1-1 Mary Ann Feathers, only grand child.
Husband: ~~Joe~~ Gabriel Feathers.

Information following from: Not Given.
21-37 LOUIS LAPONSE, dead, no heirs.

Information following from: Not Given.
22-37 O-GE-NE-WAY, dead, no heirs.

Information following from: Peter Kesis Chief & Joe Jackson, Dec 5/08, St. Jacques.
23-37 PE-MAW-SAY-QUAY, dead.
Wife: Name not given.
23-37-1 Joe Jackson #2, age ~~45~~ 33, P.O. St. Jacques, see 66-35.
Wife: Margaret Jackson, age 29, P.O. St. Jacques, see 66-35, no children.
23-37-2 Jane Slone, age 36, P.O. Ford near Escanaba Mich.
Husband: Name not given, white.
23-37-2-1 Cecil Slone, age 18.
23-37-2-2 Harold Slone, age 14.
23-37-2-3 Clyde Slone, age 9.
23-37-2-4 Hazel Slone, age 11.
~~23-37-3 Maggie Peterson, age 26, P.O. Ford near Escanaba Mich.~~
~~Husband: Tom Peterson, white.~~

Information following from: Not Given.
24-37 NAW-QUAY-AW-CO-TO-QUAY, dead.
Wife: Name not given.
24-37-1 James Leo, age 62, P.O. Stonington, (cripple) single, no children.
24-37-2 Name nor sex given, dead, no heirs.

Page 38
Northport Band
Chief WAW-SAY-QUOUM

Note: Charlott Minginn not completed 29-38. Better identification wanted for 37-38.

Information following from: Not Given.
1-38 WAW-SAY-QUO-UM (GEORGE), age 92, P.O. Northport.
Wife: Name not given, dead.
1-38-1 Thresa Yanot, age 65, P.O. Sutton's Bay.
Husband: I-Yaw-Nut or Joe Yanot, see 19-41.
1-38-2 Mary Stevens, dead.
Husband: Name not given.
1-38-2-1 Joe Stevens P.O. Pashabetown, see 19-44.
1-38-2-2 Mary Ann Francis, age 30, see 5-40.

Husband: Frank Francis.
1-38-2-2-1 Joe Francis, age 6.
1-38-2-2-2 Lena Francis, age 2.

1-38-3 George Waw-Say-Quo-Um Jr., age 57, P.O. Northport.
Wife: Julia (Kah-Ge-Gay-Be) Waw-Say-Quo-Um, age 55, P.O. Northport.
1-38-3-1 Nancy Waw-Say-Quo-Um, age 27, P.O. Northport.
1-38-3-2 Alice Waw-Say-Quo-Um John, age 25, P.O. Northport.
Husband: Amos John, age 34, P.O. Northport.
1-38-3-2-1 Annie John, died Apr/08 lived 10 hours, 2nd roll.
1-38-3-3 Daniel Waw-Say-Quo-Um, age 18.
1-38-3-4 Sarah Waw-Say-Quo-Um, age 9.

1-38-4 Sarah (Waw-Say-Quo-Um) ~~Shondayse~~ Shaw-Wan-Day-Se, age 55, P.O. Northport, see 20-38.
Husband: Louis Shaw-Wan-Day-Se, age 51, P.O. Northport R.F.D.
1-38-4-1 Jonah Shaw-Wan-Day-Se, age 28, P.O. Genoa Nebr.
1-38-4-2 Jessie Shaw-Wan-Day-Se, age 16, P.O. Northport.
1-38-4-3 Dennis Shaw-Wan-Day-Se, age 8, P.O. Northport.

1-38-5 Annie (Waw-Say-Quo-Um) Redbird.
Husband: John Redbird, see 21-23 & 1-45, P.O. Northport.

1-38-6 Eliza (Waw-Say-Quo-Um) Louis, age 44, P.O. Northport.
Husband: John Louis, age 38, see 27-28.
1-38-6-1 George Louis, age 13.
1-38-6-2 Mary Louis, age 8.

1-38-7 Louis Waw-Say-Quo-Um, age 38, P.O. Honor.
Wife: Angeline Wah-Say-Quoum or Way-A-She, age 22, died May 28, 1907, a Grand River Ind. Said to have drawn with Potts, off.
1-38-7-1 Daniel Waw-Say-Quo-Um, age 5 mos., died May 28, 1907.

1-38-8 Frank Waw-Say-Quo-Um, age 35, P.O. Northport.
Wife 1st: Name not given, dead.
Wife 2nd: Elizabeth (She-She-Bonga or Way-A-She) Waw-Say-Quo-Um, age 39, P.O. Northport, see 4-38.
1-38-8-1 Louisanna Waw-Say-Quo-Um, age 6.
1-38-8-2 Mitchell Waw-Say-Quo-Um, age 16, lives with George Waw-Say-Quo-Um Sr.

Information following from: Not Given.

2-38 SHAW-SHAW-WAN-NAY-BEECE GEORGE.
Wife: Name not given.
2-38-1 Mary ~~Nady~~ Nadae or Nado, age 70, P.O. ~~Bellaire~~ Alden Mich.

Husband: George Nady, dead, see 7-23.

2-38-1-1 Sam ~~Nady~~ Nadae, age 41, P.O. ~~Bellaire~~ Alden Mich.

Wife: Name not given, dead.

2-38-1-1-1 George Nadae, age 16, P.O. Haskell Inst. Lawrence KS.

2-38-1-1-2 Wallace Nadae, age 13, P.O. Haskell Inst. Lawrence KS, see 8-63.

2-38-1-1-3 Clarence Nadae, age 11, P.O. Alden Mich, with father.

2-38-1-1-4 Emory Nadae, age 9, P.O. Seque Mich, with grandmother, see 54-27.

2-38-1-2 Anna Willis, age 43, P.O. ~~Bellaire~~ Elk Rapids Mich, husband dead, no children.

2-38-1-3 Eli Nadge, age ~~40~~ 37, P.O. Acme Mich.

Wife: Elizabeth (Sonihbird) Nadge, see 44-43.

2-38-1-3-1 Annie Nada, age 2, born Jany 15, 1907 1st roll.

2-38-1-4 William Nadge, age 30, , P.O. ~~Bellaire~~ Alden Mich, ~~not married~~ separated.

Wife: Sarah Medawes, see 12-51.

2-38-2 ~~She-~~Me-Sho-Do-No-Quay, dead, P.O. ~~Cross V~~.

Husband: Augustus Ne-Saw-Waw-A-Quot, P.O. Cross Village.

2-38-3 Daughter, name not given, dead.

Husband: ________ Shomin.

2-38-4 Key-So-Quay, dead, husband & children in Canada.

2-38-5 James Madagame ~~O-Ge-Ma-Ge-Do~~ ~~O-GeMaw-Ke-Do~~, age 55,

P.O. Northport.

Wife: Annie Madagame, nee Waw-Kay-Zoo, age 44, P.O. Northport, niece of 9-25, see 2-45.

2-38-5-1 Katie Bailey, age 22, P.O. Honor, see 3-59.

Husband: Robert Bailey, age 24, see 3-59.

2-38-5-1-1 Nicholas Bailey, age 4.

2-38-5-1-2 Jesse Bailey, age 2.

2-38-5-2 David Madagame, age 19, P.O. Gill's Pier Mich., not married.

2-38-5-3 Rosa Madagame, age 15, P.O. Northport.

2-38-5-4 Edmund Madagame, age 10, P.O. Northport.

2-38-5-5 Josie Madagame, age 7, P.O. Northport.

2-38-6 Mrs. Peter Sha-Sha-Quay, see 39-57, is a Grand river Indian, see card left at office in Northport.

Information following from: Not Given.

3-38 PAYSON WOLF, dead.

Wife: Mary Jane (Smith) Wolf, dead.
3-38-1 Arvilla A. Emerson, age 54, P.O. Philadelphia Pa.
Husband: W. C. Emerson, white.
3-38-1 Roy Emerson, age 24, P.O. Philadelphia, Pa.
3-38-2 Ettta S. Wilson, age 50, P.O. Indianapolis.
Husband: Wesley Wilson, white.
3-38-3 Charles F. Wolfe, age 48, P.O. Chicago Topographical Union #16.
Wife: Name not given.
3-38-3-1 William Wolfe, age 27, P.O. Chicago.
3-38-4 Edwin A. Wolfe, age 46, P.O. Chicago 303 – 30 St.
3-38-5 Jessie W. Brabant, age 42, P.O. White Eagle Okla.
3-38-6 Allen Burnside Wolfe, age 40, P.O. 303 – 30th Chicago Ills.
Wife: Name not given.
3-38-6-1 Roy Wolfe, age 17, P.O. Detroit.
3-38-6-2 Fred Wolfe, age 15, P.O. Detroit.
3-38-6-3 Claire Wolfe, age 14, P.O. Omena Mich.
Note: Children live with grandmother who has been appointed their guardian Saddie P. Wright 257 Theodore St. Detroit.
3-38-7 Mary Jane Wolf, age 38, P.O. Traverse City Mich.
3-38-8 Mabel Helen Wolfe, age 36, P.O. 10 – Oak Grove St. Minneapolis Minn.
3-38-9 Clara C. Joyce, age 35, P.O. 10 Oak Grove St. Minneapolis Minn.
Husband: Charles W. Joyce, white.
3-38-9-1 Dorothy Joyce, age 8.
3-38-9-2 Lucille Joyce, age 5.
3-38-10 Stella M. Champney, age 33, P.O. Traverse City Mich.
Husband: Name not given, white, separated.
3-38-10-1 Donald Champney, age 14.
3-38-10-2 Donna Mary Champney, age 12.

257 Theodore St.

Detroit, Mich
June 16, 1909

Mr. Horace B. Durant
Petoskey Mich
Dear Sir:

It is quite probable that you already have the names of the children of whom I wrote you, from other members of this family which is one reason for my writing. As I do not want any money belonging to them diverted from their benefit. The three boys in my charge are my grandsons, children of Bernie A. Wolfe and grandsons of Payson Wolfe (whose father was Peter Wakazoo, Chief of the principal Grand Traverse band of Ottawas) and Mary

J. Smith-Wolfe daughter of Rev. Geo. W. Smith Indian Missionary of all the Grand Traverse bands in their early settlement there at Northport.

The father of these boys I suppose to be living, but we have not held any communication for many years, and for 15 years I have had this entire care and support of them being finally appointed their legal guardian by the Leelanau Co. Probate Court.

Their names and ages are as follows:
Roy A. Wolfe 19
Frederick W. " 17
Clarence B. " 15
I think this covers necessary information requested.
Yours Respy.
Seddie P. Wright

|– *Arvilla A. Emerson*
|– *Etta S. Wilson*
|– *Charles F. Wolfe*
|– *Edwin A. Wolfe*
|– *Jessie W. Brabant*
| *born Oct 9, 1865*
|–*Birney A. Wolf*
Son |
Waub-O-Gake |– *Mi-En-Gin* |– *Payson Wolf* |– *Mary Jane Wolfe*
(Wolf) *wife* |– *Mabel H, Wolfe*
|
wife *Mary Jane* |– *Clara Belle Joyse*
Smith |
Charlotte Finequary |
or |– *Minnie S. Champney*
Charlotte Waukazoo

Jessie W. Brabant |– *Harold Wolfe Brabant*
born Oct 9, 1865 | *born April 15, 1895*
|– *Marjorie Helen Brabant*
born May 7, 1901

Information following from: Not Given.

4-38 MAW-NE-DO-GAW-BOWE or JOHN SHE-SHE-BONGA, age 77, P.O. Northport.
Wife: Name not given, dead.
4-38-1 Peter She-She-Bonga, age 57, P.O. Northport, enrolled as 34-38, see 6-38.
4-38-2 Thresa She-She-Bonga, age 55, P.O. Northport.
Husband: Mitchell Paul #1, age 55, P.O. Northport, see 20-42.
4-38-2-1 Bennett Paul, age 18, P.O. Northport.

4-38-2-2 Alex
4-38-3 Elizabeth (She-She-Bonga), P.O. Northport.
Husband: Frank Wah-Say-Quom, age 35, see 1-38.
4-38-4 Kate She-She-Bonga, age 36, P.O. Northport, single.
4-38-5 Moses She-She-Bonga, age 38, see 33-38.

Information following from: Not Given.
5-38 O-GE-MAW-KE-GE-DO, dead.
Wife: Catharine O-Ge-Maw-Ke-Ge-Do, age 75, P.O. Northport.
5-38-1 Charles O-Ge-Maw-Ke-Ge-Do, dead.
Wife: Name not given, dead.
5-38-1-1 George O-Ge-Maw-Ke-Ge-Do, age 23, P.O. Charlevoix, see 1-30.
5-38-2 Steel O-Ge-Maw-Ke-Ge-Do, age 42, P.O. Northport.
Wife: Jennie O-Ge-Maw-Ke-Ge-Do (nee Pay-Shaw-Se-Gay), age 38, P.O. Northport, see 6-41.
5-38-2-1 ~~Leslie~~ Lazrous O-Ge-Maw-Ke-Ge-Do, age 21, P.O. Northport.
5-38-2-2 William O-Ge-Maw-Ke-Ge-Do, age 19, P.O. Northport.
5-38-2-3 Sarah O-Ge-Maw-Ke-Ge-Do, age 12.
5-38-2-4 Rosa O-Ge-Maw-Ke-Ge-Do, age 9.
5-38-2-5 Joseph O-Ge-Maw-Ke-Ge-Do, age 6.
5-38-2-6 Moses O-Ge-Maw-Ke-Ge-Do, age 1, born Sept 12/07 2nd roll.
5-38-2-7 Elizabeth O-Ge-Maw-Ke-Ge-Do, age 4, died May 3, 1908 1st roll.
5-38-3 Eliza, dead.
Husband: Thomas An-Was-Key, age 53, P.O. Charlevoix, see 3-23 & 24-23, Note: had another wife by name of Eliza see 11-23).
5-38-3-1 Joseph An-Was-Key, age 20
5-38-3-2 Mary Andrews, age 30, P.O. Bay Shore.
Husband: Aram Andrews, age 35, P.O. Bay Shore, doubtful, said to be a ~~Grand River Ind.~~ Mt. Pleas. Saginaw Ind.
5-38-3-2-1 Lucy Andrews, age 13.
5-38-3-2-2 Sophia Andrews, age 7.
5-38-3-2-3 David Andrews, age 6.
5-38-3-2-4 George Andrews, age 4.
5-38-3-2-5 Rebecca Andrews, age 2.
5-38-3-3 Alice Kew-Gos-Kum, age 31, P.O. Bay Shore
Husband: James Key-Way-Cush-Cum, age 36.
5-38-3-3-1 John Key-Way-Cush-Cum, age 14, P.O. Bay Shore, see 5-24.

5-38-4 Mary Bourrasaw, age 40, P.O. Omena, see 3-42.
Husband 1st: ~~Geo. Antoine~~ Pete Antoine, lives in Hammon Okla, see 13-32.
5-38-4-1 George Antoine, age 19, P.O. Omena.
Husband 2nd: William Bourrasaw, age 53, see 12-38 & 22-38.
5-38-5 (Page & Data Missing)

Information following from: Not Given.
6-38 WILLIAM NA-GA-TO-SHING or NAY-TO-SHING, dead.
Wife: Name not given, dead.
6-38-1 George Nay-To-Shing, age 57, P.O. Northport.
Wife: Louisa Nay-To-Shing, nee Sho-Da-Se, age 40, P.O. Northport, see 8-23.
6-38-1-1 Oscar Nay-To-Shing, age 8, P.O. Northport.
6-38-1-2 Susie Nay-To-Shing, age 5, P.O. Northport.
6-38-2 Annie (Nay-To-Shing) She-She-Bonga, age 52, P.O. Northport
Husband: Peter She-She-Bonga, age 57, P.O. Northport.
6-38-2-1 Elizabeth She-She-Bonga (Nezed), age 21, P.O. Northport, not married.
6-38-3 Name nor sex given, dead, no children.

Information following from: Not Given.
7-38 PETER I-YEA-QUAW-KE-ZHICK, dead.
Wife: Name not given, dead.
7-38-1 Name nor sex given, dead, no heirs.
7-38-2 Name nor sex given, dead, no heirs.
7-38-3 Name nor sex given, dead, no heirs.
7-38-4 Nancy I-Yea-Quaw-Ke-Zhick, age 48, P.O. Gill's Pier, single, no children, see 38-38.

Information following from: Not Given.
8-38 CHARLES O-SHAW-~~WE~~-WAW-SQUAW, dead.
Wife: Name not given.
8-38-1 Simon Shaw-We-Squaw or Simon Green, age ~~68~~ 69, P.O. Charlevoix or Horton's Bay, see 17-25.

Information following from: Not Given.
9-38 ANTONIE NA-GA-TO-SHING or NA-TO-SHING, dead.
Wife: Mary Ann Na-To-Shing, age 84, died Feby 24, 1908 1st roll.
9-38-1 Name nor sex given, dead, no heirs.
9-38-2 Name nor sex given, dead, no heirs.
9-38-3 Name nor sex given, dead, no heirs.
9-38-4 Antoine Jr., dead.
Wife: Name not given.
9-38-4-1 Archie Na-To-Shing, age 7, lives with Thomas

Na-To-Shing 22-38.

9-38-5 Sophia Pa-Sha-Bay.

Husband: Gabriel Pa-Sha-Bay, see 15-42.

9-38-6 Thomas Na-T0-Shing, see 22-38.

Information following from: Not Given.

10-38 KAW-BE-MWAY-AW-SHE, dead.

Wife: Name not given, dead.

10-38-1 Sarah Pe-Don-Quot, age 58, P.O. Northport.

Husband: Name not given, see 18-45.

10-38-2 Mary Wa-An-Be-Minn-Que, age 52, P.O. Beaver Island Mich.

Husband: Joe Wa-An-Be-Minn-Que, age 60, P.O. Beaver Island Mich, see 27-38.

10-38-2-1 Sarah Wa-An-Be-Minn-Que, age 35.

10-38-2-2 Susan Agosa, age 28, P.O. Beaver Island St. James.

Husband: Peter Agosa, see 8-20.

10-38-2-3 Agnes Smith, age 6, adopted, P.O. Beaver Island.

10-38-3 John Cobb or Kaw-Be-Mway-Aw-She, age 50, P.O. Omena. Mich.

Wife: Jane Cobb, nee ~~Ogosa~~ Agosa, age 47, P.O. Omena Mich

10-38-3-1 James Cobb, age 22, P.O. Beaver Island Mich.

10-38-4 Louis Cobb, age 36, P.O. Omena.

Wife: Mary Cobb, age 23, died May 24, 1908 1st roll, see 42-43.

10-38-4-1 Alice Cobb, born May 10, 1908, died May 17, 1908 2nd roll.

Information following from: Not Given.

11-38 PAW-QUAW-GAY, dead.

Wife: Name not given, dead.

11-38-1 Aaron Paw-Quaw-Gay or Pe-Quon-Gay or Sar-Gon-Quo-To, see 32-38.

11-38-2 Name nor sex given, dead, see 35-38.

Spouse: Name not given.

11-38-2-1 Mary Coon, see 55-23, daughter of 35-38.

11-38-2-2 Jane (Pe-Quon-Gay), age 34, daughter of 35-38, separated.

Husband: Solomon ~~Tabbas~~ Tabasash, P.O. Charlevoix, see 6-23.

Information following from: Not Given.

12-38 WIN-DE-GO-WISH, dead.

Wife: Name not given, dead.

12-38-1 Name nor sex given, dead.

Spouse: Name not given.
12-38-1-1 Dominick Win-De-Go-Wish, age 19, P.O. Sutton's Bay, see 4-42.

Information following from: Not Given.
13-38 CHAW-WAY-CUSH-CUM, dead.
Wife: Name not given, dead.
13-38-1 Thresa Jacobs, age 70, see 16-40.
13-38-2 Joseph Lightssky, see 25-38.
13-38-3 Esther Wah-Buscum, age 58, P.O. Beaver Island, on 1870 roll as 37-38.
Husband: John Wah-Buscum, age 65, P.O. Beaver Island, same as Wain-Bway-Skung 22-42.
13-38-4 William Bigjoe, age 58, P.O. Omena Mich.
Wife: Name not given, dead.
13-38-4-1 Alice Jacobs, age 18, enrolled with 16-40.
13-38-4-2 Ida Jacobs, age 8, enrolled with 16-40.
13-38-4-3 John W. Bigjoe, age 10.
13-38-5 John Bigjoe, age 45, P.O. Gill's Pier.
Wife: Eliza (Allen), nee Man-Do-Wash, age ~~35~~ 40, P.O. Gill's Pier, 1st husband George Allen.
13-38-5-1 Isaac Allen, age ~~18~~ 17, P.O. Genoa Nebr.
13-38-5-2 Rosie Allen, age ~~16~~ 15, P.O. Mt. Pleasant Sch.
13-38-5-3 Bennett Allen, age ~~12~~ 13, P.O. Chilocco Okla.
13-38-5-4 Artie Bigjoe (female), age1, born Sept 17/07 2nd roll

Information following from: Not Given.
14-38 PAWN-DE-GAY-AW-SHE, dead.
Wife 1st: Name not given, dead.
Wife 2nd: Agatha Aw-Naw-Quaw-Do-Quay, age 72, see 27-42.
14-38-1 Lucy Nanego, age 56, P.O. Sutton's Bay.
Husband: Name not given, see 39-41.
14-38-2 Catharine Shaw-Koo, age 50, P.O. Sutton's Bay.
Husband: Thomas Shaw-Koo, see 5-41.
14-38-3 Angeline Chippeway #1, see 18-41

18/41 – 14/38
Mrs Angeline Chippeway She is the daughter of Pon de gay a she formily of North Port. Was a qua um Band. Also her sister is Mrs Peter Nanago there are the same family And her Parents are both died.
James M. Paul

Information following from: Not Given.
15-38 AISH-QUAY-KE-ZHICK JOSEPH, age 76, P.O. Northport, wife and children all dead.

Information following from: Not Given.
16-38 A-PING-GE-SHE-MO-KE or JOSEPH POM-GE-SHIG, age 76, P.O. Gill's Pier Mich.
Wife: Margaret (Kaw-Won-Ge-Do-Saw) Pom-Ge-Shig, age 79, P.O. Gills's Pier Mich.
16-38-1 Nancy Won-Ge-Zhick, age 48, P.O. Northport.
Husband: James Won-Ge-Zhick, see 7-46.
16-38-2 Rock Pom-Ge-Shig, age 35, Gill's Pier Mich, not married, no children.

Information following from: Not Given.
17-38 AISH-CAW-BOSE, dead.
Wife: Sophia, now wife of Joe Lightsky, see 25-38.
17-38-1 James Fisher, age 43, P.O. Pashabatown Sutton's Bay.
Wife: Mary (Nagonsay) Fisher, age 33, P.O. Pashabatown Sutton's Bay, see 23-42.
17-38-1-1 Archie Miller, age 12, P.O. Pashabatown Sutton's Bay, son of Mary Fisher by 1st husband.
17-38-1-2 Ella Fisher, age 9, P.O. Pashabatown.
17-38-1-3 Edwin Fisher, age 5.
17-38-2 George Fisher, age 40.
Wife: Mary Ann Shaw-Waw-day-Se, see 8-23.
17-38-3 Marian Agosa, nee Fisher, age 33, see 12-40.

Information following from: Not Given.
18-38 KIN-NE-WE-NAY-GO-ZAY, dead.
Wife: Name not given, dead.
18-38-1 Mary Jackson, age 46, P.O. Bay Shore Mich.
Husband: Joe Jackson, age 54, see 2-30.

Information following from: Not Given.
19-38 O-Gaw-Baw-O-Say-Quay, all dead, no heirs.

Information following from: Not Given.
20-38 TO-PE-NE-BE, dead.
20-38-1 Name nor sex given, dead, no heirs.
20-38-2 Sarah Shaw-Wan-Day-See, see 1-38.
Husband: Louis Shaw-Wan-Day-See.

Information following from: Not Given.
21-38 O-SHAW-WAW-SQUAG, dead.
Wife: Name not given, dead.
21-38-1 Son, name not given, see 16-38.

Information following from: James Paul Interpreter, Sept. 21/08, Northport.

22-38 THOMAS NAY-A-TO-SHING or THOMAS ANTOINE, age 60, P.O. Northport.

Wife: Name not given, dead.

22-38-1 Peter Antoine or Pete Nay-To-Shing, age 36, P.O. Hammon Oaklahoma, member of Oaklahoma tribe, ~~have not seen~~ heard from him about week ago Sept. 21/08 Durant.

22-38-2 Therese Antoine Wah-Sa-Quoum, age 32, see 26-23.

22-38-3 Mary Ann Nay-To-Shing #2, age 21, P.O. Northport, see 2-39, not married.

22-38-4 Archie Nay-To-Shing, age 7, nephew, son of Antoine Nay-To-Shing Jr., see 9-38.

Information following from: Not Given.

23-38 PE-TAW-WAW-NAW-QUOT, dead, no heirs.

Information following from: Not Given.

24-38 PAY-BONE-UNG, dead.

Wife: Name not given, dead.

24-38-1 Name nor sex given, dead.

24-38-2 Jacob Pabo #2, age 30, P.O. Horton Bay Mich, not married, no children.

24-38-3 Angeline (Pabo) Williams, age 40, P.O. Horton Bay Mich, separated.

Husband: Jonas Williams, dead, an Indian of Traverse Band.

24-38-3-1 Alioyius Williams, age 15, P.O. Tomah Indian School Wisconsin.

24-38-3-2 Marian Williams, age 13, P.O. Mt. Pleasant Indian School.

Omena Mich May 15 1909

Mr Horace B Durant
Petoskey Mich
Dear friend
I received your letter last 3 days ago. About those ages of Jonas Williams and his wife Angeline Pabo Williams. She is living at Charlevoix her first husband died years ago. So I do not know her second Husbands name And I know her. She is the daughter of John Pabo formily of North Port Was a quam band. Old John Pabo and his wife both died years ago And Angeline Pabo Williams is near as I can judge her age is about fourty 40 years old. Her brother name Jacob Pabo living at Charlevoix Michigan.

Yours Truly
James M Paul

Information following from: Not Given.

25-38 WAW-SAY-KE-ZHICK or JOSEPH LIGHTSKY, age 60, P.O. Northport.
Wife 1st: Louisa, dead.
Wife 2nd: Sophia Lightsky, nee Waw-Be-Gin-Way, age 61, P.O. Northport, formerly wife of 17-38.
25-38-1 Name nor sex given, dead.

Information following from: Not Given.
26-38 SHAW-WAW-NAW-WAW-NO-QUAY, dead.
26-38-1 Son, name not given, dead.
26-38-1-1 Lucy Won-Ge-Zhick, see 7-46.

Information following from: Not Given.
27-38 NO-PE-ME-QUAY, dead.
27-38-1 Daughter, name not given, see 2-41.
Husband: Name not given.
27-38-1-1 Joe Wa-An-Be-Nin-Que, P.O. Beaver Island, see 10-38.

Information following from: Not Given.
28-38 WAW-BE-KE-ZHICK or BEAVER, dead.
Wife: Cassie Beaver, age 67, died Aug 1908 1st roll.
28-38-1 Sophia, dead.
28-38-2 Sam, dead.
28-38-3 William, dead.
28-38-4 Mary (Beavers) Peters, age 33, see 3-51.

Information following from: Not Given.
29-38 CHARLOTT MINGUM, dead.

Information following from: Not Given.
30-38 WAY-ZHE-ON, dead.
30-38-1 Lucy (David) Won-Ge-Zhick, see 7-46

Information following from: Not Given.
31-38 MO-SE-QUAY, dead, no heirs.

Information following from: Not Given.
32-38 SAW-GAW-NAW-QUAW-BO, better known as AARON ~~PAW-QUAW-GE-GAY or~~ PE-QUON-GAY, spelled now AARON SARGONQUATTO, age 65, P.O. Omena Mich.
Wife: Susan (Allen) Sargonquatto, age 54, P.O. Omena Mich, see 2-40.
32-38-1 Lucy Andrews, age 37, P.O. Omena.
Husband: Isaac Andrews, age 27, P.O. Omena, Indian

(Ottawa), grandson of 24-60, no children.
32-38-2 Julia King, nee Sargonquatto, age 36, P.O. Omena.
Husband: Philip King, age ~~24~~ 27, Indian (Ottawa), son of 8-62
32-38-2-1 Perry King, age 5, P.O. Omena, lives with grandmother.
~~32-38-2-2 Pearl King~~
32-38-2-2 William King, born March, died March 1908, 20 days old 2nd roll.
32-38-3 Pearl Sargonquatto or Pe-Quon-Gay, age 14, Died Sept 1907 1st roll..

Information following from: Not Given.
33-38 KEY-NO-ZHE-MIG or JACOB PABO #1, age 54, P.O. Omena R.F.D.
Elizabeth (Brown) Pabo, age 51, P.O. Omena, see 10-45.
33-38-1 William Pabo, age 34, P.O. Northport.
Wife: Marceline Ance, age 28, P.O. Fox Island Wisconsin, an Ottawa, separated, see 45-43, ~~cannot locate her~~.
33-38-2 Isaac Pabo, age 21, P.O. Genoa Nebraska.
33-38-3 Ollie Pabo, age 19, P.O. Omena R.F.D.
33-38-4 Mary (~~George~~ Newton), nee Pabo, dead.
Husband: George Newton, dead.
33-38-1 Annie Newton, age 7, P.O. Omena.
33-38-2 Ella Newton, age 5.
33-38-5 Rosie (Pabo) She-She-Bon-Ga, age 28, P.O. Omena.
Husband: Moses She-She-Bon-Ga, age 38, P.O. Omena.
33-38-5-1 Casper She-She-Bon-Ga, age 6.
33-38-5-2 Lizzie She-She-Bon-Ga, age 4.
33-38-5-3 Christina She-She-Bon-Ga, age 2.
33-38-5-4 Francis She-She-Bon-Ga, born Mch 9 1908 2nd roll.

Information following from: Not Given.
34-38 SHAW-WAW-SKO-PE-NAY-SE or PETER SHE-SHE-BONGA, age 57, P.O. Northport, see 4-38 & 6-38.

Information following from: Not Given.
35-38 SHE-SAW-NAW-QUOT, dead.
Wife: Name not given, dead.
35-38-1 George Coons, see 5-23.
Wife: Mary Coons.
35-38-2 Jane Tabasosh, see 11-38.

Information following from: Not Given.
36-38 SHO-SES, all dead.

Information following from: Not Given.
37-38 MAY-AW-GO-WAY-QUAY or ESTHER WAH-BUS-CUM, age 58, P.O. Beaver Island, on 1870 roll by herself afterwards married 22-42.

Information following from: Not Given.
38-38 QUING-QUISH, dead.
38-38-1 Name nor sex given.
38-38-1-1 Nancy I-Yea-Quaw-Ke-Zhick, see 7-38.

Information following from: Not Given.
39-38 O-ME-NAW-QUOT-O-QUAY or ANGELINE MIN-QUA-TO-QUAY, age 61, P.O. Gills Pier, husband and children dead, no heirs.

Information following from: Not Given.
40-38 PETER MOC-QUA, all dead, no heirs.

Page 39
Leland Band
Chief KAY-BAY-O-SAY-DUNG

Information following from: Not Given.
1-39 KAY-BAY-O-SAY-DUNG PETER or PAUL, dead.
Wife: Name not given, dead.
1-39-1 Simon Paul, age 38, P.O. FoxIsland, no children, see 42-43.
Wife: Thresa Aishway, dead, see 4-39.
1-39-2 Agnes, dead.
Husband: Peter Sam, age 30, P.O. Glenn Haven, see 3-44.
1-39-2-1 Christina Sam, age 5, P.O. Glenn Haven.
1-39-3 Jerry Paul, age 21, P.O. Honor, see 4-39, no children.

Information following from: Not Given.
2-39 O-MOSH-KE-DAY-SE-QUAY, dead.
2-39-1 Name nor sex given, dead.
2-39-1-1 Isabelle Daniels Chippeway, age 19, P.O. Honor, see 18-41.
2-39-2 Mary Blacksmith, age 50, P.O. Cedar, see 50-52, separated.
Husband: James Blacksmith, see 20-52.
2-39-3 Annie Prickett James, age 55, P.O. Honor, see 13-44.
Husband: Peter James.
2-39-4 Nancy, dead.
Husband: Thomas Nay-To-Shing, see 22-38.
2-39-4-1 Mary Coon, nee Pe-Gon-Gay, age 36, see 11-38 & 5-23.
2-39-4-2 Jane Pe-Quon-Gay Tabasosh, see 11-38.

2-39-4-3 Mary Nay-To-Shing, see 22-38.

Information following from: Not Given.

3-39 PAY-SHE-KE-ZHICK, dead.

Wife: Name not given.

3-39-1 Margaret Isaac, age 51, P.O. Manistique, see 53-21.

Husband: Burt Isaac, see report sheet C.

3-39-1-1 John Isaac, age 35, P.O. Manistique, single.

3-39-1-2 Therese Cline, age 28, P.O. Manistique.

Husband: Name not given, white.

3-39-1-2-1 Alex Cline, born Jany 31, 1908 2nd roll.

3-39-1-3 Stephen Isaac, age 25, single, died Apr 1908.

3-39-1-4 Rosie Isaac, age 22, P.O. Manistique.

3-39-1-5 Peter Isaac, age 20, P.O. Manistique.

3-39-1-6 Joe Isaac, age 18, P.O. Manistique.

3-39-1-7 Mary Isaac, age 17, P.O. Manistique.

3-39-1-8 Maggie Isaac, age 9, P.O. Manistique.

3-39-2 Frederick Isaac Isaac, age 32, P.O. Manistique

Information following from: Not Given.

4-39 MAW-NE-DO-WAY or JOE MANITOU, age 89, P.O. Cedar City Mich.

Wife: Name not given, dead.

4-39-1 John Manitou, age 58, P.O. Cedar Mich, on roll as 7-39.

Wife: Name not given, dead.

4-39-1-1 Mary Harris, age 22, P.O. Empire Stormer.

Husband: Ray Harris, white person.

4-39-1-1-1 Infant Harris, born June 1908 2nd roll.

4-39-1-2 Gertie Manitou, age 16, P.O. Cedar.

4-39-1-3 Clara Manitou, age 14.

4-39-1-4 Louisa Manitou, age 11.

4-39-1-5 Frank Manitou, age 9.

4-39-1-6 Walter Manitou, age 7.

4-39-1-7 Minnie Manitou, age 4.

4-39-2 Name not given, dead.

Husband: ~~Simon Paul~~

4-39-2-1 Simon Paul, see 1-39.

4-39-2-2 Jerry Paul, see 1-39.

Information following from: Not Given.

5-39 KAW-BAY-O-SAY-QUAY, all dead, no heirs.

Information following from: Not Given.

6-39 JOSEPH PRICKETTE, dead.

Wife: Name not given, dead.

6-39-1 Name not given, dead.
Wife: name not given, dead.
6-39-1-1 Ida Prickett, age 10, P.O. Gill's Pier, lives (with) George Pickett, see 19-44.

Information following from: Not Given.
7-39 NAY-WAW-DAY-KE-ZHICK or JOHN MANITOU, see 4-39.

Information following from: Not Given.
8-39 SAY-GE-TOE, dead, no heirs, son of 4-39.

Information following from: Not Given.
9-39 ME-ME-NAW-SHE or DAVID PAUL, age 52, P.O. Elk Rapids Mich, wife dead, no children.

Information following from: Not Given.
10-39 NAW-SE-CUM-O-QUAY or CATHARINE MEN-DO-WASH, age 58, P.O. Sutton's Bay, now wife of 7-45.
10-39-1 Sophia Kaw-Too-Say, see 22-41.

Information following from: Not Given.
11-39 KAW-PON-KAY or JOHN SHAWKOO, age 63, died Apr22/07.
Wife: Susan Shawkoo, age 54, P.O. BoyneCity.
11-39-1 Thomas Shawkoo, age 43, P.O. Sutton's Bay, see 5-41.
11-39-2 Noah Shocko, age 23, P.O. Bay Shore, not married.
11-39-3 Mary Shocko, age 17, P.O. Boyne City.
11-39-4 Martha Shocko, age 12, P.O. Mt. Pleas. Sch.
11-39-5 Alice Shocko, age 10, P.O. Mt. Pleas. Sch.

11/39 5/41

Springvale Mich
5-17-09

Horace B. Durant
Special U.S. Indian Agent
Dear Sir.

Your letter was at hand today asking me about my parents names. I don't know my father first English name but I will give you his last Indian name Nahkaheawangue that's as near I can make it (tribe Chippewa) And my mother's name Eliza Shawcaw or her Indian name Pedabanoqua this is her first Indian name.

(2)

My first Indian name (Chingwongasawqua)

From
Mrs. Susan Shakoo,
Springvale Mich.

Information following from: Not Given.

12-39 KAW-BE-NAW, dead.

Note: These appear to ________ 2 children who _______ enrolled in 1870 ______ name of Kaw-be____________ Kaw-be-naw was a _________ Grand River Indian _______ if living today, wi________ undoubtedly give the ________ two children's names, (if living) for enrollment with him, but the chiefs & headmen of this band (page 39) say Kaw-be-naw is dead. Horace B. Durant Apl. Agt Gill's Pier, Mich Nov. 16/08. (page has torn piece missing from right side of page)

Page 40
Leland Band
Chief AU-KO-WE-SAY

Information following from: Not Given.

1-40 AU-KO-WE-SAY (AGOSA), dead, heirs are on roll of 1870 by themselves.

Wife: Name not given, dead.

1-40-1 See 8-40.

1-40-2 See 10-40.

1-40-3 See 12-40.

1-40-4 See 15-40.

Information following from: Not Given.

2-40 NAY-SHE-KAY-SHE, dead.

2-40-1 Margaret (Miller) Fisher, age 60, P.O. Elk Rapids.

Husband: James Miller or James Fisher, age 63, P.O. Elk Rapids, see 14-40.

2-40-2 Nancy Shagonaby, age 42, P.O. Omena.

Husband: Jasper Shagonaby, age 45, died Mch 29/08.

2-40-2-1 Mitchell Shaggonaby, age 23, P.O. Rex Mich, see 20-23.

2-40-3 George Allen, age 50, P.O. Mt. Pleasant.

Wife: Eliza, now wife of John Bigjoe, see 13-38.

2-40-4 Susan Sargonquatto, see 32-38.

Information following from: Not Given.

3-40 SHE-BAW-QUO-UM, dead.

Wife: Mrs. David King, age 70, P.O. Elk Rapids Mich, afterwards wife of David King deceased.

3-40-1 Name nor sex given, dead.

3-40-1-1 Sam King, age 28, Gladstone Mich, single.

3-40-2 Eliza Ance, age 41, P.O. Elk Rapids.

Husband: Peter Ance, age 45, P.O. Elk Rapids, see 41- ~~45~~15
3-40-2-1 Isaac Ance, age 10, see 10-40.
3-40-2-2 Daniel Ance, age 6, see 10-40.
3-40-2-3 George King, age 8, P.O. Elk Rapids, illegitimate.
3-40-3 Josie Cooper, died May 27-07, see 29-32.

Information following from: Not Given.
4-40 MAY-MAW-GO-WE-NAY, dead, father of 27-40.
4-40-1 Mark Memgona, see 27-40.
4-40-2 Paul Mamgona or Mamogowina, age ~~66~~ 78, P.O. San Francisco Cala. 4a Prospect Ave, no wife or children, unmarried..

Information following from: Not Given.
5-40 PAIM-WAY-WE-DUNG, dead.
Wife: Margaret, age 70, now wife of John Pedwadum.
5-40-1 Moses Francis, age 48, P.O. Sutton's Bay.
Wife: Mary (Pean) Francis, age 45, daughter of 1-34.
5-40-1-1 Frank Francis, age 27, P.O. Sutton's Bay.
Wife: ~~Marian~~ Mary Ann (Stephen) Francis, age 30, see 1-38 & 21-41.
5-40-1-1-1 Joe Francis, age 6.
5-40-1-1-2 Lena Francis, age 2.
5-40-1-2 Charles Francis, age, 22, P.O. Sutton's Bay.
5-40-1-3 Mary Francis, age 19.
5-40-1-4 Marceline Francis, age 17.
5-40-1-5 Moses Francis Jr., age 13.
5-40-1-6 Ole Francis, age 10.
5-40-1-7 Ida Francis, age 7.
5-40-2 Jacob Francis, age 46, P.O. ~~Su Petoskey~~ Bay Shore.
Wife: ~~Nancy Francis, nee Bird~~.
5-40-2-1 Eliza Francis, age 22, P.O. Namah Mich.
5-40-3 Jane Ahko, age 40, P.O. Omena.
Husband: William Ahko, age 42, see 8-40.
5-40-3-1 Mary Ahko King, died Sept/07, see 8-40.

Information following from: Not Given.
6-40 PE-NAY-SE-WE-KE-ZHICK or
PAUL PE-NAY-SE-WE-KE-ZHICK, age 83, P.O. Omena.
Wife: Name not given, dead.
6-40-1 William Paul, age 53, P.O. Omena, see 3-42.
Wife 1st : Name not given, dead.
Wife 2nd: Margaret (Poneshing), age 38, P.O. Omena, see 6-21-54, 1st husband Isaac Maishcaw.
6-40-1-1 John Maishcaw or Paul, age 21, P.O. Genoa Ind Sch.

6-40-1-2 James Maishcaw or Paul, age 19, P.O. Genoa Ind Sch.
6-40-1-3 Julia Maishcaw or Paul, age 17.
6-40-1-4 Eliza Maishcaw or Paul, age 9.
6-40-1-5 Isaac Maishcaw or Paul, age 7.
6-40-1-6 Sophia Maishcaw or Paul, age 15, died Nov/07.
6-40-1-7 Amos Paul, age 5, see 6-21-54.
6-40-1-8 Charles Paul, age 27.
Wife: Agnes or Agatha Paul (nee Shakoo), age 21, died Mch 4/08.
6-40-1-8-1 Francis Paul, age 3.
6-40-1-8-2 Mitchell Paul, born Mch 1, 1907, died Mch 18/08.
6-40-2 James Paul, age 42, P.O. Omena.
Wife: Name not given, dead, no children.

Information following from: Not Given.
7-40 KE-SIS-WAW-BAY, dead.
Wife: Name not given, now wife of John Jacobs, see 13-38.

Information following from: Not Given.
8-40 AW-KO-WE-SAY, dead.
Wife: Name not given, dead.
8-40-1 William Ahka, age 42, P.O. Omena.
Wife: Jane Ahka, nee Francis, age 41, see 5-40, daughter of wife of 13-41.
8-40-1-1 Mary Ahka, age 22.
Husband: Louis King, an Indian, see 8-62 & 30-23 & 2-44.
8-40-2 Name nor sex given, dead, no heirs.

Information following from: Not Given.
9-40 NAY-ONG-GAY-BE or PETER NAONGGABAY, age 63, P.O. Omena.
Wife: Sophia Naonggabay, nee Agosa, age 60, P.O. Omena, on roll with him in 1870.
9-40-1 Catharine Pewash, age 44, P.O. Omena, 2nd wife of Sam Pewash.
Husband: Sam Pewash or Sam O-Ge-Maw-Ke-Ge-Do, age 43, see 6-46.
9-40-1-1 George Pewash, age 20, P.O. ~~Om~~ Bay Shore Mich.
Wife: Alice Black, age 17, see 4-30.
9-40-1-2 Joe Pewash, age 18, P.O. Omena.
9-40-1-3 William Pewash, age 16, P.O. Petosky
9-40-1-4 Ambrose Pewash or Ambrose Naonggabay, age 15,

P.O. Omena.
9-40-1-5 Hattie Pewash, age 13.
9-40-1-6 Thresa Pewash, age 10.
9-40-2 Eliza Shawanah or Naquoum, age 36, P.O. Horton Bay Mich.
Husband 1st : Peter ~~Tapekeah~~ Tepkeah, see 22-41.
9-40-2-1 Joseph Tepekeah, age 18.
9-40-2-2 Lucy Tepekeah, age 10.
9-40-2-3 Lillie Tepekeah, age 8.
Husband 2nd: George Shawanah or Naquoum, age 29, P.O. Horton Bay Mich, died Apr 1908.
9-40-2-4 Susie Shawanah, age 3.
9-40-3 Louisa Waw-Say-Ke-Zhick, age 28, P.O. Charlevoix.
Husband: Name not given, see 11-23, separated.
9-40-3-1 Annie Naonggabay, age 10.

Information following from: Not Given.
10-40 KE-WAY-TO-NAW-QUO-UM or ALBERT AGOSA, age 72, P.O. Northport.
Wife: Charlotte Agosa, age 78, P.O. Northport.
10-40-1 John Agosa, age 44, P.O. Northport.
Wife: ~~Mary Ance St~~, Pottawatomie
10-40-1-1 Moses Agosa, age 7, P.O. Northport.
10-40-2 Sarah Mendowash, age 39, P.O. Northport.
Husband: Joseph Mendowash, age 30, P.O. Northport, son of 7-45, no children.
10-40-3 Robert Agosa #1, age 36, P.O. Northport, no wife or children.
10-40-4 Mary Ann (Ance).
Husband: Peter Ance, ~~Pottawatomie~~, see 41-15.
10-40-4-1 Isaac Ance, age 10, P.O. Northport, lives with Albert Agosa.
10-40-4-2 Daniel Ance, age 6, P.O. Northport, lives with Albert Agosa.

Information following from: Not Given.
11-40 ME-SE-NAW-SKO-DAY-WAY, dead.
Wife: Name not given, dead.
11-40-1 George Sands, age 46, P.O. Omena.
Wife: Lucy Sands, age 42, died May 2/08.
11-40-1-1 Thomas Sands, age 25, P.O. Omena.
11-40-1-2 Joseph Sands, age 24, P.O. Omena.
11-40-1-3 Eliza Sands, age 22, P.O. Omena.
11-40-1-4 Lucy Sands, age 20, P.O. Omena.
11-40-1-5 Amos Sands, age 18, P.O. Omena.
11-40-1-6 Archie Sands, age 15, P.O. Omena.
11-40-1-7 Charles Sands, age 12, P.O. Omena.

11-40-1-8 John Sands, age 10, P.O. Omena.
11-40-1-9 Benjamin Sands, age 8, P.O. Omena.
11-40-1-10 Alford Sands, age 5, P.O. Omena.
11-40-1-11 William Sands, age 3, P.O. Omena.
11-40-2 Name nor sex given, dead, no heirs.

Information following from: Not Given.
12-40 DAVID AW-KO-WE-SAY or AGOSA, age 76, P.O. Omena Mich.
Wife: Mary, dead.
12-40-1 Jacob Agosa, age 54, P.O. Omena, drew with Pottawatomies.
Wife: Maggie (Chappies) Agosa, age 25, Canadian Indian.
12-40-1-1 Emma Ella Agosa, born Aug 14, 1907.
12-40-2 Robert D. Agosa, age 46, P.O. Traverse City, a Tailor, drew with Pottawatomies.
Susan Owner, daughter of 25-23, no children.
12-40-3 Paul Agosa, age 33, P.O. Omena, drew with Pottawatomies.
Wife: Marian Agosa, nee Fisher, age 33, see 17-38.
12-40-3-1 Clara M. Agosa, age 6.
12-40-3-2 Esther S. Agosa, age 4.
12-40-3-3 Lena Agosa, age 3.
12-40-3-4 Elsie Agosa, age 2.
12-40-3-5 Donald Agosa, age 7 months, born March 1908 2nd roll.

Information following from: Not Given.
13-40 AIN-NE-WAISH-KEY or MITCHELL ENIWESSKY or ANWASKY, age 80, P.O. Suttons Bay.
Wife: Sophia Eniwesky, age 73, on 1870 roll with husband.
13-40-1 Joe Anwaskey or Eniwesky, age 55, P.O. Suttons Bay.
Wife: Name not given, dead.
13-40-1-1 William ~~Eniwesky~~ Anawasky, age 31, P.O. Suttons Bay.
Wife 1st : Louisa Yanott, dead.
Wife 2nd: Angeline Eniwasky, age 29, P.O. Suttons Bay, see 3-41.
13-40-1-1-1 Lena Eniwasky, age 3 months, died Sept 10/08 2nd roll.
13-40-1-1-2 Henry Eniwasky, age 10. see 19-41.
13-40-1-1-3 Lucy Eniwasky, age 7, see 19-41.
13-40-1-2 Josephine Davenport, age 30, P.O. Suttons Bay, separated now living with James Breaksmith, see 20-52.
Husband: William Davenport, age 31, P.O. Cross Village, see 104-22.
13-40-1-2-1 Eliza Davenport, age 10, pay to father.

13-40-1-2-2 Lizzie Blacksmith, born July 26, 1907 2nd roll, see 20-52.

13-40-1-3 Charles Eniwesky, age 17, P.O. Suttons Bay.

13-40-2 John, adopted by & paid with in 1870, 19-44.

13-40-3 Name nor sex given, dead, no heirs.

Information following from: Not Given.

14-40 JAMES FISHER or JAMES MILLER, enroll as Miller, age 63, P.O. Kewadin or Rapid City.

Wife: Margaret Fisher, age 60, on 1870 roll with husband, see 2-40.

14-40-1 Rosie Miller, age 38, P.O. Kewadin.

Husband: Amos Fox, see 15-45.

14-40-2 Solomon Miller, age 35, P.O. Kewadin.

Wife: Agatha Nanego, see 39-41.

14-40-3 John Miller, age 33, P.O. Elk Rapids, not married.

14-40-4 Lillian Miller, age 31, P.O. Petosky, not married.

14-40-5 James Lyman Miller, age 29, P.O. North Forks North Dakotah, coming home soon, single.

14-40-6 Henrietta Miller, age 27, P.O. Traverse City, works for Robert Agosa.

14-40-7 Margaret Miller, age 25, said to be at Haskell Ind. Sch.

14-40-8 Fannie Laura Miller, age 23, said to be at Haskell Ind. Sch., recent graduate of Chilocco.

14-40-9 Silas W. Miller, age 16, Haskell Inst. Lawrence Ks.

14-40-10 George Lyman Miller, age 13, Chilocco Ind. Sch.

Information following from: Not Given.

15-40 GEORGE AW-KO-WE-SAY or AGOSA, died May 15/08.

Wife: Mary Ann George Agosa, age 57, P.O. Omena, with husband in 1870.

15-40-1 Name nor sex given, dead, no heirs.

15-40-2 Name nor sex given, dead, no heirs.

Information following from: Not Given.

16-40 JOHN J. BATTISE or JOHN JACOBS, age 58, P.O. Omena.

Wife: Thresa Jacobs, age 70, P.O. Omena, see 33-52 & 7-40, 1st husband John Kesiswawbay.

16-40-1 Jane K. Cobb, nee Ogosa, age ~~36~~ 47, P.O. Omena, child by Thresa and 1st husband.John Kesiswawbay.

Husband: John Cobb, see 13-10-38.

16-40-1-1 James Cobb.

16-40-2 Alice Jacobs, age 18, P.O. Genoa Ind School, adopted, grandchild of William ~~Chaw~~ Key-Way-Cush-Cum 13-13-38.

16-40-3 Ida Jacobs, age 8, P.O. Omena, adopted, grandchild of William ~~Chaw~~ Key-Way-Cush-Cum 13-13-38.

Information following from: Not Given.
17-40 KEY-WAY-SE-MO-QUAY, dead.
Wife: Name not given, dead.
17-40-1 Name nor sex given, dead, no heirs.
17-40-2 Eliza Antonie, age 57, Omenna, husband dead and no children.

Information following from: Not Given.
18-40 SAW-GAW-CHE-WAY-SAY-QUAY, dead, no heirs.

Information following from: Not Given.
19-40 O-NIP-SE-QUAY, dead, no heirs.

Information following from: Not Given.
20-40 O-MAW-SE-QUAY (female), dead, after 1870 married Chief Tay-Baw-Se-Ke-Zhick 1-46.
20-40-1 Name nor sex given, dead.

Information following from: Not Given.
21-40 SHONG-QUAY-SHE-QUAY, dead, no heirs.

Information following from: Not Given.
22-40 KAW-WAY-GO-MO-AH or WILLIAM BIRD, age 64, P.O. Suttons Bay Mich.
Wife: Elizabeth Bird, age 64, P.O. Suttons Bay Mich, with husband 1870, see 6-42.
22-40-1 Susan Bird, age 33, P.O. Suttons Bay, not married.
22-40-2 Catharine Dean, see 7-51.
Husband: Daniel Dean, see 7-51.

Information following from: Not Given.
23-40 KEY-WAY-CUSH-CUM, dead.
23-40-1 Mitchell Anawasky, see 13-40.

Information following from: Not Given.
24-40 PE-NAY-BAW-TO-QUAY, dead.
24-40-1 Son, dead, see 11-40, for heirs see George Sands 11-40.

Information following from: Not Given.
25-40 NAY-WAW-CHE-KE-ZHICK, dead, no heirs.

Information following from: Not Given.
26-40 PAY-BE-SHAY-QUAY (female), dead.
26-40-1 Name nor sex given.

26-40-1-1 Agnes (Petosky) Taylor, age 43, P.O. Petosky, see 10-26.
26-40-1-2 Mary (Petosky) Hinds, age 37, , P.O. Petosky, see 10-26.

Information following from: Not Given.
27-40 MARK MAY-ME-GO-NON or MARK MAMAGONA, age 68, P.O. Elk Rapids Mich Kewadin.
Wife: Eliza (Paul) Mamagona, age 57.
27-40-1 James Mamagona, age 37, P.O. Kewadin Mich, not married, no children.
27-40-2 Benjamin Mamagona, age 35, P.O. Kewadin, not married, no children.
27-40-3 Francis Mamagona, age 29, P.O. Kewadin Mich, not married, no children.
27-40-4 George Mamagona, age 20, P.O. Ann Arbor Law Sch. Univ. Mich.
27-40-5 Robert Mamagona, age 16, P.O. Haskell Ind. School.

Information following from: Not Given.
28-40 KEY-WAY-ON-QUOT-O-QUAY, dead, no heirs.

Information following from: Not Given.
29-40 MEN-DAW-WAW-BE, dead, no heirs.

Information following from: Not Given.
30-40 NE-GE-GWAW-BAW-NO-QUAY, dead.
30-40-1 Name nor sex given.
30-40-1-1 Jennie O-Ge-Maw-Ke-Do, see 16-6-41

Information following from: Not Given.
31-40 JACOB NAW-O-GO-NAY-BE, age 73, P.O. Omena.
Wife: Alice Naw-O-Go-Nay-Be, age 60, P.O. Omena, on roll 1870 with husband, no children.

Page 41
Chief NAW-O-QUAY-KE-ZHICK

Information following from: Not Given.
1-41 NAW-O-QUAY-KE-ZHICK, dead.
Note: Wife & all heirs dead so say all the Old Inds. At Pashabatown who are of the same band – Durant Spl Agt.

Information following from: Not Given, Nov 21/08, Beaver Island.
2-41 O-GAW-BAY-WAY, female, dead.

2-41-1 Joe Wa-An-Be-Nim-Que, age 60, P.O. Beaver Island, see 10-38.
2-41-2 Maggie Hamilton, age 52, P.O. Beaver Island St. James.
Husband: Name not given, dead.
2-41-2-1 Louis Hamilton, age 28, P.O. Beaver Island, single.
2-41-2-2 Mathew Hamilton, age 16, P.O. Beaver Island.
2-41-3 Louis, dead, no heirs.
2-41-4 Theresa, dead, no heirs.
2-41-5 Catharine, dead.
Husband: Name not given, dead.
2-41-5-1 Mitchell Andrews, age 35, P.O. Beaver Island St. James, single, see 24-60.
2-41-5-2 Isaac Andrews, age 27, see 32-38 & 24-60.
2-41-5-3 Benedict Andrews Kingbird, age 25, P.O. Omena Mich, see 24-60 & 41-43.
2-41-5-4 Madeline, dead.
2-41-5-4-1 Enos Andrews, age 2, see 24-60.
2-41-6 Nancy, dead.
Husband: Antoine Bird, now married to Sophia Chippeway, see 12-45.
2-41-6-1 See 12-45.
2-41-6-2 See 12-45.
2-41-7 John, dead.
Wife: Angeline Wabinimkee, age 39, P.O. Beaver Island.
2-41-7-1 Peter Wabinimkee, age 23, P.O. Beaver Island, see 14-34 for wife & children.
2-41-7-2 Simon Wabinimkee, age 21, P.O. Beaver Island.
Wife: Nancy Wabinimkee #1, age 19, OK-D.
2-41-7-2-1 John Wabinimkee, age 2, died Oct/08.
2-41-7-3 Josephine Wabinimkee, age 16.
2-41-7-4 Elias Wabinimkee, age 14.
2-41-7-5 Nancy Wabinimkee #2, age 12.
2-41-7-6 Julius Wabinimkee, age 10.
2-41-7-7 Ida Wabinimkee, age 5.
2-41-7-8 Jane Wabinimkee, born June/08, 2nd roll.

Information following from: Not Given, Sept 25/08, Pashbatown.
3-41 PAY-BAW-SAW, dead.
Wife: Name not given, dead.
3-41-1 Mary ~~Nadowegesa~~ Agosa, age 60, P.O. Cross Village.
Husband 1st : Name not given, dead.
Husband 2nd: Name not given, dead.
3-41-1-1 Sarah Francis, see 8-20.
Husband: Joe Francis.
3-41-1-2 Angeline (Troshe) Anawasky, age 29, see 8-20.

Husband 1st : Name not given.
3-41-1-2-1 Edmund Troshe, age 14, lives with mother Angeline Anawasky.
3-41-1-2-2 Mary Troshe, age 3, lives with mother Angeline Anawasky.
Husband 2nd: William Anawasky, age 31, P.O. Suttons Bay, see 13-40.
~~3-41-2~~ Blank no entry?
3-41-3 Andrew Tabasaw, dead.
Wife: Name not given, dead.
3-41-3-1 Enos Tabasaw, age 28, P.O. Suttons Bay, wife dead, no children.
3-41-3-2 Bennett Tabasaw, age 20, P.O. Suttons Bay.
3-41-4 Mary Ann Nadowegesa, age 47, P.O. Suttons Bay.
Husband: Name not given, dead, was brother of her 1st sister (husband) they married brothers.
3-41-4-1 Frank Nadowegesa, age 24, P.O. Suttons Bay, not married.
3-41-4-2 Rosie Nadowagesa, age 17, P.O. Suttons Bay.
3-41-5 Sophia, dead.
Husband: Name not given, dead.
3-41-5-1 Antoine Chippewqay, age23, see 19-41.
Wife: Susan Yanot.
3-41-5-2 John Chippeway, age 20, P.O. Suttons Bay, see ~~3-41~~ 46-43.

Information following from: Not Given, Sept 25/08, Pashabatown.
4-41 WAY-GE-ZHE-GO-ME, dead.
Wife 1st : Name not given, dead.
Wife 2nd: Madeline Shaw-Non-Gay, died July 4/08.
4-41-1 Julia Shako, age 47, see 22-41.
Husband: William Shako, see 22-41.
4-41-1-1 Katie Shako, age 13.
4-41-1-2 Joe Shako, age 11.
4-41-1-4 Mary Shako, age 7.
~~4-41-1-5 Julia Shako.~~
4-41-2 Nancy, dead.
Husband: Andrew Shako, age 50, P.O. Suttons Bay.
4-41-2-1 Mary James, age 23, see 15-42.
Husband: Levi James, age 25, see 18-13-44.
4-41-2-1-1 Delia James, age 7.
4-41-2-1-2 Annie James, age 3, died Apr 1908.
4-41-2-2 Agatha or Agnes Paul, age 21, died Mch 4, 1908, for husband & children see 6-40.
4-41-3 Name nor sex given, dead, no heirs.

4-41-4 Name nor sex given, dead, no heirs.
4-41-5 Jennie Pashabay, age 29, P.O. Suttons Bay.
Husband: ~~Gabriel~~ Benjamin Pashabay, age 33, see 15-42.

Information following from: Not Given, Sept 25/08.
5-41 PONTIAC, dead.
Wife: Name not given, dead.
5-41-1 Catharine, dead, see 14-41.
Husband: Name not given, dead.
5-41-1-1 Christina Negonegezhick, age 40, P.O. Bay Shore, see 14-41.
Husband: Joe Negonegezhick, age 44, died ~~Sept~~ 1908 7, see 12-24.
5-41-1-1-1 Rosie Negonegezhick, age 16, P.O. Bay Shore, not married.
5-41-1-1-1-1 John Negonegezhick, born Sept/07 2nd roll, 14-41 gives date of birth Apr 4, 1908.
5-41-2 Sophia Pontiac, age 62, P.O. Suttons Bay.
Husband: John Shawkoo, dead, see 11-39.
5-41-2-1 Thomas Shawkoo, age 43, P.O. Suttons Bay, see 11-39 & 41-43.
Wife 1st : Name not given, dead.
Wife 2nd: Catharine, see 14-38.
5-41-2-1-1 Antoine Shawkoo, age 10.
5-41-2-2 Samule Pontiac, age 32, P.O. Suttons Bay.
Wife: Lucy Pontiac, nee Chippeway, age 29.
5-41-2-2-1 Agnes Pontiac, born May 18/07, died May 21/07 2nd roll.
5-41-3 Elizabeth Smoke, P.O. Bay Shore, dead.
Husband: John Smoke, P.O. Bay Shore, dead, see 11-30.
5-41-4 Emma (Pontiac) Mitchell, age 38, P.O. Suttons Bay.
Husband 1st : William Bourassaw, see 3-42.
5-41-4-1 Caroline Bourssaw, age 16, P.O. Mt. Pleasant Sch.
5-41-4-2 Annie Bourssaw, age 14, P.O. Mt. Pleasant Sch.
Husband 2nd: Enos Mitchell, died Dec 1906 off.
5-41-4-3 Samuel Mitchell, age 12, P.O. Mt. Pleasant School.
5-41-4-4 Joe Mitchell, age 10, P.O. Mt. Pleasant School.
5-41-4-5 Louis Mitchell, age 3, P.O. Bay Shore Mich, with father's mother Mary Ann Kewanekezhick 1-30.
5-41-5 Name nor sex given, dead.

Information following from: Not Given.
6-41 PAY-SHAW-SE-GAY, dead.
Wife: Name not given, dead.

6-41-1 Jennie O-Ge-Maw-Ke-Do, age 38, see 5-38.
Husband: Steel O-Ge-Maw-Ke-Do, see 5-38.
6-41-2 Name nor sex given, dead, no heirs.
6-41-3 Name nor sex given, dead, no heirs.
6-41-4 Name nor sex given, dead, no heirs.

Information following from: Not Given.
7-41 O-TISH-QUAY-YAW, female, dead.
7-41-1 Eliza or Lizzie Sands, age 54, P.O. ~~Charlevoix~~ Bay Shore.
Husband: Alfred Sands, dead.
7-41-1-1 Rosie John, age 21, P.O. Bay Shore.
7-41-1-2 Name nor sex given, dead.
7-41-1-2-1 Nellie Taylor Webster, age 14, P.O. Mt. Pleasant Sch, see 29-32.
7-41-2 Name nor sex given, dead, no heirs.
7-41-3 Name nor sex given, dead, no heirs.
7-41-4 Name nor sex given, dead, no heirs.

Information following from: Not Given.
8-41 KAW-WE-TAW-O-SAY, dead, heirs all dead.

Information following from: Not Given, Sept 25/08.
9-41 NAY-NE-AW-SHE, dead.
Wife: Name not given, dead.
9-41-1 Name nor sex given.
9-41-1-1 ~~Mary Ann Prickett.~~
~~Husband: dead.~~
9-41-1-1-1 Ida Prickett, age 10, P.O. Gill's Pier Mich.
9-41-2 Joe Neniashe, see 12-45.

Information following from: Not Given.
10-41 NAW-O-QUAY-GE-ZHE-GONSE or LOUIS CHIPPEWAY, dead.
Wife: Name not given, dead.
10-41-1 Thresa, dead, no children, no heirs.
10-41-2 Angeline Chippeway, now wife of John Anawaskey, see 19-44.
10-41-3 Name nor sex given, dead, no heirs.

Information following from: Not Given.
11-41 CHING-QUAY, dead.
Wife: Be-Nay-Ge-She-Go-Quay, daughter of 47-43, dead.
11-41-1 William Ching-Quay, age 35, P.O. ~~Torch Lake~~ ~~Mackinaw Is~~ ~~Manistique~~ Namah Camp 10.
Wife: Mary Ching-Quay, nee Sagato, age 32, see 15-36.
11-41-1-1 William Ching-Quay Jr., age 2.

11-41-2 Mrs. Antoine Pean, age 30, see 1-34.

Information following from: Not Given.
12-41 O-NAY-NAW-GO, dead.
Wife: Name not given, dead.
12-41-1 Name nor sex given, dead, no heirs.
12-41-2 Name nor sex given, dead, no heirs.
12-41-3 Name nor sex given, dead, no heirs.
12-41-4 Angeline (Nanego) Waw-Say-Ke-Zhick, age 44, P.O. Sutton's Bay.
Husband: Charles Waw-Say-Ke-Zhick, age 57, P.O.Sutton's Bay.
12-41-4-1 Joe Waw-Say-Ke-Zhick, age 25, P.O. Sutton's Bay, no married.
12-41-4-2 Mary Waw-Kay-Zoo, age 23, P.O. Sutton's Bay.
Husband: Amos Waw-Kay-Zoo, age 33, P.O. Sutton's Bay, see 2-45.
12-41-4-2-1 Mary Waw-Kay-Zoo, age 2, P.O. Sutton's Bay.
12-41-4-3 ~~John~~ Solomon Waw-Say-Ke-Zhick, age 13, P.O. Sutton's Bay.
12-41-4-4 John Waw-Say-Ke-Zhick, age 2, P.O. Sutton's Bay.

Suttons Bay
Mich
May 22, 09
my father his name Paul Wasacishik and my mather Mary Regatawabe. my father his wife my name Chrs Wasagishit I am Ottawa Indian.
yours truly
Charles Wasagishit
Suttons Bay Mich

Information following from: Not Given.
13-41 PE-TWAY-WE-TUNG or JOHN PEDWADUM, age 70, P.O. Pashabatown.
Wife 1st : Name not given, dead.
Wife 2nd: Margaret Pedwadum, nee Agosa, age 70.
13-41-1 Louisa Pedwadum, age 27, P.O. Suttons Bay, not married.
13-41-2 Andrew Pedwadum, age 25, P.O. Suttons Bay, single.
13-41-3 Joseph Pedwadum, age 33, Suttons Bay.
Wife: Elizabeth Pedwadum, nee Chippeway, age 38, see 18-41, no children.
13-41-4 Thresa Akin, age 31, P.O. ~~Rapid City~~ Barker's Creek Mich.
Husband: Stephen Aken, see 5-46.

Information following from: Not Given.
14-41 KE-CHE-PE-NAY-SE, dead.
Wife: Catharine Ching-Quaw, age 60, died Feby/08.
14-41-1 Christina Negonegezhick, age 40, P.O. ~~Charlevoix~~ Bay Shore
Husband: Joe Negonegezhick, age ~~56~~ 44, see 5-41 & 12-23.
14-41-1-1 Rosie Negonegezhick, age 20, died Sept 14/0~~8~~7
14-41-1-1-1 John Negonegezhick, born Apr 4, 1908.
14-41-2 Name nor sex given, dead.
14-41-3 Name nor sex given, dead.

Information following from: Not Given.
15-41 SOPHIA NAW-NE-GO-WE, dead.
15-41-1 Name nor sex given, dead.
15-41-2 Name nor sex given, dead.
15-41-2-1 Bennett Stephen, age 17, P.O. Suttons Bay, see 2-
42
15-41-3 Name nor sex given, dead.

Information following from: Not Given.
16-41 PE-NAY-SE-WOW-NO-QUAY, dead.
16-41-1 John Pedwadum, age 70, 13-41.
16-41-2 Name not given, female, dead, no heirs.
16-41-3 Louis Shomin, dead.
Wife: Name not given, dead.
16-41-3-1 William Shomin, age 25, P.O. Mt. Pleasant, see 42-41.
Wife: Mary Shomin, age 16, see 42-41.

Information following from: Not Given.
17-41 MAW-CHE-WE-TAW, dead.
Wife: Name not given, dead.
17-41-1 Sampson Blackman, age 40, Suttons Bay.
Wife: Lucy Blackman, nee Shomin, age 29, P.O. Suttons Bay, see 35-20.
17-41-1-1 Julia Blackman, age 13, died June 11, 1907.
17-41-1-2 Annie Blackman, age 10.
17-41-1-3 Louis Blackman, age 8.
17-41-1-4 Jennie Blackman, age 4.
17-41-1-5 Agatha Blackman, born Sept 9, 1908, too late for any roll, do not enroll.
17-41-2 Joseph Blackman, age 26, P.O. Rapid City.
Wife: Eliza Blackman, nee Mark, see 10-46.
17-41-3 Name nor sex given, dead.

Information following from: Not Given, Ind. Camp Honor.

18-41 JOSEPH KE-CHE-O-JIB-WAY or JOSEPH CHIPPEWAY, dead.
Wife: Name not given, dead.
18-41-1 Joseph Chippeway, dead.
Wife: Mary Ann Chippeway, P.O. Charlevoix, no children.
18-41-2 Louis Chippewa, see 10-41, children are dead.
18-41-3 Samuel Chippeway, P.O. Suttons Bay.
Wife:Angeline Chippeway see 14-38.
18-41-3-1 Angeline Ance, see 8-42.
18-41-3-2 Enos Chippeway, see 45-43.
18-41-3-3 Lucy Chippeway Pontiac, 5-41.
18-41-3-4 Jennie Chippeway, age 20, P.O. Mt. Pleas. Sch.
18-41-3-5 Lucile Chippeway, age 17.
18-41-3-6 Martin Chippeway, age 4.
18-41-4 Joseph Chippeway #2 (Second Joseph), dead.
Wife: Name not given, dead.
18-41-4-1 Angeline Chippeway, age 35, P.O. Pashabatown, not married.
18-41-4-1-1 John Anse, age 7, P.O. Pashabatown, illegit.
18-41-4-2 Sophia Bird, age 44, P.O. Pashabatown.
Husband: Antoine Bird, age 47, P.O. Pashabatown.
18-41-4-3 Elizabeth Pedwadum, age 38, P.O. Pashabatown, no children.
Husband: Joe Pedwadum, age 33, P.O. Pashabatown, see 13-41.
18-41-4-4 Philip Chippewa, age 34, P.O. Pashabatown, see 15-42.
Wife: Katie Chippewa, (Paychaba), age 34, no children, separated, see 15-42.
18-41-5 Moses Chippeway, dead, no wife or children.
18-41-6 Maggie (Chippeway) Agosa.
Husband: Name not given, dead.
18-41-6-1 ~~Marian~~ Mary Ann (Agosa) ~~Mixemo~~ Mick-Se-Mong, age 32, P.O. Cross Village, see 36-43.
Husband: Caspar Mick-Se-Mong, see 42-21.
18-41-6-1-1 William Mixemo, age 11.
18-41-7 Andrew Chippeway, age 60, P.O. Honor.
Wife: Mary Ann, white, not entitled to enrollment.
18-41-7-1 William Chippeway, age 37, P.O. ~~Keystone Mich~~ Traverse City Route 7 Box 69.
Wife: Christina Chippeway, nee Wabminike, age 28, P.O. Traverse City Route 7 Box 69.
18-41-7-1-1 John Chippeway, age 12.
18-41-7-1-2 Isabelle Chippeway, age 8.
18-41-7-2 Frank Chippeway, age 30, P.O. Honor.

Wife: Nancy Chipppeway, nee Bailey, age 18, daugh of Henry Bailey, see 14-50.
18-41-7-2-1 Nettie Chippeway, born 1908 NB 2nd roll.
18-41-7-3 Matilda Deverney, age 27, P.O. Honor.
Husband: Jacob Deverney, age 32, see 4-59.
18-41-7-3-1 Dave Deverney, age 10.
18-41-7-3-2 Mary Deverney, age 7.
18-41-7-3-3 Delia Deverney, age 3.
18-41-7-3-4 Annie Shiding, age 24, P.O. Honor Mich.
Husband: John Shiding, age 31, of Traverse band look up at Suttons Bay grand father's name; Kaw-Kaw-She.
18-41-7-3-4-1 Fred Shiding, age 7.
18-41-7-3-4-2 Matilda Shiding, age 5.
18-41-7-3-4-3 Alice Shiding, age 3.
18-41-7-3-4-4 Lawrence Shiding, age 2.
18-41-7-3-5 Caroline Weese, age 23, P.O. Honor.
Husband: Frank Weese, white.
18-41-7-3-5-1 Francis or Frayman Weese, age
5
18-41-7-3-5-2 Clara Weese, age 3.
18-41-7-3-6 Clara Pero or Pereault, age 22, P.O. Traverse City.
Husband: Louis Pero or Pereault, white.
18-41-7-3-6-1 Josephine Pero or Pereault, age 5
18-41-7-3-6-2 Ethel Pero or Pereault, age 3.
18-41-7-3-6-3 Wilford Pero or Pereault, born ~~Novem~~ Sept 1907 NB 2nd roll.
18-41-7-3-7 John Chippeway, age 21, P.O. Honor.
Wife: Isabella Daniels, age 19, an Ottawa of Traverse Band, see 2-39, undisname Peter James.
18-41-7-3-8 Albert Chippeway, age 18, not married, P.O. Honor.
18-41-7-3-8 Eddie Chippeway, age 16, not married, P.O. Honor.
18-41-7-3-8 Henry Chippeway, age 14, not married, P.O. Honor.
18-41-7-3-8 Bennett Chippeway, age 12, not married, P.O. Honor.
18-41-8 Daniel Chippeway, age 57, P.O. Suttons Bay.
Wife: Christina Chippeway, see 21-46.
18-41-8-1 Louis Chippewa, age 25, P.O. Genoa Nebr.
Wife: Maggie (Paro) Chippewa, age 23, P.O. Suttons Bay, see 8-42, Enroll by herself with dead child,

separated form husband.

18-41-8-1-1 Edwin Chippewa, age 2, died Sept 20/08 1st roll.

18-41-8-2 Mary Chippeway, age 20, P.O. Suttons Bay.

18-41-8-3 Dominick Chippeway, age 19, P.O. Suttons Bay.

18-41-8-4 ~~B~~ Daniel Chippeway Jr., age 17, P.O. Suttons Bay.

18-41-8-5 Rosie Chippeway, age 14, P.O. Suttons Bay.

18-41-9 Mary (Chippeway) Shanabinasse, age 55, P.O. Suttons Bay.

Husband: Isaac Shanabinasse or Isaac Southbird, see 44-43.

18-41-9-1.

June 9th 1909
Dear Sir. I have Received your Letter here today. And understanding it about your wanto of in doutabout my Wife Indianname her name before I merrid her was Christene Wabinemikee and her Father was called Mr. John Wabinemikee. And her mother's name was Maggie. And same usto call her Margurate Hanry She wa Ottawa to. And my wife's Father was belong to Ottawa Indian Tribe.
Yours TrulyWon. Chippeway.
Traverse City R7 Box 69

Information following from: Not Given.

19-41 I-YAW-NUT or JOE YANOT, age 73, P.O. Suttons Bay.

Wife: Thersa Waw-Say-Quo-Um, age 65, see 1-38.

19-41-1 Frank Yanot, age 40, P.O. Suttons Bay, separated enroll children with mother.

Wife: Madeline Yanot, nee Ance, see 8-42.

19-41-1-1 Jane Yanot, age 15.

19-41-1-2 Silas Yanot, age 13.

19-41-1-3 Annie Yanot, age 7.

19-41-1-4 Eddie, age 9 mos., born Dec/07 2nd roll.

19-41-2 ~~Susan~~ Louisa Anawasky.

Husband: William Anawasky, age 32, P.O. Sutton's Bay, see 13-40.

19-41-2-1 Henry Anawasky, age 10.

19-41-2-2 ~~Ros~~ Lucy Anawasky, age 7, ~~died Oct/07 1st roll~~.

~~19-41-2-3 Lena~~

19-41-3 Susan Chingway, ag 19, P.O. Suttons Bay.

Husband: Antoine Chingway, age 23, no children.

Information following from: Not Given.

20-41 KYE-YOSH-KOOSE, all dead no heirs.

Information following from: Not Given.

21-41 PE-NAY-SE, dead.

Wife: Name not given, dead.
21-41-1 Mary Ann Francis, age 30, P.O. Suttons Bay, see 5-40.
21-41-2 Joe Stephens, age 34, P.O. Sutton's Bay, see 19-44.

Information following from: Peshibatown, Sept 25/08.
22-41 PE-NAY-SE-WAW-NAW-QUOT of ShawKoo.
Wife: Name not given, dead.
22-41-1 Catharine Mendowash, age58, P.O. Suttons Bay, see 10-39 & 7-40.
Husband 1st : Name not given, dead.
22-41-1 Sophia Kawtoosay, age 41, by 1st husband, see 10-39.
Husband: Peter Kawtoosay, age ~~40~~.
22-41-1-1 Pason Kawtoosay, age 23, P.O. Sutttons Bay
22-41-1-2 Rosie Kawtoosay, age 17, P.O. Suttons Bay, not married.
22-41-1-2-1 Alex Chingway.
22-41-1-3 Elizabeth Kawtoosay, age 16.
22-41-1-4 Agnes Kawtoosay, age 10.
22-41-1-5 Edwin Kawtoosay, age 2.
Husband 2nd: Louis Mendowash, age 66, P.O. Suttons Bay.
22-41-2 Susan (Shawkoo) ~~Naquoum~~ Nawquom, age 57, P.O. Suttons Bay.
Husband: Joe Nawquom, age 56, P.O. Suttons Bay, see 49-43 and 9-23.
22-41-2-1 Margaret Nesha, age 24, P.O. Cross Village.
Husband: Name not given.
22-41-2-1-1 Name nor sex given.
22-41-2-2 George Nawquoum, age 22.
Wife: Eliza Nawquoum.
22-41-2-2-1 Susie Nawquoum, died Apr 3, 1908, see 9-40.
22-41-3 Simon Shawkoo, age 54, P.O. ~~Suttons Bay~~ Boyne City.
Wife: Name not given, separated, see 30-23.
22-41-4 William Shako, age 52, P.O. Suttons Bay.
Wife: Julia Shako, age 47, see 4-41.
22-41-5 Andrew Shako, age 50, see 4-41.
Wife 1st : Name not given, children see 4-41.
Wife 2nd: Mary Shawkoo, married Sept 21st 1908, see 15-42, no children yet

Information following from: Not Given.
23-41 MAY-CAW-DAY-AW-NIN-NE, dead.
Wife: Name not given, dead.
Note: On roll 1870 by themselves & they & families may be found on 42-41.

Information following from: Not Given, Sept 25/08.
24-41 O-GAW-BAY-AW-BAY-NO-QUAY, dead.
24-41-1 Mary Ann Ance, age 58, P.O. Suttons Bay.
Husband: Antoine Ance, P.O. Suttons Bay, see 41-15, same as Anthony Anse, no children.

Information following from: Not Given.
25-41 O-GE-MAW-KE-GE-DO or SAMUEL CHIPPEWAY, age 62, P.O. Suttons Bay, for wife & family see 18-41.

Information following from: Not Given.
26-41 FRANCIS BLACKMAN, dead.
Wfe: Name not given, dead.
26-41-1 Name not given, dead, no heirs.
26-41-2 Name not given, dead, no heirs.

Information following from: Not Given.
27-41 O-WAN-O-GE-MAW, dead.
Wfe: Name not given, dead.
27-41-1 Name not given, dead, no heirs.
27-41-2 Name not given, dead, no heirs.
27-41-3 Name not given, dead, no heirs.
27-41-4 Agatha Bemos, age 28, P.O. Elk Rapids, see 4-61.

Information following from: Not Given.
28-41 WAW-WE-YEA-KE-ZHICK or JACOB FRENCHMAN or JACOB BENJAMIN, age 70, P.O. Bay Shore.
Wife: Madeline Sainwick, age 56, P.O. Goodheart, see 31-28
28-41-1 Name not given, dead, no heirs.
28-41-2 Name not given, dead, no heirs.

Information following from: Not Given.
29-41 CATHARINE, see 18-28.
Husband: Name not given, dead.
29-41-1 Name not given, dead, no heirs.
29-41-2 Name not given, dead, no heirs.

Information following from: Not Given, Sept 25/08, Pashabtown.
30-41 ME-CHAW-KE-GWAW-NAY-AW-SHE, dead.
Wife: Margaret Mark, age 58, P.O. Elk Rapids, her 2nd husband Joe Mark, dead, died Feby 22/08 ist roll, brother of Peter Mark, see 10-46.
30-41-1 Name nor sex given, dead.
30-41-1-1 Susan Van, age 16, P.O. Elk Rapids Mich.
Husband: Jesse Van, white.

30-41-1-1-1 Ambrose Van, age 2, born Jany 1/07 1st roll.

Information following from: Not Given.
31-41 O-TISH-QUAY-GE-ZHE-GO-QUAY, dead.
31-41-1 Sophia Aniwassky, age 73, see 13-40.

Information following from: Not Given.
32-41 PAY-ME-SAY, dead, no heirs.

Information following from: Not Given.
33-41 JOHN B. SHAW-WAW-NON-GAY, dead, no heirs

Information following from: Not Given.
34-41 WAY-GE-SHE-GO-MES, dead.
Wife: Name not given, dead.
34-41-1 Moses Ice, P.O. Genoa Sch., Nebr, ~~dead~~ said to be dead drowned look up.

DEPARTMENT OF THE INTERIOR
UNITED STATES INDIAN SERVICE

Genoa Indian School,
Genoa Nebraska,
Mr Horace Durant, Spec Agent,
Petosky Michigan,

Dear Sir:-

Yours received and hasten to reply will say I did Know as Indian Boy A little older than myslf whose name was Moses Ice, his Indian name was (Agatchie). It is possible the name is not spelled correctly, but that was the way he pronounced it, The last I knew of him he started for the Lawrence School, Haskell Institute. Lawrence Kansas. Begging to remain respectfully yours I am yours respectfully

Genoa Nebraska,
% Gov School,

L. Chippewa

DEPARTMENT OF THE INTERIOR
M-209-R UNITED STATES INDIAN SERVICE
Haskell Institute,
Lawrence, Kansas,
May 17, 1909

Mr. Horace B. Durant,
Special Agent,
Petoskey, Michigan.

Dear Sir:

I am in receipt of your letter of the 14th inst. Relative to the whereabouts of an Indian boy by the name of Moses Ice and in reply to same have to say that such aboy came to this school and said that he wished to enroll but deserted before he had been on the grounds twelve hours. We have heard nothing whatever of him since that time.

Very respectfully,
H.B.Peairs
Superintendent

ALB. *Per A. L. Bowdler*

Information following from: Not Given.
35-41 KE-BAW-GAW-NAW-QUOT, dead, no heirs.

Information following from: Not Given.
36-41 SHAW-WAW-NO-QUAY, female, dead, no heirs.

Information following from: Not Given.
37-41 AISH-QUAY-GAW-BO-QUAY, dead.
Wife: Name not given, dead.
37-41-1 Name not given.
Husband: Louis Mitchel or Louis Waw-Be-Gay-Kake, see 9-28.
37-41-1-1 ~~Louisa~~ Emma Waw-Be-Gay-Kake, age 20, P.O. Bay Shore.
37-41-1-2 ~~Alec~~ William Waw-Be-Gay-Kake, age 17, P.O. Bay Shore.

Information following from: Not Given.
38-41 KE-CHE-O-QUAY, female, age 75, P.O. Suttons Bay Petoskey Pellston, separated.
Husband: John B. ~~Thruse~~ Thrusho, see 51-43.
38-41-1 Casper Thrusho or Trosho, age 36, P.O. Pellston Mich.
Wife: Name not given, dead, see 51-27.
38-41-1-1 Julius Thrusho, age 17, P.O. Pellston Mich, see 27-30.

Information following from: Not Given.
39-41 MAY-MAW-E-GAY PETER, dead.
Wife: Name not given, dead.
39-41-1 Name not given, dead.
39-41-2 Peter Nanego, age 62, P.O. Sutton's Bay, nephew but enrolled in 1870 with 39-41.
Wife" Lucy Nanego, daughter of 14-38.
39-41-2-1 Agatha Miller, age 24, P.O. Sutton's Bay.

Husband 1st: David Naquoum, age 35, separated, see 16-23.
39-41-2-1-1 Julius Naquoum, age 6
39-41-2-1-2 Louis Naquoum, age 4
39-41-2-1-3 Edward Naquoum, age 3
39-41-2-1-4 Charles Naquoum, age 2, 1st roll.
Husband 2nd: Solomon Miller, age 35, see 14- 40.
N.B. These two children Louis & Edward Naquoum, live with and are supported by, Peter Nanego, the grandfather & their shares should be paid to him. HBDurant Spl. Agt. Sept 26/08.
39-41-2-2 William Nanego, age 11.

Information following from: Not Given.
40-41 ME-ZHAW-QUAW-DO-QUAY, dead, no heirs.

Information following from: Not Given.
41-41 SHE-BAW-TE-GO-QUAY, dead, no heirs.

Information following from: Not Given.
42-41 E-TO-WAY-MAY or ISAAC BLACKMAN, age 61, P.O. Pashabatown.
Wife 1st: Name not given, dead.
Wife 2nd: Name not given, dead, see 16-41.
Wife 3rd: Rosie Blackman, white, off 1st husband Ah-She-Day-Qwa.
42-41-1 Jennie Blackman, age 36, P.O. Sutton's Bay, no children.
42-41-2 John Blackman, age 34, P.O. Sutton's Bay, wife dead, no children living.
42-41-3 Mitchell Blackman, age 32, P.O. Sutton's Bay.
Wife: Agnes Blackman, nee Aiken, granddaughter of 5-46.
42-41-3-1 Allen Blackman, born March 15, 1907 2nd roll.
42-41-3-2 Celia Blackman, infant, died March 1908, born After Mch 1, 1907.
42-41-4 Edward Blackman, age 26, P.O. Sutton's Bay, single.
42-41-5 Mary Blackman – Shomin, age 16, P.O. Mt Pleasant Sch, see 16-41.
42-41-6 William Shomin, age 25, P.O. Mt Pleasant Sch, see 16-41, his mother was wife of 42-41, not married, son of Rosie Blakman by Ah-She-Day-Qwa.
42-41-7 Annie (Helen) Blackman, age 13, P.O. Sutton's Bay.

Pashawbytown, Mich. 3/16 1909
Horace B. Durant
Petoskey, Mich
Dear Fried,

Your to me and kind letter was received yesterday. Of Jacob Benjamin his Indian name is Wah we ye gejek, his father name was Tah ta geje gwe um mothers name was Shaw ah no qwa they Christian or English name are not known or remembered.
Their Chief was Nah o qwe gezik in this village.
Jacob Benjamin or Frenchman use to call him here may be that the was his name is written in the old enrollment. How near are you through will you please let me know and when you come plete the you work?

Yours Truly,
Address it to
Mike Blackman
Omena Mich

Look up on Traverse roll Chief p. ~~41-42~~ 42-41 OK Jacob Frenchman D.

Information following from: Not Given, Sept 25/08.
43-41 A-PE-TAW-KE-ZHICK, dead.
Wife: Name not given, dead.
43-41-1 Frank Jacobs, age 40, P.O. Suttons Bay, wife dead, no children.

Page 42
Chief NAY-WAW-DAY-KE-ZHICK

Information following from: Not Given.
1-42 NAY-WAW-DAY-KE-ZHICK, dead.
Wife: Name not given, dead.
1-42-1 Name nor sex not given, dead.
Spouse: Name not given.
1-42-1-1 Louis Nay-Waw-Day-Ke-Zhick, age 20, P.O. Beaver Island.
1-42-1-2 Matthew Nay-Waw-Day-Ke-Zhick.
1-42-2 Name nor sex given, dead, no heirs.

Information following from: Not Given.
2-42 KAW-KAW-KOW-CHAW, dead, Trasverse Band.
Wife: Name not given, dead.
2-42-1 Joe McKeese, age ~~44~~ 47, P.O. ~~Pashabatown~~ Omena, see 21-42.
Wife: Annie (Paul) McKeese, age 40, see 17-42 & 21-42.
2-42-1-1 David McKeese, age 19, P.O. Omena.
2-42-1-2 Dennis McKeese, age 17, P.O. Omena.
2-42-2 Raphael, dead.
Wife: Rosie Raphael, P.O. Fox Island, see 19-42.
2-42-2-1 Mitchell Raphael, age 26, P.O. Fox Island, see 19-42.
Wife: Name not given, dead.

2-42-2-1-1 Eliza Jane Raphael, age 5, P.O. Fox Island.
2-42-2-1-2 Tena Raphae;, age 4, P.O. Fox Island.
2-42-2-2 Peter Raphael, age 24, P.O. Fox Island.
2-42-2-3 Ambrose Raphael, age 20, P.O. Fox Island.
2-42-2-4 Joseph Raphael, age 19, P.O. Fox Island.
2-42-2-5 Annie Raphael, age 18, P.O. Fox Island.
2-42-3 Mary Ann Stephens, age 43, P.O. Suttons Bay.
Husband: Name not given, dead.
2-42-3-1 Bennett Stephens, age 17, P.O. Suttons Bay.
2-42-4 Gabriel McKeese, age 38, P.O. Hackley, Wisconsin.
Wife: Madeline McKeese, nee Oliver, see 30-42, no children.
2-42-5 Mary Antoine, age 55, died Sep 16 1907, should be oldest child.
Husband: Name not given, dead.
2-42-5-1 John (Antoine) known as Shiding, see 16-41 & 18 -41.
2-42-5-2 Alex Antoine, age 19, P.O. Honor.
2-42-6 Name nor sex given, dead.

Information following from: Not Given.
3-42 MRS. PETER BOURASSA, dead, age 69 P.O. Suttons Bay.
Wife: Name not given, dead.
3-42-1 Wm. Bourassa, spelled Boursaw, age 53, P.O. Omena.
Wife 1st : Emma nee Pontiac.
Wife 2nd : Mary (O-GE-MAW-KE-DO) see 5-38, age 39, P.O. Omena.
2-43-1-1 Caroline Bourassa, age 16.
2-43-1-2 Annie Bourassa, age 14.
2-43-1-3 Benjamin Bourassa, age 8.
2-43-1-4 Esther Bourassa, age 4.
3-42-2 Peter Boursaw, age 43, P.O. Omena.
2-43-2-1 Bennett Boursaw, age 16, P.O. Omena.
3-42-3 Madeline Paul
Husband: William Paul, see 6-40.
2-43-3-1 Charles Paul, age 27, see 6-40.

Information following from: Not Given.
4-42 E-TAW-WAW-CAW-ME-GO, dead.
Wife: Name not given, dead.
4-42-1 Name not given, dead, no heirs.
4-42-2 Name not given, dead, no heirs.
4-42-3 Thresa Comego Mamawigeshig or Theresa Miller, age 55, P.O. Suttons Bay.
Husband: John Mamawigeshig or John Miller, age 69, P.O. Suttons Bay, (white).

4-42-3-1 Peter Smith, age 22, P.O. Suttons Bay
4-42-4 Sophia Windogowish
Husband: Name not given.
4-42-4-1 Dominick, age 19, P.O. Suttons Bay, see 12-38.
4-42-5 ThomasEdward, age 39, P.O. Suttons Bay.
4-42-6 Name not given, dead, no heirs.
4-42-7 Name not given, dead, no heirs.

Information following from: Not Given.
5-42 PE-SAY-NO-QUAY (f)
The 5 children enrolled with this woman are enrolled with 12-45 who was their adopted father after death of mother 5-42.

Information following from: Not Given.
6-42 DANIEL AW-KO-WE-SAY
Wife: Name not given, dead.
6-42-1 Sophia Nowonggaby, age 60, P.O. Omena, see 9-40.
6-42-2 Margaret Pedwadum, see 13-41.
6-42-3 Name not given, dead.
6-42-4 Elizabeth Bird, age 64.
Husband: Wm Bird, see 22-40.

Information following from: Not Given.
7-42 PAY-BAW-ME-SAY, dead.
Wife: Name not given, dead.

Information following from: Not Given.
8-42 PETER ANCE, Travrse Band.
Wife: Mary Ance, age 68, P.O. Suttons Bay.
8-42-1 Simon Ance, age 50, P.O. Suttons Bay.
Wife: Angeline Ance nee Chippewa, age 45, P.O. Suttons Bay, see 18-41 and also 16-42.
8-42-1-1 Casper Ance, age 25, P.O. Rapid City.
Wife: Susan Ance, P.O. Rapid City.
8-42-1-1-1 Cecelia Ance, age 2.
8-42-1-1-2 Raphael Ance, born July 6/08 2nd roll.
8-42-1-2 Wm Ance, age 20, P.O. Suttons Bay.
8-42-1-3 Moses Ance, age 18.
8-42-1-4 Christina Ance, age 13.
8-42-1-5 Mary Ann Ance, age 6.
8-42-1-6 Joseph Ance, age 2.
8-42-1-7 Peter Ance, age 7, died June 1908.
8-42-2 ~~Mary Ann~~ Marian Parow, age 46, P.O. Suttons Bay.
Husband: Mitchell Parow, age 58, P.O. Suttons Bay, see 11-31.

8-42-2-1 Alex Parow, age 25, P.O. Suttons Bay.
Wife: Lucy Hinman, age 21, see 2-56, no children.
8-42-2-2 Margaret Parow, age 23, P.O. Suttons Bay.
Husband: Louis Chippewa, see 18-41.
8-42-2-2-1 Name not given, died Sept 20/08, 1st roll.
8-42-2-3 Banatin (f) Paro, age 15, P.O. Suttons Bay.
8-42-2-4 Olive Paro, age 14.
8-42-3 Philaman (P. Ance) (Fr)ancis, age 44, P.O. Suttons Bay.
Husband: Leo Francis, age 60, see 29-41 and 18-28.
8-42-3-1 Wm Francis or Wm Ogenotego, see 61-21 & 3-20 & 18-28
8-42-4 Mitchell Ance #2, age 38, P.O. Suttons Bay.
Wife: Delia (Oliver) Ance, age 27, P.O. Suttons Bay.
8-42-5 Madeline Yanot, age 35.
Husband: Frank Yanot, age 40, see 19-41.
8-42-6 John Ance, age 27, P.O. Suttons Bay, single.

Mrs Susan Ance
My age 21 years on last Jan 8, 09
Born on Jan 8 1888
Cecilia Ance
Age 2 years on last ~~F~~ July 20 1908
Born on July 20 1906
Raphael Ance
Age 10 months old on
May 19 1909

Father name Peter Mark
Mother name Mrs. Annie Mark

Mrs. Susan Ance
Alden Mich
May 17 1909

Information following from: Not Given.
9-42 WAY-DO-NE-MO-AW, dead.
Wife: Name not Given dead.
9-42-1 Name not given, dead.

Information following from: Not Given.
10-42 JOHN B.ANCE, dead, father of Louis Ance.
Wife: Name not given,dead.
10-42-1 Name not given, dead.

Information following from: Not Given.

11-42 AUSH-E-TAY-YAW or MARGARET NABINEGA, age 66, P.O. Suttons Bay, Traverse Band.

Husband: John Nabinega, age 80, P.O. Suttons Bay, on 1870 roll as Ne-Be-Ne-Gwaw-Nay-Be.

11-42-1 Margaret, dead.

Husband: Chas. Way-Way-Se-Ma, P.O. ~~Leland, or Provemont~~ Glen Arbor, see 4-44.

11-42-1-1 Mitchell Way-Way-Se-Ma, died Aug/07, see 4-44.

11-42-1-2 John Way-Way-Se-Ma, age 18, see 4-44.

11-42-1-3 Christina Caffron, age 29, P.O. Traverse City RFD#.

Husband: Wm J. Coffron, age 34, off white.

11-42-1-3-1 John Coffron, age 9, Traverse City RFD#.

11-42-1-3-2 Isabelle Coffron, age 7, Traverse City RFD#.

11-42-2 Name not given, dead.

Information following from: Not Given.

12-42 JOHN BATTISE or MESANABY, ddead, Traverse Band.

Wife: Sophia Saggasega Sah-Ga-Se-Gay, age 56, P.O. Omena.

12-42-1 Susan Mesanaby, age 40, P.O. ~~Omena~~ Baker's Creek, Mich.

Lives with Benj. ~~Ambwayseum~~ Wahbuscum, see 22-42 no children.

Information following from: Not Given.

13-42 ME-SHE-BE-SE-QUAY (f), dead.

Husband: No name given.

13-42-1 Susan Mesanby, age 40, P.O. Omena, Mich, see 12-42.

13-42-2 Mary Saw-gau-se-gay, dead.

Husband: Chas. Deverney, dead.

13-42-2-1 Hattie (Deverney) Krogima, age 32, P.O. Cross Village, see 23-20.

13-42-2-2 Joe Deverney Sawgawsegaw, age 35, P.O. Bay Shore, known as Joe Gibson, see 12-26.

13-42-2-3 Moses King, age 34, see 10-46.

13-42-2-4 Louis Macea or Massey, age 30, P.O. Cheboygan.

13-42-2-5 Stephen (Deverney), known as Steve Munson, age 29, P.O. Elk Rapids or Cross Village,See 4-44, 16-45.

Wife: ~~Annie~~ Helena Munson nee Taylor, see 17-20, no children.

Information following from: Not Given.

14-42 THERESA, dead.

Husband: No name given.

14-42-1 Bennett Bourrassaw, age 16, P.O. ~~Sutton~~ Omena, see 3-42.

Information following from: Not Given.
15-42 GABRIELPAY-SHAW-BAY, died Sept 17/07 1st roll, Traverse Band.
Wife: Sophia (Na-To-Shing), age 65, P.O. Suttons Bay, daughter of 9-38.
15-42-1 Mary Shawkoo, age43, P.O. Suttons Bay.
Husband 1st : Frank Windigowish, dead.
Husband 2nd: Andrew Shawkoo, age 50, just married Sept 21/08, see 22-41.
15-42-1-1 Eli Paul, age 18, P.O. Suttons Bay.
15-42-2 Kate Chippeway, age 34, P.O. Suttons Bay, separated.
Husband: Philip Chippeway, age 34, P.O. Suttons Bay, see 18-41.
15-42-3 Benjamin Payshawbay, age 33, P.O. Suttons Bay.
Wife: Jennie Payshawbay nee (Shawnongga), age 29, P.O. Suttons Bay.
15-42-3-1 Gracie Payshawbay, age 7.
15-42-3-2 Gladys Payshawbay, born Sept April 17, 1907 2nd roll.
15-42-4 Joe Payshawbay, age 24, P.O. ~~Su~~ Genoa Sch.
15-42-5 Frank Payshawbay, age 21, P.O. Suttons Bay.

Information following from: Not Given.
16-42 PAW-KE-CAW-NAW-NO-QUAY
16-42-1 Payrick Shawwebenayse, age 51, see 18-41 & 8-42.
16-42-2 Angeline Ance,age 45, see 18-41 & 8-42.
Note: These two wereon 1870 roll with grandmother.

Information following from: Not Given.
17-42 ME-SHE-ME-NAW-NAW-QUOT, age 72, P.O. Suttons Bay.
Wife: Name not given, dead.
17-42-1 Name not given, dead.

Information following from: Not Given.
18-42 SAW-GAW-NAW-QUAW-DO or MITCHELL ANCE, age 65, P.O. Elk Rapids.
Wife: Mary Ann Ance nee Bourassaw, age 64.
18-42-1 Etta Hattie (Ance) Gould, age 41, P.O. Elk Rapids, Mich, not married but living together as an and wife
Husband: Augustua ~~Gold~~ Gould, age 36, (Undoubtably an Ottawa Ind, but cannot findfamilyconnection as his mother is dead & father is white Durant), see 9-37.
18-42-1-1 ~~Annie~~ Josephine Gould, age 11.
18-42-1-2 Amos Gould, age 9.
18-42-1-3 Clara Gould, age 7.
18-42-1-4 Charles Gould, age 4.

18-42-2 Thomas Ance, age 31, died Jany 9/08, not married, no children.

18-42-3 Eliza (Ance) Anderson, age 38, died May 27/08.

Husband: Alex Anderson (white man), P.O. Elk Rapids, Mich.

18-42-3-1 Fred Anderson, age 16, P.O. Elk Rapids, Mich.

18-42-3-2 Cecelia Anderson, age 2, P.O. Elk Rapids, Mich.

18-42-4 Louisa (Ance) Bird, age 35, P.O. Elk Rapids.

Husband: Joe Bird, age 31, P.O. Elk Rapids, undoubtably an Ottawa mother still living in Canada mother an Ottawa, father a Canadian. But, Joe Bird says himself that he drewmoney with Canadian Indians,nine years ago. Durant Oct 3/08 Elk Rapids.

18-42-4-1 Julius Bird, age 3, P.O. Elk Rapids.

18-42-5 Antonia Ance, age 25, P.O. Elk Rapids.

18-42-6 Clara Ance, age 27, P.O. Bellaire Mich RFD#1.

Husband: Charles Finch (white).

18-42-6-1 Francis Finch, age 4.

18-42-6-2 Florence Finch, age 3.

18-42-6-3 Rosannah Finch, age 2.

18-42-7 John Ance, age 22, P.O.Elk Rapids, not married.

18-42-8 Sampson Louis Ance, age 19, P.O. Elk Rapinds.

Information following from: Not Given.

19-42 NE-BE-NAY-QUAY or MARY NEBENAQUAY, age 74, P.O. Suttons Bay, not married, Traverse Band.

19-42-1 Rosie Raphael pronounced “Rawfeel”, age 44, P.O. Fox Island.

Husband: Name not given, dead.

19-42-1-1 Mitchell Raphael, age 26, 2 children see 2-42.

19-42-2 Agnes Pean, ~~died Sept 07~~

Husband: James Pean, age 40, P.O. High Island, see 1-34.

Information following from: Not Given.

20-42 KAW-GAW-AW-SO-WAY-QUAY, Traverse Band.

Wife: Name not given, dead.

20-42-1 Mitchell Paul, age 55, P.O. Northport, see 4-38.

Information following from: Not Given.

21-42 ANDREW AW-BWAINCE or ANTONY PAUL, age 59, P.O. Northport, Traverse Band.

Wife: Name not given, dead.

21-42-1 Annie McKeese, age 40, P.O. Pashabatown Mich.

Husband: Joe McKeese, age 44, P.O. Pashabatown Mich, son of 17-2-42.

21-42-1-1 David McKeese.

21-42-2 Eliza Greensky, age 37, P.O. Traverse City.
Husband: Pepegway Greensky.
21-42-2-1 Louis Paul, age 22, P.O.Genoa Sch. Nebr, takes name of grandfather.
21-42-3 Mitchell Paul #2, age 29, P.O. Northport, see 5-38.
Wife: Nancy (O-Ge-Waw-Ke-Ge-Do), age 29, P.O. Northport, see 5-38.
21-42-3-1 Winnie Paul,age 5.
21-42-3-2 Edith Paul, age 2.
21-42-4 Jennie Paul, age 17, P.O. Northport

Information following from: Not Given.
22-42 WAIN-BWAY-SKUNG or JOHN WAH-BUSCUM, age 65, Traverse Band.
Wife: Esther (Chaw-Way-Cush-Cum) age 58, P.O. Beaver Island, see 13-38.
22-42-1 Angeline Deverney, age 50, Grand River, see 4-59.
22-42-2 Benjamin Wahbuscum, age 46, P.O. Barker's Creek, Mich.
Wife: Susie Wahbuscum nee Mesanaby,age 40, see 12-42, no children.
22-42-3 Mitchell Wahbuscum, age 34, P.O. Genoa Sch. Nebr Tailor at Sch., married?

Information following from: Not Given.
23-42 ANTONIE NE-AW-NE-SAY or NAGOUSE, age 63, P.O. Suttons bay.
Wife: Angeline Negounesay, age 60, with husb. In 1870, see 51-43.
23-42-1 Mary Fisher, age 33, P.O. Suttons Bay, see 17-38.
23-42-2 Madeline Shashagay, age 23, P.O. Gills Pier, no children.
Husband: Louis Shashagay, age 26.
23-42-3 Thos. Nagousay, age 17, P.O. Suttons Bay.
23-42-4 Stephen Nagonsay, age 15.

Information following from: Not Given.
24-42 KAW-BAY-WON, dead.
24-42-1 Name not given, dead, no heirs.

Information following from: Not Given.
25-42 NAW-GAW-NE-SAY.
Wife: Name not given, dead.
Note: No heirs so further says Antoine Negousay who is present HBDurant Spl Agt Sept 26/08 Pashabatown, Mich.

Information following from: Not Given.
26-42 O-TWA-WAW-QUAY (f), dead,died June 1908 1st roll.

Husband: Name not given, dead.
26-42-1 Name not given, dead.
26-42-2 Angeline Skibogosh, age 48, P.O. Elk Rapids RFD#1, no children.
Husband: Jeremiah Skibogosh, age 62, P.O. Elk Rapids RFD#1.

Information following from: Not Given.
27-42 AGATHA or AGABAIL AW-NAW-QUAW-DO-QUAY,age 72, P.O. Suttons, see 14-38, no children, Traverse Band.
Husband: Name not given, dead.

Information following from: Not Given.
28-42 NAW-GAW-NE-GAW-BOWE, dead, wife dead, no heirs.

Information following from: Not Given.
29-42 O-TISH-GUAY-AW-BAW-NE-QUAY or MAGGIE TUSH-QUAYAH BE-NO-QUAY, age 78, P.O. Suttons Bay, Traverse Band, no children.
Wife: Name not given, dead.

Information following from: Not Given.
30-42 ME-SHE-WAW-QUAY, dead.
Wife: Name not given.
30-42-1 Joe Oliver, age 61, P.O. Suttons Bay.
Wife 1st: Mary Ann Oliver, age 63, now living at High Island, see 16-34.
Wife 2nd: Thresa Oliver, age 60, P.O. Suttons Bay.
30-42-1-1 Madeline McKeese, age 38, P.O. Hackley, Wisconsin.
Husband: Gabriel McKeese, see 2-42.
30-42-1-2 Angeline Keway,age 36, P.O. Elmira Mich.
Husband: Ben Keway, P.O. Elmira Mich.
30-42-1-2-1 Julius Keway, age 17.
30-42-1-3 Delia Ance, age 28, Elmira Mich, separated from husband Mitchell Anc, no children..
30-42-1-4 Moses Oliver, age 26, P.O. Suttons Bay, not married.
30-42-1-5 Henry Oliver, age 18, P.O. Suttons Bay.
30-42-1-6 Rosa Oliver, age 21, died Mch 6/07, not married.
30-42-1-6-1 Mary Oliver, born Sept 9, 1906, died Sept 1907.
30-42-1-7 Mary Ann Oliver,age 15, P.O. Suttons Bay.
30-42-1-8 Mary Oliver, age 12, P.O. Suttons Bay.
30-42-1-9 Joe Oliver Jr, age 38, P.O. Charlevoix, see 6-23 &

16-34. This man & his wife wereenrolled with the head of this family in 1870 Durant Spl Agt Sept 25/08.

Information following from: Not Given.
44-42 MRS. FRANCIS SAW-GAW-NAW-QUAW-DO known now as
MARY ANN AGOSA, age 62, P.O. Cross Village.
Husband: Francis Saw-Gaw-Naw-Quaw-Do
44-42-1 Joseph Saw-Gaw-Naw-Quaw-Do, age 46, see 47-21 & 28-20

Information following from: Not Given.
45-42 FRANCIS NUG-SHA-GAW, should be MISH-SHA-GAW or
MICHIGAN. Note: This number was a woman enrolled under husband's name. The husband is enrolled as "Me-Zhaw-Gaw" or Michigan as 55-35 Beaver Island Band, & his children were enrolled with mother on this sheet. Nov 21/08 Beaver Island Durant Spl Agt.
45-42-1 Francis Michigan, age 49, P.O. ~~Bay Shore~~ Pellston.
Wife: Name not given, dead.
45-42-1-1 Moses Michigan, age 24, P.O. Middle Village, single.
45-42-1-2 Solomon Michigan, age 22, P.O. Middle Village.
45-42-2 Susan Cupe or Susan Gibson, age 47, P.O. Bay Shore, Mackinaw Band, separated, no cildren.
Husband: Joe Cupe or Joe Animekeway, P.O. Pt. St. Ignace, see 6-12.
45-42-3 William Michigan, known as Wm Gibson, age 46, P.O. ~~Bay Shore~~ Pellston, separated from wife and living with another woman..
Wife: Mary Gibson nee Ko-Se-Quot, age 41, P.O. Goodheart, ~~niece~~ daugh of ~~30-58~~ 2-28.
45-42-3-1 Thresa Gibson, P.O. Pellston.
Husband: Jasper ~~Cinsaway Cinaway~~ Assinaway, age 27, see 8-28.
45-42-3-1-1 John Assinaway, age 3.
45-42-3-1-2 Titus Assinaway, age 1, born Oct 1907.
42-3-2 Hattie Gibson, age 20, P.O. ~~Boyne City~~ Bay Shore, see 14-25.
Husband: ~~John M.~~ Jonas Micksabay, age 32.
31-42-3-2-1 Julius Micksabay,age 2.
Note: Enroll these (following) children with mother who supports them.
45-42-3-3 Ida Gibson, age 12, Harbor Springs Sch.
45-42-3-4 Agnes Gibson, age 10, Harbor Springs Sch.
45-42-3-5 Cecelia Gibson, age 8, Harbor Springs Sch.
45-42-3-6 Bagil Gibson (m), age 6, Harbor Springs Sch.

45-42-3-7 Alvina Gibson (f), age 4, Harbor Springs Sch.

45-42-4 Susan Josie Michigan, age 38, P.O. Cross Village, no children.
Husband: Bennett Shingawkose, see 30-20.

Information following from: Not Given.
46-42 MARY PAY-SHAW-BE-NO-QUAY, cannot be identified by any of the Inds. Now living, of the same band HBDurant Spl Agt.

Page 43
Chief ME-SAW-ZEE

Information following from: Not Given.
31-43 ME-SAW-ZEE, dead, no heirs.

Information following from: Not Given.
32-43 NE-BE-NA-YAW-BO-WE, dead , no heirs.

Information following from: Not Given.
33-43 JOHN MEN-DOW-WAW-BE. Note: Has not been heard from for years, went to Canadayears ago.No heirs so far as can be ascertained from all the old Indians around Pashabatown & Suttons Bay, Durant Spl Agt Pashabatown, MichSept 24, 1908.
Wife: Name not given, separated.

Information following from: Not Given.
34-43 MAW-DWAY-SAW-GE-NUM, dead, no heirs.

Information following from: Not Given.
35-43 AW-WAW-ZHE-ME-GAY-QUAY, dead.
35-43-1 Name not given, dead, no heirs.

Information following from: Not Given.
36-43 MICHAEL AW-KO-WE-SAY or AGOSA
Wife: Name not given, dead.
36-43-1 Name not given, dead.
Husband: Name not given, dead.
36-43-1-1 Mary Ann Mick-Se-Mong, age 32, P.O. Cross Village, see 77-21.

Information following from: Not Given.
37-43 KAW-NE-SAY-QUAY, dead, no heirs.

Information following from: Not Given.
38-43 ME-SAY-NE-QUAY, dead, no heirs.

Information following from: Not Given.
39-43 WAW-SAW-BE-KAY-ZOO, dead, no heirs.

Information following from: Not Given.
40-43 PAW-QUAW-GE-NIN-NE, dead,no heirs.

Information following from: Not Given.
41-43 O-GE-MAW-PE-NAY-SE.
Wife: Catharine Shawkoo, Thos. Shawkoo age 43, see 5-41.
41-43-1 Thos. Kingbird, age 30, P.O. Suttons Bay, see 24-60.
Wife: Benedicta Kingbird nee Andrews,age 25, see 24-60 & 2-41.
41-43-1-1 Enos Andrews, age 2, see 24-60, adopted son of sister of Benedicta Kingbird, see 2-41.

Information following from: Not Given.
42-43 KEY-SHE-ZHE-WAY or GEORGE SISHWAY, age 65, P.O. Honor, Traverse Band.
Wife: Mary (Kay-Ta-Say) Sishway, age 60, on roll with him in 1870.
42-43-1 Thresa (Tenese) (dead).
Husband: Simon Paul, age 38, P.O. Fox Island, see 1-39.
42-43-2 Julius Sishway or Ke-She-Way, age 37, P.O. Hackley, Wisconsin will be atFountain Box 61.
Wife: Martha Cogswell, daugh. of Joe Cogswell, age 32, see 23-54.
42-43-2-1 Levi Sishway.
42-43-2-2 Celia Sishway.
42-43-3 Esther Amboskey, age 24, P.O. Honor,nochildren.
Husband: Pete Amboskey or Wahbustum, age 37, P.O. Honor, see 22-42.
42-43-4 Mary (Sishway) Cobb, died May 23, 1908, 1st roll.
Husband: Louis Cobb, age 33, P.O. Honor, see 10-38.
42-43-4-1 Alice Cobb, 2 days old, died May 13/08 2nd roll.
42-43-5 George Sishway, age 18, see 47-43.

Information following from: Not Given.
43-43 JOHN NE-SO-GOT, dead, no heirs.

Information following from: Not Given.
44-43 ISAAC SHAW-WE-NE-PE-NA-SE, spelled now SHAWABINASSE or known as ISAAC SOUTHBIRD, age 65, P.O. Suttons Bay.
Wife: Mary (Chippeway) Shawabinasse, age 55.

44-43-1 John Southbird, age 38, P.O. Suttons Bay, single, no children.
44-43-2 Mitchell Southbird, age 27, P.O. Suttons Bay, single, no children.
44-43-3 Elizabeth Nady, age 25, P.O. Acme.
Husband: Eli Nady, age 40 37, P.O. Acme, Mich., see 2-38, his 1st wife died July/08, was not living with her.
44-43-3-1 Annie Nady, age 2.
44-43-4 Stephen Southbird, age 23, P.O. Suttons Bay, not married.
44-43-5 Albert Southbird, age 15, P.O. Suttons Bay.
44-43-6 Margaret Southbird, age 12, P.O. Suttons Bay.
44-43-7 Julia Southbird, age 17, died June 17, 1908 1st roll.

Information following from: Not Given.
45-43 LOUIS ANSE (spelled now ANCE), age 60, P.O. Northport, Mich.
Wife: Maggie Ance, age 57, P.O. lives on Fox Island.
45-43-1 Lizzie Ance Chippeway, age 35, P.O. Northport, (Fox Island).
Husband: Enos Chippeway, age 40, P.O. Northport, (Fox Island).
45-43-1-1 Josephine Chippeway, age 6.
45-43-1-2 Ben Chippeway, age 3 mos, died Mch 1908.
45-43-2 August Ance, age 32, P.O. Sutton's Bay.
Wife: Christine Raphael Ance, age 24.
45-43-2-1 Fred Ance, age 7.
45-43-2-2 Luke Ance, age 4.
45-43-2-3 Mabel Ance, age born Dec 15/07.
45-43-3 Maseline Ance Pabo, age 28, P.O. Fox Island, separated, no children.
Husband Wm Pabo, see 33-38, P.O. Fox Island.
45-43-4 Ben Ance, dead.
Wife: Janetta (Olliver) Ance, age 30, P.O. Fox Island,16-34, her mother is Mary Ann (She-No-Din) (Olliver) of High Island.
45-43-4-1 Julius Ance, age 5, live with grandfather, Louis Ance.
45-43-4-2 Emeline Ance, age 3.
45-43-5 Abbie Ance Andrew, age 18, P.O. Fox Island Northport.
Husband: John Andrew, age 23, P.O. Fox Island Northport, son of Mary Ann (She-No-Din) (Olliver), see 16-34, of High Island.
45-43-5-1 Alice Andrew, age 4, lives with grandfather Louis Ance.
45-43-5-2 Ivan Andrew, age 3.

Information following from: Not Given.

46-43 PAW-GO-NAY-GE-ZHE-GO-QUAY.
Wife: Name not given.
46-43-1 Son, name not given, dead.
Wife: Sophia, see 3-41.
46-43-1-1 John Gingway, see 3-41.
46-43-2 Dead, no heirs.
46-43-3 Dead, no heirs.

Information following from: Not Given.
47-43 O-KITCHE-GE-ZHE-GO-QUAY, Traverse Band.
Husband: Name not given, a Wisconsin Ind.
47-43-1 Be-Nay-Ge-She-Go-Quay
Husband: Ching-Quay, see 11-41.
47-43-1-1 Wm Ching-Quay, age 35, P.O. Torch Lake, now Manisque, see 11-41.
Wife: Name not given.
47-43-1-1-1 Name not given.
47-43-2 George Shisway,age 65,P.O. Honor, see 42-43.
47-43-3 Dead, mother of 46-43 and 42-43 who have separate sheets, Durant.

Information following from: Not Given.
48-43 ISAAC NE-SO-GOT, dead, no heirs.

Information following from: Not Given.
49-43 MITCHELL, dead.
Wife: Susan (Shaw-Koo) Nawquoum, age 57, P.O. Suttons Bay, npw wife of Joe Naw-Quoum, see 22-41.
49-43-1 Name not given, dead, no heirs.

Information following from: Not Given.
50-43 KE-WAY-TE-NO-QUAY, dead, (two children enrolled under this head). These were two children one the wife of Dav Chippeway Christine Chippeway, see 18-41 & 21-46, the other is Agnes Pete wife of George Pete a Grand River Ind, see 19-54, HB Durant Spl Agt, Sept 28/08 Pashabatown.

Information following from: Not Given.
51-43 JOHN TOO-TO-CHOW.
Wife: Name not given.
51-43-1 John B. Trosho or Thrush, age 70, P.O. Pellston, as 51-27, see 38-41.
51-43-2 Lucy Duverney, age 49, P.O. Petoskey, see 36-55.
Husband: John Duverney, see 36-55 and 32-26, Grand River Band.

51-43-3 Therese Peshabay, age 72, died June 11, 1908, see 7-25.
Husband: Name not given, dead.
51-43-3-1 Eliza (Daily) Key-Way-Ken-Do, age 40, P.O. Petoskey, see 11-26 & 7-25.
Husband: Name not given, dead.
51-43-3-1-1 Daniel Waw-Sa-Ke-Zhick, age 7, P.O. Harbor Spgs. Sch., see 11-26.
51-43-3-1-2 Lizzie Ke-Way-Ken-Do, age 3, P.O. Petoskey, see 11-26.
51-43-3-1-3 David Ke-Way-Ken-Do, age 15, P.O. Mt. Pleas. Sch., see 11-26.
51-43-4 Louis Too-To-Chow, see as 52-27.
51-43-5 Angeline Ne-Gaw-Ne-Say, age 60, see 23-42.

Page 44
Chief KEY-WAY-CUSH-CUM

Information following from: Not Given.
1-44 KEY-WAY-CUSH-CUM, Traverse Band.
Wife: Name not given, dead.
1-44-1 Jackson Key-Way-Cush-Cum, P.O. G;en Haven, see 3-44 for family.
1-44-2 Ne-Gon-Ge-Wah, age 56, P.O. ~~Cats Creek~~ Star City, Mich ~~Cadallac~~.
Husband: Name not given, Grand River Band.
1-44-2-1 Sophia Lucy Fransway nee Petwaquedum, age 38, P.O. ~~Cadallac~~ Star City.
Husband: ~~Pete Deverdow~~
1-44-2-1-1 Alice Fransway, age 14, P.O. in school at Mt. P.
1-44-2-1-2 Janie Fransway, age 12, P.O. in school at Mt. P.
1-44-2-1-3 John Fransway, age 8, P.O. in school at Mt. P.
1-44-2-1-4 Ida Fransway, age 5, P.O. in school at Mt. P.
Note: Alice, Janie and John drew with Potts but Ida did not.
1-44-2-2 Elizabeth Mitchell, age 32, P.O. Star City, see 6-62
1-44-2-2-1 John Baptiste, see 16-6-62.
1-44-3 Naw-Da-Ge or Janie Shaw-Naw-Nay-Se-Gay, P.O. Star City, see 16-6-62, Grand River Band.
Husband: George Shaw-Naw-Nay-Se-Gay or (Shaw-Waw-Naw-Se-Gay), see 16-6-62, Grand River Band.
1-44-4 Charles or Charley Key-Way-Cush-Cum, wife and children all

dead and not named.

1-44-5 Name not given, no children.

1-44-6 Name not given, went to Canada & was marriedsomewhere in Walpole Island.

Information following from: Not Given.

2-44 MAW-ME-WAY-KE-ZHICK, dead.

Wife: Name not given.

2-44-1 Name not given, dead.

2-44-1-1 Philip King, see 32-28 & 8-62.

2-44-1-2 Louis King, see 8-40 & 30-23.

2-44-2 Name not given, dead, no heirs.

2-44-3 Name not given, dead, no heirs.

Information following from: Not Given.

3-44 WAH-BE-GUAW-NAY or JACKSON KEY-WAY-CUSH-CUM, age 78, P.O. Glen Haven, Mich, Traverse Band.

Wife: Maggie Jackson, age 70, P.O. Glen Haven, Mich.

3-44-1 Maggie Jackson, age 49, P.O. Glen Haven.

Husband: Pete Lahay, separated, see 22-54 & 8-61.

3-44-1-1 Geo Lahay, age 26, P.O. Honor, son-in-law of Peter James, see 18-13-44.

3-44-1-1-1 Oscar Lahay.

3-44-1-2 Charles Lahay, age 23, P.O. Charlevoix, not married.

3-44-1-3 Peter Lahay, age 18, P.O. Glen Haven.

3-44-2 James Jackson, age 47, P.O. Glen Haven., no children.

3-44-3 George Jackson, age 45, died Sept 22/07 1st roll.

Wife: First name not given Jackson nee James, age 30, P.O. Glen Haven, ~~daughter of~~ sister of Peter James.

3-44-3-1 Daniel Jackson, age 6.

3-44-3-2 Estelle Jackson, age 4.

3-44-3-3 Antoine Jackson, age born Apr 12/08 2nd roll.

3-44-4 Bonapart Jackson, age 38, P.O. Glen Haven or Cross Village, not married.

3-44-5 Mike Jackson, age 36, P.O. Cross Village.

Wife: Christina Jackson, age 26, P.O. Cross Village, see 13.

3-44-5-1 Joseph Jackson, age 9, lives with Mary Ann Stone.

3-44-5-2 Cecelia Jackson, age 1, born Aug 1907.

3-44-6 Peter Jackson, age 23, P.O. Glen Haven, not married.

3-44-7 Jessie Jackson, age 21, P.O. Glen Haven, Mich.

Husband: Peter Sam, age 40, P.O. Glen Haven, Mich, see 1-39.

3-44-7-1 Christina Sam, age 6, see 1-39.

3-44-7-2 Mary Sam, age born Aug 18/08, not on any roll.

3-44-8 Wah-Say-Quah Jackson, age 25, P.O. Provemont bet. Cedar

City & Leland.
Husband: John Way-Se-Mah, age 30, see 4-44.
3-44-8-1 Moses Way-Se-Mah, age 12
3-44-8-2 Lula Way-Se-Mah, age 10
3-44-8-3 Josie Way-Se-Mah, age 8
3-44-8-4 Margaret Way-Se-Mah, age 7
3-44-8-5 Catharine Way-Se-Mah, age 2

Glen Haven
Mich
May 12-1907

Dear Sir.

I received you letter today and you asked me the name and I will send the names Well his
English name
Jackson Kewagoskum
Indian name
Wabegona Kewagoskum
and wife name
English
Maggie Kewagoskum
Indian name
Pedegashewa Kewagoskum

Well I would like to find out how are you make it
I suppose you near done
I would like to find out if you please let me know right way
Good by
Yours Truly
Peter Sam

Information following from: Not Given.
4-44 WAY-WAY-SE-MAW or JOHN WAY-WAY SE MAW, age 80, P.O. Provemont.
Wife: Mary Ann Way-Way-Se-Maw, age 70-, on 1870 roll with husb.
4-44-1 Charles Way-Way-Se-Maw, age 40, P.O. Glen Arbor, see 11-42.
Wife: Name not given, dead.
4-44-1-1 Mitchell Way-Way-Se-Maw, age 20, died Aug/07 1st roll.
4-44-1-2 John Way-Way-Se-Maw, age 18, P.O. Mich. State Prison, at Jackson.
4-44-1-3 Christina Coffrow, age 29, P.O. Keystone, Mich, P.O. Traverse City RFD #7.

Husband: Wm J. Coffrow, age 34, an Ottawa Ind. mother is Mrs. Andrew Chippeway, for children see 11-42..

4-44-2 Louise Munson, age 20, P.O. Glen Arbor, separated from husb.

Husband:Steve Munson, age 29, P.O. Cross Village, 2nd wife Helen Taylor see 17-20, mother Mary Na-Na-Da-We-Quay.

4-44-2-1 Joseph Munson, age 3, enroll with mother.

4-44-3 Name not given, dead.

Information following from: Not Given. Sept 25/08

5-44 KE-KAW-ME-SQUAW-BAW-NOS-KAY, Traverse Band.

Wife: Name not given, dead.

5-44-1 Name not given, dead.

5-44-2 Name not given, dead.

Husband 1st : Foster Robinson

Husband 2nd: Geo. Peters, see 3-51.

5-44-2-1 Christina Robinson

5-44-2-2 Lucy

5-44-2-3 Sarah

5-44-2-4 John W. Robinson, age 25, P.O. Northport, not married.

5-44-2-5 Moses Peters, age 20, P.O. Horton Bay, Mich., see 9-24.

~~Note: Grandchild of enrolled with #3 p.58 Grand River wishes card.~~

Information following from: Not Given.

6-44 WAW-BE-WIN-DE-GO.

Wife: Name not given, dead.

6-44-1 Name not given, P.O. Charlevoix

Information following from: Not Given.

7-44 SAY-MIN-GWA-BAY.

Wife: Mary Wah-Be-No-Quay, age 68, P.O. Provemont.

7-44-1 Wm Jake, age 39, P.O. Provemont, Mich, living together.

Wife: Sarah Prickett, age 41, P.O. Provemont, see 26-46.

7-44-1-1 Edwin Jake, age 2.

7-44-1-2 Mary Jake, 20 days old, died March 10/08, 2nd roll. Parents not married & child not enrolled Durant Spl Agt.

7-44-1-3 Payson Kah-Tah-Sa, age 23, see 22-41.

Note: or similar balance of her children see Susan Precketts name on another card & when found erase these notes, 19-44.

7-44-2 Nancy Paul, age 16, P.O. Provemont, adopted child, mother & father Inds & are dead, with Mary Wah-Be-No-Quay.

Information following from: Not Given.
8-44 PE-NAY-SE-WE-KE-ZHICK or GEORGE CASE, age 60, P.O. East Lake near Manistee, Mich.
Wife: Mary Ann Case ~~nee~~, age 50, with husb in 1870.
8-44-1 Eliza Case Fox, age 31, P.O. Lemmon Lake.
Husband: John Fox, white.
8-44-1-1 Joe Crampton, age 15, see 20-53.
8-44-2 Wm Case, age 24, P.O. East Lake, single.

Information following from: Not Given. Jany 9/09
9-44 NA-BE-NAY-KE-ZHICK, dead, has only one daughter living who is now wife of George Norton (or Wm Norton).
Wife: Name not given.
9-44-1 Alice Judson, Grand River Band, P.O. at Honor, Mich.
Husband: Wm Newton or Norton, see 25-55.
9-44-1-1 James Judson, see 22-54.

Information following from: Not Given.
10-44 PE-TWAY-WE-TUM, dead.
Wife: Margaret Pewaywedum ~~dead~~, age 60, P.O. Star City, Mich.
10-44-1 Lucy Sansway or Fransway, age 38, P.O. Star City, Mich, see 20-64 & 4-51, she now liveswith Levi Cawburn, see 4-51.
Husband: Levi Fransway, for children see 20-64.
10-44-2 Elizabeth Petwaywedum or Mitchell, age 32.
Husband: Name not given.
10-44-2-1 John Baptiste or John Shaw-Waw-Nay-Se-Gay, born Aug 29/07 2nd roll.

Information following from: Not Given.
11-44 NAW-O-KE-ZHICK, dead, died of small pox.
Wife: Name not given, dead.
11-44- 1 Name not given, dead.
Note: No one knows whether there are any heirs of this family or not. Hey lived near Manistee the last that was heard from them & the man & his wife died of small pox. Durant Spl Agt Sept 28/08 Pashabatown.

Information following from: Not Given.
12-44 KAW-WE-TAW-KE-ZHICK, dead.
Wife: Name not given, dead.
12-44-1 Name not given, dead, no heirs.

Information following from: Wm Deverney, Inter. At Honor.
13-44 NIN-GAW-SO-ME or JAMES, Traverse Band.

Wife: Name not given.
13-44-1 Johnson James.
13-44-2 Peter James, age 52, P.O. Honor, same as 17-44.
Wife: Annie Pricket, age 55, see 2-39, has sister Mary Blacksmith Cedar City.
13-44-2-1 Levi James, age 28, P.O. Honor.
Wife: Mary Shako James, age 23, belongs to Traverse Band 4-41.
13-44-2-1-1 Delia James, age 7.
13-44-2-1-2 Annie James, age 3, died April 1908 1st roll.
13-44-2-2 Wallace, age 23.
13-44-2-3 Johnson James, age 21.
13-44-2-4 Louisa Lahay, age 19.
Husband: Geo Lahay, age 24.
13-44-2-5 Elizabeth James, age 11.
13-44-2-6 Lucy James, age 9.
13-44-2-7 Julia James, age 7.
13-44-3 Henry James, age 48, P.O. Honor.
Wife: Mary Pay-Qus-Tusk James, age 35, see 3-58.
13-44-3-1 Jim James, age 19.
13-44-3-2 Thomas James, age 16.
13-44-3-3 Lottie James, age 10.
13-44-3-4 Amos James, age 7.
13-44-4 Nancy Jackson, P.O. Grand Haven.
Husband: Geo Jackson, died Sept 1907, 1st roll, NB a Traverse Ind., children see 3-44.

Information following from: Not Given.
14-44 SHING-GO-NAY-CAW-SE, Traverse Band.
Wife: Angeline Newton, age 56, Honor, was wife of Wm Newton, see 25-55.
14-44-1 Name not given.
Wife: Name not given, dead.
14-44-1-1 Annie Newton, age 9, P.O. Northport.
14-44-1-2 Ella Newton, age 7, P.O. Northport.
14-44-2 Julia Wah-Sa-Quom,age 38, P.O. Honor.
Husband: Thos. Wah-Sa-Quom, age 41, P.O. Honor, (a Traverse Ind son of Peter), see 26-23.
14-44-2-1 Alice Wah-Sa-Quom,age 14.
14-44-2-2 Elizabeth Wah-Sa-Quom,age 9.
14-44-2-3 John Wah-Sa-Quom,age 4.
14-44-2-4 Anna Wah-Sa-Quom,age 2.

Information following from: Not Given.

15-44 NAY-GE-WAW-NO-QUAY, dead, no heirs.

Information following from: Not Given.
16-44 NAW-O-QUAY-KE-ZHICK, dead, no heirs.

Information following from: Not Given.
17-44 KAY-BAY-O-SAY or PETER JAMES, see himself & family on sheet 13-44.

Information following from: Not Given.
18-44 AW-WAW-TIN, dead, no heirs.

Information following from: Not Given.
19-44 NAW-WE-KE-CHE-GAW-ME-QUAY, Traverse Band.
Wife: Name not given, dead.
19-44-1 Name not given, dead.
Husband 1st : Name not given, dead.
Husband 2nd: Joe Prickett, see 6-39.
19-44-1-1 George Prickett, age 48, P.O. Gills Pier, Mich.
Wife: Sarah Prickett nee Naw-Skaw, age 46, see 26-46 & 7-44.
19-44-1-1-1 Sophia Prickett Stevens, age 24, P.O. Pashabatown, Mich, see 1-38 & 21-41.
Husband: Joe Stevens, age 34.
19-44-1-1-1-1 John Stevens, age 3.
19-44-1-1-2 Mary Prickett, age 18.
19-44-1-1-3 Saml. Prickett, age 9.
19-44-2 John Anawaskey, age 53, P.O. Northport, adopted son,father 13-40.
Wife: Angeline Anawaskey nee (Chippeway) ,age 44, see 10-41.
19-44-2-1 Basil Anawaskey, age 23, P.O. Northport, not married.
19-44-2-2 Moses Anawaskey, age 21, P.O. Northport.
19-44-2-3George Anawaskey, age 19, P.O. Northport.
19-44-2-4 Rosie Anawaskey, age 12, P.O. Northport.

Information following from: Not Given.
20-44 WAY-WIND-DAW-BUN, dead, (a child), no heirs.

Information following from: Not Given.
21-44 SAMUEL KAW-GE-GAY-BE, see 3-58.
Note: Enroll as a Traverse Ind. Of the Ottawa & Chippewa Tribe. It appears that in 1870 he was enrolled twice: once as #3 p. 58 & also as #21 p. 44 – but was not paid on page 58 but was paid under #21 p. 44.

Durant Spl Agt Sept 28/08.

Page 45
Chief KAY-ZHE-QUAW-NE-GAY

Information following from: Not Given.
1-45 KAY-ZHE-QUAW-NE-GAY, Traverse Band.
Wife: Name not given, dead.
1-45-1 Joseph Redbird, age 66, P.O. Northport, see 6-45.
1-45-2 John Redbird, age 52, P.O. Honor.
Wife: Annie Waw-Say-Quom, age 50, P.O. Honor, see 1-38.
1-45-2-1 Wallace Redbird, age 23.
1-45-2-2 Enos Redbird, age 13.
1-45-3 William Redbird, age 48, P.O. Honor, wife dead, no children.

Information following from: Not Given.
2-45 JOHN B. WAW-KAY-ZOO spelled WAUKAZOO, age 80, P.O. Northport.
2-45-1 Moses Waukazoo, age 49, P.O. Honor.
Wife: Name not given, dead.
2-45-1-1 Jos. Waukazoo #2, age 19, P.O. Honor.
2-45-1-2 Calvin Waukazoo, age 17, P.O. Honor.
2-45-1-3 Ella Waukazoo, age13.
2-45-1-4 Henry Waukazoo, age 10.
2-45-2 Annie Waukazoo, age 44, P.O. Gills Pier.
Husband: James Madagome, see 2-38 for children.
2-45-3 Amos Waukazoo, see 12-41.
Wife: Mary Waukazoo (nee Waw-Say-Ke-Zhick).

Information following from: Not Given.
3-45 STEPHEN NE-SAW-ON-WAW-SO-WE-NAY or STEPHEN REDBIRD.
Wife: Name not given, dead.
3-45-1 Simon Redbird, P.O. Genoa School, see 21-23.

Information following from: Not Given.
4-45 O-ME-GE-SE-QUAY, dead, sisterof Stephen Redbird 21-23, for heirs see 18-45.

Information following from: Not Given.
5-45 MAW-CHE-KE-ZHE-GO-QUAY, dead, mother of Louis Mendowash, see 7-45.

Information following from: Not Given.
6-45 AW-BE-TWA-QUOUM or JOSEPH REDBIRD, age 66, P.O.

Northport, Traverse Band.
Wife: Name not goven, dead.
6-45-1 Name not given, dead.

Information following from: Not Given.
7-45 MEN-DO-SKUNG or LOUIS MENDOWASH, age 66, P.O. Suttons Bay, Mich, Traverse Band.
Wife 1st: Name not given, dead.
Wife 2nd: Catharine, see 22-41, on roll 1870 as 10-39.
7-45-1 WingMendowash, age 39, P.O. Northport.
Wife 1st: Name not given, dead.
Wife 2nd: Lucy (Jacobs) Mendowash, age 38, P.O. Northport, daugh of 16-4-62, 1st husband Simon Shokoo, P.O. Northport, son of #30 p 23, for children see 30-23..
7-45-1-1 Della Mendowash, age 16, P.O. Mt Pleasant Sch.
7-45-1-2 Esther Mendowash, age 14, P.O. Mt Pleasant Sch.
7-45-1-3 Mary Mendowash, age 8, P.O. Mt Pleasant Sch.
7-45-1-4 John Mendowash, age 6.
7-45-2 Joe Mendowash, age 30, P.O. Northport, for family see 10-40.
7-45-3 Eliza Bigjoe, age 40, see 13-38.
Husband: John Bigjoe.

Information following from: Not Given.
8-45 WAW-BE-ME-QUAY, dead.

Information following from: Not Given.
9-45 KE-ZHE-GO-QUAY, dead, no heirs.

Information following from: Not Given.
10-45 MIN-DAY-ME, dead.
10-45-1 Elizabeth Min-Day-Me, see 33-38.

Information following from: Not Given. Sept 25/08
11-45 NAW-CHE-GE-NE-WAY, known as JOHN ~~AGECHA~~ AGACHE,age 70, P.O. Omena, Traverse Band.
Wife: Mrs. John Agache, age 70, died May 1907, see 19-45, no children.

Information following from: Not Given. Sept 25/08
12-45 KAW-GE-ZHE-QUOUM.
Wife: Name not given, dead, Note: tis was her 2nd husband, by her 1st husb. She had children.
12-45-1 Wm Bird, see 22-40.
12-45-2 Name not given, dead.
12-45-2-1 Paynick Shaw-Wab-E-Na-Say (male), age 51, P.O.

Suttons Bay, see 16-42.
Wife: Jane, no children.

12-45-3 Threse.
Husband: Name not given, dead.
12-45-3-1 Bennett Bourrasaw, age 16, see 3-42.

12-45-4 Mary She-No-Din, P.O. Beaver Island, see 12-46.

12-45-5 Nancy Poulier (pronounced Pouillot), age 53, P.O. St James P.O. Mich or Bay Shore, same as Nancy Bird 7-30, separated.
Husband 1st : PeterPoulier, French, off.
Husband 2nd: Jacob Francis, see 7-30.

12-45-6 Samuel Bird, age 49, P.O. Suttons Bay.
Wife: Delia Bird nee Agosa, age 48, P.O. Suttons Bay, no children ,dauh of wife of 13-41.

12-45-7 Antoine Bird, age 47, P.O. Suttons Bay, see also 2-41.
Wife 1st: Name not given, dead.
Wife 2nd : Sophia Bird nee Chippeway, see 18-41.
12-45-7-1 John Bird, age 26, P.O. Suttons Bay Beaver Island see 2-41, single, child by 1st wife.
12-45-7-2 Caroline Wah-Be-Ne-Me-Ke, age 24, P.O. Beaver Island P.O. St James, separated.
Husband: John Smith or John Wah-Be-Ne-Me-Ke, age 25, see 26-34.
12-45-7-2-1 Agnes Wah-Be-Ne-Me-Ke, age 6.
12-45-7-2-2 Annie Wah-Be-Ne-Me-Ke, age 3.

12-45-8 ~~Sophia~~ Lucy Neniashe, age 44, P.O. Suttons Bay, enroll separately.
Husband: Joe Neniashe, age 48, no children, see 9-41.

Information following from: Not Given.
13-45 AISH-QUAY-BE, no heirs.

Information following from: Not Given.
14-45 GEORGE AISH-KE-BUG, dead, no heirs.

Information following from: Not Given.
15-45 AMOS AWBUAINCE or AMOS FOX, age 52, P.O. ~~Kewadin~~ Rapid City, Mich RFD Box 79, Traverse Band.
Wife: Rosie (Miller), age 38 daughter of 15-14-44.
15-45-1 Wm Fox, age 21, P.O. Rapid City.
15-45-2 Jesse Fox, age 19, P.O. Rapid City.
15-45-3 Ella M. Fox, age 17, P.O. Rapid City.
15-45-4 Fred Fox, age 15, P.O. Rapid City.
15-45-5 Benjamin Fox, age 12, P.O. Rapid City.
15-45-6 Lillian Fox, age 9, P.O. Rapid City.
15-45-7 Mary Fox, age 6, P.O. Rapid City.

15-45-8 Lottie Fox, age 5.
15-45-9 Fred Fox, age 2.
15-45-10 Rosabelle, born July 25, 1908.

Information following from: Not Given.
16-45 PE-TAW-NE-QUOT-O-QUAY known as MARY NAH-NAH-DA-WE-QUA, age 64, P.O. Suttons Bay, Traverse Band.
Husband: Name not given.
16-45-1 Mary Mexcenena, age 48, see 12-31.
16-45-2 Steven Munson, age 24, P.O. X Village.
Wife 1st: Name not given, separated, see 4-44.
Wife 2nd: ~~Annie~~ Helena Taylor, see 17-20.
16-45-2-1 Joe Munson, age 3, enroll with Louisa Munson 4-44

Information following from: Not Given.
17-45 JOSEPH WAY-TOS, dead, no heirs.

Information following from: Not Given.
18-45 PAW-GE-GAY-NAW-NAW-QUOT or JOSEPH PE-DON-QUOT, age 66, P.O. Northport,Traverse Band.
Wife: Sarah Pe-Don-Quot, age 58, on roll in 1870 with husband.
18-45-1 Julius Pe-Don-Quot, age 18, P.O. Northport, not married.
18-45-2 Eliza Pe-Don-Quot,age 13, P.O. Northport.

Information following from: Not Given.
19-45 NE-GAW-NO-BE-QUAY, age 70, died May 1907, afterwardsmarried to John Agache, 11-45.

Page 46
Chief TAT-BAW-SE-KE-ZHICK
Elk Rapids

Information following from: Not Given.
1-46 TAT-BAW-SE-KE-ZHICK.
Wife: Name not given.
1-46-1 George Ta-Baw-Se-Ke-Zhick (or George Chief), age 45, P.O. Kewadin.
Wife: Nancy, see 19-60, no children.
1-46-2 James Ta-Baw-Se-Ke-Zhick, age 26, P.O. Rapid City, not married.
1-46-3 Paul (Ta-Baw-Se-Ke-Zhick) or George, age ~~28~~ 32, P.O. Petosky.
Wife: Susan Georgie, age 44, see 21-26 for children.

Information following from: Not Given.

2-46 WAW-BOSE.

Wife: Name not given, dead.

2-46-1 ~~Ja~~ Frank Wahbose, dead, died Mch 29/07.

Wife: Jane Waboose, P.O. Rapid City,see 10-46.

2-46-1-1 Martha Waboose, age 6, P.O. Rapid City.

2-46-1-2 George Waboose, age 3, P.O. Rapid City.

2-46-1-3 Agnes Waboose, age 21, P.O. Petoskey, single, child by 1st wife, see 21-26.

2-46—2 George Wahbose, dead, no children.

Information following from: Letter to Susan Ogetanaquot, Kenneth, Mich., c/o Chambers Bro. Camp. Kenneth Dec 29, 1908.

3-46 O-GE-DON-QUOT (GABRIEL), dead, Traverse Band.

Wife: Susan Ogetanaquot, age 65, P.O. Kenneth, Mich.c/o Chambers Bro Camp.

3-46-1 Mitchell Ogetanaquot, age 48, P.O. Goodheart, Mich.

Wife: Name not given, dead, see 10-28.

3-46-1-1 Wm Ogetanaquot, age 24, P.O. Goodheart.

3-46-1-2 Joe Ogetanaquot, age 8, P.O. Goodheart.

3-46-1-3 Thomas Ogetanaquot, age 2, P.O. Goodheart.

3-46-2 John Ogetanaquot, age 46, P.O. ~~Oequeoc, Mich~~ Kenneth, Mich., single, not married, see 9-32.

3-46-3 George Ogetanaquot, age 44, P.O. ~~Millersburg, Mich.~~ Kenneth, Mich., single.

3-46-4 ~~Peter~~ Newton Ogetanaquot, age 36, P.O. ~~Millersburg.~~ Kenneth, Mich., single.

3-46-5 Frank Ogetanaquot, age ~~28~~ 34, P.O. , P.O. ~~Millersburg.~~ Kenneth, Mich., single.

3-46-6 Mary (Ogetanaquot) Arnot, dead.

Husband: Bert Arnot - - a white man, P.O. Millersburg.

3-46-6-1 Ed Arnot, age 14.

3-46-6-2 AmandaArnot, age 12.

3-46-6-3 Jane Arnot, age 9.

3-46-6-4 Mary Arnot, age 7.

Dec 28/08
H.B. Durant U.S. AgentKenneth Mich

Dear Sir

I sent you our names & we just move here at Kenneth Mich. My husband die 8 years ago . I have big Family.
Mrs Susan Ogetanaquet
My Family
George Ogetanaquet
John Ogetanaquet

Newton Ogetanaquet
Frank Ogetanaquet
Edmund Ogetanaquet
Miss Mandy Ogetanaquet
Mary Ogetanaquet

Jane Ogetanaquet
And don't put one my Boy name his at Goodhart Mich. Mitchell Ogetanaquet and we are Ottawa & Chippwa Indian. Born in Antrim Co- Elk Rapids Mich and we also have one Indian Stay with us he come from at Beaver Island his name is Kenewanba Pashinnabe. And his Family at Beaver Island, Mich and if you did not get the names. His Family you Let him knew and you will find these names alright

Our address
Mrs Susan Ogetanaquet
Indians
Kenneth P.O.
Mackinac Co Mich
c/o Chambers Bro Camp

Information following from: Not Given.
4-46 WAW-BE-SKAW, dead, Traverse Band.
Wife: Name not given, dead.
4-46-1 Susie O-Ge-Don-Quot, age 65, P.O. Ocqueoc Kenneth Mich, `see 3-46.
4-46-2 John Wabskah, age 61, P.O. Elk Rapids, not married & no children.
4-46-3 Baw-Pe-Tway or Peter White, age 58, P.O. Elk Rapids, see 11-46.
4-46-4 Naw-Ge-Sho-Ge-Shay 12-46.

Information following from: Not Given.
5-46 A-KEN, dead.
Wife: Name not given.
5-46-1 Stephen ~~Hagan (formally A-Ken)~~ A-Ken, age 58, P.O. ~~Elk Rapids~~.
Wife: Thresa (Pedwadum) A-Ken, are 31, P.O. Barker's Creek, Mich., see 13-41.
5-46-1-1 Agnes Blackman, age 24.
Husband: Mitchell Blackman, see 42-41 for children.
5-46-1-2 Mary A-Ken, age 22, P.O. Mt Pleasant Sch.
5-46-1-3 Delia A-Ken, age 18, P.O. Mt Pleasant Sch.
5-46-1-4 Tillie A-Ken,age 8, P.O. Barker Creek.
5-46-2 Name not given, dead.

5-46-2-1 Lucy Ogemahgegedo, age 27, P.O. Horton's Bay, see 9-46.

5-46-3 Name not given, dead.

Information following from: Not Given.

6-46 O-GE-MAW-KE-GE-DO, Traverse Band.

Wife: Name not given.

6-46-1 Moses O-Ge-Maw-Ke-Ge-Do, age 57, P.O. Omena.

Wife: Name not given, dead.

6-46-1-1 Mary ~~Peter~~ Assineway, age 35, P.O. Middle Village, Mich.

Husband: Peter Assinneway, see 16-28 for children.

6-46-1-2 Thomas O-Ge-Maw-Ke-Ge-Do, age 30, P.O. Petoskey, separated.

Wife: Mary Ann Naw-We-Go-Zhe-Go nee (~~Nawgezhick~~), see 10-46.

6-46-1-3 Alice White, age 26, see 11-46.

6-46-2 David O-Ge-Maw-Ke-Ge-Do, age 50, P.O. Omena.

Wife: Margaret O-Ge-Maw-Ke-Ge-Do, age 50, P.O. Omena, see 7-51.

6-46-2-1 Simon O-Ge-Maw-Ke-Ge-Do, age 2, P.O. Omena.

6-46-3 Henry O-Ge-Maw-Ke-Ge-Do, age 48, P.O. Omena, not married, no children.

6-46-4 Samuel O-Ge-Maw-Ke-Ge-Do or Sam Pewash, age ~~37~~ 43, P.O. Omena.

Wife: Catharine O-Ge-Maw-Ke-Ge-Do or Pewash, nee Naongaby, see 9-40 for children.

Information following from: Not Given.

7-46 AW-WAW-NAW-KE-ZHICK, Traverse Band.

Wife: Name not given, dead.

7-46-1 James Won-Ge-Zhick, age 55, P.O. Northport.

Wife: Nancy (Pow-Ge-Zhick), age 48, P.O. Northport, see 16-38.

7-46-1-1 John Won-Ge-Zhick, age 31, P.O. Cheboygan Brutus Mich., see 15-31.

Wife: Mary (   ).

7-46-1-1-1 Cecelia Won-Ge-Zhick, age 8.

7-46-1-1-2 Agnes Won-Ge-Zhick, age 6.

7-46-1-1-3 Irene Won-Ge-Zhick, age 5.

7-46-1-1-4 Esther Won-Ge-Zhick, born Sept 1907.

7-46-1-2 David Won-Ge-Zhick, age 20, P.O. Northport.

7-46-1-3 Levi Won-Ge-Zhick, age 18, P.O. Northport.

7-46-1-4 Anna Won-Ge-Zhick, age 10, P.O. Northport.

7-46-1-5 Archie Won-Ge-Zhick, age 8, P.O. Northport.

7-46-2 Peter Won-Ge-Zhick, age 37, died Apr 15/07.
Wife: Lucy (David), age 38, P.O. Ripid City, daugh of 30-38.
7-46-2-1 Wm Won-Ge-Zhick, age 20, P.O. Mt Pleasant Sch.
7-46-2-2 Jacob Won-Ge-Zhick, age 16, P.O. Mt Pleasant Sch.
7-46-2-3 Catharine Won-Ge-Zhick, age 10, with mother.
7-46-2-4 Louis Won-Ge-Zhick, child died Apr 1907 a few days after father, born after Mch. 1/07.

Information following from: Not Given.
8-46 FRANCIS AW-WAW-NAW-QUOT, dead, no heirs.

Information following from: Not Given.
9-46 ENOS O-GE-MAW-KE-GE-DO.
Wife: Name not given, dead.
9-46-1 Charles O-Ge-Maw-Ke-Ge-Do, spelled now O-Ge-Mah-Ge-Ge-Do, or Charles Enos, age 33, P.O. ~~Charlevoix~~ Hortons Bay.
Wife: Lucy O-Ge-Mah-Ge-Ge-Do nee A-Ken, age 27, see 5-46.
9-46-1-1 Eliza O-Ge-Mah-Ge-Ge-Do, age 10.
9-46-1-2 Jessie O-Ge-Mah-Ge-Ge-Do, age 8.
9-46-1-3 Rosie O-Ge-Mah-Ge-Ge-Do, age 6.
9-46-1-4 Susan O-Ge-Mah-Ge-Ge-Do, age 2, died jany 1908.
9-46-1-5 Agnes O-Ge-Mah-Ge-Ge-Do, born Feby 22/08 2nd roll.
9-46-2 Name not given,dead, no heirs.
9-46-3 Name not given,dead, no heirs.

Information following from: Not Given.
10-46 NAW-WE-GO-ZHE-GO or PETER MARK, age 78, P.O.Kewadin or Rapid City, Traverse Band.
Wife: Name not given, dead.
10-46-1 Alfred Mark, age 34, P.O. Bradley, Mich.
Wife: Nancy Mark nee Walker, ~~a Pott~~, see 12-53.
10-46-2 Jane (Mark) Waboose, see 2-46.
Husband: Frank Waboose, died Mch 29/07, see 2-46.
10-46-3 David Mark, age 30, P.O. Rapid City, not married.
10-46-4 ~~Josep~~ Lillie Mark King, age 26, P.O. Rapid City.
Husband: Moses King, age 34, see 13-42, grandson of Mrs. David King,see 3-46.
10-46-4-1 Beatrice King, age 9.
10-46-4-2 Lucius King, age 6.
10-46-4-3 George King, age 2.
10-46-4-4 Joshua King, born Oct 23, 1907 1st roll.
10-46-4-5 Leander King, age 3, died Sept 1/07.

10-46-5 Josie Mark, age 24, P.O. Harrisburg Philadelphia Pa 2235 N 33rd St., not married.

10-46-6 Eugene Mark, age 22, P.O. Pellston, Mich.

10-46-7 Susie Mark Ance, age 20, P.O. Rapid City Alden, Mich.
Husband: Caspar Ance, see 8-42.

10-46-8 Marian Mark, age 18, separated, see 6-46.
Husband: Thomas O-Ge-Maw-Ke-Ge-Do.

10-46-9 Eliza Mark, age 16, P.O. Rapid City.
Husband: Joe Blackman, age 26, see 17-41.
10-46-9-1 Mary Blackman, born ~~Mch 28~~ Apr 28, 1908 2nd roll

10-46-10 ~~Wm Mark~~

10-46-11 Francis Mark, age 12, P.O. Chiloceo, Okla. Ind Sch.

10-46-12 Rosie Mark, age 9, P.O. Chiloceo, Okla. Ind Sch.

Rapid City
Michigan
June 17-09

Dear Sir.-
I rec'd your letter this week asking of Josie Mark.
Address. This is
Miss Josie Mark
2235 N. 33 rd. St.,
Philadelphia,
Penna.
Yours Resp.
Peter Mark

Information following from: Not Given.

11-46 BAW-PE-TWAY or PETER WHITE, age 58, P.O. ~~Elk Rapids~~ Kewadin, Mich., Traverse Band.
Wife 1st: Name not given, dead.
Wife 2nd: Mary White nee Borden, white, off.
11-46-1 John H. White, age 38, P.O. Omena.
Wife: Alice White nee O-Ge-Ge-Ma-Do, age 26, granddaugh of 6-46.
11-46-1-1 Louisa White, age 4.
11-46-1-2 Robert Whit, age 3.
11-46-1-3 Columbus White, born Sept 16/08, Do not enroll.
11-46-2 Joseph White, age 14, P.O. Mt Pleasant, Mich.
11-46-3 Jesse White, age 9, P.O. Tomah Sch Wis, adopted child, an Ottawa (Mich) Indian, mother was Louisa King ~~nee~~ daugh of 7-46.

Information following from: Not Given.

12-46 NAW-SHO-GE-SHAY, Traverse Band.

Wife: Mary She-No-Din, age 53, P.O. Beaver Island, she now wife of Joe She-No-Din or Bundy White, age 45, an Ottawa Ind., see 16-34.

12-46-1 Eliza Nady, age 29, died July/08, share to be paid to her mother Mary She-No-Din as heir.

Husband: Eli Nady, separated from wife

Information following from: James M. Paul Interpreter Oct 2/08 Elk Rapids, Mich.

13-46 KIN-NE-SHE-WAY, dead.

Wife: Mary Kin-Ne-She-Way, age 90, P.O. Kewadin (Information by Mary), no children and no heirs.

Information following from: Not Given.

14-46 KE-ME-WAW-NISH-CUM.

Wife: Name not given, dead.

14-46-1 So Ne-So-Kat, see 32-46.

Information following from: Not Given.

15-46 ME-KE-NOC, dead.

Wife: Name not given, dead.

15-46-1 No entry made?

15-46-1-1 Rosie Johnson, age 30, P.O. Rapid City.

Husband: Sampson Johnson, off Saginaw Indian.

15-46-1-1-1 Alice Johnson, age 15, P.O. Mt Pleasant Ind Sch.

15-46-1-1-2 Minnie Johnson, age 12.

15-46-1-1-3 George Johnson, age 8.

Information following from: Not Given.

16-46 NAW-O-QUAY-KE-ZHICK.

Wife: Name not given, dead.

16-46-1 Name not given, dead, no heirs.

16-46-2 Name not given, dead, no heirs.

16-46-3 Sophia Naw-Quay-Ge-Zhick, age 50, P.O. Alden, Mich., see 21-32.

Information following from: Not Given.

17-46 O-ME-ME or JOHN OMEME, age 58, P.O. Kewadin.

Wife: Name not given, dead.

17-46-1 Name not given, dead, no heirs.

Information following from: Not Given.

18-46 CHARLES FISHER, dead.

Wife: Name not given.
18-46-1 Name not given, dead, no heirs.

Information following from: Not Given.
19-46 SAW-GAW-CHE-WAYO-SAY.
Wife: Name not given, dead.
19-46-1 Name not given, dead, no heirs.
19-46-2 Name not given, dead, no heirs.

Information following from: Not Given.
20-46 KEY-WAY-DIN, dead.
Wife:Name not given, dead.
20-46-1 Name not given, 25-46.
20-46-2 Name not given, 35-46.

Information following from: Not Given.
21-46 PAY-PAW-ME-SAY, Traverse Band.
Wife: Name not given, dead.
21-46-1 Margaret Pay-Paw-Me-Say, age 55.
Husband: Rodney Negake, Grand River Band, see 11-52.
21-46-2 Christina Pay-Paw-Me-Say, age 50, P.O. Suttons Bay Omena, see 18-41.
Husband: Dan Chippewa, an Ottawa, see 18-41.
21-46-3 Catharine Pay-Paw-Me-Say.
Husband: Geo Heneman, P.O. Fern, Mich., see 8/2/56, Grand River Band.
21-46-3-1 Wm Heneman, age 25, P.O. Petoskey, married, Grand River Band.
21-46-4 Agnes Pay-Paw-Me-Say Pete, Grand River Band, see 19-54.
21-46-5 Angeline Wabbinimkee, age 39, P.O. Beaver Island, see 2-41

Information following from: Not Given.
22-46 PE-MAY-NAW-GO-QUAY, dead.
Wife: Name not given, dead.
22-46-1 No entry made?
22-46-1-1James Miller or James Fisher, see 14-40.

Information following from: Not Given.
23-46 JOSEPH.
Wife: Name not given.
23-46-1 Mary Ann Fisher, age 30, P.O. Kewadin, no children.

Information following from: Not Given.
24-46 O-SAW-WAW-NAW-ME-QUAY, age 85, P.O. Elk Rapids, Mich.
(Very old & feeble) & wants Jacob Anderson to look after payment as

he doesnot know anything about money & is afraid to trust others. He has no living relative. Durant

Information following from: Not Given.
25-46 MARGARET KEY-WAY-DIN, age 88, P.O. Rsapid City, Mich., no heirs and no children.

Information following from: Not Given.
26-46 NAW-SCOW or EDWARD NASKAW, age 89, P.O. Elk Rapids, Traverse Band.
Wife 1st: Name not given, dead.
Wife 2nd: Mary Ann Naskaw, age 39, see 6-31 & 20-32.
26-46-1 Name not given, dead.
Husband: Thomas Fisher, age 60, P.O. Bay Shore, Mich.
26-46-1-1 Moses Fisher, age 30, P.O. ~~St. Ignace~~ Bay Shore, Mich., wife & child dead.
26-46-1-2 Susan (Fisher) Greensky, age 27, P.O. Bay Shore.
Husband: Geo Greensky, age 23, P.O. Bay Shore, see 24-23.
26-46-1-2-1 Elsie Greensky, age 5.
26-46-1-2-2 Leonard Greensky, born Nov 3, 1907, died Sept 14, 1908 2nd roll.
26-46-2 Sarah Prickett, see 19-44.
26-46-3 Angus Naw-Scow spelled Naskaw, age 44, P.O. Elk Rapids.
Wife: Mary Naskaw, age 52, daugh of 20-32.
26-46-1-4-1 Joe Isaac #2, age 14, P.O. Mt Pleasant Sch, adopted, (goes by name of Joe Naskaw) (index both and refere to both).
26-46-4 Thomas Naskaw, dead, no heirs.
26-46-5 Elijah Naskaw, age 38, P.O. Kewadin, Mich.
Wife: Maggie Naskaw, died Apr 6/08.
26-46-5-1 Christiana Naskaw, age 13, P.O. Kewadin, Mich.
26-46-5-2 Thomas Naskaw, age 11, P.O. Kewadin, Mich.
26-46-6 Jane White, age 35, P.O. Hackley, Wis.
Husband: John White, a Menominee Ind.
26-46-6-1 Annie White, age 12.
26-46-7 Isaac Naskaw, age 29, P.O. Kewadin.
Wife: Rosie Naskaw nee Ching-Gwaw, age 35, P.O. Kewadin, no children.

Information following from: Not Given.
27-46 O-CHICK-E-SAW, dead, no heirs.

Information following from: Not Given. Oct 3 Elk Rapids

28-46 PE-ME-QUAY, dead, no heirs.

Information following from: Not Given. Oct 3 Elk Rapids.
29-46 SE-BEE-QUAY, dead, no heirs.

Information following from: Not Given.
30-46 MAY-WAW-WAW-CHE-WON, age 70, P.O. Kewadin, Mich., now wife of 32-46.

Information following from: Not Given.
31-46 PAY-ME-KEY, dead.
Wife: Name not given.
31-46-1 Margaret Key-Way-Din, see 25-46.

Information following from: Not Given.
32-46 NE-SO-KAT known as JACOB SOGOT, age 75, P.O. Kewadin, on roll as 30-46, no children.

Information following from: Not Given.
33-46 GO-BAY-AW-BAW-NO-QUAY, dead, no heirs.

Information following from: Not Given.
34-46 PE-NAW-SE.
Wife: Lucy Penawse, age 56, P.O. Kewadin, see 4-23, no children, no heirs..

Information following from: Not Given.
35-46 LOUIS KE-SHAW-TAW or KESHATA, age 60, P.O. Rapid City.
Wife: Name not given, dead, see note on 52-27.
35-46-1 Mary Ann Jacko, age 39, P.O. Rapid City, Mich.
Husband: Alex ~~Shapot~~ Jocko, off, a Canadian Indian.
35-46-1-1 Paul Alexander, age 17, P.O. Mt Pleasant Sch Rapid City.
35-46-1-2 Sam Alexander, age 11.
35-46-1-3 Sarah Alexander, age 5.
35-46-1-4 Entice Alexander, age 2.
35-46-1-5 Mitchell Alexander, born Aug 31/08, do not enroll.
35-46-2 Elliott Keshata Maning, age 36, P.O. Rapid City.
Husband: Wm Maning, white off.
35-46-2-1 Bowers Maning, age 8.
35-46-2-2 Bird Maning, age 2.
35-46-3 Lucy Thomas (nee Keshata), age 35, P.O. Rapid City, see 52-27.
Husband: Joe Thomas, age 40, Ind of Ottawa Tribe, son of Mary Thomas Pabo, see 9-24 Charlevoix.

35-46-3-1 Rennie Thomas, age 4.
35-46-4 Peter Keshata, age 26, P.O. Rpid City.
Wife: Susie Keshata nee E-Do-We-Go-Na-By, no children, an Ottawa Ind & entitled to enrollment.

Page 49
Chief NE-BE-NAY-KE-ZHICK
Grand River

Information following from: Not Given.
1-49 NE-BE-NAY-KE-ZHICK, dead.
Wife: Name not given, dead.
1-49-1 Geo, dead, on roll as 4-49.
1-49-2 Wm, on roll as 9-49.
1-49-3 Mary Louis McDagnot, dead.
Husband: Name not given, dead.
1-49-3-1 Susan, dead.
1-49-3-2 Lucy Battice, age 39, P.O. Lattin, Mich, see 7-49.
Husband: Francis Battice, age 31, P.O. Lattin, Mich, see 6-59, (or Frank Mitchell).
1-49-3-3-1 Sophia Wah-Bin-Divetto, age 25, P.O. Walkerville, Mich.
Husband: Pete Wah-Bin-Divetto.
1-49-3-3-1-1 John Wah-Bin-Divetto.
1-49-3-3-2 Mary Williams, age 22, (single, P.O. Lattin, Mich.
1-49-3-3-3 LouisWilliams, age 15.
1-49-3-3-4 Wm Williams, age 12, adopted by Andrew Light, Millerton, Mich.
1-49-3-3-5 Mary Battise, age 10, died Jany 17/08.
1-49-3-3 Julia McDaquot, age 37, P.O.Fountain, Mich., no children, see 7-49.
1-49-3-4 Christel, dead.
Husband: Name not given, dead.
1-49-3-4-1 Joe Cubayasha, age 15, P.O. Lattin, Mich., lives with Mrs. Jas. J. Cogswell.
1-49-3-4-2 Elizabeth Cubayasha, age 16, P.O. Lattin, Mich., lives with Mrs. Jas. J. Cogswell.
1-49-3-5 Agust, on roll as 10-49.
Spouse not given.
1-49-3-6 Gertie Wabsis, dead.
Husband: Name not given, dead.
1-49-3-6-1 Jacob Wabsis.
Wife: Mary Wabsis, for children see 28-52.

1-49-3-6-2 John Wabsis.
Wife: Mary Wabsis, see 28-52.
1-49-3-7 Mitchell Louis or Richard Louis, age 59, P.O. Elbridge,Mich- P.O. Lattin, on roll as 20-49.
1-49-3-2 (mis numbered) Domniceke Louis, dead, on roll as 5-49.
1-49-3-8 John Louis, dead.
Wife: Mary Louis, age 57, P.O. Lattin, Mich., see 6-50
1-49-3-8-1 Nancy Pego, age 24, see 5-62.
1-49-3-8-2 Amy Akins, 20, P.O. Lattin, Mich.
Husband: Louis Akins, dead, died Nov/07.
1-49-3-8-2-1 James Akins, born Feby 20/07.
1-49-3-8-3 George Domniceke, age 6, grandson of 5-49, son of Geo Louis 36.
1-49-3-9 Peter Louis or Nebrnaykezhick, age 49, P.O. Lattin, Mich.
Wife 1st: Name not given, dead.
1-49-3-9-1 Louis Louis, age 29, P.O. Lattin, Mich.
Wife 1st: Gertie (Shay-Go-Nay-Be) now wife of Chas Perrissiansee 23, see 2-54, Honor Copernish, Mich., Diverney Dt.
1-49-3-9-1-1 Maggie Louis, age 9.
Wife 2nd: Sophia (Cogswell) Louis, granddaugh of 11-54.
1-49-3-9-1-2 Blanche Louis, age 2.
1-49-3-9-1-3 Mildred Louis, born May 11/08.
Wife 2nd: Name not given, dead,no children.
Wife 3rd: Jennie Louis, age 35, P.O. Lattin, Mich., no children, see 20-50 & 19-50, daughter of James Blacksmithby 1st wife. Durant.
1-49-3-10 Name not given, dead, no heirs.
1-49-3-11 Name not given, dead, no heirs.
1-49-3-12 Name not given, dead, no heirs.
1-49-3-13 Name not given, dead, no heirs.
1-49-3-14 Name not given, dead, no heirs.

Note: Ask him if his wife's father is living & where & if she has any brothers & sisters & who they are & where?

Hart, Mich.
May 18 1907

Horace Durant

Dear Sir.

I received your letter was ask about why is name Jennie B, Smith her fasther Ottawa and mother Ottawa.

Father James B. Smith.

Yours truly
Peter Lewis
Nebenaykezhick
Lattin, Mich.

Information following from: Not Given.
2-49 PAY-ME-WAW-WAW or CAREY.
Wife: Jessie.
2-49-1 Charles Carey.
Wife 1st: Julia.
2-49-1-1 Isaac Carey, age 28, single.
Wife 2nd: Catharine.
2-49-1-2 Thomas Carey, age 18, P.O. Hart #4.
2-49-2 Nancy Bailey, age 50, wife of Jacob Bailey 7-50, see children with husb., see 2-58 & 6-56.
2-49-3 Mary Smith, age 48, P.O. Lattin.
Husband: Wm Smith, grandchild of 13-64.
2-49-3-1 Fred Smith, age 28, P.O. Lattin, see 5-48.
Wife: Jennie Louis Smith, see 1-49.
2-49-3-1-1 CatharineSmith, age 4.
2-49-3-1-2 Leo Smith, age 3.
2-49-3-2 Jane Smith Newton, age 24, P.O. Lattin, separated from Husb. John Newton.
2-49-3-2-1 Moses Newton, age 4, see 13-64.
2-49-3-3 Augustine Smith, age 19, P.O. Lattin.
2-49-3-4 Julia Smith, age 16, P.O. Lattin.
2-49-4 Louis Carey.
Wife: Nancy Compaux Me-Niese, P.O. Freesoil.
2-49-4-1 Paul Carey, age 13.
2-49-4-2 Albert Carey, age 12.
2-49-4-3 Pearl Carey, age 11.
2-49-4-4 James Carey, age 10.
2-49-4-5 Lizzie Carey, age 9.
2-49-5 John Carey, age 41, P.O. Hart #4.
Wife: Name not given, white.
2-49-5-1 A. J. Carey, age 20, not married.
2-49-5-2William Carey, age 18.
2-49-5-3Maria Carey, age 12.
2-49-6 Eliza Carey Pierson, age 34, P.O. Hart #4.
Husband: Name not given, white.
2-49-6-1 Frank Pierson, age 17.
2-49-6-2 Harry Pierson, age 11.
2-49-6-3 Goldy Pierson, age 8.

2-49-6-4 Clyde Pierson, age 5.

Information following from: Not Given.
3-49 A-SE-BUN or SKINHORN.
Wife: Mary.
3-49-1 Charles Skinhorn.
Wife 1st: Name not given, dead.
Wife 2nd: Key-Way-Ah- Ge-Wan, age 57, P.O. Hart, daugh of ~~Shab-Wa-Ba-Se-Gay~~ Shab-Wa-Se-Gay or Cabmosa, see 2-59.
3-49-1-1 John Skinhorn (dead) no child.
3-49-1-2 Edward Skinhorn, age 29, P.O. Freesoil.
Wife: Mary Albert Skinhorn, age 27.
3-49-1-2-1 Chas Skinhorn, age 5.
3-49-1-2-2 Lydia Skinhorn, age 3.
3-49-1-2-3 Isaac Skinhorn, born Dec 27, 1907.
3-49-1-3 Katie Antoine, age 27, P.O. ~~Free East Lake Manistee Co.~~
Husband: Moses A. Antoine,age 28, P.O. Harlin, Manistee Co, see 2-50.
3-49-1-3-1 Sylvester Antwine, age 5.
3-49-1-3-2 Rosie Antwine, age 2.
3-49-1-3-3 NancyAntwine, born June 11, 1908 2nd roll.
3-49-1-4 Mary Ke-Quom, age 23, see 3-50.
3-49-1-5 John Skinhorn, age 18, by 2nd wife.
3-49-2 Philip Skinhorn, children are dead.
3-49-3 George Skinhorn, age 44, P.O. ~~Freesoil~~ Hart.
Wife 1st: Name not given, dead.
Wife 2nd: Martha (Nodin) age 35, now wife Chas Thomas, see 25-55.
3-49-3-1 A-Se-Bunor Coon Skinhorn, age 8, (enroll with Marth Thomas) see 25-55.
3-49-4 Betsy Aken, dead.
Husband 1st: Antoine Wah-Ba-Se-Gay, dead.
Husband 2nd:Jas Aken, P.O. Hart, see11-54.
3-49-4-1 Lydia Wah-Ba-Se-Gay, known as Edith Robinson.
3-49-4-2 Wm Wah-Ba-Se-Gay
3-49-4-3 Louis Aken, died Dec 1907.
3-49-4-3-1 Jas. Aken, born ~~Aug~~ Feby 20 1907.

Information following from: A. L. Eness Grand Rapids Mch26/09.
4-49 GEO NE-BE-NAY-KE-ZHICK or GEO LOUIS, dead.
Wife: Name not given, dead.
4-49-1 Louis T. Eness, age 50, P.O. 538 Scribner St. Grand Rapids, Mich.

Wife 1st: Name not given, white.
Wife 2nd: Name not given, white.
4-49-1-1 Eleanor Eness, age 15, P.O. Los Angeles, Cal, by 1st wife..
4-49-1-2 Nellie Eness, age 12, P.O. Los Angeles, Cal., by 1st wife.
4-49-2 Joseph D. Eness, age 48, P.O. Olivette, Mich.
Wife: Name not given, white.
4-49-2-1 Clara Eness, age 18.
4-49-2-2 Melvin Eness, age 7.
4-49-3 Wm Eness, age 44, P.O. 674 Hall St Grand Rapids, Mich.
Wife: Name not given, white, same address as father, married, husb white, no child..
4-49-3-1 Hazel Eness, age 17.
4-49-3-2 George Eness, age 14.
4-49-3-3 Ruth Eness, age 10.
4-49-3-4 Wm Eness, died May 1908.
4-49-4 Amos L. Eness, age 42, P.O. 603 Scribner, Grand Rapids Mich.
Wife: Name not given, white.
4-49-4-1 Bernard Eness, age 12.
4-49-4-2 Edward Eness, age 8.
4-49-4-3 Robert Eness, age 3, died Feby 23/09.
4-49-4-4 Elenor A. Eness, born Oct 18/08 off.
4-49-5 Henry Eness, age 39, P.O. 559 Cass Ave. Gd. Rapids Mich.
Wife: Name not given, white.
4-49-5-1 Marguerite Eness, age 12.
4-49-5-2 Marie Eness, age 10.

Wm Eness family
William born Sept 1890 – died May 1908
Hazel " Feb 1892
George " June 1894
Ruth " Mar 1897

Henry Eness family
Marguerite born Feb 1896
Marie " June 1899

Joseph Eness family
Clara Eness born Sept 1890
Melvin Oct 1902

Lewis Eness family
Eleanor born Nov 1889

Nellie Mar 1894

Amos Eness family
Harold born Nov 1894
Bernard Oct 1896
Edward Dec 1901
Robert Aug 1905

Information following from: Not Given.
5-49 DOMINEKE (LOUIS), dead.
Wife: Helen Louis, age 70, P.O. Lattin, Mich., see 6-50.
5-49-1 Joe Louis (dead), see 7-52.
5-49-2 Angeline Louis.
Husband: Louis Cogswell, P.O. Walkerville, Mich., see 11-54.
5-49-3 Mary Robinson (nee Louis), P.O. Dighton, Mich., see 1-49.
Husband: Chas Robison, age 48, an Ottawa Ind., se e 3-59.
5-49-4 Maggie Louis Seaman, age 39.
Husband: Jack Seaman, see 15-54.
5-49-5 Eliza Louis, dead.
Husband: Name not given, dead.
5-49-5-1 Name not given, see 33-54.
5-49-6 George Louis, age 36, P.O. Honor, Mich.
Wife: Name not given, now wife of Cobb Crampton, see 3-52 & 7-53
5-49-6-1 John Louis, age 7.
5-49-6-2 Geo Dominick, age 6, this child is adopted by grandmother see Mary Louis 5-62 & 1-49.
5-49-7 Henry Louis, age 33, died March 1907, no wife nor child.
5-49-8 Frank Louis, age 30, P.O. Lattin, Mich.
Wife: Mary Bananas Louis, age 28, see 2-50.
5-49-8-1 Eliza Louis, age 5.
5-49-8-2 Annie Louis, age 2.
5-49-9 Sylvester Louis, age 28, P.O. Mt Pleasant Sch, single.
5-49-10 Amy Louis Seaman, see 15-54.
5-49-11 Jennie Louis Smith, age 24, P.O. Lattin, Mich.
Husband: Fred Smith, age 28, see 2-49.
5-49-11-1 Catharine Smith, age 4.
5-49-11-2 Leo Smith, age 2.

Information following from: Not Given. Custer 2/18/09
6-49 KE-WAY-GOSH, dead.
Husband: No entry.
6-49-1 Mrs James Halfaday, age 66, see 19-49 & 3-59.
James Halfaday, a Pott Ind.
6-49-2 Joe Pete or Joe Pe-Nay-Se-Wan-Quot, age 52, P.O. Custer #2,

see 14-52.
Wife: Mary Pe-Nay-Se-Wan-Quot, age 23, nee Ke-Way-Quoum.
6-49-2-1 Lizzie Pe-Nay-Se-Wan-Quot, age 12.
6-49-2-2 Lazon ~~Elias~~ Pe-Nay-Se-Wan-Quot (male), age 8.
6-49-2-3 Angeline Pe-Nay-Se-Wan-Quot (girl), age ~~2~~ 3.
6-49-2-4 Benedict Pe-Nay-Se-Wan-Quot, born July/08.
6-49-3 Mary Robinson Medahko, age 44, see 21-52, P.O. Millerton.
Husband: Henry Medahko, see 21-42 & 3-59.
6-49-4 Rosie (Robison) Pete, age 35, see 2-46 & 3-59.
Husband: Chas Pete or Chas Key-Way-Quoum, see 14-54 for children.

Information following from: Not Given. Custer 2/19/09
7-49 CHAW-BAW-QUAY, dead.
Wife: Name not given, dead.
7-49-1 Lucy Battice, age 39, see 1-49.
Husband: Francis Battice or Frank Mitchell, see 1-49.
7-49-2 Julia McDaquot, age 37, see 1-49.

Information following from: Not Given.
8-49 WAW-BAW-SE-GAY.
Husband: No entry.
8-49-1 Betsy, dead.
Husband 1st: Waw-Baw-Se-Gay, dead
8-49-1-1 Edith Robinson, age 42, see 6-62 for husband and family..
8-49-1-2 William Waw-Baw-Se-Gay or Wm Petoskey, age 39, P.O. Hart, single & unmarried.
Husband 2nd: James Aken, living, see 2-58.
8-49-1-3 Louis Aken.
8-49-1-3-1 James Aken, born Feby 20/07 1st roll, see 1-49.

Information following from: Not Given.
9-49 WM NE-BE-NAY-KE-ZHICK or WM LOUIS.
Wife: No entry.
9-49-1 James Louis, age 42, P.O. Cadillac or Starr City, see 23-52.
9-49-2 Moses Louis.
Wife: No entry.
9-49-2-1 Name not given, Boy Louis, age 13, P.O. in Canada.
9-49-3 Angeline Louis Mosaw, age 38, Hamilton, Mich.
Husband: Alex Mosaw.
9-49-3-1 Josephine Mosaw, age 24.
9-49-3-2 Elizabeth Mosaw, age 21.

9-49-3-3 Tracy Mosaw, age 15.
9-49-3-4 John Mosaw, age 13.
9-49-3-5 Thomas Mosaw, age 9.
9-49-3-6 Florence Mosaw, age 8.
9-49-3-7 Mary Mosaw, age 6.
9-49-3-8 William Mosaw, age 5.
9-49-3-9 Adam Mosaw, age 4.
9-49-3-10 Louis Mosaw, age 2.
9-49-3-11 Joe Mosaw, too late.

Hamilton Mich

May 10/09
Department of Interior
Washington

Dear Sir

Your letter at hand of Inquiry and will send the same. Of my children Josiphine 24 Lisabeth 21 Tracy 15 Johnie 13 Joe 16 months Tohmas 9 years Florence 8 years
Mary 6 " " Wiliam 5 years Adam 4 yrs Lewis 1 ½

My Broth as Moses is dead 3 year ago he has one Boy 13 year old in Canada but I cant tell you what his name is
This is all

Mrs Angeline Masaw

Star City Mich
Mussaukee County
May 19, 1909

Mr. Horace B. Durant:

In answer to your letter will say, I do not know this man Moses. Only I have heard that I have a brother by that name. His address then, ten years age was Alleganac Mich. How big a family he has got I do not know, for I have never seen him.

Yours Truly
Mr. James Louis

Information following from: Not Given.
10-49 A-QUET, daughter of 1-49, dead.
Husband 1st: Seth Robinson, (dead) white.
Husband 2nd: Chas Wabsis, dead.
10-49-1 Ed Robinson #2, age 45, P.O. Tustin RFD #2 Box 74, see ~~12-49~~ & 5-49.

Wife: Name not given, white.
10-49-1-1 Ella Sprauw, age 23, P.O. Tustin RFD #3, Mich, (husb white) 1 child born Sept 1907.
10-49-1-2 Carrie Larson, age 21, P.O. Muskegon, Mich (Laundry Co).
10-49-1-3 Lena Robinson, age 19, P.O. Tustin, Mich Route 2 Box 74.
10-49-1-4 Sadie Robinson, age 16.
10-49-1-5 Glenn Robinson, age 13.
10-49-1-6 Arthur Robinson, age 10.
10-49-1-7 George Robinson, age 7.
10-49-1-8 Ardith Robinson, age 4.
10-49-2 Jake Wabsis, age 36, see 28-52.
10-49-3 John Wabsis, age 31, see 28-52.

Horace B. Durant
Indian Agt Petoskkey Mich

Bradley Jan 11 09

Mr Durant Sir
In regard to my sister Josey mark I do not know her present address the last I knew was Chicago
Alferd Mark
Information following from: Not Given.

Information following from: Not Given. Custer 2/19/09
11-49 JOSETTE, dead & MARTIN, dead , no descendants.

Information following from: Not Given.
12-49 NAW-BAW-GAW-WE-NUM or SARAH THEODORE, age 65, P.O. Freesoil lives near Hamlin Lake, see 27-59.

Information following from: A. L. Eness 4-49 Mch 16/09 Grand Rapids, Mich.
13-49 MRS RIX ROBINSON, dead.
Husband: Rix Robinson, dead.
13-49-1 John R. Roinson, dead, see 18-54.
Wife: Name not given, white, dead.
13-49-1-1 James Robinson, dead, last heard of was at Grand Rapids.
13-49-1-2 Eva Robinson, dead, no heirs,

Information following from: Not Given. Ben Trombly, a Brother, also the Pentroater Indians. Petrosky Dec 16/08

14-49 MARY TROMBLY & NIECE, sister of Mrs Rix Robinson 13-49. Said to be living in State of Washington & has children, (Information fully corroborated) . Cannot get into communication with her, Durant Spl Agt.

May 14th 1909
Custer Mich

Mr. H. B. Durant
Dear Sir you ask me to information to Mary Trombly last time we hear from her She was in Indian tertory we lost the letter that we got from her We don't know her address it Been six years sence we herd from her I don't know where shes dead or live
Lewis McClellan

Letter B Louis McClellan May 7

Pellston, Mich., *May 1st* 1909

Horace B Durant
Special U.S. Indian Agent

Dear Sir
I do not know where Mary Trombly is or wether one of them I believeheard of them for quitea while.
I should think you cant find them out by writing to Louis McClellane to them Mason Co Mich.
Yours Truly
BenjaminThrombly
Pellston Mich

Information following from: Not Given. Custer 2/19/09
15-49 EMILY TROMBLY, dead.
Husband: Name not given, white.
Notes: Married & moved west Indians do not remember much about this woman or where she is, or whether living or dead. Durant Later: Some of the old people men & women say that Emily Trombly was burned to death, by her clothing catching fire Durant.

Information following from: Not Given.
16-49 WAW-BE-SKE-NIM or NANCY AGAHGO, age 67, P.O. Chief Lake, daugh of 12/27/59.
Husband: Geo Agaho, see 12-52.

Information following from: Not Given. Custer 2/19/09
17-49 JOSEPH TRUCKEY, Indians do not recall any member by this name. The only Truckey's they mean are Antoine & Frank Truckey, see 26-57 Durant Cannot get track of him & he is not enrolled Durant Spl Agt.

Information following from: Not Given. 2/18/09
18-49 MRS NAW-TAY, dead.
    Husband: Naw-Tay.
    18-49-1 Mrs Geo Robinson, age 75, P.O. GrandHaven, Said to have descendants in Grand Haven & Charlevoix, see 20-57.
    18-49-2 Wm Naw-Tay, dead, see 27-57 for children.

Information following from: Not Given.
19-49 CHING-GUAW-O, (MRS. JAS. HALFADAY), age 66, see 6-49.
    Husband 1st: Name not given, dead, age 66, P.O. Millerton, Mich.
    Husband 2nd: James Halfday, (off) a Pott.
    19-49-1 Margaret Pokagon, age 36, P.O. Millerton, Mich see 24-53.
        Husband 1st: Name not given, dead.
        Husband 2nd: Chas. Pokagon, (off) Pott.
        19-49-1-1 Andrew Foster or Hineman, age 20, P.O. Millerton, see 19-53.
            Wife: Clara Eaton Hineman, age 17, Daugh of Sam Eaton, Honor, Mich.
            19-49-1-1-1 David Hineman, born Mch 23/08 2nd roll.
        19-49-1-2 Martha Foster or Hineman, age 18, P.O. Sac & Fox Sch Toledo Iowa.
        19-49-1-3 Julia Hineman, age 16, P.O. Millerton, Mich.
        19-49-1-4 Amy Hineman, age 14, P.O. Millerton, Mich.
        19-49-1-5 Clark Hineman, age 10, P.O. Sac & Fox Sch Iowa.
        19-49-1-6 Simon Pokagon, age 8.
        19-49-1-7 Angeli Pokagon, age 7.
        19-49-1-8 Louisa Pokagon, age 3.

Grand River Band
Sophia (wife) 3-56
Husb_(Robt Aken) 3-58
Newaygo Mich
May 10 1909

Dear Sir

Mr Durant I have received your letter askin me my fathe & mother name I can not give you there correct ages of my Parents. They both Ottawa Drod many Payment in grand Haven & grand Rapids.
My father is alex Aiken or Indian name lixer Lamorandin also my mother is maiden name Sophia Tagquessung Tagwassung her father is name James Tagquessung or Lawernce.
My wife is name Julia Lewis her maden name her father Richard Lewis or Nebenaygezhick Bonnegyegak former chief Ottawa Band.

Enrolled

Ages

Robert Aiken or Lamorandin

My age 36 June 1909
My wife age 31 Apr 2 1907
My Louisa Aiken 14 March 29 1909
Clarence Aiken 10 April 29 1909
Alex Aiken 8 Dec 9th 1908

Information following from: Not Given.
20-49 MICHAEL NE-BE-NAY-KE-ZHICK or RICHARD LOUIS, age 59, P.O. Lattin, Mich.
Wife: Name not given, dead.
20-49-1 Julia Akin, age 32, P.O. Newaygo, Mich, see 21-54.
Husband: Robt. Aiken, see 3-56 & 3-58.
20-49-2 Helen Louis Bailey, age 26, P.O. Lattin, Mich.
Husband: Bonaface Bailey,see 17-52.
20-49-2-1 Sophia Bailey, age 10.
20-49-2-2 Susie Bailey, age 9.
20-49-2-3 Julia Bailey, age 5.
20-49-2-4 Rosie Bailey, born May/07.
20-49-3 Augustus Louis, age 25.
Wife: Julia Louis (Negake), age 20, see 11-52.
20-49-3-1 Fred Louis, born Mch 6/072nd roll.
20-49-4 Mary Battise, age 19, P.O. Fern, Mich.
Husband: Louis Battise at Fern, Mich, see 6-59.
20-49-4-1 David Battise.
20-49-5 George Louis, age 18, P.O. Lattin, Mich, single.

Information following from: Benj. Trombly, a brother Petoskey Dec 26/08
21-49 THERESA TROMBLY, dead.
21-49-1 Frank Genia, age 40, P.O. Chicago, (formerly lived in State of Washington. If found would know about Mary Trombley, see 14-49 D. Cannot locate im, cousin his know where he is Durant, see latter on 29-59.

Page 50
Chief MAW-BEECE
Grand River

Information following from: Not Given. Mount Pleasant, Michigan
1-50 MAW-BEECE, (CAUBMOSAY) or WALKER, dead.
Wife: Theresa Walker or Caubmosay, age 83, P.O. Mt. Pleasant.
1-50-1 Name not given, dead.
1-50-1-1 J Maw-Beece Walker or Maw-Beece Way-Me-Ge-Wance, age 32, P.O. Mt Pleaasant, see 9-58.

1-50-2 Paul Walker (Caubmosay), age 52, P.O. Rosebush, Mich.
Wife 1st: Name not given, dead.
Wife 2nd: Name not given, Saginaw Ind.
1-50-2-1 James Walker, age 27, P.O. Mt Pleasant, single.
1-50-3 Chas Walker, age49, P.O. Mt Pleasant.
Wife: Name not given, Saginaw Indian.
1-50-3-1 Lillian Walker, age 13, Mt Pleasant.
1-50-4 Name not given, dead.
Husband: John Pego, age 46, see 2-62 & 3-56.
1-50-4-1 Henry Pego, age 22, P.O. Mt. Pleasant, single.
1-50-4-2 Elizabeth Pego, age 18, P.O. Mt. Pleasant.
1-50-4-3 ~~Jussie~~ Jesse Pego, age 17, P.O. Mt. Pleasant.
1-50-4-4 Eunice Pego, age 12, P.O. Mt. Pleasant.
1-50-5 Jacob ~~Pego~~ Walker, age 35, P.O. Redby, Minn., separated.
Wife 1st: Name not given, dead.
Wife 2nd : Saginaw Ind. Jennette Strong (a Saginaw Ind) , P.O. Mt. Pleasant.
1-50-5-1 Archie Walker, age 10.

Information following from: Mary Jackson et al Weidman Jany 19/09
1st Sheet
2-50 NAW-GAW-NE-QUO-UNG.
Wife: name not given, dead.
2-50-1 Julia Bananas, age 48, see 2nd sheet.
Husband: See next sheet.
2-50-2 Me-Non-Quay or Minnie Antoine, age 57, P.O. East Lake, Mich.
Husband: Ambrose Antoine, age 65, see 4-31, an Ottawa Ind. of Little Traverse Band, died Aug 13, 1908.
2-50-2-1 Moses Antoine, age 28, P.O. ~~Copemish~~ Harlan, Mich.
Wife: Kate (Skinhorn), daugh Chas Skinhorn see 3-49 for children.
2-50-2-1-1 Sylvester Antoine, age 5.
2-50-2-1-2 Rosie Antoine, age 3.
2-50-2-1-3 Annie Antoine, age 2 months.
2-50-2-2 Isaac Antoine or Ambrose, age 25, P.O. East Lake.
Wife: Mary Medahko, age 20, see 11-50.
2-50-2-2-1 Charles Antoine, age 1, born May 17/1907 2nd roll.
2-50-2-3 Eliza Kelsey, age 30, P.O. Fountain, Mich.
Husband: Joe Kelsey, see 5-61, 3 children.
2-50-2-4 Mary Hinman, age 20, P.O. Copemish.
Husband: Gus Hinman, see 2-56, one child.
2-50-3 Wah-She-No-Quay Mary Jackson, age 58, ~~Widower~~ P.O. ~~Mt~~

~~Pleasant~~ Remus.
Husband: Moses Jackson, Saginaw Indian.
2-50-3-1 Mary Otto, age 28, P.O. Weidman.
Husband: Name not given, Saginaw Ind.
2-50-3-1-1 Alice Otto, age 8.
2-50-3-1-2 Elizabeth Otto, age 5.
2-50-3-1-3 Henry Otto, age 3.
2-50-3-2 Anna Jackson, age 20, P.O. Remus, Mich.
2-50-3-3 May Jackson, age 18.
250-3-4 John Jackson, age 16.

2nd Sheet
2-50-1 James Bananas, age 60, P.O. Lattin, see 16-62.
Wife 1st: Name not given, dead no children, no heirs.
Wife 2nd: Julia Bananas, age 48, daugh of 2-50.
2-50-1-1 Maggie Bananas, age 20, P.O. Lattin, enroll children with mother.
Husband: Pete Alexander, separated, see 12-32.
2-50-1-1-1 Ella Alexander, age 8.
2-50-1-1-2 Sophia Alexander, age 6.
2-50-1-1-3 Jessie M. Alexander, age 3.
2-50-1-2 Mary Louis, age 28, P.O. Lattin.
Husband: Frank Louis, see 1-49 for children.
2-50-1-3 Amy Bananas, age 19, P.O. Lattin.
2-50-1-4 Samuel Bananas, age 17, P.O. Lattin.
Note: This family cannot be traced to the 1870 roll but the oral testimony of James Cogswell, Rodney Onegake, Jacob Bailey, Shay-Go-Nay-Be, and many others, James Bananas family are Ottawas of the Grand River Band, doubt that he is entitled to be enrolled.

Horace Durant
Spl. Ind. Agent

Aug 11, 1908
Elbridge township
Michigan
Indian Church House

Later: James Bananas is son of wife of 14-60 & half brother of Chas. Coby, so says the latter at Cross Village. Durant

Information following from: Not Given.
3-50 PE-TO-BICK or JOSEPH BAILEY, dead.
Wife 1st: Name not given.
3-50-1 Sam Bailey or Sam Wick 20-54.
Wife 2nd: Name not given, dead.

3-50-2 Solomon Bailey or Pe-Dah-Sha, age 61, P.O. Honor, Mich., married & see 3-59 for children.
3-50-3 Sarah Bailey Crampton, living.
Husband: John Crampton, P.O. Crystal Valley, see 7-53, married & has family.
3-50-4 Fannie Bailey Ke-Quom, dead.
Husband: Name not given, dead.
3-50-4-1 Joseph Ke-Quom, age 33, P.O. Custer.
Wife: Angeline, see 2-54 & 15-52.
3-50-4-2 Alex Ke-Quom, age 32, P.O. Hart #2.
Wife: Mary Ke-Quom, see 3-49.
3-50-4-2-1 Fannie Ke-Quom, age 8.
3-50-4-2-2 ALex Ke-Quom, age 4.
3-50-4-2-3 Mabel Ke-Quom, born Oct 16/07 2nd roll.
3-50-4-3 Emma Ke-Quom Battise, age 29, P.O. Hart.
Husband: Mitchell Battise, see 6-59 for children.
3-50-4-4 Susan Ke-Quom Micko
Husband: Jas Micko, age 27, P.O. Hart, see 15-55 for children.
3-50-4-5 Elizabeth Ke-Quom Bailey, age 24, P.O. Honor, Mich., see 20-54.
Husband: Louis Bailey, an Ottawa.
3-50-4-5-1 Sarah Bailey.
3-50-5 Agnes Bailey Akins, age 38, P.O. Honor Empire Junc., see 2-58.
Husband: Jacob Akins.
3-50-5-1 George Wakefield, age 20, P.O. Empire Junc.
3-50-6 Katie Bailey Battise, age 33, P.O. Hart, married no children.

Information following from: Not Given.
4-50 SE-BE-QUAY.
Husband, Name not given, dead.
4-50-1 John Gecick – speeling given by John Himself, or (Ke-Zhick), age 55, P.O. Chief lake.
Wife: Elizabeth, a Pott.
4-50-1-1 Lucy Baker, age 22, P.O. Copemish, Drew with Potts. with mother who was Pott.
Husband: Joe Baker., see 29-59.
4-50-1-1-1 Julia Baker, born Apr 8/08.
4-50-1-2 Jack Gecick, age 19, Drew with Potts. With mother who was Pott.
4-50-1-3 Tice Gecick, age 16, Drew with Potts. With mother who was Pott.
4-50-1-4 Waso Gecick, age 14, Drew with Potts. With mother who was Pott.

4-50-1-5 Nancy Gecick, age 9.
4-50-1-6 Thomas Gecick, age 6.
4-50-2 Girl, name not given, dead, no descendants.

Information following from: Not Given. Custer 2/18/09
5-50 ANTOINE CAUB-MO-SAY, dead.
Wife: Name not gven, dead.
5-50-1 Name not given, dead, no descendants.

Information following from: Not Given.
6-50 CHING-GWOW.
Wife: Name not given, dead.
6-50-1 Helen Louis, age 70, P.O. Lattin.
Husband: Dominick Louis, see 1-49 for children.
6-50-2 Gertie Wab-Bin-Dwetto.
Husband: Hank Wab-Bin-Dwetto, see 11-58 & 7-52.
6-50-3 George Ching-Gwow or Ching-Won, age 48, P.O. Lattin.
Wife: Mary Ching-Won, age 41, daugh of Seth Wright.
6-50-3-1 Thresa Ching-Won, age 23, P.O. Lattin, not married.
6-50-3-2 Chas. Ching-Won, age 21, P.O. Lattin.
Wife: Emma Me-Dah-Koo, age 17, see 11-50 for child.
6-50-3-3 Peter Ching-Won, age 16.
6-50-3-4 John Ching-Won, age 9.
6-50-3-5 Antony Ching-Won, age 6.

Information following from: Not Given.
7-50 PAW-GAW-CHE-QUAY or PAH-GUTCH-QUAY-AGAHGO, age 75, P.O. Lattin, enroll her by herself.
Husband 1st: Battise Bailey 2-58.
7-50-1 Jacob Bailey, age 55, P.O. Lattin.
Wife: Nancy Bailey, age 42, daugh of 2-49.
7-50-1-1 Delos Bailey, age 28, P.O. Lattin, not married.
7-50-1-2 Andrew Bailey, age 22, P.O. Lattin, not married.
7-50-1-3 Mary Negake, age 19.
Husband: Henry Negake, see 11-52., no children.
7-50-1-4 Amy Bailey, age 17, P.O. Lattin.
7-50-1-5 Maggie Bailey,age 15, P.O. Lattin.
Husband 2nd: Name not given.
7-50-1-6 Wm Pay-Ba-Me, age 45, P.O. Lattin, see 6-56 & 5-61.
Wife: Angeline Naw-Kay-O-Say or Kelsey, age 45.
7-50-1-6-1 Peter Pay-Ba-Me, age 26, P.O. Lattin, see 11-54.
Wife: Susan Cogswell Pay-Ba-Me, age 28.
7-50-1-6-1-1 Annie Pay-Ba-Me, age 3, lives

with grandfather.

7-50-1-6-2 Philip Pay-Ba-Me, age 16, P.O. Lattin.

7-50-1-6-3 John Pay-Ba-Me, age 11, P.O. Lattin.

~~adopted child: Annie Pay-Ba-Me child of~~

Information following from: Not Given.

8-50 KAW-GE-SHE-SHE or JAMES CAUB-MO-SAY.

Wife: Elizabeth Ching-Wash, age 61, P.O. Fountain, daugh. of 1-62.

8-50-1 James Battise (or Battice) or James Wa-Ba-Se-Wa, age 50, P.O. Freesoil, adopted.

Wife: Name not given.

8-50-1-1 Bert Battice, age 17.

8-50-1-2 Moses Battice, age 14.

8-50-1-3 William Battice, age 11.

8-50-2 Grandchild: Cleveland Ching-wash, age 13, enroll with Elizabeth, grandson of 1-62

8-50-3 Angeline (Caub-Mo-Say) Chippeway, age 49, P.O. Luther, Mich.

Husband 1st: Geo Hall, dead, see 2-60, 2 children.

8-50-3-1 Mary Hall Thomas, age 28, see 2-60 & 17-56.

8-50-3-2 Susan (Hall) Fisher, age 25, see 2-60.

Husband: Name not given, Saginaw Indian off.

8-50-3-2-1 Thos. Fisher, born Mch/08.

Husband 2nd: Paul Elliot, dead, no children.

Husband 3rd: Alex Chippeway, a Pott. off, (Alex Chippeway is a half brother of Jos. Cushway by same mother, a Pott.)

8-50-4 A brother see 14-63.

Information following from: Not Given.

9-50 MAY-TWA-WAY or JOHN NE-GAKE, see 11-52.

Information following from: Not Given.

10-50 KAW-KAW-NE, dead, no descendants.

Information following from: Not Given.

11-50 ME-TAW-KOO.

Wife: No entry.

11-50-1 Wm Medahko, see 21-52.

11-50-2 Charles Medahko, age 61, P.O. Millerton.

Wife: Lizzie Shay-Go-Nay-Be, age 45, daugh of Wm see 6-54.

11-50-2-1 Amy or Emma Medahko, age 16, P.O. Lattin.

Husband: Charley Ching-Won, age 21, see 6-50.

11-50-2-1-1 Frank Ching-Won, born Feby/08 2nd roll.

lives with grandparents.
11-50-2-2 Wm Medahko, age 4.

1st husband of Lizzie Shay-Go-Nay-Be above:
John Key-Way-Quom, age 49,P.O. Brutus, see 6-54.
1 Angeline Key-Way-Quom, age 23.
Husband: Joe Ke-O-Quom, see 3-50 & 15-52.
2 Mary Ambrose or Antoine, age 18, P.O. Manistee.
Husband: Isaac Ambrose or Antoine, P.O. East of East Lake, see 2-50.
2-1 Chas Ambrose, born ~~July/07~~ May/07 2nd roll.

Information following from: Not Given.
12-50 SHAW-BOO, dead.
Wife: No entry.
12-50-1 Mary Ann Chittigoo, age 60, P.O. Pinconning.
Husband 1st: Name not given, dead.
Husband 2nd: Name not given, Saginaw Ind.
12-50-1-1 Mary Elk, age 30, P.O. Mt Pleasant #6, Saginaw Indians.
Husband: John Matts, white, P.O. Gaylord, Mich.
12-50-1-1-1 Maggie Matts, age 12, P.O. Gaylord, Mich., with father.
12-50-1-1-2 Martha Matts, age 13, P.O. Gaylord, Mich., with father.
12-50-2 Alice Anderson, age 52, see 13-55.

Note: Confirmed by Grand River Inds. At Custer Feby 18/09 Durant.

Note: Mary Ann Chittigo's daughter & grandchildren are to be enrolled as Saginaw Inds & not as Grand River Inds. Durant.

Report: Mary Ann Chittig's was not enrolled with her father in 1870 as a member of the Grand River Band. Her father lived with the Grand River Band near Pentwater & she has lived since childhood among the Saginaw Inds. She was living in 180 & was entitled to be enrolled at that time with her father, but for some reason, (probably because she was not living with his band) was not enrolled.
It is her desire to now be enrolled with the Grand River and will relinquish all claims as a member of the Saginaw Band.

Horace B. Durant
Spl Ind Agt

At Mary Ann Chittigo's house Near Pinconning Mich Jany 27/09

Information following from: Not Given.

13-50 WM CAUBMOSAY'S WIFE, dead, no descendants.

Information following from: Not Given.
1st Sheet:
14-50 FRANCIS BAILEY, dead.
Wife: Name not given, dead.
14-50-1 BattisteBailey, see 2-58, 1870 living.
14-50-2 Joseph Bailey or Pe-To-Bick, see 3-50, 1870.
14-50-3 Henry Bailey or Pay-~~Qush~~-Quay, see 4-62 1870.
14-50-4 Name not given, dead,
Wife: Name not given, dead.
14-50-4-1 Henry Bailey Jr., age 45, P.O. Custer, see 2nd sheet following.
2nd Sheet:
14-50-4-1 Henry Bailey Jr., age 45, P.O. Custer

~~Note: Younger brother of John Baptise No 32 1870 roll Henry Bailey's father & mother were dead in 1870 & not on that roll, but he lived with his grandfather Francis Bailey, & was probably enrolled with his family, but Francis Baily's name is not on 1870 roll under that name. He was probably enrolled under an Ind. Name which cannot be remembered. I am satisfied beyond Doubt that Heny Bailey & family is entitled to enrollment & will enroll him subj. to approval. Horace B. Durant, Spl. Agt.~~
~~The above is corroborated by~~

Wife: Teresa Bailey, nee Do-Ne-Gay, age 40, P.O. Custer, Mich., on roll with 7-61. 187 Chief No 14., No 7 is her father.
14-50-4-1-1 Antoine Bailey, age 13.
14-50-4-1-2 Cornelius Bailey, age 11.
14-50-4-1-3 Louis Bailey, age 6.

Note: Francis Bailey's name has been found as No 14 p. 50 1870 roll Durant

Wife 1st: Mary Wakefield Bailey, now Aikens, age 39.
14-50-4-1-4 Martha Hall, age 24, P.O. Custer #2 Honor Mich, see 2-60.
Husband: Name not given.
14-50-4-1-4-1 Milo Hall, age 3/
14-50-4-1-4-2 Sarah Hall, age 2.
14-50-4-1-5 Charles Bailey,age 22, P.O. Custer #2

Honor Mich, unmarried.
14-50-4-1-6 Nancy Bailey, age 20.
Husband: Frank Chippewa, Traverse Band, see 18-41..
14-50-4-1-6-1 Nettie Chippewa, age 3 mos, born May/08.
14-50-4-1-7 Lizzie Bailey, age 18, P.O. Mt Pleasant Sch or Custer #2.

Information following from: Not Given. Custer 2/18/09
15-50 ME-SE-NAY-BE-QUAY, dead.
Husband: No Entry.
15-50-1 Elizabeth Memberto, 80, see 13-50.
Husband: Joe Memberto, age 74, see 9-54.

Information following from: Not Given. Custer 2/18/09
16-50 AW-QUAY-NE-WAY, dead, no descendants.

Information following from: Not Given. Custer 2/18/09
17-50 O-ZHE-GAW-BO-WE-QUAY, dead.
Husband: No entry.
17-50-1 Maggie Peters Thomas, age 42, P.O. Honor, see 21-50, now living with Chas Pego 24, see 5-62.

Information following from: Not Given. Custer 2/18/09
18-50 AW-ME-NE-QUAY, dead, no descendants.

Information following from: Not Given. Custer 2/18/09
19-50 O-WIS-TE-AWE or JAMES SMITH, age 50, P.O. Leland, Mich.Carp River or try Kewadin. Look up through children on Traverse sheets, Has not lived among Grand River Indians for 30 years. Is said to be yet alive & has family. Durant
Wife: No entry.
19-50-1 James Louis, age 35, see 1-49.
Wife: No entry.
19-50-1-1 Peter Louis, see 1-49.

Later: Identified as James Blacksmith 45 Sutton's Bay, see enrolled by himself as here on also see 20-52.

Information following from: Not Given.
20-50 AW-SE-GOONSE or RODNEY NEGAKE, see his family on 11-52.

Information following from: Not Given.
21-50 PAY-CAW-NAW-SE-GAY or JIM PETERS, age 68, P.O. Luther,

Mich.
Wife: Jane Peters, age 60, on roll with him in 1870.
21-50-1 Maggie (Peters) Thomas, age 42, P.O. Honor, see 17-50.
Husband: Louis Thomas, age 53, P.O. Freesoil, see 17-56, Separated.
21-50-1-1 Fred Thomas, age 29, P.O. Luther.
21-50-1-2 Bert Thomas, age 18, P.O. Luther.
21-50-1-3 Katie Thomas, age 16, P.O. Luther.

Information following from: Not Given. Custer 2/18/09
22-50 ARCHIE KAW-YAW, dead, a son of 12-50"Shaw-Boo".
Wife: Name not given, dead.
22-50-1 Name not given, dead, no heirs.

Information following from: Not Given.
23-50 NE-GON-CAUG-MO-SAY.
Husband 1st: Name not given, dead.
Husband 2nd: Len Robinson, white.
23-50-1 Mary Robinson.
Husband: Luke Wah-Bin-Duetto, see 7-52.
23-50-2 Wm Robinson, age 39, P.O. ~~White Hall near Muskegon or Montegue~~ Chicago, single. Montague Feby/09 D.

June 21st 1909
Mr Horace B. Durant
U.S. Special Indian
Agent
Dear Sir
In reply of your inquiry I'll. Say in regards of Willie Robinson my Brother he is in Detroit I don't know his address. He is my half Brother on my Mother's side he is a grand River Indian all right enough the some Band I belong to.
Yours Respectfully
Mrs Mary Wabindute
Waker Ville Mich

Page 51
Chief ME-TAY-WIS
Grand River

Information following from: Not Given.
1-51 ME-TAY-WIS JOE, died June 1908.
Wife 1st: Name not given.
Wife 2nd: Thresa Me-Tay-Wis or De-No-Quay, age 74, P.O. Fountain, same as Men-Daw-No-Quay, see 13-51.
1-51-1 Louis Me-Tay-Wis or Medowis, age 60, P.O. Allegan Co.

Bradley, Mich or Dorr, Mich, on roll as 12-51, son by 1st wife..

1-51-2 Sophie or (Key-Way-Aw-Bum) see 26-51, P.O. Fountain.

Husband: Charles Hickey, age 70, see 23-53 for child.

1-51-3 Peter or Pean Medawis, age 50, P.O. Bradley or Dorr, see 5-53

Wife: Margaret Medawis, see 21-64 & 26-53.

1-51-3-1 Johnson Medawis, age 28, P.O. Bradley, separated.

Wife: Bertha Medawis nee Mosher, age 19, P.O. Bronson, Mich, see 20-53.

1-51-3-1-1 Clarence Medawis, age 3, with father.

1-51-3-1-2 Josephine Medawis, age 2, born Aug 1907, with mother.

1-51-3-2 Ellen Sprague, age 31, P.O. Bradley.

Husband: Selkirk Sprage, age 28, see 25-53, no children.

1-51-3-3 Mary Medawis, age 20, P.O. Hamilton, single.

1-51-3-4 Anna Medawis, age 17, P.O. Hamilton, single.

1-51-4 Annie (or Paw-Shaw-Baw) Smith.

Husband: Joe Smith, see 7-55

Information following from: Not Given. Mount Pleasant, Michigan Jany 18/09

2-51 NO-TE-NO-KAY (3 children)

2-51-1 (Son) name not given, dead, see 12-32.

Wife: No entry.

2-51-1-1 Peter Alexander, age ~~35~~ 39 P.O. Bradley, see 12-32.

Wife: MinnieAlexander, see 2-55.

2-51-1-1-1 Rosie Alexander, age 2, born Summer 1907 Aug/07.

2-51-2 Elizabeth Isaac, age 50, see 4-53.

2-51-3 Annie Ostie, age 46, see 10-53.

Information following from: Not Given.

3-51 AW-BE-NAW-BE or JON PETERS.

Wife: Name not given, dead.

3-51-1 George Peters, age 42, P.O. Gills Pier, Mich.

Wife: Mary (Beaver) Peters, age 33, P.O. Gills Pier, Mich, see 28-38.

3-51-1-1 Julius Peters, age 3.

3-51-1-2 Annie Peters, age 8 months, born Apr 1/07 2nd roll, died Dec28/07.

3-51-2 Name not given, dead.

Wife: Name not given, dead.

3-51-2-1 Isaac Peters, age 19, P.O. Manistee, not married.

Information following from: Not Given.
4-51 WAUB-SIN.

Wife: Won-Qua, dead, granddau 19-51.

4-51-1 Levi Camburn or Levi Zoondah, age 41, P.O. Star City.

Wife: Name not given, dead.

Now living with Lucy Sausway, see 20-64.

4-51-1-1 Willie Camburn, age 14.

4-51-1-2 Rosie Camburn, age 12.

4-51-1-3 Lyne Camburn, age 9.

4-51-1-4 Amy Camburn, age 6.

Note: Levi and oldest son drew with the Potts, but other children did not.

Note: No other children living and left no living descendants.

Information following from: Not Given. Custer 2/18/09
5-51 JACOB KEY-O-CUSH-CUM, dead.

Wife: Name not given, dead.

5-51-1 Name not given, dead, no heirs.

5-51-2 Jacob Shaw, dead.

Wife: No entry.

5-51-2-1 Adam Shaw, age 23, P.O. Chippewa Station, Mich.

5-51-2-2 Lizzie Shaw, age 16, P.O. Mt Pleasant Sch.

Chippewa Station Mich.
Jan 23 1909

Sir

a few lines to let you know that there is one young man here that belongs to grand River Indians his name is Adam Shaw. He has a Sister in School at Mt Pleasant their Father name was Jcob Shaw he is dead.

From Charles Jackson
Chippewa Sta

Adam Shaw is living With me and is. His age 23 years

Note on letter: John Fransway says this boy is a Grand River lived at Pentwater.

Information following from: Not Given. Custer 2/18/09
6-51 AISH-KE-BAW-GAW-SUNG, dead.

Wife: Name not given, dead.

6-51-1 Name not given, dead.

6-51-2 Wm Daniels, age 45, P.O. Freesoil.

Wife: Angeline Daniels, age 28, see 22-53.

Information following from: Not Given.
7-51 WAW-BE-GUANCE.
Wife: Name not given, dead.
7-51-1 Margaret O-Ge-Maw-Ke-Ge-Do, age 50, P.O. Omena.
Husband: David O-Ge-Maw-Ke-Ge-Do, see 6-46.
7-51-2 Daniel Dean, age 33, P.O. Omena, separated.
Wife: Catharine (Bird) Dean, age 31, P.O. Suttons Bay, ~~an Ottawa Ind. Undoubtedly entitled to enrollment~~, separated, Traverse Band, daughter of 22-40.
7-51-2-1 Angus Dean, age 12.
7-51-2-2 Ambrose Dean, age 9.
7-51-2-3 Frank Dean, age 7.
7-51-2-4 Grace Dean, age 5.
Note: These children live with Grandfather: Wm Bird 22-40 enroll them separately with mother Catharine Dead, nee Bird.

Information following from: Not Given. Custer 2/19/09
8-51 SE-BE-QUAY, dead.
Husband: No entry.
8-51-1 Mary Fitch, age 35, P.O. Custer #2, see 9-55.
Husband: Amos Fitch, age 46, see 9-55.

Information following from: Not Given.
9-51 O-SAW-O-BICK, brother to 13-51.
Wife: No entry.
9-51-1 Peter James or O-Saw-Bick, age 42, P.O. ~~South Boardman, Kalkaska Co.,~~ Ashton Mich, no wife or children.
9-51-2 Kah-Gep.
Husband: Dan ~~Babett~~ or Dan Jones, age 30, P.O. lives at Mt Pleasant, an Ottawa Indian, see 3-64.
9-51-2-1 Harry Jones, 10, P.O. Mt Pleasant #6.
9-51-2-2 Jerome Jones, age 8, P.O. Mt Pleasant #6.

Information following from: Not Given. Custer 2/18/09
10-51 PAW-KEY-CAW-NAW-NAW-QUOT, dead, no heirs.

Information following from: Not Given. Custer 2/18/09
11-51 KEY-WAY-DE-NO-QUAY, dead.
Husband: No entry.
11-51-1 Name not given, dead, no heirs.
11-51-2 Jane Mitchell, age 48, see 3-52

Lattin Mich

May 17 09

Dear Sir

You letter Recd will now Anss. My father name and only in Indian name father Kok,non,quet 80 years old

Mother Key wa de no quay 70yr old father lived around Luther Mich he did there about 10 yrs

Mother died at Freesoil about 11 years Father Chief Wob be ga Kecke this is all and best Ican do yours Truly

Good bye

Mrs Jane Mitchell

Lattin P.O.

Oceana Co, Mich

Per L Louis

Information following from: Lucy Andrews Bradley Feby/09

12-51 LOUIS ME-TAY-WIS (MEDAWIS), age 60, P.O. Dorr, Mich, see 1-51.

Wife: Lydia Medawis, age 52, P.O. Dorr, Mich.

12-51-1 Martha Pi~~d~~geon, age 38, P.O. Dorr, Mich.

Husband: James Pigeon, age 45, ~~a Pott~~, see 9-53.

12-51-1-1 Sarah Pigeon, age 20, P.O. Dorr, single.

12-51-1-2 Jennie Pigeon, age 14.

12-51-1-3 George Pigeon, age 8.

12-51-1-4 Lena Pigeon, age 3.

12-51-1-5 Levi Pigeon, born Dec Nov/08 too late.

12-51-2 Mary Ann Pigeon, age 40, P.O. Dorr.

Husband: John Pigeon, age 40, see 9-53.

12-51-2-1 Wallace Pigeon, age 10.

12-51-2-2 Louis Pigeon, age 8.

12-51-2-3 Wm Pigeon, age 6.

12-51-2-4 Joseph Pigeon, age 4.

12-51-2-5 Hannah Pigeon, born Apr 1908.

12-51-3 Nancy Foster, age 32, P.O. Bradley.

Husband: James Foster, see 10-53.

12-51-3-1 John Foster, age 6.

12-51-4 Sarah Nada, age 22, P.O. Dorr, separated.

Husband: Wm Nada, may be same as Wm Nade 2-38 (yes the same – has brothers Sam & Eli), Traverse Band, no children.

12-51-5 Eliza Pigeon, age 21, P.O. Dorr.

Husband: Sampson Pigeon, age 35, see 26-53.

12-51-5-1 Rosie Pigeon, age 4.

12-51-5-2 Gladys Pigeon, age 2.

12-51-6 Henry Medavis, age 14, P.O. Dorr.

Information following from: Not Given.
13-51 MEN-DAW-NO-QUAY or THERSEDENOQUAY, age 77, P.O. Fountain, see 1-51, was 2nd wife of Chief Metaywis, for children see 1-51.

Information following from: Not Given. Custer 2/19/09
14-51 PAY-BAW-ME-GAW-BOWE, dead.
Wife: Name not given, dead, no descendants.

Information following from: Not Given. Custer 2/19/08
15-51 KUM-ME-GO-QUAY, dead, has a daughter at Omena, probably enrolled with Traverse, whose father is PeterMaishcaw 59 Omena see 1-55. Durant.

Information following from: Not Given.
16-51 SHING-GO-KEY, dead, Inds. at Custer do not remember this man by this name, Can't identify him. Durant.

Information following from: Not Given.
17-51 NO-DIN.
Wife: Nancy Hall Peters, age 60, P.O. Fountain, no children, see 2-60, husband John Peters 60 Fountain, drew with Potts & parents Potts Says so himself. Durant
17-51-1 Name not given, dead, no heirs.

Information following from: Not Given.Custer 2/19/09
18-51 KEY-O-CUSH-CUM, dead, no descendants, father of 5-51.

Information following from: Not Given. 2/19/09
19-51 KAY-SHE-SHAW-WAY-QUAY, dead, no descendants.

Information following from: Not Given. Custer 2/19/09
20-51 O-TISH-PAY, dead, no descendants, had no children.

Information following from: Not Given.
21-51 SHAW-BWOS, dead.
Husband: No entry.
21-51-1 See 7-51
21-51-1-1 See 7-51.

Information following from: Not Given. Custer 2/19/09
22-51 WALK-SHE-QUAY, dead, no descendants.

Information following from: Not Given.
23-51 PAY-BONE-UNG, dead, no heirs, a brother of Way-Be-Guance 7-51.

Information following from: Not Given. 2/19/09
24-51 KAW-BE-ME-NE-GAW-NE, ddead, no heirs, blind, never married.

Information following from: Not Given. 2/19/09
25-51 O-GAW-BAY-YAW, dead.
Husband: No entry.
25-51-1 Maggie Walker Wind, age 45, see 8-26.
Husband: Robt Genereaux or Robt Nodin, age 45, see 19-55.

Information following from: Not Given.
26-51 KEY-WAY-AW-BUM or SOPHIA nee MEDAVIS, age 54, see 1-51.
Husband: Chas. E. Hickey, age 70, P.O. Fountain, enrolled with wife in 1870 as head of family, see 23-53.

Information following from: Not Given. 2/19/09
27-51 KEY-CHE-CHE-WAW, dead, no children.

Information following from: Not Given. 2/19/09
28-51 MAW-TAY-KE-O-KISH-CUM, dead, no heirs.

Page 52
Chief AISH-KE-BAW-GOSH
Grand River

Information following from: Not Given.
1-52 AISH-KE-BAW-GOSH.
Wife: Name not given, dead, no children.

Information following from: Not Given.
2-52 PO-NE-SAY, son of 31-52.
Wife: Name not given, dead, all children dead except.
2-52-1 Rosie Po-Ne-Shing, age 35, P.O. Walkerville, no children.
Husband: Pete Po-Ne-Shing.

Information following from: Not Given.
3-52 PAW-GE-TO-GO-QUAY.
Husband 1st : Name not given, dead.
3-52-1 Ne-Zette Compaux.
Husband: Pay-Me-Saw-Aw or Pete Compaux, see 5-58 ch of 11.
3-53-1-1 Nancy Pontiac, P.O. Freesoil, now wife of Mitchell Ninise, see 5-58 chf 11.
3-52-2 Elizabeth Williams, age 68, P.O. Lattin.
Husband: Name not given, dead.

3-52-2-1 Mary Ching-Waw, age 41, see children 6-50.
3-52-2-2 John Williams, age 36, P.O. Lattin, for wife & child see 2-61.
3-52-3 James Norton, age 60, P.O. Upper Peninsala, no children.
3-52-4 Richard Albert, P.O. Freesoil, see 37-52.
3-52-5 Wm Norton, see 25-55, P.O Honor Northport, (same as Wm Newton)
Husband 2nd: Name not given.
3-52-6 Mary Louis, age 57, P.O. Lattin, for husb & children see 1-49.
3-52-7 Maw-Ge-Aw-Quo-Do-Quay, age 55, P.O. Lattin.
Husband: Name not given, separated, no children.
3-52-8 James Mitchell, age 53, P.O. Lattin.
Wife 1st: Mary, Trombly, dead, see 22-55.
3-52-8-1 Chris Mitchell, age 29, P.O. Lattin.
Wife: Nancy Ke-Ga-Ke Mitchell, age 20.
3-52-8-1-1 Mary Mitchell, age 3.
3-52-8-1-2 John Mitchell, age 25, P.O. Lattin, not married.
3-52-8-1-3 Annie Mitchell, age 22, P.O. Lattin, not married.
3-52-8-1-4 Archie Mitchell, age 19, P.O. Lattin.
3-52-8-1-5 Frank Mitchell, age 13, P.O. Lattin.
Wife 2nd: Jane Mitchell nee Paw-Caw-Non-Quot, age 48, P.O. Lattin.
3-52-8-1-6 Angeline Mitchell, age 6.
Children by 1st husband of Jane Mitchell:
1 Pete Negake, age 23, see 11-52, single.
2 Eliza Negake, age 16.
3 Nancy Mitchell, age 20.
Husband: Chris Mitchell.
3-1 Mary Mitchell.
3-52-9 Susan Mitchell Koon.
Husband: Wm Koon, age 49, P.O. Lattin, see 6-56.
3-52-9-1 Mitchell Koon, age 24, P.O. Lattin, not married.
3-52-9-2 Mary Koon (Ne-Gake) Shay-Wab-Be-No.
Husband 1st: Joe Ne-Gake, see 11-52.
3-52-9-2-1 Mich-E-Ga-Kake (m), age 8 yrs, address not known, supposed to be with Angeline Ne-gake at Brutus, Mich.
Husband 2nd : Pete Shay-Wab-Be-No, see 29-52
3-52-9-2-2 Minnie Shay-Wab-Be-No, age 3.
3-52-9-2-3 Annie Shay-Wab-Be-No, age 6 mos, born Jany 29/08.
3-52-10 Ah-Qua-She (f).
Husband: Joe Fox.

3-52-10-1 Thresa Amy Fox, age 26, P.O. Lattin.
Husband: Cobb Compton, see 7-53 for children.

Information following from: Not Given. Elbridge Aug 10.
4-52 PAY-SHAW or MRS. JOHN WILLIAMS.
Husband: John Williams (Squqy-Ge-Zhick), dead.
4-52-1 ~~Angeline~~ Mary Williams.
Husband: Mike Sho-Min, P.O. Cross Village, Traverse Ind., see 79-21.
4-52-1-1 Angeline Sho-Min, P.O. Cross Village.
4-52-1-2 Joseph Sho-Min, P.O. Cross Village.
4-52-2 John Williams, age 43, P.O. Walkerville.
Wife: Angeline Williams nee Bailey, age 43, see 9-54.
4-52-2-1 Peter Williams, age 18.
4-52-2-2 James Williams, age 16.
4-52-2-3 John Williams, age 14.
4-52-2-4 Philip Williams, age 10.
4-52-2-5 Paul Williams, age 15 months, May 19, 1907 2nd roll.

Information following from: Shagonaby family at Freesoil Aug 23/08
5-52 KEY-ME-WANCE.
Wife: Name not given, dead.
5-52-1 Mary Shagonaby, age 49, P.O. Freesoil,see 2-54.
Note:: All other children are dead.

Information following from: John Wah-Bin-Dwitto Custer Feby 17/09
6-52 AW-GE-WE-NAW or JAKE SOLOMON, age 70, P.O. Manistee, died Feby 3/09.
Wife: Name not given, dead.
Note: as no relations living except 7-52 John Wah-Bin-Dwetto, a brother.
Note: Further questioning of John shows that Jake Solomon had children who married & left children, & that at least one of these now live in Isabella Co, Mich, name Wah-Say-Quoum. Durant.
Note: Said to be Geo Mendoka (18) a grand child at Haskell Sch or at Honor or Mt Pleasant Sch.
6-52-1 Name not given, dead.
6-52-1-1 Geo Mengoka or Geo Wezoo, age 18, ~~Pott~~.
6-52-2 Name not given, dead, ~~no heirs.~~
6-52-2-1 James Wah-Say-Quoum or James Lelbis, age ~~35~~ 42, P.O. Star City, see 23-52.
6-52-3 Name not given, dead.

Athens Mich May 21-09
My dear Friend

Mr. Horace B. Durant
Special U. S. Ind Agent
Petoskey Mich.
I was very much please to here from you again.
George W. Mandoka is worker for me now. My nephew.
He is the son of Joseph Mendoka and Eliza Nee Eliza Solomon. She is a daughter of Jacob Solomon one who dead last winter.
Mrs. Eliza Mendoka

Dead about 5 or 6 or more years go.
George WezooMendoka said his address Bradley Michigan
The otherperson I know not who he is.
I will retain you letter and will try find him with out much trouble.
My wife wish to know when you will be ready to pay off.

If you wish to have any body to help you to pay of ro. As a witness I would be glad to work for you.
Yours Truly
Sam Mandoka

Information following from: Not Given.
7-52 WAH-BIN-DAW-GAW-NAY or JOHN WAH-BIN-DWITTO, age 64 yrs old, P.O. Custer, Mich.
Wife 1st: Wah-She-No-Quab.
Wife 2nd: Martha, age 69yrs, no children.
7-52-1 Luke Wah-Bin-Dwetto, age 35, Walkerville, Mich.
Wife: Mary, formally wife of Joe Louis.
7-52-1-1 Julia Louis, see 1-49.
7-52-1-2 Willie Wah-Bin-Dwetto, age 16
7-52-1-3 Maud Wah-Bin-Dwetto, age 14.
7-52-1-4 Philip Wah-Bin-Dwetto, age 11.
7-52-1-5 Rosie Wah-Bin-Dwetto, age 4.
7-52-1-6 Amos Wah-Bin-Dwetto, born Oct 18/07.
7-52-2 Sophia Wah-Bin-Dwetto, P.O. living Sales Sch. House Walkerville.
Husband: James Cogswell, children see 11-54.
7-52-3 Pete Wah-Bin-Dwetto, age 24 yrs, P.O. Sales Sch House Walkerville.
Wife: Sophia, (dau of Pe-An-No).
7-52-3-1 John Wah-Bin-Dwetto, age, born Mch 24/07.
7-52-4 Houk Wah-Bin-Dwetto, age 25, P.O. Sales Sch House Walkerville.
Wife: Name not given, no children.
7-52-5 Charles Wah-Bin-Dwetto, age 21 yrs, P.O. Sales Sch House Walkerville, no married, no children.

~~(His name pronounced Wah-bin-dwetto, now but I am Satisfied from his statements and that if others that he is the same person carried on 1870 roll in Aw-ke-be-mo-say-o Band as #4 P. 68 was twice married. 1st wife dead. wah-she-no-quab by her he had 10 children, 5 living & 5 dead.)~~

Information following from: David Fox
8-52 MAW-CHE-WE-TAW, dead.
Wife: Name not given, dead
Note: has 2 children livingone at Hamilton& one at Pentwater but Fox does not know names. Durant

Information following from: Not Given.
9-52 MAW-SHE-GO-NA-BE, (Elbridge)

Information following from: Not Given.
10-52 O-SHAW-WAW-SKO-PE-NAY-SE or SAM MARSH, age 65, P.O Freesoil, son 4-58 chf. # 11.
Wife: Name not given, dead.
10-52-1 Joe Marsh, age 40, P.O. Freesoil.
Wife: Alice Marsh, age 33, P.O. Freesoil, see 5-60, daugh of Wm Rozette, niece of Charley Joe, 1st husband Sampson Robinson.
10-52-1-1 Jacob Robinson, age 17.
10-52-1-2 Sarah Marsh, age 10.
10-52-1-3 Chas. Marsh, age 8.
10-52-1-4 Wm Marsh, age 3.
10-52-1-5 Susan Marsh, born ~~Jul~~ Jun 14/08.

Information following from: Not Given. Elbridge
11-52 O-NAY-GAKE.
Wife 1st: Elizabeth Memberto, see 9-54.
11-52-1 Rodney O-Nay-Gake or Aw-Se-Goonse or Rodney Ne-Gake, age 61, P.O. Lattin, see 20-50.
Wife: Margaret Ne-Gake, daughter of Pay-Baw-Me-Say 21-46.
11-52-1-1 Mary Stone, age 26, P.O. ~~Lattin~~ Cobmosa.
Husband: Neal Stone, age 35, grandson of Chief 11-58, son of 13-58.
11-52-1-1-1 Elizabeth Stone, age 9.
11-52-1-1-2 James Stone, age 7.
11-52-1-1-3 Joseph Stone, age 5.
11-52-1-1-4 Moses Stone, age 2.
11-52-1-2 Henry Ne-Gake, age 23, P.O. Lattin.

Wife: Mary Bailey Ne-Gake, Ind. see 7-50, no children

11-52-1-3 Julia Louis, age 20, P.O.Lattin.

Husband: Gus Louis, son of 20-49.

11-52-1-3-1 Fred Louis, born Mch 6/07.

11-52-1-4 Annie Ne-Gake, age 18, P.O. Lattin, not married.

11-52-1-5 William Ne-Gake, age 15, P.O. Lattin.

11-52-1-6 Frank Ne-Gake, age 12, P.O. Lattin.

11-52-2 John O-Nay-Gake or Ne-Gake, age 58, P.O. Lattin,see 9-50

Wife: ~~Angeline~~ Tah-Wah-Quah Bailey Ne-Gake, Ind, age 57, see 4-62, no children.

11-52-2-1 James Ne-Gake, age 8, adopted.

11-52-3 Mary Pe-Ne-Shing, for her children & this family see21-54.

Wife 2nd: Angeline Ne-Gake, age 52, P.O. Brutus.

11-52-4 Joe Ne-Gake.

Wife 1st: Name not given, now wife of James Mitchell, see 3-52.

11-52-4-1 Pete Ne-Gake, age 19, P.O. Lattin.

11-52-4-2 Nancy Mitchell.

Husband: Chris Mitchell, see 3-52.

11-52-4-2-1 Mary Mitchell, age 3.

Wife 2nd: Mary Koon-Now, wife of Pete Shag-Wah-Be-No, see 3-52.

11-52-4-3 Micb-E-Gay-Kake, age 8, see 3-52 & 7-3-52.

11-52-5 Mitchell Ne-Gake, said to be living on north shore of Michigan Escanaba, Information too indefinitive.

11-52-6 Susan Shaw-Waw-Non-Quot (f), at Brutus, see 29-31, Traverse Band.

11-52-7 James Ne-Gake, age 36, P.O. Allenville, Mich.

11-52-8 Madeline (Key-Way-Quom) Shaw-Waw-Naw-Se-Gay, age 20, P.O. Charles, Mich, now wife of Steve Bumaway or Bunang.

Husband: Peter Shaw-Waw-Naw-Se-Gay, see 8-31,P.O. Pine River.

11-52-8-1 Cecelia ~~Key-way~~ Shaw-Waw-Naw-Se-Gay, age 5, enroll with Angeline Ne-Gake

Information following from: Not Given.

12-52 WE-ZO or GEO. AGAHGO, age70, P.O. Chief Lake Mich.

Wife 1st: Name not given, dead.

Wife 2nd: Nancy Agahgo, age 67, P.O. Chief Lake Mich, see 16-49 & 12-27-59.

12-52-1 Name not given, girl by 1st wife, dead.

Husband: Thos Peters, dead.

12-52-1-1 Gertie Agahgo or Gertie Peters, age 19, P.O. Chief Lake.

Husband: Clarence Jackson, not married but live together, no children.

12-52-1-2 Isaa Agahgo, age 17, P.O. Chief Lake, with grandfather.

Information following from: Not Given. Custer 2/19/09

13-52 WAY-ZHE-BE, dead, no heirs.

Husband: No entry.

13-52-1 Name not given, dead, no heirs.

Information following from: Not Given. 2/19/09

14-52 PAIN-BAW-TOE, dead.

Wife: Name not given, dead.

14-52-1 Name not given, dead, no heirs.

Information following from: Not Given.

15-52 KEY-O-QUO-UM, dead.

Wife 1st: Name not given, dead, 1 child, both dead.

Wife 2nd: Fannie Bailey, daugh of Pe-To-Bick 3-50, had 5 children, for children see Pe-To-Bick 3-50.

Information following from: Not Given.

16-52 WAW-SAISH-CAW-NO-QUAY, dead.

Husband: No entry.

16-52-1 Wm Smith, age 36, P.O. Freesoil, see 3-56.

Information following from: Not Given.

17-52 KAW-BAY-AW-SHE.

Wife: No entry.

17-52-1 Bonaface Bailey, age 30, P.O. Lattin, step child (child of wife by Jacob Bailey.

Wife: Helen Louis Bailey, age 26, see 1-49.

17-52-1-1 Sophia Bailey, age 10.

17-52-1-2 Susia Bailey, age 9.

17-52-1-3 Julia Bailey, age 5.

17-52-1-4 Rosie Bailey, born May 1907.

17-52-2 Pete Cab-A-Yausha or Kaw-Bay-Aw-Sha.

Wife: Christina.

17-52-3-1 Eliza Marie Cabayausha, age 16, P.O. Lattin.

17-52-3-2 Joseph Cabayausha, age 13.

17-52-3 Therese Cogswell, age 51, see 11-54, separated from James Cogswell, child see 11-54.

Information following from: Not Given. 2/19/09

18-52 ME-SHE-PE-SHE-QUAY, dead.

Husband: Isaac Shag-Wah-Be-No, age 60, see 29-52.
18-52-1 Pete Isaac, age 37, see 29-52.

Information following from: Not Given.
19-52 PAY-ME-SAW-AW or JOHN ~~AGAGHO~~ AGAHGO, age 60, P.O. ~~Dorr~~ Remus, Mich.
Wife: Name not given, dead, see 4-58B.
19-52-1 Name not given, dead.
Husband 1st: Henry Pego, see 2-62.
Husband 2nd: J. G. Getcher, white, P.O. Weidman.
19-52-1-1 Ward Pego,age 15, see 2-62.
19-52-1-2 Amos pego, age 12.
19-52-1-3 Chas Pego, age 8.

Information following from: Not Given.
20-52 KEY-WE-TAW-WAW-BE.
Wife: Name not given, dead.
20-52-1 James Blacksmith, age 45, P.O. Sutton's Bay (see 19-50).
Wife 1st : Mary Blacksmith, P.O. Cedar.
Wife 2nd:Now living with Josephine Davenport, age 30, P.O. Cedar, enroll by name of Davenport, see 13-40 & 1-04-22.
20-52-1-1 David Blacksmith, age 23, P.O. Cedar, not married.
20-52-1-2 Pickett Blacksmith, age 19, P.O. Genoa Sch, Nebr.
20-52-1-3 Julius Blacksmith, age 18, P.O. Petosky.
20-52-1-4 John Blacksmith, age 13, P.O.Suttons Bay, pay share to mother Mary Blacksmith.
20-52-1-5 Scott Blacksmith, age 10, P.O. Genoa, pay share to mother Mary Blacksmith.
20-52-1-6 Sampson Blacksmith, age 8, P.O. Cedar, pay share to mother Mary Blacksmith.

Information following from: Not Given.
21-52 MAY-DWAY-BAW-GO or WM MEDAHKO, age 65, P.O. Millerton.
Wife 1st: Name not given, dead.
Wife 2nd: Mary Medahko, age 44, P.O. Millerton, see 6-49 & 11-50.
21-52-1 Moses Medahko, age 28, P.O. Millerton.
Wife: Julia (Trombly) Medahko, age 20, see 15-56.
21-52-1-1 Mary Ann Medahko, age 6.
21-52-1-2 Louis Medahko, age 5.
21-52-1-3 Mabel Medahko, age 3.
21-52-2 Joe Medahko, age 26, P.O. Millerton.
Wife: Kate (Pete) Medahko, age 20, P.O. Millerton, see 9-54.
21-52-2-1 Jacob Medahko, age 4 mos, born March 15/08.
21-52-3 Isaac Medahko, age 24, P.O. Millerton.
Wife: Lizzie (Cogswell) Medahko, age 18, see 11-54, daugh

of Louis Cogswell.
21-52-3-1 Infant Medahko, born June 1908 2nd roll.
21-52-4 James Medahko, age 19, P.O. Millerton, not married.
21-52-5 Sophia Medahko, age 17.
21-52-6 Veronica Medahko, age 14.
21-52-7 Jerome Medahko, age 12.
21-52-8 Rosie Medahko, age 9.
21-52-9 Nancy Medahko, age 6.

Information following from: Not Given. 2/19/09
22-52 A-GAW-GAW, dead, father of John Agahgo.
Wife: No entry.
22-52-1 Name not given, dead, no heirs.

Information following from: Not Given.
23-52 KE-SHE-YAW-SE-NO-QUAY.
Husband 1st: Wm Ne-Be-Nay-Ke-Zhick or Louis, see 1-9-49.
Husband 2nd: David Fox or How-De-Do, lives at ~~Bradley~~ Hartford Mich, see 5-11-53.
Note: Only child by 1st husband.
23-52-1 James Lewis, age 43, P.O. Star City, see 9-49.
Wife: Mary Lewis, a Pott off, P.O. Star City, see also 6-52.
23-52-1-1 Jacob Lewis, drew Pott, age 18, P.O. Star City.
23-52-1-2 John Lewis (did not draw), age 12, P.O. Star City.
23-52-1-3 Josephine Lewis (did not draw), age 12, P.O. Star City.
23-52-1-4 Richard Lewis (did not draw), age 12, P.O. Star City.
23-52-1-5 Mabel Lewis (did not draw), age 12, P.O. Star City.
23-52-1-6 Phillip Lewis (did not draw), born Aug 4, 1908.
Note: was separated from 1st husband in 1870.
23-52-2 Adam Fox, age 28, lives at Bradley, Mich, not married, father is How-De-Do, see 5-11-53.

Information following from: Not Given.
24-52 PE-TAY.
Wife: Name not given, dead.
24-52-1 ~~Ke-O-Quom, dead.~~
24-52-2 Jim Peters, see 21-50.
24-52-3 John Peters, not enrolled he says he drew with the Potts.
Wife: Nancy Hall Peters, 3-17-51.

Information following from: Not Given.
25-52 GEORGE STONEMAN.
Wife: Mary, new wife of David H. Elliott, see 3-55.

Information following from: Not Given.
26-52 SHAY-GO-NAY-BE or GEO. SHAY-GO-NA-BE, age 88, P.O. Lattin.
Wife 1st: Name not given, dead, no children.
Wife 2nd: Mary Man-Do-Kin Shay-Go-Na-Be, age 70, see 22-55.
Child by her 1st husbandLouis Trombly.
26-52-1 Mary Mitchell, dead, wife of James Mitchell, children see 3-52.

Information following from: Not Given.
27-52 NAY-YAW-WAW-SUNG or JOHN WESLEY, age 67, P.O. Freesoil.
Wife: Mary Wesley, age 56, P.O. Freesoil, on roll with husb, in 1870.
27-52-1 ~~Amy Wesley~~ Lizzie Wilson, age ~~41~~ 32, P.O. Freesoil.
Husband: ~~David~~ James Wilson, age 36, died Aug 1907.
27-52-1-1 Rogers Wilson, age 13.
27-52-1-2 Chas. Wilson, age 11.
27-52-1-3 Wm Wilson, age 9.
27-52-1-4 Nancy Wilson, age 4.
27-52-1-5 Sarah Wilson, born July 1907 2nd roll.
27-52-2 Frank Wesley, age 22, P.O. Freesoil, not married.
27-52-3 Amy Wesley, age 14, P.O. Freesoil.

Information following from: Not Given.
28-52 NAW-WE-CAW or CHAS WAH-BE-SIS, dead.
Wife 1st: Name not given, dead.
Wife 2nd: Gertie, daugh of 1-49.
Child by 1st wife:
28-52-1 William Wah-Be-Sis, age 46, P.O. Brutus.
Wife 1st: Mary Wah-Be-Gay-Kake, separated, see 1-58, P.O. Pentwater or Elbridge.
Wife 2nd: Julia (McClellan) Alexander Wah-Be-Sis, age 33, P.O. Brutus, 1st husb. Moses Alexander, see 29-59 & 12-32.
28-52-1-1 Paul Wah-be-Sis, age 10, see 1-58, enroll with mother.
28-52-1-2 George Wah-be-Sis, age 8, see 1-58, enroll with mother.
28-52-1-3 ~~Rosie~~ Lucy Wah-be-Sis, age 12, see 1-58, enroll with mother.
Children by 2nd wife:
28-52-2 Jacob Wab-Be-Sis, age 36, P.O. Walkerville.
Wife: Name not given, dead see 1-1-49.
28-52-2-1 Charles Wab-Be-Sis, age 11, see 9-54.
28-52-2-2 Lizzie Wab-Be-Sis, age 9, see 9-54.
28-52-2-3 Agnes Wab-Be-Sis, age 5, see 9-54.

28-52-3 John Wah-Be-Sis, age 31, P.O. Walkerville.
Wife: Mary Wah-Be-Sis, nee Poneshing, age 35, see 21-54.
28-52-3-1 Alex. Poneshing, age 5, adopted, see 21-54.

Information following from: Not Given.
29-52 ME-SHE-KAY or ISAAC SHAY-WAW-BE-NO, age 60, P.O. Lattin or ~~Freesoil~~.
Wife 1st: Name not given, dead, was 18-52.
29-52-1 Pete Shay-Wab-No, age 37, P.O.Lattin.
Wife: Mary Shay-Wab-No (nee Koon), see 11-52.
29-52-1-1 Minnie Shay-Wab-No, age 3 years.
29-52-1-2 Annie Shay-Wab-No, age 6 mos, born Jany 29/08.
Wife 2nd: Mary (Memberto) Shay-Wab-Be-No, see 9-54, dead.
29-52-2 Lizzie Shay-Wab-No, age 18.
29-52-3 Maud Shay-Wab-No, age 29, wife of Wm Coon,see 8-56.
29-52-4 Angeline Shay-Wab-No,age 16.

Information following from: Not Given. 2/19/09
30-52 AW-WAW-NE-KE-ZHICK,dead.
Wife: No entry.
30-52-1 John Robinson, age 25, P.O. Northport or Honor, see 5-44, saw him at Northport& have him on some sheet. Durant.

Information following from: Not Given.
31-52 NE-SHE-NAW-BAY-QUAY.
Husband: Name not given, dead.
31-52-1 Po-Ne-Say, see 2-52.
31-52-2 Sosette.
31-52-2-1 Thresa Cogswell, see 11-54 for child & 17-52.
31-52-2-2 Bonaface Bailey, for children see 17-52.
31-52-2-3 Pete Cab-Ay-An-Sha, for children see 17-52.
31-52-3 Ching-Go-Che-Wah.
Husband: Chas Wab-Sis, dead, see 28-52.
31-52-3-1 WmWab-Sis.

Information following from: Not Given.
32-52 JOSETTE,dead, no descendants except old people who are enrolled by themselves.

Information following from: Not Given.
33-52 O-TAW-WAW-QUAY & JOHN BATTISTE, dead, Traverse Band, living, known as John Jacobs, preacher at Northport, see 16-40 & 13-38.

Information following from: Not Given.

34-52 NE-GAW-NE-QUAY or NANCY WARD, age 80, P.O. Mt Pleasant, see also 6-53.

Husband: _____ Ward.

34-52-1 Margaret Louis or Margaret Chippeway, age 36, P.O. Mt Pleasant.

Husband: Alex Louis or Alexis Chippeway, age 42, separated, see 10-64.

34-52-1-1 Grace Louis, age 9.

34-52-1-2 Elizabeth Louis, age 7.

34-52-1-3 Sophia Louis, age 3.

34-52-2 Martha Ward Newton, age 32, P.O. Honor, Mich.

Husband: Ben Newton, see 25-55, age 38.

34-52-2-1 Sarah Newton, age 14.

34-52-2-2 Albert, age 1, 2nd roll born Aug 6/07.

Information following from: Not Given. 2/19/09

35-52 KEY-KE-TO-DO-QUAY, dead, no heirs.

Information following from: Not Given.

36-52 SHAW-WE-GAW.

Wife: Name not given, dead.

36-52-1 Elijah Shaw-Bos, age 30, P.O. Chief Lake, not married.

36-52-2 John Shaw-Bos, dead.

Wife: Eliza Tip-Sco, a Saginaw Ind., P.O. ~~Mt Pleasant~~ Walpole Island.

36-52-2-1 ~~Edward Marsh, age 19, P.O. Leaton, Mich.~~ off

36-52-2-2 Grace Shaw-Bos, age 8, P.O. Walpole Island.

Information following from: Not Given.

37-52 NAY-O-TAY-DAY-KE-ZHICK or RICHARD ALBERT, age 67, P.O. Freesoil.

Wife: Sab-Gotch or Mary Albert, age 53.

37-52-1 Mary Albert, age 27, P.O. Freesoil.

Husband: Ed Skinhorn, see 3-49.

37-52-1-1 Chas Skinhorn, age 5.

37-52-1-2 Lydia Skinhorn, age 3.

37-52-1-3 Naw-Qua-Ge-Zhick (m), born Jany 1908 2nd roll.

37-52-2 James Albert, age 25, P.O. Freesoil, not married.

37-52-3 Eliza Albert, age 23, P.O. Freesoil.

Husband: John Peters, age 27, see 12-7-59.

37-52-3-1 Fred Peters, age 4.

37-52-3-2 Jean Peters (m), age 2.

37-52-3-3 Frank (?) Peters, born June 1908 2nd roll.

37-52-4 George Albert, age 21, P.O. Freesoil, not married.

37-52-5 Whitney Albert, age 19, P.O. Freesoil.

37-52-6 Frank Albert, age 12.

Information following from: Not Given.
38-52 SAY-SAY-GO-NAW-QUAY, dead.
Inds. know nothing about the children. Durant.

Page 53
Chief SHAW-BE-QUO-UNG
Grand River

Information following from: Not Given.
1-53 SHAW-BE-QUO-UNG or MOSES FOSTER, dead.
Wife 1st: Name not given, dead.
Wife 2nd: Name not given, dead.
Only child:
1-53-1 Wallace Foster or Hineman.
Wife: Margaret Pokagon, age 36, P.O. Millerton, now wife of Chas Pokagon, see 19-49.

Information following from: Not Given. Bradley
2-53 ME-SAW-ZEE, dead.
Wife: Name not given, dead.
Note: All children dead & no heirs, except the one here given below.
2-53-1 Mary Cross, age 55, P.O. Bear Lake near Manistee or Honor Pier Port, Mich.
Husband: John Cross (white), no children.

Information following from: Not Given. Fountain 2/09
3-53 A-GAW-WAW, dead.
Wife: No entry.
3-53-1 Name not given, dead "4 of July".
Spouse: No entry.
3-53-1-1 Angeline (Bailey) McClellan, age 22, see 29-59 & 13-53.
Husband: Name not given, age 35, see 29-5 & 13-53.
3-53-2 Name not given, dead, no heirs.

Information following from: Not Given. Jany 18/09
4-53 SHAW-WAW-NE-KE-ZHICK, dead.
Wife: Name not given, dead.
4-53-1 Kelsey Isaac, age 60, P.O. Mt Pleasant Mich RFD #6.
Wife: Elizabeth Isaac, age 50, P.O. Mt Pleasant, see 2-51.
4-53-1-1 Edith (Isaac) Bennett, age 32, P.O. Mt Pleasant.
Husband: Daniel Bennett, a member of Saginaw Chip.
4-53-1-1-1 Grace Bennett, age 14.

4-53-1-1-2 Joseph Bennett, age 7.
4-53-1-1-3 Bessie Bennett, age 4.
4-53-1-1-4 Lyman Bennett, age 2.
4-53-1-2 Rosie Aishquaib, age 21, Mt Pleasant Route 6.
Husband: Chas. Aishquaib, age 24, see 5-64.
4-53-1-2-1 Harry Aishquaib, born Dec 25/07.
4-53-1-3 Chas Isaac, age 16, P.O. Mt Pleasant #6.
4-53-2 Mary Paul, age 45, P.O. Athens, Mich.
Husband: John Paul, Pott, dead.
4-53-2-1 John T. Paul (single), age 28, P.O. Athens.
4-53-2-2 Minnie Paul, age 16.
4-53-2-3 Howard Paul, age 12.
4-53-2-4 Dennis Paul, age 14.
4-53-2-5 Maggie Paul, age 4
4-53-2-6 Adam Paul, age 11.
4-53-2-7 Lizzie Paul, age 8.
4-53-3 Name not given, dead, no heirs.

Information following from: Not Given. Bradley
5-53 MICK-SE-NIN-NE family.
5-53-1 Sophia Johnson Shagonaby, age 57, P.O. Hamilton, see 2-54.
Husband: Joe Shagonaby, age 60.
5-53-2 Sosette Wezoo, age 55, P.O. Athens.
Husband: Thos Wezoo,a Saginaw Ind.
5-53-2-1 Agnes Pamp, age 26, P.O. Athens, husb: Pott Indian an cousin of the other Pamp enrolled.
5-53-2-1-1 Mary Pamp, age 12.
5-53-2-2 Elizabeth Wezoo, age 17.
5-53-2-3 Lucy Wezoo, age 12.
5-53-3 Margaret Medavis, age 56, P.O. Hamilton, Mich.
Husband: Pete Metavis, see 1-51.
5-53-4 James Johnson, age 41, P.O. Hamilton, live alone.
Wife: No entry.
5-53-4-1 Angeline Johnson, age 17, P.O. Mt Pleasant Sch.
5-53-4-2 Louis Johnson, age 14, P.O. Mt Pleasant Sch.
5-53-5 Name not given, dead.
Spouse: No entry.
5-53-5-1 Jennie Johnson, age 26, P.O. Athens, single.

~~Drew with Potts. but establishment that ancestry on Ottawa & Chippewa roll of 1870.~~

Information following from: Not Given. Mt Pleasant Jany 19/09
6-53 WAW-SAW-QUOUM family.
Wife 1st: Nancy Ward, age 80, Mt Pleasant, Mich.

Wife 2nd: Name not given, dead, see 34-52 & 19-55.
6-53-1 Mary Wasaquoum, dead, see 19-55.
Husband 1st: Name not given, dead.
Husband 2nd: Chas Genereaux, see 19-55.
6-53-1-1 Louis Genereaux, see 19-55.
6-53-1-2 David Genereaux, see 19-55.
6-53-1-3 Albert Genereaux, see 19-55.
6-53-1-4 Robt Genereaux or Nodin or Wind, age 45, see 19-55.
6-53-1-5 Wm Nodin or Wind, age 19, see 19-55.
6-53-2 Name not given, dead, no heirs.
6-53-3 Name not given, dead, no heirs.
6-53-4 Martha Ward, age 32, see 25-55

Information following from: Not Given.
7-53 JOHN CRAMPTON, age 76, P.O. Crystal Valley south of Fern.
Wife 1st: Eliza, daug of 3-53.
7-53-1 Foster Crampton, age 49, P.O. Custer #2.
Wife: Angeline Maw-By Crampton, age 40.
7-53-1-1 Lydia Crampton, age 22.
7-53-1-2 James Crampton, age 19.
7-53-1-3 Louis Crampton, age 17.
7-53-1-4 Lizzie Crampton, age 13.
7-53-1-5 Tom Crampton, age 7.
7-53-1-6 Martha Crampton, age 5.
Wife 2nd: Sarah Bailey Crampton, age 52, see Pe-To-Bick 3-50.
7-53-2 Cobb Crampton, age 35, P.O. Elbridge Lattin.
Wife: Thresa Amy Crampton, age 26, an Ottawa nee Fox, see 3-52.
7-53-2-1 Robert Crampton, age 3.
7-53-2-2 Chas Crampton, age 2, born June 17, 1908.
7-53-3 Annie Crampton Webb, age 26, see 16-56.
7-53-4 Wem-E-Gwon Crampton, age 17, P.O. Crystal, unmarried.

Information following from: Not Given. Mount Pleasant, Michigan
8-53 MAY-CO-TAY, dead.
Wife: Name not given, dead.
8-53-1 Sam Maycotay, dead.
Wife: No entry.
8-53-1-1 Betsey Maycotay or Mackety, age 17, P.O. Mt Pleasant Sch., see 5-65.
8-53-1-2 Albert Maycotay, age 19, P.O. Athens, Mich.
8-53-2 James Maycotay, dead.

Information following from: Not Given. Bradley

9-53 WAW-BE-ME-ME or PIDGEON.
Wife: No entry.
9-53-1 Lucy Stevens, age 50, P.O. Dorr, Pott.
Husband: Alex Stevens.
9-53-1-1 Peter Stevens, age 10.
9-53-1-2 Joseph Stevens, single, age 25.
9-53-2 James Pigeon, age 45, P.O. Dorr,see 12-51, Pott.
9-53-3 John Pigeon, age 40, P.O. Dorr, Pott.
Wife: Mary Ann Pigeon nee Medavis, see 12-51 for children.
9-53-4 Jennie Pigeon, dead.
Husband: Sam Mendoka's 1st wife, off.
9-53-4-1 Guy Mendoka, age 19, Mt Pleasant Sch.

Information following from: Not Given. Custer Aug/08 Bradley Feby/09
10-53 DAVID K. FOSTER.
Wife: Ellen Foster, age 64, P.O. Bradley, on 1870 roll with husb.
10-53-1 Chas. Foster, age 47, P.O. ~~Petosky~~ Boyne City, not married.
10-53-2 Lincoln Foster, age 46, P.O. Bradley, npt married.
10-53-3 James Foster, age 37, P.O. Bradley.
Wife: ~~Mary Foster~~ Nancy (Medavis) Foster, age 32, P.O. Bradley, Ottawa, see 12-51.
10-53-3-1 John Foster, age 6.
10-53-4 Lucy Foster Andrew, age 32, P.O. Bradley.
Husband: John Andrew, Saginaw Ind.
10-53-4-1 Wayne Andrew, age 2, P.O. Bradley.
10-53-5 Hinman Foster, age 28, P.O. Bradley.
Wife: Maggie (Walker) Foster, age 18, see 12-53.
10-53-5-1 Fred Foster, born Apr 3/07.
Adopted daughter of family of David K. Foster:
10-53-6 Annie Ostie, age 46, P.O. Hart #2, see 4-56 & 2-59.
Husband: Pete Ostie.
10-53-6-1 Adam Ostie, age 25, P.O. Hart #2.
10-53-6-2 Martha Ostie, age 20, P.O. Hart #2.
10-53-6-3 Martin Ostie, age 16, P.O. Hart #2.
10-53-6-4 James Ostie, age 10, P.O. Hart #2.
Note: Her father & mother were dead in 1870 & she lived with Family of D. K. Foster. She is undoubtedly entitled to enrollment, by looks & by testimony of many of the tribe. Durant Spl. Agt.
Later: She is daughter of 2-51.

Information following from: Not Given.
11-53 HOW-DE-DO or DAVID FOX, age 60, P.O. Hartford, Mich.
Wife 1st: Name not given, see 23-52.
Wife 2nd: Mary Fox, age 55, P.O. Hartford, Mich., see 3-56, Ottawa Ind, blonged to ~~Pete Foster~~ Newaygo Band.

11-53-1 Adam Fox, age 28, P.O. Ada, Mich, by 1st wife, ~~only child~~ & not married.

11-53-2 Mary Fox, age 20, P.O. ~~Haskell Inst Lawrence, Ks~~ somewhere in Wisconsin, single.

11-53-3 Jacob Fox, age 17, P.O. Hamilton, Mich.

Note: a letter from Glenn E. Warner atty, Paw Paw, mich, says David Fox has three other children: Mary Ann Fox 10, Paul Jackson Fox 7, Martha Jackson Fox 4, step children, see 3-56. Durant

Information following from: Not Given.

12-53 MAY-SE-TAY,dead.

Wife: Betsy Walker, age 70, P.O. Bradley, Mich.

12-53-1 Solomon Walker, age 42, P.O. Bradley.

Wife: Name not given, dead.

12-53-1-1 Maggie Foster, age 18, see 10-53.

Husband: Name not given, see 10-53.

12-53-1-1-1 Fred Foster, see 10-53.

12-53-2 Mary Mendoka, age 37, P.O. Athens, Mich.

Husband: Saml. Mandoka, age 42, P.O. Athens, Mich, Pott.

12-53-2-1 Ida Bush, age 23, P.O. Bradley.

Husband: Name not given, Pott off.

12-52-2-1-1 Isabelle Bush, off, born Feby/09.

12-53-2-2 Grover Mendoka,age 12, P.O. Athens, Mich.

12-53-2-3 Austin Mendoka, age 10, P.O. Athens, Mich.

12-53-2-4 Betsy Mendoka, age 8.

12-53-2-5 Homer Mendoka, age 5.

12-53-2-6 Charlotte Mendoka, born July 1908 2nd roll.

12-53-3 George Walker, age 34, P.O. see 5-64.

12-53-4 Nancy Marks, 32, P.O. Bradley.

Husband: Alfred Mark, age 34, P.O. Bradley, see 10-46.

12-53-4-1 Albert Mark, age 12, P.O. Genoa Nebr.

12-53-4-2 Robert Mark, age 10, P.O. Genoa Nebr.

12-53-4-3 Stephen Mark, age 8.

12-53-4-4 Jennie Mark, age 13.

12-53-4-5 Angeline Mark.

12-53-4-6 Peter Mark, born Jany/08 2nd roll.

12-53-5 Jacob Walker, age 30, P.O.Bradley, single.

12-53-6 Hiram Walker, age 24, P.O. Walthill, Nebraska.

Wife: Name not given, western Ind.

12-53-6-1 Melvin Walker, age 2.

12-53-7 Caroline (Walker) Mendoka, age 51, P.O. Bradley, which should be numbered 1st, no children.

Husband: Joe Mandoka, off Pott.

12-53-8 Angeline, dead.

Husband: Joe Mendoka, same fellowas above who married his

1st wife a sister.
12-53-8-1 Joe Mendoka Jr, age 23, P.O. Bradley, single.

WALTHILL PHARMACY
CHESTER A. BOUGHN, PROP.
←----------→
Drugs, Stationary, Paints, Oils,
NEWS STAND

WALTHILL, NEB. *6/15 1909*

Horace B Durant
Petosky Mich
Dear Sir:
In reply to your to your communication of June 8 would say that I am member of Ottawa & Chippewa Indians. My name Hiram Walker, age 24yrs. I have one child living Marion Walker, age 18 mos. and one child (Jonas) dead (1/1907). My father John Walker is dead and my mother Betsy Walker is at present living inBradley Mich.
Brothers & Sisters names are as follows, Jacob Walker, Solomon Walker, Geo. Walker, Nancy Mark, Mary Mendoka, Cawhill Mendoka, their residences at present are unknown to me, but believe thay are in the Vicinity of Bradley.

Yours truly
Hiram Walker

Information following from: Not Given.
13-53 PAY-QUAY-NAY-SKUNG or AMOS WAKEFIELD, age 75, P.O.Custer #2.
Wife 1st: Mary, dead.
13-53-1 Mary Wakefield Bailey Akins, age 39yrs, P.O. Honor, Mich.
Husband 1st: Henry Bailey, see 14-56.
Husband 2nd: Stephen ~~or Joseph~~ Akins, P.O. Honor Mich.
Children byAikins:
13-53-1-1 Emma Aikins
13-53-1-2 Amy Aikins, age 6 yrs.
13-53-2 Daniel Wakefield, dead.
Wife: Agnes Bailey, dau Jos Bailey.
13-53-2-1 George Wakefield, age 20.
Wife 2nd: Eliza.
13-53-3 Joseph Wakefield, age 30, P.O. Genoa Sch home Custer #2.
13-53-4 Annie McClellan.
Husband: James McClellan, age 35, an Ottawa, his 2nd wife Angeline see 3-53.
13-53-4-1 Sampson McClellan, age7.

~~13-53-5 Daniel Wakefield~~

Information following from: Not Given. Bradley
14-53 NAY-CHE-WIN-NE-QUOT, dead..
 14-53-1 Name not given, dead.

Information following from: Not Given.
15-53 SQUAW-JAW-UNG or JOS. ELLIOT.
 Wife: Name not given, dead, was the mother of 23-53.
 15-53-1 Chas Hickey, see 23-53.
 15-53-2 Rufus Hickey, dead.
  Wife: Name not given, dead.
  15-53-2-1 Dan Hickey, age 50, P.O. Georgia bay.

Fountain Mich
May 13 aD 1909
Mr H. B. Durant
I with these few line to you to day inform you I received you wil and letters a few days ago right abut Dan Hickie now I will try to tell you he was at that time he was ten years of age that time he was with his grand mother at that time the lest Payments was made his grand mothers name

Now I will give you I don't know he say have wife I do not know how many children got son with to him ask him if he has wife I give you his Pot office

Dan Hickey
Colling Let PO
Canada Ont

Mr HB Durant now let me say to you. Ask you four news about you work I have here good money thing I hafe I will him inform you at one more.
Yours Truly
C. E. Hickey
Fountain PO
Mason Co
Mich
RFD No 9

Information following from: Not Given. Bradley
16-53 NAW-MAY-GUSE, dead.
 Wife: Name not given, dead.
 16-53-1 Name not given, dead, no heirs.

Information following from: Not Given. Bradley
17-53 USH-TAY-QUOT, dead.

Wife: Name not given, dead.
17-53-1 Name not given, dead, no heirs.
17-53-2 Name not given, 24-53.

Information following from: Not Given. Fountain 2/09
18-53 NIN-NE-ME-KE-WAW, dead.
Wife: Name not given, dead, no children.

Information following from: Not Given.
19-53 WAW-WE-ES-TOE.
Wife 1st : Name not given, dead.
~~Wife 2nd: Martha Be-in Eaton, Age 60, P.O. Honor see field notes #14-4-61~~
19-53-1 Sampson Eden or Eaton, age 41, P.O. Honor.
Wife1st: Sarah She-Be-She-Quay Eden
Wife 2nd: No entry.
Wife 3rd: Martha Eaton, age 48, P.O. Honor, see 6-60.
19-53-1-1 Clara Eden Hinman, age 17, P.O. Honor.
Husband: Andrew Hinman or Andrew Foster, see 19-49.
19-53-1-1-1David Hinman, age 5 mos, born ~~Apr/08~~ Mch 23/08, see 19-49.
Note: No other living children and they left no children.

Information following from: Not Given. Bradley
20-53 ME-SHAW-QUAW-DO-QUAY, dead.
Husband 1st: No entry.
Husband 2nd: Ed Kekeck, see 21-64.
20-53-1 Emma Mackey, age 35, P.O. Hamilton, now Paw Paw.
Husband: Steve Mackey, age 50, a Pott off, see 22-65.
20-53-1-1 Paul Mackey, age 12.
20-53-1-2 Elsie Mackey, age 10.
20-53-1-3 Silas Mackey, age 8.
20-53-1-4 Sawbick Mackey, age 6.
20-53-1-5 Josiah Mackey, age 1.
20-53-2 Phoebe Pamp, age 23, P.O. ~~Bron~~ Athens, Mich.
Husband" George Pamp, a Pott off.
20-53-2-1 Elliot Pamp, age 7.
20-53-2-2 Warren Pamp, age 2.
20-53-3 Name not given, dead.
Husband: ~~Ed Kekeck~~, white, see 21-64.
20-53-3-1 Andrew Mosher, see 21-64.
20-53-3-2 Bertha Medavis, age 19, see 21-64.
20-53-4 Name not given, dead.
Husband:Ed Crampton, Traverse Band.

20-53-4-1 Joe Crampton, age 15, see 8-44, lives at Manistee(see Pe-Nay-Se-Way-Ke-Zhickat Manistee look on Geo. Case's card Traverse Band & try to find child Isabella, Mich.

Information following from: Not Given. Bradley
21-53 AW-ZHE-WAW-QUO-DO, dead.
Wife: No entry.
21-53-1 ~~Paul~~ Isaac Paul, age 41, P.O. Walpole Island, Canada near Algonac, Mich.
Wife: Name not geiven, dead.
21-53-1-1 Walter Paul age 14.
21-53-1-2 Grace Paul age 11.
21-53-1-3 Alfred Paul age 9.
21-53-1-4 Alma Paul age 7.
21-53-1-5 Roland Paul age, 5.
21-53-2 Elliot Paul, age 34, P.O. ~~Walpole Island~~ Chatham, Ontario.
Wife: Name not given, negro.
21-53-2-1 Mary Paul, age 1½ , second roll.
21-53-3 Susan Paul, dead, no children.

Department of the Interior.
UNITED STATES INDIAN SERVICE
HORACE B.DURANT
Special U.S. Indian Agent
Petoskey, Mich.

NOT CALLED FOR RETURNED

Mr. Elliott Paul
Clatham,
Ontario

Information following from: Not Given. Custer 2/19/09
22-53 SIMON DOMINEKE or SEYMORE DOMINEKE, age 54, P.O. Fountain, see 26-54.
Wife: Sophia Domineke, age 70, P.O. Fountain, step dau of 11-54.
22-53-1 Angeline Dominnek Daniels, age 28, P.O. Freesoil, see ~~26-54~~
Husband: Wm Daniels, age 45, P.O. Freesoil, son of 6-51.
22-53-1-1 Charley Daniels, age 3 4.
22-53-1-2 Eliza Daniles, age 2.

Information following from: Not Given.
23-53 SAY-GAW-QUAY-NONG or CHAS. HICKEY, age 72, P.O. Fountain RFD #2.
Wife: Sophia Key-Way-A-Bin, age 54, daugh of 1-51.

Information following from: Not Given. Bradley
24-53 WALLACE USH-TAY-QUOT, dead.
Wife: No entry.
24-53-1 Margaret Pokagon,age 36, see 19-49.

Information following from: Not Given. Bradley Feby/09
25-53 MRS SPRAGUE, dead.
Husband: No entry.
25-53-1 Selkirk Sprague, dead, single.
25-53-2 Alice Sprague Johnson or Jackson, age 47, P.O. Bradley, Mich.
Husband: James Johnson, age 40, P.O. Bradley, Mich, ~~(Pott off)~~, see 5-53, 1-51 & 25-53.
25-53-2-1 Selkirk Sprague, age 28.
25-53-2-2 Henry Sprague, age 24, single.
25-53-2-3 James Sprague, age 22, single.
25-53-2-4 Jacob Sprague or Jacob Jackson Jr., age 20, a child by Jacob Jackson, see 3-65.
25-53-2-5 Adam Sprague, age 18.
25-53-2-6 Rosie Sprague, age 11.
25-53-3 David Fox, on roll as 11-53.
25-53-4Lydia Medavis, see 12-51.

Information following from: Not Given. Bradley Feby/09
26-53 WM WE-WE-SAY or PIGEON, dead.
Wife: Name not given, now Pete Medavis' wife see 1-51.
26-53 Sampson Pigeon, P.O. Dorr, only child, see 12-51.

Information following from: Not Given. Fountain Feby/09
27-53 SAY-SAY-GOW, dead.
Wife: Name not goven, dead.
27-53-1 Name not given, dead, no heirs.

Information following from: Not Given. Bradley 2/09
28-53 ME-NASE, dead, no heirs.

Page 54
Chief PAY-BAW-ME
Grand River

Information following from: Not Given. Custer 2/18/09
1-54 PAY-BAW-ME, dead.
Wife: Name not given, dead.
1-54-1 Name not given, dead, no heirs.

Information following from: Wm Shaygonaybe Freesoil Aug/08
2-54 SHAY-GO-NAY-BE WM, age 92, P.O. Hart, Mich.
Wife 1st: Name not given, dead.
Wife 2nd: Name not given, dead.
By 1st wife:
2-54-1 Joe Shaygonaybe, age 60, P.O. Hamilton, Mich.
Wife: Sophia Shaygonaybe nee Johnson, age 57, see 5-53.
2-54-1-1 John Shaygonaybe, age 28, P.O. Hamilton, single.
2-54-1-2 Wm Shaygonaybe #2, age 27.
Wife: Name not given, a Pottawatomie.
2-54-1-2-1 Francis Shaygonaybe, age 3.
2-54-1-2-2 Charles Shaygonaybe, born Dec 1907.
2-54-1-3 George Shaygonaybe, age 23, P.O. Hamilton, single.
2-54-1-4 Lydia Birch, age 20, P.O. Bradley, Mich (Husb: ~~a Pott~~, no children, see 38-65)
2-54-1-5 Isaac Shaygonaybe, age 13.
2-54-2 William Shaygonaybe, on 1870 roll as 11-61.
Wife: Name not given, dead.
2-54-2-1 Nancy Trevan, age 20, (Detroit, Mich, 730 Medburg Ave, husband a Negro, no children.
2-54-2-2 Eunice Shaygonaybe, age 17, P.O. Haskell Inst. Lawrence, Kans.
2-54-2-3 Joshua Shaygonaybe, age 14, P.O. Haskell Inst.
2-54-2-4 Angeline Shaygonaybe age 11, P.O. Haskell Inst.
2-54-3 Louis Shaygonaybe, age 58, P.O. Hart, Mich.
Wife: Nancy Shaygonaybe, age 50, see 14-54.
2-54-3-1 Elizabeth Shaygonaybe, age 21, single.
2-54-3-2 Martha Shaygonaybe, age 17, single.
2-54-4 William (or Francis) Shaygonaybe, age 52, P.O. Freesoil
(Note: The father says he had two sons by name of William.)
Wife: Mary Shaygonaybe, see 5-52.
2-54-4-1 Elizabeth Robinson, age 29.
Husband: Sampson Robinson, see 6-61.
2-54-4-2 Gertie Deverney, age 27.
Husband: Chas Deverney, see 4-59, P.O. Copewish.
2-54-4-2-1 Maggie Deverney, age 8.
2-54-4-2-1 George Deverney, age 5.
2-54-4-2-1 Lucy Deverney, age 3.
2-54-4-3 Angeline Theodore, age 25, P.O. Freesoil, separated from Chas Theodore see 10-61 & 27-59, np child.
2-54-4-4 Susan Walker, age 23, husb: Louis Walker, see 8-26 Traverse Band.
2-54-4-5 Joe Shaygonaybe, age 19, P.O. Freesoil.
2-54-4-6 Nancy Shaygonaybe, age 16, P.O. Mt Pleasant

School.
2-54-4-7 Peter Shaygonaybe, age 14, P.O. Mt Pleasant School.
2-54-4-8 Sophia Shaygonaybe, age 10, P.O. Freesoil.
2-54-4-9 John Shaygonaybe, age 6, P.O. Freesoil.
2-54-4-10 Paul Shaygonaybe, age 4, P.O. Freesoil.
2-54-5 John Shaygonaybe, age 45, P.O. Millerton, Mich.
Wife: Alice Shaygonaybe nee Aiken, age 33, see 2-58.
2-54-5-1 Philip Shaygonaybe, age 12.
2-54-5-2 Solomon Shaygonaybe, age 10.
2-54-5-3 Christina Shaygonaybe, age 8.
2-54-5-4 Julia Shaygonaybe, died May 6/08.
2-54-5-5 Eli Shaygonaybe, age 3.
2-54-5-6 Dominick Shaygonaybe, died Sept 28/07.
2-54-6 Moses Shaygonaybe, age 47, P.O. Walkerville.
Wife: Mary, dead, children see 15-54.
2-54-7 Lizzie (Shaygonaybe) Medahko, age 45, P.O. Millerton.
Husband 1st: John Ke-Way-Quom, see 6-54, separated.
2-54-7-1 Angeline Ke-Way-Quom, age 23, P.O. Brutus, Mich, see 11-50.
Husband: Joe Ke-O-Quom 2-50.
Husband 2nd: Chas Medahko, see 11-50.
2-54-7-2 Wm Medahko.
2-54-8 Pete Shaygonaybe, age 34, P.O. Walkerville.
Wife: Margaret Skinhorn, age 34, see 2-59.
2-54-8-1 Minnie Shaygonaybe, age 11.
2-54-8-2 Enos Shaygonaybe, age 5 (m).
2-54-8-3 Jesse Shaygonaybe, age 3 (m).

Information following from: Grand River.
3-54 JOHN B. PA-CA-NA-BA-NO, dead.
Wife: Name not given, dead.
3-54-1 Paw-Caw-Naw-Baw-No, see 15-54.
3-54-2 Peter Paw-Caw-Naw-Baw-No, see 19-54.
3-54-3 Pean Paw-Caw-Naw-Baw-No, see 33-54.

Information following from: Custer 2/18/09.
4-54 PE-NAY-SE-WE-KE-ZHICK, dead.
Wife: Name not given, dead.
4-54-1 Name not given. Children all dead, no heirs.
4-54-2 Isaac Lewis, dead. See 11-30. He married Julia Smoke, a member of Traverse Band, who is now living & is said to have a child by her now living Inds. here do not know the name but it is supposed to be identified with Julia Smoke, in Traverse Band. Durant Later: see 11-30.
Wife: Julia Smoke, dead. See 11-30.

4-54-2-1 Angeline Louis, age 17, Grand River.
4-54-2-2 Joseph Louis, age 11, Grand River.
4-54-3 Name not given, dead.
Husband: Mitchell Battise, see 6-59, no children by this marriage.
4-54-4 Daughter, name not given, who went to Kawkawlin.

Information following from: Grand River.
5-54 WILLIAM MAW-CAW-DAY-O-QUOT or MCDAQUETT, age 81, P.O. Custer #2.
Wife: Mary Aish-Quay-O-Say, age 76, living, daughter of chief of that name #8.
5-54-1 Charles Maw-Caw-Day-O-Quot (McDaquett), age 49, P.O. Custer #2.
Wife: Mary (Twombly) McDaquett, age 35.
5-54-1-1 Anne McDaquett, age 16.
5-54-1-2 Jessie McDaquett, age 8.
5-54-2 Julia McDaquett Alexander, age 37.
Husband: Bonapart Alexander, age 49.
5-54-2-1 Margaret Alexander, age 10.
5-54-2-2 Louis Alexander, age 5.
5-54-2-3 Mitchell Alexander, age 3.
5-54-3 Name not given, dead, no heirs.
5-54-4 Name not given, dead, no heirs.

Information following from: Not Given.
6-54 KAW-BAY-KE-ZHE-GO-QUAY, dead.
Husband: Name not given.
6-54-1 John KeyWay-Quom, age 49, P.O. Brutus.
Wife: Lizzie Shay-Go-Nay-Be, see 11-50 now wife of Charles Medahko.
6-54-1-1 Veronica KeyWay-Quom, age 16, P.O. Brutus.
6-54-1-2 Louisa KeyWay-Quom, age 11, P.O. Brutus.
6-54-1-3 Coletta KeyWay-Quom, age 8, P.O. Brutus.
6-54-1-4 William KeyWay-Quom, age 2, P.O. Brutus.
6-54-2 Sophia, age 50, see 19-54, 68-54.
Husband: John Peta, see 19-54.

Information following from: Custer 2/18/09.
7-54 SKIN-NEECE, dead.
Wife: Name not given, dead.
7-54-1 Name not given, children all dead. (?)
Spouse: Name or sex not given.
7-54-1-1 Joe Green, age 23, P.O. Fountain. Single.

Information following from: Not Given.
8-54 WAW-BE-SKAY-SHE-QUAY, dead.
Husband: Name not iven, dead.
8-54-1 Joseph Key-Way-Quoum, dead, see 27-54.
Wife: Angeline, dead.
8-54-1-1 Isaac Key-Way-Quoum, age 35, P.O. Petoskey, see 27-54.
8-54-1-2 Katie Ke-Zhe-Go-Way, P.O. Brutus, Mich., half sister of Isaac, see 24-59 & 9-31.
8-54-2 Pete Key-Way-Quoum, P.O. Millerton, see 14-54.
Wife: Name not given.
8-54-2-1 Name not given.
8-54-2-2 Name not given.
8-54-2-3 Name not given.
8-54-2-4 Name not given.
8-54-3 Lizzie.
Husband: William Shay-Go-Nay-Be, P.O. Freesoil, see 2-54 & Children.
8-54-4 Susan.
Husband: Sa-Gie
8-54-4-1 Paul Sa-Gie, P.O. Millerton.
Wife: Mary Cogswell Sa-Gie, see 23-54.
8-54-5 Martha.
Husband: John Fox, all children dead.
8-54-6 Paul Key-Way-Quoum.
Wife: Name not given, dead.
8-54-6-1 Sophia, see 19-54.
Husband: Pete.
8-54-6-2 Jack Key-Way-Quoum, P.O.Brutus.

Information following from: At Elondge church house Aug 10/08.
9-54 MWAY-AW-BAW-TOO or JOSEPH MEMBERTO, living age 74, P.O. Walkerville. Lives with
Wife 1st : Name not given, dead.
9-54-1 Name not given, dead, no children.
9-54-2 Name not given, dead, no children.
9-54-3 George Memberto, age 42.
Wife: Mary Memberto, nee Key-aw-Day-Way, daughter of 12-54.
9-54-3-1 Jerome Memberto, age 18.
9-54-3-2 Wiilliam Memberto, age 16.
9-54-3-3 Gertie Memberto, age 13.
9-54-3-4 Philippe Memberto, age 10.
9-54-3-5 Lyda Sherote or George Memberto, age 7. Lives with Joe Mitchell's family & the father wants her enrolled

with Joe Mitchell, see 6-59 & 3-50.
9-54-3-6 Rosie Memberto, died Aug 1906.
9-54-4 Mary
Husband: Isaac Shag-Wab-No, age 60, P.O. Freesoil. 1st wife dead.
9-54-4-1 Lizzie Shag-Wab-No, P.O. Freesoil.
9-54-4-2 Maud Shag-Wab-No, P.O. Freesoil.
9-54-4-3 Angeline Shag-Wab-No, P.O. Freesoil.
Child by Isaac Shag-Wab-No and 1st wife:
9-54-4-4 Pete Shag-Wab-No, age 60, P.O. Lattin, see 3-52 & 29-52.
Wife: Mary Coon.
9-54-4-4-1 Name not given.
9-54-4-4-2 Name not given.
9-54-5 Margaret
Husband: George Saw-By, no children.
Wife 2nd: Elizabeth Memberto, age 80, living, nee Caub-Mo-Say, sister 5-50 & 13-50
9-54-6 William Memberto, not married, no children.
9-54-7 Mary Memberto.
Husband: Jacob Wabsis, age 36, P.O. Walkerville, son of 28-52.
9-54-7-1 Charles Wabsis, age 11.
9-54-7-2 Lizzie Wabsis, age 9.
9-54-7-3 Agnes Wabsis, age 5.
9-54-8 Angeline Bailey Williams, age 43, see 4-52.
Adopted son of Joseph Memberto:
9-54-9 Mitchell Memberto, age 27, P.O. Walkerville, grandchild of Elizabeth Memberto.

Information following from: Custer 2/18/09.
10-54 WAW-BAW-BE-QUAY or MAGGIE BAILEY, age 80, P.O. Custer #2, formerly wife of 19-54, now wife of 4-62.
10-54-1 John Pete, age 57, see 19-54.
10-54-2 George Pete, see 19-54.

Information following from: Elbridge Aug 10.
11-54 KAW-GE-SHE-QUO-UM or JAMES COGSWELL.
Wife 1st : Name not given, dead, no children.
Wife 2nd: Name not given, dead.
11-54-1 Joseph Kaw-Ge-She-Quo-Um or Joe Cogswell, living, P.O. Fountain, see 23-54.
11-54-2 James Kaw-Ge-She-Quo-Um or James Cogswell, age 52, P.O. Walkersville.
Wife 1st : Thresa Cogswell, (sparated), age 51, P.O. Lattin,

see 17-52. Children all dead except:
11-54-2-1 Margaret Louis, age 11, by Richard Louis, sparated.
Wife 2nd: Sophia Wah-Bin-Dwetto Cogswell, age 49.
11-54-2-2 Leo Cogswell, age 5.
11-54-2-3 Maud Cogswell, born Mch 1908. Adopted child of Louis Cogswell
11-54-3 Louis Kaw-Ge-She-Quo-Um or Louis Cogswell, age 48, P.O. Walkersville.
Wife 1st: Name not given, dead, daughter of 27-65.
11-54-3-1 Susie Pay-Baw-Me.
Husband: Peter Pabame.
11-54-3-1-1 Annie Pay-Baw-Me, age 3.
11-54-3-2 Mitchell Cogswell, age 26, P.O. Millerton.
Wife: Martha Bailey, age 16, daughter of Maggie Bailey.
11-54-3-2-1 Stephen Cogswell, born Apr 18/07.
11-54-3-3 Helen Akins, age 24, P.O. Lattin.
Husband: James Akins, age 48?
11-54-3-3-1 Jacob Akins, age 5.
11-54-3-4 Sophia Louis, age 22.
Husband: Louis Louis, see 1-49.
11-54-3-5 Lizzie Me-Dah-Ko, age 20.
Husband: Isaac Me-Dah-Ko, P.O. Millerton.
11-54-3-6 Mary Pete, age 18, P.O. Millerton.
Husband: Gustavus Pete, P.O. Millerton.
Wife 2nd: Leta Cogswell, age 23, died Mch 9/08.
11-54-3-7 Benjamin Cogswell, age 5.
11-54-3-8 Delia Cogswell, age 3.
11-54-3-9 Maud Cogswell, born Mch/08. Now adopted by James Cogswell, see above.

Information following from: Not Given.
12-54 KEY-WAW-DAY-WAY, dead.
Wife: Name not given, dead.
12-54-1 George Key-Waw-Day-Way, age ~~45~~ 47, P.O. ~~Mancelona~~ Alden, Mich., ~~not known if~~ married ~~or not~~.
Wife: Name not given, is now wife of Charles Bailey of Millerton, Mich, see 2-58.
12-54-1-1 Louis Joseph, age 20, see 2-58.
12-54-2 Martha Key-Waw-Day-Way Andrews, age 41, P.O. Missankie, Mich., see 28-54.
Husband 1st: Mike Seymour, dead.
12-54-2-1 Peter Seymour,age 18, single, P.O. Missankie.
Husband 2nd: Dan Andrews, no children.
12-54-3 Angeline Key-Waw-Day-Way Swagon, age 35, P.O.

Wateman,Michigan near Remus.
Husband: Samuel Swagon, not of these Indians.
12-54-3-1 Jane Swagon, age 15.

Information following from: Custer 2/18/09.
13-54 MARY, dead, no heirs.

Information following from: Not Given.
14-54 PE-AW-NO or PETER KEY-WAY-QUOUM.
Wife: Lizzie Key-Way-Quoum, age 75, P.O. Millerton, on roll 1870 with husband.
14-54-1 Charles Pete or Charles Key-Way-Quoum, age 46, P.O. Millerton.
Wife: Prosie (Robinson) Key-Way-Quoum, see 6-49.
14-54-1-1 Pe-Ano Key-Way-Quoum, Jr., age 24, P.O. Millerton.
Wife: Sarah Davis, age 19.
14-54-1-1-1 Henry Key-Way-Quoum, born Mch 1908.
14-54-1-2 Augustus Key-Way-Quoum or Augustus Pete, age 21, P.O. Millerton.
Wife: Mary Cogswell Key-Way-Quoum, age 18, daughter of Louis Cogswell, no children.
14-54-1-3 Maggie Key-Way-Quoum Sam, age 19.
Husband: George Sam or George Pay-Quo-Tush, see card?
14-54-1-3-1 John Sam, age 3.
14-54-1-3-2 Mary Ann, born Aug 1908.
14-54-1-4 Mitchell Key-Way-Quoum or Pete, age 16, P.O. Millerton.
14-54-1-5 Annie Key-Way-Quoum, age 14.
14-54-1-6 Josie Key-Way-Quoum, age 12.
14-54-1-7 Julia Key-Way-Quoum, age 10.
14-54-1-8 John Key-Way-Quoum, age 6.
14-54-1-9 Arthur Key-Way-Quoum, born Aug 1908, 2nd roll.
14-54-2 Maggie Bailey, age 29, P.O. Millerton, see 2-58.
Husband 1st: George Joseph, P.O. Petoskey, cannot find him by that name.
14-54-2-1 Louis Joseph, age 19, P.O. Millerton, see 2-58.
14-54-2-2 Martha Joseph Cogswell, age 16, separated, see 2-58 enroll with mother.
Husband 2nd : Charles Bailey, age 48, son of Battise Bailey.
14-54-2-3 Eliza Bailey, age 12.
14-54-2-4 Peter Bailey, age 2.
14-54-3 Rosie Light, age 39, P.O. Millerton.
Husband: Andrew Light,age 38, son of 15-59.

14-54-3-1 Billy Light or William Williams, age 12, see 1-49.
14-54-4 Nancy, age 50.
Husband: Louis Shay-Go-Nay-Be, see 2-54.
14-54-5 Mary ~~Joe~~ Pete or Peters, P.O. Custer #2, see 6-49.
Husband: ~~Mary~~ Joe ~~(Shaw-Way-No)~~ Peano Peters, age 52.
14-54-5-1 Michael Peter, age 8, see 6-49.
14-54-5-2 Name not given, see 6-49.
14-54-5-3 Name not given, see 6-49.

Information following from: Not Given.
15-54 PAW-CAW-NAW-BAW-NO.
Wife: Angeline Paw-Caw-Naw-Baw-No, died May 1908.
15-54-1 Jack Seaman or Paw-Caw-Naw-Baw-No, age 49, P.O. Crystal.
Wife: Amy Louis Seaman, granddaughter of Chief 1-24.
15-54-1-1 Glenn Louis, age 13 mos.
15-54-2 Charles Seaman or Paw-Caw-Naw-Baw-No, age 38, P.O. Crystal.
15-54-3 James Seaman or Paw-Caw-Naw-Baw-No, age 36, P.O. Crystal.
Wife: Margaret, age 39, granddaughter of Chief 1-49.
15-54-3-1 James Seaman, Jr., age 19.
15-54-3-2 Annie Seaman, age 14.
15-54-3-3 Hannah Seaman, age 6.
15-54-4 Mary Shay-Go-Nay-Be.
Husband: Moses Shay-Go-Nay-Be, P.O. Hart, see 2-54.
15-54-4-1 Cecelia Shay-Go-Nay-Be, age 17.
15-54-4-2 Martha Shay-Go-Nay-Be, age 15.
15-54-4-3 Sophia Shay-Go-Nay-Be, age 13.
15-54-4-4 Rosa Shay-Go-Nay-Be, age 10.
15-54-4-5 Thomas Shay-Go-Nay-Be, age 6.
15-54-4-6 George Shay-Go-Nay-Be, age 4.

Information following from: Custer 2/18/09.
16-54 NAY-NAW-GO-NAY-BE, dead.
Wife: Name not given, dead.
16-54-1 Sophia Robinson, dead, see 6-62.
Husband: Name not given.
16-54-1-1 Nancy Robinson, see 6-62.
16-54-1-2 AgnesRobinson, see 6-62.
16-54-2 Name not given, dead.

Information following from: Joe Cogswell,et al.
17-54 JOSEPH TOUCHEY, dead.
Wife: Name not given, dead.

17-54-1 Mary Cross, age 55, P.O. Honor, Mich.
Husband: John Cross (white) off, see 2-53, no children.
17-54-2 Louisa Touckey, dead.
Husband: Name not given, married a Touckey, dead.
17-54-2-1 Frank Touckey, age 30, P.O. Traverse City, works for Oval Dish Co.

Information following from: Not Given.
18-54 JOHN R. ROBINSON, dead, no heirs.
Wife: Name not given.

Information following from: Not Given.
19-54 PETER PAW-CAW-NAW-BAW-NO.
Wife: Maggie Bailey, age 80, living now wife of Henry Bailey, see 4-62 & 10-54.
19-54-1 John Pete or Paw-Caw-Naw-Baw-No
Wife: Sophia Pete, niece of 21-54, granddaughter of 8-54 and daughter of 6-54.
19-54-1-1 Mobis Pete, age 30, P.O. Mt. Pleasant Sch employer, unmarried.
19-54-1-2 Charles Pete, age 24, P.O. Custer #2.
19-54-1-3 Jesse Pete, age 17, P.O. Mt. Pleasant Sch.
19-54-1-4 Charlotte, age 7, P.O. Custer #2.
19-54-2 George Pete, age 46, P.O. Millerton,Mich.
Wife: Agnes Joseph, age 45, Traverse, see 21-46.
19-54-2-1 Jacob Pete, age 24, P.O. Fountain, not married.
19-54-2-2 Catharine Pete Me-Dah-Ko, age 21.
Husband: Joe Me-Dah-Ko, see 21-52.
19-54-2-2-1 Jessie Me-Dah-Ko, born Mch/08.
19-54-2-3 Angeline Pete, age 17.
19-54-2-4 Alex Pete, age 13.
19-54-2-5 Joe Pete, age 10.
19-54-2-6 Esther Pete, age 3.
Note Bottom of Page: No children by Bailey

Information following from: Not Given.
20-54 SAM WICK or SAM BAILEY, age 66, P.O. Honor, Mich.
Wife 1st: Lucy Elliott Bailey, age 61, P.O. Honor, separated, 37-55.
Wife 2nd: Nancy Bailey, died May 1908.
Sam Bailey: He says he never had any children by either wife but his 1st wife (Lucy Elliott) says that Charles Bailey is her child by Sam Bailey. So I here enroll the name of Lucy Elliott's children, whether by Sam Bailey or any other. HBDurant Spl Agt Aug 26/08 Honor, Mich.
20-54-1 Charles S.Bailey, age 41, P.O. Honor.

Note: Adopted child of Sam Bailey: his father is white, his mother Lizzie Lahay, living near Hamlin Lake.
20-54-2 Louis Bailey, age 23, P.O. Honor.
Wife: Elizabeth Key-O-Quoum, age 24, daughter of John Key-O-Quoum, sister of Alex & Joe Key-O-Quoum.
20-54-2-1 Samuel L. Bailey, born June 28, 1908.

Information following from: Elbridge Aug 10.
21-54 PO-NE-SHING or JOSEPH PO-NESHING, age 64, P.O. Walkerville.
Wife: Mary Ne-Gake, dead.
21-54-1 Alex Po-Ne-Shing.
Wife: Julia, now wife of Robert Akins, Ind., Newaygo, children dead.
21-54-2 Margaret Paul, P.O. Northport, Mich.
Husband 1st: Isaac Maish-Caw, Grand River.
21-54-2-1 John Maish-Caw, age 22, P.O. Genoa Sch.
21-54-2-2 James Maish-Caw, age 20, P.O. Northport.
21-54-2-3 Julia Maish-Caw, age 18, P.O. Northport.
21-54-2-4 Eliza Maish-Caw, age 10, P.O. Northport.
21-54-2-5 Isaac Maish-Caw, age 8.
Husband 2nd: William Paul, P.O. Northport, Traverse
21-54-2-6 Amos Paul, age 5.
21-54-3 Peter Po-Ne-Shing, age 37, P.O. Walkerville.
Wife 1st : Name not given, dead.
21-54-3-1 William Po-Ne-Shing, age 12.
21-54-3-2 Peter Po-Ne-Shing, age 11.
21-54-3-3 Alex Po-Ne-Shing, age 5.
Wife 2nd: Rosie Po-Ne-Say or Po-Ne-Shing, daughter of 2-52, no children.
21-54-4 Mary Wah-Be-Sis, age 35, P.O. Walkerville.
Husband: John Wah-Be-Sis, age 31, see 28-52.
21-54-4-1 Alex Po-Ne-Shing, adopted, same as 21-54-3-3 above, enroll with John Wah-Be-Sis.
21-54-5 Louis Po-Ne-Shing, age 33, P.O. Walkerville, not married.
21-54-6 Maud Po-Ne-Shing, age 23, P.O. Walkerville, not married.
21-54-7 Joseph Po-Ne-Shing, age 18, P.O. Walkerville.
21-54-8 James Po-Ne-Shing, age 16, P.O. Walkerville.

Information following from: Not Given.
22-54 JAMES JUDSON, age 64, P.O. Chief Lake, Browntown, Mich.
Wife 1st: Name not Given, dead.
22-54-1 Elizabeth Judson, dead.
Husband 1st: William Russett, dead.
22-54-1-1 Mary Russett, age 17, P.O. Chief Lake.
Husband 2nd: Pete Lahe or Lahay, age 45, P.O. ~~Escanaba,~~

Mich or Beachwood, Mich.

22-54-1-2 Edward Lahe, age 16, P.O. Chief Lake.

Wife 2nd: Name not given, Traverse, see 25-55.

22-54-2 Julia Judson, age 18, P.O. Freesoil, see 25-55.

Information following from: Not Given.

23-54 JOSEPH KAW-GE-SHE-QO-UM or JOE COGSWELL, age 62, P.O.Fountain RFD #61.

Wife 1st: Name not given, dead.

23-54-1 Eliza Skinerhorn, ~~age 40, P.O. Elbridge~~, dead.

Husband: George Skinerhorn, age 44, see card 3-44. Children all deceased.

23-54-2 John Cogswell, age 38, P.O. (Elbridge) Walkerville, no wife or children.

23-54-3 Mary Ann Sa-Gie.

Husband: Paul Sa-Gie, see 5-59.

23-54-4 Martha Ke-She-A-Way or Shisway, age 32, P.O. Hackley, Wisconsin, but will be at Fountain box 61.

Husband 1st: ~~Peter~~ Louis Thomas, an Indian of Isabella.

23-54-4-1 Charles Thomas, age 6, P.O. Bear Creek, near Chief Lake.

Husband 2nd : Julius Ke-She-A-Way, age 37.

23-54-4-2 Levi Ke-She-A-Way, age 4.

23-54-4-3 Celia Ke-She-A-Way, age 2.

23-54-5 Henry Cogswell, age 21, twin, P.O. Genoa Sch. Nebr.

23-54-6 Lucy Cogswell Houseman, age 21, twin, P.O. Walkerville.

Husband: Name not given, white.

23-54-6-1 Floyd Houseman, age 2.

Wife 2nd: Julia McClure, age 44, granddaughter of 28-60.

23-54-7 Mary Cogswell, age 13, P.O. Fountain.

Information following from: Not Given.

24-54 DAVID MAW-CAW-DAY-O-QUOT, dead.

Wife: Elizabeth McKensie or McDaquett, white, living, P.O. Freemont, Mich.

24-54-1 Eva McDaquett or Maw-Caw-Day-O-Quot, P.O. Freemont, Mich. Mrs. Eva Congdon Brunswick., Mich.

Brunswik
~~Freemont~~, Mich

Horace B. Durant
Petoskey, Mich.

Dear Sir:

As I have been informed and have all ready read some of your letters and truly believe you tobe the <u>right</u> agent it is with the utmost confidence I write you to explain it to me.

I am an Indian. My maiden name was Mac Daquoitte and am of course interested in what I have all ready heard.

Please let me hear from you soon.

Yours Truly
Mrs. Eva Congdon
Brunswick, Mich

Lois:
Mrs Congdon, nee McDaquob or Maw-caw-da-quot on Grand River Band. If She is already enrolled, notify her. If not try to connect her by correspondence. Durant

Information following from: Custer 2/18/09.
25-54 KAW-GE-GAY-MEIG, dead.
Wife: Name not given, dead, nochildren.

Information following from: Custer 2/19/09.
26-54 KEY-WAY-AW-SHE, dead.
Wife: Name not given, dead.
26-54-1 Name or sex not given.
26-54-1-1 Seymore or Simon Domineke, age 54, see 22-53.

Information following from: Not Given.
27-54 JOSEPH KEY-WAY-QUOUM, dead.
Wife: Name not given, dead, see 24-59.
27-54-1 Isaac Key-Way-Quoum, age 39, P.O. Petoskey, see 24-59.
Wife: Alice Key-Way-Quoum, age 36, P.O. Petoskey, Traverse, see 28-26, no children.
27-54-2 Kate Ke-Zhe-Go-We, age 32, step daughter, Traverse, see 9-31.

Information following from: Not Given.
28-54 CHARLOTTE, dead.
28-54-1 Martha Key-Wan-De-Way, P.O. Ston City or Missanke, Mich, see 12-54.

Information following from: Custer 2/18/09.
29-54 NAW-ME-ME-GAY now SOPHIA DOMINEKE, age 70, P.O. Fountain, Mich, see 22-53.

Information following from: Custer 2/19/09.
30-54 O-CHE-BWAW, dead, grandmother of James & Jos Cogswell.

Information following from: Custer 2/19/09.
31-54 O-TISH-QUAY-AW-BAW-NO-QUAY,dead.
31-54-1 Maggie Bailey, age 80, see 4-62 & 10-54.
Husband: Henry Bailey, Sr., see 4-62 & 19-54

Information following from: Custer 2/19/09.
32-54 KE-SHE-GO-QUAY, dead.
32-54-1 Angeline Shomin, P.O. X Village, Traverse, see 19-20 & 66-21.
32-54-2 Joe Shomin, P.O.Bear Island,Traverse, see 19-20.

Information following from: Not Given.
33-54 PETER PAW-CO-NAW-BE-NOW or PEAN, died July 16/08.
Wife 1st: Amanda Moon, dead.
33-54-1 Nelie White, age 26, P.O. Muskegon, Mich, see 3-59.
Wife 2nd: Eliza Louis, dead.
33-54-2 May Pete or Paw-Co-Naw-Be-No, age 15, P.O. Harbor Springs, Bdg. Sch Catholic.
Wife 3rd: Eliza Genereaux Paw-Co-Naw-Be-No, P.O. Fountain, Mich, daughter of 6-55.
33-54-3 ~~Elsie~~ Edna Paw-Co-Naw-Be-No, age 3, P.O. Fountain, Mich.
33-54-4 Jennie Janie Paw-Co-Naw-Be-No, age 1 ½ , P.O. Fountain, Mich.

Page 55
Chief MAISH-KEY or MAISH-CAW
Grand River

Information following from: Not Given.
1-55 MAISH-CAW, chief, dead.
Wife: Name not given, dead.
1-55-1 Name not given, dead.
1-55-2 Name not given, dead.
1-55-3 Name not given, dead.
1-55-4 Peter Maish-Caw, age 59, P.O. Omena, see 29-55.
Wife: Name not given, died May 5/08, see 4-62

Information following from: Custer 2/20/09.
2-55 PE-TO-WE-KE-ZHICK, dead.
Wife: Name not given.
2-55-1 Name or sex not given.
2-55-1-1 Minnie Ke-Wa-Ge-Won, age 25, P.O. ~~Salem or Dorr or Millerton~~ Bradley, Mich, see 22-57.
Husband: Pete Alexander, age 29, see 2-51, 12-32

& 6-58.

2-55-1-1-1 Rose Alexander, born summer of 1907 (~~Sept~~) Aug.

Information following from: Not Given.

3-55 DAVID H.ELLIOTT, age 72, P.O. Fountain.

Wife: Mary, age 65, was wife of George Stoneman in 1870, see 25-52., no heirs.

Information following from: Custer 2/20/09.

4-55 AISH-KE-BAW-GE-NE-GAY or AMOS GREEN, dead.

Wife: Name not given, dead.

4-55-1 Name not given, dead, no heirs.

4-55-2 Name not given, dead, no heirs.

Information following from: Custer 2/20/09.

5-55 PO-NE-BWAW, wife dead, no heirs.

Information following from: Not Given.

6-55 WILLIAM GENEREAUX, age 65, P.O. Fountain.

Wife: Betsey Generaux, age 55, P.O. Fountain, enrolled with husband in1870, see 12-55 & 21-57. Had 9 all (children) are dead except 2 the dead ones left no heirs. See below for marriage with 1st husband.

6-55-1 Eliza Paw-Caw-Naw-Ba-No, age 35, P.O. Fountain.

Husband: Pean or Peter Paw-Caw-Naw-Ba-No, died July 19/08, see 35-54.

6-55-1-1 Edna Paw-Caw-Naw-Ba-No, age 3, P.O.Fountain.

6-55-1-2 Janie Paw-Caw-Naw-Ba-No, age 1 ½ , born Nov 1906.

6-55-2 Ella Generaux, age 23, P.O. Fountain, separated.

Husband: ~~Pete Paw-Caw-Naw-Ba-No Joe, died July 16/08 see 23-54~~ John or John David,age 25, P.O. Millerton.

6-55-2-1 John Joe John or John Dvid, age 5, P.O. Fountain, with mother.

6-55-2-2 Andrew David, age,1 ½ , P.O. Born Nov/06.

Husband 1st of Betsey Generaux:

Peter J. Lawrence, dead.

6-55-2-3 Solomon Lawrence, age 45, P.O. Millerton.

Wife: Eliza Davis Lawrence nee Peters, age 40, a Saginaw off, see 21-57.

6-55-2-3-1 Mary Lawrence, age 10.

6-55-2-3-2 Emma Lawrence, age 6.

6-55-2-3-3 Peter Lawrence, age 4.

Note: & other children see 21-57.

Information following from: Not Given.
7-55 JOHN SMITH, dead.
Wife: Mary Smith, living, P.O. Custer, Mich, now wife of Amos Fitch, see 12-08, 9-55 & 8-51.
7-55-1 Martha Smith Alexander, age 44.
Husband: Name not given, dead, no children.
7-55-2 Joseph Smith, age 38.
Wife: Annie Medavis Smith, age 30, daughter of Joe Medavis.
7-55-2-1 Elizabeth Smith, age 12.
7-55-2-2 Rosie Smith, age 8.
7-55-2-3 Agnes Smith, age 5.
7-55-2-4 Moses Smith, age 3.
7-55-2-5 David Smith, age 2
7-55-3 Matilda Smith, age 30, unmarried, no children..
Husband 2nd: Amos Fitch, husband of Mary Smith, living, age 46, see 9-55.
7-55-4 Thomas Fitch, age 17.
7-55-5 Nancy Fitch, age 13.
7-55-6 Daughter, name not given.
7-55-6-1 John Alexander or John Pete, illegitimate child of deceased daughter of Amos Fitch. Father's surname is Pete.
7-55-6-2 Alice King, adopted daughter of deceased daughter of Amos Fitch:father is Joe King, living, an Ottawa, see 9-55 & 12-58.

Information following from: Custer 2/20/09.
8-55 LOUIS GENERAUX, JR., dead.
Wife: Name not given, see 11-23.
8-55-1 Levi Generaux, age 40, P.O. Petoskey, see 11-23.
Wife: Rena Smith Generaux, age 18, P.O. Petoskey, see 11-23, 11-55 & 12-59.

Information following from: Not Given.
9-55 JOSEPH ELLIOTT, dead, blind.
Wife: Name not given, dead, no children.
9-55-1 Amos Fitch Ah-Be-Naw-Be, living, age 46, married & family Adopted by Elliott, lives at Custer. His father: Ah-Be-Naw-Be, died before 1870, mother: Mary Mish-E-Gay-Ka-Ke-Quay 38-57 Roll 1870.
Wife 1st: Name not given, dead.
9-55-1-1 Annie Fitch, died Mch 19, 1908, age 21 when died.
9-55-1-1-1 Alice King, age 2, living with Amos Fitch, see 12-58.
9-55-1-1-2 John Pete, age 3, living with Martha

Alexander, see 7-55.
Wife 2nd: Mary Fitch Smith, widow of John Smith, 7-55 roll 1870 , see 12-58.
9-55-1-2 Thomas Fitch, age 17, living.
9-55-1-3 Nancy Fitch, age 14, living.

Information following from: Custer 22/20/09.
10-55 NAW-KAY-O-SAY or ISAAC BENNETT, dead.
Wife: Name not given, dead.
10-55-1 Name not given, dead, no heirs.

Information following from: Not Given.
11-55 LOUIS GENERAUX SR., dead.
Wife: Name not given.
11-55-1 Name not given, see 8-55.
Wife: Name not given, see 11-23, now wife of Enos Petoskey.
11-55-1-1 Levi L. Generaux, age 45, P.O. Petoskey, see 11-23 & 12-59. Ok D 2/19/09 Custer.

Information following from: Custer 2/20/09.
12-55 ME-SHE-BE-SHE,dead.
Wife: Name not given, dead.
12-55-1 Betsey Generaux, age 65, see 6-55.
Husband: William Generaux, age 55, see 6-55.

Information following from: Not Given.
13-55 AISH-KE-BAW-GO-WE-QUOT or PETER ANDERSON, age 70, P.O. Chief Lake, Mich.
Wife 1st: Name not given, dead.
Wife 2nd: Name not given,dead.
13-55-1 Mary (Anderson) Hennessy, age 29, P.O. Muskegon 136 Wood Ave, separated.
Husband: Name not given, white.
13-55-1 Ed Hennessy, age 9.
13-55-2 Susie Hennessy, age 12.
13-55-3 Thomas Hennessy, age 5.
Wife 3rd: Alice Anderson Won-Quay, age 52, see 12-50 & 18-55.
13-55-2 Sarah Smith, age 30, P.O. Chief Lake.
Husband: Joe Smith, age 41, P.O. Chief Lake, sonof 3-5, see 18-55.
13-55-2-1 Solomon Smith, age 13.
13-55-2-2 John Smith, age 8.
13-55-2-3 Delia Smith, age 4.
13-55-2-4 Allie (son) Smith, age 2.

Information following from: Custer 2/20/09.
14-55 WILLIAM MAY-DOSH, dead.
Wife: Name not given.
14-55-1 John Williams, see 2-61 & 3-52.

Information following from: Not Given.
15-55 WILLIAM ELLIOTT or MICKO, age 64, P.O. Fountain, see 3-56 & 7-62.
Wife 1st: Name not given, dead.
Wife 2nd: Name not given, dead.
15-55-1 James Micko, age 27, P.O.Lattin.
Wife: SusanKe-Quoum, age 25, see ~~5-52~~ & 3-50.
15-55-1-1 John Micko, age 6.
15-55-1-2 Arthur Micko, age 4.
15-55-1-3 Martha Micko, age 14 mos.
Wife 3rd: Martha Jackson, age 34, P.O. Fountain, daughter of 26-51.
15-55-2 Albert Elliott, age 5.
15-55-3 Susan Elliott, age 3.
15-55-4 Thomas Elliott, age 2.
15-55-5 Charity Elliott, born Dec 22/07.

Information following from: Custer 2/20/09.
16-55 E-TAW-WAW-GE-WON, dead.
Wife: Name not given, dead.
16-55-1 Charles Hickey 23-53.
16-55-2 Name or sex not given, dead, no heirs.

Information following from: Custer 2/20/09.
17-55 SARAH JANE REPETT, dead, no heirs.

Information following from: Custer 2/20/09.
18-55 ANDREW M. FITCH, dead.
Wife: Alice Anderson, age 52, P.O. Chief Lake,, husband now 13-55.
18-55-1 Sarah Smith, age 30, P.O. Chief Lake, see 13-55 & 21-55.

Information following from: Not Given.
19-55 CHARLES GENERAUX, age 60 living, P.O. ~~Bear Creek near Peacock, near Manistee~~ Fountain.
Wife 1st: Name not given, dead.
19-55-1 Nancy Josiah, age 38 living, P.O. Custer #2.
Husband: Name not given, dead.
19-55-1-1 Margaret Josiah, age 22, P.O. Custer #2.
19-55-1-2 John Josiah, age 18, P.O. Custer #2.
19-55-1-3 Annie Josiah, age 12, P.O. Custer #2.
19-55-1-4 Jacob Josiah, age 9, P.O. Custer #2.

19-55-1-5 Sophia Josiah, age 7, P.O. Custer #2.
19-55-1-6 William Josiah, age 5, P.O. Custer #2.
19-55-1-7 James Josiah, age 2.
19-55-2 Eva Generaux Hineman, age 36.
Husband 1st: Peter Bailey, dead.
19-55-2-1 Lucy Bailey, age 16, P.O. Custer #2.
19-55-2-2 Philip Bailey, age 14, P.O. Custer #2.
19-55-2-3 Mary Bailey, age 10, P.O. Custer #2.
Husband 2nd: George Hineman, age 60, Ottawa.
19-55-2-4 Angeline Hineman, age 8.
Wife 2nd: Mary ~~Kasis~~ Wasacum, dead, see 6-53, an Ottawa.Children by Charles Generaux her 2nd husband:
19-55-3 Louis Generaux, age 16, P.O. Scottville #1.
19-55-4 David Generaux, age 14, P.O. Custer #2.
19-55-5 Albert Generaux, age 7, P.O. Fountain.
Children by 2nd husband name not given, dead, see 25-51:
25-51-1 Robert No-Din, P.O. Honor, Mich, see 25-51. Also goes by name of Robert Wind or Robert Generaux, wife see card of Peter Walker.
25-51-2 William No-Din, P.O. at Genoa Sch.
Wife 3rd: Mary Kay-Wis Generaux, age 60, an Ottawa. No children by Charles Generaux her 2nd husband.
Children by 1st husband name not given, see 3-56:
3-56-1 Joe David, age 25, P.O. Fountain, see 6-55.
3-56-2 Nancy David, age 18, P.O. Custer #2.
3-56-3 Martha David, age 14, P.O. Fountain.

Information following from: Custer 2/20/09.
20-55 WALK-SHE-QUAY, dead.
20-55-1 Lucy Elliott Bailey, see 20-54.

Information following from: Custer 2/20/09.
21-55 MAW-CAW-DAY-O-SAY, dead.
Wife: Name not given, dead.
21-55-1 Andrew Fitch, dead, see 18-55 & 13-55.
Wife: Name not given.
21-55-1-1 Sarah Smith, see 18-55 & 13-55.

Information following from: Custer 2/20/09.
22-55 NE-DAW-WAY-QUAY or MARY SHY-GO-NAY-BE, age 70, P.O. Lattin.
Husband: George Shay-O-Nay-By, age 88, see 26-52.
22-55-1 Mary Mitchell, see 3-52 & 26-52.

Information following from: Custer 2/20/09.

23-55 MAY-WE-SHAW-WAY, dead, wife dead and no heirs.

Information following from: Custer 2/20/09.
24-55 SHAW-GAY-SHE, dead, wife dead and no children.

Information following from: Not Given.
25-55 WAW-WAW-CHE-NO-DIN or WILLIAM ~~NODIN~~ NEWTON, age 62, P.O. Honor.

Wife: 1st: Martha, dead.

25-55-1 Ben Nodin or Newton, age 38, P.O. Honor, Mich.

Wife: Martha Ward, age 32, mother an Ottawa (Ne-Gon-Quay) father a white man, see 6-53.

25-55-1-1 Sarah Nodin, age 14.

25-55-1-2 Albert Nodin, age 1, born Aug 6/07.

25-55-2 Martha (Nodin) Thomas, age 35, P.O. Freesoil, see 3-49.

Husband: Charles Thomas, see 17-56 & 31-57.

25-55-2-1 John Thomas

25-55-2-2 Asebun Thomas or Coon Skinhorn, age 8, see 3-49.

25-55-2-3 Mary Thomas, age 1, born May 1907 2nd roll.

25-55-2-4 Elizabeth Thomas, born June 1908 2nd roll.

25-55-3 John Nodin (Newton), age 33, P.O. Freesoil.

Wife: Jennie Smith, ~~nee Louis see 1-49~~, separated, daughter of William Smith, see 13-6.

25-55-3-1 Moses (Nodin) Newton, age 5, child lives with mother.

Wife 2nd: Alice (Nodin or Newton) Judson, age 58, P.O. Freesoil, Traverse. Her 2nd husband is Jim Judson, P.O. Bear Creek, see 22-54. Her child by 2nd husband:

22-54-1 Julia Judson, age 21, P.O. Freesoil, not married see 22-54.

Wife 3rd: Angeline Shilo, age 56, Traverse, see 14-44.

Information following from: Custer Feby 18/09.
26-55 KAW-GAW-BAISH-QUAM or GEORGE ~~CROCKEY~~ CROKEY, age 63, P.O. Fountain.

Wife: Ke-She-Go-Quay or Mrs. George Crokey, age 58, no children.

26-55-1 ~~John Griffin~~ Jacob Crane or Jacob Daniels or Jacob Griffin, age 22 P.O. Lives in Isabella Co Wise, Mich, adopted child, see 27-60.

Information following from: Custer 2/20/09.
27-55 LOUIS KE-SHE-O-CUM, dead, wife dead, no heirs.

Information following from: To Eunice Baily May 1/09 Horace B. Durant Special U.S. Indian Agent.
28A-55 NAH-BAH, dead, see 3-59 & 28-55.

.28A-55-1 Eunice Bailey, age 53, P.O. Stormer, Mich, see 28-55.
Husband: Solomon Bailey, age 61, P.O. Stormer, see 3-50
28A-55-1-1 Francios Bailey, age 17, P.O. Stormer.
28A-55-1-2 Robert Bailey, age 23, P.O. Stormer.
Wife: Katie Bailey, age 22, P.O. Stormer.
28A-55-1-2-1 Nicholis Bailey, age 3, P.O. Stormer, see 3-59..
28A-55-1-2-2 Jesse Bailey, age 2, P.O. Stormer.
Note: Charity green arm only Daughter I Ever Had in the World the one I send you before yours truly Eunice Bailey.

Information following from: Not Given.
28-55 JOSEPH ELLIOTT JR., dead.
Wife: Eunice Robinson Bailey, age 53, P.O. Honor Stormer, Mich, 2nd husband Solomon Baily, see 3-50 & 3-59.
28-55-1 Charity Greenarm Smith, died Apr/07 off, husband white no children.

Letter to her May/09
April 30 09
Special U.S. Indian agent
Horace B, Durant Dear Sir your Letter comes at hand april 27. I will now tell you my Daughter was Born 1871 in May. She got one pament at Last pamant. Her name was before She was married Charity greenarm and She never have no children after she was married Charity of Smith and she Died in 1907 in Last april. Seems to me By right I am the one ought to have that her money. Yours truly
Eunice Bailey
Sormer Po Benzie Co Mich
Write her & ask for all of her child'n especially the name of ones at Charlevoix.

May 23/09

Stormer Mich

Horace B Durant – Dear Sir you mantion my Daughter Charrity HusBand he Lives in Benzie county one mile from home to work now he is Down to Hollan, mich now to Peel Bark.

We are going there too to work for this Summer.
Yours &truly
Eunice S. Bailey

Information following from: Custer 2/20/09.
29-55 TAY-BAIN-DOWN or PETER MAISH-CAW, age 59, P.O. Omena.

Wife: Angeline (Bailey) Maish-Caw, died May/08, for children see 4/62 & 1-55.

Information following from: Custer 2/20/09.
30-55 CHE-GAW-ME-QUAY, dead, no heirs.

Information following from: Custer 2/20/09.
31-55 PAY-BE-SHAY, dead, no heirs.

Information following from: Custer 2/20/09.
32-55 MAW-OH, dead, no heirs.

Information following from: Custer 2/20/09.
33-55 MICK-WE-NIN-NE, dead, no heirs.
Wife: Name not given, now wife of George Shay-Go-Nay-Be.

Information following from: Custer 2/20/09.
34-55 PETER CO-TAY, dead, no heirs.

Information following from: Custer 2/20/09.
35-55 NAY-TAW-ME-NE-SAY, dead.
35-55-1 Name not given, dead, no heirs.
35-55-2 Name not given, dead, no heirs.

Information following from: Not Given.
36-55 JOHN DUVERNEY, age 62, P.O. Petoskey.
Wife 1st: Angeline Pesney, Traverse, P.O. Bay Shore, see 22-42, separated from Duverney now lives with Simon Pesney or Simon Peters see 41-26.
Wife 2nd: Lucy Duverney, age 49, P.O. Petoskey, daughter of 51-43.
36-55-1 John Duverney, age 22, P.O. Petoskey, single.
36-55-2 Oldest child, name not given, dead, no heirs.
36-55-3 Ida Duverney, age 18, P.O. Petoskey, now with sister at Pawhuska, Okla, single no children.
36-55-4 James Duverney, age 11, P.O. Petoskey.
36-55-5 Rose Duverney Tolley, age 31, P.O. Pawhuska, Okla.
Husband: Name not given, white.
36-55-5-1 Stella May Tolley, age 4, P.O. Pawhuska, Okla.

Pawhuska, Okla
June - 12 - 09

Horace B. Durant
Special U.S. Indian Agent

Dear Sir

Received your letter. I am a member of the Ottawa and Chippewa Indians. My parents are John and Lucy Duvernay. Brothers John age 23 and Jimmie age 11. Sister Ida 18.

I am 30 years of age and have a little daughter Stella May Tolley aged 5 years Hope this is satisfactory. When do you think the Indians will get their payment.

Yours Truly
Mrs. Rose Tolley

Information following from: Custer 2/20/09.
37-55 PE-TAW-QUOT-O-QUAY or LUCY BAILEY or LUCY ELLIOTT, age 61, see 20-54.
Husband 1st: Sam Bailey, separated, see 20-54.
37-55-1 Charley Bailey #3, age 41

Page 56A
Chief AISH-QUAY-O-SAY
Grand River

Information following from: Fountain Feby/09.
1-56A AISH-QUAY-O-SAY, dead.
Wife: Name not given, dead.
1-56A-1 Mary McDaquett, age 76, see 5-54, Ok D 2/09.

Information following from: Not Given.
2-56A TUSH-QUAY-AW-BAW-NO, dead.
Wife: Name not given, dead.
2-56A-1 Eliza Hineman Ke-Quoum, dead.
Husband: Joe Ke-Quoum, no children.
2-56A-2 George Hineman, age 60, P.O. Lattin (Fern), se on 1870 roll as 10-56A.
Wife 1st: Catharine Pay-Baw-Me, dead
2-56A-2-1 William Hineman, age 25, P.O. Charlevoix.
~~2-56A-2-2 Mary Hineman.~~
2-56A-2-2 Levi Hineman, dead.
2-56A-2-3 Charles Hineman, dead.
Wife 2nd: Eva Generaux, age 36 now wife of Charles Generaux, see 19-55.
2-56A-2-4 Lucy Hineman, age 16, not married.
2-56A-2-5 Phillip Hineman, age 14.
2-56A-2-6 Mary Hineman, age 10.
2-56A-2-7 Angeline Hineman, age 8.
2-56A-3 Smith Hineman, age 52, P.O. Freesoil.
Wife: Lizzie Maw-By, age 42, see 2-56B
2-56A-3-1 Gus Hineman, age 22.

Wife: Mary Antoine, age 19, sister of Isaac & Moses Antoine.

2-56A-3-1-1 David Antoine, age 2, ~~born Nov/06~~.

2-56A-3-2 Lucy Hineman, age 21, Traverse, see 8-42.

Husband: Alex Parow, Traverse.

2-56A-3-3 Martha Hineman, age 18.

2-56A-3-4 Elizabeth Hineman, Age 15.

Information following from: Not Given.

3-56A KAY-WIS, dead.

Wife: Name not given, dead.

3-56A-1 Mary Generaux, age 60, P.O. Fountain.

Husband: Charles Generaux, 19-55.

Note: for chld'n by her 1st husband see 19-55.

3-56A-2 Maggie Kay-Wis, dead, no children.

Husband: William Micko as Elliott, P.O. Fountain, see 7-62 & 15-55.

3-56A-3 Joe Kay-Wis or Joe Smith #2, age 41, P.O. Chief Lake.

Wife: Sarah Fitch Anderson Smith, age 30, P.O. Chief Lake, see 13-55.

3-56A-3-1 Solomon Smith, age 13.

3-56A-3-2 John Smith, age 8.

3-56A-3-3 Delia Smith, age 4.

3-56A-3-4 Allie (son), age 2.

3-56A-4 William Kay-Wis Smith, age 36, P.O. Freesoil..

Wife: Mary Joe, age 32, see 5-60, daughter of Charley Joe.

3-56A-4-1 Lillie Smith, age 11.

3-56A-4-2 Robert Smith, age 9.

3-56A-4-3Wallace Smith, age 6.

3-56A-4-4Mattie Smith, age 4.

3-56A-4-5Annie Smith, age 2.

Information following from: Fountain 2/09.

4-56A AISH-TAW-AW-SUNG, dead.

Wife: Name not given, dead.

4-56A-1 Ella Bailey, age 47, P.O. Honor, see 4-62.

4-56A-2 Lucy Moby, age 44, see 2-56B.

Husband: James Moby.

4-56A-3 Pete Aish-Taw-Aw-Sung, dead.

Wife: Annie Ostie, age 46, see 10-53 & 2-51.

4-56A-4 Name or sex not given, dead.

Information following from: Fountain 2/09.

5-56A SHAW-BWAY-WAY, dead.

Wife: Name not given, dead.

5-56A-1 Name not given, dead.
Wife: Nancy Josiah, age 38, see 19-55.
5-56A-2 Name not given, dead, no heirs.
5-56A-3 Name not given, dead, no heirs.
5-56A-4 Name not given, dead, no heirs.

Information following from: Not Given.
6-56A KE-SIS-WAY-BAY, dead.
Wife: Name not given, dead.
6-56A-1 Nancy Bailey, see 2-49.
Husband: Jacob Bailey, see 2-58.
6-56A-2 William Koon, age 47, P.O. Lattin.
Wife 1st: Name not given, dead.
6-56A-2-1 Mary Koon Shag-Wab-Mo, living.
Husband: Shag-Wah-Mo, see 29-52.
6-56A-2-2 Mitchell Koon, age 24, P.O. Lattin, no children, see 3-52.
Wife 2nd:Name not given, dead.
6-56A-2-3 Gertie Wah-Bin-Dwetto, age 19, P.O. Walkerville.
Husband: Hank Wah-Bin-Dwetto, age 25, no children, see 7-52.
Wife 3rd: Maud Shay-Wah-Be-No Koon, age 28, P.O. Lattin, see 29-52.
6-56A-2-1 Mary Koon, age 11.
6-56A-2-2 Peter Koon, age 8.
6-56A-2-3 Amy Koon, age 5.
6-56A-2-4 Vern Koon, age 2.
6-56A-3 Angeline Pay-Baw-Me, age 45, P.O. Lattin.
Husband: William Pay-Baw-Me, see 7-50.

Information following from: Fountain 2/09.
7-56A AW-ZHE-WAY-KE-ZHICK, dead.
Wife: Name not given, dead.
7-56A-1 Son name not given, see 12-56.

Information following from: Fountain 2/09.
8-56A ME-SQUAW-NAW-QUOT or SOPHIA BAILEY, age 75, now wife of Battise Bailey, see 2-58.

Information following from: Fountain 2/09.
9-56A AISH-QUAY-GO-NAY-BE.
Note: Indians do not recall this name. Durant

Information following from: Not Given.
10-56A SHAW-NAW-WE-KAW-WAW or GEORGE HINEMAN, age 60,

see 2-56A & 21-46. For wife and children see 2-56A.

Information following from: Fountain 2/09.
11-56A SHAW-KO, dead, no heirs.

Information following from: Not Given.
12-56A QUEEN-QUO-AW-GAY, dead, son of 7-56A.
Wife: Name not given, dead.
12-56A-1 Name not given dead.
Husband: Johnson Green, see 10-58.
12-56A-1-1 Julia Green, age 13, see 10-58, 4-61 & 22-59.

Information following from: Fountain 2/09.
13-56A THERESA, dead.
13-56A-1 Name or sex not given, dead.
13-56A-1-1 Thomas Peters, age 17, see 3-50.
13-56A-2 Name or sex not given, dead.

Information following from: Fountain Feby/09.
14-56A JOSEPH, dead & NAW-CO-MO-QUAY, dead.
Note: Joseph had one child which is dead but left ~~a grandchild which is dead~~ no heirs.
Note: The above information is given me by George Clucky, enrolled as # 26 p. 55, 1870 roll by name of Kaw-Gay-Bush-Quaw and he & his wife are the only ones who know of the identity of these parties. He says Joseph was a brother of Aish-Quay-O-Say. Chief # 1 p. 56, said Joseph also having the English name of John Collins & the Naw-Co-Mo-Quay was a small girl lived with him when he first came to this country from Canada.
All of the above information controverts the statements of Joseph Cushway, of Fern, Mich, who claims to be the "Joseph" mentioned on this card. Horace B Durant U.S. Spl. Ind. Agt. Fountain Feby/09
Those present & whom the above statement was made to me are: Charles Generaux, William Generaux, Charles Hickey, James & Joe Cogswell & George Clucky & their wives, at the home of Joe Cogswell. Durant

Disputed information follows
14-56A JOSEPH (CUSHWAY) & NAW_CO_MO_QUAY, his sister.

Joseph Cushway, living, age 59, P.O. ~~Fern~~ Custer RFD #2, drew with the Potts.
Wife: Name not given, Pottawatomi.
14-56A-1 Martha Cushway Rider, age 39, P.O. Scottville RFD #2.
Husband: Name not given, white.

14-56A-1-1 Joseph Rider, age 16.
14-56A-1-2 John Rider, age 15.
14-56A-1-3 Leo Rider, age 13.
14-56A-1-4 Niley Rider (son), age 12.
14-56A-1-5 Myrtle Rider, age 10.

14-56A-2 Nora Cushway Bushaw, age 36, P.O. Custer RFD #2.
Husband: Name not given,white.
14-56A-2-1 Joseph Bushaw, age 15.

14-56A-3 Mary Cushway Wilson, ~~age 34.~~ Dead.
Husband: Name not given, white.
14-56A-3-1 James Wilson, age 12.
14-56A-3-2 Maud Wilson, age 10.
14-56A-3-3 Mary Wilson, age 8.
14-56A-3-4 Raymond Wilson, age 3.
Note: P.O. Custer RFD #2 children live with grandfather.

14-56A-4 Clara Cushway Bushaw, age 31, P.O. Custer RFD #2.
Husband: Name not given, white.
14-56A-4-1 William Bushaw, age 12.
14-56A-4-2 Veronica Bushaw, age 10.
14-56A-4-3 Louis Bushaw, age 8.
14-56A-4-4 Margaret Bushaw, age 6.
14-56A-4-5 Pearl Bushaw, age 2 mos.

14-56A-5 Charles Cushway, age 27, P.O. Custer RFD #2, not married
14-56A-6 James Cushway, age 25, P.O. Custer #2, not married.
14-56A-7Annie Cushway, age 18, P.O.Custer #2, not married.

NAW-CO-MO-QUAY, dead, sister of Joseph 14-56A.
Husband: Name not given, dead, Pottawatomie.
Child: Elizabeth Alexis, age 34, has not been heard of for 2 or 3 years but was working at Haskell & went to school there.

Pages 56B & 57
Chief PAY-NAY-SE
Grand River

Information following from: Bradley.
1-56B PE-NAY-SE, dead, wife deand and no heirs.

Information following from: Not Given.
2-56B KUSH-KE-MAW-NE-SAY or JOE MAW-BY or MOBY, age 75, P.O. Carrs Mich.
Wife: Susan Maw-By, age 76, P.O. Carrs Mich, her 2nd husband. (See below for her children by 1st marriage).
2-56B-1 James Maw-By or Moby, age 47, P.O. Honor.
Wife: Lucy (Ah-She-Te-Ah-Sin) Moby, age 44, P.O. Honor.

2-56B-1-1 Mitchell Moby, age 18, P.O. Honor.
2-56B-1-2 Mary Ann Moby, age 15, P.O. Honor.
2-56B-1-3Nancy Moby, age 14, P.O. Mt Plesant Sch.
2-56B-1-4 Emma Moby, age 13.
2-56B-1-5 Frank Moby, age 12.
2-56B-1-6 Andrew Moby, age 10.
2-56B-1-7 John Moby, age 7.
2-56B-1-8 Eunice Moby, age 5.
2-56B-1-9 Henry Moby, age 1, born June 1/07 2nd roll..

2-56B-2 Elizabeth Hineman, age 43, P.O. Freesoil.
Husband: Smith Hineman, age 52, P.O. Freesoil, see 2-56A.
2-56B-2-1 Gus Hineman, age 24, P.O. Copenish.
Wife: Mary Hineman, age 20, daughter of 2-50.
2-56B-2-1-1 David Hineman, age 2.
2-56B-2-2 Lucy Hineman, age 21, P.O. Freesoil.
2-56B-2-3 Martha Hineman, age 18, P.O. Freesoil.
2-56B-2-4 Alice Hineman, age 15, P.O. Freesoil.

2-56B-3 Angeline Maw-By Crampton, P.O. Fern.
Husband: Foster Crampton, see family with Crampton, drew with Potts, see 7-53.

2-56B-4 Joe Maw-By Jr., age 39, P.O. Millerton.
Wife: Mary Maw-By nee Lake, age 39, sister of Pete Lake, see 8-61
2-56B-4-1 Rosie Maw-By, age 16.
2-56B-4-2 Lizzie Maw-By, age 13.
2-56B-4-3 David Maw-By, age 11.
2-56B-4-4 Mary Maw-By, age 8.
2-56B-4-5 Catharine Maw-By, age 5.

2-56B-5 Mary Maw-By Hall, dead.
Husband: Eddie Hall, P.O. Starr City, see 2-60.
2-56B-5-1 Joe Hall, age 12, enroll with Nancy Peters, his aunt, his father's sister, who lives at Fountain, wife of John Peters.

SUSAN MAW-BY or MOBY and her marriage to 1st husband.
Husband: Name not given, dead.
Child 1: Polly Sands, age 58, P.O. Algonac.
Husband: Name not given, dead.
1-1 Lydia Riley, age 32, P.O. Walpole Island Algonac Mich.
Husband: Name not given, Canadian Ind.
1-1-1 Lila Riley, age 5.
1-2 Silas Sands, age 27, 3 children.
1-3 Lizzie Sands, age 25, single.
1-4 Walter Sands, age 21, single.
Note: All draw from Canadian gov't Polly Sands admits this, Durant

Walpole Island Mch/09.

Information following from: Lydia Sands Riley, Algonac June 10/09.
2-56B KUSH-KE-MAW-NE-SAY – Supplemental compare with original sheet 2-56 (Autor Comment: Immediately preceeding) & add this to it. Durant
Wife: Name not given.
2-56B-1 Polly Sands, age 55, P.O. Walpole Island Canada Algonac, Mich.
Husband: Name not given.
2-56B-1-1 Lydia Riley, age 29.
Husband: Name not given, Canadian.
2-56B-1-1-1 Nora Riley, age 2, off.
2-56B-1-2 Silas Sands, age 27.
Wife: Name not given, Canadian.
2-56B-1-2-1 Homer Sands, age 2, off.
2-56B-1-3 Lizzie Sands Greenbird, age 27.
Husband: Name not given, Canadian.
2-56B-1-3-1 Daisy Greenbird, age 8.
2-56B-1-4 Walter Sands, age 22, P.O. Walpole Island Canada Algonac, Mich, off.
Note: All draw in Canada.

Information following from: David Fox & wife Paw Paw Mch/09.
3-56B JAMES TAY-GWAW-SUNG, dead.
Wife: Name not given, dead.
3-56B-1 Peter Tay-Gwaw-Sung, on roll as 21-57.
3-56B-2 Sophia Tay-Gwaw-Sung, dead.
Husband: Name not given, dead.
3-56B-2-1 Robert Aiken, P.O. Newaygo, see 21-54, 20-49 & 3-58.
3-56B-2-2 Thomas Aiken, P.O. Newaygo, married and has family.
3-56B-2-3 Jacob Aiken #2, age 43, P.O. Newaygo, married and has children.
3-56B-3 Elizabeth Aiken, dead, see 3-56B.
Husband: Name not given.
3-56B-3-1 John Pego, P.O. Armstrong Creek, Forest Co., Wis.
Wife: Name not given, dead.
3-56B-3-1-1 Name not given.
3-56B-3-1-2 Name not given.
3-56B-3-2 Levi Pego, age 26, P.O. Armstrong Creek,see 2-62 & 1-50, single.
3-56B-4 Julia Aiken, dead.

Husband: ______ McDaquot, dead, he married a sister of his 1st wife & by her had a child, see 3-56B-5-1 below.

3-56B-4-1 ~~Enos~~ Esau McDaquot, age 20, P.O. Pentwater on near there.

3-56B-5 Catharine Aiken, dead.

Husband: ______ McDaquot, dead, see note on 3-56B-4 above.

3-56B-5-1 Thomas McDaquot, P.O. Pentwater.

3-56B-6 Niase Aiken (son), dead.

3-56B-7 Name or sex not given, dead.

3-56B-8 Nancy Aiken, dead, no heirs.

3-56B-9 Name or sex not given, dead, no heirs.

3-56B-10 Mary or Hariet Aiken Fox, age 50, see 11-53.

Husband 1st: Moses Jackson, dead, see 10-59.

Husband 2nd : David Fox, age 59, P.O. Hartford, Mich, see 11-53.

3-56B-10-1 Adam Fox, see 11-53.

3-56B-10-2 Mary Fox.

3-56B-10-3 Jacob Fox.

Note: Children of David by another wife: Martha Solomon, dead, daughter of Jacob Solomon, who died in Feby/09.

3-56B-10-4 Agnes Fox, dead.

Husband: Frank Bush, ~~dead~~ P.O. Bradley, Pott. off.

3-56-10-4-1 Louis Jackson, age 14, P.O. ~~Petongay~~ Petoskey, lives with aunt: Mary McMullen or McClellem, nee Jackson.

3-56B-10-4-2 Martha Jackson, age 5, lives with David Fox or Martha Fox

3-56B-10-5 Mary ~~McMullen~~ Makamenaw ~~or Mary McClellem~~, nee Jackson, P.O. (Petoskey) Pellston, see 10-59 & 7-26.

Husband: ~~Paul~~ Peter Makamenaw.

3-56B-10-5-1 Paul ~~McMullen~~ Makamenaw or Paul Fox, age 7, lives with David Fox.

3-56B-10-5-2 Agnes Makamenaw.

3-56B-10-5-3 Louise Makamenaw.

Information following from: Newaygo Feby/09.

4-56B SHAW-WAW-NE-KE-ZHICK, dead.

Wife: Adeline (McClellan) Echtinaw, age 70, P.O. Newaygo.

4-56B-1 Mary Laffarty, age 53, P.O. Holton, Mich, enrolled in 1870 with 29-56.

Husband:Name not given, white.

4-56B-1-1 Addie Lafferty, age 33, P.O. Muskegon Mich, single.

4-56B-1-2 Ruth Lafferty Benson, age 30, P.O. Muskegon.
Husband: Name not given, white, P.O. 66 Yuba St.
4-56B-1-2-1 Vivian M. Benson, age 11 mo., born Sept/07, 2nd roll.
4-56B-1-3 James Lafferty, age 26, P.O. Muskegon, Mich.
Wife: Name not given, white.
4-56B-1-3-1 Violet Lafferty, age 2.
4-56B-2 William McClellan, age 52, P.O. Fife Lake, wife name not given, white, no children.
4-56B-3 George McClellan, age 50, P.O. Fife Lake, Mich.
Wife: Name not given, white
4-56B-3-1 Gertie McClellan, age 13.
4-56B-3-2 Herbert McClellan, age 11.
4-56B-3-3 Gladys McClellan, age 4.
4-56B-4 Frank McClellan, age 48, P.O. Harrietta, Mich, wife name not given, white, no children.
4-56B-5 Herbert McClellan, age 44, P.O. Fife Lake, single.
4-56B-6 Ingar (McClellan) Thompson, age 42, P.O. Newaygo.
Husband: Name not given, white.
4-56B-6-1 Frossard Thompson (son), age 15.
4-56B-6-2 Lizzie Thompson, age 13.
4-56B-6-3 Roy Thompson, age 11.
4-56B-6-4 Clifford Thompson, age 8.
4-56B-6-5 Irwin Thompson, age 4.
4-56B- 7 Rachel McClellan, age 32, P.O. Grand Rapids, single, has not been heard from her for 3 years.
4-56B- 8 Levi McClellan, age 29, P.O. Newaygo.
4-56B- 9 Ida Thompson, age 27, P.O. Big Raapids, Mich.
Husband: Name not given, white.
4-56B-9-1 Herbert Thompson, age 8.
4-56B-9-2 Arthur Thompson, age 3.

Information following from: To Mrs Frances Carver Holland Mich Apr/09 Gd. Haven Feby/09 Letter from Mrs Frances Carver Apr/09.
5-56B NO-BWAY-QUOM or GEORGE SHASHAQUAY, dead.
Wife: Mary Snay Wongon, age 69, P.O. Saugatuck.
5-56B-1 William Shashaquay, age 47, P.O. Holland, Mich 307 W 15th St.
Wife: Name not given, white.
5-56B-1-1 Anna E. (Shashaquay) Hacklander, age 21.
Husband: _______ Hacklander, white.
5-56B-1-1-1 Elizabeth Hacklander, born July/06 1st roll.
5-56B-1-1-2 Louise Hacklander, born Sept 19/08 off
5-56B-1-2 Joseph P. Shashaquay, age 19, P.O. Holland, Mich

307 W 15th St.

5-56B-1-3 Theresa E. Shashaquay, age 16, P.O. Holland, Mich 307 W 15th St.

5-56B-1-4 Mary F. Shashaquay, age 13, P.O. Holland, Mich 307 W 15th St.

5-56B-1-5 Agnes J. Shashaquay, age 11, P.O. Holland, Mich 307 W 15th St.

5-56B-1-6 Henry W. Shashaquay, age 7, P.O. Holland, Mich 307 W 15th St.

5-56B-2 Frances Carver, age 33, P.O. Holland, Mich 337 W 16th St.

Husband: Name not given, white.

5-56B-2-1 George Carver, age 9.

5-56B-3 Maggie Mitchell, age 26, P.O. Sangatuck Mich.

Husband: _______Mitchell, ~~white~~ Indian.

5-56B-3-1 Benjamin Mitchell, age 5, born Aug 17.

5-56B-3-2 Evelen Mitchell, age 3, born June 20.

5-56B-4 Joseph P. Shashaquay, dead.

Wife: Name not given, white.

5-56B-4-1 William Shashaquay, age 9.

5-56B-4-2 Chester Shashaquay, age 7.

5-56B-4-3 Clarence Shashaquay, age 5.

5-56B-4-4 Margaret Shashaquay, age 3.

Information following from: ~~Inquire as to identity~~ Identity Established D.

6-56B JOSEPH MICK-SAW-BAY, dead.

Wife: Name not given, dead.

6-56B-1 Margaret Scanlon, age 51, P.O. Grand Haven.

Husband: _________ Scanlon, white.

6-56B-1 Marian Scanlon,age 24, P.O. Grand Haven, single.

6-56B-2 Catharine Ellman, age 20, P.O. Grand Haven.

Husband: ______ Ellman, white.

6-56B-2-1 Francis Charles Ellman, born Jan 23/08 2nd roll.

6-56B-2-2 Name or sex not given, born 1909 too late.

6-56B-3 William Scanlon, age 18, P.O. Grand Haven.

6-56B-4 Margaret Scanlon Jr., age 16, P.O. Grand Haven.

6-56B-5 Thomas Scanlon, age 14, P.O. Grand Haven.

6-56B-6 Frank Scanlon, age 12, P.O. Grand Haven.

6-56B-7 John Scanlon, age 10, P.O. Grand Haven.

6-56B-8 Fred Scanlon, age 8, P.O. Grand Haven.

6-56B-2 Kate Mick-Say-Bay, dead, no heirs.

6-56B-3 Angeline Awsegenock, see 14-56.

Grand Haven, Mich
Apr. 22, 1909

Horace Durant:

In reply too yours of the 22nd I will hire state that the baby was born the (23rd) twenty third of Jan. 1908. I also have had a recent birth of an older boy born the (27th) twenty seventh of Feb 1909.
Francis Charles Ellmann born Jan 23rd 1908.
Thomas George Ellmann born Feb. 27th 1909.

Your truly
Mrs. F.C.Ellmann
Grand Haven, Mich.

Information following from: Mrs Charles Webb.
7-56B MRS. DANIEL HYDE, dead.
7-56B-1 Daniel Hyde, age 64, P.O. Chippewa Lake Big Rapids (six miles west).
Wife: Name not given.
7-56B-1-1 Arthur Hyle, age 34, P.O. Hamilton Montana.
7-56B-1-2 Agnes Hyle ~~Chippeway~~, age 32, P.O. Chippewa ~~Lake~~ Sta.
7-56B-1-3 Cora Hyle, age 29, P.O. Grand Rapids.
7-56B-1-4 Clarence Hyle, age 30,P.O. GrandRapids.
7-56B-1-5 Fred Hyle, age 25.
7-56B-1-6 Stephen Hyle, age 22, P.O. Chippewa Lake.
7-56B-1-7 Lydia Hyle, age 20, P.O. Chippewa Lake.
7-56B-1-8 Maggie Hyle, age 15, P.O. Chippewa Lake.
7-56B-2 Francis Hyde, P.O. Hamilton, Montana.
Note: Write Daniel Hyde what has become of the other 2 children enrolled with his mother in 1870's. D
Note: Information from Daniel Hyde in attached letter.
7-56B-3 Name or sex not given, dead.

Chippewa Lake
mecosta County Mich
may 23 1909

mr horace durant
Dear sir Petoskey mich
I received your letter of the 19 I am married have a wife eight children my wifes name is aloria m Hyde she is fifty years old her father & mother had no Indian name her maden name was baker they were of English decent.
I am sixty four years old Adress Daniel C Hyde Chippewa Lake Mecosta Co Mich

those are the names and address of my children
Arthur H Hyde age 34 years Hamilton Montana
agnes Hyde Chippewa Lake mich age 32 years
cora Hyd grand rapids mich age 29 years
clarance Hyde grand rapids mich age 30 years

fred Hyde Chippewa Lake mich age 25 years
steven Hyde Chippewa Lake mich age 22 years
lydia Hyde Chippewa Lake mich age 20 years
magie Hyde Chippewa Lake mich age 15 years

Chippewa Lake mich
June 20 1909
mr horace B Durant
Petoskey mich
Dear sir my oldest sister name unice she is dead
next Amanda she is dead
next marinda she is dead
my brother in hamilton Montana his name is frances hyde
I bleave this all you asked for
yours truly
Daniel Hyde
Chippewa Lake mich

Information following from: John Snay Gd Haven.
8-56B MRS SOOT SNAY, dead. This family are all children of Mrs Soot Snay.
8-56B-1 Joe Snay, age 63, P.O. Saugatuck, Mich.
Wife: Name not given, white.
8-56B-1-1 Laura Snay, age 20.
8-56B-1-2 Joe Snay Jr., age 16.
8-56B-1-3 George Snay, age 10.
8-56B-1-4 John Snay, age 5.
8-56B-1-5 Maynard Snay, born Summer of 1908 X? Aug 27 off.
8-56B-2 Theresa C. Snay, age 51, P.O. Grand Rapids, Mich 210 N Prospect St., single.
8-56B-3 John Snay, age 61, P.O. Grand Rapids.
Wife: Name not given, white.
8-56B-3-1 Fannie Marks, age 34, P.O. Grand Rapids 207 7th Ave.
Husband: Name not given,white.
8-56B-3-1-1 Edwin Marks, age 6.
8-56B-3-1-2 Mary Marks, age 4.
8-56B-3-2 Jannie Snay, age 32, P.O. Grand Rapids 207 7th, single.
8-56B-4 Eliza Snay, dead, no heirs.

Information following from: Louis Speidle Grand Haven Feby/09 This name Spider has been identified as meaning the same as Speidle; wrongfully spelled in 1870. Durant.

9-56B MRS JACOB SPIDER, dead.

Husband: Jacob Speidle, white, P.O. Lexington, Mich.

9-56B-1 Louis Speidle, age 47, P.O. Grand Haven, Mich.

Wife: Name not given, white.

9-56B-1-1 Grace Speidle, age 21, P.O. Grand Haven, Mich.

9-56B-1-2 Louis Speidle Jr., age 19, P.O. Grand Haven, Mich.

9-56B-1-3 Marian Speidle, age 17.

9-56B-1-4 Margaret Speidle, age 6.

9-56B-2 Julia Jones, age 45, P.O. ~~Kingsley~~ South Boardman ~~or Fife Lake~~ Mich.

Husband:Ed Jones, white.

9-56B-2-1 Jacob Spaulding, age 25.

9-56B-2-2 Lena Patrick, age 23.

9-56B-2-3 Dolly Wilson, age 20.

9-56B-2-4 Francis Spaulding, age 16.

9-56B-3 Mary Hammond, age 45, P.O.Klondike, Mich.

Husband: Name not given, white, P.O. Hesperia RFD #3 Bx 110.

9-56B-3-1 Nora Hammond, age 25, P.O. Hesperia RFD #3 Bx 110.

9-56B-3-2 Elizabeth Hammond, age 22, P.O. Hesperia RFD #3 Bx 110.

9-56B-3-3 Annie Hammond, age 19, P.O. Hesperia RFD #3 Bx 110.

9-56B-4 Emma Garlick, age 42, P.O. Grand Haven, Lafayette Sh.

Husband: Name not given, dead.

9-56B-4-1 Minnie Alexander, age 23, P.O. Grand Haven, Lafayette Sh.

Husband: Name not given, white.

9-56B-4-1-1 Evaline Alexander, age 3, P.O. Grand Haven, Lafayette Sh.

9-56B-4-2 Name or sex not given, dead.

9-56B-4-3 Clarence Garlick, age 21, P.O. Grand Haven, Lafayette Sh.

9-56B-4-4 Edith Lehman ~~Backleg~~, age 19, P.O. Grand Haven, Lafayette Sh., no children.

Klondike Mich April 26th 1909
H B Durant Agent. Dear Sir. You requested me to write you the names ages & Addresses of my children for the Ottawa & Chippewa pay roll. First. Miss Nora Hammond age 25 years. Second Miss Elizabrth Hammond age 22 years third Miss Annie Hammond age 19 years. All their Addresses are.

Mrs Mary Hammond
Hesperia RFD No3 Box 110 Mich

South Boardman
May 5 1909. Mr Horace Durant Dear Sir your leter of May 1st received. My Childrens Father name was George Spaulding he was my First husband my Girles are all married But One.
Mrs Ed Jones

1909
South Boardman
Mich april 26
Mr Horace B Durant
Dear Sir. Yours of the 22nd received was very glad to hear Frome you in regard to my Indian Clame I was Born on Grand river Ottawa Co mich in 1858: and I was 51 years Old. the First of this month April my mother was a Ottawa Indian woman and Belonged to that Band and I lived thare until I was 16 years Old. My mothers name was Tommace Speidal my mother dyed in Ottawa Co near Grand have. I have 4 Children a Son Jacob Spaulding age 25 years. Lenia panick age 23 years. Dally Wilson age 20 Francis Spaulding age 16 years, her address is South Boardman mich the rest of the Children live in Travers City Mich. I will clowse now By thanking you For your favor.
Mrs Ed Jones South
Boardman mich.

how did these children get names of Spaulding?
Letter to her may 1/09 D

Information following from: Not Given.
10-56B AKEN RESSETT, dead.
Wife: Was daughter of Tong-Quish or Joe Elliott.
Note: There were two "Charleys" in this family.
10-56B-1 Charley Russett or Akin, age 55, P.O. ~~Dorr Allegan Co~~ Hamilton, Mich.
Wife: Kate.
10-56B-1-1 Clara Russett, age 4.
10-56B-1-2 Ida Bush, age 20, P.O. Bradley, no children.
10-56B-2 Charley Joe, see 5-60.
10-56B-3 William Aiken, dead, see 5-60.
10-56B-4 John Fox, age 40, P.O. Grand Haven, son by an Ind wife of Aken Russett.
Wife: Name not given, white.
10-56B-4-1 Sadie Wartleboer, age 20.
Husband: Name not given, white.
10-56B-4-1-1 Anna Wartleboer, age 2.
10-56B-4-1-2 Cecil Wartleboer, born Feby/09 off.
10-56B-4-2 Grace Fox, age 21, P.O. Grand Haven, single.

My Mothers Chief she drawed under last Was (genagusgesick).

Alder May 25 1909
Mr Horace Durant

Dea Sir I received word from my Sister Mrs Henrietta Ridley who Resides in Volney Mich you was't taking names of the Remoing tribe of Ottowa Indians and as I am one them I felt as though I would like to hear from you. My Mother is Mrs James Anderson of Brooks Township Newaygo Mich I live here by her she cannot write or would write you a letter I Have 2 children Boys John R. Richardson age 16 the 21 of March Arthur C Richardson age 8 the 12 of June my maiden name was Emma E Anderson.

My Mothers maiden name Betsey Sharlol I also have one Brother and One Sister In the State of Washington Hoping you will consider this worthy of an answer I I wait your reply address Mrs Emma Richardson Alder Washington

Interlochen Mich
May 12-09

Mr Horace B Durant
Petoskey Mich
Dear Sir
the ages of My children
Myrtle Anderson 7 year June 19-09
Marshall Anderson 5 years May 1st - 09
Could you give me my information as to where we will Be called to assemble
your very Respectfully
James Anderson Interlochen

Heafer Ark May Th 17 1909
Mr Horace B Durant
Dear Sir in reply to yours of May to 8 Mr Durant I am Married But no Children.
Mr Durant will you please let me know when they pay off be a bout that time and whear are they going to pay in Newaygo and oblige
yours truly
Norman Anderson

Information following from: Not Given.
13-56B MRS WALLACE LARAWAY, dead.
Husband: Wallace Larraway, white, engineer for Stuart White in Gd. Rapids.
Note: Children said to be living in Grand Rapids, ask A.J. Emlaw.
13-56B-1 Alice Shriver, P.O. Grand Rapids Diamond St.
Husband: Rudolph Shriver, white.
13-56B-2 Eva Laraway, Dressmaker Monroe St. Grand Rapids.

Information following from: Ask about identity Identity fully established D.
14-56B LOUIS SAW-GAW-NE-QUO-UM or LOUIS AW-SE-GE-NOCK, age 61, P.O. Benton Harbor, Mich.

Wife: Angeline Aw-Se-Ge-Nock, age 61, P.O. Benton Harbor, Mich, daughter of 6-56 sister to Maw-Che-We-Taw, see 33-28.

14-56B-1 Name or sex not givn, dead, no heirs.

14-56B-2 Name or sex not givn, dead, no heirs.

14-56B-3 Mitchell Ossiginac, age 38, P.O. Benton Harbor, single.

14-56B-4 Lucy Ossiginac, age 35, P.O. Benton Harbor

14-56B-5 William Ossiginac, age 23, P.O. Holland, Mich.

Wife: Name not given, wite, P.O. Holland, Mich.

14-56B-5-1 Robert Ossiginac, age 3.

14-56B-6 Frank Ossiginac, age 19, P.O. Benton Harbor.

Note: Louis Awsegenock married a daughter of his mother's 2nd husband by by his 1st wife. Durant

Information following from: Benjamin Trombly, a brother Petoskey Dec 26/08 & also Millerton, Aug/08.
15-56B LOUIS TROMBLY, dead.

Wife 1st: Mary Shay-Go-Nay-Be, see 26-52.

15-56B-1 Mary McDaquett, age 35, see 5-54.

15-56B-2 Rosa Collins, age 34, P.O. Mt Pleasant Rosebush #2.

Husband: Richard Collins, (Chippewa) Swan Creek Ind off

15-56B-2-1 Georgia Collins, age 12.

15-56B-2-2 Samuel Collins, age 11.

15-56B-2-3 Esther Collins, age 9.

15-56B-2-4 Dawson Collins, age 2.

15-56B-3 Maggie Peters, age 28, P.O. Duluth, Minesota 225 W 4th St.

Husband: Ernest Peters, ~~Chippewa~~ off Saginaw.

15-56B-3-1 Roy Peters, age 6.

15-56B-3-2 Ernest Peters, age 3.

15-56B-3-3 Morris Peters, age 2.

15-56B-4 Julia Me-Doc-O, age 25, P.O. Millerton, Mich.

Husband: Moses Me-Doc-O or Me-Taw-Kee, age 28, son of 11-50, see 21-52.

15-56B4-1 Mary Ann Me-Doc-O, age 6.

15-56B4-2 Louis Me-Doc-O, age 5.

15-56B4-3 Mabel Me-Doc-O, age 3.

Wife 2nd: Elizabeth Trombly, age 60, P.O. Custer RFD #2 daughter of 3-54.

225 W. 4th St.
Duluth, Minn.
April 27-09

Mr. Horace B. Durant
Petoskey, Mich.
Dear Sir:
Your of the 22nd at hand. In reply to your request in reference to my fathers and mothers names they are as follows
Louis Trombley, dead
Elizabeth Trombley, Fern, Mich.
And the names of and ages of my children are.
Roy G. Peters, six years old
Ernest D. Peters three " "
Maurice R. Peters two " "
All living with me.
If it is convenient I would liketo know if theChippewas of Mich. are going to draw money also Mr. Peters is a Chippewa and was born near Mt Pleasant, Mich
He is one of the few Indians from there that never drew any money from the Govt. I would also appreciate to have an Idea as to the amount we will receive per. And about when.
Thanking youin advance
I remain Respectfully
Mrs E. Peters

Information following from: Not Given.
16-56B MRS CHARLES WEBB or SOPHIA ALEXIE or SOFHIA AW-NE-ME-QUOM, age 70, P.O. Honor, was wife of John Pego.
Husband: John Pego, dead, see 5-62 & 14-62, also 33-57.
16-56B-1 John Webb, age 49, P.O. Honor.
Wife 1st: Mrs Carrie Hendrickson, P.O. Holton, Mich RFD. #2
16-56B-1-1 age 17, P.O. Muskegon Holton, Mich R.F.D. #2.
Wife 2nd : Annie Webb, age 26, ~~daughter of Sarah Bailey Crampton~~ granddaughter of Joe Bailey 3-50, see 7-53.
16-56B-1-2 Audie Webb, age 4,
16-56B-1-3 Eliza Webb, born Dec. 25/1907.
16-56B-2 Henry Webb, dead, died in Wis.
Wife: Lela, white, P.O. Norment, North Carolina.
16-56B-2-1 John Webb, age 9.
16-56B-2-2 Michael Webb, age 7.
16-56B-3 Charles Pego, see 5-62 & 14-62.

Boardman, N. C. June 14th, 1909.

Mr. Horace B. Durant,
Special U. S. Indian Agent.,
Petoskey, Mich.
Dear Sir, -

Replying to your favor of June 9th, regarding the family of Henry Webb, deceased, will say that his father, Charles Webb, now deceased, and Sophia, his wife, had two boys. Brother and Henry, deceased. John lives at Stormer, Mich., and sofar as I have been able to learn his mother lives with him there. She afterwards married ---------- Pego. They had one boy Charles who is a half-brother of John and Henry. The last I heard from Charles he was living with his brother John and mother at Stormer. Henry Webb, deceased, was injured on the Butters Lumber Co., logging railroad on the 19th of December, 1901, and died the same day. Am not positive as to the day of his death, but he was buried on the 20th. He left a widow Lela who is still unmarried (that is myself) and two boys, Jack who was nine years old Dec. 27th, 1908 and Mike who was seven years old Sept. 4th, 1908.

I trust that this information will be all that you desire, but will be glad to furnish anything further in my knowledge.

Yours Truly, Lela Webb Norment N.C.

Information following from: Not Given.
17-56B AW-WAW-NAW-QUOT or THOMAS, dead.
Wife: Mary Aw-Waw-Naw-Quot or Mary Thomas, age 72, P.O. Ashton, Mich.
17-56B-1 Louis Thomas, age 56, P.O. Fountain.
Wife: Mary Smith, dead, an Ottawa.
17-56B-1-1 Charley Thomas, age 36, P.O. Freesoil.
Wife: Martha, 4 children indicated but no names given, see 25-55..
17-56B-2 William Thomas, age 30, P.O. Ashton.
Wife: Mercy Hall Thomas, she 1-62, said to have drawn with Potts., see 22-60.
17-56B-2-1 Lewis Thomas, born Oct/1906, died Mar 1/08, see 30-60.
17-56B-3 Thomas Thomas, age 23, P.O. Ashton, not married.
17-56B-4 Moses Thomas, age 16, P.O. Freesoil.

Information following from: John B Perrissian family Grand Haven Feby/09.
18-56B MRS PETER DUVERNEY & daughter's child, both dead.
18-56B-1 Mary Duverney, dead.
18-56B-1-1 Minnie,, dead.
18-56B-1-1-1 Pearl Stevens, age 18, P.O. Whitehall.

Information following from: Grand Haven Feby/09.
19-57 AZH-QUAY-TAW-GAW or JOSEPH SHA-SHA-QUAY, dead.
Wife: Name not given, dead, was a daughter of Mrs Soot Snay 8-56B.
19-57-1 Louise, dead.
Husband: Name not given, white.
19-57-1-1 James Williams, age22, P.O. Saugatuck, Mich,

single.
19-57-2 Name not given, dead, no heirs.

Information following from: Mrs George Robinson Mount Pleasant, Michigan Grand Haven Feby/09.

20-57 MRS GEORGE ROBINSON, age 75, P.O. Grand Haven 5 miles up river on south side, see 10-49.
Wife: Name not given, white.
20-57-1 Ellen Crandell, age 60, P.O. Grand Rapids, 38 Goodrich St.
Husband: Name not given, white.
20-57-1-1 Albert Crandell, age 32, Grand Rapids 80 Wealthy Ave.
Wife: Name not given, white.
20-57-1-1-1 Winnie Crandell, age 14.
20-57-1-1-2 Lester Crandell, age 10.
20-57-1-2 Nora Cloverton, age 30, Grand Rapids 38 Goodrich St.
Husband: Name not given, white.
20-57-1-2-1 Lester Cloverton, age 7.
20-57-1-2-2 Name/sex not given, age 1 1/2., 2nd roll.
20-57-1-3 Mark Crandell, age 27, P.O. Grand Rapids 106 Ellsworth Ave, separated.
Wife: Jesse Crandell, white.
20-57-1-3-1 Percy Crandell, age 4.
20-57-1-3-2 Earl Crandell, age 6.
20-57-1-4 Luke Crandell, age 26, P.O. 4th AveGd Rapids, Mich.
Wife: Name not given, white.
20-57-1-4-1 Hazel Crandell, age 3.
20-57-1-5 John Crandell, age 24, P.O. Chestnut St Gd Rapids Mich, wife name not given white and no children.
20-57-1-6 Pearl Crandell (son), age 22, an actor travels.
20-57-1-7 Eber Crandell (son), age 20, P.O. Goodrich St. Gd Rapids.
20-57-1-8 Hazel Crandell, age 14, P.O. Goodrich St. Gd Rapids.
20-57-2 Edward Robinson #3, age 58, P.O. Glenn Haven.
Wife: Name not given, dead.
20-57-2-1 Charles Robinson #2, age 35, P.O. Glenn Haven ~~(write)~~ (U.S. Life Saving Station Sleeping Bear Point)
Wife: Name not given, white.
20-57-2-1-1 Ed Robinson Jr., age 14 P.O. Glenn Haven.
20-57-2-1-2 Charles Robinson, age 12.

20-57-2-1-3 Frances Robinson, age 10.
20-57-2-1-4 Kenneth Robinson, age 8.
20-57-2-1-5 Lyle Robinson, age 6.
20-57-2-1-6 Dale Robinson, age 4.

20-57-3 Eunice Robinson, dead.
Husband: Thomas Hancock, white, P.O. Grand Rapids.
20-57-3-1 Clarence Hancock, age 20, P.O. Grand Rapids.
20-57-3-2 Guy Hancock, age 18, P.O. Grand Rapids RFD1.
20-57-3-3 Ernest Hancock, age 15, P.O. Grand Rapids RFD1
20-57-3-4 Mamie Hancock, age 13, P.O. Grand Rapids.
20-57-3-5 Millie Hancock, age 11, P.O. Lacota, Mich, lives with Mrs Jay Gibson.

20-57-4 George Robinson, age 50, P.O. Grand Rapids 129 Wealty Ave.
Wife 1st: Name not given, white, dead.
20-57-4-1 Myrtle Pego, P.O. Remus, Mich, see 2-62.
20-57-4-2 Fred Robinson, age 28, P.O. Stanbury, Missouri.
Wife: Name not given, white.
20-57-4-2-1 Bela Robinson (son), age 7.
20-57-4-2-2 Harley Robinson, age 5.
20-57-4-2-3 Marie Laura Robinson, age 3.
20-57-4-3 Chauncey Robinson, age 25, P.O. Grand Haven, Mich, single.
Wife 2nd: Name not given.
20-57-4-4 Clarence Robinson, age 14.
20-57-4-5 Mary Robinson, age 13.
20-57-4-6 Harold Robinson, age 10.

20-57-5 William Robinson, age 48, P.O. ~~Marion~~ Ceder Rapids, Iowa 1530 N. 4th St.
Wife: Name not given, white.
20-57-5-1 Dwight Robinson, age 23, Saratoga, Wash. (~~Montana~~), single.
20-57-5-2 Garnett ~~Pitzer~~ Pitcher (dau), age 22 Iowa(~~Marion~~).
20-57-5-3 Gaylord Livingston (dau), age 20 Cedar Rapids Iowa (~~Marion~~) 219 N 2nd St West.
Husband: Name not given, white.
20-57-5-3-1 Howard D. Livingston, age 1, born Jan/08.
20-57-5-4 Mary E. Robinson

20-57-6 Frank Robinson, age 46, P.O. Grand Rapids 205 Market St.
Wife: Name not given, white.
20-57-6-1 William Robinson, age 15, P.O. Grand Rapids 205 Market St..
20-57-6-2 Walter Robinson, age 13, P.O. Grand Rapids 205 Market St..

20-57-6-3 Maud Robinson, age 11.
20-57-6-4 John Robinson, age 9.
20-57-6-5 Earmel Robinson, age 4.
20-57-6-6 Caroline Robinson, age 2, P.O. Blind School, Milwaukee..

20-57-7 Annie Tripp, age 32, P.O. Grand Haven RFD1
Husband: Name not given, white.
20-57-7-1 Claud Tripp, age 14.
20-57-7-2 Laura Tripp, age 3.

20-57-8 John Robinson, age 30, P.O. Grand Rapids Mich Curve St.
Wife: Name not given, white.
20-57-8-1 Percy Robinson, age 4.

20-57-9 Jesse Robinson, age 28, P.O. Grand Rapids Mich Curve St.
Wife: Name not given, white.
20-57-9-1 Olive Robinson, age 6.

20-57-10 Ida ~~H~~ Tappan, age 40, P.O. Bangor, Mich.
Husband: Name not given, white.
20-57-10-1 Lee Tappan, age 24, Bangor, Mich, single.
20-57-10-2 Caddie Pitzer, age 22, name of husband not given and is white, no children.
20-57-10-3 Louise Tappan, age 18, Bangar, Mich.

Glen Haven Mich
April 21 1909
Horace B. Durant

Dear Sir,

As I have been told, you are going to make Indian payments, and, have been looking up most of them, and as they have passed me here at Glen Haven I felt it my duty to write you for a little information, as my father draws a payment and think I and my children are also entitled to it. I will write names on opposite side.

My name
Charles Robinson
Children Edward "
Chas. "
Frances "
Kenneth "
Lyle "
Dale "

Kindly write me information.
You find stamped envelope in my letter.
Very Respectfully
Charles Robinson

Glen Haven Mich.
United States Life Saving Station Sleeping Bear Point.

over

Mr Charles Robinson		*age 35 yr May 5 1909*
Edward	"	*age 15 yrs March 11/1909*
Chas	"	*age 12 yrs June 20/1908*
Girl Frances	"	*age 10 yrs Nov 25/1908*
Kenneth	"	*age 7 yrs July 12/1908*
Lyle	"	*age 5 yrs Sept 10/1908*
Dale	"	*age 3 yrs Oct 17/1908*

Mr Charles	*was*	*born*	*the*	*yr*	*1874*
Edward	"	"	"	"	*1894*
Chas	"	"	"	"	*1896*
Frances	"	"	"	"	*1898*
Kenneth	"	"	"	"	*1901*
Lyle	"	"	"	"	*1903*
Dale	"	"	"	"	*1906*

Dear Sir:
Please give the ages of yourself & children
Very respectfully
Horace B. Durant
Special U.S. Indian Agent
Apr 29/09

Stanberry Mo.
Jun 14 1909

Horace B. Durant
Petoskey Mich
Dear Sir
I willcomply with your request of June 9.
Fathers name. Geo. W. Robinson
Mothers " Clara (deceased)
Brothers " Chancey
Sisters " Mrs Myrtle Pego
I will be 30 the 13 of July, and my children ages are, Bela 9 Harley 6 Laura 4 Nera 1 month.
yours truly
Fred Robinson
Stanberry, Mo.

Information following from: John Duverney Mobis Lawrence.
21-57 PETER TAY-GWAW-SUNG or PETER LAWRENCE, dead.

Wife 1st: Name not given.
Wife 2nd: Betsey Generaux, age 55, P.O. Fountain, see 6-55 & 12-55.
21-57-1 Solomon Lawrence, age 45, P.O. Millerton.
Wife: Eliza Davis, nee Peters, age 40, P.O. Millerton, Saginaw Ind
21-57-1-1 Mary Lawrence, age 10.
21-57-1-2 Emma Lawrence, age 6.
21-57-1-3 Peter Lawrence, age 4.
21-57-2 Madeline Lawrence, dead, no heirs.
21-57-3 Moses Lawrence, age 35, P.O. Charlevoix (Wm Scogy's Camp)
Wife: Mary, age 38, same as Mary Petoskey, see 106-22, 1st husband Eson Petoskey.
21-57-3-1 Frank Lawrence, age 3, born June/08 died Sept/08
21-57-4 Frank Lawrence, age 32, P.O. Freesoil.
Wife: Mary Compeau, separated, see 5-58, three children indicated but not named, youngest on 2nd roll.
21-57-5 Sophia Lawrence, age 14, P.O. Harbor Springs School.

Horace B. Durant
Petoskey
Mich

Sturgeon Bay
Mich
June 22-1909

Dear Sir.
I received your letter about two weeks ago And I answered about that what you ask me.
My sister Mary E. Petoskey their or not married with Mobis Lawrence their just staying together. I'm ~~it~~ telling ~~the~~ you the truth, what you ask me.
Yours Truly
Mr. Mitchel S. Nanagos
Sturgeon Bay Mich.
Over
Say Mr Horace B. Durant
Will you kind and Please look for me work there in Petoskey some in Hotel to do some wash dishes or peel Potatoes I if you find one know will you PleaseMy name is Mr Mitchel S. Nanagos.

Information following from: David Fox Paw Paw.
22-57 KIN-NE-QUAY, dead.
Husband: Moses Ke-Way-Ge-Won, age 77, living, see 13-62 & 6-58.
22-57-1 Name or sex not given, dead
22-57-1-1Minnie Ke-Way-Ge-Won, P.O. Custer.
Husband: Peter Alexander, see 2-55, 12-32 & 6-58.

Information following from: Not Given.
23-57 MRS. CHARLES GENIA, dead, a daughter of Trombly.

Husband: Charles Genia, white, P.O. Soldier's Home, Grand Rapids, write & ask where child is.

23-57-1 Frank Genia, age 35+, P.O. Milwaukee or Chicago, see 21-49. Cannot find him. Durant June 3/09.

may 11 rockton ill
Dear Sir drop a few lines regards leter frank genia is my first coson where he is i don't know Henry genia my Brother i don't know where he is me i ant seen him 15 years Hord eny thing of him no Body knows troby mrs mary Osgood rockton ill

Information following from: Not Given.
24-57 ELI DUVERNEY, dead.
24-57-1 Dixie Duverney (dau).
Notes: Cannpt trace child. Durant Grand Haven Feby/09
Mary Thompson at Montoy at Whitehall is an aunt & may know. So says John Duverney May 18/09.

Information following from: Louis Speidle Gd Haven Feby/09.
25-57 MRS JACOB POOLE, dead, a sister of Mrs Jacob Speidle 9-56B.
Husband: Jacob Poole.
25-57-1 Name or sex not given, dead, no heirs.
25-57-2 Name or sex not given, dead, no heirs.
Note: Mrs. Jacob Poole's own children are dead leaving no heirs: The two children enrolled with her in 1870 were children of her sister Mrs Jacob Speidle (or Spidir) 9-56B see that sheet for all of children of Mrs Jacob Spider.

Information following from: Joe Cogswell Mch/09.
26-57 ANTOINE TOUCKEY, dead.
Wife: Name not given, dead.
26-57-1 Name or sex not given, dead.
26-57-1-1 Name or sex not given, dead, no heirs.
26-57-2 Name or sex not given, dead, no heirs.

Information following from: Not Given.
27-57 WILLIAM NAW-TAY, dead.
Wife: Name not given.
27-57-1 Henry ~~Nauty~~ Naw-Tay, ~~age 40, P.O. Grand Haven~~ dead.
Wife: Name not given, white, Died young.
27-57-2 Mary Swartz, age 43, P.O. Charlevoix, Mich.
Husband: Dan Swartz, white.
27-57-2-1 Grace E. Geneit, age 26, P.O. Charlevoix, Mich.
Husband: Name not given.
27-57-2-1-1 Alvina D. Geneit, born April 23. 1907.

27-57-2-2 Etta Gill, age 23.
Husband: Name not given.
27-57-2-2-1 Dorothy I. Gill, age 3.
27-57-2-2-2 Alfred A. Gill, born Jan 16, 1909 too late.
27-57-2-3 ~~Mary~~ Marion A. Swartz, age 19, single.
27-57-3 William Nontay, age 39, P.O. Grand Haven No 9 Clinton St
Wife: Name not given, white.
27-57-3-1 May Nontay, age 14.
27-57-3-2 Lawrence Nontay, age 11.
27-57-3-3 Louis Nontay, age 5.
27-57-4 Lillie Bourassaw, age 30, P.O. Charlevoix ~~Northport~~.
Husband: Louis Bourassaw, age 29, ~~at Light House, Fox Island, maybe an Indian~~, Mackinaw, son of Louis G & Josephine Bourissaw, see 51-14.

Enrolled Acknowledged D.

Grand Haven Mich
April 28 1909

Dear Sir.
Receiveda letter from my sister Mrs D. E. Bourissaw from Charlevoix stating, that you wanted my family names and ages. my name is Wm Noantay I am 39 years born May the 7 the year of 1870. my wife Kate Noantay 36 years born Oct 2 the year of 1873.
my daughter May Noantay 15 years born in May 25 in year of 1894
son Lawrence Noantay 11 years born Oct 30 the year 1898
son Louis Noantay 5 years born in Jan 22 year of 1904.
Yours Respectfully
Mr Wm Noantay
No 9 Clinton st Grand Haven Mich

Information following from: Wm Badeux, Muskegon Grand Haven Feby/09.
28 SHEET #1:
28-57 MICHAEL BEDDOE, age 52, P.O. Freemont Center, Mich.
Wife: Jennie F., white, off.
28-57-1 Emma M. Beddoe, age 18.
28-57-2 Mitchell Beddoe, age 12.
28-57-3 Thelma Beddoe, age 8.

Ask about brother Geo Baddaux in Minnesota letter May 1/09.

Freemont Mich
April 24 1909

Dear Sir I received your leter and i will give his Adress it is Eva Bonce Femont Mich RFD i fond to his and told his she has 3 Children but a don't know the ages Can you tell Me everything When they Will Drow the Money as i Wold like to Move a Way i Will give My Trailer i and 52 past May.

My Name Mitchell Badaux My Wiefs Jenie F Badaux 3 Children
Emma M Badaux 19
Mistell J Badaux 18
thellna L Badaux 9 in May

28 SHEET #2:
28-57 GEORGE BEDDOE now BADEAUX, age 60, P.O. Brainard, Minn
103 NE Pine.
Wife: Name not given, white.
28-57-1 Eleanor Doty, age 38.
28-57-2 Daisy Thabes, age 36.
28-57-3 William B. Badeaux, age 33.
28-57-4 Annie L. Goryh, age 31.
28-57-5 George Irving Badeaux, age 20.

Brainerd May 18-1909

H.B.Durant, Peloske Mich
Ddepartment of the Interior D.C.

Dear Sir:

M reply to yours of 5/18 – will state – May 20/ will be Sixty two this coming August. My family consist of Wife and five children, the eldest Mrs Eleanore Doty is thirty nine years old (39) Mrs Daisy A. Thabes thirty – Seven (37) Mrs Annie L Gough – thirty two (32) Willard B. Badeaux thirty four (34) Geo Irving Badeaux twenty one (21). Please address all communications tomy addres 103 – N.E. Pine Brainerd Minn.

Yours Respectfully
Geo Badeaux

Information following from: Not Given.
29-57 JOSEPH BADDOE & niece, dead.
Wife: Name not given, dead.
29-57-1 Ed Baddoux, 35, P.O. Holton, Mich, single.
29-57-2 Victor Baddoux, age 28, P.O. Chicago, wife's name not given, she is white, no children.
29-57-3 Eva Bonce, P.O. ~~Holton, or~~ Freemont RFD.
26-57-4 Mary Lafferty, niece, see 4-56.

Information following from: William Badaux Muskegon Feby/09.
30-57 WILLIAM BEDDOE or BADAUX, dead.
Wife 1st: Name not given, white.
Wife 2nd: Name not given, white, living, P.O. Muskegon.
30-57-1 Lena Martin, age 40, Elgin, Ill

Husband: Name not given, white.
30-57-1-1 ~~George~~ Genevieve Martin, age 15.
30-57-1-2 Donald Martin, age 13.
30-57-2 Rose Dacher Gatechair, age 38, P.O. Elgin, Ill, husband name not given, no children.
30-57-3 William Badaux, age 32, P.O. Muskegon, Mich, single.
30-57-4 Perry Badaux, age 28, P.O. Muskegon, Mich.
Wife: Name not given, white.
30-57-4-1 Perry Badaux Jr., age 3.
Author Note: No indication of which child was born by which wife.

Elgin Ill.
June 16, 1909.

Horace B. Durant;
Dear Sir;
In reply to yours of June 9, would say that my name before marriage was Miss Lina B. Badeaux. My parents are Mr~~s~~ & Mrs. Wm Badeaux. Brothers, Pierr Badeaux and Wm Badeaux Jr. My sister, was Miss Rose Badeaux, now Mrs. Lewis Gatechair. My age is 44, My children Miss Genevieve B Martin is 17 years of age and Donald Martin 14 yrs. I shall probably be in Muskeon during the summer, with my parents, so whatever further communication you may have with me please address Me at My father's address.
Mrs. Lina B. Martin
17 Palmer St. Muskegon Mich

Information following from: Not Given.
31-57 NE-GON-NE-KE-ZHICK or LEWIS THOMAS, age 53, P.O. Free Soil, see 3-61A.
Wife 1st: Mary Smith, dead.
31-57-1 Charley Thomas, age 33, P.O. Free Soil.
Wife: Martha Newton or Nodin, age 40, P.O. Free Soil.
31-57-1-1 Mary Thomas, age 1, born Aug/07 2nd roll.
31-57-1-2 Infant Thomas, age 1 mo, girl born July/08 NB 2nd roll.
31-57-2 William Thomas, age 28, P.O. Ashton Mich, see 17-56.
Wife: Mary Hall Thomas, age 35, see 2-60 & 8-50.
31-57-2-1 ___ Thomas, age 3, died Mch 1st/08 NB 1st roll.
31-57-3 Thomas Thomas, age 22, P.O. Ashton, Mich, single.
31-57-4 Moses Thomas, age 15, P.O. Ashton, Mich, single.
Wife 2nd: Margaret Peters, age 40, P.O. Honor, separated, no children by this wife, see 17-50 & 21-50.

Information following from: Grand Haven.
32-57 KAW-BE-NAW, dead, no children

Information following from: Charles Webb.
33-57 ALIXSIE ST. PIERRE, dead.
Husband: None given.
33-57-1 Mrs. Charles Webb, on 1870 roll by that name, see 15-56A for children.
33-57-2 Mary Wah-Be-Gay-Kake, see 1-58, husband dead & name not given.
33-57-3 Antoine St. Pierre, on 1870 roll as 34-57.

Information following from: Mrs Charles Webb a daughter Mch/09.
34-57 ANTOINE ST. PIERRE, dead, no heirs.

Information following from: Grand Haven Feby 23/09.
35-57 JOSEPH CHING-GWAW, dead, no heirs.

Information following from: Benjamin Trombly Nov 24/08 Dec 26/08.
36-57 BENJAMIN TROMBLY, age 65, P.O. Bay Shore.
Wife: Rose Trombly, age 30, P.O. Bay Shore, Traverse, see 23-23.
36-57-1 Therese Trombly, age 76, P.O. Bay Shore Pellston.
Note: This is an adopted child of Indian parents. Right name is Esther Gilbert, see 19-28.
36-57-2 Grace Trombly, age 4 6.

Information following from: Not Given.
37-57 KEY-SHE-GE-WAW
Note: Indians do not recall this name. Durant Grand Haven Feby/09

Information following from: Not Given.
38-57 MAW-CHE-AW-SE-GAY-QUAH, dead.
Husband: Name not given.
38-57-1 Amos Fitch or Ah-Be-Naw-Be, lived wit hJoseph Elliott.
38-57-2 Sah-Wah-Be-Non-Quay (sex not given)

Information following from: James Paul, Interpreter Northport.
39-57 PETER SHAW-SHAW-GWAY-SHE spelled now SHO-SHO-GUAY, age 63, P.O. Gill's Pier, Mich.
Wife: Margaret (Ma-Da-Go-Me), age 50, P.O. Gill's Pier, Mich, a Traverse Ind, see 2-38.
39-57-1 Louis Sho-Sho-Guay, age 28, P.O. Gill's Pier.
Wife: Madeline (Nah-Gon-Say), age 27, Gill's Pier.
39-57-2 Alex Sho-Sho-Guay, age 18, P.O. Genoa Sch. Nebr.
39-57-3 Francis Sha-Sha-Guay, age 9, 1st roll, died June 10, 1907.

Information following from: Not Given.

40-57 ROBERT SHAW-SHAW-GWAY-SHE, dead, see 11-61.

Information following from: Not Given.
41-57 MINNIE DUCHESNE now MRS MINNIE VAN ZEE, P.O. Holland, Mich, moved from Holland to Grand Rapids. Husband (name not givn) kept a saloon in Holland.

Information following from: Gd Haven Feby/09.
42-57 SHAW-WAW-DAY-QUAY, dead, no heirs.

Information following from: Mary Vandenberg Grand Haven Feby/09.
43-57 NELLIE VANDERBURGH, ~~P.O. Grand Haven~~ dead, ~~daughter of John B. Perret see~~ daughter of Mary Duverney, deceased.
    Husband: ________ McClellan.
    43-57-1 Minnie, dead.
        ~~Husband: Will Hall, white P.O. Muskegon.~~
        ~~43-57-1-1 Pearl Steorns, age 18, P.O. White Hall,~~ child by another husband (married to 18-56B).
    43-57-2 Eva McClellan Bieneman, age 25, P.O. Kenosha, Wis.
        Husband: Name not given, white.
        43-57-2-1 James Bieneman, age 4.
        43-57-2-2 Jack Bieneman, age 2.
    43-57-3 William McClellan known as William Vandenberg, age 20, P.O. Grand Have Mich. Two unnamed children died without issue.

Information following from: Gd Haven Feby/09.
44-57 HELEN CURTIS, dead, no heirs.

Information following from: Not Given.
45-57 PETER ST. PETER'S family.
    Author Note: No information sheet(s) found for the family.

Page 58A
Chief PAY-QUO-TUSH
Grand River

Information following from: Custer 2/19/09.
1-58A PAY-QUO-TUSK, dead.
    Wife: Name not given, dead.
    1-58A-1 Name not given, dead.
        Husband: George Baker, see 29-59.
        1-58A-1-1 Joe Baker, age 19.
        1-58A-1-2 Adam Baker

& others see 29-59.
1-58A-2 Name or sex not given, dead.
1-58A-3 Name or sex not given, dead.

Information following from: Not Given.
2-58A BATTISE BAILEY, age 84, P.O. Custer No2.
Author Note: no indication which wife iis mother of which child.
Wife 1st: Name not given, dead.
Wife 2nd: Sophia Bailey nee Ke-Ne-Sway, age 75, see 8-56A.
2-58A-1 Jacob Bailey, age 50, P.O. Walkerville.
Wife: Nancy Carey, see 2-49.
2-58A-1-1 Delos Bailey, age 28, not married.
2-58A-1-2 Andrew Bailey, age 22, not married.
2-58A-1-3 Mary Bailey, age 19.
Husband: Henry Negake, no children.
2-58A-1-4 Annie or Amy Bailey, age 17.
2-58A-1-5 Maggie Bailey #2, age 15.
2-58A-2 Charley Bailey #1, age 47, P.O. Millerton.
Wife 1st: Name not given, dead.
2-58A-2-1 Sophia McClellan, age 27, P.O. Custer #2.
Husband: James McClellan, for children see 29-59.
Wife 2nd: Maggie or Angeline (Pete) Bailey #1, age 30, see 3-53.
2-58A-2-2 Eliza Bailey, age 12.
2-58A-2-3 Peter Bailey, age 2.
2-58A-2-4 Infant Bailey, born Aug 13, 1908, off do not enroll.
Children by 1st husband of Maggie Pete Bailey.
Husband 2nd: George (Pete) Joseph, at Petoskey (see 14-54), cannot find George Joseph by that name. Durant.
14-54-1 Louis Joseph, age 19, P.O. Millerton.
14-54-2 Martha Joseph, age 17, P.O. Millerton.
Husband: Michael Cogswell, separated, see 11-54.
2-58A-3 Mary Bailey, left home when 6 years old & has not been seen – went down Missis. R. to Missouri. Information too indefinite to enroll.
2-58A-4 Peter Bailey, dead.
Wife: ~~Abbie~~ Eva Bailey, now wife of George Hineman, see 19-55, 2-56 & 21-46.
2-58A4-1 Lucy Bailey, age 14, P.O. Custer.
2-58A4-2 Philip Bailey, age 12, P.O. Custer.
2-58A4-3 Mary Bailey, age 8, P.O. Custer.
2-58A-5 David Peter Pete, age 6, adopted, (father Peter Pete), lived with Bailey since child entited to enrollment.

Information following from: Not Given.

Note: William was not paid on Grand River but was on Traverse.

3-58A SAMUEL KAW-GE-GAY-BE or SAMUEL PAY-QUO-TUSH, age 65, P.O. Chief Lake, Travers, see 21-44, Drew with Potts himself only.

Wife 1st: Name not given, dead.

3-58A-1 William Pay-Quo-Tush or William Sam, age 47, P.O. Fountain.

Wife: Nancy Micko, age 47, sister of William Micko, P.O. Fountain.

3-58A-1-1 George Pay-Quo-Tush, age 23, P.O. Fountain.

Wife: Maggie Pe-An-O Sam, age 19, see 14-54 for children.

3-58A-1-1-1 John Pay-Quo-Tush, age 3.

3-58A-1-1-2 Mary Ann Pay-Quo-Tush, born Aug/1908 NB 2nd roll.

3-58A-1-2 Eunice Sam, age 16, lives with William Sam.

Husband: James Pete, separated, see 19-54.

3-58A-1-2-1 Mary Pete, born Nov 9, 1907 NB 2nd roll.

3-58A-2 Pete Quo-Mo-Quay or Mary Pay-Quo-Tush James, P.O. Honor.

Husband: ~~John~~ Henry James, P.O. Honor, Traverse, for children see 13-44.

3-58A-3 Maggie Sam or Agnes Robinson, age 15, P.O. Chief Lake, adopted, daughter of John Robinson an Ottawa living in Oceana Co near Knox's Mill, see 6-62.

3-58A-4 Joseph Sam, age 47, P.O. Chief Lake, Mich, adopted grandson of 5-44.

Wife: Jane Sam, age 50, (see 2-58).

3-58A-4-1 Charles Thomas or Charles Sam, age 9, adopted whose ~~father~~ mother dead. His mother was a daughter of Joseph Cogswell. He now goes by the name of Charley Sam.

Wife 2nd: Wew-Te-Quo-She-Qua or Elizabeth Pay-Quo-Tush, age 65, P.O. Chief Lake, see 26-59.

May 13 1909

Dear Sir

I give you the name of my Father and mother my Fathers name Sam Kahgegoba my mother Mary ~~Ogahbageshegogy~~ Ogahbagshegoquay my mother died 80 years ago my Father live that is all you can find the on Kewagoskhom Chief that is all I want you to tell me when you get don't this matter I want you tell me the truth

Your truly

Julia Wahsayquoumge

NorthPort mich

Information following from: 2/19/08.
4-58A NAW-WE-KE-GE-GO-QUAY, dead.
Note: Indians do not remember who her children are. Durant.

Information following from: Not Given.
5-58A MRS. DAVID SMITH or MRS. LYDIA ARMSTRONG, age 79, P.O. Montagne, Mich.
Wife 1st: ______ Smith, white, dead.
Wife 2nd: George Armstrong, white, dead, see 7-58.
5-58A-1 Sarah Robinson, age 51, P.O. Montague.
Husband: Mack Robinson, white.
5-58A-1-1 George Robinson, age 22, P.O. Montague, wife name not given, white, no children..
5-58A-1-2 Edna Robinson, age 16.
5-58A-1-3 Evaline Irene Robinson, age 10.
5-58A-1-4 William Robinson, age 12, adopted, see 3-59.
5-58A-2 Martha Robinson, age 49, P.O. Montague, Mich.
Husband: Name not given, white.
5-58A-2-1 Lizzie Keho, age 32, P.O. Chicago, Ills 531 E 50 Place.
Husband: Name not given, white.
5-58A-2-1-1 James Keho, born Dec 1907.
5-58A-2-2 Fred Robinson, age 29, P.O. Montague, single.
5-58A-2-3 Oliver Robinson, age 27, P.O. Montague, single.
5-58A-2-4 Jerome Robinson, age 27, P.O. Montague, Mich.
Wife: Name not given, wife.
5-58A-2-4-1 Oliver Robnson Jr., age 6.
5-58A-2-4-2 Elenor Robinson, age 4.
5-58A-2-4-3 Mary Robinson, born Mch 1908.
5-58A-2-5 Lydia Robinson, age 25, P.O. Montague, single
5-58A-2-6 Margaret Robinson Aley, age 22, Montague, husband name not given white, no children.
5-58A-2-7 Jessie Robinson, age 15, single.
5-58A-3 George Armstrong, age 43, P.O. Shattack, Okla.
Wife: Name not given, white.
5-58A-3-1 Gertrude Armstrong, age 18, P.O. Shattack, Okla, single.
5-58A-3-2 Lydia Armstrong #2, age 13.
5-58A-3-3 Dora Armstrong, age 12.
5-58A-3-4 Elizabeth Armstrong, age 10.
5-58A-3-5 Eddie Armstrong, age 8.
5-58A-3-6 Esther Armstrong, age 4.

Information following from: 2/19/09.

6-58A KEY-WAY-GAW-BO-WE, dead.
6-58A-1 Mary Wah-Bin-Dwetto, see 7-52.
Husband: Luke Wah-Bin-Dwetto, see 7-52.

Information following from: Custer 2/19/09.
7-58A QUAY-SE-MO-QUAY, dead.
7-58A-1 Pete Anderson, see 13-55.
7-58A-2 Jacob Anderson, see 14-58.
7-58A-3 Mrs. David Smith, see 5-58 1870 Roll.

Information following from: Not Given.
8-58A JOHN PAY-QUO-QUSK, dead.
Wife: Name not given, dead.
Note: No living descendants Ok D 2/19/09.

Information following from: Not Given.
9-58A WAW-ZHOW or JOHN WAY-ME-GWAS, age 60, P.O. Chief Lake.
Wife 1st: Name not given, dead.
9-58A-1 Maw-Beece or Maw-Beece Walker, P.O. Mt Pleasant, Mich, single, see 1-50.
Wife 2nd: Helen, now wife of William Chetfield Mt. Pleasant, a Saginaw Indian.
Wife 3rd: Jennie Hineman Way-Me-Gwas, age 48, daughter of Wallace Hineman, see 1-53. Children by her 1st husband John Theodore are: (see 27-59)
1 Ben Theodore, age 23.
2 Nelson Theodore, age 19.
3 Maggie Theodore, age 17.
4 James Theodore, age 14.
5 Paul Theodore, age 11.

Information following from: Not Given.
10-58A SHAW-WAW, dead, no heirs.

Information following from: Custer 2/19/09.
11-58A ME-TE-MO-SAY-GAW, dead, no descendants.

Information following from: Custer 2/19/09.
12-58A ME-SE-WAY-BE-QUAY, dead.
12-58A-1 Mary Smith Fitch, see 7-55.
Husband: Amos Fitch, see 7-55 & 9-55.
12-58A-2 Name not given, dead.
Husband: ________ King, dead.
12-58A-2-1 Joe King, age 23, P.O. Freesoil.
Wife: Name not given, dead, was daughter of Amos

Fitch, see 9-55 & 4-60.

12-58A-2-1-1 Alice King, age 2, lives with Amos Fitch, see 9-55.

12-58A-2-2 Watson King, see 4-60 & 34-60.

12-58A-2-3 John King, see 4-60 & 34-60.

Information following from: Custer 2/19/09.

13-58A MIN-SE-NO-SCAW, dead, never married.

Information following from: Information from head of family.

14-58A NE-GAW-NAW-NAW-QUOT or JACOB ANDERSON, age 60, P.O. Elk Rapids.

Wife 1st : Sarah Aiken, dead.

14-58A-1 Edward Anderson, age 32, P.O. Elk Rapids, Traverse.

Wife: Thresa (Round Sky) Anderson, age 26, P.O. Elk Rapids, granddau of 6-44.

14-58A-1-1 Eddie Anderson, age 8, P.O. Elk Rapids.

14-58A-1-2 Lucy Anderson, age 6, P.O. Elk Rapids.

14-58A-1-3 Thomas Anderson, age 5, P.O. Elk Rapids.

14-58A-1-4 Lizzie Anderson, age 1, March 23/07 Sept 28 NB 2nd roll.

Wife 2nd: Name not given.

Wife 3rd: Stella Anderson, age 56, P.O. Elk Rapids, an Ind of Cross Village ban, see 15-20.

Page 58B
Chief WAW-BE-GAY-KAKE
Grand River

Information following from: Not Given.

1-58B WAW-BE-GAY-KAKE ~~or JOSEPH~~, dead

Wife: Name not given, dead.

1-58B-1 Rosie Way-Be-Gay-Kake, dead, 1st wife of Joseph Memberto, children see 9-54.

1-58B-2 George Way-Be-Gay-Kake, dead, no wife or child.

1-58B-3 Joe Way-Be-Gay-Kake, dead, same as 9-58.

Wife: Mary Way-Be-Gay-Kake, age 73, P.O. Lattin, a sister of Mrs.. Charles Webb 16-56B.

1-58B-3-1 Joseph Way-Be-Gay-Kake, age 48, P.O. Lattin, no wife or child, crippled.

1-58B-3-2 Mary Wah-Be-Sis, age 32, P.O. Lattin.

Husband: Name not given, see 28-52.

1-58B-3-2-1 Lucy Wah-Be-Sis, age12.

1-58B-3-2-2 Paul Wah-Be-Sis, age 10.

1-58B-3-2-3 George Wah-Be-Sis, age 8.

1-58B-3-3 Louis Way-Be-Gay-Kake, age 27, P.O. Lattin.

Wife: Lizzie Battise Way-Be-Gay-Kake, age 18, sup said she drew with Potts..

1-58B-3-3-1 Alex Way-Be-Gay-Kake, born March 1908 NB 2nd roll.

1-58B-4 William Way-Be-Gay-Kake, dead, see 13-58.

1-58B-5 Mary Cogswell, dead, husband Joe Cogswell, see 23-54.

1-58B-6 Lucy Louis, dead, husband Mitchell Louis, see 20-49.

Information following from: James Aken Lattin Aug/08 Jacob Aken #2 Petoskey Dec 1/08.

2-58B AKEN LAMARANDIERE, dead.

Wife 1st: Name not given, dead, 1 child 3-58.

Wife 2nd: Mary, dead.

2-58B-1 Thade Akins (son), dead, no children.

2-58B-2 Steve Akins, age 70, P.O. Honor.

Wife 1st: Name not given.

2-58B-3-1 Jacob Akens #1, age 40.

Wife: Agnes Bailey, see 3-50, no children.

2-58B-3-2 Andrew Akins, age 35, P.O. Ashland, Wis.

Wife 2nd : Mary (Bailey) Wakefield Akens, age 40, see 13-53 & 14-50.

2-58B-3-3 Amy Akins, age 6.

2-58B-3 Jane (Akins) Sam, age 50, P.O. Bear Creek, Manistee Co, see 3-58.

2-58B-4 James Akin, age 48, P.O. Lattin.

Wife 1st: Betsey Skinhorn, dead

Wife 2nd: Helen Cogswell Akin, see 11-54.

Author Note: No indication which wife is mother of which child.

2-58B-4-1 Louis Akin, died Nov 1907.

Wife: Amy Louis, age 20, P.O. Elbridge, Lattin, Mich, see 1-49.

2-58B-4-2 Jacob Akin #3, age 5.

2-58B-5 Sarah (Akin) ~~Gluett~~ Gruett, age 45, P.O. Mt. Pleasant, Mich.

Husband: Name not given, Saginaw Indian.

2-58B-5-1 Ambrose Stone, age 23, P.O. Mt. Pleas., see 13-58.

2-58B-5-2 Paul Gruett, age 9, P.O. Mt. Pleas., see 13-58.

2-58B-6 No information given.

2-58B-7 Charles, dead, not married.

2-58B-8 Mitchell, dead, not married.

2-58B-9 Margaret, dead, not married.

Petoskey Mich
Horace B. Durant, Newaygo Mich

Special U.S. Indian Agent May 10, 1909
Dear Sir,-
You wanted to know how many children I had and their ages
And my father's name was Lexie Lamorandiere.
And my mother's name was Sophia Tag-ques-sung maiden name .
And their ages not known.
My nationality is Ottawa. "continued below"

Louie Aiken	*Age*	---	*22*
Bud Aiken	*Age*	---	*20*
Fred Aiken	*Age*	---	*15*
Lawrence Aiken	*Age*	---	*11*
Gkadys Aiken	*Age*	---	*9*
Geneva Aiken	*Age*	---	*7*
Thomas Aiken Jr.	*Age*	---	*2*

Father Thomas Aiken. Sr. Lamorandieres
My wife's is a white women.
We do not know where Louie Aiken is at present. Send his mail to Nevaygo, Mich.,
Yours Truly
Thomas Aiken
My father's name was Alex Aiken.
My mother's name was Sophia Lawrence.

Information following from: Jacob Lamarandiere or Jacob Aiken #2 Petoskey Dec 1/08.
3-58B ALEXIE LAMARANDIERE, dead.
Wife: Name not given, dead.
3-58B-1 Jacob Aiken #2, age 43, P.O. Newaygo Mich, see 3-56.
Wife: Name not given, white.
3-58B-1-1 Daniel Aken, age 19, P.O. Newaygo Mich.
3-58B-1-2 Dorsey Aken, age 16, P.O. Newaygo.
3-58B-1-3 Dora Aken, age 13, P.O. Newaygo.
3-58B-1-4 Delsie Aken, age 11, P.O. Newaygo.
3-58B-1-5 Daisy Aken, age 8, P.O. Newaygo.
3-58B-1-6 Douglas Aken, age 6, P.O. Newaygo.
3-58B-2 Mary, dead.
Husband: Charles Pego, age ~~40~~ 24, P.O. Elbridge, son of John Pego, see 5-62, has 2 children by 1st wife.
3-58B-3 Lucy, dead.
Husband: William Battise or William Deverney, see 4-59. For 2nd wife see 4-59.
3-58B-3-1 Charles Deverney, age 23, see 2-54 & 4-59.
3-58B-4 Susan, dead, no children.
3-58B-5 Nesette, dead, no children.

3-58B-6 Thomas Aken, age 41, P.O. Newaygo.

Wife: Name not given , white.

3-58-6-1 Louis Aken, age 22, P.O. Grand Rapids, single.

3-58-6-2 Bud Aken, age 20, P.O. Newago, single.

3-58-6-3 Fred Aken, age 15, P.O. Newago.

3-58-6-4 Lawrence Aken, age 11, P.O. Newago.

3-58-6-5 Gladys Aken, age 9, P.O. Newago.

3-58-6-6 Geneva Aken, age 6, P.O. Newago.

3-58-6-7 Thomas Aken, age 1, born July 25, 1907.

3-58B-7 Robert Aken, age 39, P.O. Newago.

Wife: Julia (Poneshing), age 32, see 21-54 & 20-49.

3-58B-7-1 Louisa Aken, age 13.

3-58B-7-2 Clarence Aken, age 9.

3-58B-7-3 Alex Aken, age 7.

May 10 1909

Newaygo Mich

Dear Sir Horace B Durant Special U.S. indian Agent I received your letter here other day i now answer it you ask me my children ages, and also my father and my mothers They wore ottawa tribe indian. They ar both dead. They been dead for some time. My mother is maden is ~~Sophia~~ name Sophia Tag-ques-sung or Lawrence in English Better known is sophia Aiken. My father is name Alex Lamorandiere or Alex Aiken Better known. Now my children names aare as follows.

Daniel Aiken	*age*	*19*
Dorsey Aiken	*age*	*16*
Dora Aiken	*age*	*14*
Dalcie Aiken	*age*	*11*
Dasy Aiken	*age*	*8*
Dougles Aiken	*age*	*6*

And now my wife is a white woman I belong to ottawa.

Yours Truly

Jacob Lamorandiere Better known is Jacob Aike Newaygo mich

Information following from: Not Given.

4-58B PAY-CHE-KE-ZHICK, dead.

Author Note: No indication given which wife is mother of which child.

Wife 1st: Name not given, dead.

Wife 2nd: Name not given, dead.

4-58B-1 Sam Marsh, age 65, P.O. Freesoil.

Wife: Name not given, dead, see 10-52.

4-58B-2 Charles Marsh, age 60.

Wife: ~~Eliza Tipsco Saginaw Indian, dead~~ dead.

4-58B-2-1 Dan Marsh, age 30, P.O. Bear Lake, see 4-61.
4-58B-2-2 Charles Marsh, dead.
Wife: Eliza Tipsco. A Saginaw Ind. off.
4-58B-2-2-1 Edward Marsh, age 19, P.O. Leaton, Mich.
4-58B-2-2-2 Grace ~~Agohgo~~ Shawbose, age 8, P.O. Walpole Island or Mt. Pleasant, Child of Eliza Tipsco by John ~~Agohgo~~ Shawbose, see 36-52
4-58B-3 Anderson Marsh, dead.
Wife: Name not given, dead.
4-58B-3-1 James Marsh, age 22, P.O. Freesoil, not married.
4-58B-4 Name not given, dead.
Husband: John Agohgo, P.O. Dorr, Mich, see 19-52.
4-58B-5 Name or sex not given, dead, no heirs.

Information following from: Not Given.
5-58B PAY-ME-SAW-AW or PETER COMPAUX, age 80, P.O. Freesoil.
Wife: Name not given, dead.
5-58B-1 Nancy Pontiac Ninise, age 39, P.O. Freesoil, see 7-65.
Husband 1st: Henry Pontiac.
5-58B-1-1 George Ninise, age 19, P.O. Freesoil, right name George Pontiac goes by name of Ninise.
Husband 2nd: ______ Casey, dead.
5-58B-1-2 Paul Casey, age 14, P.O. Freesoil.
5-58B-1-3 Albert Casey, age 12, P.O. Freesoil.
5-58B-1-4 Abbie Casey, age 10.
5-58B-1-5 James Casey, age 8.
5-58B-1-6 Elizabeth Casey, age 6.
Husband 3rd: Mitchell Ninise, age 31, P.O. Freesoil, Canadian Ind. off. Note: NB Mitchell Ninise is not a Grand River but probably belongs to some of other bands up north. Do not carrie until family is found.
5-58B-1-7 George Ninise (Nin-Eece), age 3.
5-58B-1-8 Josie Ninise, age 2.
5-58B-1-9 Jessie Ninise, age 9mos,born Nov 2 1907 NB 2nd roll.
5-58B-2 Otto Compeaux, age 36, P.O. Freesoil.
Wife: Maggie Josiah, age 22, daughter of Frank Josiah, dead, see 19-55.
5-58B-2-1 Paul Compeaux, died Nov 1/07 N.B. 1st roll.
5-58B-3 Mary Lawrence, age 29, P.O. Freesoil.
Husband: Frank Lawrence, P.O. Freesoil, see 21-57.
5-58B-3-1 Sarah Lawrence, age 7.
5-58B-3-2 Madaline Lawrence, age 3.
5-58B-3-3 Lizzie Lawrence, age1, born Jany 1907.

* Freesoil Inds do say Mitchell Ninise's parents were Grand River Inds but left here & went North.

Peter Alexander Age 29
Father – William Alexander.
Mother – Bimasawckwe Mesinebekwe
Wife – Minnie Alexander
her father Joseph Kiwegwan ←Kewaygewon
her mother Nejigabawekwe Betawegejik ← Petwagezhick HBD
Your childrens names 1 Rosie Alexander 20 mo.
and ages 2 Frances Alexander 6 wks.

Information following from: Not Given.
6-58B KEY-WAY-CHE-WON MOSES, age 77, P.O. Bradley, Mich.
Wife: Name not given, dead, see 13-62.
6-58B-1 Joseph Key-Way-Che-Won, dead.
Wife: Name not given, dead.
6-58B-1-1 Minnie or Mary Ann (Key-Way-Che-Won) Alexander , age 26, P.O. Bradley.
Husband: Pete Alexander, age ~~35~~ 29, see 12-32 & 2-51.
6-58B-1-1-1 Rosie Alexander, age ~~21~~ born Aug 21/07.
6-58B-2 Name or sex not given, no heirs.

Information following from: Not Given.
7-58B AWW-ZHE-WAY-KE-ZHICK, dead, wife dead not named, no heirs.

Information following from: Mount Pleasant, Michigan.
8-58B AW-ZHONCE, dead.
8-58B-1 Dick Richards or Aish-Ga-Bay, age 70, P.O. Weidman, single.
8-58B-2 ~~Mrs Moses~~ Mary Jackson, see 2-50.
Report: Dick Richards, being 70 years old, it is puzzling to me that he was not enrolled by himself as the head of a family in 1870, altho I am unable with the assistance of himself & many of the older Indians of the same band, to so locate him, and, as he and all affirm that he is a Grand River Indian & drew an allotment as such, he is therefore enrolled. Horace B Durant Spl. Agt, Jany 19/09-: Weidman, Mich.

Information following from: Not Given.
9-58B NE-SAW-KEE, dead, see 1-58.

Information following from: Not Given.
10-58B ME-SKO-GWON, dead, no heirs.

Information following from: Not Given.
11-58B MAW-CHE-O-QUIS or JOE FOX, dead.
Wife: Name not given, dead.
11-58B-1 Name or sex not given.
11-58B-1-1 Gertie Wah-Bin-Dwetto, see 12-58.

Information following from: Not Given.
12-58B QUAW-QUAW, dead.
Husband: Name not given, dead.
12-58B-1 Joe Fox, dead, on roll as 11-58.
Wife: Name not given, dead.
12-58B-1-1 Gertie Koon, now the wife of Hank Wah-Bin-Dwetto, see 11-58.
12-58B-2 Mary Elliott, P.O. Fountain, husband David Elliott 3-55, no children.
12-58B-3 Henry Fox, age 56, P.O. Lattin, no wife or child.

Information following from: Not Given.
13-58B WILLIAM WAW-BE-GAY-KAKE or STONE, dead.
Wife 1st: Elizabeth, dead.
13-58B-1 Shon-Yap, dead.
13-58B-2 Rosie, P.O. Petoskey, see 2-26 & 4-26.
Husband: Enos Ke-Way-Ge-Zhick, Traverse Band, see 4-26.
13-58B-3 Elizabeth, dead.
Husband: Pete Po-Ne-Shing, see 21-54.
13-58B-4 Neal Stone, age 35, P.O. Cobmosa.
Wife: Mary Ne-Gake, see 11-53.
13-58B-4-1 Elizabeth Stone, age 9.
13-58B-4-2 James Stone, age7.
13-58B-4-3 Joseph Stone, age5.
13-58B-4-4 Moses Stone, age 2.
Wife 2nd: ~~Lizzie Gluett~~ Sarah Gruett, living neat Mt. Pleasant.
Husband: Ambrose Stone, age 24, P.O. ~~Stomer's probably at Lawrence Sch heard gone in May 1908 Empire June Mich~~ Mt. Pleasant, unmarried,

Information following from: Not Given.
14-58B WAW-BE-TUNG-GWAY-SE, dead, child dead, no heirs.

Information following from: Not Given.
15-58B ME-SAW-CAW-ME-GO-QUAY, dead, no heirs.

Page 59
Chief PAY-SHAW-SE-GAY
Grand River

Information following from: Not Given.
1-59 PAY-SHAW-SE-GAY, dead.
Wife: Name not given, dead.
1-59-1 Name or sex not given, dead, 15-59.
1-59-1-1 Andrew Light, age 38, see 15-59 for wife & child.
1-59-2 Name or sex not given, dead.

Information following from: Not Given.
2-59 SHAW-BWAW-SE-GAY or GEORGE.
Wife: Name not given.
2-59-1 Pay-Baw-Me, dead, never married, sex not given.
2-59-2 Thresa ~~SeKinshe~~ Skinhorn, age 57, P.O. Cob-moosa East of Lattin.
Husband: Charles Skinhorn, dead.
2-59-2-1 Margaret Shay-Go-Nay-Be, age 33, P.O. Cob-moosa.
Husband: Pete Shay-Go-Nay-Be, see 2-54.
2-59-2-1-1 Minnie Shay-Go-Nay-Be.
2-59-2-1-2 Name not given.
2-59-2-1-3 Name not given.
2-59-2-2 John Skinhorn, age 17, P.O. Cobmoosa.
2-59-3 Angeline Shaw-Bwaw-Se-Gay, dead, no children.
2-59-4 Margaret Shaw-Bwaw-Se-Gay, dead, no children.
2-59-5 Mary Shaw-Bwaw-Se-Gay, dead, no children.
2-59-6 Susan Shaw-Bwaw-Se-Gay, dead, no children.
2-59-7 Simon Shaw-Bwaw-Se-Gay, dead.
Wife: Maud Shag-Wab-No, in Mt Pleasant & married again.
2-59-7-1 Pete Shaw-Bwaw-Se-Gay, age 20, in Mt Pleasant School.
2-59-8 Gus Shaw-Bwaw-Se-Gay, dead, no children.

Department of the Interior,
United States Indian Service,
Mount Pleasant Indian School,
Mt. Pleasant, Mich., May 21, 1909.

Mr. Horace B. Durant,
Special U. S. Indian Agent,
Petoskey, Michigan.

Dear Sir:

Your letter of the 19th instant, asking whether we have a man in school here at Mt. Pleasant by the name of PeteShawbwawsegay, at hand.

In reply I would say that we have no manin school of that name. The nearest to it is a boy, fourteen years of age, by the name of Peter Shagonaby. His mother is Mrs. Mary Shagonaby of Freesoil, Michigan. Some of the puples here, who know the family, say that boy's father and mother are living together at the present time, so I hardly think she will be the person you are looking for.

Very respectfully,
R. A. Cochran Superintendent

R.I.B.

Information following from: Not Given.
3-59 MRS. HENRY ROBINSON, dead, sister of John B Perrissier 4-49.
Husband 1st: Peter Deverney, dead, white.
3-59-1 Sophia Deverney Parr, age 65, P.O. Elbridge.
Husband: Name not given, white.
3-59-1-1 Mary Ann Bodewell, age 32, P.O. Compeau Grand Rapids near Drum HBR, two children indicated but no names given.
3-59-1-2 Sam Deverney, age 27, P.O. Silver Beach, Wash, no children.
3-59-1-3 Lizzie Wilson, age 30, P.O. Montague Mich.
Husband: Name not given, white.
3-59-1-3-1 Setha Wilson, age 7.
3-59-1-3-2 Mary Wilson, age 2.
3-59-1-3-3 William ~~Wilson~~ or William Robinson, age 12, father unknown, lives with Sarah Robinson, see 5-58.
Husband 2nd: David Moaw, dead, white.
3-59-2 ~~Nellie White~~ Sarah Green, age 47, P.O. ~~Muskegon~~ Hart.
Husband: Name not given, ~~white,~~ dead.
3-59-2-1 George Green, age 31, P.O. Lattin.
Wife: Name not given, white.
3-59-2-1-1 Charlotte Green, age 4.
3-59-2-1-2 George Green, age 4 mos, Mch/08.
3-59-2-2 Josie France, age 28, P.O. ~~Lattin~~ Hart #1.
Husband: Name not given, white.
3-59-2-2-1 Earl France, age 12.
3-59-2-2-2 William France, age 9.
3-59-2-2-3 May France, age 6.
3-59-2-2-4 Elmer France, age 5.
3-59-2-2-5 Dorothy France, age 4.
3-59-2-2-6 Clarence France, age 2.
3-59-2-3 Charles Green, age 26, P.O. Lattin.
Wife: Name not given, white.
3-59-2-3-1 Gerald Green, age 3.
3-59-2-3-2 Ione Green, age 10 weeks, born May/08 NB 2nd roll.
3-59-2-4 Carrie Bell, age 18, Hart #1, husband name not given, white.

3-59-3 Henry Moaw, age 45, P.O. Scottville, Mich, no children.

~~Husband 3rd: Henry~~

3-59-4 Amanda Garrison nee Moaw, dead.

Husband: Name not given, white.

3-59-4-1 Nelly White, age 26, P.O. Muskegon.

Husband: Name not given, white, see 33-54write for children, several children indicated .

Husband 3rd: Henry Robinson, white, his 2nd Wife.

3-59-5 Mabel Rummer, age 42, P.O. Hart.

Husband: Name not given, white.

3-59-5-1 Clyde Rummer, age 22.

3-59-5-2 Claud Rummer, age 20.

3-59-5-3 Maud Rummer, age 16.

3-59-5-4 Laura Rummer, age 14.

3-59-5-5 Owen Rummer, age 12.

3-59-5-6 Cecil Rummer, age 10.

3-59-5-7 Katie Rummer, age 8.

3-59-5-8 Fannie Rummer, age 4.

3-59-5-9 Ethel Rummer, age 2.

3-59-6 Kate Ryeson, age 37, P.O. ~~Nook-seh-K~~ Washington.

Husband: Ira Ryeson, white.

3-59-6-1 Leanna Ryeson, age 14, P.O. Lawrence Whatcome Co. Wash.

3-59-6-2 Wilbur D. Ryeson, age 13.

3-59-6-3 Fannie S. Ryeson, age 11.

3-59-6-4 Charles S. Ryeson, age 9.

3-59-6-5 Madge Ryeson, age 7, letter 5/29/09.

Husband 3rd: Henry Robinson, white, by his 1st wife.

Wife 1st: Nah-Bah, dead, an Ottawa, died before 1870.

1 Eunice Bailey, age 53, P.O. Honor Mich.

Husband: Solomon Bailey, see 28-55.

1-1 Charity Greenarm, died Apr/07 see 3-50.

1-2 Robert Bailey, age 24, P.O. Honor.

Wife: Katie (Ma-Dah-Ge-Me) Bailey, age 22, see 2-38.

1-2-1 Nicholas Bailey, age 4.

1-2-2 Jesse Bailey, age 2.

1-3 Francis Bailey, age 16.

2 Edward Robinson #1, age 50, P.O. Hart #4.

Wife: Name not given, white.

2-1 Winnie Bell Robinson, age 15, P.O. Hart #4.

3 Charles Robinson #1, age 48, Dighton near Cadallac.

Wife: Mary Louis, age 40, daughter of 1-49, see 5-49.

3-1 William Robinson, age 19, P.O. Dighton.

3-2 Cora Robinson, age 16.

3-3 Yetabelle Robinson (dau), age 10.
3-4 Gertie Robinson, age 7.
3-5 Vernie Robinson (son), age 4.
3-6 Clarence Robinson, age 2.

Children by 1st husband of Nah-Bah or Mrs. Henry Robinson. Husband 1st: Name not given, dead.

1 Agnes Halfday, age 66, P.O. Millerton.
Husband: James Halfday, P.O. Millerton, see 19-49.
1-1 Name or sex not given.

2 Joseph Petis or Pe-Na-Se-Waw-Quot, age 52, P.O. Custer R.R.2, see 6-49 & 14-54.
Wife: Mary Key-Way-Quom, age 32, daughter of 14-54.
2-1 Lizzie Petis, age 13.
2-2 Elias Petis, age 6.
2-3 Angelie Petis, age 3.
2-4 Benedict Petis, age 6 weeks, born July/08.
Children by 1st husband of Mary Key-Way-Quom, husband name not given.
1 Mary Me-Dah-Ko, P.O. Millerton.
Husband: William Me-Dah-Ko, see 21-52 for 8 indicated children.
2 Rosie Pete, age 35, P.O. Millerton.
Husband: Charles Pete, children see 6-49 & 14-54.

Ansd May 4th
Lawrence Wash
April the 29 1909

Mr Horace B Durant
Special US Indian Agent
Dear Sir, in slosed you will find my age and the ages and address of my Children for which you wanded for the Ottaway and Chippewa pay Roll
Miss Leanna Ryason born Sept the 21 1895
Wilbur D Ryason, born Dec the 6 1896
Fannie S Ryason born Oct the 25 1898
Charles S Ryason born May the 28 1900
Miss Madge Ryason born Dec the 9 1902
Mrs Kate Ryason born Mar the 24 1872
Address Lawrence
Mrs Kate Ryason Whatcome Co Wash

Letter to her May 1/09 D ask her about her sister Kate Ryeson
April the 24 1909

Horace B Durant dear sir as you wonted the names of my Children i will try and write them well i have nine of them the Oldest One is Clyde E Remmer age 23 he is marred and got one Child three months Old
Moud Remmer age 14
Laura Remmer age 15
Oren Remmer age 13
~~D~~ Cecil Remmer age 11
Katie Remmer age 9
fannie Remmer 5
Ethel Remmer 3 frm
Mrs Mable Remmer Hart Mich
We all get Our mail at Hart at the same place

Department of the Interior,
United States Indian Service,

Petoskey, Mich
June 8/09

Mr. Sam Duverney,
Silver Beach, Wash
Dear Sir:-

Your name has been given me as belonging to the Ottawa and Chippewa Indians of Michigan if you do will you please confirm same by sending me the names of your father & mother & addesses of your brothers & sisters.

Will you please send this information at once to complete the pay roll & oblige.

Yours truly,
Horace B. Durant,
Special U.S. Indian Agent B

Larsons Mich
June 17th 09

Horace B. Durant
Special U.S. Indian Agent
Sir,

In reply to your letter asking me about my belonging to the Ottawa and Chippewa Indians I do. My father's name as well as he is unknown to me, but if necessary I could get it from mother, Mothers Name Mrs. Sophia B Parr address Hart Mich c/o M. Rummer Sisters Names Mrs. Bert Bodwell Mrs Jack Wilson Adress unknown
Father is dead never remember seeing him, raised by Mr. and Mrs. H. L. Robinson Mr. H. S. Robinson still lives in Hart Mich. Hoping this reply is satisfactory as to my identity, if not let me know.

And oblige
Sam Duverney

Information following from: at Honor Lumber Camp William Perrissien, Inter.

4-59 JOHN B. PERRISSIEN, age 85, P.O. at daughter's Mrs. Vandenberg 619 Monroe St. Grand Haven.
Wife: Madeline Perrissien, died Apr 10, 1908, on roll 1870 with husband.
4-59-1 John Perrissien, age 59, P.O. Honor, wife name not given, dead, no children.
4-59-2 Patrick Perrissien, age 57, P.O.Hart.
Wife: ~~Delia~~ white.
4-59-2-1 Ed Perrissien, age 33, P.O. Honor, no children.
4-59-2-2 Mary Neff, age 30, P.O. 2912 Aberdeen Ave. Hoqueam Wash. State.
Husband: Name not given.
4-59-2-2-1 George Neff, age 10.
4-59-2-2-2 Ed Neff, age 8.
4-59-2-2-3 Martha Neff, age 6.
4-59-2-2-4 William Neff, age 4.
4-59-2-3 Sarah Hill, age 27, P.O. Walkerville Mich.
Husband: Name not given.
4-59-2-4-1 Merna Hill, age 8.
4-59-2-4 Henry Perrissien, age 25, P.O. Elbridge, single.
4-59-2-5 Pearl Perrissien, age 23, P.O. Elbridge, single.
4-59-2-6 Roy Perrissien, age 15, P.O. Elbridge.
4-59-2-7 William Perrissien, age 10.
4-59-3 William Perrissien or William Duverney, age 52, P.O. Honor.
Wife 1st: Lucy, dead.
4-59-3-1 Jake Duverney, age 32, P.O. Honor, by another wife who lives near Pellston.
Wife: Matilda Chippeway, age 27, Traverse, see 18-41.
4-59-3-1- 1 Dave Duverney, age 10.
4-59-3-1- 2 Mary Duvernaey, age 7
4-59-3-1- 3 Delia Duverney, age 3.
4-59-3-2 Charles Duverney, age 27, P.O. Copemish, see 2-54.
Wife 2nd: Angeline, Traverse, see 22-42
4-59-3-3 Levi Deverney, age 16.
4-59-3-4 Josephine Duverney, age 13.
4-59-3-5 John Deverney, age 12.
4-59-3-6 William Deverney Jr., age 9.
4-59-3-7 Moses Deverney, age 4.
4-59-3-8 Frank Deverney, age 2.
4-59-4 Mary Vandenburg, age 45 living, P.O. 619 Monroe St. Grand Haven, ~~see 43-50~~.
Husband: Name not given, dead.

~~4-59-3-1 Annie, dead, P.O. Whitehall Muskegon.~~
~~Husband: White.~~
~~4-59-3-1-1 Pearl Steven, age 18, P.O. Whitehall, child by other husband.~~
4-59-3-1 Madeline Gardner, age 28, P.O. Grand Haven.
Husband: Name not given, white.
4-59-3-1-1 Louis Gardner, age 8, P.O. Grand Haven
4-59-3-1-2 Prissilla Gardner, age 6, P.O. Grand Haven.
4-59-5 Isaac Perrissien or Piasha or Piasien, age 35, has not been heard from for last 15 or 20 years went to Wisconsin, near Monacoe Junction worked from one place to another.

Hart Mich R4
May 16 1909
Mr Durant/Mary Neff address is 2912 Aberdeen ave Hoquram Wash
Edd Perysian quick Otsego Co Mich
Henry Perysian Alanson Emmet Co Mich
Sarah Hill Walkerville Ocana Co Mich
Pirl Perysian Hart Mich and Will and Roy that is at home yet this is my famley and thare address but my brother Isaac i don't know enything about whare he is Patrick Perysian

Information following from: Not Given.
5-59 O-ZHE-GE-NE-GAW-GAW or SAGIE, dead.
Wife: Name not given, dead.
5-59-1 Paul Sagie or Paul Kay-Bay-O-Say, age 38, P.O. Walkerville, see 9-59.
Wife: Mary Ann Cogswell Sagie, age 36, P.O. Walkerville, daughter of Joe Cogswell, see 23-54. See Note on 9-59 Durant.
5-59-2 Name or sex not given, dead.
5-59-3 Name or sex not given, dead.

Information following from: Not Given.
6-59 JOHN BATTISE, dead.
Wife 1st: Name not given, dead.
6-59-1 Louis Battise, age 55, P.O. Custer #2.
Wife: Mary Battise, age 19, grand daughter of Chief #1.
6-59-1-1 David Battise, age 2.
6-59-2 Mitchell Battise, age 53, P.O. Walkerville.
Wife 1st: Angeline Shay-Go-Na-Be, dead.
6-59-2-1 Joe Mitchell, age 33, P.O. Hart.
Wife: Katie Bailey, age 33, P.O. Hart, Ind see 3-50, no children.
6-59-2-1-1 George Memberto, adopted see 9-54.

6-59-2-2 Frank Mitchell, age 29, P.O. Lattin.
Wife: Lucy Mitchell or Frances Battise, see 1-49, no children.

Note: Louis, Joe, Moses & Benedict Battise & their families drew with Potts. Mithell Battise & his family did not, so say James Cogswell. Durant.

Wife 2nd: Angeline Hickey Battise, dead.

6-59-3 Joe Battise, age 45, P.O. Custer #2.
Wife: Mary Daniels, age 28, granddaughter of 6-5, no children

6-59-4 Moses Battise, age 38, Custer No 2, see 5-61.
Wife 1st: Flora Kelsey, age 18, not married to Battise but lived with him, also has a child by him.
6-59-4-1 Angeline Battise, age 2.
Wife 2nd: Nancy Kelset or Naw-Kay-O-Say, age 36.

6-59-5 Benedict Battise, age 30, Custer #2, see 5-61.
Wife: Alice Kelsey, age 28, no children.

Information following from: Not Given.

7-59 CHAW-SHAW-WAW-NAY-BEECE, dead.
Wife: Name not given, dead.
7-59-1 Lizzie Peters, dead.
Husband: Peter Espien, see 10-61 for children.
7-59-2 Daniel Peters, dead, unmarried.
7-59-3 Maggie Peters, dead.
7-59-4 Mary Peters, dead.
7-59-5 John Peters, age 27, P.O. Freesoil.
Wife: Eliza Albert, age 23, daughter of Richard Albert, see 3-52 & 37-52.
7-59-5-1 Fred Peters, age 4.
7-59-5-2 James Peters, age 2.
7-59-5-3 Frank Peters, born June 14, 1908 2nd roll NB.

Information following from: Not Given.

8-59 SAMUEL, dead.
Wife: Name not given, dead.
8-59-1 ~~Eliza Antoine Kelsey, age 3~~ Name or sex not given, Dead, no heirs.
8-59-2 Name or sex not given, dead, no heirs.

Information following from: Not Given.

9-59 LOUIS KAY-BAY-O-SAY, family, dead.
Wife: Name not given, dead.
9-59-1 John Kay-Bay-O-Say, not married and no children.
9-59-2 Paul Kay-Bay-O-Say or Paul Sagie, age 40, P.O. Hart #4, see 5-59 & 23-54.

Wife: Mary Cogswell, age 32, daughter of Joe Cogswell.
9-59-2-1 Louis Kay-Bay-O-Say, age 15.
9-59-2-2 Frank Kay-Bay-O-Say, age 5.
9-59-2-3 Fred Kay-Bay-O-Say, age 2, born May 21/07 2nd roll NB.

Note: Some mistake about wives of: Paul Kay-Bay-O-Say & Paul Sagie. Are these two "Pauls" one & the same? Yes! These are the same. Durant 2/19/09, identified by head men.

Information following from: Not Given.
10-59 MOSES AW-ZHE-WATCH or JACKSON, dead.
Wife: Name not given, now wife of David Fox.
10-59-1 Agnes, dead, no children.
10-59-2 Mary Makomenaw, age 30, Traverse, see 7-26 & 3-56.
Husband Peter Makomenaw.

Information following from: Not Given.
11-59 AW-NO-WAY-QUAY's children, all dead, no heirs.

Information following from: Not Given.
12-59 CHARLES DUVERNEY, dead.
Wife: Name not given.
12-59-1 John Duverney, age 62, P.O. Petoskey, see 36-55.
12-59-2 Louisa Duverney Keway, age 59, P.O. Petoskey, see 11-23.
Husband 1st: Louis Genereaux Jr., dead.
12-59-2-1 Levi Genereaux, age 37, P.O. Petoskey.
Wife: Name not given, white, ~~nochildren~~.
12-59-2-1-1 Lena Smith or Rena Genereaux Smith, age 18, P.O. Muncie Ind. 120 N. frankin St., see 8-55 & 11-55.
Husband: Name not given, white.
12-59-2-1-1-1 Manetto Smith, age 2.
Husband 2nd: Benjamin Keway #1, age 60, P.O. Beaver Isld 35-32, a member of Traverse band..

Muncie Indiana May 10, 1909

Mr Horace B Durant
Petoskey Michigan
Dear Sir:-
In reply to the attached.
I herein submit the information sought.
My fathers name is Levi Genereaux
My name is Mrs Erelena Genereaux Smith
My childs name is Manetho Hiawatha Smith
His age is two years, My adress

Mrs Erelena Genereaux Smith
120 N Franklin St. Muncie Ind.

Information following from: Not Given.
13-59 KEY-ZHE-GO-PE-NAY-SE.
Note: Cannot locate him. Durant.

Information following from: Not Given.
14-59 NON-GO-SAY, all dead, no heirs.

Information following from: Not Given.
15-59 KEY-ME-WON, dead, son of Chief 1.
Wife: Name not given, dead.
15-59-1 Andrew Light, age 38, P.O. Millerton, see 1-59.
Wife: Rosie, see 14-54.
15-59-1-1 William Light or William Williams, age 12, adopted see 1-49.

Information following from: Not Given.
16-59 AW-NE-ME-KE-QUAY, dead.
16-59-1 Name or sex not given, see 5-59.
16-59-1-1 Paul Sagie, see 5-59.

Information following from: Not Given.
17-59 SHA-AW-SE-NO-QUAY
Author Note: No information contained in the file.

Information following from: Not Given.
18-59 JOHN B. ME-NO-MAW-NE, all dead, no heirs.

Information following from: William Petoskey & Grand River Inds. who referred me to Petoskey.
19-59 MRS. WILLIAM KEY-SHAW-TAY or MARTHA GROUNDY, died Apr 20, 1908, see 19-23.
Husband 1st: William Hot or William Key-Shaw-Tay, dead
Husband 2nd: Louis Grandain or Groundy, white, sole heir, P.O. Petoskey Mich.
19-59-1 Daughter, name not given, dead, no heirs, which husband was father was not indicated.

Information following from: Not Given.
20-59 MATHEW MCGULPHIN, all dead, no heirs.

Information following from: Not Given.
21-59 PE-TAW-BUN, all dead, no heirs.

Information following from: Not Given.
22-59 PE-NAY-SE-QUAY, dead.
22-59-1 Name or sex not given, dead.
22-59-2 Name not given, dead.
Husband: Johnson Green, P.O. Honor, see 12-56 & 4-61.
22-59-2-1 Julia Green, age 13, see 10-58.

Information following from: Not Given.
23-59 AIN-ME-WE-KEESE, all dead, no heirs.

Information following from: Not Given.
24-59 ANGELINE, dead.
24-59-1 Isaac Ke-Way-Quoum, age 39, see 27-54 & 8-54

Information following from: Not Given.
25-59 WAW-KASE
Note: Cannot trace this man. Durant.

Information following from: Not Given.
26-59 A-BWAY-QUO-UM, dead.
Wife: Elizabeth Pay-Quo-Tush, now wife of Samuel Pay-Quo-Tush, all children by this husband dead, see 3-58A.

Information following from: Not Given.
27-59 KEY-WAY-NE-GOW-NE-QUAY.
Husband: Name not given, died before 1870.
27-59-1 Wah-Be-Ske-Min Nancy #2, age 67, P.O. Copenish now at Freesoil waiting enrollment, see 16-49.
Husband: George Agago, age 70, see 12-52.
27-59-2 Sarah Theodore, age 65, P.O. Freesoil, on roll as 12-49.
Husband: Name not given, dead.
27-59-2-1 John Theodore, age 48, P.O. Freesoil, Mich, see 5-60.
Wife 1st: Marian, P.O. Charlevoix.
27-59-2-1-1 Charles Theodore, age 26, P.O. Freesoil, Mich, separated from Angeline Shay-Go-Na-By see 2-54.
Wife: Laura Espien Theodore, age 19, see 10-61A, no children.
Wife 2nd: Jennie Wallace We-Me-Ge-Bweece, P.O. Freesoil, see 9-58A.
27-59-2-1-2 Benjamin Theodore, age 23, not married.
27-59-2-1-3 Nelson Theodore, age 19, not married.
27-59-2-1-4Maggie Theodore, age 17, not married.

Wife 3rd: Jennie Antone Theodore, age 31, P.O. Freesoil, Mich.
27-59-2-1-5 Louis Theodore, age 5, not married.
27-59-2-1-6 Harry Theodore, age 2.
27-59-2-1-7 Bessie Theodore, age 6 mos, born Jany 29/08 NB 2nd roll.
Children of wife 3rd: Jennie Antone Theodore by her 1st husband are:
Husband 1st: Charles Isaac, dead.
Note: Enroll with family of John Theodore.
27-59-2-1-8 Ellen Isaac Theodore, age 11, P.O. at Mt Pleas. Sch.
27-59-2-1-9 Christina Isaac Theodore, age 8, P.O. Freesoil.
27-59-3 James Manitous, dead.
Wife. Name not given, dead, was No 22-60 1870 roll.
27-59-3-1 William Manitous,
age 28, P.O. Ludington Camp Arcadia, Hamlin Lake, not married, see 22-60 & 13-61A

Information following from: W.J. Masqueskey Mich State Prison Mch 23/09.
28-59 KAW-ME-SQUAW-SE-GAY or THOMAS HENRY or W. J. MASQUSKEY, age 53, P.O. #8130 Mich State Prison Jackson, Mich.
Wife: Sarah Northrup, white, P.O. Muskegon Mich.
28-59-1 Sarah Masqueskey, age 19, single.
~~Note: Said to have died at Georgian Bay. Durant 2/19/09 Custer.~~
28-59-2 Frank Masqueskey, age 16.
Note: Cannot locate his children. Durant.

Board Of Control	*John C. Wenger, Deputy Warden*
T. C. Quinn, President, Caro	*Rev. John M. Shank, Chaplain*
T. J. Navin, Detroil	*Geo. R. Stone, Clerk*
Geo. W. Merriam, Hartford	*A. H. Pickett, Warden's Secretary*

MICHIGAN STATE PRISON
A. N. ARMSTRONG
WARDEN

Office of
The Deputy Warden

Jackson, Mich., Nov. 10th, 1908

Mr. Horace B. Durand,
Special Indian Agent.
Washington, D. C.

Dear Sir:-

Regarding the Claim of William Jones Masquskey, referred to in letter of April 13th., 1905, (Finance 27035-1905), I desire to state that this party is a member of the Ottawa Tribe instead of the Pottawatomie's, as inferred to in previous letter, and at present an inmate of the Michigan State Prison. Masquskey has a wife and three children living.

Very respectfully,
John C. Wenger Deputy Warden

Department of the Interior,
Office of Indian Affairs,
Washington.

Petoskey, Mich
May 4/09

Post Master
Muskegon, Mich
Dear Sir:

An Indian by the name of Thomas Henry who also goes by the name of W. J. Masqueskey now in Michigan State Prison tells me he has a wife and three children in Muskegon. The wife's maiden name was Northrup. Can you ascertain if they are in Muskegon now and their address there.

Yours truly
Horace B. Durant,
Special U.S. Indian Agent. Per B

Mr Durant,
Dear Sir
Have made every effort to locate parties but cannot be found.
Very respectfully P.P.Schnorbach P.M.

I hope you will help me out about this matter.
Please excuse me this if I have made mistake by written this.
Respt Yours
8130 W.J.Masquskey
Jackson Mich
Cofa M.S.P. to Warden of Prison

that which who I am. And I was Born in the city of Grand Rapids of Kent County Michigan; at the 17 th day of March 1856 and I'm 53 years old. And reall Indian name's Komasquskey; Also the English is William Jones Komasquskey

Now Presen I am an Inmate of the Michigan State Prison also I got wife and 3 cchildren, and my family now cannot be Located of Grand Rapids.

further which I Said. My Father's name Wobbena=inggo he was chippewa Tribe and he was one of member of Chief Passhaw=Sak-gays Bands of Early of Grand River Band of the Ottawa and chippewas Tribe and

These of ~~Two~~ Two Tribes of the Grand River Bands and Grand Rapids Black skin Tribes and the chief Mr=noon-day, the government of the United States, they moved those 2 Tribes to the forther north of the given them no later 1857- to oceana, co. of Indian Reservation of the Lands of the situation ~~of you~~ Township of albridge Oceana County Michigan.
So my Parents- they moved to Muskegon county Mishigan to the white River, they died, and my father dead in 1867 and at Muskegon. My mother she's been dead in 1869 in White Riiver; also my Sisters and one Brother they are all dead,

our – Old Chief Passhaw-Sak-gay. he was the chief at the Indian Reservation of Town of alberidge oceana county. at the last we received of our money from the government of the United States, in the Spring the yeat of May 22th 1872.

My mother's she is Ottawa Tribe; We have been Living in that Reservation of Township albridge about 15 years But we Life there in 1874 of Oceana county

Michigan, to coming back to Grand Rapids again 1875 to 1899.

Jackson Michigan
Marh 1st 1909
Mr Horace B. Durant
Department of the Interior
Office of Indian Affairs
Washington, D.C.
My Dear Sir

I Desire to Express to you, of my Statement for the Interest, that fact you have Shown in my favor, for your working for those 2 Tribes.

For this reason why I had to Trying of Best I could of Statin my acknowledgement for the Establishing of my Identity, as so far I understanding your reports,
Also I had no attorney to do this for me. So I had to do this for myself. And to Including with these whose all ready being Taken of census, and all over the county, to making Lists of the names of the Ottawa and Chippewa. Now who are Entitled to Share in the $130,000

Information following from: Custer Aug/08 Feby/09.
29-59 LOUIS WAY-WE-DE-QUO-UNG, or LOUIS MCCLELLAN, age 70, P.O. Custer #2.
Wife: Christina McClellan, age 76, Custer #2.
29-59-1 James McClellan, age 38, P.O. Custer #2
Wife 1st: Eliza, dead.
Wife 2nd: Annie, dead
Wife 3rd: Angeline (Bailey) McClellan, age 22, see 3-53 & 2-58, 1st husband Peter Pete, child David Pete see 2-58.
Author Note: No indication given which wife is the mother of

which child.
29-59-1-1 Julia McClellan, age 12.
29-59-1-2 Sampson McClellan, age 7, enroll with Amos Wakefield 13-53.
29-59-1-3 Christina McClellan, age 4.
29-59-1-4 Maggie McClellan, age 2.
29-59-1-5 Grace McClellan, age 1.
29-59-2 Julia McClellan Alexander Wah-Be-Sis, age 33, P.O. Pellston, Mich, see 28-52.
Husband 1st: Name not given, separated.
Husband 2nd: Moses Alexander, see 12-32 Traverse Band.
29-59-2-1 Katie Alexander, age 12, P.O. Harbor Spgs. Sch, also known as Katie Osgood having been adopted by Mary Osgood see below, Traverse.
29-59-2-2 Francis Alexander, age 10, Traverse.
29-59-2-3 Benjamin Alexander, age 6, Traverse.
Children of 1st husband of wife: Christina Baker McClellan.
Husband 1st: _______ Baker, dead.
1 George Baker, age 58, P.O. Copemish, Mich, see 9-62.
Wife: Name not given, dead.
1-1 Joe Baker, age 19, P.O. Copemish, Mich, see 1-58A.
Wife: Name not given, Pottawatomie, see 4-50.
1-2 Adam Baker, age 17, P.O. Copemish.
Wife: Sarah (Griffith) Baker.
1-2-1 Charles Baker, born Aug/08 too late.
1-3 Henry Baker, age 15.
1-4 Christina Baker, age 12, see 9-62.
2 Maggie Baker Burns, dead.
Husband: Mike Burns, white.
2-1 George Burns, was in Spanish War & has not been heard From, off Information too indefinate.
2-2 Theresa Burns Stamford, age 24, P.O. Scottville, Mich
Husband: _______ Burns, white.
2-2-1 George Stamford, age 12.
2-2-2 Mary Stamford, age 9.
Children of 2nd husband of wife: Christina Baker Genia McClellan.
Husband 1st: _______ Genia, dead.
1 Henry Genia, address unknown, heard he was in California, Information too indefinite nothing established by correspondence, Durant off.
2 Mary (Genia) Osgood, age 40, P.O. Rockton, Ills.
Husband: D. W. Osgood, white, P.O. Rockton, Ill, no children.

Katie PO is at present –Harbor Springs Michigan
Rockton Ills April 22 1909

Horace B Durant
us Special Ind agent
Your letter of the 17th inst is, read Mary Osgood is the aunt of Katie Osgood & is an Indian belonged to the ottawa Tribe and is a claimant entitled to a Share of the money to be distributed among the ottawa Tribe. Marys Maiden name was genia and christina McClellan is her Mother whose first husbands name was Baker who died then her mother married genia who died then her Mother Married McClellen Katie will be 11 years old on the 23rd day of June 1909. Mary Osgood is Katie aunt has no children of her own isa sister of Julia Alexander and is 45 years old she says her Post office is Rockton Winnebago Co. Ills. Katies PO address is Harbor Springs Michigan. She is or was sent there by adopted Parents Daniel W & Mary Osgood to attend the Frances can School Derkins Supt. She was adopted by the Osgoods about 5 years ago under the order of the county Court of Winnebago Co. and was sent to this School by her adopted Parents. Katie was in a bad way when adopted but has been made something of since adopted and away from her mother who is a hard working Wash woman now what I want to know is the steps necessary to be taken to obtain this money, the amount going to Mary Osgood and Katie and when It will be paid &c I enclose a statement of the facts in pencil please answer soon

Respectfully yours
C Bentley

P.S. do not pay Katie Share to her mother Julia Alexander but to Katie or her adopted Parent or guardian.

Ansd Apr 17/09 Durant

Rockton Ills April 14 1909
Horace B Durant Special Agent &c

On behalf of Mary and D W Osgood adopted parents of Katie Osgood an Indian child of of Julia Alexander. I write you for information under a letter recd from Interior Dept Indian affairs directing me so to do this adopted child is now at Franciscan Fathers Harbor Springs Michigan at school D Eckins Supt this Indian child Katie is about 11 years old and is entitled to a Share in the distribution of the Money going to the Ottaway and Chippewa Indians we understand she has been enrolled and is entitled or her adopted Parents to a Share of the funds appropriated to these Indians Mary Osgood is an Aunt of Katie what the adopted parent desire know is whose is her share payable deed what Steps are necessary to be taken to get It will you kindly inform me all the matter soon
this Indian child was adopted under the Laws of this State by the adopted Parents under an order of the County Court of Winnebago Co Ills

Respectfully yours
C Bentlsy for Mary & D W Osgood

PS by mistake I wrote to John Francis Jr ok Dupt

Copemish Mich

May 24/19

Dear Sir

Well sir her father is name Mr Griffon and her mother is maggie thomas is Ottawa Indian Grand River Band and her father is ded long time ago

From Mr George Baker
Copemish

May 24th 1909

Mr Durant

You ask me where Henry Genia I hear he is dead long time ago when he was about 14 years old when he died Please tell me how Near you though How soon we will get our Pay Drop me line soon yours truly

Lewis McClellanon

Information following from: Petoskey Dec 26/08.
30-59 MARGARET TROMBLY, dead.
Husband: Name not given, white.
Note: Said to be mother of Benjamin & Louis & Mry & Theresa Trombly, see 36-57, 15-56, 14-49 & 21-49. OK D.

Page 60
Chief KAW-GAY-GAW-BO-WE
Grand River

Information following from: Not Given.
1-60 KAW-GAY-GAW-BO-WE, dead.
Wife: Name not given, dead.
1-60-1 Cornelius Hall, No 18-60.
1-60-2 Mary Hall, P.O. Fountain, see 8-60.
1-60-3 Name or sex not given, see No 2-60.

Information following from: by Tuttle Aug/08 by Durant Mch/09.
2-60 TAY-BAW-SE-KE-ZHICK-WAY-UM or JOE HALL, dead.
Wife: Name not given, dead.
2-60-1 George Hall, dead.
Wife 1st: Name not given, dead.
Wife 2nd: Angeline Caub-Mo-Say Chippeway, see 8-50.
Author Note: No indication which wife was the mother of which child.
2-60-1-1 Spencer Hall or Pete Zoondah, age 35, P.O. Star City, Mich.
Wife: Name not given, a Pottawatomie,children dead.
2-60-1-2 Mary Hall Thomas, age 28, P.O. Leroy, Mich, no

children, see 17-56.
Husband: William Thomas
2-60-1-3 Susan Hall Fisher, age25, P.O. Ashton, Mich or Luther, Mich.
Husband: John Fisher, a Saginaw Indian, off.
2-60-1-3-1 Thomas Fisher, born May1908
2-60-2 Nancy Hall Peters, age 60, P.O. Fountain, Mich, nochildren, see 17-51.
2-60-3 Eddie Hall, age 33, P.O. Star City.
Wife 1st: Mary, dead.
2-60-3-1 Joseph Hall, age 13, lives with Nancy Hall Peters, P.O. at Fountain, see 17-51.
Wife 2nd : Martha Bailey, age 22, P.O.Fountain, Mich, see 14-50, separated.
2-60-3-2 Milo Hall, see 14-50.
2-60-3-3 Sarah Hall, see 14-50.

Information following from: Not Given.
3-60 PE-NAY-SE-WAW-BE, dead, no descendants.

Information following from: Not Given.
4-60 TO-TOGE-TOO, dead.
Wife: Name not given, dead.
4-60-1 Name or sex not given, dead, 34-60.
4-60-1-1 Watson King, age 25, P.O. Freesoil, single.
4-60-1-2 Joe King, age 23, son in law of Amos Fitch, see 9-55, 12-58A & 34-60
4-60-1-3 John King, age 17, P.O.Freesoil.
4-60-2 Name or sex not given, dead.
4-60-3 Name or sex not given, dead.

Information following from: Not Given.
5-60 TONG-GUISH or JOE ELLIOTT, dead.
Wife: Name not given, dead.
5 SHEET #1:
5-60-1 Name not given, dead.
Husband 1st: Name not given.
5-60-1-1 Charley Joe or Charley Russett, see below.
5-60-1-2 William Aiken or Russett.
Wife: Name not given, dead.
5-60-1-2-1 Alice Marsh, age 33.
Husband: Joe Marsh, see 10-52.
5-60-1-2-2 George Rozette or Rosett or Russett, age 23, P.O. Freesoil, not married.
Husband 2nd: Ching-Gaw-Quo-Um or Aiken, dead, see 7-60.

5-60-1-3 Lucy Cloud, age 50, P.O. ~~Oscoda or Lake Harbor~~, Alvin, Mich, see 7-60.

Husband: John Cloud, off a Saginaw.

5-60-1-3-1 Alice Cloud Williams, age 26, P.O. Alvin, Mich.

Husband: Sam Williams, a Saginaw Ind off.

5-60-1-3-1-1 Paul Williams, age 7.

5-60-1-3-1-2 Riley Williams, age 9.

5-60-1-3-1-3 Jessie Williams, age 3.

5-60-1-3-2 Susan Cloud, age 15.

5 SHEET #2:

Note: Children all dead except Charley Joe who lived with Elliott & when Father's name was Akin (Ind. name) his mother was wife of Tong-Guish before after she married Aiken

(Grand children or of children of Tong-Guish.)

5-60-1 Charley Joe, age 54, P.O. Lexington RFD #4 Live on Hamlin Lake.

Wife: Lizzie Joe, age 50, P.O. Lexington RFD #4.

Children by 1st husband of wife Lizzie Joe:

Husband 1st: Thomas Antoine.

1 Jane Antoine Theodore, age 31, P.O. Freesoil.

Husband: John Theodore (I) , see 27-59 & 9-58.

1-1 Ellen Theodore.

1-2 Christina Theodore.

1-3 Louis Theodore.

2 Thresa (Antoine) Wasaquaum, age 28, P.O. Charlevoix Mich.

Husband: Isaih Wasaguaum (I). see 26-23, Traverse.

2-1 Name or sex not given.

2-2 Name or sex not given.

2-3 Name or sex not given.

Children by 2nd husband of wife Lizzie Joe:

Husband 2nd : Henry Genia.

3 James Genia Joe or James Genia, age 26, P.O. Freesoil #4.

4 Mary Smith, age 24, P.O. Freesoil.

Husband: William Smith (I), age 30, see 3-56 & 16-52

Children by 3rd husband of wife Lizzie Joe:

Husband 3rd: Charley Joe.

5 Eddie Joe, age 8.

Department of the Interior,
Office of Indian Affairs,
Washington.

Petoskey, Mich.
May 7 09

Mrs Jennie Theodore
Freesoil, Mich.
Dear Madam:-
Will you kindly givethe names (English & Indian) of your father and mother for the Ottawa and Chippewa pay roll and oblige.
Yours truly,
Horace B. Durant
Special U.S. Agent. Per B
My fathers was Thomas Enturine Indian Wa ge she go ma
My mothers before her marriage Lizzie Case Indian She bah

Information following from: Not Given.
6-60 AIN-NE-ME-KE-WAY, dead.
Wife: Name not given, dead.
6-60-1 Martha Eaton, age 48, P.O. Honor.
Husband: Sampson Eaton, age 41, see 19-53.

Information following from: Not Given.
7-60 CHING-GAW-QUO-UM, dead.
Wife 1st: Name not given, died Nov 1907 1st roll, Charley Joe's mother.
Wife 2nd: Martha Pe-Nay-Se-Wah-Bun.
7-60-1 Lucy Cloud, age 50, P.O. ~~Oseoda Mich~~ Alvin, see 5-60.

Information following from: Not Given.
8-60 PE-NAY-SE-WAW-NAW-QUOT or JOHN HALL, dead.
Wife: Name not given, dead.
8-60-1 Mary Hall, age 45, P.O. Fountain, never married (blind).

Information following from: Not Given.
9-60 PAY-SHE-QUAW-MO-QUOSH, dead, never married.

Information following from: Not Given.
10-60 AIN-NE-MWAY-WAY, alldead, no heirs.

Information following from: Not Given.
11-60 AW-SAW-MAY-KE-ZHICK, all dead, no heirs.

Information following from: Not Given.
12-60 ADDISON C. SHAW, dead.
Wife: Name not given, dead.
12-60-1 Name not given, dead.
Husband: David Ching-Wash, age 58, P.O. Harbor Spings, see 1-62.
12-60-1-1 Samuel Ching-Wash.

12-60-1-2 Charles Ching-Wash.

Information following from: Not Given.
13-60 KEY-WAY-CUSH-CUM, dead, children all dead, no heirs.
Wife: Tah-Be-Dah or Sarah King, living, age 75, P.O. Custer, Mich.

Information following from: Not Given.
14-60 NE-O-BE, dead.
Wife: Name not given, dead.
14-60-1 Charles Coby, age 60, P.O. Cross Village.
Wife: Name not given, dead.
14-60-1-1 Robert Coby, age 18, P.O. Cross Village.
14-60-1-2 Lucy Coby, age 16, P.O. Cross Village.
14-60-1-3 Sam Coby, age14, P.O. Cross Village.
14-60-1-4 John Coby. Age 12, P.O. Cross Village.
14-60-2 Name or sex not given, dead, no heirs.
Note: The wife of Ne-O-Be is also the mother of James Bananas 2-50.

Information following from: Custer 2/19/09.
15-60 ME-SKO-TAY-SE-MIN, all dead, no heirs.

Information following from: Not Given.
16-60 AW-BE-TAW-SE-GAY, all dead, no heirs.

Information following from: Not Given.
17-60 O-GE-MAW-PE-NAY-SE, all dead, no heirs.

Information following from: Not Given.
18-60 NE-GAW-NE-SAY or CORNELIUS HALL, age 63, P.O. Star City.
Wife: Florence Ne-Be-Nay-Se Ne-Gaw-Me-Say, dead, enrolled with husband in 1870.
18-60-1 Isaac Hall, age 39, P.O. Star City.
Wife: Name not given, dead, drew with Potts.
18-60-1-1 Edward Hall, age 13, P.O. Star City.
18-60-1-2 Allice Hall, age 12, P.O. Star City.
18-60-1-3 Eliza Hall, age 10, P.O. Star City.
18-60-1-4 David Hall, age 7, P.O. Star City.
18-60-1-5 Joseph Hall, age 6, P.O. Star City.
18-60-1-6 Deliah Hall, age 3, P.O. Star City.
Note: Children did not draw with the Potts. Tuttle.
18-60-2 Other children all dead, and left no children.

Information following from: Not Given.
19-60 PE-TAW-WAW-NAW-QUOT, dead.
Wife: Nancy Pe-Taw-Waw-Naw-Quot Ta-Baw-Se-Ke-Zhick, age 65,

P.O. Kewaden, now wife of George Ta-Baw-Se-Ke-Zhick or George Chief 1-46.

19-60-1 Sophia Key-Wah-Day-Way, age 39, P.O. Alden, Mich
Husband: George Key-Wah-Day-Way, age 47, see 12-54.
19-60-1-1 Rosie Key-Wah-Day-Way, age 15.
19-60-1-2 Eliza Key-Wah-Day-Way, age 3, diedSept 17/08.
19-60-1-3 John Key-Wah-Day-Way, age 9.
19-60-1-4 Mary Key-Wah-Day-Way, born Dec 25, 1907 2nd roll.

Information following from: Not Given.
20-60 PAY-SHAW-NAW-QUOT, dead, no heirs.

Information following from: Not Given.
21-60 SHAY-YAW, dead.
Note: Last heard from this Ind was at Omena, Mich, & died there. Do not know what became of the Child. Durant 2/19/09

Information following from: 2/19/09.
22-60 WAY-ZHE-O-QUAY, dead.
Husband: None given.
22-60-1 Name or sex not given, dead.
22-60-2 William Manitous, age 28, P.O. Hamlin Lake, single.

Information following from: 2/19/09.
23-60 SAW-GOTCH, all dead, no heirs

Information following from: Not Given.
24-60 KEY-CHE-CHE-WAW, dead.
Wife: Name not given, dead.
24-60-1 Name not given, dead, no heirs.
24-60-2 John Andrews, dead.
Wife: Name not given, dead.
24-60-2-1 Isaac Andrews, Traverse, see 32-38.
24-60-2-2 Mitchell Andrews, age 38, Beaver Island, not married, see 2-41.
24-60-2-3 Benedicta Kingbird, age 25, P.O. Pashabatown, see 2-41.
Husband: Thomas Kingbird, 41-43.
24-60-2-4 Madeline Andrews, age 22, P.O. Omena, Mich, Died May 30/08.
24-60-2-4-1 Enos Andrews Kingbird, age 2, father unknown, see 2-41 & 41-43.
Note: This share should be paid to Benedicta Kingbird, sister of Madeline Andrews.

Information following from: Not Given.
25-60 MO-SAY-QUAY, dead, no children.
Husband: Jack Foster, white, dead.

Information following from: Not Given.
26-60 AW-KO-ZHAY or JOHN PETERS, dead.
Wife: Name not given, dead.
26-60-1 Charles Peters, age 24, P.O. Lusher.
Wife: Name not given, dead.
26-60-1-1 John Pete, lives with Martha Alexander see 9-55.
(one child) ~~Owen an Ottawa Ind of one of the Northern bands.~~

Information following from: Rosebush Jany 21.
27-60 PAY-BAW-ME-SAY, dead.
Wife: Name not given, dead.
Father of Charles Crane dead.
27-60-1 Charles Crane or Scott Crane, age 29, P.O. Rapid City, see 32-60, born at Custer, single, ist cousin of George Peters 3-51.

Notes:

Probably same as "Scott" Crane.
~~Scott Crane dead, died near Custer not same as Charles Crane~~.
There was another Scott Crane acousin, who died near Custer. Durant Custer 2/19/09.
Am satisfied from oral testimony of members of tribe that he is entitled to enrollment though cannot trace his family connection. Durant Spl Agt, Oct 3/08 Elk Rapids, Mich.
Later: identified with this sheet. Durant.
27-60-2 Jacob Crane, age 27, P.O. Wise, Mich, see 26-55, Saginaw Indian, ½ brother?
Confirmed 2/19/09 Custer. Durant

Information following from: Not Given.
28-60 PAW-QUA-CHE-QUAY, age 99, P.O. Fountain, see 2-61.
Husband 1st: John Joseph, dead.
28-60-1 John Joseph or John Doe, age 47, Fountain, single, no children.
28-60-2 Name not given, dead.
Husband: __________ McClure.
28-60-2-1 Julia McClure Cogswell, wife of 23-54.
28-60-2-2 Christina Fisher, dead.
Husband: Name not given, white.
28-60-2-2-1 Joe Fisher, age 21, P.O. Honor.

Wife: Martha Bailey, age 19, see 4-62.
28-60-2-2-1-1 Adam Fisher, ~~age 18~~ dead.
28-60-2-3 Charles McClure, dead, adopted by 9-64.
Wife: None given.
28-60-2-3-1 Jennie McClure, age 16, P.O. Mt Pleasant Sch.
Husband 2nd: Name not given, dead.

Information following from: Not Given.
29-60 PIN-DE-GOSH-SHE-WAY, all dead, no heirs.

Information following from: Not Given.
30-60 TOW-O-KO-NE or GEORGE HALL, dead.
Wife 1st: Name not given, dead.
30-60-1 Spencer Hall or Pete Zoondah, age 35, P.O. Star City, he drew with Potts under the name of Peter Zoondah.
Wife: Julia Hall, is a Pott.
30-60-1-1 Phoebe Hall, age 4 2, died Jul 24/08.
Wife 2nd: Angeline Caub-Mo-Sy, age 48, P.O. Mt. Pleasant, Chippeway, daughter of 8-50.
30-60-2 Mercy Hall Thomas, age 28, P.O. Doane Siding near Ashton.
Husband: William Thomas, age 31, P.O. Doane Siding near Ashton, see 31-57.
30-60-2-1 Lewis Thomas, age 4 3, died in April, 1908, see 8-50 & 17-56.
30-60-3 Josaphine Hall, age 25, P.O. Beal City near Mt. Pleasant.

Information following from: Not Given.
31-60 PE-TAW-BUN, dead.
Note: Indians do not know what became of child. Durant 2/19/09.

Information following from: Not Given.
32-60 WAW-SAW-TIN-NO-QUAY, dead.
32-60-1 Charles (or Scott) Crane, age 29, P.O. Rapid City, see 27-60.
32-60-2 Name or sex not given, dead, no heirs.

Information following from: 2/19/60.
33-60 CAW-GAW-GOOSE, dead, no descendants.

Information following from: Not Given.
34-60 PAW-WAY-WE-TUNG or THOMAS KING, dead.
Wife: Name not given, dead.
34-60-1 Watson King, see 12-58 & 4-60.
34-60-2 Joe King, see 12-58 & 4-60.
34-60-3 John King, see 12-58 & 4-60.

Information following from: 2/19/09.
35-60 KEY-SHAY-SEE, dead, no descendants.

Page 61A
Chief NAW-GAW-NE-QUO-UNG
Grand River

Information following from: Not Given.
1-61A NAW-GAW-NE-QUO-UNG, all dead and no heirs.

Information following from: Not Given.
2-61A KAW-BAY-O-MAW, dead.
Wife: Pe-Gotch-Quay, age 99, living, P.O. Fountain, very old on roll alone in 1870 28-60.
Husband 1st: Name not given.
Husband 2nd: Wis-Go-Mack, dead.
Author Note: No indication which husband is the father of which child.
2-61A-1 John Joseph, age 47, P.O. Fountain, no children, see 28-60.
2-61A-2 Name or sexnot given, dead.
2-61A-2-1 Julia Cogswell.
Husband: Joe Cogswell, see 28-60 & 23-54.

Information following from: Not Given.
3-61A NAW-O-QUAY-GE-ZHE-GO-QUAY, dead.
Husband 1st: Name not given, (Ind), dead.
3-61A-1 Louis Thomas, age 70, P.O. ~~Traverse City~~ Freesoil FRD #2, see 31-57. ~~Cannot find him. Durant.~~
Husband 2nd: William Barnhart, dead.
3-61A-2 George Barnhart, age 51, Ludington,Mich.
Wife: Name not given, white.
3-61A-2-1 William Barnhart, age 22, P.O. Ludington, not married.
3-61A-2-2 Joe Barnhart, age 18.
3-61A-2-3 George Barnhart, age 16.
3-61A-2-4 Edmund Barnhart, age 13.
3-61A-2-5 Matthew Barnhart, age 11.
3-61A-2-6 Ambrose Barnhart, age 9.
3-61A-2-7 Lillian Barnhart, age 8.
3-61A-3 Mary Compeau Craig, age 49, P.O. Ludington.
Husband 1st: Joe Compeau, dead.
3-61A-3-1 James Compeau, age 29, P.O. Ludington #4.
Wife: Eliza Lahaye Compeau, age 31, see 6-61.
3-61A-3-1-1 Benjamin F. Lahaye, age 29(?).

3-61A-3-2 Benjamin Compeau, age 20, P.O. Ludington, not married, see 6-61.
3-61A-3-3 Lillian Compeau, age 18, P.O. Ludington, see 6-61.
3-61A-3-4 Bessie Compeau, age 16, P.O. Ludington.
Husband 2nd: Oscar Craig (white).
3-61A-3-5 Oscar Craig, age 7, P.O. Ludington.
3-61A-4 Lillian La Fromway, age 36, P.O. Ludington, Mich.
Husband: Ambrose Fromway, white.
3-61A-4-1 Harry Fromway, age 9.
3-61A-4-2 Gladys Fromway, age 6.
3-61A-4-3 Fred Fromway, age 3.

Hamlin Lake Mich
May 22 th 1909

Dear Sir you inquing about Louis Thomas he at this Place up head the this Lake
Address Free Soil Mich R.F.D. 2
Care Joe Fortier
Geo. Barnhart

Information following from: Grand Rive put on other sheet & compare.
4 SHEET #1
4-61A AIN-NE-ME-KE-WAY, dead
Wife: Name not given, dead.
4-61A-1 Name not given (dau), dead.
4-61A-1-1 Nancy (Generaux).
4-61A-1-2 Abbie.
4-61A-2 Name not given (dau), P.O. Copemish.
4-61A-3 Name not given, dead.
Wife: Name not given, dead.
4-61-3-1 James Bemos, age 34, P.O. Elk Rapids.
Wife: Agatha Bemos, age 28, Traverse, see 27-41.
4-61A3-3-1-1 ~~Serlonyer Sagonac (dau), age 7~~ dead 4 yrs ago.
4-61A3-3-1-2 Amos Sagonac, age 9, P.O. Mt Pleas. Sch.
4-61A3-3-1-3 Joseph Bemos, age 4 Died Apr 14/07.
4-61A3-3-1-4 Marie Bemos, age 3.
4-61A3-3-1-5 Edwin Bemos Born Mch 1908 2nd roll.
4-61A-3-2 Name not given, dead.
Husband: Dan Marsh, P.O. Bear Lake, see 4-58.
4-61A-3-2-1 Eunice Marsh, age 12, P.O. Harbor Springs School.

4 SHEET #2 at Copemish

4-61A AIN-NE-ME-KE-WAY or BEMIS, dead
Wife: Name not given, dead.
4-61A-1 John Bemis, dead, not married.
4-61A-2 Jennie Bemis, dead, not married.
4-61A-3 Martha Bemis, age 60, P.O. Honor.
Husband 1st: James Zoondah, see 14-65 look up.
Husband 2nd: Jacob Anderson.
Husband 3rd: John Ching-Wash, dead.
Husband 4th: ~~Sampson Eden~~ Henry Shaw-Naw-Hay-Se-Gay.
Husband 5th: Sampson Eden.
Note: Never had any children by any husband.

Information following from: Not Given.
5-61A KAY-KAY-KAW-ME, all dead, no heirs.

Information following from: Not Given.
6-61A PE-ANE or PETER ROBINSON, dead.
Wife 1st: Name not given, dead.
Wife 2nd: Nancy Robinson, Died May 20, 1908 N.B. 1st roll.
6-61A-1 Marian Robinson Lahaye, dead.
Husband: Ephraim Lahaye, dead.
6-61A-1-1 Lottie Allard, age 33, P.O. Ludington RFD #4.
Husband: Pete Allard, white.
6-61A-1-1-1 Alex Ching-Wash, age 8, P.O. Ludington RFD #4.
6-61A-1-1-2 Irene Allard, age 1, P.O. Ludington, Born Feby 11/07 NB 2nd roll.
6-61A-1-2 Eliza Compeaux, age 31, P.O. Ludington RFD #4.
Husband: James Compeaux, see 3-61.
6-61A-1-3 ~~Geo~~ Alma Olk, age 27, P.O. Ludington RFD #4.
Husband: William Olk, white.
6-61A-1-3-1 Estelle Olk, age 7.
6-61A-1-3-2 Leona Olk, age 6.
6-61A-1-3-3 George Olk, age 4.
6-61A-1-3-4 Mildran Olk, age 2.
6-61A-1-3-5 Rosaline Olk, Born Jany 13/08 NB 2nd roll.
6-61A-1-4 George Lahaye, age 25, Ludington #4.
6-61A-1-5 William Lahaye, age 21, Ludington #4.
6-61A-1-6 Alice Lahaye, age 18, Ludington.
6-61A-1-7 Francis Lahaye, age 16..
6-61A-2 Sampson Robinson, age 42, P.O. Freesoil.
Wife 1st: Maggie Walker, no children.
Wife 2nd: Lizzie Lahaye, no children.
Wife 3rd: Alice Marsh.

6-61A-2-1 Jacob Robinson, age 17, P.O. Freesoil.
Wife 4th: Elizabeth Shagonaby, age 30, daughter of Francis Shagonab, 2-54.
6-61A-2-2 Mary Robinson, age 11, P.O. Mt Pleasant Sch..
6-61A-2-3 Lincoln Robinson, age 5.
6-61A-2-4 Rosanna Robinson, Born Mch. 29, 1907 – Died Nov. 14, 1907 NB 2nd roll.
6-61A-2-5 Chester Robinson, Born Mch 8, 1908 NB 2nd roll.

Freesoil Mich June 23rd 1909
Hon. Horace B. Durant
St. Ignace, Mich.
Dear Sir.
I hope I will hear from you by return mail, in regard to the whole number of the following bands
Grand River, Traverse,
Mackinac, Sault Ste Marie
Also other bands, and you likely could tell near when the funds to be distributed among the Ottawa and Chillewa Indians.
Please. Answer.
I, am, Your Very Respectfully
Sampson Robinson
Freesoil, Mich.

Information following from: Not Given.
7-61A NIN-DO-NE-GAY, dead.
Wife: Name not given.
7-61A-1 Joseph Do-Ne-Gay, dead, lived around Custer.
Wife: Name not given, dead, see Medavis, all children dead.
7-16A-2 Louis Do-Ne-Gay, dead, livedaround Custer, wife and children dead.
7-61A-3 John Do-Ne-Gay, dead when 15 yrs and unmarried.
7-61A-4 Thresa Do-Ne-Gay Bailey, living, see wife of Henry Bailey, belonging to family of 14-50.

Information following from: Not Given.
8-61A WAY-WIN-DAW-QUAW-DO-QUAY, dead.
Husband: Ephriam Lahey, dead, see trs #3 & #10 & #11 (?)
8-61A-1 Libbie Lawson, P.O. Beechwood.
Husband: J. J. Lawson, Postmaster, P.O. Beechwood, Iron Co. Mich, no children.
8-61A-2 Lizzie Lahey, P.O. Grand Rapids Mich, not married.
8-61A-3 Pete Lahey, age 45, P.O. Beechwood, Mich ~~Wisconsin~~.
See 3-44 & 22-54.
8-61A-4 Mary Lahey Mawby.

Husband: Joe Mawby (an Ind), see2-56 & 22-54.

Beechwood, Iron Co. Mich
May 21 1909
Horace B Durant
Petoskey
Sir
Cant knowe anyting aboutLezze Lahey she as Only a halfe Sister of Eunce
I have always been working out and out knowe em.
I am not a caller of Lahey he as my Step Father my Father and Mother are Ottawa my age as about 50. I am a Pure Ottawa Indian, Never have Bee Anything to be gat or if any Our ever have gat anything in my Name. Please Let Know
My Inds and Name Horswergee
Name Miss Lebby Scott c/o JJLarson

Department of the Interior,
Office of Indian Affairs,
Washington.

Petoskey, Mich.
May197 09

Mrs. J. J. Lawson.
Beechwood, Mich
Dear Madam:-
Will you please tell me if your sister Lizzie Lahey has ever been married if she has, her name, age and present address.
Also if she has any childrentheir names, ages addresses etc also please give me your age for the Ottawa and Chippewapayroll and oblige.
Yours truly,
Horace B. Durant
Special U.S. Indian Agent. PerB

Information following from: Not Given.
9-61A JOSEPH DONEGAY, dead, wife dead, had 2 children all dead unmarried.
Note: relation of Henry Bailey's wife Thresa Donegay Bailey see 7-61.

Information following from: Not Given.
10-61A MAY-YAW-O-BAY or PETER ESPIEW, age 72, P.O. Freesoil Mich
Wife 1st: Name not given, dead.
10-61A-1 Jane Coon, age 37, P.O. Freesoil
Husband: Joe Coon, age 47, P.O. Freesoil, father William Coon. Note: Write Joe Shagonagbe at Hamilton who lived

with Joe Coon.

10-61A-1-1 James Coon, age 19, P.O. Freesoil ~~see 6-56~~.

10-61A-1-2 Anthony Coon, age 17.

10-61A-1-3 Martha Coon, age 9.

10-61A-1-4 Angeline Coon, age 7.

10-61A-1-5 Frank Coon, age 5.

10-61A-1-6 Rosie Coon, Born Dec 1, 1907 NB 2nd roll.

Wife 2nd: Lizzie Chaw-Shaw-Waw-Nay-Beece, dead, dau. of 7-59.

10-61A-2 Laura Espiew, age 21, P.O. Freesoil, no children.

Husband: Charles Theodore, age 26, see 27-59 & 2-54.

10-61A-3 Edward Espiew, age 11.

10-61A-4 Elmer Espiew, age 9.

10-61A-5 Janet Espiew Battise.

Husband: James Battise.

Information following from: Not Given.

11-61A WAW-BE-NE-BE-QUAY (F), dead, mother of #10 & #3.

Husband 1st: Name not given, dead.

Husband 2nd: Name not gven, dead.

11-61A-1 ~~Libbie~~ Harriet Shaw-Quay, age 63, P.O. Ludington.

Husband 1st: Frank Froew, white, dead.

11-61A-1 Henry Shaw-Quay, age 35, P.O. Ludington, child by 1st husband but taken name of 2nd husband his step father.

Husband 2nd: Robert Shaw-Quay, dead, see 40-57.

11-61A-2 Joe Shaw-Quay, age 31.

11-61A-2 Marsha Shaw-Quay, age 27.

11-61A-2 Eunice Shaw-Quay, age 18.

11-61A-2 Name not given, died without heirs.

Information following from: NB said to have been with Canadian Indians.

12-61A JOSEPH MISH-E-GAY-KAKE, dead.

Wife: Name not given, dead.

12-61A-1 Martha Mish-E-Gay-Kake (Snake), living P.O. Cap-croker Canada near.

12-61A-1-1 Charlotte Mish-E-Gay-Kake.

~~Note: Joseph Mish-e-gay-kake is a brother of Sarah King, or Tah-be-dah, living Custer, Mich. She claims enrollment & undougtedly entitled but cannot find a husband or her name on 1870 roll~~

Horace B Durant

Her husband was Key way o cushaw or Chas. King, dead. See 13-60 Key-way-cush-cum.

Information following from: Not Given.

13-61A MAW-NE-DONSE or JAMES MANITOUS, dead.

Wife: None given.
13-61A-1 William Manitous, age 28, see 27-59.

Information following from: Not Given.
14-61A SHAW-WAW-NE-WAY-WAY-GE-WON, dead.
Wife: None given.
14-61A-1 Eliza Antoine Kelsey, age 33, see 5-61 & 2-50.
Husband: Joe Kelsey

Information following from: Not Given.
15-61A MAW-BEECE, dead, no children.

Information following from: John Wahbindwetto Henry Bailey Chas Genereaux Joe Cogswell JamesCogswell Sampson Robinson.
16-61A PAY-BE-SHAY, dead, no heirs.

Page 61B
Chief MAISH-KE-AW-SHE
Grand River

Information following from: Not Given.
1-61B MAISH-KE-AW-SHE, dead.
Wife: Name not given, dead.
1-61B-1 Randall Kelsey, age 71, see 5-61.

Information following from: Not Given.
2-61B KAY-GWAY-DAW-SUNG, dead, wife & children all dead. Uncle of John Williams, only child of parents but has ½ sister on mother's side, mother living see 3-52.
2-61B-1 John Williams #2, age 36, P.O. Lattin.
Wife: Nancy Pontiac Williams, age 32, daughter of 7-65.
2-61B-1-1 Pontiac Williams, age 12.
2-61B-1-2 Alex William Williams, age 8, see 14-55.
2-61B-1-3 Joe Williams, age 6.
2-61B-1-4 Henry Williams, age 3.
2-61B-1-5 Cecelia Williams, age 1, born July 19, 1907 NB 2nd roll.
2-61B-2 Mary Ching-Gwan, age 41, P.O. Lattin.
Husband: George Ching-Gwan, see 6-50 for children.

Information following from: Not Given.
3-61B KIN-NAY-BICK, dead.
Wife: Name not given, dead.
3-61B-1 Mary Kay-Kake (Ke-Keck), age 50, see 6-61A.
Husband: Isaac Kay-Kake, age 57, see 1-64 & 21-64, no

children..
Note: No other children.

Information following from: Not Given.
4-61B SHAW-WAW-NE-PE-NAY-SE, dead.
Wife: Name not given, dead.
4-61B-1 Johnson Green, age 40, P.O. Copemish.
Wife: Name not given, dead.
4-61B-1-1 Julia Gree, age 13, see 12-56 & 22-59.
4-61B-2 Paul Green, age 27, P.O. Hamilton, no children.

Information following from: Not Given.
5-61B NAW-KAY-O-SAY or RANDALL KELSEY, age 71, P.O. Custer #2.
Wife: Name not given, dead.
5-61B-1 Angeline Pay-Ba-Ma, age 47, P.O. Hart, see 6-56.
Husband: William Pay-Ba-Ma, an Ottawa, see 7-50.
5-61B-1-1 Pete Pay-Ba-Ma, age 26, P.O. Hart RFD.
Wife: ~~Josephine~~ Susan, granddaughter of 11-54.
5-61B-1-1-1 Annie Pay-Ba-Ma, age 3.
5-61B-1-2 Philip Pay-Ba-Ma, age 17, P.O. Hart.
5-61B-1-3 John Pay-Ba-Ma, age 11, P.O. Hart.
5-61B-2 Joseph Kelsey or Naw-Kay-O-Say, age ~~45~~ 47, P.O. Fountain.
Wife 1st: Name not given, dead.
5-61B-2-1 Flora Kelsey, age 18, P.O. Custer #2, see 6-59, has 1 child name not given.
5-61B-2-2 John Kelsey, age 16, P.O. Custer #2.
Wife 2nd: Eliza Kelsey, age 33, daughter of Ambrose Antoine, see 14-61.
5-61B-2-3 George Kelsey, age 13.
5-61B-2-4 Lizzie Kelsey, age 7.
5-61B-2-5 Esther Kelsey, age 4.
5-61B-2-6 Bessie Kelsey, age 2, born Sept 1906.
5-61B-3 Nancy Kelsey Battise, age 36, see 6-59.
Husband: Mose Battise, P.O. Custer #2, no children.
5-61B-4 Alice Kelsey Battise, age 28, P.O. Custer #2.
Husband: Benedict Battise, see 6-59, no children.

Information following from: Bradley.
6-61B AW-ME-KOONSE JR., dead.
Wife: Mary Ke-Keck, see 3-61B, 21-64 & 1-64.

Information following from: Not Given.
7-61B AW-BE-ME-QUAW, age 69, P.O. Lattin.
Husband 1st: Name not given, dead.
Husband 2nd: Seth Wright, dead.

Author Note: No indication given which husband was the fatherof which child.

7-61B-1 Mary Ching-Gwon, age 41, see 2-50.

Husband: George Ching-Gwon, see 2-50 & 3-52.

7-61B-2 John Williams #2, age 36, P.O. Lattin.

Wife: Nancy (Pontiac) Williams, see 7-65, 2-61 & 3-52.

7-61B-2-1 Pontiac Williams, age 13.

7-61B-2-2 ~~Joe~~ William Williams, age 11.

7-61B-2-3 Joe Williams, age 6.

7-61B-2-4 Hank or Henry Williams, age 4.

7-61B-2-5 Poc-To-G0-Quay or Cecelia Williams, age 1, Born July or Aug 1907 NB.

Information following from: Bradley Feby/09.
8-61B O-BE-MAW-CHE-WON, all dead, no heirs.

Information following from: Not Given.
9-61B O-PE-TAW, all dead, no heirs.

Information following from: Not Given.
10-61B O-TAW-SHE-TAY-WEN.

Author Note: No information contained in file.

Information following from: Not Given.
11-61B PEM-PAW-TAW-BE or WILLIAM SHAY-GO-NAY-BE, dead, wife dead, for family see 2-54.

Page 62
Chief CHING-GWA-SHE
Grand River

Information following from: Not Given.
1-62 CHING-GWA-SHE, dead.

Wife 1st: Name not given, dead.

Wife 2nd: Name not given, dead.

Author Note: No indication given which wife is mother of which child.

1-62-1 Elizabeth Chingwash, age 61, P.O. Fountain, see 8-50.

Husband: Name not given, dead, see 2-60 & 8-50.

1-62-2 David Chingwashe, age 58, P.O. Harbor Springs.

Wife 1st: Name not given, dead, step father 9-34, see 12-60.

1-62-2-1 Samuel Chingwas, age 28, P.O. Harbor Springs, not married.

1-62-2-2 Charles Chingwas, age 25, P.O. Tomah Sch Wis.

1-62-2-3 William Chingwas, age 18, P.O. Harbor Springs.

1-62-2-4 Angeline Chingwas, age 16, P.O. Mt Pleas Sch.
1-62-2-5 Cecelia Chingwas, age 13, P.O. Mt Pleas Sch.
1-62-2-6 Lucy Chingwas, age 11, Harbor Springs.
Wife 2nd: Isabella Chingwash nee Smith, age 45.
Note: Children by 1st husband:
1-62-2-7 Ella Petoskey, age 28, P.O. Carlisle Ind Sch, Traverse.
1-62-2-8 Cornelius Petoskey, age 25, P.O. Howell, Mich, Traverse.

1-62-3 Catharine Saw-Ge-Waw, P.O. Star City, see 61-33, no children.
Husband: Domineke Saw-Ge-Waw, see 6-33, separated.

1-62-4 Mary Ching-Gwa-She, dead.
Husband: None given.
1-62-4-1 Sah-Qus-Ah or Sarah Petosky, age 30, P.O. Petoskey
Husband: ~~Julius~~ Huron Petoskey, age 24, see 14-26, Traverse.
1-62-4-2 ~~Sig-A-Nack or Thomas Meine~~ or Blackbird, age ~~15 28~~, P.O. Petoskey.
1-62-4-3 Daisy Meine, age 18, P.O. Tomah Sch. Wis.
1-62-4-4 Joe Meine, age 14, P.O. Petoskey.

1-62-5 Sarah Ching-Gwa-She, dead.
Husband: Name not given, dead.
1-62-5-1 Ching-Gwa-She or George Peters #2, age 31, P.O. Petoskey.

1-62-6 Ke-So-Quay, dead.
Husband: John Brown, a Saginaw.
1-62-6-1 Ida Brown, age 6, P.O. Sogonning, Mich.
1-62-6-2 Simon Brown, age 6, P.O. Sogonning, Mich.
1-62-6-3 Bessie Brown, age 6, P.O. Sogonning, Mich.
Note: Information from headmen at Sogonning confirm by asking David Chingwasheat Harbor Springs.

Information following from: Henry Pego Nancy Stafford Mount Pleasant Michigan Letter from Mrs Nancy Stafford Feby 11/09 confirming record B.

2-62 MWAY-AW-BAW-TOE or MO-A-PUT-TO or HENRY PEGO, age 66, P.O. Remus, Mich.
Wife 1st: Name not given, dead.
Wife 2nd: Name not given, ~~dead~~.
Wife 3rd: Lucy Pego, Saginaw Indian whose grandmother was 22-64, but wose mother married a Saginaw Indian & drew with Saginaw's.
Author Note: No indication which wife was the mother of which child. Also Not certain if there were 3 or only 2 wives.
2-62-1 John Pego, age 46, see 1-50.
Wife: Name not given, dead.

2-62-2 Moses Pego, dead.
Wife: Name not given, dead.
2-62-2-1 Lizzie Pego, age 17, P.O. Mt Pleasant Sch.
2-62-2-2 James Pego, age 13, P.O. Mt Pleasant Route 1.
2-62-3 Nancy Stafford, age 41, P.O. ~~Armstong Creek, Wis~~ Bemidji, Minnesota.
Husband: Allison Stafford, age 45, white.
2-62-3-1 Sylvia J. Stafford, age 18, P.O. Bemidji, Minn.
2-62-3-2 Airs L. Stafford, age 15.
2-62-3-3 Hannah M. Stafford, age 13.
2-62-3-4 Name or sex not given, dead.
2-62-3-5 Name or sex not given, dead.
2-62-4 Enos Pego, age 28, P.O. Remus, Mich.
Wife: Myrtle Pego, age 24, see 20-57.
2-62-4-1 Hazel D. Pego, born June 14, 1907 2nd roll.
2-62-5 Levi Pego, age 26, Armstrong, Wis, single.
2-62-6 ~~John~~ Ward Pego, age 15, see 19-52.

Armstrong Creek Wis.
May 15/09

Horace B Durant
~~Washington~~ Petoskey Mich
Dear Sir.
In reply to yours of May 8/09 will say children and my age. John Pego 48
Henry Pego age 22 armstrong Creek, Wis
Elizabeth Pego ag – 19 on June 16/09 Mt Pleasant Mich
Jessie Pego – age – 17- Mt Pleasant Mich
Eunice Pego- age 31- address Armstrong Creek Wis
Yours truly
John Pego

Department of the Interior,
United States Indian Service,
Petoskey, Mich.,
June 8/09

Mr Levi Pego,
Armstrong Creek, Wis.
Dear Sir:-
Your name has been given me as belonging to the Ottawa& Chippewas of Michigan if you are will you please confirm same by sending me the names of your parents, names & addresses of your brothers & sisters also ages of yourself and family.
Please send at once to complete the roll and oblige.
Yours truly,

Horace B. Durant
Special U.S. Indian Agent. B

Henry Pego – Remus Mich
Elizabeth Pego – Dead
Mrs Nancy Stafford, Nymore Minn
John Pego, Armstrong Creek Wis
Enos Pego Remus Mich
My age 31 years I am single
Levi Pego, Armstrong Creek Wis

Information following from: Fountain 2/09.
3-62 NE-OBLE, all dead, no heirs.

Information following from: Not Given.
4-62 PAY-QUAY or HENRY BAILEY SR., age ~~86~~ 83, P.O. Custer #2.
Wife 1st: Name not given, dead.
4-62-1 Angeline Bailey, died May 1908.
Husband: Peter Maish-Caw, P.O. Northport, son of chief by that name, see 1-55.
4-62-2 Tah-Wah-Quah, age 57, see 11-52.
Husband: John Ne-Gake, P.O. Lattin.
4-62-3 James Bailey, age 56, P.O. Honor, see 4-56.
Wife: Ella Bailey, age 47.
4-62-3-1 Marsha Bailey, age 19.
Husband: Joe Fisher, age 26, see 28-60.
4-62-4 Charles Bailey, dead, no children.
~~Wife 2nd: Margaret, no children.~~
Wife 2nd: Maggie Bailey, on 1870 roll as 10-54, formerly wife of Peter Paw-Caw-Maw-Baw-No see 19-54.

Information following from: Not Given.
5-62 O-PE-GO, dead.
Wife: Name not given, dead.
5-62-1 John Pe-Go or O-Pe-Go, dead, on roll as 14-62.
Wife 1st : Name not given, dead.
Wife 2nd: Name not given, see 16-56.
Author Note: No indication which wife is mother of wich child.
5-62-1-1 Bert Pego, age 33, P.O. Lattin.
Wife: Nancy Louis, see 1-49, no children.
5-62-1-1-1 Susan Theodore Pego, age 14, P.O. Honor, see 12-62, adopted, Father John Theodore mother Ida Ching-Gwaw-She granddaughter of chief #16.
5-62-1-2 Charles Pego, age 24, P.O. Honor, see 14-62,

married name of wife not given..

5-62-2 James Pego, age 45, P.O. Lattin.

Wife 1st: Name not given, dead.

5-62-2-1 Amy Pego, dead, not married no children.

5-62-2-2 Lucy Pego, dead, not married no children.

5-62-2-3 Annie Pego, dead, not married no children.

Wife 2nd: Sarah Williams Pego, age 34, (father: William Fox or William Pe-Waw-No (?) mother Waw-Be-Nah-Kaw-She-Qua (?))

5-62-2-4 Benedict Pego, age 6, P.O. Lattin.

Children by 2nd wife Sarah Williams Pego and her 1st husband.

Husband 1st: Frank Bailey, living, see 27-65.

1 Eunice Bailey, age 16, P.O. Lattin, see 27-65.

2 Madeline Bailey, age 13, P.O. Lattin, see 27-65.

3 George Bailey, age 11, P.O. Lattin, see 27-65.

Note: Enroll with Sarah Pego.

Information following from: Not Given.

6 SHEET #1

6-62 SHAW-NAW-NAY-SE-GAY or STEPHEN ROBINSON, dead.

Wife: Mary, see Sheet #2 following.

6-62-1 Peter Robinson, dead, no children.

6-62-2 John Robinson, age 39, P.O. Hart.

Wife 1st: Sophia Peters, dead.

6-62-2-1 Nancy Robinson, age 19, P.O. Cath. Sch. Harbor Springs.

6-62-2-2 Agnes Robinson, age 14, P.O. Fountain, lives with Sam Pay-Quo-Tush known as Maggie Sam.

Wife 2nd : Edith Wah-Bah-Se-Gay Robinson, age 42, see 8-49.

6-62-2-3 Philip Robinson, age 10.

6-62-2-4 Cora Robinson, age 9.

Note: Says John Robinson is a half brother of Steve Robinson, father of John Robinson is a white man, but had same mother.

6 SHEET #2

6-62 SHAW-NAW-NAY-SE-GAY, dead.

Wife: Mary Ann (Ching-Gwaw-She) Shaw-Naw-Naw-Se-Gay, age 69, P.O. Star City, daughter of Chief #16 ~~see 6-62~~.

6-62-1 George Shaw-Naw-Naw-Se-Gay or Shaw-Waw-Naw-Se-Gay, age 47, P.O. Star City.

Wife: Janie Key-Way-Quo-Cum Shaw-Naw-Naw-Se-Gay, age 46, P.O. Star City, see 1-44, Traverse, no children by this marriage.

6-62-1-1 John Shaw-Naw-Naw-Se-Gay, age 23, P.O. Star City, single, child by former marriage father unknown,

Traverse.

6-6-1-2 John Baptiste, born Aug 29, 1907, see 1-44, Traverse.
Note: This is a child of John Baptiste and Elizabeth Mitchell see 1-44 but was adopted by and lives with ~~Henry~~ George Shaw-Naw-Naw-Se-Gay at Star City. Tuttle see 10-44.

6-62-2 Henry Shaw-Naw-Naw-Se-Gay, age 40, P.O. Star City, wife and children not named and all dead.

6-62-3 Name not given, dead, no children.

Information following from: Not Given.
7-62 AW-ME-KOONSE family, dead.
Wife: Name not given, dead.
7-62-1 William Micko or William Elliott, age 64, see 15-55.
Wife: Marsha Micko, see 26-51.
7-62-2 Nancy Sam, age 47, see 3-58.
Husband: William Sam or William Pay-Quo-Tush, see 3-58.

Information following from: Not Given.
8-62 SHE-MAW-GAW, dead.
Wife: Name not given, dead.
8-62-1 Name or sex not given, dead.
8-62-2 Philip King, age 24, see 32-38, Traverse.
8-62-3 Louis King, age 24, P.O. Omena, see 8-40, no children.
Wife 1st : Mary King, dead, Traverse
Wife 2nd: Sophia King nee She-Koo, age 20, P.O. Omena, see 3-23, Traverse.

Information following from: Not Given.
9-62 JOSEPH PAY-QUO-TUSH, dead.
Wife: Name not given, dead.
9-62-1 Name not given, dead.
Husband: George Baker, see 29-59.
9-62-1-1 Henry Baker.
9-62-1-2 Christina Baker.

Information following from: Not Given.
10-62 MAW-SE-NAY, wife and children names not given, all dead, no heirs.

Information following from: Not Given.
11-62 QUA-MIX-SE-QUAY, all dead, no heirs.

Information following from: Not Given.
12-62 PE-SKO-NOTE, dead.
Wife: Name not given, dead.

12-62-1 Name or sex not given, dead.

12-62-1-1 Susan Theodore or Susan Pego, see 5-62.

Information following from: Not Given.
13-62 WAW-BE-NE-BE-QUAY, dead.

13-62-1 Moses Ke-Way-Che-Won, age 71, see 6-58

Information following from: Not Given.
14-62 AW-NE-ME-QUO-UM, dead.

Wife 1st: Name not given, dead.
Wife 2nd: Mrs. Charles Webb or Sophia Alixe or Sophia Aw-Ne-Me-Qo-Um, P.O. Honor, see 16-56.
14-62-1 Bert Pego, age 33, see 5-62.
14-62-2 Charles Pego, see 5-62.

Fountain, Mich.
May 19, 1909

Horace B. Durant,
Petoskey, Mich.
Dear Sir:-

Received your letter the 13th. Julia McDaquot single 37 years in Fountain and Julia McDaquot the wife of Bonaparte Alexander at Custer R.F.D.#2, are not the same person the are cousins.

Lucy Hauseman live in Walkerville, Oceana Co.
Zita Cogswell the wife of Louis Cogswell is an ottawa her father is name is Frank Bailey and he is up to Star City her mother name is Maude Wabindato.

Charlies Pego his wife are separated they had one child the child is dead. Charlies is by himself now and he's about 28 years old he get his mail in Lattin, Oceana.Co. Mich And I would like to get my day wages on account those names.

Yours Truly
Joe Cogswell
Fountain Mich. Bx 61

Hart Mich
May 13 1909
Horace B. Durant
Dear Sir, your letter was received yesterday Im here near Hart. Thos King and I havnt been to lattin for two or three Weeks, now. I Will be twenty Seven years old the 25th of June and my Fathers name is John Pego and his age that I don't know But I think he was Some Where about 70 years old. When he died, he been dead over twent Six years ago and my mother name Sophia Pego. But She go by the name now of Webb, and her age is between 70 or 75 years old and Family that I ant got. I was Within one and half mile Where you Was, eases camp at Honor last fall. I am Staying here With my Brother

Bert Pego oh Say Will you Please tell me the amt of money that going to be divide among us if you Please

yours truly
Chas Pego
Hart Mich Route Box 15

Information following from: Not Given.
15-62 PO-KE-BE, dead, no heirs.

Information following from: Not Given.
16-62 NAW-BAW-NAY-NOSE or JAMES BANANAS, see 2-50 & 14-60.

Information following from: Not Given.
17-62 ME-TAY-QUAY, dead, no heirs.

Information following from: Not Given.
18-62 O-TAW-WAW-QUAY now John Ne-Go-Ke's wife, age 57, see 4-62 & 11-52.

Information following from: Not Given.
19-62 SAW-GAW-SE-GAY, dead.
Wife: None given.
19-62-1 Name or sex not given, dead.
Spouse: Not Given.
19-62-1-1 Cleveland Chingwash, see 1-62 & 8-50.
19-62-1-2 ~~Alex~~ Chingwash, age 8, see 6-61.

Information following from: Not Given.
20-62 PE-SHE-KEENSE, names wife and children not given and all dead, no heirs.

Information following from: Not Given.
21-62 MAY-DWAY-WAY, dead, son in law of 1-62, wife and child dead, no heirs.

Page 63
Chief AW-KE-BE-MO-SAY
Grand River
Thunder Bay
Oscoda
AuSable
Pinconing
Sagoning

Information following from: Thomas Johnson, Edward Johnson & Several Indians, Joe Bradley, Interpreter Pinconning.
1-63 AW-KE-BE-MO-SAY, dead.
    Wife: Name not given, dead.
    1-63-1 Thomas Johnson, age 60, P.O. Sagoning.
        Wife: Name not given, dead.
        1-63-1-1 James Johnson, age 26, Sagoning Haskell Inst.
        1-63-1-2 Martha Johnson, age 19, P.O. Sagoning.
    1-63-2 Edward Johnson, age 50, P.O. Sagoning.
        Wife: Name not given, Saginaw Indian, no children.

Information following from: Oscoda Jany 29.
2-63 KAY-TAW-GE-GO-NAY-BE, dead.
    Wife: Mary J. Peters, age 65, P.O. Alvin, Mi
    2-63-1 Lucy Greensky, age 46, P.O. Alvin, Mich.
        Husband: Simon Greensky, a Saginaw Ind., off.
        2-63-1-1 John Greensky, age 20, P.O. Alvin Chicago, Ills 4312 Calumet Ave.
        2-63-1-2 Naomi Greensky, age 18, Carlisle, Pa.
        2-63-1-3 Peter Greensky, age 16, Alvin.
        2-63-1-4 Daniel Greensky, age 13, P.O. Alvin.
        2-63-1-5 Lucy Greensky, age 24, P.O. Alvin.
    2-63-2 Julia Noonday, age 30, P.O. Alvin Mich.
        Husband: Lyman Noonday, Saginaw Ind, off.
        2-63-2-1 Agnes Noonday, age 7.

4312 Calumet Ave
Chicago Ill
June 10/09

Horace B Durant Agt.
Petoskey Mich

Dear Sir:

Your favor of the 10th inst, is at hand.

In reply I shall take the greatest of pleasure in giving you the confirmation about the matter my father bellongsto the tribe of Chippewa. Mother being Ottawa.

It is true that I belong to the both tribes. But I desire to have my name be on father's tribe.

The names of my parents are as fallows- Mother Lucy, Father Simon Greensky. Brothers, Peter & Daniel.

My sister Naomi- her address is, Indian School, Carlise Penna. Thanks for your kindness.

Yours very truly,
John Greensky

Information following from: head men of this band Sagoning Jany 27/09.
Author Note: This family was originally 3-63 on the 1870 but fields in file labeled 4-63with no explination given.
4-63 QUAY-KE-CHE-WON, dead.
Wife: Name not given, dead.
4-63-1 Name or sex not given, dead, no heirs.
4-63-2 Name or sex not given, dead.
Spouse: Not given.
4-63-2-1 Wesley James, age 18, P.O. Pinconning Carlisle.
4-63-2-2 Peter James, age 14, P.O. Pinconning ~~Carlisle~~ Chilocco School.
4-63-3 Thomas James, age 40, P.O. Sagoning.
Wife: Name not given, Saginaw Ind.
4-63-3-1 Iland James, age 17.
4-63-3-2 Mabel James, age 15.
4-63-3-3 Nora James, age 13.

Information following from: Not Given.
Author Note: See preceeding author note under 4-63. No information regarding this family contained in the file.
4-63 WAW-BIN-DAW-GAW-NAY

Information following from: Sagoning Jany 27/09
5-63 NAY-WAW-DAY-KE-ZHICK, P.O. Wolverine near Grayling, said to be William Isaac, has no family, wrote to Detriot pension Agency for his present address. June June 8/09 Durant probably John Isaac's brother see 6-63.

17579 NL#2 Ctf 348099 – Pr K 1 Mich V.S.S. 12 – 4 Mar 07 on 10" Died Mar- 07 Rep. Aug 28/07 (PM) no Acc'd issued in case.
U.S. Pension Agcy Detroit, Michigan Received Jun 9-1909
Isaac add at date of last pay't Horton Bay- Mich

Department of the Interior,
United States Indian Service,
Wolverine, Mich.
June 8/09
U. S. Pension Agent
Detriot, Mich.
Dear Sir:

I am engaged in making a roll of the Indians of Michigan, and desire to ascertain the present address of one Wm Isaac, who formerly lived at Wolverine, Mich.

It is said, here, that he is a pensioner, and, if so, you can probably inform me of his present address.

Kindly give me this information addressing me at Petoskey, Mich and should his Indian name be of record in your office, give me that also.

Very respectfully
Horace BDurant
Spl. Ind. Agent Petoskey, Mich

Died in March, 1907 O.A. James U.S. Pension Agent Detroit, Mich.

Information following from: Not Given.
6-63 NAY-DAW-NAW-QUAY-DO-QUAY, dead.
Husband: None given.
6-63-1 Name or sex not given, dead, has one child who is enrolled as a Saginaw.
6-63-2 John Isaac, age 57, P.O. Pinconning, probably 5-63 Not 5-63 Durant.
Wife: Name not given, a Saginaw Indian.
6-63-2-1 Daniel Isaac, age 30, P.O. Pinconning.
Wife: Name not given, Saginaw Indian.
6-63-2-1-1 Louise Isaac, age 7.
6-63-2-1-2Johnson Isaac, age 5.
6-63-2-1-3 Guy Isaac, age 4.
6-63-2-1-4 David Isaac, age 2.
6-63-2 James Isaac, age 26, P.O. Pinconning, single.
6-63-3 Silas Isaac, age 24, P.O. Pinconning.
Wife: Name not given, a Saginaw Ind.
6-63-3-1 Walter Isaac, age 2.
6-63-4 Mark Isaac, age 22, P.O. Pinconning.

Information following from: head men Sagoning Januy 27/09.
7-63 TAY-BAW-QWAW-SUNG, dead.
Wife: Name not given, dead.
7-63-1 Name or sex not given, 11-63.
7-63-2 Name or sex not given, dead.
7-63-2-1 Elijah Tad-Gwa-Sung, age 28, Alvin, Mich.

Information following from: headmen Nancy Ottawa Pascoby Sagonong Jany 27/09 Hubbard Lake Alpena, Mich June 9/09.
8-63 PAY-SHE-GO-BE or JAMES TAY-SHE-GO-BE (PASCOBY), age ~~55~~ 60, P.O. ~~Oscoda~~ Hubbard Lake near Aipena, Mich.
Wife: ~~Saginaw Indian~~ Nancy (Ottawa) Pascoby, age 55, says her father was Augustus Ottawa & she has sister at Petoskey or Elk Rapids (probably 19-26) Durant.
8-63-1 ~~No children~~ Isaac Pascoby, age 38, P.O. Oscoda, no children.
Child by 1st husband of wife:
Husband 1st: Sampson Nadae, P.O. Elk Rapids or Kewagdin.

8-63-2 Emory (Pascoby) or Nadae on roll sheet 2-38 as Wallace Nadae, lives with mother Nancy Ottawa, on Traverse roll.

Information following from: headmen Sagoning Jany 27/09.
9-63 WAW-BE-MAW-ING-GUN, dead, wife and children names not given, all dead.

Information following from: Not Given.
10-63 NAY-WAW-DAY-GE-ZHE-GO-QUAY.
Author Note: No information regarding this family contained in the file.

Information following from: John Tadgwasung St Ignace Jany 6/09, Mount Pleasant, Michigan Confirmed & @ Sagoning Jany 27/09.
11-63 SAW-GAW-NIN-WA-BE or JOHN TAD-GWA-SUNG, age 68, P.O. ~~St Ignace~~ Alvin, Mich near Oscoda.
Wife: Louisa Tad-Gwa-Sung, age 60.
11-63-1 Levi Bourassaw, age 10, son of 61-16 (Mackinaw Band) adopted by John Tad-Gwa-Sung.
~~11-63-2 Elijah Tad-Gwa-Sung, age 28, P.O. Alvin, Mich.~~

Information following from: Not Given.
12-63 PAW-SAW-GE-MAW
Author Note: No information regarding this family contained in the file.

Information following from: headmen Sagoning Jany 27/09.
13-63 O-GAW-BAY-GE-ZHE-GO-QUAY, dead, no heirs.

Information following from: Joe Johnson Pinconning Jany 27/09.
14-63 KE-WAY-DE-NAW-QUO-UM or JOSEPH BUCKWHEAT or JOE JOHNSON, age 80, P.O. Sagoning.
Wife: Mary Johnson or O-Tish-Quay-Ke-Zhick-Go-Quay, age 59, said to be a daughter of Ne-Saw-waw-quot, see ~~1-32~~ 2-24 on roll as 22-24, no children..

Page 64
Chief ME-TAY-O-MIG
Grand River

Information following from: Not Given.
1-64 ME-TAY-O-MIG, dead.
Wife: Name not given, dead.
1-64-1 Name or sex not given, dead, no heirs.
1-64-2 Name or sex not given, dead, no heirs.

1-64-3 Isaac Kay-Kake, age 57, P.O. Hamilton, Mich, a brother of 21-64 but raised by Me-Tay-O-Mig 1-64, nephew.
Wife: Mary Kay-Kake, age 50, see 3-61, no children
Note: Amos Fitch, Wah-bin-dwetto, John Baptiste say that all the band of Me-tay-o-mig drew with Potts, in the last payment about 2 or 2 yrs ago.

Information following from: Not Given.
2-64 JAMES O-GE-MOS, dead.
Wife: Name not given, dead.
2-64-1 Name or sex not given, 15-64.
2-64-2 George O-Ge-Mos, age 45, P.O. ~~Armstrong Creek~~ Wabeno, Wisconsin c/o T. A. Richardson.
Wife: Name not given, dead, Pott, no children.
2-64-3 Name or sex not given, dead, no heirs.
2-64-4 James Jackson O-Ge-Mos, age 56, P.O. Coleman #2.
Wife: Mary O-Ge-Mos, Saginaw Indian, off.
2-64-4-1 May Fisher, age 34, Mt Pleasant.
Husband: Name not given, Saginaw Indian, a mail carrier.
2-64-4-1-1 Elmer Fisher, age 8.
2-64-4-1-2 ~~Margaret~~ Marvin Fisher, age 6.
2-64-4-1-3 Edmund Fisher, age 4.
2-64-4-2 Fred Jackson, age ~~36~~ 32, P.O. Wise, Mich, single.
2-64-4-3 Clara Jackson, age 11, P.O. Coleman.
2-64-4-4 Sarah Belle Jackson, age 9, P.O. Colemen.
2-64-4-5 Elijah Jackson, age 5.
2-64-4-6 (unreadable name and age)
2-64-5 Sarah Peters, age 50, P.O. Beal City, Mich, see 4-64.
Husband: Name not given, dead.
2-64-5-1 Mary (Peters) Neyonce, age 24, P.O. Beal City.
Husband: Name not given, Saginaw Indian, no children.
2-64-5-2 Wesley Peters, age 19, Beal City, single.

Wabeno, Wis., Feb. 17th 1909

Mr. Horace Durant,
Special U.S. Indian Agent,
Mount Pleasant, Mich.
Dear Sir:-
Yours of Jan. 22nd received some time ago, from Amstrong Creek, Wis. My address now is Wabeno, Wis. % T.A. Richardson.
My wife who was a Pottawatomie died#, my son whom I adopted is a Pottawatomie now 12 year of age name Ope-mon-ga.

My brother Jim Ogemos lives in Coleman Mich. and when I last saw him he had 6 children. When writing me please address Geo. Ogemos Care of T.A. Richardson Wabeno, Wis.
Yours Resp.

His
Geo. X Ogemos
Mark
Per. J.A. Richardson

P.S. If you a need a quick answer from Geo. Please address me as Geo. Is several miles from P.O. T.A.R.

Information following from: Mount Pleasant, Michigan.
3-64 PE-TAW-QUO-AW-MO-QUAY, dead.
Husband: None given.
3-64-1 Charlotte Thomas, age 55, P.O. Mt pleasant #6.
Husband: None given.
3-64-1-1 Dan Jones, age 27, P.O. Mt Pleasant #6.
Wife: Name not given, dead.
3-64-1-1-1 Harry Jones, age 10.
3-64-1-1-2 Jerome Jones, age 8.
3-64-2 Name or sex not given, dead, no heirs.
3-64-3 Name or sex not given, dead, no heirs.

Information following from: Mt Pleasant, Michigan.
4-64 PAW-TWAY-WE-TUNG, dead.
Wife: Name not given, dead.
4-64-1 Henry Peters, dead.
Wife: name not given, dead.
4-64-1-1 James Peters, age 23, P.O. Beal City, Mich, single.
4-64-2 Isaac Peters, dead.
Wife: Sarah Peters, age 50, Beal City, see 2-64.
4-64-3 William Peters, age 48, P.O. Mt Pleasant #6.
Wife: Elizabeth Peters, age 49, Saginaw Indian off.
4-64-3-1 Amelia Peters, dead, no children.
4-64-3-2 James Peters, dead.
4-64-3-3 Eliza (Peters) Jackson, age 19, P.O. Mt Pleasant #6.
Husband: Arthur Jackson, Saginaw Indian off.
4-64-3-3-1 Clayton Jackson, age 1 7mos, Born May 3/07 2nd roll.
4-64-4 Frank Peters, age 44, P.O. ~~Beal~~ Mt Pleasant #6.
Wife: Name not given, Swan Creek Indian, no children by this marriage.
Child by 1st husband of wife.
Husband 1st: Watson Chippeway, see 10-64.
1 Philip Chippeway, see 10-64.

Information following from: Not Given.
5-64 AISH-QUAIB, dead.
Wife: Name not given, dead.
5-64-1 Mrs. Peter Bennett or Persilla, dead.
Husband: Peter Bennett, Saginaw Indian off.
5-64-1-1 David Bennett, age 42, P.O. Mt Pleasant #6.
Wife: Betsy Bennett, age 34, see ~~6-64~~ 24-64.
5-64-1-1-1 Peter Bennett, age 14.
5-64-1-1-2 Delia Bennett, age 10.
5-64-1-1-3 Helen Bennett, age 8.
5-64-1-1-4 Dollie Bennett, age 5.
5-64-1-1-5 James Bennett, age 2.
5-64-2 Name or sex not given, dead, no heirs.
5-64-3 Moses Aish-Quaib, a ge 53, P.O. Rosebush #3.
Wife: Susan Aish-Quaib, Saginaw Ind off.
5-64-3-1 Julia Walker, age 30, P.O. Rosebush #3.
Husband: George Walker, age 34, see 12-53.
5-64-3-1-1 Floyd M. Walker, age 7.
5-64-3-1-2 Pearl Walker, age 5.
5-64-3-2 Charles Aish-Quaib, age 24.
Wife: Rosie Aish-Quaib, age 21, see 4-53 for children.
5-64-3-3 Sarah Aish-Quaib, age 19, P.O. Rosebush #3.
5-64-3-4 Priscilla Aish-Quaib John, age 17, P.O. Rosebush #3.
Husband: Name not given, Saginaw Chip (off).
5-64-3-4-1 Name not given, age 1 month, born Dec/08 too late.
5-64-3-5 Ella Aish-Quaib, age 13.

Information following from: Mount Pleasant, Michigan.
6-64 NAY-AW-BE-TUNG, dead.
Wife: Name not given, dead.
6-64-1 Name or sex not given, 24-64.
6-64-2 Name or sex not given, dead, no heirs.
6-64-3 Name or sex not given, dead, no heirs.

Information following from: Not Given.
7-64 KE-ZHICK, dead, all children dead, no heirs.

Information following from: Mount Pleasant, Michigan.
8-64 SOLOMON CHE-NE-WAY, dead.
Wife: Wife: Name not given, dead.
8-64-1 Name or sex not given, was married & lived in Pinconning or Elk Lake & may have children living.

8-64-2 Name or sex not given, dead.
8-64-3 Name or sex not given, dead.
8-64-4 Name or sex not given, dead.
Note: Could not get trace of them at Pinconning. Durant.
Note: John Franssway say's Solomon Cleneway never had any children of his own. Those enrolled with him must have been his step children, two girl's living – Ogewaw Co. one of them Viz:
1 Betsy Jacobs, age 62, P.O. Round Lake, Mich.
Husband: Name not given, Saginaw.
1-1 George Jacobs, age 31.
1-2 John Jacobs, age 29.
1-3 Jackson Jacobs, age 25.
1-4 Jennie Jacobs, age 27.
1-5 Dan Jacobs, age 23.
1-6 Nancy Jacobs, age 21.
2 Nellie David, age 59, P.O. Round Lake, Mich.
Husband: John David, Saginaw Ind. off.
2-1 Benson David, age 24.
2-2 William David, age 22.
2-3 John David, age 20.
2-4 Tom David, age 18.
2-5 Levi David, age 16.
Note: The information in note confirmed, but it is believed that Betsy Jacobs & Nellie David are now considered Saginaw Inds.- and it is doubtful if they should be enrolled as Ottawas & Chippewas. Durant.

Information following from: Not Given.
9-64 WAIN-ZHE-KE-TAW-SO, dead.
Wife: Name not given, dead.
9-64-1 Charles McClure, dead, adopted.
Wife: Name not given, dead.
9-64-1-1 Jennie McClure, age 16, P.O. Mt Pleasant Sch, see 28-60.
9-64-2 Name not given, dead.
Wife: Emma Walker, Saginaw Indian off.
9-64-2-1 Frank McClure, age 24, P.O. Rosebush #1.
9-64-2-2 Rose Jackson, age 19.
Husband: Name not given, Saginaw Ind.
9-64-2-2-1 May Jackson, Born May 1, ~~1909~~ 1908.
9-64-3 Name or sex not given, 27-64.
9-64-4 William McClure, age 56, P.O. Lattin, see 13-64 for wife & child.

Information following from: Mount Pleasant, Michigan.
10-64 AW-BE-TAW-SUNG, dead.

Wife: None given.

10-64-1 William Chippeway, age 50, died July 4/08.

Wife: Mary Chippeway, age 48, P.O. Mt Pleasant #6, Saginaw off.

10-64-1-1 Walter Chippeway, age 15, P.O. Mt Pleasant #6.

10-64-1-2 Eliza Chippeway, age 14, P.O. Mt Pleasant #6.

10-64-1-3 Dewey Chippeway, age 10, P.O. Mt Pleasant #6.

10-64-2 Watson Chippeway, dead.

Wife: Name not given, now wife of Frank Peters & Swan Creek Ind. see 4-64.

10-64-2-1 Philip Chippeway, age 25, P.O. Mt Pleasant #6, single.

10-64-3 Alexander Chippeway or Alex Louis, age 42, ~~Chippewa, Wa Mt P~~ Wiedman.

Wife: Margaret Chippeway, age 35, see 6-53 & 34-52

10-64-3-1 Grace Chippeway, age 12.

10-64-3-2 Elizabeth Chippeway, age 10.

10-64-3-3 Sophia Chippeway, age 4.

Information following from: Mount Pleasant, Michigan.

11-64 KE-ZHE-GO-QUAY, dead.

Husband: None given.

11-64-1 Name or sex not given, 17-64.

11-64-2 William, dead, no heirs.

11-64-3 Name not given, dead.

Husband: David Rodd, Saginaw Indian.

11-64-3-1 Susan Jackson, age 30, P.O. Rosebush, Mich.

Husband: John Jackson, Saginaw Indian.

11-64-3-1-1 Eliza Jane Jackson, age 11.

11-64-3-1-2 Wilmer Jackson, age 8.

11-64-3-1-3 Bert Jackson, age 5.

11-64-3-1-4 Agnes Jackson, age 2

11-64-3-1-5 Edward Jackson, Born Aug 18/08 too late.

Information following from: Not Given.

12-64 PAY-SHE-NIN-NE-QUAY.

Author Note: No information contained in the file for this family.

Information following from: Not Given.

13-64 ME-NOW-QUOT, dead.

Wife: Name not given, dead.

13-64-1 Saus-Sway 20-64.

13-64-2 William Smith or McClure, age 56, P.O. Lattin, Mich.

Wife: Mary (Carey) McClure, age 48, see 2-49.

13-64-2-1 Fred Smith, age 28, P.O. Lattin.

Wife: Jennie (Louis) Smith.
13-64-2-1-1 Catharine Smith, age 4.
13-64-2-1-2 Leo Smith, age 3.
13-64-2-2 Jane (Smith) Newton, age 24, P.O. Lattin, Mich.
Husband: John Newton, see 25-55.
13-64-2-2-1 Moses Newton, age 4.
13-64-2-3 Augustine Smith, age 19, P.O. Lattin, Mich.
13-64-2-4 Julia Smith, age 16, P.O. Lattin, Mich.

Information following from: Mount Pleasant, Michigan.
14-64 QUAY-CO-CHE, dead.
Wife: None given.
14-64-1 Louis Quay-Co-Che, age ~~44~~ 47, P.O. Mt Pleasant #1, single.
14-64-2 Name or sex not given, dead, no heirs.

Information following from: Betsy Shawagon Mount Pleasant, Michigan Jany 19/09.
15-64 SHAW-WE-NE-KE-ZHICK-GO-QUAY or BETSEY SHOWAGON, age 59, P.O. Weidman.
Husband: Joe Wabinaw, see 30-65.
15-64-1 Joseph Pearnew or Payono #1, age 38, see 24-64 & 33-65, no children.
15-64-2 John Shaw-We-Gon or William Waw-Be-Gay-Keke, age 17, P.O. Weidman, see 6-65.
15-64-3 Sam Shaw-We-Gon, age ~~34~~ 36, P.O. Weidman.
Wife: Angeline Shaw-We-Gon, age 36, P.O. Weidman.
15-64-3-1 Jennie Shaw-We-Gon, age 16, P.O. Weidman.
15-64-4 Smith Shaw-We-Gon, age 34, P.O. Weidman, single, living with Julia Andrews, age 27, see 24-64.
15-64-5 Name not given, (dau), dead.
Husband: John Solomon or Solomon Pay-Me-Saw-Dung, Saginaw Ind. off.
15-64-5-1 Agnes Solomon, age 13, P.O. Mt Pleasant Sch.
15-64-5-2 Esther Solomon, age 11, P.O. Mt Pleasant Sch, cripple with father.
15-64-5-3 Sam Solomon, age 9, P.O. Mt Pleasant Sch.

Information following from: Mount Pleasant, Michigan.
16-64 PE-TAW-WAW-NAW-QUOT, dead, child dead, no heirs.

Information following from: Chiefs Mount Pleasant, Michigan Jany 18/09.
17-64 WAY-WE-NOW-SHE, dead.
Wife: Name not given, dead.
17-64-1 James Jackson, age 22, P.O. Genoa Ind School, single.

Information following from: Mount Pleasant Jany 18/09.
18 SHEET #1
18-64 NE-BAW-MO-QUAY or MRS ELIZA TROMBLY, age 58, P.O. Frost Lake Edwards, no children.
Note: Confirmed by letter from her Feby 22/09. Durant.

18 SHEET #2
Note: Forwarded to Mrs Trombly Feby 13/09 Returned (Recd Mch 1/09) D.
18-64 NE-BAW-MO-QUAY or MRS ELIZA TROMBLY, age 58, P.O. Edwards.

Mr. Horace B. Durant *Feb 22 1909*
Sir received your Letter an answer will Sey I am full Member Ottawa & Chippewas Grand River Band Chief Me=tay-0-mig *no children*
Mrs Eliza Trombly

Information following from: Mount Pleasant, Michigan.
19-64 AW-NE-ME-QUOUM, dead, no heirs.

Information following from: John Fronssway at his home – Admits he and his family drew with Pottawatomies. Durant Jany 19/09 Mount Pleasant, Michigan.
20-64 SAUS-SWAY ~~or JOHN HAWK~~ or JOHN FRONSSWAY, age 78, P.O. My Pleasant #6, see 13-64.
Wife: Name not given, dead, Saginaw Indian.
20-64-1 Lizzie Jackson, age 44, P.O. Frost Lake, Edwards.
Husband: Name not given, Saginaw Ind., no children.
20-64-2 Levi Saus-Sway or Fronssway, age 37, P.O. Mt Pleasant #6.
Wife: Lucy Saus-Sway, age 28, P.O. Star City, separated, now lives with Pete Zoondah or Levi Zoondah or Levi Cawbury, see 4-51, no children, see also 10-44
20-64-2-1 Alice Saus-Sway, age 14, P.O. Mt Pleasant Sch.
20-64-2-2 Jennie Saus-Sway, age 12, P.O. Mt Pleasant Sch.
20-64-2-3 John Saus-Sway, age 11, P.O. Mt Pleasant Sch.
20-64-2-4 Ida Saus-Sway, age 8, P.O. Star City, with mother.
20-64-3 Douglas Saus-Sway or Fronssway, age 18, P.O. Mt Pleasant Sch.

Information following from: Mount Pleasant, Michigan Hamilton Feby/09.
21-64 KAY-KAKE or EDWARD KAY-KAKE, age 55, P.O. Hamilton, Mich.
Wife 1st: Name not given, dead.
Wife 2nd: Name not given.
21-64-1 John Ke-Keck (nephew), age 40, P.O.Walpole Island Canada, off.

Note: This man I saw at Walpole Isle – says he is 43 yrs & was born in Canada – has land on Walpole Isle & is a Canadian. Durant Spl Agt Walpole Isle Canada June 11/09.

21-64-2 Name not given, dead.
  Husband: _______ Mosher, (white)
  21-64-2-1 Andrew Mosher, age 19, P.O. Genoa Sch.
  21-64-2-2 Bertha Mosher, age 21, see 1-51.
    Husband: Johnson Medavis.
    21-64-2-2-1 Clerence Medavis, age 3.
    21-64-2-2-2 Josephine Medavis, Born Aug 6/08, 1-51 born Aug/07.

Information following from: Mount Pleasant, Michigan.
22-64 O-GAW-BAY-ISH-CAW-MO-QUAY, dead.
  Husband: None given.
  22-64-1 Nezette, dead, no heirs.
  22-64-2 Name or sex not given, dead.
    Spouse: Not given.
    22-64-2-1 Lucy Pego, age 52, wife of 2-62, Saginaw off.
    22-64-2-2 Betsey Waynee, P.O. Pinconning or Bay City or Kawkawlin, Saginaw off.
      Husband: Name not given, Saginaw Ind.
      Note: Enroll with Saginaw

Information following from: Mount Pleasant, Michigan.
23-64 AW-GE-WE-KE-ZHICK, dead, no heirs.

Information following from: William Smith Mount Pleasant, Michigan.
24-64 WAW-BE-PE-NAY-SE or WILLIAM SMITH, age 65, P.O. Mt Pleasant #6.
  Wife: Name not given, dead.
  24-64-1 Betsy (Smith) Bennett, age 34, see 5-64.
  24-64-2 Jane (Smith) ~~Payne~~ Peyono, age 29, P.O. Mt Pleasant #6.
    Husband: Joseph Peyono, see 33-65, no children
  24-64-3 Julia (Smith) Andrews, age 27, P.O. Mt Pleasant #6, see 15-64.
    Husband: Frank Andrews, age 29, P.O. Mt Pleasant #6, Saginaw off.
    Note: No children by this husband.
    24-64-3-1 Elmer Andrews, Born Aug 29/07.
  24-64-4 Adam Smith, age 24, P.O. Mt Pleasant #6, single.
  24-64-5 Louisa Smith, age 17, P.O. Mt Pleasant #6.

Information following from: Rosebush (Chiefs) Jany 21/09 Mount Pleasant, Michigan.

25-64 PO-QUAW-KE-NE-GAW, dead, no heirs.

Information following from: Rosebush Jany 29/09 Mount Pleasant, Michigan.
26-64 WAW-SAW-QUOM, dead.
Wife: Name not given, dead.
26-64-1 Jennie McClure, age 16, P.O. Mt Pleasant Sch, see 9-64 & 28-60.

Information following from: Mount Pleasant, Michigan.
27-64 PAY-SHE-KE-ZHICK or HENRY MCCLURE, age 60, P.O. Frost Lake Edwards Mich.
Wife: Caroline McClure, age 56, P.O. ~~Ogem~~ Frost Lake Edwards Mich, a Saginaw Ind. off, no children.

Page 65
Chief A-KEN-BELL
Grand River

Information following from: Marsha Pinnance & husb: Jany 19/09 at their house near Weidman, Mich Mount Pleasant, Michigan.
1-65 A-KEN-BELL, dead.
Wife 1st: Name not given, dead.
Wife 2nd: Nancy Wah-Be-Kaw-Ne-Quay A-Ken-Bell, age 93, P.O. Weidman #2.
1-65-1 Martha Pinnance, age 52, P.O. Weidman, Do not enroll.
Husband: Name not given, Canadian Indian.
Note: Drew money with Canadian Indians and was living in Canada in 1870, both husband, wife & their children drew money in Canada. (N.B. Their own statements). Jany 19/09 Durant SplAgt.
Later: Walpole Isld Canada, June 11/09. This woman also appeared before me here for enrollment & her status is as stated on the attached supplemental sheet 1-65. Durant Spl Agt.
1-65-2 Name not given, dead, was 2nd wife of 33-65.
Husband: Name not given.
1-65-2-1 Joseph Peyano #2 or Joe A-Ken-Bell, age 27, P.O. Weidman, Mich #2, see 33-65.

1 SUPPLEMENTAL SHEET by Marth Penance Walpole Isle June 11/09.
1-65 A-KEN-BELL.
1-65-1 Martha Penance, age 53, P.O. Walpole Isl.
Note: The woman claims to be a daughter of Akenbell by his 1st wife – she says she has no brothers or sisters, but had a half

sister, now dead – who has a child now living at Weidman – named Joe Akenbell – about 30 yrs old . She says akenbell was thrice married & his present widow is Wah-be-kaw-ne-qua – If the above information corresponds with what is now on original sheet 1-65, enroll her – Subject to note below. Note: This woman has lived at Walpole Isle ever since she was… (Author Note: remainder of sentence unreadable) Horace B. Durant Special U.S. Indian Agent.

1-65-1-1 Mary Wah-Dee, age 30.
Husband; Name not given, Canadian.
1-65-1-1-1 Lizzie, age 15.
1-65-1-1-2 Clerence, age 13.
1-65-1-1-3 John, age 11.
1-65-1-1-4 Clara, age 9.
1-65-1-1-5 Norlis, age 8.
1-65-1-1-6 Gertie, age 6.
1-65-1-1-7 Geraldine, age 4.
1-65-1-2 Elijah Penance, age 26.
1-65-1-3 Nancy Penance, age 24.
1-65-1-4 Justin Penance, age 15.
1-65-1-5 Mitchell Penance, age 13.

Information following from: Not Given.
2-65 ME-SAW-BAY.
Note: Cannot trace this family.

Information following from: Athens Mch/09.
3-65 MAW-CAW-DAY-WE-NUM, dead.
Wife: None given.
3-65-1 Mong-Go-Quay, dead, no heirs.
3-65-2 Henry Jackson, dead, no children.
3-65-3 Jacob Jackson #1, age 49, P.O. Athens.
Wife: Alice (Sprague), now wife of James Johnson, see 5-53 & 25-53.
3-65-3-1 Jacob Jackson Jr or Jacob Sprague, age 20, see 25-53
3-65-4 Lucy King, age 45, P.O. Freesoil.
Husband: Thomas King, no children.

Information following from: James David a ~~brother~~ son Athens Mch/09.
4-65 KAW-WE-TAW-KE-ZHICK, dead.
Wife: Name not given, dead.
4-65-1 James David or 5-65.
4-65-2 Sarah Isaac or 15-65.
4-65-3 Mackie or 22-65.
4-65-4 Naw-O-Quay-Saw-Mo-Quay or 38-65, dead.

4-65-5 Silas or 25-65, dead.
Wife: Name not given, dead.
4-65-5-1 Lucy Alexis, P.O. Hartford.
Husband: Charles Alexis or Charles Rapp, Pott off.
4-65-5-1-1 Name or sex not given, age 7, drew with Potts.
4-65-5-1-2 Name or sex not given, age 6, drew with Potts.
4-65-5-1-3 Name or sex not given, drew with Potts.

Information following from: James David & Sam Mendoka James David says all drew with Potts – by letter from James David & in person at Athens Mch/09.
5-65 AW-ZHE-TAY-AW-SUNG or JAMES DAVID, age 68, P.O. Athens Mich.
Wife: Sarah David, age 66.
5-65-1 Moses David, dead, no children.
5-65-2 SusanDavid, dead.
Husband: Sam Meckety, dead, P.O. ~~Ath~~, see 8-53.
5-65-2-1 Albert Mackety, age 21, P.O. Athens, single, see 8-53.
5-65-2-2 Betsy Mackety, age 19, P.O. Athens, single, see 8-53.
5-65-3 Ida David, dead.
Husband: Thomas Mackey, dead, not same name as Mackety.
5-65-3-1 Frank Mackey, age 14.

Information following from: Mount Pleasant, Michigan.
6-65 ME-SHE-GAY-KAKE, dead.
Wife: None given.
6-65-1 Name or sex not given, dead, no heirs.
6-65-2 Name not given, dead.
Wife: Betsey Showagon, age 56, P.O. Weidman, see 15-64.

Information following from: Nancy Williams, Henry Williams, James Williams, Lattin, Mich Aug/08 Rosebush Jany 21/09 Mount Pleasant, Michigan.
7-65 PONTIAC, dead.
Wife: Name not given, dead.
7-65-1 Henry P. Pontiac, age 49, P.O. Rosebush.
Wife: Nancy Compean Ninish, age 39, separated, see 5-58.
7-65-1-1 George Pontiac, age 19, see 5-58.
7-65-2 James W. Pontiac, age 46, Rosebush.
Wife: Mary, Saginaw Ind.
7-65-2-1 Melinda Pontiac, age 11.

7-65-2-2 Grace Pontiac, age 8.
7-65-2-3 Amelia Pontiac, age 6.
7-65-2-4 Jesse Pontiac, age 4.
7-65-2-5 Cecelia Pontiac, age 2.

7-65-3 Jane Williams, age 44, P.O. Loomis, Mich.
Husband: Lyman Williams, Saginaw Ind off.
7-65-3-1 Lillie Williams, age 14, off see note.
7-65-3-2 Elizabeth Williams, age 11, off see note.
7-65-3-3 Sarah Williams, age 9, off see note.
7-65-3-4 Joseph Williams, age 5, off see note.
Note: Father wants the children enrolled as Saginaw Indians. Durant Spl Agt Jany 21/09.

7-65-4 Nancy Pontiac Williams, age 32, P.O. Lattin, Mich.
Husband: JohnWilliams #2, see 2-61.

Ansd Mch 1/09 Durant

Rosebush Mich
Feb 3 09

Commissary of Indian Affairs
Washington DC ~~Feb~~

Dear sir:- Excuse me of writing you a letter, I want my children to go with me Mr Durant the Indian Agent Did take our names alright

But, my man ~~is~~ has not a sound mind and memory (Lyman William) he wet before Durant and scratched all my children's names
I am sure if you'll tell Mr Durant to put the names back again he will do it at once I would like to know it some time this beforehe'll return to Washington D.C.

Children's name Lillie Williams
Elizabeth "
Sarah "
Joseph "
Frank " 5 weeks old the youngest of all.

I am yours very Respectfully
Jane Williams

Information following from: at Chippewa.

8-65 AW-BE-TAW-SE-GAY or FRANK JACKSON, dead.
Wife: Name not given, dead.
8-65-1 Charley Jackson, age 38, P.O. Chippewa, Mich, is a grand child of 29-65.
Wife: Mary Jackson (maiden name), age 34, P.O. Chippewa, Mich, see 17-65.
8-65-1-1 Alice Jackson, age 12, P.O. Chippewa.
8-65-1-2 Minnie Jackson, age 8, P.O. Chippewa.
8-65-1-3 Aw-Be-Tos-Ke Jackson, age 5, P.O. Chippewa.

8-65-1-4 Me-Sho-To-Quay Jackson, age 2, Born April 2, 1906.

8-65-1-5 Nabel, Born April 6/08.

Note: Thonk Chas. Jackson had one brother & sister.

8-65-2 Shay-Zhose or Julia Thomas, age 36, P.O. Crooked Lake or Lake Station.

Husband: Fred Thomas, is a Saginaw Indian.

8-65-2-1 John Thomas, age 10, P.O. Crooked Lake or Lake Station.

8-65-3 Ka-Bash-Mo-Quay or Mrs Carrie Auguste, age 34, supposed to live somewhere in Indiana. Connot trace or locate. Durant.

Enroll Mrs Auguste
Chippewa Sta June 9 1909

Dear Sir

Just received your letter. Well one of my sisters has one boy. James Solomon age 16 years her Address Mrs Julia Thomas Lake Sta Mich Now my other Sister I don't know Where she is, the last time I herd from her they lived at South Bend Indiana that was in march 1903 but of seen a man last Summer in Clar he told me that they had six Children I have never seen them. I havtseen her but once since 1882 that was before she was married. When I seen her thay must be around Allegan Co if not in South Bend Ind Mrs Julia Thomas age 36 Lake Station Clare Co Mich Mrs Carrie Augustr about 34 years I am not sure. From

Charley Jackson
Chippewa Station

Information following from: Saml Mandoka Athens.

9-65 O-WAW-NE-KEY JOHN, dead.

Wife: None given.

9-65-1 Johnson O-Waw-Ne-Key, age ?, P.O. near Dowogiac, said to be dead: no family see attached letter. Durant Spl Agt.

Note; Nadeau-Kaw – another brother, write Edson Watson, Supt. Ind Sch Nadeau Ks.

Department of the Interior,
United States Indian Service,

Pottawatomie Agency, Kansas,
Nadeau, June 12, 1909.

Horace B. Durant,
Petoskey, Mich:
Dear Sir:

In reply to your letters of May 19, and June 4, 1909, I desire to state that, after inquiry from all known sources, we have been unable to find any one who knows anythingabout O-waw-ne-key or knows any one by that name.
Very respectfully,
Edson Watson Superintendent.

Athens Mich. June 8, 1909
Mr. Horace B. Durant.
Petoskey Mich
They was a man name John Owannekey. But not Johnson. He has been dead over Thirty (30) years, leave no family.
Mr. James David said he never draw Ottawa payment. How more you don taken up names. When will commence pay off.
Sam Mandoka

Athens Mich June 9-1909
Mr. Horace B. Durant
Dear Sir
Mr. David has reca;; again the matter of Johnson Owannekey He stated that he used to call himself as a John or Johnson Owannekey.
This is a seam man we reffance to yesterdays letter I think he is a very man you seeking for.
He has a dead Sister left Three Children.
She perhaps not on the roll of Ottawa
Yours
Sam Mandoka
Get the names of the 3 children of his dead sister. Durant

Information following from: Mount Pleasant, Michigan.
10-65 NE-BE-NAW-SHE, dead.
10-65-1 Name not given, 33-65.

Information following from: John Fronssway March 16/09.
11-65 SAW-GAW-SE-GAY, dead.
Wife: Name not given, dead.
11-65-1 Name or sex not given.
Spouse: Not given.
11-65-1-1 Susan Jackson, age 35, P.O. Mt Pleas.
Husband: John Jackson, Saginaw off, see 11-64.

Information following from: John Fronssway March 16/09.
12-65 QUAY-QUAY-CHE-ME, dead, no heirs.

Information following from: Mount Pleasant, Michigan.
13-65 KEY-GAW or SAMUEL FISH, age 80, P.O. Weidman.

Wife: Name not given, dead.
13-65-1 Name not given, dead.
Husband: Name not given, dead (Saginaw)
13-65-1-1 Mary Neyome #2, age 15, P.O. ? Mt Pleasant Sch.
13-65-1-2 Mike Neyome, age 10, P.O. ? Mt Pleasant Sch.
13-65-2 Jennie Neyome, age 34, P.O. Weidman.
Husband: Name not given, dead (Saginaw).
13-65-2-1 Thomas Neyome, age 1 ½ , Born July 1907.
13-65-3 Julia Fish, age 23, single.
13-65-4 George Fish, age 21, single.

Information following from: Not Given.
14-65 NING-GO-TWAY or JIM ZOONDAH ~~or SAM ZOONDAH~~, 73+, P.O. Star City.
Wife 1st: Name not given, dead.
14-65-1 Maud ~~Sundah~~ Zoondah Kelsey, dead.
Husband: Joe Kelsey, lives at Custer did not know his Indian name so I could not trace him back.
14-65-1-1 John Kelsey, age 17?, P.O. Custer, see 5-69.
14-65-1-2 Flora Kelsey, age 18.
Note: Children live with father at Custer. Tuttle
Note: ~~Sun-Dah~~ Zoondah drew with the Potts.
Wife 2nd : Name not given, dead, no children.

Information following from: Sarah Isaac & her brother James David.
15-65 KAW-BAISH-CAW-MO-QUAY or SARAH ISAAC, age 66, P.O. Bradley, Mich.
Husband: Thomas Isaac, dead.
15-65-1 This child was not her child but her sister's child, see 38-65.

Information following from: Not Given.
16-65 AW-ZHE-WAW-BE-ME.
Note: Cannot trace this man through any Indians of the Gd. River Band. Durant.
Note: John Duverney says he remembers the name, that he used to live near Ludington & afterwards went to Isabella Co- but does not know anything about him or his family. Durant Apr/09

Information following from: at Chippewa.
17-65 MOOSE-E-QUAY or NANCY JACKSON, age 80, P.O. Chippewa (East of Reed City on P.M.), Died June 12/09.
Husband 1st: Name not given, dead.
Note: Children by 1st Husband are all dead leaving no descendants.
Husband 2nd: Frank Jackson, dead.
17-65-1 Mary Jackson, age 34, P.O. Chippewa

Husband: Charles Jackson, see 8-65 for children.
Husband 3rd: Name not given, all dead.

Information following from: John Fronssway Mch/09.
18-65 PE-NAY-SE-WAW-BE-QUAY, dead, sister of A-Ken-Bell, Chief.
Husband: None given.
18-65-1 Name not given, dead, no heirs.

Information following from: John Fronssway Mch/09.
19-65 AW-MIN-NE-WAY-QUAY, dead.
Husband: Jale Shawbose, a Saginaw.
19-65-1 Dan Shawbose, age 41, Mt Pleasant #6.
Wife: Name not given, dead.
19-65-1-1 Betsey Shawbose, age 14.
19-65-1-2 Ida Shawbose, age 11.
19-65-2 Name or sex not given, dead, no heirs.
19-65-3 Name or sex not given, dead, no heirs.
19-65-4 Name or sex not given, dead, no heirs.
19-65-5 Harry Shawbose, age 23, P.O.Mt Pleasant #6.
19-65-6 Julia Shawbose, age 20, single.
19-65-7Westbrook Shawbose, age 19.

Information following from: Mount Pleasant, Michigan.
20-65 AW-BE-WAY-QUOUM, dead.
Wife: Name not given, dead.
20-65-1 Name or sex not given, dead, no heirs.
20-65-2 Name or sex not given, dead, no heirs.
20-65-3 Mary Silas, age 22, P.O. Leaton, Mich.
Husband: Name not given, Saginaw Indian.
20-65-3-1 Thomas Silas, Born July20, 1907.

Information following from: John Fronssway.
21-65 SOLOMON, dead, name of wife not given dead, no children.

Information following from: Not Given.
22-65 MACKIE or MACKIE DAVID, dead, son of 4-65.
Wife: Name not given, dead, 20-53.
22-65-1 Emma (David) Mackey, age 39, P.O. Hamilton, see 20-53.
Husband: Steve Mackey, a Pott off, see 20-53 for children.
22-65-2 See 20-53 – all same family as 20-53.

Information following from: Not Given.
23-65 O-TAY-ZHE's son.
Note: Cannot trace this man. Durant.

Information following from: Not Given.
24-65 PE-NAY-SE-QUAY's son.
Note: Cannot trace this child. Durant.

Information following from: Not Given.
25-65 TAW-BAW-SOSH, son of4-65.
25-65-1 Name or sex not given, see 4-65.

Information following from: John Fronssway Mch 16/09.
26-65 PAY-MAW-ME, dead.
Wife: Julia Paymame, age 68, P.O. Alvin, Mich.
26-65-1 William Pay-Maw-Me, age 35, P.O. Oscoda, has two children in Oscoda ask Jake Shawbose, Mt Pleasant. Durant see letter from Jake Shawbose.
26-65-2 Amos Pay-Maw-Me, age 32, P.O. ~~Oscoda~~ Alvin, Alcona Co.
26-65-3 Elijah N. Pay-Maw-Me, age 17, P.O. Alvin.

26 SUPPLEMENTAL SHEET sent to Wm & Amos Paymawme Oscoda, Mich June 15/09 Durant Alvin June 18th Alvin Mich.
26-65 (father), dead.
Wife: (mother) Julia Pamance, age 68, P.O. Alvin.
26-65-1 William Pay-Maw-Me, age 35, P.O. Alvin Alcona Mich.
26-65-2 Amos Pay-Maw-Me, age 32, P.O. Alvin Alcona Mich.
26-65-3 Elijah N. Pamance, age 17, P.O. Alvin Alcona Mich
Note: The head of family is dead. The wife is a Saginaw. The others drew with Potts. Durant Horace B. Durant Special U.S. Indian Agent.

Letter to them June 15/09 Durant

Mt Pleasant Michigan
May 24th 1909

H. B. Durant
At Petoskey
Dear Sir yours of Letter the 19 09 is at hand. And in reply your requesting Me concerning too children of Pay-Maw-Me and will advise you and you will find them in the Pay roll of Potawatomies Tribe Dec 24 the 1904
William Pay-Maw-Me and his Brother who are living at Ocoda Amos Pay-Maw-Me
Your truly
Jacob Shawbose Mt Pleasant R.F.D. not

Information following from: Not Given.
27-65 SAUS-SWAY or FRANK BAILEY, age 69, P.O. Fountain.
Wife: Name not given, dead.
27-65-1 Setah Cogswell, age 23, died Mch 9, 1908 NB 1st roll.
Husband: Louis Cogswell, see 11-54 for children.

Wife 2nd: Name not given, separated, living now wife of James Pego – Viz: Sarah Williams Pego – see 5-62.

27-65-2 Eunice Bailey, age 16, ~~Walkerville or~~ Lattin, see 5-62.

27-65-3 ~~Martha~~ Madeline Bailey, age 13, P.O. Lattin, see 5-62.

27-65-4 George Bailey, age 11, P.O. Lattin, see 5-62.

Information following from: Mount Pleasant, Michigan Jany 18/09.

28-65 PE-NAY-SE-WE-KE-ZHICK, dead, no heirs.

Information following from: at Chippewa.

29-65 SHAY-ZHOSE or JULIA THOMAS, age 36, see 8-65.

Husband 1st : Solomon Fisher, dead, Saginaw Indian, P.O. Lake Station.

29-65-1 James Fisher or Charles Bobish or Charles Jackson or James Solomon, age 15, P.O. Crooked Lake Mich.

Note: Information from John Fronssway Mch 16/09 D Confirmed.

Husband 2nd: Name not given, no children.

Information following from: Mount Pleasant, Michigan.

30-65 O-BAW-NE-BAW-SE-NO-QUAY or DELIA WABINAW, age 70, P.O. Weidman.

Husband: Name not given, Saginaw Ind.

30-65-1 Joe Wabinaw, age 46, P.O. Weidman

Wife: Betsey Shawagon, see 15-64 for children.

Information following from: Not Given.

31-65 WAY-ME-GWANCE.

Note: Cannot trace this man. Durant.

Information following from: Note: Drew with Potts but established their ancestors names in Ottawa & Chippewa roll of 1870.

32-65 JOHN BAPTISTE or WAW-BAW-SWAY, living age 60, P.O. Custer, Mich.

Wife: Mary Smith Baptiste, age 58, ~~Burt~~ Furgus, Mich, Swan Creek Black River Saginaw Ind, living in Isabella Co Mt Pleasant.

32-65-1 Joseph Baptiste or Waw-Baw-Sway, age 30, P.O. lives in ~~Minnisota~~ Signer, Wisconsin~~, not married~~.

Wife: Emma.

32-65-1-1 Lawrence Baptiste, 2nd roll.

Note; Write letter about family.

32-65-2 Ira Baptiste or Waw-Baw-Sway, age 19, P.O. living Mt Pleasant Sch Fergus, Mich.

32-65-3 Lizzie Baptiste or Waw-Baw-Sway, age 11, P.O. living Mt Pleasant Sch Fergus, Mich.

Note: John Baptiste & Elizabeth Mitchell have an illegitimate child, which was adopted by George Shaw-naw-nay-se-gay, lives at Star City. Tuttle

Note: This card confirmedat Rosebush. Jany 21/-0 Durant.

Signor Wis.
May 26-1909

Horace B. Durant,
Petoskey, Mich;
Dear Sir:-
There is just my wife and one child Lawrance Battus Age 2 yrs wife Emma Battus Age 23 yrs Joseph Battus Age 31 yrs.
Yours truly
Joseph Battus

Information following from: Mount Pleasant, Michigan.
33-65 PE-NAW-SEE-MAW-QUOUM, dead.
Wife 1st: Name not given, ~~dead~~ living, see 15-64.
33-65-1 Joseph Peyono, age 38, see 24-64.
Wife: Jane, no children.
Wife 2nd: Name not given, dead, was a daughter of A-Ken-Bell 1-65.
33-65-2 Joseph Peyono #2, age 29, P.O. Weidman, Mich #2, see 1-65, single.

Information following from: Not Given.
34-65AW-BE-TAW-SEE-WAY-QUAY.
Note: Cannot trace this woman. Durant.

Information following from: James David Sam Mandoka Athens Mch/09.
35-65 KE-NE-QUAY, dead, child also dead, no heirs.

Information following from: James David Sam Mandoka Athens Mch/09.
36-65MONG-GO-QUAY, dead, daughter of 3-65, child also dead, no heirs.

Information following from: James David Sam Mandoka Athens.
37-65 PAW-YEASE, dead.
Wife: Mary Solomon or Mary David, age 85, P.O. Hamilton, no heirs.

Information following from: James David a brother Athens Mch/09.
38-65 NAW-O-QUAY-SHAW-MO-QUAY, dead.
Husband: None given.
38-65-1 Henry Birch, age 28, P.O. Bradley.
Wife: Lydia Birch, age 20, nee Shaygonaybe, see 2-54. No children.

Information following from: Not Given.
39-65 MARTHA HOLT's child.
Note: Cannot trace this child. Durant.

www.ingramcontent.com/pod-product-compliance
Lightning Source LLC
Chambersburg PA
CBHW060546280326
41932CB00011B/1411
9780788455810